Courts and Judges

The International Library of Essays in Law and Society
General Editor: Austin Sarat

Titles in the Series

Law and Religion
Gad Barzilai

Police and Policing Law
Jeannine Bell

Law and Society Approaches to Cyberspace
Paul Schiff Berman

Law and Families
Susan B. Boyd and Helen Rhoades

Rhetoric of Law
Marianne Constable and Felipe Gutterriez

Law in Social Theory
Roger Cotterrell

Ethnography and Law
Eve Darian-Smith

International Law and Society
Laura Dickinson

Legal Lives of Private Organizations
Lauren Edelman and Mark C. Suchman

Courts and Judges
Lee Epstein

Consciousness and Ideology
Patricia Ewick

Prosecutors and Prosecution
Lisa Frohmann

Intellectual Property
William T. Gallagher

Human Rights, Law and Society
Lisa Hajjar

The Jury System
Valerie Hans

Regulation and Regulatory Processes
Robert Kagan and Cary Coglianese

Race, Law and Society
Ian Haney Lopez

Crime and Criminal Justice
William T. Lyons, Jr.

Law and Social Movements
Michael McCann

Colonial and Post-Colonial Law
Sally Merry

Social Science in Law
Elizabeth Mertz

Sexuality and Identity
Leslie J. Moran

Law and Poverty
Frank Munger

Rights
Laura Beth Nielsen

Governing Risks
Pat O'Malley

Lawyers and the Legal Profession, Volumes I and II
Tanina Rostain

Capital Punishment, Volumes I and II
Austin Sarat

Legality and Democracy
Stuart A. Scheingold

The Law and Society Canon
Carroll Seron

Popular Culture and Law
Richard K. Sherwin

Law and Science
Susan Silbey

Immigration
Susan Sterett

Gender and Feminist Theory in Law and Society
Madhavi Sunder

Procedural Justice, Volumes I and II
Tom R. Tyler

Trials
Martha Merrill Umphrey

Courts and Judges

Edited by

Lee Epstein

Washington University, USA

ASHGATE

Published by
Ashgate Publishing Limited
Gower House
Croft Road
Aldershot
Hants GU11 3HR
England

Ashgate Publishing Company
Suite 420
101 Cherry Street
Burlington, VT 05401-4405
USA

Ashgate website: http://www.ashgate.com

British Library Cataloguing in Publication Data
Courts and judges. – (The international library of essays
in law and society)
1. United States. Supreme Court 2. Courts – United States
3. Judicial power – United States 4. Judicial process –
United States 5. Judges – United States
I. Epstein, Lee, 1958–
347.7'3

Library of Congress Cataloging-in-Publication Data
Courts and judges / edited by Lee Epstein.
p. cm. — (International library of essays in law and society)
Includes bibliographical references.
ISBN 0-7546-2475-7 (hbk. : alk. paper)
1. Judges—United States. I. Epstein, Lee, 1958– II. Series.

KF8775.A75.C68 2005
347.73'1—dc22

2005043567

ISBN 0 7546 2475 7

Printed in Great Britain by The Cromwell Press, Trowbridge, Wiltshire

Contents

Acknowledgements

The editor and publishers wish to thank the following for permission to use copyright material.

Blackwell Publishing Ltd for the essays: Bryon J. Moraski and Charles R. Shipan (1999), 'The Politics of Supreme Court Nominations: A Theory of Institutional Constraints and Choices', *American Journal of Political Science*, **43**, pp. 1069–95. Copyright © 1999 the Midwest Political Science Association; Forrest Maltzman and Paul J. Wahlbeck (1996), 'Strategic Policy Considerations and Voting Fluidity on the Burger Court', *American Journal of Political Science*, **90**, pp. 581–92; Melinda Gann Hall (1987), 'Constituent Influence in State Supreme Courts: Conceptual Notes and a Case Study', *Journal of Politics*, **49**, pp. 1117–24; Thomas G. Walker, Lee Epstein and William J. Dixon (1988), 'On the Mysterious Demise of Consensual Norms in the United States Supreme Court', *Journal of Politics*, **50**, pp. 361–89; Micheal W. Giles and Thomas G. Walker (1975), 'Judicial Policy-Making and Southern School Segregation', *Journal of Politics*, **37**, pp. 917–36; Gerald N. Rosenberg (1999), 'African-American Rights After *Brown*', *Journal of Supreme Court History*, **24**, pp. 201–25.

Cambridge University Press for the essays: Charles M. Cameron, Albert D. Cover and Jeffrey A. Segal (1990), 'Senate Voting on Supreme Court Nominees: A Neoinstitutional Model', *American Political Science Review*, **84**, pp. 525–34. Copyright © 1990 The American Political Science Association, published by Cambridge University Press, reprinted with permission; C. Herman Pritchett (1941), 'Divisions of Opinion among Justices of the U.S. Supreme Court, 1939–1941', *American Political Science Review*, **35**, pp. 890–98. Copyright © 1941 The American Political Science Association, published by Cambridge University Press, reprinted with permission; Glendon A. Schubert (1958), 'The Study of Judicial Decision-Making as an Aspect of Political Behavior', *American Political Science Review*, **52**, pp. 1007–25. Copyright © 1958 The American Political Science Association, published by Cambridge University Press, reprinted with permission; Jeffrey A. Segal (1984), 'Predicting Supreme Court Cases Probabilistically: The Search and Seizure Cases, 1962–1981', *American Political Science Review*, **78**, pp. 891–900. Copyright © 1984 The American Political Science Association, published by Cambridge University Press, reprinted with permission; Sheldon Goldman (1966), 'Voting Behavior on the United States Courts of Appeals, 1961–1964', *American Political Science Review*, **60**, pp. 374–83. Copyright © 1966 The American Political Science Association, published by Cambridge University Press, reprinted with permission; Walter F. Murphy (1959), 'Lower Court Checks on Supreme Court Power', *American Political Science Review*, **53**, pp. 1017–31. Copyright © 1959 The American Political Science Association, published by Cambridge University Press, reprinted with permission; Gretchen Helmke (2002), 'The Logic of Strategic Defection: Court-Executive Relations in Argentina Under Dictatorship and Democracy', *American Political Science Review*, **96**, pp. 291–303. Copyright © 2002 The American Political Science Association, published by Cambridge University Press, reprinted with permission; Charles H. Franklin and Liane C. Kosaki (1989), 'Republican Schoolmaster:

The U.S. Supreme Court, Public Opinion, and Abortion', *American Political Science Review*, **83**, pp. 751–71. Copyright © 1989 The American Political Science Association, published by Cambridge University Press, reprinted with permission.

Journal of Public Law for the essay: Robert A. Dahl (1957), 'Decision-Making in a Democracy: The Supreme Court as a National Policy-Maker', *Journal of Public Law*, **6**, pp. 279–95.

Oxford University Press for the essay: Gregory A. Caldeira, John R. Wright and Christopher J.W. Zorn (1999), 'Sophisticated Voting and Gate-Keeping in the Supreme Court', *Journal of Law, Economics, and Organization*, **15**, pp. 549–72.

The University of Chicago Press for the essay: Richard A. Posner (1993), 'What Do Judges and Justices Maximize? (The Same Thing Everybody Else Does)', *Supreme Court Economic Review*, **3**, pp. 1–41.

The Yale Law Journal Company for the essay: Frank B. Cross and Emerson H. Tiller (1998), 'Judicial Partisanship and Obedience to Legal Doctrine: Whistleblowing on the Federal Courts of Appeals', *Yale Law Journal*, **107**, pp. 2155–76. Reprinted by permission of The Yale Law Journal Company and William S. Hein Company.

Every effort has been made to trace all the copyright holders, but if any have been inadvertently overlooked the publishers will be pleased to make the necessary arrangement at the first opportunity.

Series Preface

The International Library of Essays in Law and Society is designed to provide a broad overview of this important field of interdisciplinary inquiry. Titles in the series will provide access to the best existing scholarship on a wide variety of subjects integral to the understanding of how legal institutions work in and through social arrangements. They collect and synthesize research published in the leading journals of the law and society field. Taken together, these volumes show the richness and complexity of inquiry into law's social life.

Each volume is edited by a recognized expert who has selected a range of scholarship designed to illustrate the most important questions, theoretical approaches, and methods in her/his area of expertise. Each has written an introductory essay which both outlines those questions, approaches, and methods and provides a distinctive analysis of the scholarship presented in the book. Each was asked to identify approximately 20 pieces of work for inclusion in their volume. This has necessitated hard choices since law and society inquiry is vibrant and flourishing.

The International Library of Essays in Law and Society brings together scholars representing different disciplinary traditions and working in different cultural contexts. Since law and society is itself an international field of inquiry it is appropriate that the editors of the volumes in this series come from many different nations and academic contexts. The work of the editors both charts a tradition and opens up new questions. It is my hope that this work will provide a valuable resource for longtime practitioners of law and society scholarship and newcomers to the field.

AUSTIN SARAT
William Nelson Cromwell Professor of Jurisprudence and Political Science
Amherst College

Introduction

The Selection Criteria

Compiling a volume of twenty influential essays on courts and judges is an enterprise fraught with peril. No two scholars toiling in this field are likely to agree on a list of the top fifty, much less the top twenty. Worse still, I am not sure that I – the compiler of the list of essays included here – could replicate my own decisions.

The problem, if I dare call it that, is an embarrassment of riches. Over the past six decades or so, scholars have produced study after study that has contributed to our understanding of judges and courts. Sometimes that contribution is methodological, sometimes it is theoretical, many times it is substantive but almost always it is some combination of the three. So choosing among the hundreds, perhaps even thousands, of outstanding essays is quite a task.

I have tried to minimize it by adhering to the following criteria.

1. *Essays Only.* My contract with Ashgate Publishing states that, 'the essays should be drawn from relevant periodicals. . . . Chapters from books, even if the books are collections of essays, should not be included'. Of course I followed this rule but I do wish to point out that many of the most important contributions to the study of judges and courts come in the form of books and, to a lesser extent, chapters in edited volumes and unpublished papers. I think here of Pritchett (1941); Schubert (1965); Danelski (1979); Murphy (1964); Rosenberg (1991); Perry (1991); Tanenhaus (1963); Segal and Spaeth (1993), to name just a few. In some instances, the author(s) wrote an essay before or after publication of the book or chapter, and I was able to incorporate those (e.g. Pritchett, 1941; Rosenberg, 1999). But for many that was not the case (e.g. Perry, 1991; Segal and Spaeth, 1993), and I regret that I cannot include them here.
2. *A Focus on Courts and Judges.* The title of this volume is Courts and Judges. Since I was able to identify more than an ample number of seminal essays directly on this topic, I eliminated pieces that were even remotely peripheral. This criterion led to the exclusion of many more than a handful of papers, including two of my personal favorites: the extremely influential Priest and Klein (1984) and Galanter (1974). While both cover courts, their emphasis, it seems to me, is on litigants. Along similar lines, I excluded even landmark papers on juries, interest groups, and attorneys.[1]
3. *A Concentration on Positive, Rather Than Normative, Studies.* At the risk of greatly overgeneralizing, two types of scholars study law and courts: one that chiefly focuses on describing and analyzing observations drawn from the legal world; and the other, primarily on (normatively) theorizing about that world, offering prescriptions to change it, or both.[2] In light of the emphasis of this series, as well as my own inclination,[3] I limited my selections (with a few exceptions) to work falling into the former category. I thus excluded essays asking, for example, how judges *should* interpret statutes or whether the practice of judicial review fits compatibly with democratic principles, or were

otherwise motivated largely by normative concerns. Since many of the most influential of these works appear in book form (e.g., Scalia, 1994; Eskridge, 1994; Posner, 1985; Ely, 1980; Dworkin, 1977; Bickel, 1962), this was a less daunting task than it might appear.[4]

4. *The 'Best' Research.* When Austin Sarat, the general editor of the Law and Society series, asked me to edit this volume, he described my job as one of selecting 'twenty of the best already published essays'. It should go without saying – although I already have said as much – that I cannot imagine many scholars agreeing on a definition of 'best'. So, in the interest of full disclosure I should reveal mine. For purposes of making selections for this volume, I define 'best' as studies that changed the way we (or perhaps more accurately I) think about courts and judges.

   At the very least, this was my 'separating the men from the boys' criterion. Scores and scores of works make important contributions to the literature but far fewer are sufficiently powerful to alter perspectives about entire areas of study. Sometimes that alteration comes about by settling old and important debates but more likely – judging by the essays in this volume – it happens from opening new ones.

These are the criteria I employed but I am certain others structured my thinking as well. Those primarily come in the form of my own biases, two of which seem particularly relevant. First, while I have a joint appointment in a law school and a political science department, I am a political scientist by training. Accordingly, I am far more familiar with literature in that discipline than in virtually all others, including economics, sociology, anthropology, and psychology. No doubt my selections reflect that familiarity. Another bias is methodological in nature. I have, to be sure, made use of qualitative data and methods but I have a stronger taste for the quantitative. Again with little doubt my selections shore up that preference, though (perhaps ironically enough) the one piece I selected from my own *oeuvre* (Walker, Epstein and Dixon, 1988) relies less on numerical evidence and statistical analysis than most others I have included.

The Volume's Organization and Contents

If there is one word that characterizes the study of courts and judges it is diversity – diversity in the kinds of questions scholars raise, the theories they invoke, and the methodologies they use to assess the implications of their theories. Given this mix, it would be, on the one hand, a nearly Quixotic task to incorporate even the 'best' articles representative of the range of research in a single book, that would necessitate a much larger volume, perhaps even two or three. On the other hand, despite the multiplicity of specific research questions, theories, and methodologies, analysts of courts and judges have coalesced around perhaps a half dozen general substantive concerns. For purposes of organizing this volume, I fold them into four: judicial selection and retention, judicial decision making, constraints on judicial power, and the role of courts in democracies.

In what follows, I briefly describe each topic, and offer some rationale for the essays I selected to represent them. Along the way, I also provide citations to related work that space limitations prevent me from including but nonetheless may be of interest.

The Selection and Retention of Judges

Of all the difficult choices confronting societies when they go about designing legal systems, among the most controversial are those pertaining to judicial selection and retention: how ought a nation select its judges and for how long should those jurists serve?[5] Indeed, some of the most fervent constitutional debates – whether they transpired in Philadelphia in 1787 (Farber and Sherry, 1990) or in Moscow in 1993–4 (Hausmaninger, 1995) – over the institutional design of the judicial branch implicate not its power or competencies; they involve who would select and retain its members. It is thus hardly surprising to find an immense amount of scholarship on questions pertaining to judicial selection and retention, ranging from the primarily normative (e.g., Garrow, 2000; Oliver, 1986) to the chiefly empirical (e.g., Segal, Cameron and Cover, 1992; Martinek, Kemper and Van Winkle, 2002), to work falling between the two (e.g., Davis, 2005; Epstein et al., 2005; Choi and Gulati, 2002).

In choosing among the many contenders for inclusion here, I limited myself mainly to the empirical (though with the occasional normative implication) and then to two central substantive questions: what explains the selection (and rejection) of judges and what effect(s) do rules governing selection and retention have on the types of men and women who will serve and, in turn, the decisions they, as judges, will make? As to the first, my choice of Cameron, Cover and Segal (1990) is, I think, an obvious one. It may not be the earliest study to attempt to explain why the American Senate confirms some Supreme Court nominees and rejects others but it is the first to elaborate and systematically assess a theoretical account of confirmation politics in the United States. Briefly, it operates under the assumption that electorally oriented senators vote on the basis of their constituents' 'principle concerns in the nomination politics' (Cameron, Cover and Segal, 1990, 528). Those concerns primarily (though not exclusively) center on whether a candidate for the U.S. Supreme Court is (1) qualified for office and (2) sufficiently proximate to the senator in ideological space. An analysis of data drawn from the votes of individual senators over the twenty-two nominations between 1953 and 1987 supports the account.

To say that Cameron and his colleagues made a critical contribution to a line of inquiry of concern to multiple fields and disciplines is hardly to overstate the case. Scholars studying other executive appointments have liberally drawn on its insights (e.g., Routh, 2004; Nixon, 2001; Krutz, Fleisher and Bond, 1998; King and Riddlesperger, 1996; Hammond and Hill, 1993); secondary accounts in the judicial and legislative fields regularly report its results (e.g., Baum, 2004; Smith et al., 2003); and, it has been a centerpiece of normative debates, particularly in the legal literature, about the confirmation process.

And, yet, however important the Cameron et al. effort, it never explicitly addresses the question of why so many appointments to the Supreme Court are relatively uncontroversial. That task falls to Moraski and Shipan (1999), which I also incorporate in pages to follow. These scholars point to two possible answers: the Senate simply defers to the President or the President, knowing that the Senate must confirm his choice, takes senators' preferences into account when he makes nominations. The first is unlikely in light of the Cameron et al. study and, in fact, it is the second that the data tend to reflect: When the President and the Senate share preferences over the future direction of the judiciary Moraski and Shipan show that the President is relatively free to appoint a nominee of his choice; but when they are distant, as Moraski and Shipan also demonstrate, the President must move toward the Senate if he wants to see his nominee confirmed.

Seen in this way, Moraski and Shipan (1999) is a bridge between the two questions of primary concern here: it speaks to why candidates for judgeships are (un)successful and to how the rules affect choices made by political actors on whom to nominate to the Court; after all, without the constitutional mandate of senatorial 'advise and consent', the President would be free to appoint anyone he deemed desirable to the Court. But it is Hall (1987a), the final paper included in this section, that addresses directly the link between rules and decisions eventually made by judges. What she explores is the intersection between the votes jurists cast and the methods used to choose them in the individual U.S. States, most of which elect their judges.[6]

Hall's findings, though limited to one court, may merely seem to confirm what many analysts had long suspected: that elected judges act in sophisticated fashion, making decisions that echo popular sentiment and not necessarily their own policy or jurisprudential preferences (see, e.g., Gryski, Main and Dixon, 1986; Vines, 1962; Watson and Downing, 1969). On the other hand, the Hall study went some distance toward reinvigorating this area of inquiry, prompting both its author and others to conduct deeper and more rigorous investigations into the effect of selection and retention rules on the choices judges make (e.g., Brace and Hall, 1993, 1997; Croly, 1995; Hall, 1987b, 1992; Hall and Brace, 1992; Pinello, 1995; Tabarrok and Helland, 1999).

Judicial Decision Making

That formal rules work to structure judicial decisions is certainly a promising avenue for future research – especially for work outside the United States, where variation in the mechanisms for the selection and retention of judges abound.[7] But truth be told most empirical studies of decision making have emphasized other factors that may effect judicial choices – though no one factor more so than judges' ideology or policy preferences.

Perhaps the emphasis on ideology reflects the genesis of modern-day inquiries into judicial decision making: C. Herman Pritchett's work on the the justices of the (Roosevelt) U.S. Supreme Court (Pritchett, 1941, 1948). As readers will see, Pritchett asked deceptively simple questions: If judges were merely 'declaring' the law rather than making it, why did they so often disagree?[8] How, in interpreting the same legal provisions, could they consistently reach different conclusions on important questions of law? When Pritchett concluded that the usual explanations – primarily those rooted in the primacy of precedent – could not provide intellectually acceptable responses, he turned to the answer offered by Jerome Frank and the other legal realists (e.g. Rank, 1930; Llewellyn, 1951): judges are 'motivated by their own preferences'. Pritchett, however, did not see preferences as mere whims but as opinions, often as deeply thought out as they were felt.

Pritchett's work marked a new beginning, and not an end, to social-scientific inquiry into the legal process. Today, social scientists invoke a range of approaches to the study of judicial decision making – both in the United States and abroad. Some reflect Pritchett's emphasis on ideology, while others are rather distinct in their theoretical underpinnings.

Among scholars following in Pritchett's footsteps, few are more prominent than Glendon Schubert. Just as virtually all students of courts and judges have read Pritchett's *The Roosevelt Court* (1948), many if not all are familiar with Schubert's (1965) *The Judicial Mind*. Since I cannot include this classic book here, I take the next best step and incorporate a related, classic essay, Schubert (1958). This is a mainstay on graduate syllabi at least in part, I suspect, because it deepens Pritchett's emphasis on political preferences in ways theoretical, substantive, and methodological. So, for example, while Pritchett (at least to my knowledge) did not write much on how courts set their agendas, Schubert devotes attention to this crucial topic – or what he calls the Certiorari Game. This part of his 1958 paper is a precursor to the more sophisticated analysis conducted by Caldeira, Wright and Zorn (1999), which I include here as well. A multitude of scholars may have written on the subject of agenda setting between Schubert and Caldeira et al.,[9] but it is Caldeira, Wright and Zorn (1999), I believe, that represents the final word on the subject – at least for now.

Methodologically too Schubert's work advanced Pritchett's project. While Pritchett made use of data in his research (see, e.g., the work I include here, Pritchett, 1941), Schubert went one step further developing innovative methods for analyzing that data. Of course some of those techniques no longer figure prominently in contemporary work but Schubert's willingness to experiment encouraged others to do the same. Of these subsequent efforts, I can imagine no single one more influential than Segal's (1984) 'Predicting Supreme Court Decisions Probabilistically: The Search and Seizure Cases'. While this paper built on ideas in the Schubert (1958) article, as well as in work by Kort (1957) on the role of facts in judicial decisions, it more than pushed them along; it brought to the study of courts and judges a now-ubiquitous class of statistical tools (those enabling researchers to model the outcomes of courts cases), as well.

Pritchett and Schubert – and later Segal (1984) and Segal and Spaeth (2002) – generally confined their work to the U.S. Supreme Court and then to explaining judicial decisions vis-à-vis the political ideologies of judges. Other early students of courts and judges, however, turned to different tribunals and, as I just noted, to different (albeit related) theories of judging. Sheldon Goldman (1966; 1973; 1975), for example, was among the first to study federal intermediate appellate courts.[10] Taking his cues largely from Pritchett, Schubert, and a handful of others, Goldman too explored the extent to which judges' ideology affected their votes but he went further, investigating whether judges' demographic or background characteristics also infiltrate their decisions. As readers will see, he concluded that 'party affiliation was . . . associated with voting behavior' but that 'other demographic variables, such as religion, socio-economic origins, education, and age' were not.

The Goldman (1966) study thus makes a central contribution to the study of judging for any number of reasons but two deserve emphasis here. First, it was among the first to move beyond the Supreme Court. And while I cannot say that its effect was immediate – another three decades or so elapsed before scholars began studying the federal circuit courts in force (see, e.g., Revesz, 1997; Klein and Morrisroe, 1999; Segal, Cameron and Songer, 1995; Merritt, 2001; Sheehan and Mishler, 1992; Songer, Davis and Haire, 1994; Songer, Segal and Cameron, 1994; Spriggs and Wahlbeck, 1995) – it stands as a landmark in the field.

Second, Goldman was one of only a handful of works at the time to contemplate the importance of judges' backgrounds on their decisions.[11] Goldman, of course, found little effect but that did not prevent others from continuing the hunt (e.g., Tate, 1981; Tate and Handberg, 1991; Ulmer, 1986; Brudney, Schiavoni and Merritt, 1999). Since I can hardly include all of the many efforts along these lines I selected just two (Giles and Walker, 1975; Sherry, 1986), and for two different reasons at that. One is a famous paper by Giles and Walker (1975),[12] which attempts to 'explain the policy choices made by Southern federal judges in race relations cases' (p. 919) – a subject of considerable interest in the United States. As part of that exercise, the authors examined a range of social background variables but found only one – whether a judge went to school in the South – to hold any explanatory power.

Giles and Walker's then is not a study that lends much credence to theories emphasizing a judge's personal attributes. But the same cannot be said of Sherry's 'Civic Virtue and the Feminine Voice in Constitutional Adjudication'. Written in 1986, 'Civic Virtue' brought to light a background characteristic that did not – owing to a lack of women on the bench – figure into much earlier work: a judge's sex.

When Sherry suggested that female judges may speak in 'a different voice', she created quite a stir. Scores of scholars undertook follow-up studies (e.g., Segal, 1997; Aliotta, 1995; Davis, Haire and Songer, 1993; Walker and Barrow, 1985; Gruhl, Spolm and Welch, 1981; Allen and Wall, 1993); and even Sandra Day O'Connor, the first woman appointed to the U.S. Supreme Court, chimed in. O'Connor took issue with Sherry's conclusions, as did some subsequent papers (compare, e.g., Gruhl, Spolm, and Welch 1981 and Allen and Wall 1993). But Sherry's work nonetheless stands as a path-breaking, albeit controversial, study if only because it renewed scholarly interest in the analysis of judges' backgrounds and attributes (see, e.g., Ashenfelter, Eisenberg and Schwab, 1995; Brudney, Schiavoni and Merritt, 1999; Schneider, 2001; Sisk, Heise and Morriss, 1998).

No less controversial is yet another approach to judging – and one that has developed a growing following in recent years: strategic analysis (Epstein and Knight, 1998; Gely and Spiller, 1990; Spiller and Gely, 1992; Maltzman, Spriggs and Wahlbeck, 2000; Maltzman and Wahlbeck, 1996; Cross and Tiller, 1998). While shades of this account appear in both Pritchett (1961) and Schubert (1958) it remained for Walter F. Murphy, a student of Pritchett's, to bring it to prominence. Murphy (1962; 1964) begins with the same general premise as did Pritchett and Schubert – justices are single-minded seekers of policy – but he added nuance to that rather stark (and pehaps crude) idea. Specifically, to Murphy, if jurists truly care about etching their policy preferences into law, then they may be willing to modulate their views to avoid an extreme reaction from either their colleagues or external actors. Judges, on this account, would rather hand down a ruling that comes close to, but may not exactly reflect, their preferences than, in the long run, see other actors completely override their decisions.

Unfortunately, I cannot include Murphy's most important work along these lines here: *Elements of Judicial Strategy* is a book, not an essay. What I do instead is incorporate three modern day manifestations of his strategic analysis. One is the Caldeira, Wright and Zorn (1999) essay I mentioned earlier. The second is a classic paper by Richard Posner (1993), which asserts that 'Judges are rational, and they pursue instrumental and consumption goals of the same general kind and in the same general way that private persons do' (p. 39). The third, by political scientists Forrest Maltzman and Paul J. Wahlbeck (1996), runs along similar lines but focuses explicitly on judges as policy maximizers. Following Murphy's (1964) and later Epstein and Knight's (1998) lead, Maltzman and Wahlbeck argue that judges can only achieve their policy goals by attending to the preferences of their colleagues and the actions they expect them to take.

Constraints on Judicial Power

These last three works but especially Maltzman and Wahlbeck (1996) and Caldeira, Wright and Zorn (1999) focus attention on how judges interact with their colleagues. What strategic approaches also suggest, as I imply above, is that judges who wish to make efficacious decisions must take into account – in addition to the preferences and likely actions of their colleagues – various limitations or constraints imposed by forces external to their tribunals (e.g., Gely and Spiller, 1990; Spiller and Gely, 1992; Vanberg, 1998; Eskridge, 1991b,a; Epstein, Knight and Martin, 2001; Helmke, 291–303).[13]

Those external forces take many different forms: politicians in the states, for example, can refuse to implement judicial decisions, thereby rendering them inefficacious; and 'the public' too may play a role in limiting judicial power. But scholars toiling in this area tend to focus on two others: the extent to which higher courts can impose limits on lower courts (the 'hierarchy of justice') and the degree to which the checks and balances inherent in systems of shared power can constrain judges ('separation of powers').

Beginning with the first, while it seems to be the case that lower court judges are no less interested in etching their values into law than those on higher courts (see, e.g., Sunstein, Schkade and Ellman, 2004), they face a substantial constraint in their quest to do so – the possibility of sanctioning from a higher court. To the extent that supreme courts cannot hire, fire, promote, demote, financially reward, or penalize members of trial or intermediate courts, that sanction can take only one form: reversal. But such is apparently sufficient to restrain judges of lower courts from acting on their sincere preferences – or so argue Cross and Tiller (1998). Their highly influential study, which I include here, asserts that the presence of a 'whistleblower' on the court – a judge 'whose policy preferences differ from the majority's and who will expose the majority's manipulation or disregard of the applicable legal doctrine' to a higher court – can constrain his or her colleagues from behaving in accord with their own preferences.

Hence, in the Cross and Tiller study the hierarchical structure imposes limits on lower courts from tribunals above them (see also, e.g., Segal, Cameron and Songer, 1995; Songer, Segal and Cameron, 1994; Cameron, Segal and Songer, 2000; Sunstein, Schkade and Ellman, 2004). But that same structure can also work the other way, as Murphy's 1959 seminal paper, which too appears in the page to follow, indicates: Lower-court judges can hamper the commands of higher courts by avoiding, limiting, or even defying them – as many did with the U.S. Supreme Court's desegregation decisions. Or, as one observer noted in 1941: '[Many] precedents have been rejected through the stratagem of distinguishment; others have been the subject of conscious judicial oversight. As a consequence, judicial discretion among inferior judges is not so confined and limited as legal theorists would have it' (Comment, 1941, 1448–1449). That these words continue to resonate today seems beyond doubt. Indeed, it was only a few short years ago that a lower court (in *Hopwood v. Texas*, 1996) took the dramatic step of defying the U.S. Supreme Court's landmark decision in the affirmative action case of *Regents of the University of California v. Bakke* (1978).

Seen in this way, the limitation imposed by the hierarchy of justice 'comes full circle', as Murphy (1959, 1031) wrote. 'The Supreme Court must take into account the reaction of inferior judges', he continued 'and lower courts must attempt to divine the counter-reaction of the Supreme Court.' We might say the same of the second major constraint – that imposed by the separation-of-powers system. Although some scholars belie the importance of this limit – Segal and Spaeth (1993), for example, claim that, under certain institutional conditions (e.g., the existence of life tenure, the lack of superiors in the judicial hierarchy, and the dearth of political ambition) judges on high or constitutional courts will be free to ignore the desires of elected actors – most scholars believe otherwise. Just as Murphy (1961) and Pritchett (1962) argued some thirty years ago, contemporary analysts assert that judges must take into account the preferences of legislators if they are to achieve their goals. That is because legislators and executives can take many steps to punish 'errant' courts, thereby making it difficult for them not just to achieve policy goals but to develop or maintain some level of legitimacy, as well. Certainly this is true in the American statutory context in which Congress and the President can overturn judicial interpretations of laws (see the important paper in this volume by Eskridge, 1991a).

But what of constitutional interpretation? While legislatures and executives typically cannot pass legislation to overturn decisions reached by courts on constitutional grounds, they can (and have) used the Senate's confirmation power to select certain types of judges, enacted constitutional amendments to reverse decisions or change Court structure or procedure, impeached judges, withdrawn Court jurisdiction over certain subjects, altering the selection and removal process, required extraordinary majorities for declarations of unconstitutionality, allowed appeal from the Supreme Court to a more 'representative' tribunal, removed the power of judicial review, slashed the budget, and altered the size of the Court.[14]

This list of weapons pertains directly to the American context. Even more radical steps have been taken elsewhere, as Helmke (291–303, 292) points out in fascinating insights on the Argentine judiciary:

> In many parts of the developing world, judges face threats far greater than simply having their decisions overturned. In such contexts, sanctions range from impeachment, removal, and court-packing to criminal indictment, physical violence, and even death. Compared to American justices, who serve an average of 16.3 years on the bench, in Argentina in the post-Perón period, the average length of tenure has been a mere 5.6 years. Although judges stepped down for a variety of reasons throughout each of the three governments, multiple resignations clustered at the end of both the military and the first democratic government of Alfonsin suggest that incoming governments in Argentina routinely get rid of their predecessors' judges despite constitutional guarantees.

Helmke proceeds to show, as readers will see, that Argentine judges respond to these potential threats by 'strategically defecting', that is, by ruling against the existing regime once it begins to lose power.

The Roles of Courts in Democracies

As the discussion thus far suggests, scholars have spilt no shortage of ink investigating the correlates of judicial decisions and the constraints on the ability of judges to make them – so much ink in fact that they often neglect to ask questions about the impact of judicial decisions or, even more broadly, about the the role(s) courts play in democratic societies.

The three pieces I include in this section – Dahl (1957), Rosenberg (1999), and Franklin and Kosaki (1989) – remind us why these are important, if not critical, questions to ask. For even though they tackle different substantive dimensions of the problem, intriguingly enough they reach the same general conclusion: Courts may not be wholly ineffective organizations within their societies but neither are they as influential as some observers claim.

The first of the trio, Robert Dahl's 'Decision Making in a Democracy', draws attention to Bickel's (1962) 'countermajoritarian difficulty': Given America's fundamental commitment to a representative form of government, why should its citizens allow a group of unelected officials – federal judges – to override the wishes of the people, as expressed by their elected officials? Dahl attempts to address this question via the 'ruling regime' thesis: Because the political preferences of Supreme Court justices will never be substantially out of line with those of the existing lawmaking majorities, the justices will usually reach decisions consistent with preferences of the elected branches. The primary reason for this, on Dahl's account, is quite simple: Vacancies occur on the Court on the average once every twenty-two months, giving the president ample opportunity to restaff and reshape the bench. Exceptional circumstances do occur; but, Dahl claims, judges usually cannot – or will not – run counter to the policies of the ruling coalition. They can only fashion specific policies within the general framework of the dominant coalition's goals or, at considerable risk, make new policy when the alliance has not yet arrived at a consensus.

To be sure, Dahl's analysis has its fair share of critics. Helmke's (2002) study of Argentina suggests that it does not fit courts there. And Casper (1976) has argued that Dahl's conclusion fails to capture accurately certain eras in American history (see also Epstein, Knight and Martin, 2001). But Dahl also has his supporters, of which we might count Gerald Rosenberg as one.

Like Dahl, Rosenberg is interested in assessing the role courts – but especially the American Supreme Court – play in a democratic society. Rather than asking, 'Are courts majoritarian or counter-majoritarian branches of government', however, Rosenberg centers his research on what may be the heart of the matter: 'Are courts effective policy makers?', 'Can courts bring about social change?' His answer, first explicated in the landmark *The Hollow Hope* (1991) and later in the paper I include here, is generally no: courts cannot generate large-scale social change unless the ruling regime supports them. So, for example, Rosenberg claims that *Brown v. Board* (1954) produced little integration in public schools in the South until Congress, at the insistent urging of the President and the broader civil rights movement, had enacted the Civil Rights Act of 1964. This statute put the federal spending power and criminal laws behind desegregation. Then the Voting Rights Act of 1965 utilized federal authority to allow blacks to use their right to vote to retire state and federal officials who wished to continue governmentally imposed racial discrimination. It was these laws, according to Rosenberg, and not *Brown*, which furthered the cause of civil rights.

Rosenberg's conclusion came as something of a surprise to scholars of the day – many of whom long believed that courts could generate meaningful social change and, in fact, held *Brown*, in particular, as a prime exemplar.[15] But perhaps Rosenberg's finding should not have been so startling. Long ago, students of the presidency concluded that the White House can seldom bring about lasting changes in public policy.[16] Success typically requires not only strong presidential action, but also new legislation – including, very importantly, appropriation – from Congress, enthusiastic enforcement from administrative agencies, sympathetic treatment from courts, and, not least, the active support of politically skilled interest groups. Public policy is almost always the product of a process, a series of actions and reactions, not of a single decision by a legislative, executive, or judicial institution. And this interactive process starts – or sometimes even stops – with the action of an interest group or one of the formal political institutions.

It is for similar reasons that Franklin and Kosaki's (1989) findings also fall short of surprising. These researchers too are interested in the role of courts in democratic societies but their emphasis is on public opinion. Specifically, they ask whether judges can act as 'republican schoolmasters', conferring legitimacy on the position they favor. The answer, as it turns out, is that they generally cannot. Rather than move the public toward their decisions, Franklin and Kosaki report that courts have a polarizing effect. So, for example, citizens who were pro-choice prior to the Supreme Court's decision in *Roe v. Wade* (1973), which legalized abortions, grew even more supportive of the right to choose; citizens who were pro-life before *Roe* too became more resolute in their views.

Franklin and Kosaki's study focused on abortion but follow-up research on the death penalty reaches much the same conclusion: both supporters and opponents became even more adamant in their respective views after the U.S. Supreme Court's decision in *Furman v. Georgia* (1972), which held that existing death penalty laws in the United States violated the constitution. In other words, rather than unifying the public *against* capital punishment, the Court's decision further divided Americans (Johnson and Martin, 1998). (Worth noting is that after *Furman* many state legislatures rewrote their laws in an effort to conform to the decision. Four years later, in *Gregg v. Georgia*, the justices upheld most of these new laws but *Gregg* generated virtually no change in public opinion: Americans became no more or less likely to support the death penalty, nor did they grow more polarized.)

At the end of the day, then, the readings in this section combine to show that a judicial ruling, like an executive decision or legislative act, is only one element in a complex battle that often begins in the private sphere, is waged in various political arenas, and will return to those arenas – if, indeed, it ever completely leaves them – after judges have had their say. Furthermore, it is likely that most important issues will also reappear in the courts for fresh decisions, and do so not once but several times before they are finally settled, forgotten, or, what is most likely, superseded by new problems of public policy.

Notes

1 Caldeira, Wright and Zorn (1999), which I do include, incorporate interest groups into the analysis but in the context of judicial decision making.

2 This is, in fact, a gross generalization. Most empirical work proceeds from theory; and many more than a few scholars move between the empirical and the prescriptive. I think here, to take but one example, of Tiller and Cross (1999), in which the authors analyze voting on the U.S. Court of Appeals for the District of Columbia. Based on that investigation, Tiller and Cross offer a 'modest proposal': eradicating the practice of randomly assigning judges to circuit court panels and instead 'assigning panels with reference to the party of the appointing President' (p. 228).

3 This is just one bias that influenced my decisions; I discuss others in the text.

4 There are, of course, exceptions – including Frankfurter (1947), Bork (1971), Wechsler (1959) – to cite just a few.

5 I adapt this and the next few sentences from Epstein and Knight (2004).

6 By the American Judicature Society's tally, in 21 states judges serving on courts of last resort are initially elected to office either on a partisan (8 states) or non-partisan (13) ballot; in all 21 judges must appear on a ballot of one form or another to retain their position. Six states enable their governor (4) or their legislature (2) to appoint their high court judges; and, in many instances to reappoint them. Just 1 of the 6 (New Hampshire) gives its justices life tenure but only until they reach the age of 70. The remaining 23 states employ some version of the 'Missouri' or merit plan. These plans differ from state to state – and substantially differ in some instances – but usually they call for an election after a year or two of service, in which the name of each new judge is put on the ballot with the question whether he or she should be retained in office. If the voters reject an incumbent, another

'merit' candidate replaces him or her. If elected, the judge then serves a set term, at the end of which he or she is eligible for reelection.

7 While many nations, typically those using the civil law system, have developed similar methods for training and choosing ordinary judges, they depart from one another rather dramatically when it comes to the selection of constitutional court justices. In Germany, for example, justices are selected by Parliament, though six of the 16 must be chosen from among professional judges. In Bulgaria, one-third of the justices are selected by Parliament, one-third by the President, and one-third by judges sitting on other courts. Moreover, in some countries with centralized judicial review, justices serve for a limited period of time. In South Africa, for instance, they hold office for a single 12-year term, in Italy a single nine-year term. In others, including the Czech and Korean Republics, justices serve for a set, albeit renewable, term.

8 Indeed, Pritchett's early work actually derives from a simple empirical observation; namely, that beginning in the 1930s and 1940s dissents accompanied many Supreme Court decisions. For an attempt to explain why dissent rates skyrocketed during this period, see Walker, Epstein and Dixon (1988), also included in this volume. The authors provide a graph illustrating the marked increase that Pritchett observed.

9 A small sample of the extant literature includes Armstrong and Johnson (1982); Baum (1979); Boucher and Segal (1995); Brenner (1979); Brenner and Krol (1989); Caldeira and Wright (1988, 1990); Caldeira, Wright and Zorn (1999); Krol and Brenner (1990); McGuire and Caldeira (1993); Palmer (1982, 2001); Perry (1991); Provine (1980); Schubert (1962, 1959); Smith (1999); Songer (1979); Tanenhaus (1963); Teger and Kosinski (1980); Ulmer (1972); Ulmer, Hintze and Kirklosky (1972); Ulmer (1983, 1984); Lawless and Murray (1997); Estreicher and Sexton (1984); Linzer (1979); Estreicher and Sexton (1986); Berlage (1984); Hartnett (2000); Hellman (1985); Long (1984); Sturley (1989); Tiberi (1993); Baker (1984); Cordray and Cordray (2001).

10 Howard (1977, 1981) too was another important scholar to focus on courts of appeals early on.

11 Other early works include, for example, Nagel (1961); Ulmer (1970, 1973); Tate (1972).

12 The author's name is spelled incorrectly on the paper included here. His name is Micheal Giles.

13 This general idea, as I suggest in the text, too flows from work by Murphy (1962), as well Pritchett (1961), both of whom tell a tale of shrewd judges – judges who anticipate the reactions of *other relevant actors* and take those reactions into account in their decision making.

14 I adopt this list from Rosenberg (1992).

15 Rosenberg's work on the Court, like Dahl's, has its share of critics and supporters. For an example of the latter, see McCann (1994). For recent work also critiquing *Brown*, see Klarman (2004); Ogletree (2004); Bell (2004).

16 I adopt the next few sentences from Murphy et al. (2005).

References

Aliotta, Jilda M. (1995), 'Justice O'Connor and the Equal Protection Clause: A Femine Voice?', *Judicature*, **78**, pp. 232–5.

Allen, David W. and Diane E. Wall (1993), 'Role Orientations and Women State Supreme Court Justices', *Judicature*, **77**, pp. 156–65.

Armstrong, Virginia and Charles A. Johnson (1982), 'Certiorari Decisions by the Warren and Burger Courts: Is Cue Theory Time Bound?', *Polity*, **15**, pp. 141–50.

Ashenfelter, Orley, Theodore Eisenberg and Stewart J. Schwab (1995), 'Politics and the Judiciary: The Influence of Judicial Background on Case Outcome', *Journal of Legal Studies*, **24**, pp. 257–81.

Baker, Stewart A. (1984), 'A Practical Guide to Certiorari', *Catholic University Law Review*, **33**, pp. 611–32.

Baum, Lawrence (1979), 'Judicial Demand-Screening and Decisions on the Merits: A Second Look', *American Politics Quarterly*, **7**, pp. 109–19.

Baum, Lawrence (2004), *The Supreme Court*, 8th ed., Washington, D.C.: CQ Press.

Bell, Derrick (2004), *Silent Covenants: Brown v. Board of Education and the Unfulfilled Hopes for Racial Reform*, New York: Oxford University Press.

Berlage, Derick P. (1984), 'Pleas of the Condemned: Should Certiorari Petitions from Death Row Receive Enhanced Access to the Supreme Court?', *New York University Law Review*, **59**, pp. 1120–49.
Bickel, Alexander M. (1962), *The Least Dangerous Branch of Government: The Supreme Court at the Bar of Politics*, Indianapolis: Bobbs-Merrill.
Bork, Robert H. (1971), 'Neutral Principles and Some First Amendment Problems', *Indiana Law Journal*, **47**, pp. 1–35.
Boucher, Robert L. and Jeffrey A. Segal (1995), 'Supreme Court Justices as Strategic Decision Makers: Aggressive Grants and Defensive Denials', *Journal of Politics*, **57**, pp. 824–37.
Brace, Paul and Melinda Gann Hall (1993), 'Integrated Models of Dissent', *Journal of Politics*, **55**, pp. 914–35.
Brace, Paul and Melinda Gann Hall (1997), 'The Interplay of Preferences, Case Facts, Context, and Rules in the Politics of Judicial Choice', *Journal of Politics*, **59**, pp. 1206–31.
Brenner, Saul (1979), 'The New Certiorari Game', *Journal of Politics*, **41**, pp. 649–55.
Brenner, Saul and John F. Krol (1989), 'Strategies in Certiorari Voting on the United States Supreme Court', *Journal of Politics*, **51**, pp. 828–40.
Brudney, James I., Sara Schiavoni and Deborah Jones Merritt (1999), 'Judicial Hostility Toward Labor Unions? Applying the Social Background Model to a Celebrated Concern', *Ohio State Law Journal*, **60**, pp. 1675–771.
Caldeira, Gregory A. and John R. Wright (1988), 'Organized Interests and Agenda Setting in the U.S. Supreme Court', *American Political Science Review*, **82**, pp. 1109–128.
Caldeira, Gregory A. and John R. Wright (1990), 'The Discuss List: Agenda Building in the Supreme Court', *Law & Society Review*, **24**, pp. 807–36.
Caldeira, Gregory A., John R. Wright and Christopher J. Zorn (1999), 'Sophisticated Voting and Gate-Keeping in the Supreme Court', *Journal of Law, Economics, & Organization*, **15**, pp. 549–72.
Cameron, Charles M., Albert D. Cover and Jeffrey A. Segal (1990), 'Senate Voting on Supreme Court Nominees: A Neoinstitutional Model', *American Political Science Review*, **84**, pp. 525–34.
Cameron, Charles M., Jeffrey A. Segal and Donald R. Songer (2000), 'Strategic Auditing in a Political Hierarchy: An Informational Model of the Supreme Courts Certiorari Decisions', *American Political Science Review*, **94**, pp. 101–16.
Casper, Jonathan D. (1976), 'The Supreme Court and National Policy Making', *American Political Science Review*, **70**, pp. 50–63.
Choi, Stephen and Mitu Gulati (2002), 'A Tournament of Judges?', *California Law Review*, **92**, pp. 299–322.
Comment (1941), 'The Attitude of Lower Courts to Changing Precedents', *Yale Law Journal*, **50**, pp. 1448–59.
Cordray, Margaret Meriwether and Richard Cordray (2001), 'The Supreme Court's Plenary Docket', *Washington and Lee Law Review*, **58**, pp. 737–94.
Croly, Steven P. (1995), 'The Majoritarian Difficulty: Elective Judiciaries and the Rule of Law', *University of Chicago Law Review*, **62**, pp. 689–791.
Cross, Frank B. and Emerson H. Tiller (1998), 'Judicial Partisanship and Obedience to Legal Doctrine: Whistleblowing on the Federal Courts of Appeals', *Yale Law Journal*, **107**, pp. 2155–75.
Dahl, Robert A. (1957), 'Decision-Making in a Democracy: The Supreme Court as a National Policymaker', *Journal of Public Law*, **6**, pp. 279–95.
Danelski, David J. (1979), 'The Influence of the Chief Justice in the Decisional Process', in *Courts, Judges, and Politics*, ed. Walter F. Murphy and C. Herman Pritchett. 3rd ed, New York: Random House.
Davis, Richard (2005), *Electing Justice: Fixing the Supreme Court Nomination Process*, New York: Oxford University Press.
Davis, Sue, Susan Haire and Donald R. Songer (1993), 'Voting Behavior and Gender on the U.S. Courts of Appeals', *Judicature*, **77**, pp. 129–33.
Dworkin, Ronald. M. (1977), *Taking Rights Seriously*, Cambridge, MA: Harvard University Press.
Ely, John Hart (1980), *Democracy and Distrust*, Cambridge, MA: Harvard University.
Epstein, Lee and Jack Knight (1998), *The Choices Justices Make*, Washington, D.C.: CQ Press.
Epstein, Lee and Jack Knight (2004), 'Courts and Judges', in *The Blackwell Companion to Law and Society*, ed. Austin Sarat, Malden, MA: Blackwell.

Epstein, Lee, Jack Knight and Andrew D. Martin (2001), 'The Supreme Court as a (Strategic) National Policy Maker', *Emory Law Journal*, **50**, pp. 101–29.
Epstein, Lee, Jeffrey A. Segal, Nancy Staudt and René Lindstadt (2005), 'The Role of Qualifications in the Confirmation of Nominees to the U.S. Supreme Court', *Florida State University Law Review*, forthcoming.
Eskridge, Jr., William N. (1991a), 'Overriding Supreme Court Statutory Interpretation Decisions', *Yale Law Journal*, **101**, pp. 331–417.
Eskridge, Jr., William N. (1991b), 'Reneging on History?: Playing the Court/Congress/President Civil Rights Game', *California Law Review*, **79**, pp. 613–84.
Eskridge, Jr., William N. (1994), *Dynamic Statutory Interpretation*, Cambridge, MA: Harvard University Press.
Estreicher, Samuel and John Sexton (1984), 'A Managerial Theory of the Supreme Court's Responsibilities: An Empirical Study', *New York University Law Review*, **59**, pp. 681–822.
Estreicher, Samuel and John Sexton (1986), *Redefining the Supreme Court's Role*, New Haven: Yale University Press.
Farber, Daniel A. and Suzanna Sherry (1990), *A History of the American Constitution*, St. Paul, MN: West.
Frank, Jerome (1930), *Law and the Modern Mind*, New York: Brentano's.
Frankfurter, Felix (1947), 'Some Reflections on Reading Statutes', *Record of the Association of the Bar of the City of New York*, **2**, pp. 213–37.
Franklin, Charles H. and Liane C. Kosaki (1989), 'Republican Schoolmaster: The U.S. Supreme Court, Public Opinion, and Abortion', *American Political Science Review*, **83**, pp. 751–71.
Galanter, Marc (1974), 'Why the "Haves" Come Out: Speculations on the Limits of Legal Change', *Law & Society Review*, **9**, pp. 950–97.
Garrow, David J. (2000), 'Mental Decreptitude on the U.S. Supreme Court: The Historical Case for a 28th Amendment', *University of Chicago Law Review*, **67**, pp. 995–1087.
Gely, Rafael and Pablo T. Spiller (1990), 'A Rational Choice Theory of Supreme Court Decision Making with Applications to the State Farm and Grove City Cases', *Journal of Law, Economics, & Organization*, **6**, pp. 263–300.
Giles, Michael W. and Thomas G. Walker (1975), 'Judicial Policy-Making and Southern School Desegregation', *Journal of Politics*, **37**, pp. 917–36.
Goldman, Sheldon (1966), 'Voting Behavior on the United States Courts of Appeals, 1961–1964', *American Political Science Review*, **60**, pp. 374–83.
Goldman, Sheldon (1973), 'Conflict on the U.S. Courts of Appeals, 1965–1971: A Quantitative Analysis', *University of Cincinnati Law Review*, **42**, pp. 635–58.
Goldman, Sheldon (1975), 'Voting Behavior on the United States Courts of Appeals Revisited', *American Political Science Review*, **69**, pp. 491–506.
Gruhl, John, Cassia Spolm and Susan Welch (1981), 'Women as Policymakers: The Case of Trial Judges', *American Journal of Political Science*, **25**, pp. 308–22.
Gryski, Gerard S., Eleanor C. Main and William J. Dixon (1986), 'Models of State High Court Decision Making in Sex Discrimination Cases', *Journal of Politics*, **48**, pp. 143–55.
Hall, Melinda Gann (1987a), 'Constituent Influence in State Supreme Court: Conceptual Notes and a Case Study', *Journal of Politics*, **49**, pp. 1117–24.
Hall, Melinda Gann (1987b), 'An Examination of Voting Behavior in the Louisiana Supreme Court', *Judicature*, **71**, pp. 40–46.
Hall, Melinda Gann (1992), 'Electoral Politics and Strategic Voting in State Supreme Court', *Journal of Politics*, **54**, pp. 427–46.
Hall, Melinda Gann and Paul Brace (1992), 'Toward an Integrated Model of Judicial Voting Behavior', *American Politics Quarterly*, **20**, pp. 147–68.
Hammond, Thomas and Jeffrey Hill (1993), 'Deference or Preference: Explaining Senate Confirmation of Presidential Nominees to Administrative Agencies', *Journal of Theoretical Politics*, **5**, pp. 23–59.
Hartnett, Edward A. (2000), 'Questioning Certiorari: Some Reflections Seventy-Five Years after the Judges' Bill', *Columbia Law Review*, **100**, pp. 1643–738.
Hausmaninger, Herbert (1995), 'Towards a "New" Russian Constitutional Court', *Cornell International Law Journal*, **28**, pp. 349–86.

Hellman, Arthur D. (1985), 'Case Selection in the Burger Court: A Preliminary Analysis', *Notre Dame Law Review*, **60**, pp. 947–1050.
Helmke, Gretchen (2002), 'The Logic of Strategic Defection: Court Executive Relations in Argentina Under Dictatorship and Democracy', *American Political Science Review*, **96**, pp. 291–303.
Howard, J. Woodford (1977), 'Role Perceptions and Behavior in Three U.S. Courts of Appeals', *Journal of Politics*, **39**, pp. 916–38.
Howard, J. Woodford (1981), *Courts of Appeals in the Federal Judicial System: A Study of the Second, Fifth, and District of Columbia Circuits*, Princeton, NJ: Princeton University Press.
Johnson, Timothy R. and Andrew D. Martin (1998), 'The Public's Conditional Response to Supreme Court Decisions', *American Political Science Review*, **92**, pp. 299–310.
King, James D. and James W. Riddlesperger (1996), 'Senate Confirmation of Cabinet Nominations: Institutional Politics and Nominee Qualifications', *Social Science Journal*, **33**, pp. 273–85.
Klarman, Michael J. (2004), *From Jim Crow to Civil Rights: The Supreme Court and the Struggle for Racial Equality*, New York: Oxford University Press.
Klein, David and Darby Morrisroe (1999), 'The Prestige and Influence of Individual Judges on the U.S. Courts of Appeals', *Journal of Legal Studies*, **28**, pp. 371–91.
Kort, Fred (1957), 'Predicting Supreme Court Cases Mathematically: Analysis of the Right to Counsel Cases', *American Political Science Review*, **57**, pp. 1–12.
Krol, John F. and Saul Brenner (1990), 'Strategies in Certiorari Voting on the United States Supreme Court', *Western Political Quarterly*, **43**, pp. 335–42.
Krutz, Glen S., Richard Fleisher and Jon R. Bond (1998), 'From Abe Fortas to Zoë Baird: Why Some Presidential Nominations Fail', *American Political Science Review*, **92**, pp. 871–81.
Lawless, Robert M. and Dylan Lager Murray (1997), 'An Empirical Analysis of Bankruptcy Certiorari', *Missouri Law Review*, **62**, pp. 101–34.
Linzer, Peter (1979), 'The Meaning of Certiorari Denials', *Columbia Law Review*, **79**, pp. 1227–600.
Llewellyn, Karl N. (1951), *The Bramble Bush*, New York: Oceana.
Long, Thomas J. (1984), 'Deciding Whether Conflicts with Supreme Court Precedent Warrant Certiorari', *New York University Law Review*, **59**, pp. 1104–19.
Maltzman, Forrest, James F. Spriggs, II and Paul J. Wahlbeck (2000), *Crafting Law on the Supreme Court*, Cambridge: Cambridge University Press.
Maltzman, Forrest and Paul J. Wahlbeck (1996), 'Strategic Policy Considerations and Voting Fluidity on the Burger Court', *American Political Science Review*, **90**, pp. 581–92.
Martinek, Wendy L., Mark Kemper and Steven R. Van Winkle (2002), 'To Advise and Consent: The Senate and Lower Federal Court Nominations, 1977–1998', *Journal of Politics*, **64**, pp. 337–61.
McCann, Michael W. (1994), *Rights at Work*, Chicago: University of Chicago Press.
McGuire, Kevin T. and Gregory A. Caldeira (1993), 'Lawyers, Organized Interests, and the Law of Obscenity: Agenda-Setting in the Supreme Court', *American Political Science Review*, **87**, pp. 717–28.
Merritt, Deborah Jones (2001), 'Stalking Secret Law: What Predicts Publication in the United States Courts of Appeals', *Vanderbilt Law Review*, **54**, pp. 71–121.
Moraski, Brian J. and Charles R. Shipan (1999), 'The Politics of Supreme Court Nominations: A Theory of Institutional Choice and Constraints', *American Journal of Political Science*, **43**, pp. 1069–95.
Murphy, Walter F. (1959), 'Lower Court Checks on Supreme Court Power', *American Political Science Review*, **53**, pp. 1017–31.
Murphy, Walter F. (1962), *Congress and the Court*, Chicago, IL: University of Chicago Press.
Murphy, Walter F. (1964), *Elements of Judicial Strategy*, Chicago, IL: University of Chicago Press.
Murphy, Walter F., C. Herman Pritchett, Lee Epstein and Knight Jack (2005), *Courts, Judges, and Politics*, 6th ed., New York: McGraw-Hill.
Nagel, Stuart S. (1961), 'Political Party Affiliations and Judges' Decisions', *American Political Science Review*, **55**, pp. 843–50.
Nixon, David C. (2001), 'Appointment Delay for Vacancies on the Federal Communications Commission', *Public Administration Review*, **61**, pp. 483–92.
Ogletree, Charles J. (2004), *All Deliberate Speed Reflections on the First Half-Century of Brown v. Board of Education*, New York: Norton.

Oliver, Philip D. (1986), 'Systematic Justice: A Proposed Constitutional Amendment to Establish Fixed, Staggered Terms for Members of the United States Supreme Court', *Ohio State Law Review*, **47**, pp. 799–834.

Palmer, Barbara (2001), 'The "Bermuda Triangle?" The Cert Pool and Its Influence over the Supreme Court's Agenda', *Constitutional Commentary*, **18**, pp. 105–20.

Palmer, Jan (1982), 'An Econometric Analysis of the U.S. Supreme Court's Certiorari Decisions', *Public Choice*, **39**, pp. 387–98.

Perry, H.W. (1991), *Deciding to Decide: Agenda Setting in the United States Supreme Court*, Cambridge, MA: Harvard University Press.

Pinello, Daniel R. (1995), *The Impact of Judicial Selection Method on State Supreme-Court Policy*, Westport, CT: Greenwood.

Posner, Richard A. (1985), *The Federal Courts*, Cambridge, MA: Harvard University Press.

Posner, Richard A. (1993), 'What Do Judges and Justices Maximize? (The Same Thing Everybody Else Does)', *Supreme Court Economic Review*, **3**, pp. 1–41.

Priest, George L. and Benjamin Klein (1984), 'The Selection of Disputes for Litigation', *Journal of Legal Studies*, **13**, pp. 1–55.

Pritchett, C. Herman (1941), 'Divisions of Opinion among Justices of the U.S. Supreme Court', *American Political Science Review*, **35**, pp. 890–98.

Pritchett, C. Herman (1948), *The Roosevelt Court*, New York: Macmillan.

Pritchett, C Herman (1961), *Congress Against the Supreme Court*, Minneapolis, MN: University of Minnesota Press.

Provine, Doris Marie (1980), *Case Selection in the United States Supreme Court*, Chicago: University of Chicago Press.

Revesz, Richard L. (1997), 'Environmental Regulation, Ideology, and the D.C. Circuit', *Virginia Law Review*, **83**, pp. 1717–72.

Rosenberg, Gerald N. (1991), *The Hollow Hope*, Chicago, IL: University of Chicago Press.

Rosenberg, Gerald N. (1992), 'Judicial Independence and the Reality of Political Power', *Review of Politics*, **54**, pp. 369–98.

Rosenberg, Gerald N. (1999), 'African-American Rights After Brown', *Journal of the Supreme Court Historical Society*, **24**, pp. 201–25.

Routh, Stephen R. (2004), 'The Contingency of Senate Consent: A Study of the Determinants of Roll Call Confirmation Voting on Executive Branch Appointments, 1945–1996', *Social Science Journal*, **41**, pp. 67–82.

Scalia, Antonin (1994), 'The Dissenting Opinion', *Journal of Supreme Court History*, **1994**, pp. 33–4.

Schneider, Daniel M. (2001), 'Empirical Research on Judicial Reasoning: Statutory Interpretation in Federal Tax Cases', *New Mexico Law Review*, **31**, pp. 325–51.

Schubert, Glendon (1958), 'The Study of Judicial Decision-Making as an Aspect of Political Behavior', *American Political Science Review*, **52**, pp. 1007–25.

Schubert, Glendon (1959), 'The Certiorari Game', in *Quantitative Analysis of Judicial Behavior*, ed. Glendon Schubert, New York: Free Press.

Schubert, Glendon (1962), 'Policy without Law: An Extension of the Certiorari Game', *Stanford Law Review*, **14**, pp. 284–327.

Schubert, Glendon (1965), *The Judicial Mind: The Attitudes and Ideologies of Supreme Court Justices 1946–1963*, Evanston: Northwestern University Press.

Segal, Jeffrey A. (1984), 'Predicting Supreme Court Decisions Probabilistically: The Search and Seizure Cases', *American Political Science Review*, **78**, pp. 891–900.

Segal, Jeffrey A., Charles M. Cameron and Albert D. Cover (1992), 'A Spatial Model of Roll Call Voting: Senators, Constituents, Presidents, and Interest Groups in Supreme Court Confirmations', *American Journal of Political Science*, **36**, pp. 96–121.

Segal, Jeffrey A., Charles M. Cameron and Donald R. Songer (1995), 'Decision Making on the U.S. Courts of Appeals', in *Contemplating Courts*, ed. Lee Epstein, Washington, D.C.: CQ Press.

Segal, Jeffrey A. and Harold J. Spaeth (1993), *The Supreme Court and the Attitudinal Model*, New York: Cambridge University Press.

Segal, Jeffrey A. and Harold J. Spaeth (2002), *The Supreme Court and the Attitudinal Model Revisited*, New York: Cambridge University Press.
Segal, Jennifer A. (1997), 'The Decision Making of Clinton's Nontraditional Judicial Appointees', *Judicature*, **80**, p. 279.
Sheehan, Reginald S. and William Mishler (1992), 'Who Wins on Appeal? Upperdogs and Underdogs in the United States Courts of Appeals', *American Political Science Review*, **36**, pp. 235–58.
Sherry, Suzanna (1986), 'Civic Virtue and the Feminine Voice in Constitutional Adjudication', *Virginia Law Review*, **72**, pp. 543–616.
Sisk, Gregory C., Michael Heise and Andrew P. Morriss (1998), 'Charting the Influences on the Judicial Mind: An Empirical Study of Judicial Reasoning' *New York University Law Review*, **73**, pp. 1377–500.
Smith, Kevin H. (1999), 'Justice for All? The Supreme Court's Denial of Pro Se Petitions for Certiorari', *Albany Law Review*, **63**, pp. 381–425.
Smith, Steven S., Jason M. Roberts and Ryan Vander Wielen (2003), *The American Congress*, Boston, MA: Houghton Mifflin.
Songer, Donald R. (1979), 'Concern for Policy Outputs as a Cue for Supreme Court Decisions on Certiorari', *Journal of Politics*, **41**, pp. 1185–94.
Songer, Donald R., Jeffrey A. Segal and Charles M. Cameron (1994), 'The Hierarchy of Justice: Testing a Principal-Agent Theory of Supreme Court-Circuit Court Interactions', *Journal of Politics*, **38**, pp. 673–96.
Songer, Donald R., Sue Davis and Susan Haire (1994), 'A Reappraisal of Diversification in the Federal Courts: Gender Effects in the Courts of Appeals', *Journal of Politics*, **56**, pp. 425–539.
Spiller, Pablo T. and Rafael Gely (1992), 'Congressional Control of Judicial Independence: The Determinants of U.S. Supreme Court Labor-Relations Decisions, 1949–1988', *RAND Journal of Economics*, **23**, pp. 463–92.
Spriggs, II, James F. and Paul J. Wahlbeck (1995), 'Calling it Quits: Strategic Retirement on the Federal Courts of Appeals', *Political Research Quarterly*, **48**, pp. 573–97.
Sturley, Michael F. (1989), 'Observations on the Supreme Court's Certiorari Jurisdiction in Intercircuit Conflict Cases', *Texas Law Review*, **67**, pp. 1268–75.
Sunstein, Cass R., David Schkade and Lisa Michelle Ellman (2004), 'Ideological Voting on Federal Courts of Appeals: A Preliminary Investigation', *Virginia Law Review*, **90**, pp. 301–54.
Tabarrok, Alexander and Eric Helland (1999), 'Court Politics: The Political Economy of Tort Awards', *Journal of Law & Economics*, **42**, pp. 157–87.
Tanenhaus, Joseph et al. (1963), 'The Supreme Court's Certiorari Jurisdiction: Cue Theory', in *Judicial Decision Making*, New York: Free Press.
Tate, C. Neal (1972), 'Social Background and Voting Behavior in the Philippine Supreme Court, 1901–1968', *Lawasia*, **3**, pp. 317–38.
Tate, C. Neal (1981), 'Personal Attribute Models of Voting Behavior of U.S. Supreme Court Justices', *American Political Science Review*, **75**, pp. 355–67.
Tate, C. Neal and Roger Handberg (1991), 'Time Binding and Theory Building in Personal Attribute Models of Supreme Court Voting Behavior, 1916–88', *American Journal of Political Science*, **35**, pp. 460–80.
Teger, Stuart and Stuart Kosinski (1980), 'The Cue Theory of Supreme Court Certiorari Jurisdiction: Further Consideration of Cue Theory', *Journal of Politics*, **42**, pp. 834–46.
Tiberi, Todd J. (1993), 'Supreme Court Denials of Certiorari in Conflict Cases: Percolation or Procrastination?', *University of Pittsburgh Law Review*, **54**, pp. 861–92.
Tiller, Emerson H. and Frank B. Cross (1999), 'A Modest Proposal for Improving American Justice', *Columbia Law Review*, **99**, pp. 215–34.
Ulmer, S. Sidney (1970), 'Dissent Behavior and the Social Background of Supreme Court Justices', *Journal of Politics*, **32**, pp. 580–98.
Ulmer, S. Sidney (1972), 'The Decisions to Grant Certiorari as an Indicator to Decision On the Merits', *Polity*, **4**, pp. 429–47.
Ulmer, S. Sidney (1973), 'Social Background as an Indicator to the Votes of Supreme Court Justices in Criminal Cases', *American Journal of Political Science*, **17**, pp. 622–30.

Ulmer, S. Sidney (1983), 'Conflict with Supreme Court Precedents and the Granting of Plenary Review', *Journal of Politics*, **45**, pp. 474–8.
Ulmer, S. Sidney (1984), 'The Supreme Court's Certiorari Decisions: Conflict as a Predictive Variable', *American Political Science Review*, **78**, pp. 901–11.
Ulmer, S. Sidney (1986), 'Are Social Background Models Time-Bound?', *American Political Science Review*, **80**, pp. 957–68.
Ulmer, S. Sidney, William Hintze and Lois Kirklosky (1972), 'The Decision to Grant or Deny Certiorari: Further Considerations on Cue Theory', *Law & Society Review*, **7**, pp. 637–50.
Vanberg, Georg (1998), 'Abstract Judicial Review, Legislative Bargaining, and Policy Compromise', *Journal of Theoretical Politics*, **10**, pp. 299–326.
Vines, Kenneth N. (1962), 'Political Functions on a State Supreme Court', in *Tulane Studies in Political Science: Studies in Judicial Politics*, ed. Kenneth N. Vines and Herbert Jacob, Vol. 8, New Orleans: Milane University.
Walker, Thomas G. and Deborah J. Barrow (1985), 'The Diversification of the Federal Bench: Policy and Process Ramifications', *Journal of Politics*, **47**, pp. 596–617.
Walker, Thomas G., Lee Epstein and William J. Dixon (1988), 'On the Mysterious Demise of Consensual Norms in the United States Supreme Court', *Journal of Politics*, **50**, pp. 361–89.
Watson, Richard A. and Rondal G. Downing (1969), *The Politics of Bench and Bar: Judicial Selection under the Missouri Nonpartisan Court Plan*, New York: Wiley.
Wechsler, Herbert (1959), 'Toward Neutral Principles of Constitutional Law', *Harvard Law Review*, **73**, pp. 1–35.

Part I
The Selection and Retention of Judges

[1]

SENATE VOTING ON SUPREME COURT NOMINEES: A NEOINSTITUTIONAL MODEL

CHARLES M. CAMERON
Princeton University
ALBERT D. COVER
JEFFREY A. SEGAL
State University of New York
Stony Brook

We develop and test a neoinstitutional model of Senate roll call voting on nominees to the Supreme Court. The statistical model assumes that Senators examine the characteristics of nominees and use their roll call votes to establish an electorally attractive position on the nominees. The model is tested with probit estimates on the 2,054 confirmation votes from Earl Warren to Anthony Kennedy. The model performs remarkably well in predicting the individual votes of Senators to confirm or reject nominees. Senators routinely vote to confirm nominees who are perceived as well qualified and ideologically proximate to Senators' constituents. When nominees are less well qualified and are relatively distant, however, Senators' votes depend to a large degree on the political environment, especially the status of the president.

Roll call voting in the U.S. Senate on nominees to the Supreme Court presents political scientists with an empirical puzzle and a theoretical challenge. The empirical puzzle stems from a curious pattern in the nomination politics of recent decades. In some cases, as shown in Table 1, the Senate routinely confirms the nominee. In these cases, liberal senators vote for conservative nominees and conservative senators vote for liberal nominees. For example, the most liberal members of the Senate recently voted to confirm judicial conservative Antonin Scalia. But on other occasions—including 9 of the 20 post-*Brown*-v.-*Board of Education* confirmations (see Songer 1979)—the confirmation becomes extremely contentious. In these cases many or even most senators vote against the nominee, and voting becomes ideologically polarized. The recent rejection of Robert Bork illustrates this case.

We therefore face some puzzling questions: Why are some votes consensual? Why are some votes contentious? And what determines voting decisions in both cases? Satisfactory answers to these questions must explain the apparent switching process between the consensual and conflictual votes and the variance within the conflictual votes.

Satisfactory analysis of roll call voting on Supreme Court nominees must do more than solve an empirical puzzle, however. It must also respond to the theoretical challenge raised by the "new institutional" approach to congressional policy making (McCubbins and Sullivan 1987).

The political science literature abounds with historical studies (Abraham 1974;

American Political Science Review Vol. 84

Table 1. Nominee Margin and Vote Status

Nominee	Year	President's Status[a]	Margin	Vote[b]
Warren	1954	strong	96–0[c]	consensual
Harlan	1955	weak	71–11	conflictual
Brennan	1957	weak	95–0[c]	consensual
Whittaker	1957	weak	96–0	consensual
Stewart	1959	weak	70–17	conflictual
White	1962	strong	100–0[c]	consensual
Goldberg	1962	strong	100–0[c]	consensual
Fortas 1	1965	strong	100–0[c]	consensual
Marshall	1967	strong	69–11	conflictual
Fortas 2	1968	weak	45–43[d]	conflictual
Burger	1969	weak	74–3	consensual
Haynsworth	1969	weak	45–55	conflictual
Carswell	1970	weak	45–51	conflictual
Blackmun	1970	weak	94–0	consensual
Powell	1971	weak	89–1	consensual
Rehnquist 1	1971	weak	68–26	conflictual
Stevens	1975	weak	98–0	consensual
O'Connor	1981	strong	99–0	consensual
Rehnquist 2	1986	strong	65–33	conflictual
Scalia	1986	strong	98–0	consensual
Bork	1987	weak	42–58	conflictual
Kennedy	1988	weak	97–0	consensual

[a]The president is labeled "strong" in a non-election year in which the president's party controls the Senate and "weak" otherwise.

[b]A vote is labeled "conflictual" when less than 90% of the votes cast are cast on the winning side and "consensual" otherwise.

[c]Voice vote.

[d]Vote on cloture—failed to receive necessary two-thirds majority.

Blaustein and Mersky 1978; Cole 1934; Danelski 1964; Friedman 1983; Grossman and Wasby 1972; Harris 1953; McHargue 1949; Schmidhauser 1979; Scigliano 1971; and Warren 1923) and statistical studies (Palmer 1983; Segal 1987) of Senate confirmation of Supreme Court justices. Few studies, however, address the puzzle of confirmation voting directly in terms of the roll call votes of individual senators over many confirmation votes. In fact, only three studies begin to address the puzzle at all (Felice and Weisberg 1988–89; Rohde and Spaeth 1976; Songer 1979). These studies all find evidence that the ideology of *senators* plays a role in controversial votes. By running separate models for each nominee, however, they are unable to determine to what extent the ideology or qualifications of the *nominee* affects opposition. Further, because they restrict their attention to controversial votes, they cannot explain why some votes are controversial while others are not. Songer's declaration remains true: "There have been no systematic explanations why a majority of nominations remain essentially noncontroversial" (1979, 929). Moreover, no analysis of confirmation voting has yet employed insights from the new institutionalism. In short, the empirical puzzle remains a mystery and the theoretical challenge has been left unanswered.

First, we discuss institutional issues in confirmation voting. Second, based on

Voting on Supreme Court Nominees

this analysis, we develop a spatial model of roll call voting on confirmations. Using newly generated data on nominees, we then test the theoretical model.

A Neoinstitutional Perspective on Confirmation Voting

A neoinstitutionalist perspective suggests that votes on Supreme Court nominations depend on (1) the goals the senator pursues during the confirmation process, (2) the choices confronting the senator at each stage during the sequence of votes (or "agenda") leading to a filled vacancy on the Court, (3) the foresight the senator exercises in moving from one stage to the next in a multistage agenda, and (4) the payoffs the senator receives as a consequence of his or her choices (for related references, see Krehbiel 1988).

With respect to motivation, we imagine senators asking themselves, "Can I use my actions during the confirmation process to gain electoral advantage? Or if I am forced to account for my votes, can they be used against me? What is the most electorally expedient action for me to have taken?" Hence, we follow Mayhew (1974), Fenno (1978), and Fiorina (1974) in analyzing how the prospect of explaining behavior in Washington influences the behavior of representatives. We recognize (as did Mayhew, Fenno, and Fiorina) that senators often have additional goals in mind as they make highly visible decisions. Among these goals may be furthering a vision of good public policy and enhancing power and prestige within the Senate (Dodd 1985; Fenno 1973; Kingdon 1981). But a narrower focus on the electoral connection often captures much of the motivation of senators, provides a useful base line for more complex models, and offers an attractive, direct path to the statistical analysis of confirmation roll call voting.

In light of the electoral connection, a senator is likely to view roll call voting as an opportunity for position taking and credit claiming. The senator can generally expect to gain electorally (or at least not to lose electorally) from voting as constituents wish and can expect to incur losses from flouting constituents' desires, regardless of the actual outcome of a vote. In addition, to the extent that the senator's vote actually sways the outcome, the senator may claim credit for a good outcome or receive blame for a bad one (Mayhew 1974; Weaver 1986).

Position taking and credit claiming must take place within the agenda of voting opportunities offered during the confirmation process. This agenda operates fairly simply: First, the president nominates a candidate; the Senate then votes on this candidate. If the nominee is approved, the process ends. If the nominee is rejected, the president nominates another candidate and the Senate votes on this candidate. The process continues until the seat is filled. In the twentieth century, the process has never proceeded past three votes and rarely past two.

As this agenda involves a potential series of votes, strategic voting is a possibility. For example, in an early stage of the agenda a senator might vote against a nominee constituents actually favor in order to create the opportunity to vote for an even better nominee at a later stage. Or a senator might vote for a nominee constituents oppose to block the confirmation of an even worse subsequent nominee.

Because strategic voting requires misrepresenting one's true motivation, it can present difficulties for senators compelled to explain roll call votes to their electorate. Under most circumstances, better chances for position taking and credit claiming result from what Denzau, Riker, and Shepsle (1985) call rationally nonstrategic behavior, that is, apparently sincere voting. We have suggested elsewhere (Cameron, Cover, and Segal 1989) that rationally nonstrategic voting is almost always a better choice for senators than strategic voting when casting roll call votes on nominees to the Supreme Court.

The presence of strategic voting presents major problems for regression-based approaches to roll call voting (Krehbiel and Rivers 1985, 1988). On the other hand, rationally nonstrategic voting is observationally indistinguishable from sincere voting. A statistical analysis of roll call voting in confirmation politics can therefore proceed in a straightforward way.

A Spatial Model of Confirmation Voting

What factors would electorally minded senators care about when judging the merits of Supreme Court nominees? Both the public record and common sense suggest that the public's principal concerns in nomination politics (whenever that concern becomes manifest) are the characteristics of nominees. Two characteristics in particular receive close scrutiny in hearings and in the press: (1) the nominee's professional competence and (2) the nominee's judicial philosophy. The importance of high qualifications is exemplified by the universal ridicule heaped on Senator Roman Hruska's defense of Judge G. Harold Carswell's manifest mediocrity: "Even if he [Carswell] were mediocre, there are a lot of mediocre judges and people and lawyers. They are entitled to a little representation, aren't they, and a little chance" (Baum 1981, 47). The importance of judicial philosophy is suggested by the attacks by liberals on judicial conservative Robert Bork and those by conservatives on judicial liberals Thurgood Marshall and Abe Fortas. Ideologically proximate nominees will be attractive, poorly qualified nominees unattractive, and nominees who are both ideologically distant and poorly qualified very unattractive.

In addition, the president is not a passive bystander but an active participant in the nomination process. The president has nominated a particular person to satisfy his own constituents and possibly to further his own policy objectives. Failure to send the confirmation through the Senate harms the president's prestige, his reputation for competence, and possibly his popularity and his ability to govern (Neustadt 1960; Ostrom and Simon 1985). Therefore, the president is likely to bring his political resources to bear to help his nominee. In general, the president will have more political resources to deploy—and can deploy his political resources more effectively—when his party controls the Senate and when he is not in the fourth year of his term. In addition, presidential resources are not likely to affect every senator the same way. First, the president's resources will probably carry greater impact on members of his own party. Second, presidential resources are much more likely to change a senator's votes when the senator is more or less undecided on the basis of the nominee's characteristics.

Ideology can be considered a spatial characteristic; nominee qualifications and the strength of the president are nonspatial or valence characteristics of a nominee; party status is a nonspatial characteristic of a senator. Hence, define five variables, I_j, X_{ij}, U_j, S_j, and P_{ij}. I_j is a measure of nominee j's ideology, ranging from zero (a very conservative nominee) to one (a very liberal nominee). X_{ij} measures the ideal or desired ideology for nominees held by senator i's constituents at the time of nominee j, as perceived by senator i. U_j measures nominee j's (lack of) qualifications, ranging from zero (highly qualified) to one (poorly qualified). S_j and P_{ij} measure, respectively, whether the president is strong at the time of nominee j (i.e., whether the president's party controls the Senate in a nonelection year) and whether senator i is from the

Voting on Supreme Court Nominees

same party as the president at the time of nominee j.

Slightly modifying a well-known spatial model incorporating both spatial distance and valence dimensions (Enelow and Hinich 1982; Enelow and Hinich 1984, secs. 5.1–2), senator i votes for nominee j if

$$U_j + \|I_j - X_{ij}\|^2 + U_j \cdot \|I_j - X_{ij}\|^2 - S_j - P_{ij} < D_{ij^*}, \quad (1)$$

where D_{ij^*} is the "critical distance" or value separating acceptable from unacceptable nominees and $\|I_j - X_{ij}\|^2$ is the simple squared Euclidean distance, in this case just $(I_j - X_{ij})^2$. (See Cameron, Cover, and Segal 1989 for formal definitions of "acceptable" and "unacceptable" nominees.) The inclusion of an interaction term between distance and lack of qualifications, suggesting that nominees who are both ideologically distant and poorly qualified are very unattractive to senators, follows familiar precedent in spatial models (Enelow, Hinich, and Mendell 1986).

Assume the critical distance for senator i, D_{ij^*} has two components, namely, $D_{ij^*} = \delta^* + \epsilon_{ij}$ where δ^* is a distance or value common to all senators over all nominations and ϵ_{ij} is an unobservable distance specific to each senator for each nomination. Then equation 1 can be rewritten as

$$U_j + \|I_j - X_{ij}\|^2 + U_j \cdot \|I_j - X_{ij}\|^2 - S_j - P_{ij} - \delta^* < \epsilon_{ij}. \quad (2)$$

If ϵ_{ij} is normally distributed with zero mean and variance σ^2, equation 2 may be estimated as a probit equation, to wit,

$$P(V_{ij} = 1) = \Phi(\alpha_0 + \alpha_1 U_j + \alpha_2 D_{ij} + \alpha_3 U_j \cdot D_{ij} + \alpha_4 S_j + \alpha_5 P_{ij}),$$

where $D_{ij} = |I_j - X_{ij}|^2$ and Φ is the cumulative normal probability density function.

Presidential influence may appear to enter the model linearly; but because the probit model is intrinsically nonlinear, presidential influence has a much greater impact on senators near $P(V_{ij} = 1) = .5$ than $= .0$ or 1.0, as indicated earlier.

Data

The dependent variable consists of the 2,054 confirmation votes cast by senators from the nomination of Earl Warren to the nomination of Anthony Kennedy.

To determine perceptions of nominees' qualifications and judicial philosophy we conducted a content analysis from a source that contains comparable information on each nominee since Earl Warren, statements from newspaper editorials from the time of the nomination by the president until the vote by the Senate. We selected four of the nation's leading papers, two with a liberal stance (the *New York Times* and the *Washington Post*) and two with a more conservative outlook (the *Chicago Tribune* and the *Los Angeles Times*). We note here that the data are reliable and appear to be valid.[1] Table 2 displays the ideology and qualification scores for the nominees from Earl Warren to Anthony Kennedy.

The spatial model requires a measure of senators' ideal points. Moreover, if the distance metric is to be meaningful, this measure must be comparable with that of the nominees. In the absence of a direct measure of the perceived preference of senators' constituencies about nominees' judicial philosophy, we have developed an inferential measure using senators' liberalism ratings calculated by the Americans for Democratic Action (ADA). The method we employ is based on the theory of predictive mappings in the spatial theory of voting and has been discussed at some length elsewhere (Cameron, Cover, and Segal 1989).[2]

We define a dummy variable S

American Political Science Review Vol. 84

("strong") which takes the value one when the president's party controls the Senate and the president is not in the fourth year of his term, zero otherwise. We define a dummy variable P ("party") which takes the value one when a senator is of the same party as the president, zero otherwise.

Table 3 provides summary statistics on the variables used in the model.

Table 2. Nominee Ideology and Qualification Scores

Nominee	Ideology	Qualifications
Warren	.75	.74
Harlan	.88	.86
Brennan	1.00	1.00
Whittaker	.50	1.00
Stewart	.75	1.00
White	.50	.50
Goldberg	.75	.92
Fortas 1	1.00	1.00
Marshall	1.00	.84
Fortas 2	.85	.64
Burger	.12	.96
Haynsworth	.16	.34
Carswell	.04	.11
Blackmun	.12	.97
Powell	.17	1.00
Rehnquist 1	.05	.89
Stevens	.25	.96
O'Connor	.48	1.00
Rehnquist 2	.05	.40
Scalia	.00	1.00
Bork	.10	.79
Kennedy	.37	.89

Note: .00 is the most conservative and 1.00 the most liberal score possible. .00 is the least qualified and 1.00 the most qualified score possible.

Results

The maximum likelihood estimates of the coefficients in our model may be summarized succinctly:[3]

$$P(V_{ij} = 1) = \Phi\,[\underset{(15.31)}{1.80} - \underset{(-4.44)}{1.20U_j} - \underset{(-4.50)}{1.19D_{ij}} - \underset{(-9.80)}{9.97U_j{\cdot}D_{ij}} + \underset{(8.97)}{1.39S_j} + \underset{(6.50)}{.74P_{ij}}]^3 \quad (3)$$

(MLE's/SE's are in parentheses; χ^2 = 985.9; estimated R^2 = .746; percentage correct = 93.0; and percentage improvement = 53.5.)

As the estimates in equation 3 indicate, the overall fit of the model is extremely good: the χ^2 is significant at $p < .001$; the proportion of votes explained correctly by the probit equation is 93%; the pseudo-R^2 for the equation is approximately .75; and the percentage improvement in predicted votes over the margin is a little over 53%. All of the estimated coefficients take the predicted sign, are significant at $p < .001$ or greater, and are of reasonable magnitudes.

As the results indicate, confirmation voting is decisively affected by the ideological distance between senators and nominees. Equally important, as indicated by the virtually identical parameter estimates on the U and D terms, are the qualifications of the nominee. Overwhelmingly, however, it is the interaction

Table 3. Dependent and Independent Variables

Variable	Mean	Variance	Minimum	Maximum
Vote	.850	.123	.00	1.00
Squared Euclidean distance (D)	.243	.070	.00	1.00
Lack of qualifications, 1 − Q (U)	.195	.063	.00	.89
Strong president (S)	.372	.234	.00	1.00
Same party status (P)	.500	.250	.00	1.00
Distance × lack of qualifications (UD)	.045	.011	.00	.89

Voting on Supreme Court Nominees

Table 4. Examples of Voting Probabilities

	Lack of Qualification (0 = most qualified, 1 = most unqualified)										
Ideological distance	.0	.1	.2	.3	.4	.5	.6	.7	.8	.9	1.0
.0	.96	.95	.94	.93	.91	.88	.86	.83	.80	.76	.73
.1	.95	.93	.89	.85	.79	.72	.64	.56	.47	.38	.30
.2	.94	.89	.82	.73	.61	.52	.36	.26	.14	.10	.05
.3	.93	.85	.73	.58	.41	.26	.14	.07	.03	.01	—
.4	.91	.79	.61	.41	.23	.10	.04	.01	—	—	—
.5	.89	.72	.51	.26	.10	.03	.01	—	—	—	—
.6	.86	.64	.36	.14	.04	.01	—	—	—	—	—
.7	.83	.56	.26	.07	.01	—	—	—	—	—	—
.8	.80	.47	.14	.03	—	—	—	—	—	—	—
.9	.77	.39	.10	.01	—	—	—	—	—	—	—
1.0	.73	.31	.05	—	—	—	—	—	—	—	—

Note: Examples assume a weak president and a Senator not of the president's party.

of qualifications and ideology that determines the votes of senators.

As probit estimates are not readily interpretable in terms of probabilities, we provide in Table 4 examples of voting probabilities for varying levels of ideological distance and qualifications. Senators, even opposition senators serving with a weak president, will vote for a poorly qualified nominee if the nominee is ideologically close (e.g., Southern Democrats for Clement Haynsworth). They will vote for an ideologically distant nominee if the nominee is highly qualified (e.g., liberal Democrats for Anthony Kennedy). Ideological distance, however, becomes paramount for nominees with even moderate questions concerning their qualifications. Alternatively, we could say that qualifications become paramount for nominees of even moderate ideological distance from senators.

Additionally, presidential influence and same party status have a powerful impact on voting probabilities, especially for senators who remain undecided after examining the characteristics of the nominee. For example, in the model a switch from a weak to a strong president raises to .92 the probability of a *yes* vote from a senator who was previously undecided. Similarly, same party status raises the probability of a *yes* vote from .5 to .78.

In order to solve the puzzle of confirmation voting, a model must not only explain individual votes but also correctly distinguish consensual from conflictual votes. In the sample of 22 votes, 13 are consensual and 9 are conflictual. As shown in Table 5, the model correctly identifies all of the consensual votes. It is almost as successful in identifying the conflictual votes; 7 of the 9 conflictual votes are correctly identified (78%). It fails to identify the Stewart and Marshall confirmations as conflictual; in these confirmations a group of conservative southern senators voted against the nominees. The model fails to capture the source of the senators' (apparently race-related) opposition.

The model must also account for variance in voting. A useful summary measure of the success of the model in accounting for the variation in the votes is mean absolute error. On average the model misidentifies only five votes per confirmation. Within the consensual

American Political Science Review Vol. 84

Table 5. Actual Versus Predicted *No* Votes

Nominee	Actual	Predicted
Warren	0	0
Harlan	11	25
Brennan	0	0
Whittaker	0	0
Stewart	17	0
White	0	0
Goldberg	0	0
Fortas 1	0	0
Marshall	11	0
Fortas 2	43	36
Burger	3	0
Haynsworth	55	46
Carswell	51	53
Blackmun	0	0
Powell	1	0
Rehnquist 1	26	13
Stevens	0	0
O'Connor	0	0
Rehnquist 2	33	35
Scalia	0	0
Bork	58	29
Kennedy	0	0

Note: Mean absolute error for all votes = 4.9; for consensual votes = .2; for conflictual votes = 11.6; r actual versus predicted = .91.

votes, however, the mean absolute error is almost zero. Within the conflictual votes, the mean absolute error is higher—11–12 votes. The correlation between actual and predicted *no* votes is .91.[4]

Gauging the success of the model in terms of confirmation outcomes is not a straightforward task. The vote on the Fortas nomination as chief justice was 45 *yea* and 43 *nay*, but this majority was insufficient to invoke cloture, so the nomination was defeated. Even under current rules, it is reasonable to presume that no nominee will pass with more than the 43 "nays" received by Fortas. (In fact, no nominee this century has been confirmed with more than 33 negative votes.) If we use 43 as the number of negative votes needed to ensure defeat, the model correctly predicts the outcome of every nomination except Bork's and Fortas'.

Conclusion

The model resolves the puzzle of confirmation voting straightforwardly. When a strong president nominates a highly qualified, ideologically moderate candidate, the nominee passes the Senate in a lopsided, consensual vote. Presidents have often nominated this type of candidate and consequently consensual votes have been fairly common. When presidents nominate a less well qualified, ideologically extreme candidate, especially when the president is in a weak position, then a conflictual vote is likely. Surprisingly, presidents have nominated quite a few candidates of this description, and conflictual votes occur periodically. In short, the behavior of senators emerges as sensible, predictable, and readily understandable; the real source of the puzzle in confirmation voting appears to be the behavior of presidents in choosing nominees.

Learning more about confirmation voting requires moving beyond our simple model of position taking. First, the framework assumes senators are "single-minded seekers of reelection," but we know this is not so. A more appealing framework would allow senators to trade off among competing goals in their roll call votes. In particular, to what extent do senators follow the (presumptive) desires of their constituents in confirmation votes, and to what extent do they "shirk" by voting their personal preferences? Second, future research might find it worthwhile to examine the role of interest groups in the nomination process. Finally, much more attention needs to be given to presidential selection of nominees.

In essence, we are suggesting the need to take a much more inclusive view of the nomination process. But an important issue then comes to the fore: What is properly exogenous and what is properly endogenous in the theory and models? For example, we treat the nominees' ideolo-

Voting on Supreme Court Nominees

gies and qualifications as exogenous, but presidents presumably pick their nominees with the Senate's composition at least partly in mind. In addition, public perceptions of quality and ideology could be regarded as endogenous if interested parties can affect those perceptions. And any attempt to model interest group mobilization must confront the fact that their mobilization results from calculations by the groups and therefore must be regarded as endogenous as well. Solving these problems is likely to be the major challenge facing future analysts of confirmation voting and nomination politics more generally.

Notes

We thank Renee Adwar, Yen Giang, and Regina Stephanie Good for research assistance. James M. Enelow provided many helpful and timely suggestions. This material is based upon research supported by the National Science Foundation under grant no. SES-8812935.

1. We have discussed details of the content analysis elsewhere (Cameron, Cover, and Segal 1989). The measures of ideology and qualification pass standard criteria for intercoder reliability; using π as our index (see Krippendorff 1980), results of .72 for ideology and .87 for qualifications were achieved. Both figures are significant at $p < .001$. The ideology measure also passes the most stringent measure for validity, predictive validity. For confirmed nominees this measure is highly correlated with later votes on the Court dealing with civil rights and civil liberties (Segal and Cover 1989).

2. Tests reported in Cameron, Cover, and Segal 1989 indicate that the ideal points of senators can be measured on the same metric as nominee ideology scores. Our estimates are virtually unchanged if, following Wright and Berkman (1986), we use predicted, rather than actual, ADA scores. See n. 3.

3. Using predicted rather than actual ADA scores to determine D_{ij} yields

$$P(V_{ij} = 1) = \Phi\,[\underset{(16.39)}{1.56} - \underset{(-7.84)}{1.67U_j} - \underset{(-4.19)}{1.20D_{ij}} - \underset{(-6.42)}{5.85U_j \cdot D_{ij}} + \underset{(8.65)}{.99S_j} + \underset{(4.55)}{.42P_{ij}}].$$

4. The model does not include dummy variables for individual nominees. Inclusion of such dummy variables drives the mean absolute errors to very low levels even in the conflictual votes and considerably improves prediction of outcomes. However, the substantive interpretation of these "black box" factors is not very clear and prevents predicting out of sample.

References

Abraham, Henry. 1974. *Justices and Presidents.* New York: Oxford University Press.

Baum, Lawrence. 1981. *The Supreme Court.* Washington: Congressional Quarterly.

Blaustein, Albert P., and Roy M. Mersky. 1978. *The First One Hundred Justices.* Hamden, CT: Anchor Books.

Cameron, Charles, Albert Cover, and Jeffrey Segal. 1989. "The Puzzle of Roll Call Voting on Supreme Court Nominees: A Neoinstitutional Analysis." Presented at the annual meeting of the Midwest Political Science Association, Chicago.

Cole, Kenneth C. 1934. "The Role of the Senate in Confirmation of Judicial Nominations." *American Political Science Review* 28:875–94.

Danelski, David J. 1964. *A Supreme Court Justice Is Appointed.* New York: Random House.

Denzau, Arthur, William Riker, and Kenneth Shepsle. 1985. "Farquharson and Fenno: Sophisticated Voting and Home Style." *American Political Science Review* 79:1117–34.

Dodd, Lawrence C. 1985. "Congress and the Quest for Power." In *Studies of Congress,* ed. Glenn R. Parker. Washington: Congressional Quarterly.

Enelow, James M., and Melvin J. Hinich. 1982. "Nonspatial Candidate Characteristics and Electoral Competition." *Journal of Politics* 44: 115–30.

Enelow, James M., and Melvin J. Hinich. 1984. *The Spatial Theory of Voting: An Introduction.* New York: Cambridge University Press.

Enelow, James M., Melvin J. Hinich, and Nancy Mendell. 1986. "An Empirical Evaluation of Alternate Spatial Models of Elections." *Journal of Politics* 48:675–93.

Felice, John D., and Herbert F. Weisberg. 1988–89. "The Changing Importance of Ideology, Party, and Region in Confirmation of Supreme Court Nominees, 1953–88." *Kentucky Law Journal* 77: 509–31.

Fenno, Richard. 1973. *Congressmen in Committees.* Boston: Little, Brown.

Fenno, Richard. 1978. *Home Style: House Members in Their Districts.* Boston: Little, Brown.

Fiorina, Morris P. 1974. *Representatives, Roll Calls, and Constituencies.* Lexington, MA: D. C. Heath.

Friedman, Richard D. 1983. "The Transformation in Senate Response to Supreme Court Nominations: From Reconstruction to the Taft Administration and Beyond." *Cardozo Law Review* 5:1–95.

American Political Science Review Vol. 84

Grossman, Joel B., and Stephen L. Wasby. 1972. "The Senate and Supreme Court Nominations: Some Reflections." *Duke Law Journal* 1972: 557–91.

Harris, Joseph P. 1953. *The Advice and Consent of the Senate*. Berkeley: University of California Press.

Kingdon, John W. 1981. *Congressmen's Voting Decisions*. 2d ed. New York: Harper & Row.

Krehbiel, Keith. 1988. "Spatial Models of Legislative Choice." *Legislative Studies Quarterly* 13: 259–321.

Krehbiel, Keith, and Douglas Rivers. 1985. "Congressional Roll Call Voting Strategies: Applications of a New Test to Minimum Wage Legislation." Presented at the annual meeting of the American Political Science Association, New Orleans.

Krehbiel, Keith, and Douglas Rivers. 1988. "The Analysis of Committee Power: An Application to Senate Voting on the Minimum Wage." *American Journal of Political Science* 32:1151–74.

Krippendorff, Klaus. 1980. *Content Analysis*. Beverly Hills: Sage.

McCubbins, Mathew D., and Terry Sullivan, eds. 1987. *Congress: Structure and Policy*. Cambridge: Cambridge University Press.

McHargue, Daniel. 1949. "Appointments to the Supreme Court of the United States: The Factors That Have Affected Appointments, 1789–1932." Ph.D. diss. University of California, Los Angeles.

Mayhew, David. 1974. *Congress: The Electoral Connection*. New Haven: Yale University Press.

Neustadt, Richard E. 1960. *Presidential Power: The Politics of Leadership*. New York: John Wiley.

Ostrom, Charles W., Jr., and Dennis M. Simon. 1985. "Promise and Performance: A Dynamic Model of Presidential Popularity." *American Political Science Review* 79:334–58.

Palmer, Jan. 1983. "Senate Confirmation of Appointments to the U.S. Supreme Court." *Review of Social Economy* 41:152–62.

Rohde, David, and Harold Spaeth. 1976. *Supreme Court Decision Making*. San Francisco: W. H. Freeman.

Schmidhauser, John R. 1979. *Judges and Justices*. Boston: Little, Brown.

Scigliano, Robert. 1971. *The Supreme Court and the Presidency*. New York: Free Press.

Segal, Jeffrey A. 1987. "Senate Confirmation of Supreme Court Justices: Partisan and Institutional Politics." *Journal of Politics* 49:998–1015.

Segal, Jeffrey A., and Albert D. Cover. 1989. "Ideological Values and the Votes of Supreme Court Justices." *American Political Science Review* 83: 557–65.

Songer, Donald R. 1979. "The Relevance of Policy Values for the Confirmation of Supreme Court Nominees." *Law and Society Review* 13:927–48.

Warren, Charles. 1923. *The Supreme Court in United States History*. Boston: Little, Brown.

Weaver, R. Kent. 1986. "Automatic Government: The Politics of Indexation." Brookings Institution. Typescript.

Wright, Gerald, and Michael Berkman. 1986. "Candidates and Policy in United States Senate Elections." *American Political Science Review* 80: 567–88.

Charles M. Cameron is Assistant Professor of Political Science, Columbia University, New York, NY 10027.

Albert D. Cover and Jeffrey A. Segal are Associate Professors of Political Science, State University of New York, Stony Brook, NY 11794.

[2]

The Politics of Supreme Court Nominations: A Theory of Institutional Constraints and Choices

Bryon J. Moraski, *University of Iowa*
Charles R. Shipan, *University of Iowa*

When a vacancy occurs on the Supreme Court, the president can attempt to use his power of nomination strategically in order to bring the Court in line with his own policy preferences. However, the president faces two constraints when attempting to do so. First, he may be constrained by the presence of continuing justices and the existing Court median. Second, he may be constrained by the Senate, which must approve his nominee. In this paper we develop and test a theory that examines the conditions under which a president is constrained in his choice of a nominee. Our results show that presidents can, and do, behave strategically with respect to Supreme Court nominations.

1. Introduction

In recent decades, vacancies on the Supreme Court have appeared approximately every two years. Because the Court plays such a central role in politics and policymaking, presidents place a great deal of importance on filling these vacancies with nominees who will produce a Court that looks more favorably on their agendas. Surprisingly, however, while we have learned a great deal in recent years about Senate voting on Supreme Court nominations, very little systematic analysis has been done on presidents' choices of nominees. Given the involvement of the judiciary in nearly every important area of policymaking and the centrality of the nomination process to an understanding of the checks and balances in our political system, it is imperative to understand the process by which presidents select nominees.

Here we analyze presidential choices of Supreme Court nominees. Our starting point is the observation that the Senate almost always approves Supreme Court nominees. Since the turn of the century, only four nominees have been rejected by the Senate, while fifty-five have been approved—a

Earlier versions of this paper were presented at the 1996 meeting of the Southern Political Science Association and the 1997 meeting of the American Political Science Association. We would like to thank Chris Achen, Matt Gabel, Michael Giles, John Huber, Eric Lawrence, Ed Schwartz, Jerry Sorokin, Katie Tenpas, and especially Kathy Bawn, Cary Covington, and Becky Morton for helpful comments and discussions. We also would like to thank Tim Groseclose, Greg Adams, and George Krause for providing us with ideology scores.

success rate oi greater than 93 percent.[1] Given this tremendous rate of success, we believe the important question to examine is how the president decides what kind of nominee hc should choose.

Our primary interest is in determining how the political context influences nominations. In particular, we look to see whether the existence of other political institutions, the preferences of those other institutions, and the constitutionally prescribed sequence of the process affect the president's choice. We also explore whether other factors, such as presidential popularity and years remaining in office, affect nominations. Our goal is to determine which of these factors influence the president's choice.

2. The Supreme Court and the Separation of Powers

The selection of a Supreme Court justice begins with an opening on the Court due to either the death or retirement of a justice. When a vacancy occurs, the president nominates a candidate, and the candidate is confirmed or rejected by a majority vote of the Senate. If the position of chief justice becomes vacant, the president may either nominate both a sitting justice for the position and a new associate justice, or he may nominate a new chief justice from outside the Court.[2]

Surprisingly, even though the president plays a major role in this process, most recent systematic analyses of Supreme Court nominations have focused mainly on the Senate's confirmation vote.[3] We have learned that the Senate vote is more likely to be conflictual when the nominee is less qualified or is ideologically out of step with the Senate (Cameron, Cover, and Segal 1990b). We have also seen that the timing of the nomination (Segal 1987) and the preferences of constituencies and interest groups (Overby et al. 1992; Segal, Cameron, and Cover 1992; Caldeira and Wright 1998) influence the Senate's vote. Additional evidence suggests that the ideology of the departing justice also may matter (Ruckman 1993).

[1]The four nominees rejected by the Senate were John J. Parker in 1930, Clement Haynsworth, Jr., in 1969, G. Harrold Carswell in 1970, and Robert H. Bork in 1987. Despite being rejected, these nominees all received a good deal of support when the Senate voted, ranging from Bork's 42 percent to Parker's 49 percent. In addition to these rejections, two other nominees were not confirmed by the Senate: Johnson withdrew his nomination of Abe Fortas for the position of chief justice before voting took place, and the Senate took no action on Johnson's nomination of Homer Thornberry.

[2]William Rehnquist, for example, was an associate justice when nominated and confirmed for the position of chief justice. His predecessor, Warren Burger, was not on the Court when nominated and confirmed.

[3]A wealth of descriptive material on how presidents choose from among potential nominees can be found in a number of studies. For recent examples, see Abraham (1991), Maltese (1995), and Silverstein (1994). For systematic evaluations of presidential nominations see Massaro (1978; 1990), Cameron, Cover, and Segal (1990a), Watson and Stookey (1995), and Nemacheck and Wahlbeck (1998).

These studies of the confirmation vote treat the choice of a nominee as exogenous. Put somewhat differently, although many of these studies assume that members of the Senate behave rationally in deciding how to vote, they do not make the same assumption for the president. Instead, the strategic manner in which a president might choose a nominee is ignored. Yet most nominees receive a large majority of votes, which suggests the need for a careful analysis of the *nomination* stage. Lopsided confirmation votes are almost certainly due in part to the careful consideration given by presidents to the choice of nominees, consideration given with an eye toward the confirmation vote.

How might the president behave strategically? Given the Court's key role in setting public policy, the president will want a Court that shares his ideology and thus will nominate someone who will bring the Court closer to his preferences. At the same time, however, the president is constrained by institutional features of the nomination process. First, the Senate has the power to confirm or deny the president's choice, which may force him to take the preferences of the Senate into account when nominating someone for a seat on the Court. Second, depending on the configuration of preferences of continuing justices and his own ideology, the president may not be able to shift the Court so that it completely shares his own preferences. Instead, he may be able to move it only a short distance toward his ideal point.

3. The Nomination Game

The requirement that the Senate must approve a president's nominee places a certain structure on the nomination game. In the first stage, a vacancy occurs; in the second stage, the president nominates someone to fill that vacancy; and in the third stage, the Senate votes on the president's nominee.[4] Because the president knows that the Senate will vote on his nominee, when he makes his choice he will take the preferences of the Senate into account. Given the constitutionally prescribed sequence of this game, and relying on the assumption that actors are rational and forward-looking, we can model the nomination game using the equilibrium concept of subgame perfection.[5]

[4]For reasons discussed later in this paper, we omit the Judiciary Committee from our analysis.

[5]Analyses using the same equilibrium concept to examine the president's appointment power include Nokken and Sala (forthcoming), Hammond and Hill (1993), and Snyder and Weingast (1994). Like Snyder and Weingast, we model the appointment process as occurring along a single dimension. Although some recent analyses (most notably, Nokken and Sala forthcoming) indicate that a second dimension might be empirically relevant for Supreme Court confirmation voting, previous studies have demonstrated that a single dimension provides a useful approximation of the more complicated multi-dimensional reality of the appointment process (e.g., Segal, Cameron, and Cover 1992; Cameron, Cover, and Segal 1990b). In addition, single-dimensional analyses are more

If the Senate rejects the nominee, the game ends. In other words, we treat this as a single-period game. Several arguments provide justification for focusing on a single-period game. To begin with, as our analysis demonstrates below, there are a number of interesting and testable implications that derive from a single-period model.[6] Furthermore, in order eventually to model the nomination process as a multiperiod game, it is useful first to understand the single-period game.

Most importantly, a single-period game is a very plausible representation of the nomination process. For a number of reasons, the president will not want the game to continue. The president's public approval and standing with the Senate may suffer from such a rejection. Thus, there is a loss of *political capital* associated with putting forth a nominee who is rejected. Moreover, the president has to expend this capital in a losing cause, whereas it might otherwise be spent more profitably on other policy issues. In addition, there are *time-related* costs. If his term in office is ending, the president might not get another chance to nominate someone. Alternatively, the Senate might change and become more inhospitable to his preferred nominees (e.g., the president's party often loses Senate seats at the midterm election). Finally, the president will lose time in which he could have a Court that produces outcomes more in line with his preferences. Because of these costs, he has a strong incentive to nominate someone who will be approved.

We make the following assumptions in the game. First, all players have perfect and complete information about the preferences of other actors and the sequence of the game. Second, players have Euclidean preferences. Third, the actions of players are driven by their preferences over policy, an assumption we elaborate on below. Fourth, recognizing that the size of the Court has remained at nine members for well over one hundred years, we assume that after a justice retires or dies the Court will have eight members. Fifth, we assume that if the Senate does not approve a nominee, the seat remains open, and the Court functions with eight members. Finally, in the spatial models presented below we also assume, without loss of generality, that the president's ideal point is to the left of the Court median.

The game begins when a seat opens on the Court.[7] Prior to the creation of the vacancy, the median of the nine-member Court is equal to the position

tractable, theoretically and empirically. We agree with Krehbiel's (1996) assessment that "multidimensional institutional theories are more likely to yield examples than general propositions, and as such it is difficult to discern whether or how the general properties of multidimensional choice within inter-branch institutional settings differ from the unidimensional results" (1996, 34).

[6]A single-period approach also facilitates empirical testing by narrowing the potential equilibrium predictions (Morton 1999). Allowing a game to be repeated often produces multiple equilibria, which could prevent the model from yielding clear and testable implications.

[7]We treat the existence of a vacancy on the Court exogenously. In a more complete model, vacancies could be endogenous, as some openings occur due to strategic considerations (Squire 1988; Hagle 1993).

Figure 1. Supreme Court with a Vacancy

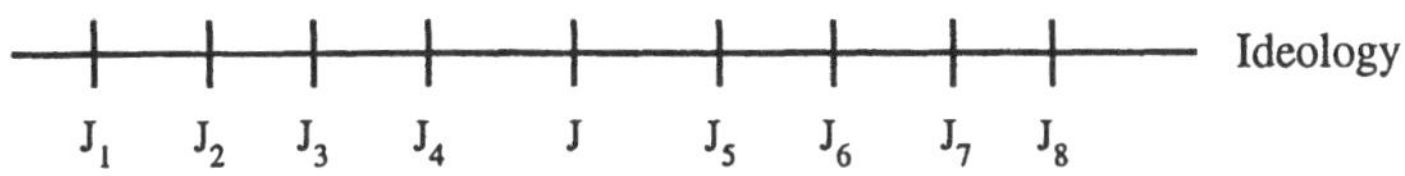

of the fifth justice. Once the vacancy occurs, however, this changes. In Figure 1, each of the eight remaining justices (J_1 through J_8) is located along a scale according to his or her ideology. Because there are now only eight members on the Court, no single justice occupies the median position. Instead, the policy outcome will be a lottery over the interval $[J_4, J_5]$, and we therefore allow the midpoint of this interval, $J = (J_4 + J_5)/2$, to be considered the Court's median after a vacancy occurs.

Once a seat opens, the president has an opportunity to nominate a potential new justice. We assume that the president, whose ideal point we denote by P, is motivated by policy concerns. Thus, he wants to move the median of the Court as close as possible to his own ideal point. In other words, the president wants to minimize the distance between P and J^*, where J^* is defined as the location of the new median if the president's nominee is approved by the Senate.[8]

Consider first what the president would do in the absence of the requirement that the Senate confirm his nominee. In such a case, of course, the president still cannot simply "choose" a new median for the Court. Rather, he is constrained by the presence of eight sitting justices. Because of these continuing justices, the new median will remain in the interval $[J_4, J_5]$, regardless of the ideological position of the nominee. More specifically, if the president chooses a nominee N such that $N < J_4$, then the new median, J^*,

[8]We do not explicitly model the process through which the Supreme Court reaches decisions; instead, we rely on the median voter on the Court to provide a proxy for its decision-making outcomes. Somewhat surprisingly, very little attention has been paid to the accuracy of using the median voter to represent the Court's policy positions. We believe that the relevance of the median voter to Court decision making deserves further attention, but here use three arguments to support its use. First and most simply, we rely on Black's median voter theorem, which holds that in a voting body whose members can be arrayed along a line with single-peaked preferences, the outcome will be the median voter. Second, although some studies have demonstrated that the chief justice can act strategically in assigning opinions (Maltzman and Wahlbeck 1996), it remains true that both the chief justice and the opinion author must take care to satisfy the median member of the Court, for without the support of that member, they cannot sustain a majority. Thus, changes in the median lead monotonically to changes in the Court's output. Finally, and most impressionistically, close observers recognize the importance of the median member of the Court. When *National Journal* recently published a list of the most important political actors in Washington, Sandra Day O'Connor and Anthony Kennedy—usually at or near the median on the Court—made the list, but Justices Rehnquist and Scalia did not. See "The Washington 100," *National Journal*, June 14, 1997.

will be equal to J_4. Similarly, if $N > J_5$ then $J^* = J_5$; and if N is located in the interval $[J_4, J_5]$, then $J^* = N$.

We maintain that the president's choice is motivated by the effect the nominee will have on the Court's median. The president will choose a nominee who, if approved, will bring the Court's median closer to his own ideal point. He can do this by choosing a nominee whose ideal point is close to his own (i.e., N = P). Thus, what is key from our perspective is that the president can achieve both of these goals—minimizing both $|P - J^*|$ and $|P - N|$—simultaneously.

Consider Figure 1, keeping in mind that for the moment we are still ignoring the role played by the Senate. If the president is located to the left of J_4, he will want to move the median to J_4 and can do so by choosing a nominee such that N = P. Similarly, if $P > J_5$, any nominee such that $N > J_5$ will move the median to J_5; and the president again will choose N = P. Finally, when the president is located in the interval $[J_4, J_5]$, choosing a nominee at his own ideal point will cause the new median to be located at his ideal point (i.e., N = P will lead to $J^* = P$).

In other words, regardless of his location relative to the existing Court median, the president can move the median toward his ideal point by choosing N = P.[9] In some cases he is constrained by the presence of the continuing justices, in the sense that he can only move the median a portion of the distance to his own ideal point. But in all cases, by choosing N = P he obtains the best possible new median.

What happens when we introduce the Senate into the model? Obviously, the president now must take into account the preferences of the Senate before deciding on a nominee. His goal will be to choose the nominee who will produce the best new median and *who also will be approved by the Senate.*[10]

Whether the Senate constrains the president, however, depends on the configuration of institutional preferences. As the model we develop in the next section demonstrates, there are three distinct *regimes,* and which variables affect the position of the nominee depends on which regime exists. In the first two regimes discussed below, the Senate and president agree on the direction of change for the median (although they may disagree on the amount). In the third regime, they disagree about even the direction of change.

[9]Choosing N = P therefore is a weakly dominant strategy for the president. The president could, of course, choose other values of N. However, by choosing N = P he not only moves the median toward his ideal point, he also increases the likelihood that future medians will be located close to his ideal point.

[10]We assume that the Senate also is motivated primarily by policy concerns and is most concerned with how the new nominee will, if confirmed, affect the median on the Court. We base this assumption on the demonstrably strong relationship between senators' policy preferences and their votes on Supreme Court nominees (see, e.g., Cameron, Cover, and Segal 1990b; Ruckman 1993).

3.1 Regime 1: Unconstrained Presidential Power

First, consider the case where S < P < J, as illustrated in Figure 2a. The president knows that if he nominates someone who shares his ideology (i.e., N = P) and that person is confirmed, then the new median will be equal to J_4. In addition, he knows that the Senate prefers any new median J^* such that $J^* < J$. Since a nominee located at P produces $J^* = J_4$, the president knows that the Senate, which prefers J_4 to J, will approve such a nominee. Of course, the Senate might prefer a nominee located closer to S than the one the president is willing to put forward. Since it prefers J_4 to J, however, the Senate's hand is forced: by rejecting the president's nominee, it would decrease its own utility. The president, by virtue of having the first move, can present the Senate with an option that, while not perfect, is one it prefers to the status quo.

More generally, in this regime the president is *unconstrained* by the Senate; by choosing a nominee at his ideal point he also moves the median closer to the Senate's ideal point. Put somewhat differently, any nominee that the president likes will create a new Court median that falls within the Senate's win set. This holds true whenever S < P < J and also usually when

Figure 2. Presidential Nominating Regimes

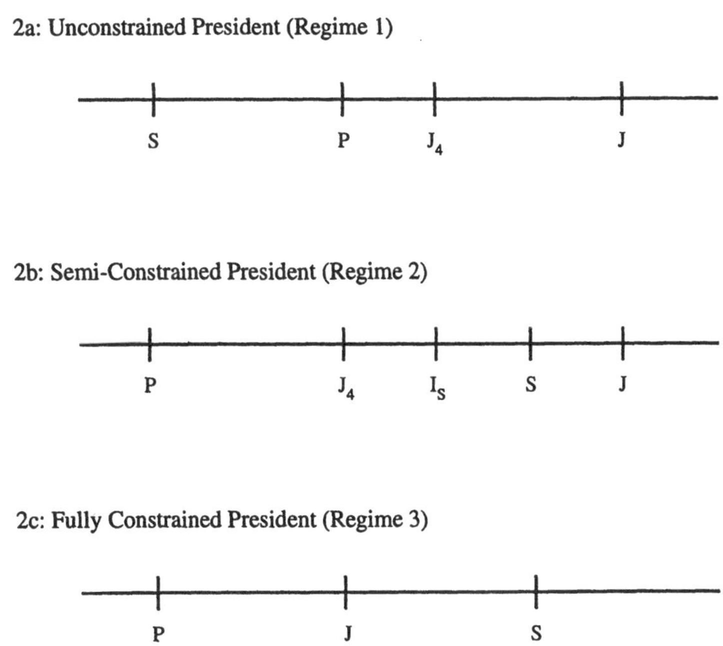

P < S < J, with the exception of the condition discussed in the next section.[11] In effect, when the president and the Senate are on the same side of the Court median, the president is almost always unconstrained by the Senate position, and N will be a function of P, but it will not be a function of S or J.

3.2 Regime 2: Semi-Constrained President

If the Senate is located closer to the median of the Supreme Court than is the president (i.e., $|J - S| < |J - P|$), the president may not have as much power as he does in Regime 1. More specifically, if $P < S < J$, $S > (J_4 + J)/2$, and $P < 2S - J$, the president will no longer be able to present the Senate with a take-it-or-leave-it offer and be confident that the Senate will take it.[12] To see this, consider Figure 2b. If the president chooses a nominee such that N = P, then the new median would be $J^* = J_4$. The Senate, however, prefers J to J^* and therefore would reject the nominee. In fact, the Senate prefers any point to the right of I_S, which is defined as $I_S = 2S - J$ and is the Senate's indifference point with respect to the Court median, to J.

As opposed to Regime 1, where the president is constrained by neither the Senate's ideal point nor the median of the Court, here the president is constrained by a combination of the two. What nominee can the president choose in order to obtain the best possible new median? Working backward, we can see that the Senate will approve any nominee that yields a median that is closer to S than is J. The president then knows that the best he can do is to choose a nominee who will produce a new median at I_S. He can do so by choosing a nominee such that $N = I_S$. Hence, in this regime, the president has to nominate someone whose position is determined by the combination of the ideal points of the Senate and the Court. He is *semi-constrained*; that is, he can choose a nominee who will bring the Court's median closer to his own ideal point, but he cannot do so by choosing N = P, and he cannot move the median all the way to J_4.

3.3 Regime 3: Fully Constrained President

Finally, the president and the Senate might be located on opposite sides of the Court's median, as depicted in Figure 2c. In this regime, the president and the Senate disagree completely about the ideological direction the Court should take. Indeed, any attempt by the president to move the median closer to his ideal point will be rebuffed by the Senate; and the Senate will never

[11]When S < P < J, P is always in the Senate's win set, and the president can always choose N = P.

[12]In other words, if the Senate is closer to J than to J^* and the president is farther from S than S is from J, then the president is semi-constrained.

see a presidential nominee who is likely to move the Court's median toward S. There is a standoff, and the only outcome that would please both the president and the Senate would be a nominee located at J. Regardless of whether the distance between J and S is small or large, as long as P and S are on opposite sides of J the president will be *fully constrained* in his ability to move the Court median closer to his ideal point.

Equilibrium Outcomes

The preceding discussion demonstrates that while P, J, and S each are important determinants of the location of N, their importance is a function of the specific configuration of preferences. More explicitly, the model demonstrates that there are three distinct theoretical regimes: one in which N is a function of P, one in which N is a function of I_S (which in turn is a function of S and J), and finally, one in which N is a function of J.

Figure 3 depicts the equilibrium outcomes as a function of the Senate median. Holding P and J constant, we see that when S < P, the outcome will be equal to P, regardless of the location of S. Similarly, when S > J, the outcome will be J, regardless of the location of S. Only when S is located to the right of $(J_4 + J)/2$ (i.e., the midpoint of the interval $[J_4, J]$) does the location of the Senate median have a direct influence on the outcome. Similar figures could be drawn in which P is allowed to vary while S and J are held constant or where J is allowed to vary while P and S are held constant. In each figure we would see that within one regime the variable of interest would have an effect on the outcome, while in the other two regimes it would not.

Figure 3. Nominee's Ideology as a Function of the Senate's Location

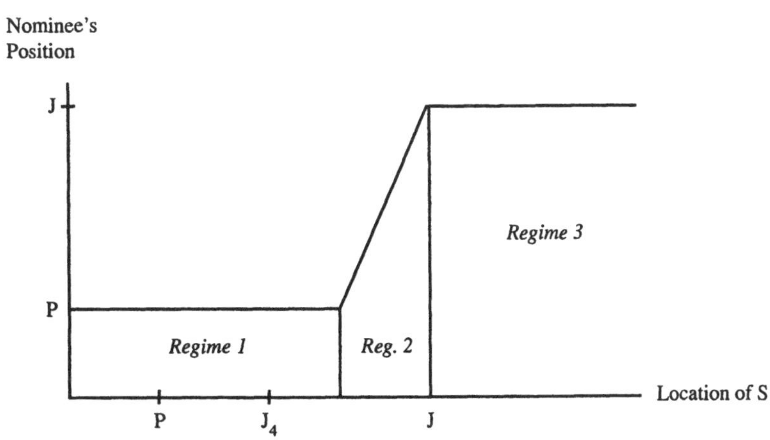

This theoretical finding—that different variables are influential in different regimes—guides our empirical approach. In particular, the theory points to the following specification of the empirical model:

$$N = \beta_0 + \beta_1 {*} D_1 {*} P + \beta_2 {*} D_2 {*} I_S + \beta_3 {*} D_3 {*} J + \varepsilon \quad (1)$$

where D_1, D_2, and D_3 are dummy variables indicating the nature of the regime.[13] As the theoretical model and the empirical specification in Equation 1 make clear, the nominee's position is affected by *either* the president's ideology *or* the Senate's indifference point *or* the Court's median. It is not, however, a function of all of these variables at the same time. Whether each variable matters depends on the location of S relative to J and P. In effect, then, this adopts the approach of switching regressions, where different independent variables matter under different conditions.[14]

4. Measuring Influences on the Nomination

To examine the choice of Supreme Court nominees, we consider all justices nominated to the Supreme Court between 1949 and 1994 (i.e., from Tom Clark through Stephen Breyer). This sample is relatively small, with only twenty-eight observations, and it is limited in time.[15] However, since these were the only nominees for whom we could obtain data for all the variables, this problem could not be avoided.[16]

Our dependent variable, which follows from our theoretical model, is the ideological position of the nominee. To operationalize this variable we use the ideology scores developed for Supreme Court nominees by Segal and Cover (1989). Segal and Cover derived these scores, which are meant to be predictive of a justice's future behavior, from a content analysis of preconfirmation editorials about the civil liberties and civil rights tendencies of the nominees. Like ADA scores, these predicted scores range from zero to

[13]More formally, $D_1 = 1$ if $S < P < N$ or if $P < S < N$, $S < (J_4 + J)/2$, and $P < I_S$, otherwise $D_1 = 0$; $D_2 = 1$ if $P < S < N$, $S < (J_4 + J)/2$, and $P < I_S$, otherwise $D_2 = 0$; and $D_3 = 1$ if $P < J < S$, otherwise $D_3 = 0$.

[14]The switching regimes regression approach is especially valuable when we do not know which regime exists (e.g., Lee and Porter 1984). In our analysis, the location of the various actors spells out which regime exists. See also footnote 29.

[15]Another potential problem is that we cannot observe all the people that a president chooses *not* to nominate. Instead, we make the reasonable assumption that the president is allowed to choose from a set of potential justices whose preferences range across the ideological spectrum. For a perceptive analysis that includes people who were considered but not nominated, see Nemacheck and Wahlbeck (1998).

[16]The limiting variable is the ideology of elected officials. ADA scores extend back to only 1947, and W-NOMINATE scores for the president extend back to roughly the same time.

one, with zero being the most conservative and one being the most liberal ideology. Table 1 presents the descriptive statistics for this variable and for other variables we discuss below.

To measure the ideology of the Senate, we use the yearly ADA scores of the median member of the Senate. We adjust these scores according to the methodology recently developed by Groseclose, Levitt, and Snyder (1999), which controls for the possibility that the ADA scale shifts and compresses or expands over time.

Measurement of presidential ideology is somewhat less straightforward. One option would be to use a dummy variable to designate a president's partisanship. We prefer to use a more differentiated measure, however, and thus use presidential ADA scores, which are computed by examining each president's positions on the votes ADA uses to calculate scores for members of Congress (Zupan 1992). As with the ADA scores for the Senate, the presidential ideology scores also range from zero to one, with zero being most conservative and one most liberal. And as with the Senate ADA scores, the presidential ADA scores are computed yearly and are adjusted.

While ADA scores and the nominees' ideology scores both can be aligned along the same zero-to-one scale, a potential problem exists. ADA scores are general measures of ideology, computed in order to demonstrate the overall liberal or conservative tendencies of each member of Congress. The nominees' scores, on the other hand, focus on civil liberties and civil rights and thus are more issue-specific than ADA scores. Yet, there are reasons to use them together. First, justices cast far more votes in civil liberties and civil rights cases than in any other policy area. Thus, a good portion of their overall ideology is comprised of these more specific scores. Second, at the congressional level, ADA scores and ACLU scores are highly correlated. Third, both types of scores represent attempts by third parties to locate political actors along a similar zero-to-one, conservative-to-liberal dimension. In the end, we maintain that it remains the best option. The only preconfirmation measures of nominees' ideologies are the civil liberties scores, and ADA scores for the Senate and president are relevant and extend farther back in time than do other issue-specific scores.

To measure the median position of the Court, we look at the median voting score on civil liberties from the Court's previous term. We compute this by looking at the voting scores of the eight continuing members of the Court and using the midpoint of the interval [J_4, J_5] as the median. For example, in 1994 Stephen Breyer was nominated to fill the seat vacated by the retirement of Harry Blackmun. Of the eight justices from the 1993 term who were retaining their seats, Justice O'Connor had the fourth highest voting score and Justice Kennedy the fifth. Since their scores were 36.2 and

Table 1. Descriptive Statistics

Variable	Maximum	Minimum	Mean	Median	Mode	Standard Deviation	Skewness Statistic
Nominee's Ideology Scores	1.00	0.00	0.45	0.45	0.50[a]	0.33	0.26
President's Ideology	0.89	-0.06	0.35	0.34	0.34[a]	0.31	0.26
Senate's Indifference Point	0.60	-0.29	0.21	0.21	0.21[a]	0.24	0.26
Court Median	0.76	0.26	0.52	0.50	0.50	0.12	0.30
President's Ideology in Regime 1	0.85	0.00	0.22	0.11	0.00	0.27	0.96
Senate's Indifference Point in Regime 2	0.59	0.00	0.01	0.00	0.00	0.17	2.74
Court Median in Regime 3	0.65	0.00	0.11	0.00	0.00	0.21	1.59
Presidential Approval	0.79	0.40	0.59	0.62	0.65	0.11	-0.15
Years Remaining in Office	1.00	0.25	0.73	0.75	0.75[a]	0.22	-0.18
Qualifications of Nominee	1.00	0.11	0.77	0.99	1.00	0.27	-1.11

[a]indicates one of multiple modes

N = 28

Note: Scores for the president and the Senate are adjusted ADA scores. These adjusted scores can take on values greater than one or less than zero. We used the full range of values in our analysis, but the results were essentially the same if we bounded these scores at zero and one.

44.7, respectively, the median we use for Breyer's appointment is 40.5, the average of these two scores.[17]

5. Empirical Analysis

Table 2 presents the distribution of nominations by regime type. Of the twenty-eight observations, the majority—eighteen, to be specific—fall into Regime 1. Three nominations (Stevens, Bork, and Kennedy) fall into Regime 2. The remaining seven nominations belong to Regime 3. The existence of nominations in each regime will allow us fully to test our theory, but the small number of observations in the second and third regimes will decrease the likelihood of obtaining statistically significant results.

As our theoretical model indicates, the location of the nominee, N, should be a function of the president's ideal point, the Senate's indifference point, and the existing median on the Court once a vacancy occurs. However, the type of regime determines which of these variables should have an effect on N. In Regime 1 we expect P to have a significant effect; in Regime 2 we expect I_S to have a significant effect; and in Regime 3 we expect J to have a significant effect.

Bivariate analysis provides initial support for our model. In Regime 1, there is a strong relationship between the president's ideology and the nominee's ideology ($r = .60$, $p < .01$). Similarly, in Regime 3, we find a strong relationship between the Court median and the nominee's ideology ($r = .76$, $p < .05$). In Regime 2 we do not find support for our theory ($r = -0.08$); this is unsurprising, given the small number of observations in this regime.

Table 3 presents the results of our switching regressions. Column 1 in this table presents the most basic and straightforward test of our model. All three of the variables have positive coefficients, as the theory predicts. Both the president's ideology in Regime 1 and the Court's median in Regime 3 differ from zero at $p < .01$.[18] Only the Senate's indifference point in Regime 2 fails to reach standard levels of significance, although here and in a range of other specifications its coefficient is in the expected direction. On the whole, the model does a good job of predicting the ideology of nominees to the Court.

Before proceeding to a discussion of alternative hypotheses and specifications, we wish to make two general points about our empirical analysis.

[17] In some cases, there were only seven continuing members on the Court when a nominee was chosen. In such cases we use the voting score of the median, or fourth, justice. In other cases, there were seven sitting justices and also one justice who had been confirmed but who had not yet established a voting record on the Court. For these cases we used the voting scores of the continuing justice along with the predicted vote of the newly confirmed justice.

[18] All significance levels we report for the theoretical variables of interest are based on one-tailed tests.

Table 2. Nominees Classified by Regime Type

Regime 1: Unconstrained President	Regime 2: Semi-Constrained President	Regime 3: Fully Constrained President
Warren	Stevens	Clark
Brennan	Bork	Minton
Whittaker	Kennedy	Harlan
Stewart		Fortas (associate)
White		Fortas (chief justice)
Goldberg		Souter
Marshall		Thomas
Burger		
Haynsworth		
Carswell		
Blackmun		
Powell		
Rehnquist (associate)		
O'Connor		
Rehnquist (chief justice)		
Scalia		
Ginsburg		
Breyer		

Note: Regime 1 occurs when $S < P < J$; Regime 2 occurs when $P < S < J$, $S > (J_4 + J)/2$, and $P < 2S - J$; and Regime 3 occurs when $P < J < S$. The same regimes occur for the mirror-images of these preference configurations (i.e., $J < P < S$ also is classified as Regime 1).

First, because ADA scores are imperfect proxies for ideology, we reran the regression shown in Column 1 (and others presented in this paper) using several other measures for ideology. Using raw (unadjusted) ADA scores produced results that were essentially the same as—or in some cases, even better than—those produced using real (adjusted) ADA scores. Adjusted W-NOMINATE scores also yielded strong support for our theory. Because no measure of ideology is perfect, scholars are better off using a variety of measures to test a theory. The similarity across different measures in our analysis demonstrates the robustness of our results.[19]

Second, the significance of our theoretical variables can be tested in two different ways. Our theory predicts that the coefficients of these variables

[19]The NOMINATE scores were rescaled from 0 (conservative) to 1 (liberal) so they would be consistent with our other measures. Using the average of a president's ideology score over the course of his term produced results that were nearly identical to those found in Column 1. Using the presidential ideology scores of Segal, Howard, and Hutz (1996), which are based on expert assessments, yielded similar results.

Table 3. Predicting the Ideology of Supreme Court Nominees

	Column 1	Column 2	Column 3	Column 4
Presidential ADA Scores (in Regime 1 only)	0.83 (0.23)	0.87 (0.25)	0.92 (0.53)	0.83 (0.25)
Senate's Indifference Point (in Regime 2 only)	0.20 (0.32)	0.06 (0.30)	0.62 (0.39)	
Court Median (in Regime 3 only)	1.18 (0.29)	1.42 (0.74)	1.23 (0.61)	0.96 (0.29)
Presidential ADA Scores (in Regimes 2 and 3)		–0.04 (0.42)		
Senate's Indifference Point (in Regimes 1 and 3)		–0.55 (0.30)		
Court Median (in Regimes 1 and 2)		0.18 (0.47)		
Presidential ADA Scores (in all Regimes)			–0.04 (0.42)	
Senate's Indifference Point (in all Regimes)			–0.55 (0.30)	
Court Median (in all Regimes)			0.18 (0.47)	
Constant	0.13 (0.10)	0.11 (0.25)	0.11 (0.25)	0.12 (0.10)
Adjusted R^2	0.41	0.49	0.49	0.31
SEE	0.26	0.24	0.24	0.28
Durbin-Watson	1.49	1.99	1.99	1.21

Numbers in parentheses are standard errors
N = 28

should be positive and significantly different from zero. In other words, our model predicts that these theoretical variables should have a positive effect on the nominee's ideology. However, our theory also predicts that a one-unit change in the relevant independent variables should produce a corresponding one-unit change in the dependent variable. To test this second prediction, the proper null hypothesis is that the coefficient is equal to one; and failure to reject this null constitutes support for our theory. Both predictions are important. We cannot simply test whether the coefficient differs from one, because a coefficient indistinguishable from one also might be indistinguishable from zero (e.g., a coefficient of 1.00 with a standard error of 2.00).

Similarly, we cannot test only whether the coefficient differs significantly from zero, since such a coefficient might be statistically distinguishable from one (e.g., a coefficient of 0.20 and a standard error of 0.04). In the remainder of the paper we will report p-values based on the null hypothesis that the coefficient is equal to zero, but we will also note whether the coefficients differ significantly from one. It is extremely important—and supportive of our theory—to note that in every instance where we find that the coefficients are significantly different from zero, we also find that they are *not* significantly different from one.[20]

Alternative Hypotheses

While the most basic test of our theoretical model is the one presented in Column 1, our theory also produces additional hypotheses. In particular, the theory not only predicts that the president's ideology should be a significant influence on the nominee's ideology in Regime 1; it also predicts that the president's ideology should *not* be a significant influence on the nominee's ideology in Regimes 2 and 3. Similarly, the Senate should play no role in Regimes 1 and 3, and the Court median should be insignificant in Regimes 1 and 2. In other words, instead of expecting that the variables for the president, Senate, and Court should be significant and positive (and equal to one) in all three regimes, the theory predicts regime-specific effects. The equation to be estimated is thus:

$$N = \beta_0 + \beta_1 * D_1 * P + \beta_2 * D_2 * I_S + \beta_3 * D_3 * J + \beta_4 * (D_2 + D_3) * P + \beta_5 * (D_1 + D_3) * I_S + \beta_6 * (D_1 + D_2) * J + \varepsilon \qquad (2)$$

where we expect β_1, β_2, and β_3 to be significant and β_4, β_5, and β_6 to be insignificant.

Column 2 in Table 3 presents the results for the alternative specification (2). Again, the results are supportive of our theory. The president's ideology is significant in Regime 1, but not in Regimes 2 and 3, and the Court median is significant in Regime 3, but not in Regimes 1 and 2. Both variables also are indistinguishable from one. Once again, the Senate's indifference point is not a significant influence on ideology in Regime 2, although it curiously produces a somewhat significant but negative coefficient for Regimes 1 and 3.

While this alternative specification follows directly from our theoretical model, a number of other hypotheses also are plausible. For example, the nominee's position might be a function of the preferences of the president, the Senate's indifference point, and the Court, irrespective of the regime. The expectation for this alternative hypothesis would be that as the ideologi-

[20]We also find that our constant term is always indistinguishable from zero, which the theory also predicts.

cal scores of any of these actors increase, so would the ideological score of the nominee.

To test this alternative hypothesis we added these three variables to Column 1 of Table 3 (i.e., we removed the parenthetical terms from the last three interactions in Equation 2). The results of this test, shown in Column 3, once again provide support for our model. The president's ideology in Regime 1 and the Court's median in Regime 3 again have coefficients that are in the predicted direction, are significantly different from zero at $p < .05$, and are also indistinguishable from one. Interestingly, the Senate's indifference point in this specification also approaches standard levels of significance ($p < .10$) and is indistinguishable from one, lending an additional measure of support to our theory.

At the same time, little support is given to the alternative hypothesis. None of the noninteracted variables are significant in the predicted direction, and a joint F-test shows that they are jointly insignificant at the .05 level.[21] These results, like those presented in the other columns, lend support to our theoretical argument and to the robustness of our results.[22] As the theory predicts, the president's choice of a nominee appears to be a function of the president's preferences in Regime 1, the Senate's indifference point in Regime 2, and the Court's median in Regime 3.[23]

[21]Furthermore, we can reject the hypothesis that these other variables are equal to one. As in the previous column, the variable measuring the Senate's indifference point was weakly significant, albeit with a negative coefficient. This implies that, for example, if $P < I_S < J$, as I_S moves to the right, the president will choose a nominee farther to the *left*. We offer no explanations for this result but simply note that it presents an opportunity for future research.

[22]Similarly, we allowed the constant to vary across regimes by omitting the constant from the estimation and instead including D_1, D_2, and D_3. None of these noninteracted regime dummy variables were significant, while the interaction of D_1 with the president's preferences and the interaction of D_3 with the Court's position remained significant at the $p < .05$ level.

[23]The text reports two of the alternative hypotheses that we tested: whether the president, Senate, and Court matter across all regimes and whether these three variables matter in regimes in which we expect them *not* to matter. We also examined a variety of other null hypotheses, including one in which the nominee's ideology is regressed on the president and Senate alone, one where it is regressed on the president and the distance between the president and the Senate, one where we include the president alone, and one where we include variables about the president's popularity and time remaining in office and the nominee's qualifications (discussed below with respect to Table 4). We also included the regime-specific theoretical variables in these models. While there were some differences across these specifications, in general the results showed that the regime-specific interaction terms were significant, and the alternative variables were not. The main exception to this occurred when we included the president in all three regimes with the three regime-specific theoretical variables. In this case, due to collinearity, nothing was significant. We discuss collinearity below. We also note that even if these alternative models had not generally produced insignificant results for variables we expect to be insignificant and significant results for variables we expect to be significant, it can be argued that none of these alternatives are well-developed enough to provide specific alternative hypotheses or theoretical interpretations.

While these results support our theory, we wish to introduce a bit of caution in interpreting them. First, standard hypothesis testing is more appropriate for testing whether a particular variable is significant (i.e., when the null hypothesis is that the variable is not different from zero) than for situations where the model holds that a variable should be insignificant. Thus, conventional levels of significance should not be used to determine whether these coefficients are indeed equal to zero, as this might result in a Type II error. One approach that social scientists take to deal with this problem is to use a more stringent test of $p < .50$ for a one-tailed test (e.g., Hall and Grofman 1990). Even according to this much more stringent test, none of the variables we expect to be insignificant turn out to be significant in a positive direction.

A second problem is more serious and has to do with collinearity between the variables. In both Columns 2 and 3, collinearity is a problem.[24] Unfortunately, two of the standard ways to fix collinearity are not plausible options—we can neither add more observations nor delete independent variables (Lewis-Beck 1995). Thus, we cannot directly address the problem of collinearity.

The primary effect of multicollinearity, of course, is to increase the size of standard errors. Thus, it provides a bias against finding significant results. We cannot know whether coefficients are indistinguishable from zero because the model is correct or because of multicollinearity and random variation producing spurious results. Therefore, it is even more surprising that our primary theoretical variables—the president in Regime 1 and the Court median in Regime 3—remain significant under a wide range of specifications. In addition, these variables remain significant for alternative measures for each variable, as noted earlier. Moreover, the variables that we do not expect to be significant also turn out to be insignificant under a wide range of specifications and operationalizations.[25] Although we cannot ignore the problems

[24]For example, the bivariate correlations range from .01 to .89. And when we regress Presidential Ideology (in Regimes 2 and 3) on the other independent variables in Column 2, we find a high adjusted R^2 (0.83). Other diagnostic tests were much more encouraging. In Columns 2 and 3 the Durbin-Watson statistic allowed us to reject the possibility of autocorrelation (in Column 1 the statistic is inconclusive). Furthermore, plotting the standardized residuals of Column 1 against its standardized predicted values demonstrates that the analysis was not driven by outliers. To complement this visual inspection of the data, we relied on Cook's distance test, which is a measure of how much the residuals of all cases would change if a particular case were excluded from the calculation of the regression coefficients. A large Cook's D indicates that excluding a case from computation of the regression statistics changes the coefficients substantially. In the case of only one observation—Stephen Breyer—did this test indicate the existence of a potential outlier. Removing Breyer from the dataset actually *improved* our results—it increased the overall fit of the model and made our theoretical variables more significant.

[25]Comparing the degrees of collinearity our theoretical variables encounter to the degrees of collinearity encountered by the variables representing the alternate hypotheses yields further support

potentially caused by multicollinearity, the stability of our results across a wide range of tests lends additional support to our findings.

In the end, how should the findings be interpreted? We will not be surprised if future theoretical work demonstrates a more important role for the president in other regimes. Because of the collinearity between the presidential variable and the other variables, it is difficult conclusively to reject this possibility. And in the next section we explore a couple ways in which the president might be able to be more influential in Regimes 2 and 3. At this point, however, the evidence suggests that the president is significant in Regime 1, and the Court median is significant in Regime 3, while these variables and the Senate are not significant in other regimes.

Reclassifying Borderline Observations

One finding from the previous columns that has not been consistent with our theory is the lack of significance of the Senate's indifference point in Regime 2. No doubt this is due, at least in part, to the small number of cases in this regime. However, it also calls for a closer examination of the three observations that occur in this regime. And it turns out that in all three cases the observations might justifiably be reclassified as belonging to one of the other regimes.[26]

First, let us look at the nomination of John Paul Stevens in 1975. At that time, President Ford's adjusted ADA score was 18, the Court's median in the wake of Justice Douglas's retirement was 51.1, and the adjusted ADA score for the Senate median was 50.2. Based on the latter two of these values, the Senate's indifference point was thus 49.3. Because Stevens's predicted vote was fairly conservative (38.0), Senate approval of his nomination would have led to a new median of 49.3. Since the Senate fell in between the existing and the potential new Court medians (i.e., J and J^*), we classified this observation as belonging to Regime 2. However, given that the new median and the Senate's indifference point are equal, and given that P is less than both S and J, we could just as well have classified Stevens as belonging to

for our theory. For example, in Column 3 of Table 3 the Regime 1 * Presidential ADA Scores variable suffers from a greater degree of collinearity (an adjusted R^2 of .87 when regressed on the other variables) than any of the nontheoretical variables, yet it is significant. Furthermore, when we use unadjusted ADA scores, collinearity decreases a great deal, yet the results remain the same.

[26]We hasten to add that we examined *all* observations to determine which, if any, classifications were borderline. Only those classified as belonging to Regime 2 were even remotely borderline—no observations classified as belonging to other regimes were close to the regime borders. Thus, we stress that we are not reclassifying Regime 2 observations in order to provide post hoc explanations for the lack of significance of the Regime 2 variable. Rather, because the theory predicts such sharp cutpoints and because there are only three cases in this regime, we believe it makes sense to examine these cases individually to see how securely they fit into Regime 2.

Regime 1.[27] More generally, any time a nomination is this close to the border of two regimes, classification of regime type is uncertain, since the ideology and voting scores should be considered to measure true preferences with some error and since any uncertainty on the part of the political actors could lead to a change in regime classification.

Examination of the Bork and Kennedy nominations similarly shows that these also could be classified differently. In both cases the Senate median is less than, but very close to, the Court median, with S = 48.2 and J = 48.6, respectively. Since the president's ideal point is much less than either of these other points, we classified these nominations as belonging to Regime 2. However, because the values for S and J are extremely close, both Bork and Kennedy could very plausibly be reclassified as belonging to Regime 3, which calls for the president and Senate to be on opposite sides of the Court median.[28]

Based on these reclassifications, we re-estimated Equation 1. In Column 4 of Table 3, Stevens is moved into Regime 1 while Bork and Kennedy are placed in Regime 3. The results again show support for our theory. Both the Court median in Regime 3 and the president's ideology in Regime 1 are significantly different from zero and indistinguishable from one.[29]

Controlling for the President's Bargaining Advantage

Several other factors outside of our model might affect the choice of a nominee. We would not, however, expect these factors, which we can think of as the president's bargaining advantage, to be important under all conditions. Rather, like the theoretically derived independent variables discussed earlier, we expect that if these variables matter, they do so only in certain regimes. We offer these as additional alternatives to our model, alternatives that derive from the descriptive and historical work on nominations.

More specifically, in Regime 1 we would not expect these other factors to matter, whereas we might expect them to matter in Regimes 2 and 3. In Regime 1, the president already can nominate someone who shares his ideology. He cannot use any political capital he might have to move the nominee closer to his own position. In Regimes 2 and 3, however, the president must choose a nominee located some distance from his own most preferred

[27]Furthermore, since the Court median and the Senate median are separated by only one percentage point, it could also be the case that J < S, or at least that actors perceive that J < S, in which case this could be classified as belonging to Regime 3.

[28]In addition, aggregate civil liberties voting scores probably understate the conservative nature of the Rehnquist Court (Baum 1995; Lee, Sandstrum, and Weisert 1996).

[29]We also performed a switching regimes regression, using LIMDEP, on this equation. This procedure similarly yielded significant results for these variables.

point.[30] Several factors might, however, enable him to choose a nominee such that $P < N < I_S$ (in Regime 2) or $P < N < J$ (in Regime 3).[31]

We propose and test three such variables: presidential approval, the president's year in office, and the qualifications of the nominee. Each of these variables was recoded for placement on the interval from zero to one. The approval ratings, which register the percentage of people approving of the president, were acquired for the month of each nomination from the Gallup Opinion Poll.[32] Gallup asked the same question in each month for each year in our sample: "Do you approve or disapprove of the way [the current president] is handling his job as president?" The descriptive literature on nominations suggests that the greater a president's popularity, the more likely he is to be able to choose a nominee closer to his own ideal point.

Similarly, the more recently a president has been elected, the more successful he should be in bargaining with the Senate. Consequently we include a variable measuring the percentage of the president's term that remains to be served. This variable takes on the value of 1 in the president's first year in office, 0.75 in the second year, and so on.

Finally, the more qualified a nominee is, the harder it will be for the Senate to reject her or him. Thus, a president will be able to nominate someone who is closer to P if that nominee is highly qualified.[33] These qualification

[30]Thus we have another example of regime-specific variables. By including the variables discussed below without interacting them with specific regimes, we would be biasing the results toward zero, since we would be mixing a regime where we expect to find no effect (Regime 1) with regimes in which an effect might exist (Regimes 2 and 3). Not surprisingly, when we did include the bargaining variables without regime-specific effects, the results were insignificant.

[31]In effect, while we do not formally model it, these factors, if important, should improve a president's position in a bargaining game with the Senate. Since the president already can nominate someone located at his ideal point when faced with a Regime 1 configuration, he need not bargain, and these factors should not be important in that regime. However, we should note that allowing these variables to matter across all three regimes did not alter the results shown below.

[32]Gallup lacked data on Reagan at the time of his nomination of Kennedy in November 1987. As a result, we used his approval rating for the last month they had it available, which was August 1987. Ratings were obtained from *The Gallup Opinion Index*, October–November 1980, Report Number 182 and *The Gallup Poll: Public Opinion*, 1981–1995.

[33]All values were rescaled to account for the location of the president. If, for example, $P < J$ in Regime 3, then we would expect an increase in popularity to *decrease* the value of N, whereas if $P > J$, then we would expect an increase in popularity to *increase* the value of N. Because the expected signs differ according to whether P is to the left or to the right of J, D_2*Approval is inappropriate. The most straightforward way to correct for the directional issue is to multiply this interaction term by the difference between P and the Court (for Regime 3) or P and the Senate's indifference point (for Regime 2). For example, for popularity the measures are D_2*Approval*$(P - I_S)$ and D_3*Approval*$(P - J)$. This controls for not only direction, but also for the distance between the president's ideal point and the other points. Equivalent changes were made for the other variables. We control for distance as well as direction because we hypothesized that, for example, a very popular president in Regime 3 located far from J could lead to a greater change in the nominee's position

scores were obtained from *The Supreme Court Compendium* (Epstein et al. 1996) and were computed in the same way as the Segal/Cover ideology scores.

The results presented in Table 4 demonstrate little systematic support for these factors.[34] It appears that in Regime 3 there is at least some reason to believe that these variables affect the choice of a nominee in the expected manner. High approval ratings, proximity to an election, and a more highly qualified nominee all seem to allow a president in Regime 3 to nominate someone whose predicted vote is on the president's side of the Court's median. However, even in this regime the results are not strong: with one-tailed tests the p-values range from .07 for approval and qualifications to .15 for years remaining in office.

Two final points are important to note here. First, we do not doubt that these factors *sometimes* matter. What we show here is that they are not systematic, regular, and significant influences on the president's choice. Second, the "Years Remaining" variable taps into what might be called the *electoral context*, whereas most of this paper has been devoted to looking at the institutional context. These results, as well as other unreported results, provide little evidence of a significant influence from the electoral context.[35]

Additional Interpretations

What additional substantive interpretations can be drawn from our results, particularly those found in Columns 1, 2, and 3 of Table 3? First, the model makes it clear that presidents are faced with different constraints at different times. Two of the first three justices that Ronald Reagan nominated were extreme conservatives (William Rehnquist and Antonin Scalia). Yet his final nominee to the bench was the relatively moderate Anthony Kennedy. One difference between these contexts was the regime. For Reagan's first three appointments, he was unconstrained (i.e., Regime 1). His party controlled the Senate, and he was able to choose any nominee he wished, know-

than a very popular president located a very short distance from J. We also tried using a signed dummy variable (e.g., instead of (P – J) we used –1 if J > P and 1 if P > J). This produced no substantive differences in the results.

[34]Because of collinearity and limited degrees of freedom, we have chosen to report these variables separately rather than together. When we include all the variables shown in Table 4 in one equation, the only variables that are significant are presidential ideology in Regime 1 and the Court median in Regime 3.

[35]We also examined whether the choice of a nominee was affected by a host of other related variables, such as whether it was a president's first term, whether he was running for re-election, whether he was in his last year in office, whether he was in his last two years in office, and whether he was an unelected president (i.e., Johnson and Ford). None of these variables were significant. Nor were variables controlling for the number of previous nominees or appointments.

Table 4. Controlling for Additional Factors in the Nomination of Supreme Court Justices

	Column 1	Column 2	Column 3
Theoretical Variables			
Presidential ADA Scores (in Regime 1)	0.80 (0.23)	0.81 (0.24)	0.78 (0.23)
Senate's Indifference Point (in Regime 2)	0.30 (1.10)	0.74 (4.53)	–0.06 (1.61)
Court Median (in Regime 3)	1.04 (0.30)	1.06 (0.32)	0.95 (0.33)
Additional Factors			
Presidential Approval (in Regime 2)	0.27 (2.23)		
Presidential Approval (in Regime 3)	0.91 (0.59)		
Years Remaining in Office (in Regime 2)		0.10 (8.50)	
Years Remaining in Office (in Regime 3)		0.53 (0.51)	
Nominee's Qualifications (in Regime 2)			–0.25 (1.86)
Nominee's Qualifications (in Regime 3)			1.00 (0.65)
Constant	0.14 (0.10)	0.13 (0.10)	0.15 (0.10)
Adjusted R^2	0.41	0.38	0.41
SEE	0.26	0.26	0.26
Durbin-Watson	1.54	1.51	1.59

Numbers in parentheses are standard errors
N = 28

ing that the Senate would be likely to approve of him or her. However, after the Senate changed hands and was controlled by Democrats after the 1986 election, Reagan was faced with a different situation. Once in Regime 3, he was no longer able to nominate an extreme conservative, but rather was constrained because the Senate's preferred point was on the other side of the Court median.

Bill Clinton, on the other hand, disappointed some Democrats by not choosing justices who were more liberal. And indeed, Stephen Breyer's prenomination record was perceived to be fairly moderate. On the other hand, Ruth Bader Ginsburg's Segal/Cover score is liberal, and even Breyer's score was far more liberal than all but one of the nominees from the previous twenty-five years. Interestingly, shortly after Breyer was approved, Clinton's party lost control of the Senate. This changed the political context to Regime 3, which would further constrain Clinton's ability to nominate a more liberal jurist.

The model also allows us to speculate on the substantive influence of regimes and of elections. If George Bush had defeated Bill Clinton in the 1992 election, Bush certainly would have chosen nominees who were more conservative than Ginsburg and Breyer. But at the same time, the nomination context instead would have been Regime 3, compelling Bush to choose a moderate nominee rather than a strongly conservative nominee. Speculating even further, if Bush had been in office when the Republicans gained control of the Senate in 1994, we would have switched back to Regime 1, where Bush would have been unconstrained. In this situation a justice like William Rehnquist might have realized that conditions were ripe for a successor who shared his ideology and that it might be a strategically opportune time to retire.

6. Discussion

Presidents view Supreme Court nominations as important policy choices. To help ensure Senate approval of their nominees and to move the policy orientation of the Court closer to their own preferences, they must take into account the preferences of the Senate and the ideology and behavior of continuing members of the Court. Our theoretical model, which is supported by our empirical results, spells out the way in which presidents engage in such strategic behavior.

One potential extension to our analysis would be to incorporate the Senate Judiciary Committee, which holds hearings on each nominee, into the theoretical model. Including this committee would change the president's calculus. No longer could he worry about only the Senate median; he would also have to worry about the committee median.[36] However, while the Judiciary Committee undoubtedly plays an important role in the confirmation process, and while the president undoubtedly takes into account the preferences of its members, the committee does *not* act as a gatekeeper. Even if the committee disapproves of a nominee, it still can send that nominee's name to the floor for a vote by the entire Senate.[37] For example, neither Clarence

[36]See Nokken and Sala (Forthcoming) for such a model.

[37]If the committee approves a nominee, it automatically sends the nomination to the floor. If the committee does not approve the nominee, it can choose whether or not to send the nomination to the floor.

Thomas nor Robert Bork won a majority of the vote within the committee, yet the nominations of both of these men were forwarded to the floor.

Instead of acting as a gatekeeper, the committee's primary role is to make a recommendation that sends a signal to the rest of the Senate. Whether the committee acts as a binding constraint and absolutely needs to be included in this analysis is therefore an open question. On the one hand, the Senate has never approved a nominee who was voted down by the committee, with Thomas's committee vote of 7-7 being the only near exception. On the other hand, the committee does not gatekeep; thus, its function is probably better handled by a model of information transmission.

Second, our paper was motivated by the observation that in this century presidents have been enormously successful in getting their nominees past the Senate. However, it is worth noting that failed nominations were more common in the nineteenth century, as were closely contested votes. Were presidential appointments in general more contentious in the nineteenth century than in this century? Did presidents treat Supreme Court appointments differently? While such questions are beyond the scope of this study, they are certainly worthy of attention. Our analysis represents a building block toward a fuller understanding of presidential appointments, but we acknowledge that future research should attempt to deal with these other sorts of questions.

Third, instead of using the median voter of the Senate, future work might consider using the member of the Senate located at the filibuster pivot. The reason for this, of course, is that the Senate can filibuster on a nomination, a tactic that the president will need to take into account. While the use of a filibuster on a Supreme Court nomination is a rare event, its infrequency does not denote its unimportance.[38]

Fourth, we believe scholars should proceed cautiously when moving from our model to any predictions about Senate voting. Even leaving aside the possibility that the president has made an error when choosing a nominee (which presidents surely have done), we would not expect all Senate confirmation votes to consist of bare majorities, which this analysis might seem to indicate. Events that happen between the president's nomination and the confirmation vote can influence the Senate's action. In the cases of Fortas and Thomas, for example, information made public subsequent to the nomination but prior to the confirmation vote undoubtedly shifted the votes of some members. In addition, individual senators might be influenced by party leaders, norms, or even something akin to a snowball effect, causing a larger than expected majority to vote for a nominee. Thus, we recognize that the Senate

[38]The 1968 nomination of Abe Fortas to the position of chief justice was withdrawn after it was filibustered in the Senate. In addition, it is entirely conceivable that Bill Clinton had the filibuster pivot (Krehbiel 1998) in mind when he nominated moderate Stephen Breyer to the bench.

might pay attention to factors other than policy positions when voting on Supreme Court nominees and recognize that incorporating such factors into future models might make for a richer analysis.

While these and other changes might be made to our theoretical model and empirical tests, we believe that our analysis sheds new light on the nominations process. There is a reason most Supreme Court nominees easily pass the Senate: presidents act strategically to choose the best nominee they can, given the constraints that they face.

Manuscript submitted March 16, 1998.
Final manuscript received March 8, 1999.

REFERENCES

Abraham, Henry J. 1991. *Justices and Presidents: A Political History of Appointments to the Supreme Court*. Oxford: Oxford University Press.

Baum, Lawrence. 1995. "Measuring Policy Change in the Rehnquist Court." *American Politics Quarterly* 23:373–382

Caldeira, Gregory A., and John R. Wright. 1998. "Lobbying for Justice: Organized Interests, Supreme Court Nominations, and the United States Senate." *American Journal of Political Science* 42:499–523.

Cameron, Charles M., Albert D. Cover, and Jeffrey A. Segal. 1990a. "Supreme Court Nominations and the Rational Presidency." Presented at the American Political Science Association Annual Meeting, San Francisco.

Cameron, Charles M., Albert D. Cover, and Jeffrey A. Segal. 1990b. "Senate Voting on Supreme Court Nominees: A Neoinstitutional Model." *American Political Science Review* 84:525–534.

Epstein, Lee, Jeffrey A. Segal, Harold J. Spaeth, and Thomas G. Walker. 1996. *The Supreme Court Compendium: Data Decisions, and Development*. 2nd ed. Washington D.C.: Congressional Quarterly Inc.

Groseclose, Tim, Steven D. Levitt, and James M. Snyder. 1999. "Comparing Interest Group Scores across Time and Chambers: Adjusted ADA Scores for the U.S. Congress." *American Political Science Review* 93:33–50.

Hagle, Timothy M. 1993. "Strategic Retirement: A Political Model of Turnover on the United States Supreme Court. *Political Behavior* 15:25–48.

Hall, Richard, and Grofman, Bernard. 1990. "The Committee Assignment Process and the Conditional Nature of Committee Bias." *American Political Science Review* 84:1149–1166.

Hammond, Thomas H., and Jeffrey S. Hill. 1993. "Deference or Preference? Explaining Senate Confirmation of Presidential Appointments to Administrative Agencies." *Journal of Theoretical Politics* 5:23–59.

Krehbiel, Keith. 1996. "Institutional and Partisan Sources of Gridlock: A Theory of Divided and Unified Government." *Journal of Theoretical Politics* 8:7–40.

Krehbiel, Keith. 1998. *Pivotal Politics*. Chicago: University of Chicago Press.

Lee, Emery G., III, Frances U. Sandstrum, and Thomas C. Weisert. 1996. "Context and the Court: Sources of Support for Civil Liberties on the Rehnquist Court." *American Politics Quarterly* 24:377–395.

Lee, Lung-Fei, and Robert Porter. 1984. "Switching Regression Models With Imperfect Sample Separation Information, With an Application on Cartel Stability." *Econometrica* 52:391–418.

Lewis-Beck, Michael S. 1995. *Data Analysis: An Introduction*. London: Sage Publications.

Maltese, John A. 1995. *The Selling of Supreme Court Nominees*. Baltimore: Johns Hopkins Press.

Maltzman, Forrest, and Paul J. Wahlbeck. 1996. "May It Please the Chief? Opinion Assignments in the Rehnquist Court." *American Journal of Political Science* 40:421–443.

Massaro, John. 1990. *Supremely Political: The Role of Ideology and Presidential Management in Unsuccessful Supreme Court Nominations*. Albany: SUNY Press.

Massaro, John. 1978. "'Lame-Duck' Presidents, Great Justices?" *Presidential Studies Quarterly*. Summer:296–302.

Morton, Rebecca M. 1999. *Methods and Models: A Guide to the Empirical Analysis of Formal Models in Political Science*. New York: Cambridge University Press.

Nemacheck, Christine, and Paul J. Wahlbeck. 1998. "The President's Choice of a Supreme Court Nominee." Presented at the Annual Meeting of the Midwest Political Science Association.

Nokken, Timothy P., and Brian R. Sala. 1999. A Spatial Interpretation of Senate Confirmations. *Journal of Theoretical Politics*. Forthcoming.

Overby, L. Marvin, Beth M. Henschen, Michael H. Walsh, and Julie Strauss. 1992. "Courting Constituents? An Analysis of the Senate Confirmation Vote on Justice Clarence Thomas." *American Political Science Review* 86:997–1006.

Ruckman, Jr., P. S. 1993. "The Supreme Court, Critical Nominations, and the Senate Confirmation Process." *Journal of Politics* 55:793–805.

Segal, Jeffrey A. 1987. "Senate Confirmation of Supreme Court Justices: Partisan and Institutional Politics." *Journal of Politics* 49:998–1015.

Segal, Jeffrey A., Charles M. Cameron, and Albert D. Cover. 1992. "A Spatial Model of Roll Call Voting: Senators, Constituents, and Interest Groups in Supreme Court Confirmations." *American Journal of Political Science* 36:96–121.

Segal, Jeffrey A., and Albert D. Cover. 1989. "Ideological Values and the Votes of U.S. Supreme Court Justices." *American Political Science Review* 83:557–565.

Segal, Jeffrey A., Robert Howard, and Christopher Hutz. 1996. "Presidential Success in Supreme Court Nominations: Testing a Constrained Presidency Model." Presented at the Annual Meeting of the Midwest Political Science Association.

Silverstein, Mark. 1994. *Judicious Choices*. New York: W.W. Norton and Company.

Snyder, Susan K., and Barry R. Weingast. 1994. "The American System of Shared Powers: The President, Congress, and the NLRB." Unpublished manuscript. Stanford University.

Squire, Peverill. 1988. "Politics and Personal Factors in Retirement from the United States Supreme Court." *Political Behavior* 10:180–190.

Watson, George L., and John A. Stookey. 1995. *Shaping America: The Politics of Supreme Court Appointments*. New York: Harper Collins.

Zupan, Mark A. 1992. "Measuring the Ideological Preferences of U.S. Presidents: A Proposed (Extremely Simple) Method." *Public Choice* 73:351–361.

[3]

Constituent Influence in State Supreme Courts: Conceptual Notes and a Case Study

Melinda Gann Hall
North Texas State University

This study examines the low rate of dissent in state supreme courts and argues that this trend might be accounted for, in part, by certain institutional arrangements. Specifically, in state supreme courts where justices are subject to re-election, perceived constituent values may suppress the expression of dissent on highly salient issues for certain types of justices. Instead of voting in accordance with their personal preferences, justices who have very strong ambitions to retain their positions, who perceive themselves to have views inconsistent with those of their constituents, and who find themselves in the minority on issues of high public visibility, may utilize the strategy of not dissenting in order to avoid being singled out for possible electoral sanction. A case study of the Louisiana Supreme Court, combining personal interviews with voting data, supports this proposition.

A significant and impressive body of literature has emerged on the correlates of decisional behavior in appellate courts. Of particular interest are the studies which examine the propensity to dissent. Although in most appellate courts dissent seems to be the exception rather than the rule, numerous factors have been identified as the causes of dissent behavior (see Peterson, 1981, for a propositional inventory of this literature). Recently, Steven Peterson (1981) summarized the findings in this area by arguing that "a disproportionate share of 'tests' is limited to the [United States] Supreme Court and . . . few of the propositions have been examined adequately" (p. 423). He further suggests that simple ideological disagreement with the majority, which might lead a judge to dissent, "may be overridden by organizational or tactical considerations" (p. 425). Like past researchers (Atkins, 1973; Atkins and Green, 1976; Songer, 1982), Peterson intimates that unanimity in decisions may not merely reflect ideological agreement among the judges but a very complex interaction of political stimuli.

This paper examines the propensity to dissent in a setting other than the United States Supreme Court—the Louisiana Supreme Court—and

*I wish to thank each of the justices of the Louisiana Supreme Court for participating in this study and also Paul Brace for his continuing encouragement and support.

argues that, indeed, certain institutional arrangements and strategic calculations seem to affect justices' voting behavior. To wit, the process of facing an electorate may have a subtle but significant impact on the way certain types of justices, who have a strong desire to retain the office and who anticipate possible electoral opposition, vote on highly salient political issues. More generally, the tendency toward unanimity or near unanimity in the decisions of many state courts of last resort may be explained, in part, by constituent influence and strategic voting.

The subject of constituent influence has been indirectly examined in the judicial selection literature. Although this research has many facets, including in-depth descriptions of how the various selection methods actually operate, assessments of the quality of judges selected by particular methods, and identification of variables explaining the adoption of each selection method, several studies attempt to ascertain whether the various methods of judicial recruitment have any effect on decision making in state courts. Without finding any connections between types of selection plans and such dependent variables as background characteristics of judges (Jacob, 1964; Canon, 1972; Watson and Downing, 1969) or a court's support for certain types of litigants (Atkins and Glick, 1974), the studies rather universally conclude that the various methods of selecting judges do not seem to make any meaningful differences in judicial decisions (see Flango and Ducat, 1979, for a summary of the empirical literature).

However, the literature on judicial recruitment has only examined aggregate voting patterns when trying to detect distinctions between selection systems. It is quite possible that aggregate voting patterns (i.e., characteristics of courts) mask important variations in individual justices' behavior. An examination of patterns in each justice's voting may be more appropriate for ascertaining, more generally, how justices of elected state supreme courts resolve the interaction between their personal political views and those of their constituents.

To anticipate some degree of constituent influence in most state supreme courts seems very reasonable. The justices of a majority of these courts are elected for specific terms, either by partisan or nonpartisan election mechanisms, and even justices of the courts chosen by "merit" are forced to face retention elections. Since most state supreme court justices are elected and are forced to appear at given intervals before the voters after having cast large numbers of votes on divisive public policy issues, it is plausible that justices may pursue voting strategies in order to maximize their chances of re-election.

However, judges, unlike other political actors, are generally perceived to make decisions on the basis of such legal constraints as laws, precedents, and constitutions, without the interplay of politics or political preferences.

Therefore, even though the most casual observers of courts recognize that judges often have extraordinary discretion in rendering decisions, judges can claim protection of the "purple curtain" and defend their choices with the shield of the law.

For judges, controversial decisions become more difficult to justify on the basis of law when they depart from the majority's decisions and vote in the minority. It can be argued that though voters may accept a legal explanation for a unanimous court's unpopular decision, the mechanism of judicial accountability is more rigidly adhered to on issues where voters have information and strong preferences and where judges have singled themselves out for criticism.

Therefore, it can be hypothesized that justices who strongly desire re-election and fear the possibility of electoral sanction will not distinguish themselves from the rest of the court by dissenting on highly salient political questions. Instead, a justice will either vote with the majority or will mask his or her disagreement in a concurrence rather than a dissent. In other words, we should see a higher level of unanimous voting relative to an overall pattern on controversial, very visible issues for certain types of justices. A limited case study of the Louisiana Supreme Court is utilized to explore this proposition.

The Louisiana Supreme Court is a seven-member state supreme court whose members are elected on partisan ballots (party label on the ballot) after open primaries for ten-year terms. Justices are chosen from specific geographic districts within the state, with two justices representing the district which includes New Orleans, the largest population center within the state. Therefore, each justice is chosen from a limited constituency and is connected to the constituency by a residency requirement. Terms on the court are staggered so that the entire court is never up for re-election at the same time. Interim vacancies are filled through appointments made by the court until elections can be scheduled within the following six months.

In-depth personal interviews were conducted in 1983 with each of the members of the Louisiana Supreme Court, with each interview lasting anywhere from several hours to all day. In order to solicit frank and candid remarks, each justice was guaranteed absolute confidentiality. As a result, the individual justices will not be associated with their specific comments or votes.

A rather wide variety of subjects was covered with each justice, but each was asked to assess the impact of facing re-election on his decision-making propensities. Of particular interest were the responses of the justices who perceived themselves to be much more liberal than their constituencies. It is, after all, in the conflict between decision makers' personal values and their constituents' preferences that the effects of elections can best be examined and understood.

During the interviews, three of the justices who identified themselves as liberals voiced very different reactions to the prospects of facing voters. Justice "A" described rather comprehensively how the process of seeking re-election affects his votes on one subset of criminal cases, the death penalty suits. This justice expressed, in general, a very strong concern for the protection of individual rights and freedoms and the necessity of courts to guard against "tyrannical majorities." In particular, he professed a personal abhorrence of executions and the death penalty, and he was also very critical of the United States Supreme Court's interpretation of the Eighth Amendment. What this particular justice indicated was a strong personal preference against the use of the death penalty.

Yet, at the same time, Justice "A" acknowledged that his perception of his constituents was that they clearly preferred the death penalty as a punishment for murder and that they would retaliate against him at election time if the justice did not reflect constituent preferences in this set of judicial decisions. Justice "A" felt that, of all the cases decided by the court, the decisions involving the death penalty were most likely to be reported by newspapers and most likely to be focused upon by opponents in campaigns. Louisiana is, of course, a state which has always provided for the death penalty and has actually executed several convicted murderers in the past few years. Since a liberal voting pattern in this highly visible and emotional set of decisions would place the justice at odds with his more conservatively oriented constituency, Justice "A" stated that he does not dissent in death penalty cases against an opinion of the court to affirm a defendant's conviction and sentence, expressly because of a perceived voter sanction, in spite of his deeply felt personal preferences to the contrary. He further acknowledged that in decisions prior to 1983, a period when the end of his term was rather distant, he had frequently dissented against the majority's upholding sentences in death cases, and he felt the public reaction was quite negative.

Justice "A" also expressed a great deal of anxiety over potentially losing his position, for which he would be running again in the upcoming few years. This justice, who seemed particularly satisfied with his office, apparently did not have the necessary years of service to draw a pension if defeated.

What Justice "A" described is the use of an uncomplicated, yet interesting and potentially effective strategy to pursue re-election. In order to minimize electoral opposition and maximize his public position, this minority justice professed to pursue a strategy of voting with the majority on issues of high public salience (e.g., the death penalty cases) and not voicing any dissent. Quite simply, although Justice "A" feels relatively free to decide most cases in line with his preferences about civil rights and liberties and other matters of public policy, this member of the Louisiana Supreme Court avoids giving ammunition to potential opponents in campaigns by not singling himself out for attention in highly visible decisions.

The other liberal justices, Justice "B" and Justice "C," when asked about voters, argued that they were relatively unconcerned with winning or losing their next elections. Although both expressed plans to run again for office and certainly claimed the desire to win, they seemed very casual about the prospect of losing. These justices have a great deal of service to the court, seemed somewhat bored with the job, and if defeated would qualify for lifetime pensions from the state. Like Justice "A," Justice "B" and Justice "C" also seemed concerned about defendants' rights but did not voice the same level of abhorrence or philosophical objections to the death penalty as Justice "A."

Both Justice "B" and Justice "C" expressed a lack of concern with constituent reaction and argued that it was their perceptions of justice which prevailed in decisions, even on high-salience issues presented to the court where their personal views were clearly in conflict with those of the voters.

TABLE 1

LIBERAL VOTING TENDENCIES OF THE JUSTICES OF THE LOUISIANA SUPREME COURT: 1980-81

CRIMINAL CASES DECIDED WITH DISSENT

JUSTICE	NO. OF VOTES CAST IN FAVOR OF DEFENDANTS' CLAIMS	% OF VOTES CAST IN FAVOR OF DEFENDANTS' CLAIMS
A	70/102	68.6%
B	59/102	57.8%
C	56/102	54.9%
D	38/101	37.6%
E	35/102	34.3%
F	31/102	30.4%
G	19/102	18.6%

In order to investigate whether the patterns each justice described are reflected in actual votes, data on all criminal decisions of the Louisiana Supreme Court with written opinion for the 1980-81 term and data on all cases in which the death penalty was given as a sentence from 1981 through June 1986 were collected from the *Southern Reporter*. A vote cast in favor of overturning a defendant's conviction or sentence was classified as a liberal vote, while a vote cast supporting a defendant's conviction or sentence was designated a conservative vote. Table 1 ranks the justices of the Louisiana Supreme Court according to their liberal voting tendencies in nonunanimous criminal decisions for 1980-81, the first term of the most recent complete natural court. As the data demonstrate, Justices "A," "B," and "C" do seem to be the most liberal justices of the Louisiana Supreme Court on criminal cases during this period. To anticipate electoral incompatibility on death penalty cases seems imminently reasonable for these justices.

If Justice "A" is pursuing a process of strategic voting according to the above prescriptions (i.e., not casting liberal dissents on highly visible decisions before a perceived conservative constituency), then for Justice "A" there should be significant differences in dissent rates between criminal cases in general and death penalty cases. Conversely, for Justice "B" and Justice "C," who did not feel pressures from their constituencies, we should see very similar levels of dissent between criminal cases overall and the death penalty cases. Table 2 presents this information.

TABLE 2

VOTING PROPENSITIES OF JUSTICES A, B, AND C

	JUSTICE A		JUSTICE B		JUSTICE C	
	ALL CRIMINAL CASES	DEATH PENALTY CASES	ALL CRIMINAL CASES	DEATH PENALTY CASES	ALL CRIMINAL CASES	DEATH PENALTY CASES
Number of liberal dissents from conservative decisions	33/127 (26.0%)	1/30 (3.3%)	16/127 (12.6%)	4/30 (13.3%)	17/127 (13.4%)	4/30 (13.3%)
Number of votes with the court majority	165/202 (81.7%)	44/45 (97.8%)	186/202 (92.1%)	41/45 (91.1%)	184/202 (91.1%)	41/45 (91.1%)
Overall number of liberal votes, including majority votes and dissents	105/202 (52.0%)	16/45 (35.6%)	91/202 (45.0%)	19/45 (42.2%)	90/202 (44.6%)	19/45 (42.2%)

As can be seen from table 2, the expectations about Justice "A"'s behavior are borne out by the data. For the death penalty cases, Justice "A" has a pronounced tendency to dissent less from conservative decisions of the court, to vote with the majority more often, and to cast fewer liberal votes than he does on criminal cases overall. In fact, the only liberal dissent Justice "A" cast in death penalty cases during the period 1981 through 1986 was cast in early 1982, and for four years Justice "A" has not expressed public disagreement with any death case decisions of the court.

As table 2 also indicates, the expectations about Justice "B" and Justice "C" are confirmed by the data. Unlike Justice "A," Justice "B" and Justice "C" do not exhibit differential voting patterns for death cases, and there is no clear evidence in the data that Justice "B" or Justice "C" responds to constituent pressures, even in such controversial cases as death penalty suits.

This look at the Louisiana Supreme Court presents some evidence that suggests that certain types of justices may, indeed, be affected by the pressures of re-election. Justices who find themselves in the court minority, who perceive themselves to have views inconsistent with those of their constituents, and who have very strong ambitions to retain their positions and fear electoral challenge, may be extremely hesitant to voice disagreement with the court's decisions on highly controversial issues of public policy. To avoid singling themselves out for criticism during the re-election process, these types of justices may suppress the expression of dissent. Whether voters and opponents are cognizant of the justices' behavior or not, certain justices seem to fear the prospect of electoral sanction and consequently alter their behavior.

Though it is impossible from a case study to speculate about the pervasiveness or significance of constituent effects in state supreme courts, this analysis does indicate that future enterprises in this area may be fruitful. It could well be the case that the extraordinary levels of unanimity or near unanimity in elected state courts of last resort are, to some extent, the result of strategic voting by justices with strong re-election ambitions. Research combining personal interviews with the examination of voting data for all the elected state supreme courts, comparing votes for each justice on different types of issues, may illuminate the process of constituent influence in these institutions. It might also be productive to look for changes over time in justices' overall patterns of voting as re-election dates approach and then become more distant. It seems quite possible that justices, as they near the time to face the electorate, will vote more in line with perceived constituent opinion on controversial issues and dissent less than if re-election is not looming on the horizon. Future research should more thoroughly investigate these intriguing possibilities.

References

Atkins, Burton M. 1973. Judicial Behavior and Tendencies Toward Conformity in a Three-Member Small Group: A Case Study of Dissent Behavior on the U.S. Court of Appeals. *Social Science Quarterly*, 54: 41-53.

Atkins, Burton M., and Henry R. Glick. 1974. Formal Judicial Recruitment and State Supreme Court Decisions. *American Politics Quarterly*, 2: 427-49.

Atkins, Burton M., and Justin J. Green. 1976. Consensus on the United States Courts of Appeals: Illusion or Reality? *American Journal of Political Science*, 20: 735-48.

Canon, Bradley C. 1972. The Impact of Formal Selection Processes on the Characteristics of Judges—Reconsidered. *Law and Society Review*, 13: 570-93.

Flango, Victor Eugene, and Craig R. Ducat. 1979. What Difference Does Method of Judicial Selection Make?: Selection Procedures in State Courts of Last Resort. *Justice System Journal*, 5: 25-44.

Jacob, Herbert. 1964. The Effect of Institutional Differences in the Recruitment Process: The Case of State Judges. *Journal of Public Law*, 13: 104-19.

Peterson, Steven A. 1981. Dissent in American Courts. *Journal of Politics*, 43: 412-34.

Songer, Donald R. 1982. Consensual and Nonconsensual Decisions in Unanimous Opinions in the United States Courts of Appeals. *American Journal of Political Science*, 26: 225-39.

Watson, Richard, and Rondal Downing. 1969. *The Politics of the Bench and the Bar*. New York: John Wiley.

Part II
Judicial Decision-Making

[4]

Divisions of Opinion Among Justices of the U.S. Supreme Court, 1939–1941

C. Herman Pritchett

"We are under a Constitution," said Charles Evans Hughes when he was governor of New York, "but the Constitution is what the judges say it is . . . " Several theories of jurisprudence have arisen which attempt to take into account this personal element in the judicial interpretation and making of law. The so-called "realistic" school has argued that law is simply the behavior of the judge, that law is secreted by judges as pearls are secreted by oysters.[1] A less extreme position was taken by the late Justice Holmes, who said: "What I mean by law is nothing more or less than the prediction of what a court will do." While these views go rather far in eliminating any idea of law as a "normative, conceptual system of rules," no one doubts that many judicial determinations are made on some basis other than the application of settled rules to the facts, or that justices of the United States Supreme Court, in deciding controversial cases involving important issues of public policy, are influenced by biases and philosophies of government, by "inarticulate major premises," which to a large degree predetermine the position they will take on a given question. Private attitudes, in other words, become public law.

More precisely, it is the private attitudes of the majority of the Court which become public law. As an inexact science, issues at law are settled by counting the noses of jurors and justices. About 150 times every term the judges of the Supreme Court announce to the world in a formal written opinion the result of their balloting on the questions raised by a legal controversy before the Court. Happily, in the great majority of these ballots the decision is unanimous. In such cases, presumably the facts and the law are so clear that no opportunity is allowed for the autobiographies of the justices to lead them to opposing conclusions. It is always possible that the members of the Court may be agreeing for different reasons, but no hint of that fact is given unless concurring opinions are written.

In a substantial number of cases, however, the nine members of the Court are not able to see eye to eye on the issues involved. Working with an identical set of facts, and with roughly comparable training in the law, they come to different conclusions. If our thesis is correct, these divisions of opinion grow out of the conscious or unconscious preferences and prejudices of the justices, and an examination of these disagreements should afford an interesting approach to the problem of judicial motivation.

---

act to provide for the Fifteenth and subsequent decennial censuses and to provide for apportionment of representatives in Congress, approved June 18, 1929, in Sec. 22 (b), provides the method which shall be employed "if the Congress . . . fails to *enact a law* apportioning Representatives among the several States," after the President has submitted a statement showing the results of applying various mathematical methods.

[1] This figure and the quotations following are taken from Francis D. Wormuth, "The Dilemma of Jurisprudence," in this Review, Vol. 35 (1941), p. 44.

These cases in which dissent is expressed are particularly deserving of study because they furnish data which are not simply the verbalizations of justices, to be handled by the typical process of interpretation, analysis, comparison, search for inconsistencies, and general legal exegesis. Instead, they contribute the tangible data of a series of yes and no votes on a variety of issues. Analysis of this voting behavior should be of value in explaining Supreme Court action, in revealing basic relationships among the justices, and, in short, in "predicting" the law.

It may be suggested that the nature of the division of opinion on the Supreme Court at any given time is a matter of common knowledge among those who follow Supreme Court thinking. In the hope, however, that a more precise analysis might have some value, the divisions of opinion in Supreme Court decisions during the past two years (the October terms, 1939 and 1940) have been analyzed. This period was one in which the membership of the Court was fairly stable. The only changes in its composition came when Butler died soon after the beginning of the 1939 term (without having participated in any cases) and was replaced by Murphy, and when McReynolds resigned during the 1940 term.

During this two-year period, dissent was registered to more than one-fourth of the decisions rendered by the Court. In the 1939 term, the rate was 30 per cent (42 dissents in a total of 140 decisions), and for the 1940 term it dropped slightly to 28 per cent (47 dissents out of 169 decisions). There were thus 89 decisions during the period in which one or more of the justices dissented, at least in part, from the conclusion reached by the majority.[2] Table I shows the extent of each justice's participation in these dissents. The judge most persistent in disagreement was McReynolds, who took a minority stand in 22 per cent of the decisions in which he participated. Justices Roberts and Hughes were next in order, with records of 18 per cent and 12 per cent respectively. On the other hand, Frankfurter found himself on the losing side in only four of the 309 decisions rendered by the Court, a fact which calls attention to the central position which he appears to occupy on the Court. It should also be noted that he was the only justice whose dissents did not increase in number from 1939 to 1940 (with the exception of McReynolds, who did not serve out the 1940 term).

[2] It should be noted that some 10 or 11 of these dissents were in "companion" cases, i.e., cases involving an issue identical with that decided in a preceding case, and requiring little or no new discussion. For statistical treatment, these cases might have been eliminated, to prevent double weight being given to divisions of opinion in a single situation. However, they have not been excluded, for various reasons, and it is not believed that any distortion has resulted from their inclusion. In two cases (61 S.C. 845, 861), there are dissents by two groups of justices involving separate aspects of the decision; these have been treated as two distinct dissents, and thus there are 91 dissents in the 89 cases.

Justices Reed, Murphy, and Stone are also shown by the data to be consistently members of the Court's majority.

TABLE I
PARTICIPATION OF SUPREME COURT JUSTICES IN DISSENTING OPINIONS, 1939 AND 1940 TERMS

Justice	*Number of Dissents*			*Opinions Participated In*	*Per Cent Dissents*
	1939	*1940*	*Total*		
McReynolds*	32	9	41	184	22
Roberts	23	31	54	300	18
Hughes	14	24	38	305	12
Black	4	15	19	306	6
Douglas	4	15	19	303	6
Stone	4	7	11	303	4
Reed	1	8	9	302	3
Murphy**	1	6	7	215	3
Frankfurter	2	2	4	309	1

* Resigned February 1, 1941.
** Began service February 5, 1940.

Of these 89 dissents, 25 were one-man affairs. McReynolds dissented alone in 13 cases, Roberts in 10, and Reed and Stone once each. In the other 64 dissents, the concurrence of two, three, or four justices in deviation from the majority view raises interesting problems of judicial interrelationships. Was there a regular pattern of dissent? Did certain justices tend to agree with each other in expressing dissent? Table II attempts to answer such questions by showing the number of times each justice joined each other justice in a dissenting opinion. A well-defined pattern of relationships was found to exist on the Court, and the names have been arranged in the table so as to bring out this relationship most clearly. Figures on the one-man dissents have been included in parentheses.

The table appears to reveal a marked division of the justices into two wings or groups. The first is composed of McReynolds, Roberts, Hughes and Stone; the other includes Murphy, Frankfurter, Black, and Douglas. With the exception of two cases, no justice in one of these groups ever joined in a dissenting opinion with a justice from the other group. While every one of the eight justices on occasion dissented in company with other members of his own bloc, in only two out of 89 dissents was there fraternization with the enemy. Both of these exceptional cases saw Roberts crossing the line to vote with Black and Douglas.[3] Justice Reed presents a special problem, since he was found in company with justices

[3] The cases are Neuberger v. Commissioner of Internal Revenue, 61 S.C. 97 (1940), and Union Pacific Rr. Co. v. U. S., 61 S. C. 1064 (1941).

from both groups. His nine dissents included four with judges from each wing, and one lone dissent. He thus appeared to have one foot in each camp.

To the extent that the above table appears to show the existence of two self-contained blocs of opinion on the Court, it obviously misrepresents the situation. The pattern of relationships which begins to emerge from the table needs to be made clearer by presenting more complete data which will show all judicial agreements, whether on the majority or minority side. Table II reveals that Frankfurter and Hughes were never in dissent together, but it does not tell us how often they agreed with each other when other justices were in dissent. Table III, consequently, is arranged to show the extent of agreement between each pair of justices in the 89 controversial cases (or rather, in so many of them as were participated in by that pair). The number of agreements is expressed in percentages of total cases participated in by each pair.

TABLE II

AGREEMENTS AMONG SUPREME COURT JUSTICES IN DISSENTING OPINIONS, 1939 AND 1940 TERMS

Justice	*McReynolds*	*Roberts*	*Hughes*	*Stone*	*Reed*	*Frankfurter*	*Murphy*	*Black*	*Douglas*
McReynolds	(13)	26	20	4	2				
Roberts	26	(10)	33	5	3			2	2
Hughes	20	33	—	10	3				
Stone	4	5	10	(1)	1				
Reed	2	3	3	1	(1)			4	4
Frankfurter						—	1	4	4
Murphy						1	—	7	7
Black		2			4	4	7	—	19
Douglas		2			4	4	7	19	—

The table reveals some interesting facts. Justices Black and Douglas are shown never to have been on opposite sides of a decision during the entire period. On the other hand, McReynolds disagreed with them in three-fourths of all the decisions in which there was division of opinion. Chief Justice Hughes was closer to Stone than to any other justice, Stone found himself most often in agreement with Frankfurter, and Frankfurter's views coincided most often with those of Murphy. The most important fact about this complex of individual relationships, however, is that it conforms to a basic underlying pattern. Examination of the table

TABLE III

AGREEMENTS AMONG SUPREME COURT JUSTICES IN CONTROVERSIAL CASES, 1939 AND 1940 TERMS
(In Percentages)

Justice	*McReynolds*	*Roberts*	*Hughes*	*Stone*	*Reed*	*Frankfurter*	*Murphy*	*Black*	*Douglas*
McReynolds	—	64	64	41	35	31	38	24	24
Roberts	64	—	75	51	45	45	39	37	36
Hughes	64	75	—	78	63	64	53	49	49
Stone	41	51	78	—	81	84	75	69	68
Reed	35	45	63	81	—	86	80	79	79
Frankfurter	31	45	64	84	86	—	91	85	84
Murphy	38	39	53	75	80	91	—	89	89
Black	24	37	49	69	79	85	89	—	100
Douglas	24	36	49	68	79	84	89	100	—

shows that with the justices ranked as they are, every member of the Court is placed next to or between the justice or justices with whom he is most completely identified in agreement, and farthest away from those with whom he has least in common. The only important exceptions to this rule are found in the McReynolds-Murphy and the Stone-Frankfurter relationships.

The division of opinion thus takes the form of the figure below, which locates the justices along a continuum from one extreme to the other according to the direction and intensity of their deviation from the normal majority position of the Court, represented by the zero point on the scale.

Deviations Expressed in Percentages

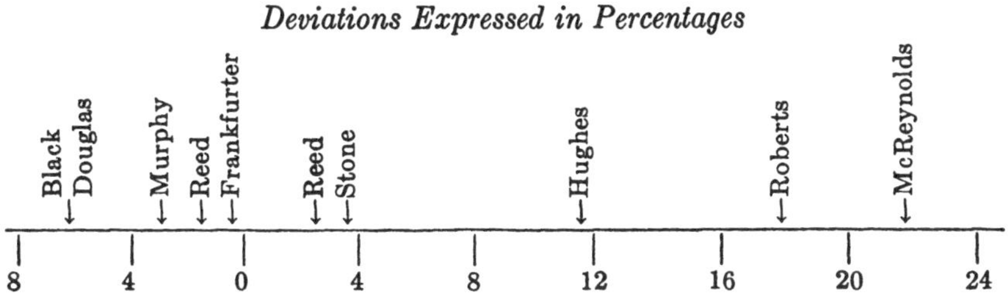

Frankfurter is closest to this point, since he dissented from only one per cent of the Court's decisions. Reed is given a position on both sides of the zero point, since his dissents were divided between the two wings. The scale makes apparent the existence of a fairly cohesive six-judge majority, most of the dissents being entered by the right-wing minority of McReynolds, Roberts, and Hughes.

This use of the term "right-wing" assumes that the division of opinion on the Court results from differences of opinion as to desirable public policy. It assumes that the above scale reflects relative "liberalism" and "conservatism" as those terms are understood by the man in the street. This assumption should be checked by an examination of the issues actually involved in the cases where dissents were filed. Did all of these cases present issues of public policy on which liberals and conservatives might well be expected to differ, or did a number of them involve "purely legal" questions? A proper answer on this point would require the setting up of elaborate criteria for distinguishing between these two kinds of issues, and application of the criteria in a detailed analysis of each case. Such an analysis has been attempted here to only a limited degree, and covering only the dissents of the 1939 term.

A case which requires a decision as to the extent of governmental powers, or presents an issue between the government and an individual, is obviously one in which the result may be affected by the judges' views on public policy. Our present stereotypes picture the conservative as anti-government (in the sense of opposing new or more effective forms of governmental control over individuals or corporations), and the liberal or New Dealer as pro-government.[4] An examination of the 1939 term's 42 dissents shows that in at least 36 an issue was presented which required the justices to vote for or against the government, to uphold or deny a government contention, to approve or disapprove an exercise of governmental authority.[5] The voting record of the justices in these 36 cases shows that in 27 the dissenters were right-wingers taking an anti-government position; in three more cases, the dissenters were left-wing justices voting for the government. Thus in 30 of the cases judicial action ran true to form.

Of the six remaining cases in this group, four saw the situation exactly

[4] The Court's newest justice, former Attorney-General Jackson, has recently commented feelingly on the "anti-government" attitude (not simply anti-New Deal) of the Court's conservative majority during the pre-deluge period of 1935–1936. See Robert H. Jackson, *The Struggle for Judicial Supremacy* (New York, 1941), p. 170.

[5] The citations are: 308 U.S. 147, 313, 331, 338, 473, 488; 309 U.S. 33, 70, 83, 106, 149, 176, 310, 331, 350, 370, 430, 517, 527, 530, 551; 310 U.S. 53, 69, 80, 88, 106, 113, 141, 150, 371, 381, 434, 534, 554, 573, 586.

reversed, with the government's support coming from the right wing.[6] The explanation is simple, however. All four were civil liberties cases (involving free speech, the right to picket, and freedom from wire-tapping), and in all four McReynolds was the lone dissenter voting to uphold government restrictions on individuals. His action was in line with the traditional conservative position on the Court. It will be recalled that in 1931 the famous free press case of Near v. Minnesota[7] brought out a perfect conservative dissenting lineup of Butler, Van Devanter, McReynolds, and Sutherland. By the 1939 term, only one of this old guard remained to take a stand against civil liberties.

In the remaining two of these 36 dissents, the vote is completely inexplicable in terms of the scale positions of the justices. One dissent was that of Justice Stone in the well-known flag salute case,[8] in which he alone maintained a strict civil liberties position in the face of the justification for the compulsory salute which the rest of the Court found compelling. The other exception came in a case presenting the thorny question of taxability of trust income, and saw Reed alone voting for the government's contention.[9] Apart from these cases, however, the judicial reaction to a "government" issue was so consistent that it must be considered a definite factor in the Court's divisions of opinion.

Examining the 42 dissents of the 1939 term from another point of view, we find 18 cases in which the Court was required to make a decision for or against "business."[10] The issue was presented in many forms—the validity of a business tax, an alleged violation of the anti-trust laws, the constitutionality of a federal or state regulatory scheme. But wherever the issue was present, the reaction pattern was consistent, support for business coming always from the conservative end of the Court. Specifically, there were 15 dissents by right-wingers taking the side of business, and three by liberals voting against a majority decision favorable to business. Again, in five cases during the 1939 term the Court was dealing with a "labor" issue, and here also the reaction was uniform.[11] There were four conservative dissents to decisions favoring labor, and one dissent by Douglas and Black from a majority decision slightly weakening the effect of a N.L.R.B. order.

[6] Schneider v. State, 308 U.S. 147 (1939); Nardone v. U.S., 308 U.S. 338 (1939); Thornhill v. Alabama, 310 U.S. 88 (1940); Carlson v. California, 310 U.S. 106 (1940). [7] 283 U.S. 697 (1931).

[8] Minersville School District v. Gobitis, 310 U.S. 586 (1940).

[9] Helvering v. Fuller, 310 U.S. 69 (1940).

[10] The citations are: 308 U.S. 165, 331; 309 U.S. 190, 280, 310, 350, 370; 310 U.S. 1, 53, 113, 141, 150, 371, 381, 434, 469, 534, 573.

[11] National Licorice Co. v. N.L.R.B., 309 U.S. 350 (1940); Paramino Co. v. Marshall, 309 U.S. 370 (1940); Thornhill v. Alabama, supra; Carlson v. California, supra; Apex Hosiery Co. v. Leader, 310 U.S. 469 (1940).

The 1939 dissents included seven cases in which state or local action was attacked as violating provisions of the federal Constitution; for example, state and local taxes were resisted as burdening interstate commerce or contrary to due process or infringing a privilege of national citizenship.[12] Here the consistent policy of the justices at the Black-Douglas end of the Court was to uphold state action, in line with the traditional liberal belief that state legislative powers should be left as unrestricted by federal constitutional limitations as possible. It may also be noted that an issue involving the extent of judicial review was raised in some form in four cases; the left-wing wanted to narrow review, and the right-wing opposed any narrowing.[13] Public operation of a power system was an issue in one case; McReynolds opposed it.[14] The rights of a debtor under the Frazier-Lemke Act were involved in another case; a liberal minority voted in his favor.[15]

One or more of the seven issues just considered was present in every one of the cases where opinion was divided during the 1939 term. In other words, none of these cases appears to present a "purely legal" question, for in each instance the observer can find a facet of the case which might offer an opportunity for the decision to be influenced by judicial views as to desirable public policy. It is not contended, of course, that the decisions were motivated wholly by the personal views of the justices, but the data clearly indicate that these views had a considerable effect in the process of making up the judicial mind.

It would be interesting to discuss the records of several of the individual justices in the light of the information which this analysis has supplied. The case of the Court's new Chief Justice is particularly worthy of notice. The participation of Justice Stone in right-wing dissents may seem strange, in view of his reputation as one of the soundest and ablest liberals on the Court. Two explanations suggest themselves. One is that he has deviated slightly to the right in his views with the passage of time. The other is that he has maintained very nearly his original position, but that the Court has with recent appointments moved so substantially leftward that views which put Stone to the left of the Court ten years ago now occasionally leave him exposed in dissent on the right. Whatever the cause, the process appears to be accelerating, for Stone's dissents with the con-

[12] McGoldrick v. Berwind-White Co., 309 U.S. 33 (1940), and two companion cases; Ford Motor Co. v. Beauchamp, 308 U.S. 331 (1939); Madden v. Kentucky, 309 U.S. 83 (1940); McCarroll v. Dixie Greyhound Lines, 309 U.S. 176 (1940); Osborn v. Ozlin, 310 U.S. 53 (1940).

[13] McCarroll v. Dixie Greyhound Lines, *supra*; Perkins v. Lukens Steel Co., 310 U.S. 113 (1940); U.S. v. Bush & Co., 310 U.S. 371 (1940); Railroad Commission v. Rowan & Nichols Oil Co., 310 U.S. 573 (1940).

[14] U.S. v. San Francisco, 310 U.S. 16 (1940).

[15] Union Joint Stock Land Bank v. Byerly, 310 U.S. 1 (1940).

servative group numbered three in the 1939 term and six in the 1940 term.

The general result of this study has been to emphasize the influence of personal attitudes in the making of judicial decisions and the interpretation of law.[16] To prevent over-emphasis on this point, it would be well to recall that even in a Court representing as wide a range of views as has been found during the last two terms, 71 per cent of the cases were decided by unanimous vote. Where there were divisions of opinion, however, they appear to be for the most part explicable in terms of the opinions of the respective judges on public policy. This conclusion hardly comes as a surprise. For few are likely to deny that justices of the Supreme Court have always, to paraphrase Justice Frankfurter, "read the laws of Congress through the distorting lenses" ground by their own experience. On the other hand, there are many who will agree that the Supreme Court's vision is better today than it has been for many years past.

C. HERMAN PRITCHETT.

University of Chicago.

Unconstitutional Legislation in Minnesota.[1] This study is concerned with certain phases of the operation of the power of the courts to declare legislative enactments unconstitutional. It is concerned with the exercise of this power rather than with the rules governing or applicable to the exercise of the power itself. For this reason, it might be thought of as a

[16] One further illustration of this point may be supplied. During the 1940 term, the Supreme Court twice had to consider problems raised by the establishment of a new terminal produce market at Kansas City, Kansas, which was promoted by the Union Pacific Railroad and the city in an evident effort to attract trade away from the existing terminal at Kansas City, Missouri. The legal questions raised in the two cases were quite different. In the first (L. Singer & Sons v. Union Pacific R. Co., 61 S.C. 254 (1940)), the question was whether Kansas City, Mo., could as a "party in interest" under the Transportation Act of 1920, seek to enjoin the construction of an extension by the railroad to serve this competing market. In this case, the city lost. In the second case (Union Pacific R. Co. v. U.S., 61 S.C. 1064 (1941), the question was whether the Elkins Act had been violated by the action of Kansas City, Kan., which, in coöperation with the railroad, had offered concessions to induce leasing of space in the new terminal. Here the court held that the act had been violated. Seven members of the court participated in both decisions, and it is interesting to note that three of the justices (Roberts, Douglas, and Black) took a position on the legal points involved which favored the new terminal in both cases, while three other justices (Stone, Hughes, and Reed) opposed it in both cases. Justice Frankfurter alone switched sides between cases, and was with the majority in both. This incident suggests that the judges decided the legal questions in terms of their attitude towards the terminal and the justifiability of this kind of competition.

[1] Assistance in the preparation of these materials was furnished by the personnel of the Work Projects Administration, Official Project No. 165-1-71-154. A research grant was received also from the Graduate School Research Fund of Indiana University.

[5]

On the Mysterious Demise of Consensual Norms in the United States Supreme Court

Thomas G. Walker
Emory University
Lee Epstein
Southern Methodist University
William J. Dixon
Emory University

The early 1940s marked a period in which the consensus norms of the Supreme Court experienced a radical and apparently permanent change. The consistent pattern of relatively high cohesion characteristic of the Court's earlier years gave way to surging rates of concurring and dissenting opinions. The present research is an examination of the factors possibly contributing to the justices' sharply increasing tendency to express their individual views rather than to defer to the opinion of the Court. Using both historical and quantitative methods, the authors evaluate the impact of the Court's discretionary jurisdiction, changing caseload, associate justice characteristics, and judicial leadership. The evidence presented points to the conclusion that in combination with other factors the leadership style introduced by Harlan Fiske Stone in 1941 had a dramatic effect on the consensus norms of the Court.

Patterns of social behavior occasionally experience abrupt changes that defy explanation by apparent cause. When precipitous deviations from the norm are experienced by politically important institutions, they should be treated not as idiopathic curiosities, but as perplexing phenomena worthy of systematic analysis.

Figure 1, which illustrates the rate of dissenting and concurring opinions on the Supreme Court since 1800, presents such a mystery.[1] From John Marshall's appointment as chief justice to the end of the Charles Evans Hughes era, the Court exhibited relatively stable, cohesive behavior. These years are marked by individual justices accepting the Court's majority opinions. Although the nation suffered through turbulent periods of war, rebel-

*The authors are indebted to Professor James Stimson for his generous assistance on this project and to the anonymous referees for their very helpful comments.

[1]Dissent is measured as the number of dissenting opinions per 100 opinions of the Court; concurrence as the number of concurring opinions per 100 opinions of the Court. These particular measures were employed because the issuance of a dissenting or concurring opinion represents behavior clearly inconsistent with traditional consensus norms. Our measures are based on data provided by Blaustein and Mersky (1978) and the *Supreme Court Reporter's* annual summaries.

lion, economic depression, and political cleavage, the high court maintained the norm of consensus. Individual expression was kept at a minimum and within a relatively consistent range. In the early 1940s, however, the conventions of the Court radically changed. The incidence of individual justices separating themselves from the majority by articulating dissenting and concurring opinions surged to unprecedented levels. Not only was the increase dramatic in magnitude, but it represented an apparently permanent alteration in the Court's decision-making regime.[2] Consider, for example, that prior to 1941 an average of 8.5 dissenting opinions were issued for every 100 majority opinions, but after 1941 that figure rose to seventy-three dissenting opinions. This evolutionary development presents the following research question: What transformed the practices of the Supreme Court from a regime in which individual views were suppressed in deference to the majority into a decision-making system in which individual expression became the rule rather than the exception?

The answer to this question is of no small consequence. C. Herman Pritchett has argued that the increase in dissenting and concurring opinions weakened the Court's "institutional ethos" (Pritchett, 1954, p. 22). The Court moved from a decision-making process based on consensus to one characterized by individual decision making, or what Justice Lewis Powell recently claimed to be decisions emanating from nine separate law offices. Ironically, this particular change is precisely what John Marshall sought to avoid when he eliminated the practice of seriatim opinions that allowed each justice to voice his individual views on every case. According to Bernard Schwartz, "if carried to its extreme, the right to concur or dissent leads back . . . to the practice . . . of *seriatim* opinions" (1957, pp. 356–57). Surely, Court norms since the 1940s approximate such a reversal; today, a decision announced by a single, unanimously supported opinion is a rarity.

Not only did the decade of the 1940s irrevocably alter the institutional norms of the Supreme Court, but the skyrocketing dissent and concurrence rates of that period radically changed the way scholars viewed the judiciary. Prior to 1941, traditional legal approaches provided satisfactory explanations for a Supreme Court whose institutional practices led to consensus decisions with relatively low levels of expressed disagreement. Pritchett was the first to recognize the scholarly implications of the Court's post-1941 abandonment of strong consensus norms. Writing in 1954, he argued, "it is precisely because the Court's institutional ethos has become so weak that we must examine the thinking of the individual justices . . ." (1954, p. 22). At Pritchett's urging, scholars such as Nagel (1961), Ulmer (1962), and Schubert (1962) initiated the exploration of factors that affect the decisions of individual judges

[2]We use the term "regime" to refer to shared norms and rules governing the actions of individuals engaged in an established collective decision-making process. Our usage is similar to that proposed by Kegley (1987) in a different context.

FIGURE 1

DISSENT AND CONCURRENCE PER 100 MAJORITY OPINIONS IN THE UNITED STATES SUPREME COURT, 1800–1981

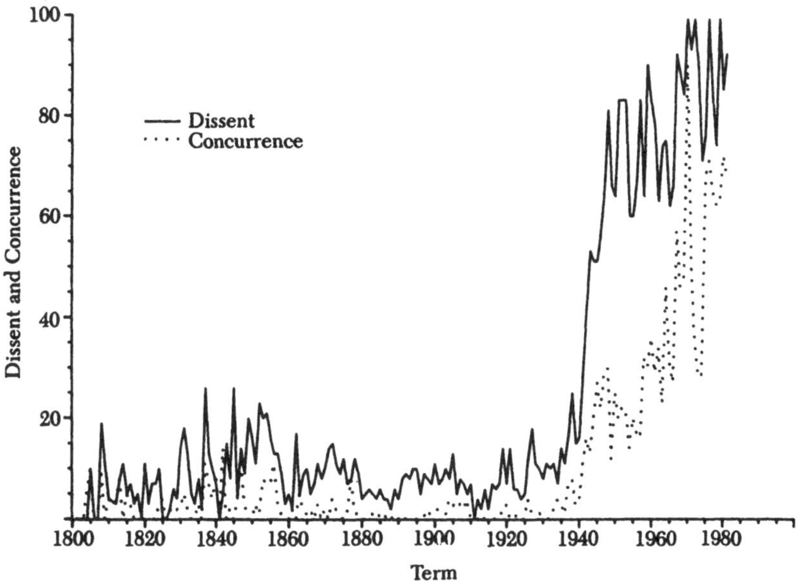

on federal and state courts. These efforts propelled the field of public law into the behavioral revolution, a theoretical perspective that continues to dominate our perceptions of the American legal system. All this, it seems, occurred because after 1941 there were huge variations in judicial voting behavior begging to be explained.

Consequently, unravelling this mystery involves confronting questions of substantial importance. Although the much studied Warren and Burger Courts have led contemporary scholars to take individual judicial expressions for granted, a mere glance at figure 1 indicates that such an assumption ignores 140 years of Court history. Whoever or whatever was responsible for the abrupt and dramatic increase in dissenting and concurring opinions not only changed the norms of the Supreme Court, but also altered the way in which an entire cohort of political scientists now view the judicial process.

How do we identify the causes of change? As any good investigator knows, the first steps in solving a mystery are to establish a list of suspects and set criteria by which to eliminate them from culpability. In creating our list we are aided by two important factors. First, we are able to determine with some precision the point at which the Court's behavioral patterns were altered. As figure 1 shows, consensus norms did not gradually erode, but were abruptly shattered. Table 1, which presents in numerical form dissent and

TABLE 1

DISSENT AND CONCURRENCE RATES, 1935–1946

Term	Dissent Rate	Concurrence Rate
1935	.14	.03
1936	.11	.01
1937	.17	.07
1938	.25	.08
1939	.15	.04
1940	.16	.03
1941	.29	.11
1942	.43	.16
1943	.54	.13
1944	.51	.20
1945	.51	.27
1946	.57	.22

For data source and methods of calculation, see footnote 1.

concurrence rates from 1935 to 1946, isolates the 1941 term, the first under Chief Justice Harlan Fiske Stone, as the turning point. This evidence allows us to focus our efforts on a particular historical period. Second, there is a body of scholarly research that has sought to identify the causes of dissent. This literature provides theoretical grounding for the identification of factors suspected to have contributed to the demise of the Court's strong consensus norm. Following these leads we have constructed a list of five possible causes and tested their viability as explanations for the Supreme Court's regime change:

1. Congressional enactment of the Judiciary Act of 1925.
2. Changes in the Court's caseload.
3. The promotion of a sitting associate to be chief justice.
4. Changes in the Court's composition.
5. The leadership of the chief justice.

THE JUDICIARY ACT OF 1925

Perhaps of all our suspected causes, most scholarly fingers point to congressional passage of the Judiciary Act of 1925. In essence, this legislation, known as the "Judges' Bill," changed the Court's docket from one of obligation to one of discretion. The statute allowed the justices to avoid hearing frivolous cases involving well-established legal issues and to concentrate instead on questions of true significance. There is reason to believe that a discretionary docket will contain a relatively large number of controversial cases that generate divisions of opinion (Halpern and Vines, 1977; Grossman and Wells, 1980, p. 232). Therefore, grounds exist to hypothesize that the

Act, which began to affect the ratio of obligatory to discretionary cases in 1927, had a permanent impact on patterns of individual judicial expression.

In an article published in 1977, Stephen Halpern and Kenneth Vines tested this expectation and concluded that the Act had "contributed" to the behavioral patterns depicted in our Figure 1.[3] Their analysis rests largely on a comparison of dissent behavior for nearly equal periods shortly before [1922–1925] and after [1927 through the first sixty-five cases of the 1929 term] passage of the statute (pp. 472–73). The results revealed a slight overall increase in dissent following the implementation of the legislation. The change occurred almost exclusively in the Court's obligatory cases (an 8.2 percent dissent rate prior to enactment and a 25.1 percent dissent rate after), leading the authors to explain that the Act eliminated appeal as a matter of right in numerous classes of cases which generally raised straightforward legal issues (1977, p. 475). The dissent rate in the Court's discretionary docket showed virtually no change (7.6 percent before the Act and 8.3 percent after). To substantiate their position further, Halpern and Vines presented a series of graphs illustrating the incidence of dissenting behavior longitudinally. From these data, the authors concluded that "1925 stands out . . . as a starting point in the evolution of a new trend of dissenting votes" (1977, pp. 479–80).

While granting the Court broad discretionary jurisdiction surely affected the nature of the institution, a closer examination of the data leads us to doubt that the Judges' Bill alone can account for the massive increases in individual judicial expression. First, the changes in the Court's ratio of obligatory to discretionary cases do not conicide with the justices' patterns of increasing dissent activity. As figure 2 demonstrates, the discretionary share of the Court's docket rose dramatically immediately following the Act and remained relatively stable thereafter, a phenomenon also observed by Halpern and Vines (1977, pp. 475–76). However, as is also readily observable in figure 2, significant escalation in both the dissent and concurrence rates did not occur until almost fifteen years later.

Second, an analysis of the terms immediately surrounding implementation of the Judges' Bill indicates, contrary to Halpern and Vines, that 1925 was not the beginning of a sustained upward trend in dissent. By focusing on that portion of figure 2 which illustrates the Court's dissent patterns for the years immediately preceding and following the 1925 statute, we readily observe that Halpern and Vines were correct in noting a slight increase in individual expression following passage. However, dissent clearly leveled off to pre-statute rates shortly thereafter and remained relatively low for another

[3] Halpern and Vines clearly indicate that their work did "not seek to explain all the causes that have produced the increased division of opinion commonly found on the high court in recent decades." Rather, they "attempted to assess to what extent and in what ways the 1925 Act may have been one of the starting points . . ." (1977, p. 472).

FIGURE 2

DISCRETIONARY JURISDICTION, DISSENT AND CONCURRENCE IN THE UNITED STATES SUPREME COURT, 1923–1981

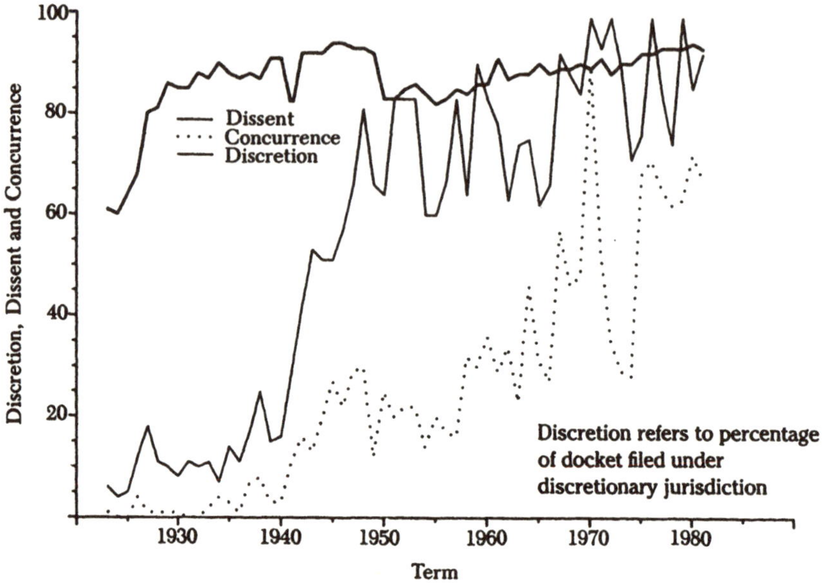

decade. Simply stated, a radical jump in dissent following 1927 is not evident. Dissent rates did not begin their major upward move until the early 1940s. We have no theoretical or empirical reason to suspect that a fifteen year lag existed between passage of the Act and its putative effect on the incidence of individual judicial expression.

Based upon this evidence, we must dismiss enactment of the 1925 statute as the primary factor in the alteration of the Court's consensus norms. Certainly, it is possible that a discretionary docket may be one factor, and a necessary one at that, in maintaining high levels of conflict once such patterns are established. Little support exists, however, for the position that the Judges' Bill alone initiated the significant elevation in individual judicial expression.

CHANGES IN THE COURT'S CASELOAD

It is reasonable to suspect that docket changes can affect the level of decision-making consensus on the Court. Two possibilities exist. First, we might anticipate that marked increases in caseload volume are associated with heightened levels of individual expression. As demands on the Court increase, the justices lose the luxury of ample time to build consensus and construct the compromises that hold the Court together. Constant pressure exists to arrive at a decision and move on to address the next case. It is no longer as advantageous to expend substantial resources to convince a dissenting or concurring justice to join the majority opinion. Second, the Court's docket can change in terms of case mix. Some issues obviously tend to provoke disagreement and others present questions attracting broad-based consensus. If the Court undergoes an abrupt alteration in the kinds of cases the public brings to it for resolution, we might witness a corresponding change in consensus levels. Both of these caseload factors can be examined as possible causes of the increased levels of individual judicial expression which began in the 1940s.

To test our first suspicion we superimposed the number of case filings each term on a graph of dissent and concurrence rates for the years 1900 to 1981. The result, which is displayed as figure 3, reveals that the increasing caseloads observed over this period are not likely to be responsible for the marked rise in individual expression occurring after 1940. In the first place, it is apparent that dissent rates are not systematically affected by caseloads since the surge in the former actually *precedes* the period of strongest growth in case filings. More generally, the shapes of the curves in figure 3 are inconsistent with the caseload hypothesis, since the extraordinary rise in

FIGURE 3

CASELOAD, DISSENT AND CONCURRENCE IN THE UNITED STATES SUPREME COURT, 1900–1981

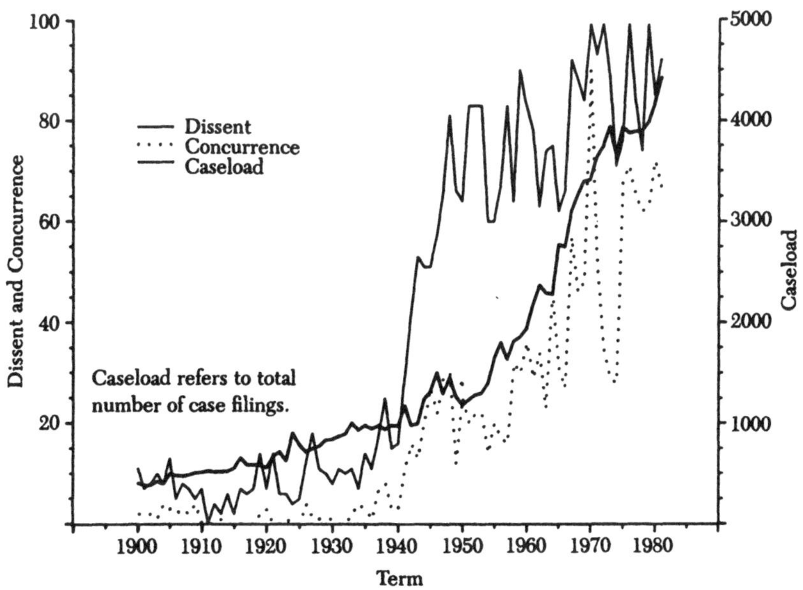

dissents and the smaller but still dramatic jump in concurrences are rather unlikely consequences of the comparatively more uniform growth in case filings. Additionally, by using the transfer function technique (Norpoth, 1986), we attempted to determine whether caseload "drove" up dissent or concurrence rates. The results corroborated our initial conclusion that the series follow independent processes. Thus, by visual consideration of figure 3, as well as results based on a more powerful analytic tool, we can conclude that caseload levels and individual expression are not causally associated with one another.[4]

Our second docket hypothesis prompts us to examine changes in case mix. Because the precipitous increase in dissent began with Harlan Fiske Stone's first term as chief justice in 1941, we can best evaluate our suspicions by taking a "snapshot" of the relationship between case mix and dissent during the last two terms of the Hughes Court (1939–1940) and the first two terms of the Stone Court (1941–1942).[5] For every case decided with a full opinion, we recorded the issue brought to the Court and the number of dissenting opinions, if any. Specifically we were looking for particular issues during the last two terms of the Hughes era that produced unusually high or low levels of dissent. If changes in case mix are responsible for the surge in dissenting opinions, we would expect the 1941–1942 Stone Court to have been faced with larger numbers of issues associated with high levels of dissent, and correspondingly fewer cases with issues associated with high levels of consensus. Such changes in case mix might be attributable to an alteration in the variety of issues the public brought to the Court or a change in the kinds of cases the justices granted review.

The results of the Hughes/Stone comparisons are illustrated in table 2. In order to control for personnel changes, the dissent data in this table are based only on justices who served during both the Hughes and Stone years. Examining the Hughes Court portion of the table, we note a rate of fifteen dissenting opinions for every 100 opinions of the Court. Anti-trust cases constituted the most dissent-prone issue (dissent rate = 43; n = 7), closely followed by issues involving banking and stocks (both dissent rates = 33, n = 6). Cases bringing questions of criminal procedure, Indian rights, the Federal Communications Commission, and maritime and patent law failed to yield any dissenting opinions. Thus, knowing that dissent behavior increased tremendously after Stone took the reins of the Court and knowing

[4]In addition to total filings as a measure of caseload, we did a similar set of analyses using "number of cases decided with full opinions" as the independent variable. There was no evidence to suggest that increasing numbers of decided cases were associated with the abrupt rise in nonmajority opinions. In fact, the number of cases decided declined over the years studied.

[5]Realizing that issues would vary tremendously from one Court era to the next, this "snapshot" view provides the best mechanism for determining the most and the least conflictual issues for this particular set of justices.

TABLE 2

ISSUES AND DISSENT: 1939–1942*

Issue	Hughes Court (1939–1940) Dissenting Opinions[a]	Hughes Court (1939–1940) n=	Stone Court (1941–1942) Dissenting Opinions[a]	Stone Court (1941–1942) n=
Anti-Trust	43	7	50	8
Banking	33	6	50	2
Stocks	33	6	33	3
Labor	27	26	43	28
Civil Liberties	25	8	38	16
Jurisdiction/Procedure	21	14	20	10
Civil Rights	20	5	0	3
Insurance	17	6	40	10
Taxes	16	86	26	51
Miscellaneous[b]	9	53	28	50
Bankruptcy	9	23	28	18
Railroads	7	14	36	11
Commerce	6	17	39	23
Criminal Rights	0	13	52	27
FCC	0	4	80	5
Indian Law	0	2	27	11
Maritime	0	2	57	7
Patents	0	8	38	16
Total	15	300	35	299

*Data collected by authors.

[a]Dissenting opinions per 100 majority opinions, counting only dissenting opinions written by justices who served on both the Hughes and Stone Courts.

[b]Includes case types appearing infrequently in both Court eras (e.g., utilities, issues involving Puerto Rico).

what case types tended to produce dissent, we would expect to find a sharp increase in the number of anti-trust, banking and stock cases during the Stone era.

Scrutiny of the Stone Court's first two terms, however, does not meet our expectations. The numbers of cases in the three most dissent-prone categories either decreased or remained relatively stable during the first two years of the Stone era. The dissent rates in these three issue categories either remained unchanged or increased slightly.

What about the consensual issues of the Hughes Court? Since certain cases acted as non-dissent stimuli during the Hughes era, we would expect to find fewer such cases during the Stone period, or, at the very least, similarly low dissent rates. Again this was not the case. Not only did cases in these categories increase in number, but every issue evoking unanimity in the Hughes Court surpassed a dissenting opinion rate of 25 during Stone's first two terms. FCC cases illustrate the most extreme example of this phenomenon, with the dissent rate moving from 0 to 80. Consider also issues of criminal rights, which failed to evince a dissenting opinion from 1939 to 1940, but increased to a rate of 52 during the 1941 and 1942 terms.

Although changes in the number of cases falling within the various issue areas were insufficient to have caused the sharp increase in conflictual behavior, it is possible that our aggregated scheme may be masking the effect of differences within issue categories. Take, for example, civil liberties cases. They doubled in number from eight during the 1939–1940 terms to sixteen during the 1941–1942 period, presenting squarely the possibility that the Stone Court was faced with more complex and/or wholly different kinds of civil liberty cases than its earlier counterpart. Based upon an examination of the twenty-four civil liberties cases, however, we must eliminate this explanation. Five of the eight Hughes Court cases involved solicitation, picketing, or loitering; nine of the Stone Court cases raised similar issues. In fact, the Jehovah's Witnesses were responsible for bringing the majority of these cases to both Courts. Even more illustrative of the parity of issues raised were the Flag Salute cases, one of which was heard in each of the two periods. The only litigation presenting substantially different civil liberties claims were the Japanese internment cases decided in the 1942 term. However, no dissenting opinions were issued in these disputes.

These data lead us to reject the notion that case mix changes ushered in the dissent-prone period after 1941. It is clearly not the case that dissent-producing issues increased in frequency concurrently with Stone's assumption of the chief justiceship, nor is it true that consensus-prone issues decreased in number. On the contrary, it appears that dissent-prone cases remained relatively stable and that the consensus-producing issues of the Hughes years began producing dissent on the Stone Court. Whoever or whatever was responsible for increasing the level of individual judicial expression beginning with the Stone years was a powerful force indeed, for it was able to produce judicial conflict over issues that during the previous two terms were associated with unanimity.

The Promotion of a Sitting Associate to be Chief Justice

Because the incidence of widespread individual expression began with the New Deal Court, the judicial selection policies of Franklin Roosevelt clearly demand attention. One of the more commonly expressed possibilities is that Roosevelt's elevation of Harlan Fiske Stone, a sitting associate justice, to be chief justice created an internal condition not conducive to consensus decision making. The rationale is that internal promotions lead to intra-Court conflict and cause acrimony prompted by jealousies or prior interpersonal conflicts (see Mason, 1968, p. 52). Inside candidates are saddled with the scars of past battles and are unable to discard them. Consequently, Stone's ability to lead the Court as a cohesive whole may have been impaired by his previous Court service.

If the hypothesis that internal promotions disrupt consensus norms is correct, we would expect that the pattern of increasing individual expression characteristic of the Stone era would also be found on the Court during the leadership years of Edward White, the only other individual to have completed a tenure as chief justice after having been promoted from a sitting associate position.[6] White, who like Stone had sixteen years of prior service as an associate justice, assumed the chief justiceship in 1910. At that time the Court was plagued with personality conflicts (Abraham, 1986, p. 206) and carried a high potential for internal divisiveness. White, however, was quickly able to overcome what on the surface appeared to be insurmountable problems. He was "plainly anxious to create an atmosphere of friendliness and to promote agreement in the disposition of cases" (Goldman, 1982, p. 262). Through the institution of various practices, White was able to maintain good relations with and among his colleagues.

It is obvious from the data examined thus far that White's efforts succeeded in maintaining the Court's consensual norms. The mean level of dissent exhibited by the Court for all years prior to White's promotion was 8.3 while during his first five years as chief justice this figure declined to 3.8. Stone's record is radically different. The Court's mean dissent rate of 8.5 before Stone's leadership ballooned to 45.2 during his five-year tenure as chief justice. Similar patterns hold for the concurrence data. We also examined trends in the Court's behavior by regressing our measure of dissent on the term number for the first five years of each internally-promoted chief justice. Because slope estimates from these regressions indicate the average annual change in dissent, large positive slopes for both Courts would lend some credence to the internal promotion hypothesis. Our results reveal the expected upward trend in dissents under Stone ($b = 4.5$; $t = 3.4$), but virtually no change during the five years following White's promotion ($b = -.25$; $t = -.37$). It is possible, of course, that the promotion of a sitting associate was an unwise decision because of particular conditions inside the Court in 1941. However, given the contradictory consequences of the White and Stone appointments, we are unable to accept the general validity of the internal promotion hypothesis.

Changes in the Court's Composition

Although the leader of any group influences the relations among its members, "it is difficult to imagine any judge, even a Marshall, dominating . . . a

[6] Conclusions put forward in this section must obviously be tentative since only two cases exist for analysis. The 1986 appointment of William Rehnquist to replace Chief Justice Warren Burger will allow us the opportunity at some future date to evaluate the internal promotion hypothesis with a third case.

Court composed of brilliant, individualistic, and strong willed . . ." justices (Murphy, 1964, pp. 40–41; but see Roper, 1965). Thus, in searching for the causes of the Court's rejection of consensus norms, we must take into account the role of the associate justices. It is quite possible that Stone was faced with a Court composed of associates who were to a significant degree "unleadable." Four possible conditions merit examination:

1. The associate turnover rate was unusually high.
2. The associates were disproportionately young and inexperienced.
3. The associates were deeply divided ideologically.
4. The associates were abnormally dissent prone.

High Turnover. We first need to address the possibility that the Stone Court experienced unusually high levels of turnover. The Supreme Court is a continuing institution averaging only one new member every two years. This gradual rate of membership change allows the institution to socialize new justices into the acceptance of its internal norms. However, a rapid and large influx of new members can disrupt the Court and stunt normal socialization processes. It is possible that the Court was faced with just such a condition, making the enforcement of traditional consensus norms impossible.

The first column in table 3 indicates the number of justices appointed during the 1941 to 1946 Stone era as well as during the tenures of the four chief justices preceding him: Melville Fuller, Edward White, William Howard

TABLE 3

ASSOCIATE JUSTICES UNDER FIVE CHIEF JUSTICES

Chief Justice	New Justices[a]	Turnover Rate[b]	Mean Age[c]	Mean Youngest/ Oldest[d]	Inexperience Index[e]
Fuller (1888–1910)	11	.50	63.9	54.0–74.4	18.8
White (1910–1921)	7	.64	63.0	53.0–75.4	26.1
Taft (1921–1930)	4	.44	66.7	57.7–84.0	16.7
Hughes (1930–1941)	7	.64	67.0	53.8–80.6	19.3
Stone (1941–1946)	4	.80	61.6	50.0–70.0	32.5

[a]Total number of associate justices added to the Court during the period from the date of a chief justice's confirmation to his death or resignation. Associates confirmed between May and September were coded as joining the Court at the beginning of the October term.

[b]Mean number of new associate justices per term.

[c]Mean age of associates calculated for each term and averaged over the tenure of the chief justice.

[d]Age of the youngest and oldest associate justice each term averaged over the tenure of the chief justice.

[e]Percentage of associate justice seats occupied by justices with three or fewer years of experience, combining all terms of a chief justice's tenure.

Taft, and Charles Evans Hughes. The number of new associates joining the Court during these periods ranged from a high of eleven under Fuller to a low of four for Taft and Stone. Turnover rates, however, place matters in a different perspective. The Court under Fuller, White, Taft, and Hughes averaged .55 new associates per term, with only modest deviations from the mean. Stone, on the other hand, experienced a turnover rate of .80, considerably higher than his four predecessors. The addition of four associate justices in a five-year period certainly carries with it the potential of creating a disruptive situation.

Youth and Inexperience. It is possible that Chief Justice Stone was asked to lead justices who were unusually young, inexperienced and resistant to the norms of the Court's old guard. One author has alluded to this problem, noting that "Stone presided over a Court consisting primarily of new, inexperienced justices" (Goldman, 1982, p. 339). And, as Pritchett claimed, the justices were not only "inexperienced," but youthful as well (1948, p. 13). It is conceivable that the comparatively large number of new justices and their relative youth presented Stone with conditions conducive to dissension that were not faced by chief justices who served before him. The third and fourth columns of table 3 portray the mean age and age ranges for the Court during the time Chief Justices Fuller, White, Taft, Hughes, and Stone served. The average age of the justices during the Stone years was the lowest of the five eras, but the differences are not substantial. Moreover, we cannot verify an argument that it was an unusually large "spread" in ages (young vs. old) that affected levels of disagreement. In fact, the range of ages during the Stone era was the smallest of the Courts examined.

High levels of inexperience may also provide conditions conducive to a breakdown in decision-making norms. Veteran group members with loyalties to existing behavioral customs must exist in sufficient numbers to inculcate less experienced members into acceptable patterns of behavior. A disproportionately inexperienced Court may have difficulty maintaining allegiance to ways of the past. For purposes of this analysis, we defined as inexperienced any justice with three or fewer full terms on the Court. This defining criterion is admittedly somewhat arbitrary since justices have individually different rates of adapting to the demands of their new positions. It seems reasonable to assume, however, that after three years on the bench a justice will be fully acclimated and can no longer be labeled as inexperienced or under the influence of a "freshman effect."

The final column in table 3 illustrates the percentage of associate justice seats occupied by inexperienced justices over the full tenures of Chief Justice Stone and his four immediate predecessors. The Stone Court associates distinguish themselves by having the highest inexperience rates of the five courts examined. When Chief Justice Stone first convened the Court in October 1941, five of the eight associate positions were filled by justices falling into the inexperienced category. Conditions such as this make the transition of decision-making values susceptible to interruption.

The Stone justices not only had a lack of experience on the Supreme Court, but an extremely low level of judicial service at any level. Of the ten men who served as associate justices under Stone, Wiley Rutledge's three years on the Court of Appeals for the District of Columbia represents the only prior appellate court experience. Consequently, Stone associates had almost no exposure to the "no dissent" traditions common to appellate tribunals. Furthermore, the backgrounds of these men were not such that they would naturally value the practice of deferring to the views of others on matters of public and legal policy. Like Chief Justice Stone, Frankfurter, Douglas, and Rutledge had devoted the bulk of their careers to university teaching, an occupation which encouraged them to articulate their individual theories of law and legal institutions. Black, Byrnes, and Burton had come to the Supreme Court directly from the United States Senate where free debate was valued. Roberts had come from private practice, and Jackson, Murphy, and Reed had been high ranking Justice Department attorneys. Consequently, the Stone Court associates not only possessed relatively low levels of Supreme Court experience, but came from occupational traditions that encouraged individual expression.

Ideological Division. The third possibility is that the associate justices were deeply divided ideologically, forcing a large amount of individual expression. To evaluate this contingency, we examined the configuration of ideological voting blocs among the justices of the Hughes and Stone Courts. We expect, of course, that all Courts are divided to some degree along ideological lines. That is, scholars have consistently found that during most eras at least two voting blocs exist: liberal and conservative. If these blocs have high degrees of internal cohesion, dissenting opinions occur at modest levels and concurring opinions are very infrequent. On the other hand, when the ideological subgroups themselves are highly fractionalized internally, dissenting and concurring opinions proliferate.

In *The Roosevelt Court*, Pritchett examined agreement scores of the Hughes and Stone Court justices in "every nonunanimous opinion" (see Pritchett, 1948, pp. 242–47). His findings are startling: between the 1931 and 1940 terms "the existence of well-defined groups, referred to as left wing and right wing, was clearly evident." That is, strong intra-bloc agreement existed. According to Pritchett, however, ". . . [A]fter 1941, a marked decline was apparent in the cohesiveness of the judicial bloc on the right, and later in that on the left" (p. 241). In sum, "In 1941, divisive forces of some kind hit the Court in full force" (p. 251). This occurred in spite of the fact that the Stone Court had the potential of being one of the most ideologically united in the history of the institution. After all, except for the seat held first by Roberts and then Burton, every Stone Court justice was an appointee of Franklin Roosevelt who placed a priority on nominating justices loyal to New Deal policies.

Pritchett's findings are certainly pertinent to our inquiry. The future Stone Court justices while serving under Hughes were not divisive within their ideological blocs. Well-defined subgroups existed, but justices of the same ideological leanings agreed. After 1941, however, agreement was not even evident within blocs of justices sharing the same ideology. Given that it is well established that judicial attitudes are stable, there is no reason to presume that beginning with the 1941 term the justices underwent radical fragmentation of their ideologies. Instead, it appears reasonable to conclude that a significant and generalized decline in norms of cohesion occurred.

This point is reinforced by examining the concurrence data. To some extent, concurrences control for ideology. That is, concurring opinions denote a general agreement with the directional outcome of a case. Standard ideological divisions do not necessarily result in increased numbers of concurring opinions. In fact, it could be convincingly argued that as ideological divisions deepen, concurring opinions should decline. A mere glance at either figure 1 or table 1, however, reveals a much different situation. As Chief Justice Stone took lead of the Court, both dissenting and concurring opinions rose dramatically. Almost overnight, the justices began expressing their personal views at extraordinarily high levels, demonstrating little compulsion to defer to the opinion of either the Court majority or of their own attitudinal subgroups. This indicates that ideology alone cannot account for the sharp rise in individual judicial expression.

Dissent-Prone Associates. The decline in the Court's consensus norms may have occurred because the Stone Court associates, regardless of ideology, were particularly prone to state positions at odds with those articulated by the Court's designated spokesmen. To test for this possibility, we examined the proportion of total dissenting votes and dissenting opinions for which the Stone Court associates were responsible before Stone assumed the leadership position. If these justices had consistently high levels of individual expression, then we would have reason to believe that consensus norms deteriorated because a particular set of judicial mavericks happened to be on the Court at a specific point in time. The findings, which are illustrated in table 4, suggest a different conclusion. If we expect each justice to carry .11 (1/9) of both categories (dissenting votes and opinions), then prior to Stone's ascension, the justices did not demonstrate particularly high propensities to dissent. Excluding Stone, only two of the future Stone associates had disproportionately high dissent rates: Roberts and Black. The Roberts case is clear-cut—he grew increasingly conflictual following the Court's 1937 shift in constitutional philosophy. Black, however, started his tenure with relatively high proportions, which declined slightly until the Stone ascen-

TABLE 4

PROPORTIONS OF DISSENTING VOTES CAST AND DISSENTING OPINIONS WRITTEN BY FUTURE STONE COURT JUSTICES, 1925–1942*

*Dissenting Votes***

	Pre-Stone-Terms																Stone Terms	
	25	26	27	28	29	30	31	32	33	34	35	36	37	38	39	40	41	42
Stone	.11	.14	.19	.08	.21	.13	.24	.20	.19	.18	.22	.03	.05	.03	.05	.05	.14	.09
Roberts						.04	.07	.04	.06	.05	.05	.09	.03	.11	.27	.26	.11	.18
Black													.17	.14	.05	.13	.13	.14
Reed														.06	.01	.07	.09	.10
Frankfurter															.02	.02	.10	.12
Douglas															.05	.13	.18	.13
Murphy																.05	.11	.15
Actual	.11	.14	.19	.08	.21	.17	.31	.24	.25	.23	.27	.12	.25	.34	.45	.71	.86	.91
Expected[a]	.11	.11	.11	.11	.11	.22	.22	.22	.22	.22	.22	.22	.33	.44	.66	.77	.77	.77
Deviation[b]	.00	+.03	+.08	−.03	+.10	−.05	+.09	+.02	+.03	+.01	+.05	−.10	−.08	−.10	−.21	−.06	+.09	+.14

*Dissenting Opinions****

	Pre-Stone-Terms																Stone Terms	
	25	26	27	28	29	30	31	32	33	34	35	36	37	38	39	40	41	42
Stone	.09	.14	.16	.23	.46	.16	.37	.29	.27	.43	.30	.00	.00	.08	.05	.15	.16	.09
Roberts						.08	.00	.05	.11	.07	.15	.11	.04	.11	.50	.34	.06	.12
Black													.32	.19	.11	.15	.23	.18
Reed														.05	.05	.07	.14	.06
Frankfurter															.00	.07	.14	.19
Douglas															.05	.11	.14	.10
Murphy																.00	.00	.15
Actual	.09	.14	.16	.23	.46	.24	.37	.34	.38	.50	.45	.11	.36	.43	.76	.89	.87	.89
Expected[a]	.11	.11	.11	.11	.11	.22	.22	.22	.22	.22	.22	.22	.33	.44	.66	.77	.77	.77
Deviation[b]	−.02	+.03	+.05	+.12	+.35	+.02	+.15	+.12	+.16	+.28	+.23	−.11	+.03	−.01	+.10	+.12	+.10	+.12

*Data depicted here represent the proportion of the Court's dissenting votes and opinions for which each of the future Stone Court justices was responsible.

**Data sources: 1925–1938 terms, annual summary, *Harvard Law Review* (1928–1939); 1939–1942 terms, Pritchett (1948).

***Data sources: 1925–1938 terms, annual summary, *Harvard Law Review* (1928–1939); 1939–1942 terms, collected by authors.

[a]Expected totals = .11 × number of justices.

[b]Deviations = total proportion − expected total.

sion. Even more interesting, perhaps, are the proportions of Justices Douglas and Frankfurter. Although both would later be known as dissenters, they were relatively quiet until 1941. Thus, the associate justices were not a particularly dissent-prone group prior to Stone's assumption of the center chair.

A final observation centers on the "bottom line" figures provided in table 4. For each Court term, we computed the total proportion of dissenting votes and opinions for which the Stone Court justices accounted and the deviation from our expected proportions (actual proportion less expected proportion), where the expected proportion equals the number of justices × .11. As is readily observable between 1926 and 1935, the two Stone Court justices generally accounted for more than their fair share of dissent solely because Stone well exceeded his expected values. This situation quickly changed as more justices were added. Between 1936 and 1940, the associates who would later staff the Stone Court cast dissenting votes at lower rates than expected. Their propensity for writing dissenting opinions was slightly elevated, but this was due primarily to the high rates exhibited by Roberts and Black. Reed, Frankfurter, Douglas, and Murphy expressed minority viewpoints at relatively low levels. If these judges possessed a desire to articulate their individual views more freely, the prevailing norms of the Court kept such tendencies in check. This situation, of course, radically changed when Stone assumed the mantle. These same generally "quiet" justices began to dissent at relatively equal, high proportions.

In sum, the Stone Court associates do not appear to have been especially divided ideologically; nor do those who initiated their service during the Hughes era seem to have been unusually prone to dissent. Yet there were ample signs that the possibility of high rates of individual expression existed. Because of their low levels of Supreme Court experience, the Stone associates had not been firmly tutored in the norms of consensus; indeed, as table 4 indicates, Frankfurter, Douglas, and Murphy had only served a short period under Chief Justice Hughes. The great turnover rate left the Stone Court with few justices who were schooled in and committed to the traditional ways and who had moved beyond the "freshman" experience. The Stone associates were relatively young. They came from the ranks of professors, senators, and private or government attorneys rather than being promoted from lower court service. Because of these conditions, the caliber of leadership and the quality of group socialization efforts carried the promise of exerting an even greater than normal impact on the future of the institution.

The Leadership of the Chief Justice

Many scholars have noted that the character of leadership provided by the chief justice has a great influence on the operating norms of the Court. Pritchett claimed that in court periods prior to the "Roosevelt Court," "there [were] vital conformist effects in the operating methods of the Court itself.

Probably the most important of these is the discussion which goes on around the judicial conference table, out of which consensus can often be achieved. The influence of a strong and skillful Chief Justice is of great importance in leading to the discovery of solutions satisfactory to all members of the Court" (1948, p. 24). In his seminal work, *Elements of Judicial Strategy*, Walter Murphy (1964) developed Pritchett's argument, suggesting that chief justices can design special tactics to "marshal" or "mass" the Court. According to Murphy, chief justices can employ an array of strategies during conference deliberations and in the opinion-assignment process to create the illusion of unanimity even when great splits of opinion exist among the justices.

Chief justices who best perform these functions have been, in the words of David Danelski, good social and/or task leaders. Social leaders are those able to "counterbalance" the "negative aspects of conference" through activity "which relieves tension, shows solidarity, and makes for agreement" (Danelski, 1980, p. 237). Task leadership, on the other hand, concentrates on the business of the Court. According to Danelski, the chief justice has the best opportunity to emerge as both a task and social leader, thus preserving his role as a "first among equals," or the most influential member of the Court. If a chief plays both roles, then the Court members should be socially cohesive, satisfied with conference, and generally less conflictual among themselves.

Since the breakdown in the Court's consensus behavior coincided with his chief justiceship, we must consider Harlan Fiske Stone a major suspect. Consequently, we need to address Stone's leadership qualities and compare them to those of his predecessors who presided over courts with much lower rates of individual expression.

The biographical and historical works on Stone are of one voice. Stone, in spite of his generally acknowledged intellectual greatness, was an ineffective leader. According to Danelski, debates in conference were heated in the Stone Court and a social leader was needed to smooth ruffled tempers, relieve tensions and maintain solidarity. The conflict was not friendly as in Taft's day; rather it was acrimonious, and, at times, descended to the level of personalities (Danelski, 1980). Others, including Mason (1958), Abraham (1986), Murphy (1964), and Wasby (1984), agree with Danelski's view.

Alpheus Mason persuasively argues that Stone was capable of bringing cohesion to the Court; he simply thought that such leadership was not only unnecessary, but harmful. In Stone's own words, "The right of dissent is an important one and has proved to be such in the history of the Supreme Court. I do not think it is the appropriate function of a Chief Justice to attempt to dissuade members of the Court from dissenting in individual cases" (1956, p. 608). Dissent, he believed, was critical because "[s]ound legal principles . . . never sprang full-fledged from the brains of any man or group of men. They are the ultimate resultant of the abrasive force of the clash of competing and sometimes conflicting ideas . . ." (1956, p. 629).

Clearly, we cannot eliminate Stone as a possible cause in the erosion of the

Court's consensus norms. Not only was he ineffective at using task and social leadership to forge consensus, but he believed that those who had been successful were detrimental to the Court. Moreover, the historical evidence suggests that no member of the quartet of twentieth century chiefs immediately prior to Stone (Fuller, White, Taft or Hughes) was as ineffective at building consensus as he, nor did any share his views on individual judicial expression.

Melville Fuller was chief justice from 1888 to 1910. By almost every available account, both by scholars and his colleagues, Fuller was an excellent social leader. He desired harmonious relations among the justices and seemed well equipped to accomplish this task because he was "blessed with conciliatory and diplomatic traits" (Goldman, 1982, p. 178). Others have noted that he was "an extraordinary Chief Justice in his relations with his colleagues" (Frank, 1958, p. 85), creating a "warmth and closeness" on the Court (Schiffman, 1969, p. 1480).

Justices certainly agreed with these scholarly assessments. According to Justice Holmes, Fuller was "extraordinary. He had the business of the Court at his fingers' ends; he was perfectly courageous, prompt, and decided . . . Fuller was the greatest Chief Justice I have ever known" (quoted in Goldman, 1982, pp. 178–79). Later, Justice Frankfurter noted that "When you're in a conference room of the Supreme Court, or en banc in a court of appeals, or at faculty meetings . . . the same kind of thing happens. Men get short of temper and humor is a great solvent. Fuller had that. He presided with great courtesy. He presided with authority, quiet authority . . ." (1963, pp. 215–16).

Chief Justice White, as discussed earlier, was promoted by President Taft from associate to chief justice in 1910, a time at which the Court was divided and difficult to lead. Yet White, perhaps well-schooled by his experience as senate majority leader, possessed the interpersonal skills to lead the Court effectively. He was blessed with a genial temperament and adroit logrolling skills (Watts, 1969) that permitted him to mend fences and reinforce the consensus norms of the Court.

Perhaps of all Stone's twentieth century predecessors, social leadership was most important to William Howard Taft. Taft went to great extremes to attain harmony on the Court. As one biographer has noted: "Taft valued congeniality and goodwill above most things, and consequently had few acrimonious relations with his professional peers. His ideological convictions very often shaped his attitude toward a colleague, but he never let differences on social and intellectual issues override his desire for harmonious personal relations" (White, 1976, p. 179). Another scholar has stated that "[h]appy working relations were not accidental. Taft went to great pains to establish *esprit de corps*" (Mason, 1969, p. 2114).

To achieve "team spirit" on the Court, Taft took a number of tacks. First, because "he hated dissenting opinions, (he) wrote very few himself and made every effort to dissuade others from writing them" (White, 1976, p. 180). He strongly believed that "important questions of law should not be broken anymore than we can help by dissents" (Murphy, 1964, p. 47). In fact, he once told Justice Clarke, "I don't approve of dissents generally, for I think in many cases where I differ from the majority, it is more important to stand by the Court and give its judgment weight than merely to record my individual dissent where it is better to have the law certain than to have it settled either way" (Murphy, 1964, p. 61). In short, Taft's views were diametrically opposed to Stone's. Second, Taft was the "most active Supreme Court lobbyist of the 20th Century" (Baum, 1985, p. 35). Among his most important lobbying activities, of course, was "frequently exerting pressure on behalf of people he wanted nominated" (Wasby, 1984, p. 93; see also Danelski, 1964). He then socialized those new justices in the "no dissent unless absolutely necessary" tradition (Danelski, 1980). Finally, when required, Taft was willing to use his opinion assignment power to reward team players and punish dissidents. Among those on the "punish" list—none other than Associate Justice Stone. In one instance, Taft sent the following message to Stone: "I voted to reverse. While this sustains your conclusion to affirm, I still think reversal would be better. But I shall in silence acquiesce. Dissents seldom aid in the right development or statement of the law. They often do harm. For myself I say: 'lead us not into temptation'" (quoted in Abraham, 1986, p. 224).

Chief Justice Hughes, Stone's immediate predecessor, joins the ranks of Fuller, White, and Taft as a highly skilled social leader. His colleagues indicated that the chief worked for sociability and harmony among the justices. Owen Roberts, in fact, claimed that Hughes's efforts resulted in "a feeling of personal cordiality and comradeship that . . . was unique in a Court so seriously divided in its review on great matters. . . ." Roberts also noted that even those justices deeply divided, such as Brandeis and Van Devanter, "were at one in their admiration and affectionate regard for their presiding officer" (1963, p. 210). The scholarly literature supports the view of Hughes's colleagues: the chief justice "was the most esteemed member of his Court" (Danelski, 1980, p. 238). As Tressolini contends, Hughes "had the ability to allay jealousies and minimize personal frictions. This was no mean accomplishment on a Court made up of strong, tough minded personalities . . ." (1963, p. 87).

Little doubt exists about Hughes's leadership. But what of his views on the value of the justices expressing their individual opinions on cases? On the surface, Hughes's writings lead us to believe that he was a major proponent of dissent. A relevant section of his 1928 book, ***The Supreme Court of the United States***, is often quoted: "A dissent in a court of last resort is an appeal to the brooding spirit of the law, to the intelligence of a future day, when a later decision may possibly correct the error into which the dissenting judge believes the Court may have been betrayed" (1928, p. 68).

Taken on its face, this passage seems to echo the views expressed by Chief Justice Stone. However, we have several reasons to suspect that upon being elevated to the chief justiceship in 1930, Hughes's perception of dissent had more in common with that of Taft than Stone. Simply stated, Hughes and Taft, as Danelski points out, both shared the "no dissent unless absolutely necessary" tradition (Danelski, 1980, p. 242; see also Schmidhauser, 1979, p. 170).

This suspicion is verified by a number of points. First, Hughes was extremely time conscious, attempting to get the most out of conference in the least amount of time. To accomplish this, Hughes provided concise summaries of each case and then presented his view in "a forceful, confident manner" (Goldman, 1982, p. 337). After that, he "controlled discussion tightly, limiting the time devoted to each case" (Baum, 1985, p. 114). Hughes's summaries and opinions "were so complete that in many cases nothing needed to be added by any of his associates" (Roberts, 1963, p. 207; see also Murphy, 1964 and Frank, 1958).

Second, Hughes was determined to present the Court to the public as a dignified and united institution (Abraham, 1986, p. 230). Hughes discouraged dissent in part because it would expose divisions within the Court to the public. In an attempt to show the ever dissenting Associate Justice Stone why he would go along with an opinion with which he disagreed, Hughes wrote, "I choke a little at swallowing your analysis, still I do not think it would serve any useful purpose to expose my views" (quoted in Abraham, 1986, p. 224).

Finally, Hughes often kept opinions for himself by joining the majority even if it meant changing his view of the case. He did this, at least in part, because he believed that he could prevent dissents and concurrences "by compromising and incorporating several different lines of reasoning in his opinion" (Murphy, 1964, p. 64). Moreover, like Taft, Hughes tried to ingratiate himself to new justices, socializing them in the no-dissent tradition (see Murphy, 1964; Goldman, 1982; Bates, 1936).

We do not question Hughes's intentions at the time he wrote his book, a period during which "dissents were usually saved for serious business . . ." (Frank, 1958, p. 127). We are suggesting, however, that when Hughes assumed the role of chief justice he, in contrast to Stone, strove for harmony among the justices. In fact, in summarizing the differences between the two, John Schmidhauser wrote, "In many respects Merlo Pusey's biography of Chief Justice Hughes and Alpheus Mason's biography of Chief Justice Stone provided polar viewpoints on the propriety of strong efforts on the part of the Chief Justice to 'mass the Court'" (1979, p. 170).

The conclusion of the historical works is further supported by quantitative evidence. Although many mechanisms exist for a chief to exert social leadership affecting consensus norms, one of the most important is his own dissent behavior. According to Stephen Wasby, "The Chief Justice's leadership is affected by the degree to which he dissents: a dissenter may exercise *policy* leadership, but exercising leadership over colleagues in the short term is difficult if one is often in dissent" (Wasby, 1984, p. 188). S. Sidney Ulmer has provided an analysis of the dissent patterns of eleven chief justices (Ulmer, 1986). Data based on a portion of his study are illustrated in table 5. They are clearly consistent with the more qualitative evidence. Chief Justice Stone's dissent rate was far greater than any of his predecessors and even exceeded the two who followed him. Chief justices serving before Stone kept their dissent to a minimum (mean = 1.8 percent); Stone voted against the majority of his Court at a rate of 13.5 percent.

Stone's behavior as chief justice was consistent with his earlier record as an associate. Referring back to his associate justice years in table 4, we find that for nine of the sixteen and ten of the sixteen terms depicted, Stone cast more dissenting votes and wrote more dissenting opinions, respectively, than would be expected. During six terms, in fact, he wrote a higher proportion of dissenting opinions than any of the other eight justices with whom he served. And as the histories of the Court tell us, he might well have cast even more dissenting votes had Chief Justices Taft and Hughes not discouraged him from doing so. Thus, when Stone ascended to the head of the Court, dissent was fully acceptable to him as an outlet for individual expres-

TABLE 5

DISSENT BEHAVIOR OF ELEVEN CHIEF JUSTICES*

Chief Justice	N of Cases	N of Chief Justice Dissents	Dissent Proportion[a]
Marshall	1187	7	.0058
Taney	1708	38	.0222
Chase	1109	33	.0297
Waite	2642	45	.0170
Fuller	4866	113	.0232
White	2541	39	.0153
Taft	1708	16	.0093
Hughes	2050	46	.0224
Stone	704	95	.1349
Vinson	723	90	.1244
Warren	1772	215	.1213

*Source: Ulmer (1986), p. 53.

[a]Number of Chief Justice dissents divided by number of cases.

sion. Furthermore, as he moved to the leadership position he experienced no changes in role orientation that caused him to modify his views on the Court's consensus norms.

The foregoing analyses led us to several conclusions. First, Stone's leadership appears to be a prime cause of the Court changing from an institution emphasizing consensus to one characterized by a high level of individual expression. In a break from the tradition of his predecessors, Stone steadfastly held that justices should be free to assert their individuality—that imposed unanimity was no virtue in developing the law. Second, Stone's attitudes were translated into action. He did not draw back from challenging the majority. He expressed his own views frequently, and by doing so gave a signal to the other members of the Court that it was perfectly permissible to engage in concurring and dissenting opinions. Furthermore, unlike his predecessors, there is no evidence that Stone engaged in any actions to enforce the traditional consensus norms of the Court or to socialize new justices into the no dissent convention. Third, Stone's views appear to have been reinforced by his lack of appreciation for the tightly run conferences of Hughes and what he believed to be the superficial harmony of the Taft years. Stone, in a sense, rebelled against the chiefs under which he had served. As Mason has best stated: "On the matter of 'massing the court,' Stone thought there was a line beyond which a Chief Justice could not, with propriety, press for compromise. He might seek unanimity by removing doubts and misunderstanding 'so far as that could be accomplished by exposition and discussion at conference.' But unanimity purchased at the cost, 'either for himself or others, of strongly held convictions' was not worth the price. A Chief Justice should recognize the 'part played in the development of law by the dissenting opinion'" (Mason, 1956, p. 575). In short, Stone boasted that "in his Court . . . conflict represented intellectual, not personal differences" (Mason, 1956, p. 591).

Discussion and Conclusions

The evidence examined in the foregoing analysis leads to the conclusion that much of the responsibility for changing the operational norms of the Court from institutional unity to permitting free expression of individual views can be attributed to the leadership of Harlan Fiske Stone. His conception of the chief justiceship radically differed from his predecessors. He rejected the "no dissent unless absolutely necessary" rule and believed that good law was the product of the clash of individually expressed positions. Importantly, Stone refused to enforce consensus expectations, always remaining a participant rather than a leader (Steamer, 1986, p. 266). He led by example in maintaining high rates of concurring and dissenting opinions.

However, it is doubtful that Stone's leadership alone can account for the abrupt alteration in Court behavior. Other conditions, which coincided with

Stone's elevation, substantially enhanced the impact of his leadership style and may have been necessary, if not sufficient, factors in producing the radical change in Court norms. The Court's jurisdiction had been largely converted to one of discretion. The associates were generally young and had relatively few years of Supreme Court experience. They had not been deeply immersed in the traditional norms of the institution; nor for that matter, of any other appellate court. Instead, they came from backgrounds in which individual articulation of views was expected and independence of thought rewarded. With the most crucial legal battles of the New Deal already won, conditions were ripe for disagreement on emerging issues. Unlike earlier leaders of the Court, Stone did not attempt to curb this tendency but granted the associate justices "permission" to disagree. Delivered from the restrictions of the past, the associates took full advantage of the chief's tolerant attitudes toward individualism.

Stone died in 1946, succumbing to a massive cerebral hemorrhage that struck immediately after he delivered his dissenting opinion in the naturalization case of *Girouard v. United States* (328 U.S. 61). Although he had served only five years in the center chair, the shortest chief justiceship since Oliver Ellsworth stepped down in 1800, Stone's tenure in that position had a remarkable impact on the institution of the Supreme Court.

Importantly, the Court did not revert to its traditional expectations following Stone's death. The norm changes introduced under his leadership were maintained in spite of immediate attempts to reverse them. Like many others, President Truman looked with disapproval on the results of the Stone years. In selecting a new chief justice, the President desired a leader to bring unity back to the Court. Truman's choice was the affable and kindly Fred Vinson (Frank, 1954). Clearly, Truman hoped that Vinson would be capable of curbing the rise of individuality among the justices. As one scholar explained: "Although Truman admired Vinson's record in government and agreed with his political philosophy, his personality was the most important factor in influencing the decision to appoint him to the High Court. His sociability and friendliness, his calm, patient, and relaxed manner, his sense of humor, his respect for the views of others, his popularity with the representatives of many factions, and his ability to conciliate conflicting views and clashing personalities and to work out compromises were qualities that Truman admired. Even more important, those personal qualities seemed to the President to fit the needs of the situation inside the Supreme Court. Dissension and dissent were on the rise . . . Vinson seemed capable of unifying the Court and thereby improving its public image" (Kirkendall, 1969, p. 2641).

Truman's hopes did not materialize. Vinson faced a Court unwilling to return to the old ways. The eight associate justices already in place when the new chief justice opened the October 1946 term represented forty-six years of experience, 74 percent of which had been served under Stone. All of the associates had spent a majority of their Court tenures under the Stone regime. Rutledge, Jackson, and Burton had served only under Stone and had no exposure to pre-Stone consensus norms. Frankfurter, Douglas, and Black, once freed from the expectations of cohesion and consensus, continued to assert their new prerogatives after Vinson's nomination. Significantly, each member of this trio had long years of service after Stone's death: Black and Douglas for more than a quarter century and Frankfurter for a decade and a half. Vinson was unable to reimpose the norm that individual views should be suppressed in deference to the majority. Instead, the Vinson Court became characterized as "nine scorpions in a bottle" (Steamer, 1986, p. 19). Successive new justices joined and were socialized into a Court with behavioral expectations quite unlike those operative in the pre-Stone years. Consequently, although Stone's term as chief justice was relatively short, his views on individual judicial expression constituted a legacy protected by his surviving associates.

Vinson's successors to the center chair did not attempt to turn back the clock. Earl Warren, Vinson's immediate replacement, may have possessed many of the necessary leadership qualities to promote cohesion. Yet Warren came to the Court directly from the political world having had no exposure to the traditional norms of the judiciary. He could hardly be expected to value pre-1941 behavioral expectations, or impose them on associate justices who were by then accustomed to readily engaging in dissenting and concurring opinions. Except for extraordinary situations, such as posed by the *Brown* case, there is little evidence that Warren expended special effort to bring about unanimity. Instead, he was primarily interested in insuring that internal disagreement was accepted by the justices without rancor (Katcher, 1967, p. 312), thus further institutionalizing the practice. By the time Warren Burger rose to the Supreme Court in 1969, the atmosphere initiated in the Stone era was more than a quarter century old and firmly rooted.

Contemporary justices accept individual expression as an established practice. Some describe dissenting behavior in rather matter-of-fact terms (see, for example, Rehnquist, 1987, pp. 302–03). Others speak of a justice's "responsibility" and "duty" to articulate views that differ from the majority (Brennan, 1985). This attitude is a far cry from earlier times when even Justice Holmes, noted for distinguishing his views from those of the majority, acknowledged "it useless and undesirable, as a rule, to express dissent" (*Northern Securities v. U.S.*, 193 U.S. 197, 400, 1904).

Hence, the long-term consequences of the regime change occurring under Stone's leadership are institutional in nature. Today we have a Supreme Court characterized by division rather than consensus. Was this a change for the better? Naturally this is a very difficult issue to address, but one upon which a great many scholars, lawyers, and judges have commented. Those who suggest that dissents and concurrences serve a negative institutional function offer the following reasons. First, individual opinions may shake public confidence in the judiciary by bringing into question the certainty of the law (Bowen, 1905; Hughes, 1928; Schmidhauser, 1979). Second, dissents and concurrences avert the Court from functioning in the most ideal way—as an "organic unit" (Swisher, 1958; Schwartz, 1957). And third, as expressed in the American Bar Association's Canons of Judicial Ethics, when individual opinions are inconsistent with past jurisprudence or are based on issues of less than fundamental importance, they tend to pervert the judicial function and weaken the development of the law. In an award-winning essay on dissents, R. Dean Moorhead noted that, "If the decisions of a court are consistently accompanied by concurring or dissenting opinions which represent attempts to substitute the impulses of the present for the wisdom of the past, the law suffers, and the only possible prediction is one of chaos" (1952, p. 884).

However, the institutionalization of individual judicial expression has received a great deal of support from other quarters. One school of thought, grounded in Jeffersonian views of the judiciary,[7] suggests that dissents and concurrences not only represent divisions of opinion within society (Douglas, 1948), but reflect democratic values as well. According to one adherent, Stanley Fuld, ". . . disagreement among judges is as true to the character of democracy, and as vital, as freedom of speech itself. . . . Indeed, we may remind ourselves, unanimity in the law is possible only in fascist and communist countries" (1962, p. 926). Thus, as Chief Justice Stone would most assuredly agree, individuals, whether they be average citizens or justices of the Supreme Court, should be free to express their views.

Scholars and justices have also argued that dissents and concurrences increase the quality of the judicial decision-making process and generally make for a more "responsible judiciary" (see Stone, 1942). One scholar contends that the mere threat of a dissent in conference helps to improve judicial decisions: "The thousands of potential but unwritten dissents and concurrences have no doubt raised the caliber of judicial opinions substantially just because they might have been written" (Stephens, 1952, p. 404).

What are the implications of this study for future research? On one level, further examination of the evolution, nature, and use of individual judicial expression is indicated. A substantial difference of opinion exists over the implications of the regime change ushered in by Stone's years in the center chair. The purpose of the present research was merely to locate the sources of that change. Studies examining its ramifications may ultimately address the question of whether history should regard Stone as a hero or a failure.

[7]For example, Jefferson disliked the decision-making process used by the Marshall Court, claiming that the Court was "cooking up opinions in conclave." Jefferson wanted the Court to return to the seriatim tradition (See Moorhead, 1952).

On another and perhaps more important level, the results of this study point to the promise offered by diachronic research designs in the investigation of the American legal system. Those who use traditional methods to explore areas of public law would never consider beginning their studies at the Warren or Burger Court eras. They have always recognized the importance of understanding the historical development of doctrinal trends. Yet, for far too long, students of the judicial process have concentrated exclusively on relatively short, discrete and contemporary periods. Certainly, longitudinal research can help us develop a richer appreciation for the Supreme Court as an institution.

References

Abraham, Henry J. 1986. *The Judicial Process*, 5th ed. New York: Oxford University Press.

Bates, Ernest S. 1936. *The Story of the Supreme Court*. Indianapolis: Bobbs-Merrill.

Baum, Lawrence. 1985. *The Supreme Court*, 2d ed. Washington: CQ Press.

Blaustein, Albert P., and Roy M. Mersky. 1978. *The First One Hundred Justices: Statistical Studies on the Supreme Court of the United States*. Hamden, CT: Archon Books.

Brennan, William J., Jr. 1985. In Defense of Dissents. Mathew O. Tobriner Memorial Lecture, University of California.

Bowen, William A. 1905. Dissenting Opinions. *Green Bag*, 17:690–98.

Danelski, David J. 1964. *A Supreme Court Justice is Appointed*. New York: Random House.

———. 1980. The Influence of the Chief Justice in the Decisional Process of the Supreme Court. In Joel B. Grossman and Richard S. Wells, eds., *Constitutional Law and Judicial Policy Making*. New York: John Wiley.

Douglas, William O. 1948. The Dissent: A Safeguard of Democracy. *Journal of the American Judicature Society*, 32:104–7.

Frank, John P. 1954. Fred Vinson and the Chief Justiceship. *University of Chicago Law Review*, 21:212–46.

———. 1958. *Marble Palace*. New York: Alfred A. Knopf.

Frankfurter, Felix. 1963. Chief Justices I Have Known. In Alan F. Westin, ed., *An Autobiography of the Supreme Court*. New York: Macmillan.

Fuld, Stanley H. 1962. The Voices of Dissent. *Columbia Law Review*, 62:923–29.

Goldman, Sheldon. 1982. *Constitutional Law and Supreme Court Decision-Making*. New York: Harper and Row.

Grossman, Joel B., and Richard S. Wells. 1980. *Constitutional Law and Judicial Policy Making*, 2d ed. New York: John Wiley.

Halpern, Stephen C., and Kenneth N. Vines. 1977. Institutional Disunity, the Judges' Bill and the Role of the Supreme Court. *Western Political Quarterly*, 30:471–83.

Hughes, Charles Evans. 1928. *The Supreme Court of the United States*. New York: Columbia University Press.

Katcher, Leo. 1967. *Earl Warren: A Political Biography*. New York: McGraw-Hill.

Kegley, Charles W. Jr. 1987. Decision Regimes and Foreign Policy Behavior. In Charles F. Herman, Charles W. Kegley, Jr., and James N. Rosenau, eds., *New Directions in the Comparative Study of Foreign Policy*. London: George Allen and Unwin.

Kirkendall, Richard. 1969. Fred M. Vinson. In Leon Friedman and Fred L. Israel, eds., *The Justices of the United States Supreme Court 1789–1969*, Vol. IV. New York: Chelsea House.

Mason, Alpheus T. 1956. *Harlan Fiske Stone: Pillar of the Law*. New York: Viking Press.

———. 1958. *The Supreme Court from Taft to Warren*. Baton Rouge: Louisiana State University Press.

———. 1968. The Chief Justice of the United States: Primus Inter Pares. *Journal of Public Law,* 17:20–60.

———. 1969. William Howard Taft. In Leon Friedman and Fred L. Israel, eds., *The Justices of the United States Supreme Court 1789–1969,* Vol. III. New York: Chelsea House.

Moorhead, R. Dean. 1952. Concurring and Dissenting Opinions. *American Bar Association Journal,* 38:821–24, 884.

Murphy, Walter F. 1964. *Elements of Judicial Strategy.* Chicago: University of Chicago Press.

Nagel, Stuart. 1961. Political Party Affiliation and Judges' Decisions. *American Political Science Review,* 55:843–50.

Norpoth, Helmut. 1986. Transfer Function Analysis. In William D. Berry and Michael Lewis-Beck, eds., *New Tools for Social Scientists.* Beverly Hills, CA: Sage.

Pritchett, C. Herman. 1948. *The Roosevelt Court.* New York: Macmillan.

———. 1954. *Civil Liberties and the Vinson Court.* Chicago: University of Chicago Press.

Rehnquist, William H. 1987. *The Supreme Court: How It Was, How It Is.* New York: William Morrow.

Roberts, Owen J. 1963. Charles Evans Hughes: The Administrative Master. In Alan F. Westin, ed., *An Autobiography of the Supreme Court.* New York: Macmillan.

Roper, Donald M. 1965. Judicial Unanimity and the Marshall Court—A Road to Reappraisal. *American Journal of Legal History,* 9:118–34.

Schiffman, Irving. 1969. Melville W. Fuller. In Leon Friedman and Fred L. Israel, eds., *The Justices of the United States Supreme Court 1789–1969,* Vol. II. New York: Chelsea House.

Schmidhauser, John R. 1979. *Judges and Justices: The Federal Appellate Judiciary.* Boston: Little, Brown.

Schubert, Glendon. 1962. The 1960 Term of the Supreme Court. *American Political Science Review,* 56:90–107.

Schwartz, Bernard. 1957. *The Supreme Court: Constitutional Revolution in Retrospect.* New York: Ronald Press.

Steamer, Robert J. 1986. *Chief Justice: Leadership and the Supreme Court.* Columbia: University of South Carolina Press.

Stephens, Richard B. 1952. The Function of Concurring and Dissenting Opinions in Courts of Last Resort. *University of Florida Law Review,* 5:394–410.

Stone, Harlan Fiske. 1942. Dissenting Opinions Are Not Without Value. *Journal of the American Judicature Society,* 26:78.

Swisher, Carl Brent. 1958. *The Supreme Court in Modern Role.* New York: New York University Press.

Tressolini, Rocco J. 1963. *Justice and the Supreme Court.* Philadelphia: J. B. Lippincott.

Ulmer, S. Sidney. 1962. The Political Party Variable in the Michigan Supreme Court. *Journal of Public Law,* 11:352–62.

———. 1986. Exploring the Dissent Patterns of the Chief Justices: John Marshall to Warren Burger. In Sheldon Goldman and Charles M. Lamb, eds., *Judicial Conflict and Consensus: Behavioral Studies of American Appellate Courts.* Lexington: University Press of Kentucky.

Wasby, Stephen L. 1984. *The Supreme Court in the Federal Judicial System,* 2d ed. New York: Holt, Rinehart and Winston.

Watts, James F., Jr. 1969. Edward Douglas White. In Leon Friedman and Fred L. Israel, eds., *The Justices of the United States Supreme Court 1789–1969,* Vol. III. New York: Chelsea House.

White, G. Edward. 1976. *The American Judicial Tradition.* New York: Oxford University Press.

[6]

THE STUDY OF JUDICIAL DECISION-MAKING AS AN ASPECT OF POLITICAL BEHAVIOR*

GLENDON A. SCHUBERT
Michigan State University

In a recent essay, Richard Snyder has stated that: "[A] paradox in political science is the lack . . . of any systematic attention to the analysis of the decision-making behavior of judges."[1] It is not my purpose to argue either for or against the particular frame of reference for decision-making analysis advocated by Snyder. I do believe, however, that he has correctly identified the approach —the analysis of judicial decision-making as an aspect of political behavior— which is most likely to command the focus of interest and activity of the coming generation of political scientists whose substantive concern is with the study of political problems in the area of our discipline traditionally known as public law.

The concept "political behavior" remains sufficiently novel within the public law fraternity to impose something of an obligation to make clear what I have in mind in using the term. I shall borrow from David B. Truman who, in a Brookings Lecture not long ago, defined the "behavioral sciences" as "those bodies of knowledge, in whatever academic department they may be found, that provide or aspire to provide 'verified principles' of human behavior through the use of methods of inquiry similar to those of the natural sciences."[2] Truman noted that the research techniques that have characterized developments in the behavioral sciences during the period since 1930 include: (1) the sample survey; (2) experimentation in group dynamics (and, in particular, sociometric analysis of interaction and influence structure in small groups); (3) communications content analysis; and (4) the theory of games.[3] I shall omit consideration of the sample survey, which is discussed, together with several examples of its application to the study of judicial behavior, in a recent paper;[4] but I shall present

* I wish to acknowledge the assistance, in supporting the research upon which this article is based, of a grant from the All-University Research Fund, and of the Bureau of Social and Political Research, both of Michigan State University. This article is a revision of a paper presented at the September, 1958, Meeting of the American Political Science Association.

[1] Richard C. Snyder, "A Decision-Making Approach to the Study of Political Phenomena," in Roland Young (ed.), *Approaches to the Study of Politics* (Evanston: Northwestern University, 1958), p. 13. *Cf.* Foster H. Sherwood, "The Role of Public Law in Political Science," *ibid.*, p. 87: "public law [has] all but disappeared as a recognized object of study for political science." Sherwood adds, p. 89, that public law, properly conceived as a body of relevant *political data*, "is within political science, and not at its borders."

[2] David B. Truman, "The Impact on Political Science of the Revolution in the Behavioral Sciences," in *Research Frontiers in Politics and Government: Brookings Lectures, 1955* (Washington: Brookings Institution, 1955), p. 203.

[3] *Ibid.*, pp. 204–208, 214.

[4] Joseph Tanenhaus, "The Uses and Limitations of Social Science Methods in Analyzing Judicial Behavior" (presented at a panel of the Annual Meeting of the American Political Science Association, September 7, 1956; mimeo., 22 pages plus footnotes and appendices.)

some uses of the other three, with the objective of illustrating the kinds of questions about judicial behavior that can be investigated with the aid of these tools. First, however, I wish to direct attention to a neglected aspect of judicial decision-making, the analysis of which requires no sophisticated methods of measurement but simply counting. None of the examples will be developed in more than a sketchy and somewhat fragmentary manner; I have attempted a fuller exposition elsewhere.[5]

I. THE ANALYSIS OF SUMMARY DECISION-MAKING

One area conspicuously neglected by political scientists is that of the summary decision-making processes of courts. I shall use the United States Supreme Court as an example. Perhaps one reason for our neglect of 90 percent of this Court's decisions is our distaste for quantification—except, of course, for the use of lawyer-like quantification such as citator systems—although the only feasible method for handling up to 2000 decisions a year is quantitative. Our attempt to understand "the Court's work" on the basis of the hundred or so cases in which decisions are accompanied by formal opinions is as inadequate as would be a description of icebergs relying only upon the visible portion above water. As Jack Peltason has pointed out, we do not limit our investigations of the legislative process to a perusal of the *Congressional Record.*[6]

Unfortunately, we cannot rely upon the official reports of the Court's summary decision-making. The data given in the Annual Reports of the Attorney General focus upon the successes of the Solicitor General as the principal litigant before the Court; and the Annual Reports of the Director of the Administrative Office of United States Courts do not supply the data needed to answer most of the important questions that might be asked about the political behavior of the Court. For example, we might well be curious as to how far a Court which has been so insistent that the summary decision-making of administrators,[7] the President,[8] and the Congress[9] shall comport with the rule of law, itself practices what it preaches. To be specific, the Judges' Bill of 1926 purports to make the Court's certiorari jurisidiction *discretionary,* while the limited appeals jurisdiction is supposed to be *obligatory.* For almost two decades, articles in the law reviews have been pointing out that the Court was in the process of making its appeals jurisdiction almost as discretionary, in practice, as certiorari jurisdiction, especially in the dismissal of appeals from state courts for "want of a substantial federal question." Any reader of these, noticing that the textbooks

[5] Glendon A. Schubert, *Quantitative Analysis of Judicial Behavior,* to be published shortly under the joint auspices of the Bureau of Social and Political Research, Michigan State University and the Free Press.

[6] Jack Peltason, *Federal Courts in the Political Process* (New York, 1955), pp. 1–2. *Cf.* Sherwood, *op. cit.*, p. 88.

[7] Peters v. Hobby, 349 U.S. 331 (1955); Hannegan v. Esquire, 327 U.S. 146 (1946).

[8] Cole v. Young, 351 U.S. 536 (1956); Youngstown Sheet & Tube v. Sawyer, 343 U.S. 579 (1952).

[9] Watkins v. United States, 354 U.S. 178 (1957); Sacher v. United States, 356 U.S. 576 (1958).

copy the statute on this point, and wanting to investigate, would soon discover that the Director reports the data on denials of certiorari, but that the analogous information about summary dismissal of appeals reposes—if anywhere—in a statistical category innocently labelled "Appeals and reviews by certiorari disposed of *on the merits*."[10] He would next discover that this category is a catch-all which includes appeals disposed of after argument as formal cases; appeals decided on the merits, both with and without argument, as per curiam cases; appeals dismissed (*i.e.*, denied review) with or (usually) without argument, by per curiam orders; and certiorari cases disposed of, both with or without argument, as formal or per curiam cases. He could not even discover the number of dismissed appeals without making an independent count directly from the case reports.

A related question has come to the attention of political scientists, no doubt due in no small meaure to Mr. Justice Frankfurter's repeated essays on the subject: whether the denial of certiorari has substantive significance. A recent law note has suggested,[11] and an analysis of four recent terms of the Court confirms that the question is broader than Frankfurter has revealed. In effect, there appears to be an equation such that the summary *denial* of certiorari (in either federal or state cases) is functionally equivalent to the summary *dismissal* of appeals from state courts which is equivalent to the summary *affirmance* on appeals from federal district counts. Moreover, there appears to be a second equation, such that *formal* reversals on appeals from federal district courts are equivalent to the *summary* reversals on appeals from state courts. I shall not attempt to prove these equations at this time, but only suggest that, if true, they relate to significant uniformities in the behavior of the Supreme Court as the administrative head of a federal system of adjudication.

II. BLOC ANALYSIS

We are all familiar with Pritchett's studies of dissenting votes and bloc affiliations on the Supreme Court. I shall not use the derisive term "box scores," which appears to be particularly popular among those political scientists whose research experience with quantitative methods begins and ends with the aphorism that "Thinkers don't count, and counters don't think." Although Pritchett's work is methodologically quite simple, he has done far more than merely to count heads. His quantitative studies have aided him in making highly perceptive and sophisticated interpretations of the voting behavior of the justices, and he has taken a long stride in the direction of a group dynamics approach to Supreme Court decision-making.

The surprising thing is that, in a profession of political "scientists," no one appears to have tried to replicate Pritchett's experiments. No one has criticized or suggested improvements in his methods,[11a] or applied them to study other

[10] Emphasis added. See, *e.g.*, the 1957 *Annual Report*.

[11] Note, *Harvard Law Review*, Vol. 69 (February, 1956), pp. 712–713.

[11a] There have been critics outside the profession; see Pritchett, *op. cit.*, fn. 13, below, pp. 189, 191, 275.

periods in the Supreme Court's history, or to study the work of other courts.

I shall confine my remarks about bloc analysis to three points. In the first place, Pritchett has used two basic kinds of tables: those which analyze paired agreement in dissent (see, *e.g.*, Figure 1); and those which present paired agreement in both assent and dissent in divided decisions, expressed as a percentage of total paired participation (Figure 2). It is also possible to construct dissent tables which focus upon marginal decisions only (Figure 3), and to construct tables of paired agreement in assent in divided decisions (Figure 4). Tables of marginal dissents reveal significant patterns of voting behavior that would

	Douglas	Black	Warren	Clark	Minton	Reed	Burton	Frankfurter	Harlan
Douglas	(19)	72	37	13	11	6	11	12	4
Black	72	(2)	37	10	6	2	2	13	2
Warren	37	37		12	3	4	3	2	
Clark	13	10	12	(2)	7	13	16	4	3
Minton	11	6	3	7		30	26	9	10
Reed	6	2	4	13	30	(5)	33	10	14
Burton	11	2	3	16	26	33	(3)	28	29
Frankfurter	12	13	2	4	9	10	28	(5)	41
Harlan	4	2		3	10	14	29	41	(6)
Total dissents:	113	82	44	41	52*	62*	79	76	61*

INDEX OF COHESION
IC[Left] = .611
IC[Center] = .489
IC[Right] = .478

FIG. 1. Dissenting Blocs on the Warren Court, 1953–1956 Terms

* Minton, Reed, and Harlan each served for less than four complete terms of the Court. Jackson, Brennan, and Whittaker, each of whom served a single term or less during the period covered, have been deleted from this computation, and also from Figures 2–4 for the same reason. Numbers in parentheses denote instances in which the justice is in "paired agreement" with himself, viz., his solo dissents.

otherwise be missed. During the 1953–1956 Terms, for instance, Clark cast his dissenting votes about equally with the left and with the right wings of the Court (Figure 1); but he was definitely affiliated with the left bloc of Black-Douglas-Warren in marginal dissents (Figure 3). Assent tables help, in the interpretation of dissent tables and tables of over-all interagreement, to determine the locus of decisive power within the Court. Libertarians may deride Clark, for instance, for the uninspired quality of his judicial writing—to say nothing of the content of his views—but bloc analysis of recent terms shows him to have been the most powerful justice on the Court—with the possible exception of the

Chief Justices—in terms of participation in winning majority coalitions,[11b] and by no means a conservative in relation to his colleagues. Bloc analysis also confirms the journalistic observation[12] that Clark votes as an acolyte to the Chief Justice on the far right of the Court under Vinson[13] and slightly left of center under Warren and immediately to his right (Figures 1–4).

In the second place, bloc identification does not need to be intuitive, but can be placed upon an objective basis by the use of standard indices to denote the

	Douglas	Black	Warren	Clark	Minton	Reed	Burton	Frankfurter	Harlan
Douglas		80	67	50	34	30	31	34	30
Black	80		77	58	44	37	36	46	31
Warren	67	77		76	54	55	53	55	42
Clark	50	58	76		64	68	65	55	46
Minton	34	44	54	64		74	61	54	49
Reed	30	37	55	68	74		71	48	51
Burton	31	36	53	65	61	71		61	65
Frankfurter	34	46	55	55	54	48	61		80
Harlan	30	31	42	46	49	51	65	80	
% of assent:	70	78	88	89	81	80	79	80	71

INDEX OF INTERAGREEMENT

II[Left] = .747

II[Center] = .673

II[Right] = .687

II(Wa-C) = .760

FIG. 2. Interagreement in Split Decisions of the Warren Court, 1953–1956 Terms, in percentages

presence and composition of blocs. In my own experiments in the use of bloc analysis, I have developed three such indices, which I offer tentatively until someone else comes up with something better. For the analysis of dissent tables, I suggest an Index of Cohesion, which is the ratio of the mean of the included dissenting pairs, in a postulated bloc, to the mean of the total dissents (for the period of time under investigation) of the included justices. It is, in other words, a decimal fraction which results from dividing the average of the dissenting participation of the included justices into the average of agreement among the included pairs. This index assumes that a justice can affect the over-

[11b] In describing Clark as "powerful," I employ the concept of "power" as defined by the Shapley-Shubik index, a probability measure of the extent to which any justice's votes were pivotal in the winning majority coalition which controlled the decisions. See below, fn. 28, *op. cit.*

[12] *Time Magazine*, Vol. LXVII, No. 26 (June 25, 1956), p. 14.

[13] C. Herman Pritchett, *Civil Liberties and the Vinson Court* (Chicago, 1954), p. 183.

all cohesion of a dissenting bloc significantly only to the extent that both his rate of interagreement with other members of the bloc, and his volume of dissent, are high. On the basis of limited empirical application, I consider an Index of Cohesion of .50 or greater to be high; .40–.49 to be moderate; and less than .40 to be low. In Figure 1, for instance, the Index of Cohesion for the Left Bloc = 1/3 (146) ÷ 1/3 (239) = .611, which is quite high.

For the analysis of assent tables, one might consider an Index of Adhesion, defined as the ratio of the mean of the included pairs to the total number of

	Douglas	Black	Warren	Clark	Minton	Reed	Burton	Frankfurter	Harlan
Douglas		26	20	10	7	2	6	6	1
Black	26		18	10	4	2	1	4	
Warren	20	18		12	2	3	3	2	
Clark	10	10	12			7	5	2	
Minton	7	4	2			9	15	5	7
Reed	2	2	3	7	9		15	4	5
Burton	6	1	3	5	15	15	.	13	14
Frankfurter	6	4	2	2	5	4	13		10
Harlan	1				7	5	14	10	
Total dissents:	34	28	24	19	22*	19*	29	20	14*

INDEX OF COHESION

IC[Left] = .610

IC[Center] = .557

IC[Right] = .587

Fig. 3. Dissenting Blocs in Marginal Decisions of the Warren Court, 1953–1956 Terms

* See Figure 1.

split decisions under investigation. This index measures the extent to which the justices combine to form a dominant majority bloc. Because of the non-participatants, the assent matrix which this index measures is not necessarily the converse of the dissent matrix for a given period. Apart from the difference in the matrices to which they apply, the Index of Adhesion differs from the Index of Cohesion in two respects: (1) the denominator of the IA is a constant for any measurement of a given matrix, while the denominator of the IC is a variable; and (2) the denominator of the IA is always much larger than the denominator of the IC, since no justice dissents all the time. (The highest level of dissent on the Supreme Court during the past decade appears to be Douglas's 51 percent during the 1952 Term.) I consider an IA of .60 or more to be high; .50 to .59 to be moderate; and less than .50 to be low. An IA of less than .50 for a pair or bloc would signify that the justices concerned had participated together in the majority in less than half of the split decisions of the Court for the period under examination. The IA for the Left Bloc in Figure 4 =1/3 (401)÷256=.522, which is moderate.

For the tables of over-all interagreement, which are expressed in percentages, the average of the ratios of the included pairs can be used as an Index of Interagreement, with .70 or better considered high, .60–.69 moderate, and less than .60 low. For the Left Bloc in Figure 2, the Index of Interagreement=1/3 (2.24)=.747, which is high.

	Douglas	Black	Warren	Clark	Frankfurter	Burton	Reed	Minton	Harlan	
Douglas		122	130	109	73	67	52	46	42	
Black	122		149	129	98	87	66	66	43	
Warren	130	149		173	135	131	102	88	64	INDEX OF
Clark	109	129	173		130	144	114	97	68	ADHESION
Frankfurter	73	98	135	130		124	83	80	79	IA[Left]=.522
Burton	67	87	131	144	124		107	90	70	IA[Center]=.545
Reed	52	66	102	114	83	107		92	36	IA(Wa-C)=.676
Minton	46	66	88	97	80	90	92		23	
Harlan	42	43	64	68	79	70	36	23		
Total assents:	141	163	209	204	176	176	135*	117*	93*	Total decisions=256

FIG. 4. Participation in the Majority in Split Decisions of the Warren Court, 1953–1956 Terms

* See Figure 1.

Although bloc analysis appears to have been applied only to the United States Supreme Court, I think that fruitful applications can be made to state courts. In order to test this notion, I have made a bloc analysis of four recent terms of the Michigan Supreme Court. The 1954–1957 Terms were chosen, because it was during this interval that Governor Williams, near the end of a decade in office, finally succeeded in placing on the Court a majority of like-minded Democrats. Bloc analysis of recent periods of the United States Supreme Court shows no relationship between partisan affiliation and bloc composition and voting behavior. In recent Terms, for instance, we find Democrat Black and Republican Warren on the left wing, and "Independent" Frankfurter and Republican Harlan on the right wing. The most interesting finding from bloc analysis of the Michigan Supreme Court was the perfect correlation between political party affiliation and bloc composition and voting behavior during the 1956 and 1957 Terms, after the Williams justices accrued in sufficient numbers to begin to take over control of the court (see Figure 5).[14] This finding, in turn, raises interesting questions about the relative impact upon judicial behavior of appointment for life as compared with election for fixed terms.

III. SCALOGRAM ANALYSIS

Scalogram analysis, or cumulative scaling, offers probably the easiest research technique to use as well as the most widely applicable of those surveyed in this paper. The method for constructing scales of judicial cases can be stated in

		Smith	Black	Edwards	Voelker	Kelly	Dethmers	Carr	Sharpe	
Smith	(Dem.)		9	9	7			1	1	
Black	(Dem.)	9	(1)	9	8			1	1	
Edwards	(Dem.)	9	9		7	1	1	1		
Voelker	(Dem.)	7	8	7						INDEX OF COHESION
Kelly	(Rep.)			1		(1)	8	11	10	IC[Left] = .830
Dethmers	(Rep.)			1		8		12	12	IC[Right] = .675
Carr	(Rep.)	1	1	1		11	12		23	
Sharpe	*	1	1			10	12	23		
Total dissents:		8	12	10	10	12	13	25	25	

FIG. 5. Dissenting Blocs on the Michigan Supreme Court, 1957 Term

* Although Sharpe originally was elected to the court as a Democrat in 1933, he was not so regarded in the mid-'fifties; nor did the Williams Administration consider that Justice Sharpe served in any sense as a spokesman for its views and policies.

terms of fixed, objective procedures, too lengthy for development here.[15] In essence, scale analysis measures the presence of a single dominant variable in a set of additional data. Assume, *e.g.*, that several related cases decided on the merits by the Court have asked questions of the justices to which they should have responded consistently if they understood the questions to relate to a single basic issue. Scalogram analysis provides a technique for arranging both the cases and the respondent justices in uniquely determined rank orders. Moreover, it can tell us both how consistent and how intense the underlying attitudes of the respective individual justices, and of the Court as a collective group, have been.

It happens that the fifteen "right to counsel" cases decided by the Supreme

[14] Majority control was not actually achieved until January 1, 1958, when Governor Williams' Attorney General, Thomas Kavanaugh, replaced expatriate-Democrat Sharpe.

[15] For a detailed explanation, see *op. cit.* above, note 5, ch. 5.

Scale Scores	Respondent's Name	Case: Smith v. O'Grady, 312 U.S. 329 (1941)	White v. Ragen, 324 U.S. 760 (1945)*	Lutz v. Ragen, 324 U.S. 760 (1945)*	Hawk v. Olson, 326 U.S. 271 (1945)	DeMeerleer v. Mich., 329 U.S. 663 (1947)*	House v. Mayo, 324 U.S. 42 (1945)*	Williams v. Kaiser, 323 U.S. 471 (1945)	Tomkins v. Missouri, 323 U.S. 485 (1945)	Rice v. Olson, 324 U.S. 786 (1945)	Carter v. Illinois, 329 U.S. 173 (1946)	Foster v. Illinois, 332 U.S. 134 (1947)	Betts v. Brady, 316 U.S. 455 (1942)	Canizio v. New York, 327 U.S. 82 (1946)	Avery v. Alabama, 308 U.S. 444 (1940)	Total votes per justice	Total inconsistencies per justice
	Scale Position:	1	2	3	4	5	6	7	8	9	10	11	12	13	14		
13	Murphy	(+)	(+)	(+)	(+)	(+)	(+)	(+)	(+)	(+)	'+')	+)	+)	'+')		13	0
13	Rutledge		(+)	(+)	(+)	(+)	(+)	(+)	(+)	(+)	+)	'+')		'+')		11	0
12	Black	('+')	(+)	(+)	(+)	(+)	(+)	(+)	(+)	('+')	+)	'+')	'+')	('−')	('−')	14	0
12	Douglas	(+)	(+)	(+)	(+)	(+)	(+)	('+')	('+')	(+)	'+')	+)	+)	(−)	(−)	14	0
9	Reed	(+)	(+)	(+)	('+')	(+)	(+)	(+)	(+)	(+)	(−)	(−)	(−)	(−)	(−)	14	0
9	Stone	(+)	(+)	(+)	(+)		(+)	(+)	(+)	(+)			(−)	(−)	(−)	11	0
8	Jackson		(+)	(+)	Y	(+)	(+)	(+)	(+)	−)	(−)	(−)	(−)	Y		10	0
6	Frankfurter	(+)	(+)	(+)	(+)	(+)	(+)	'−')	'−')	'−')	('−')	('−')	(−)	(−)	(−)	14	0
5	Vinson					(+)					(−)	(−)				3	0
5	Burton				(+)	(+)					(−)	(−)		(−)		5	0
3	Roberts	(+)	+	+			−	−)	−)	−)			('−')		(−)	9	0
1	Hughes	(+)													(−)	2	0
0	McReynolds														(−)	1	0
0	Byrnes												(−)			1	0
	Division of votes: +	8	9	9	8	9	8	7	7	6	4	4	3	2	0	122	
	−	0	0	0	0	0	1	2	2	3	5	5	6	6	8		
	Number of inconsistencies per case:	0	0	0	0	0	0	0	0	0	0	0	0	0	0		0

* Per curiam decision. $CR = 1 - \frac{0}{62} = 1.000$

Fig. 6. A Scalogram of the "Right to Counsel" Cases, 1940–1947

Court from the 1940 Term through the end of the 1947 Term[16] form that empirical rarity, a perfect scale, so I shall use it as an example (Figure 6). The cases can be arranged in an order such that, it is assumed, the cases to the left of the scale are most seriously damaging to the claimed rights and interests of the defendants, and those to the right of the scale least so. Here the question the justices are asked to answer is: "How sympathetic are you to claims of the right to counsel under the Fourteenth Amendment?" Or we can conceptualize

[16] This particular period was chosen because it includes the "source group" cases in the article by Fred Kort to be discussed below. See ftn. 20, *infra*.

the cases as raising a set of questions of this order: "Do you approve when a criminal defendant in a state court is denied counsel to the extent of *X?*" "Do you approve when he is denied counsel to the extent of $X+Y$?," "to the extent of $X+Y+Z$?"—and so on. In this particular example the cases ranged from several, to the left of the scale, in which the Court voted unanimously in favor of the defendants' claims, to the case at the right of the scale which found even Black and Douglas joining in a unanimous decision against the defendant. Murphy and Rutledge have the highest scale scores; neither of them ever voted against a right to counsel claim. Frankfurter voted, with perfect consistency, in favor of defendants in the first six cases along the scale, and against defendants in the remaining eight. We can readily rank, on the basis of their voting participation, all of the members of the Court during the eight-year period. But we can do more than this, we can also predict how they should have voted in the cases in which they did not participate.

In fact, scalogram theory postulates that, knowing the scale of cases and the scale scores of the justices, we should be able to predict all votes in all cases comprising the scale. If any justices voted inconsistently in some cases, the degree of their inconsistency can be measured by a Coefficient of Reproducibility, which is the decimal fraction resulting from the subtraction, from unity, of the number of inconsistent votes divided by the total number of votes in all cases except those decided unanimously or with a single dissenting vote.[17] It is conventional, based upon experience in analyzing other types of data, to consider a CR of .900 or better to be evidence of unidimensionality in a scale. I have followed the convention, although ultimately the question whether scales with CR's of .900 are acceptable for the analysis of Supreme Court decision-making must await considerably more experimentation than appears to have taken place to date. The CR for the right-to-counsel cases of our example was, of course, 1.000.

It may be either fool's or beginner's luck, but every hypothesis that I have tested thus far has resulted in an acceptable scale. The subject matter of these scales includes: (a) Federal Employers' Liability Act evidentiary cases since 1942; (b) aliens' claims since 1950; (c) all the split decisions of the 1936 Term—the term of the "Court-packing" controversy; (d) the right to counsel cases since 1940; and (e) the search and seizure csaes, both federal and state, since 1937. On the other hand, it is easy to state inappropriate hypotheses which lead to unacceptable scales, as the report of the experiments of a sociologist demonstrates.[18]

The matrix of the scalogram can readily include supplementary information

[17] The reason for excluding unanimous and near-unanimous decisions from the denominator of the fraction is the much greater probability that there will be no inconsistent votes in such decisions than in those in which the Court is more divided. (The CR for unanimous decisions must, of course, be 1.000.) See Warren S. Torgerson, *Theory and Methods of Scaling* (New York, 1958), p. 324.

[18] Jessie Barnard, "Dimensions and Axes of Supreme Court Decisions," *Social Forces*, Vol. 34 (October, 1955), pp. 19–27.

of considerable value in the interpretation of the data. In addition to the votes of the justices, the scalogram can show who wrote, and who joined in the majority opinion; which justices concurred and/or wrote concurring opinions; and which justices dissented and/or wrote dissenting opinions.[19]

Scalograms of judicial decisions focus attention upon the justices whose voting has been least, or most, consistent; and cases displaying inconsistent votes are pinpointed. Such clues may suggest, in the attitudes of inconsistent justices, the possible presence of a secondary variable and, as regards inconsistent cases, the additional possibility that a case has been misclassified.

I should like to offer just one more example of the kinds of hypotheses that can be tested by scalogram analysis. The Court's "official" doctrine in the right-to-counsel cases is familiar enough: that the Constitution unequivocally requires representation by counsel in state criminal trials only for capital offenses. Scalogram analysis demonstrates conclusively that the Court has been just as consistent, and just as favorable, in non-capital as in capital cases. The Court has decided $66\frac{2}{3}$ percent of the right to counsel cases involving non-capital offenses, and $62\frac{1}{2}$ percent of the capital-offense cases, in favor of defendants, and the coefficients of reproducibility for the two subscales are both very high: .962 and .972. Which among the Court's many other doctrines may be confirmed, and which may be deflated by scalogram analysis, one cannot predict on *a priori* grounds; but I am confident that cumulative scaling offers a most powerful analytic tool for the study of the Supreme Court.[20]

IV. CONTENT ANALYSIS

Content analysis can be used as the basis for more precise description of "value" as well as "fact" assertions in judicial opinions; but since no study of content analysis of judicial values has as yet been published, I shall limit my

[19] I have used the following symbols in Figures 6 to 8:

+ = Voted in favor of the defendant
– = Voted against the defendant
' ' = Wrote opinion
( ) = Joined in the Opinion of the Court
(= Joined in concurring opinion
) = Joined in dissenting opinion
Y = Did not participate in the decision (a blank cell signifies that the justice was not a member of the Court at the time the case was decided).
[ ] Denotes an inconsistent vote

For example, the composite symbol ('+') means that the justice wrote the Opinion of the Court in a case decided by a majority of positive votes. Or, if a justice joined in a dissenting opinion written by another justice, in a case decided by a negative majority (*i.e.*, voting against the defendant), the appropriate combination of symbols to signify his position would be +).

[20] For two recent reports of applications of cumulative scaling to the analysis of legislative voting, see Charles D. Farris, "A Method of Determining Ideological Groupings in the Congress," *Journal of Politics*, Vol. 20 (May, 1958), pp. 308–338 and George M. Belknap, "A Method for Analyzing Legislative Behavior," *Midwest Journal of Political Science*, Vol. 2 (November, 1958), pp. 377–402.

remarks to fact analysis. A short time ago, Fred Kort described in this REVIEW a method for content analysis of facts in a set of Supreme Court opinions, together with a mathematical formula for processing the derived numerical data.[21] He reported the results of an experiment in which he divided the right to counsel cases chronologically into two groups, and in which he predicted successfully how the Court would decide the later group of cases on the basis of his analysis of the earlier group. More recently an econometrician has sharply criticized the theoretical assumptions which might support such a method as Kort used, and Kort has replied.[22] My own views regarding this controversy have been developed elsewhere at greater length than can be set forth here.[22a] Irrespective of specific defects in Kort's method and notwithstanding any personal scepticism as to its utility, I think that Kort's venture represents a serious and thought-provoking attempt to apply content analysis and mathematical procedures to the study of judicial decision-making, and I do not see how we can avoid learning something from his efforts.

For present purposes, I shall limit my remarks to two points. First, I have applied Kort's method to the analysis of the search and seizure cases of the past two decades. I treated those decided during the first decade as what Kort terms the "source group," and I divided the decisions since 1947 into a federal test group and a state test group. I found it possible to predict from the source group (which consisted, of course, exclusively of federal cases) to the federal test group, but not to the state test group. Now, perhaps I should confess that I lumped together cases involving statutory interpretation (wire-tapping cases) and those raising constitutional issues under the Fourth (or Fourteenth) Amendments. I did this on the assumption that if, as Kort presumes, the decisions of the justices were determined by the cumulative impact of factors harmful to defendants, I could safely disregard such doctrinal nuances as the legal aftermath of the *Olmstead* case.[23] By the same token, however, it seemed not unreasonable to assume that the "facts" should speak with equal authority for Supreme Court justices whether the defendant has been tried in a state or in a federal court. This leaves me with the question: if his method is theoretically sound, why should the prediction fail so completely for the state test group?[24] I believe that Kort would reply that my assumption *is* unreasonable, since we should anticipate consistency of decisions only in regard to the application of the same rule of law. From this point of view, my experiment confirms the Court's

[21] Fred Kort, "Predicting Supreme Court Decisions Mathematically: A Quantitative Analysis of the 'Right to Counsel' Cases," this REVIEW, Vol. 51 (March, 1957), pp. 1–12.

[22] Franklin M. Fisher, "The Mathematical Analysis of Supreme Court Decisions: The Use and Abuse of Quantitative Methods," this REVIEW, Vol. 52 (June, 1958), pp. 321–338; Fred Kort, "Reply to Fisher's *Mathematical Analysis of Supreme Court Decisions*," *ibid.*, pp. 339–348.

[22a] *Op. cit.*, fn. 5 above, ch. 5, Appendix E: "Statistical Inference and Judicial Behavior: A Comment Upon the Kort-Fisher Mélange."

[23] Olmstead v. United States, 277 U.S. 438 (1928).

[24] According to the prediction, all six of the state search and seizure cases should have been decided in favor of the defendants; in fact, only one of the six was a pro decision.

own contention that the requirements of due process under the Fourteenth Amendment are substantially less rigorous than the "more specific" norms supplied by the Fourth Amendment.

The other aspect of Kort's method I shall comment upon here has to do with the relationship between Kort's results and those obtained by scalogram analysis. Kort assigns weights to both source and test group cases. Indeed, the purpose of his content analysis and mathematical operations is to arrive at a set of what he calls "composite values," or numerical weights, for the cases. His basic prediction is that all pro cases (*i.e.*, those decided in favor of defendants) will have higher weights than any of the con cases (*i.e.*, those decided against defendants); and that all cases in the test group with scores equal to or higher than that of the lowest pro case in the source group will be decided pro; conversely, all cases in the test group with scores equal to or less than that of the highest con case in the source group will be decided con. He thus arrives at a numerical scale for all of the cases under investigation.

It is possible, of course, to arrange the right to counsel cases that Kort analyzed, and the search and seizure cases that I analyzed, in a scale according to Kort's system of weights; and to compare the resulting pseudo-scales of the justices' votes with the scales obtained by direct scalogram analysis. This can be done for the entire group of right to counsel (or search and seizure) cases, and also for sub-groups such as the source and test groups. We find that the Coefficients of Reproducibility for the Kort pseudo-scales are lower than those of the direct scalograms; but several of the Kort pseudo-scales have CR's that are acceptable, and the others are in the .800's. The highest correlation between a Kort pseudo-scale and the corresponding Guttman scale appeared in the source group of search and seizure cases (Figures 7 and 8). The CR's for these scales are identical and exceptionally high—.988—with only a single (and the same) inconsistent vote appearing in each scale. The rank correlation coefficient[25] for this scale and its corresponding pseudo-scale is .920 at a confidence level of considerably better than one percent (.00004). With the exception of the state test group of the search and seizure cases, the rank correlation coefficients for the corresponding pairs of Guttman scales and Kort pseudo-scales, for the various groupings of right to counsel and search and seizure cases, all were .765 or better at confidence levels of not less than .0002. Moreover, I believe that slight modifications in Kort's method would result in an even closer numerical approximation of cumulative scales.

These findings suggest two conclusions: (1) Kort's method worked success-

[25] I used Kendall's tau (beta) formula, which takes tied ranks into consideration, for the computation of these rank correlation coefficients. The formula is:

$$\tau_b = \frac{S}{\sqrt{\{\frac{1}{2}n(n-1) - T\}}\sqrt{\{\frac{1}{2}n(n-1) - U}}; \; T = \tfrac{1}{2}\sum_t t(t-1); \; U = \tfrac{1}{2}\sum_u u(u-1).$$

For an explanation of the method, see Maurice A. Kendall, *Rank Correlation Methods* (London: Chas. Griffin, 1948 ed.), pp. 4–5, 17–18, 25–27, 40–43. The formula is presented at p. 26.

Scale Scores	Respondent's Name	Weiss v. U.S., 308 U.S. 321 (1939)	Nardone v. U.S., 308 U.S. 338 (1939)	Nardone v. U.S., 302 U.S. 379 (1937)	U.S. v. Di Re, 332 U.S. 581 (1948)	McDonald v. U.S., 335 U.S. 451 (1948)	Johnson v. U.S., 333 U.S. 10 (1948)	Trupiano v. U.S., 334 U.S. 699 (1948)	Goldstein v. U.S., 316 U.S. 114 (1942)	Goldman v. U.S., 316 U.S. 129 (1942)	Davis v. U.S., 328 U.S. 582 (1946)	Zap v. U.S., 328 U.S. 624 (1946)	Harris v. U.S., 331 U.S. 145 (1947)	Scher v. U.S., 305 U.S. 251 (1938)	Total votes per justice	Total inconsistencies per justice
	Scale Position:	1	2	3	4	5	6	7	8	9	10	11	12	13		
12	Frankfurter	(+)	('+')		(+)	(+)	(+)	(+)	+)	+)	'+')	'+')	'+')		11	0
12	Murphy				(+)	(+)	(+)	('+')	'+')	'+')	+)	+)	'+')		9	0
12	Rutledge				(+)	(+)	(+)	(+)			'+')	+)	+)		7	0
12	Jackson				('+')	('+'	('+')	(+)			Y	Y	'+')		5	0
9	Stone	(+)	(+)	(+)					+)	+)				(−)	6	0
7	Douglas	(+)	(+)		(+)	('+')	(+)	(+)	(−)	(−)	('−')	('−')	(−)		11	0
5	Black	(+)	(+)	(+)	[−]	+	−	−)	(−)	(−)	(−)	(−)	(−)	(−)	13	1
4	Burton				(+)	'−')	−	−			(−)	(−)	(−)		7	0
4	Reed	(+)	Y		(+)	−)	−	−	(−)	(−)	(−)	(−)	(−)	(−)	11	0
3	Hughes	(+)	(+)	(+)										(−)	4	0
3	Butler	(+)	(+)	(+)										(−)	4	0
3	Roberts	('+')	(+)	('+')					('−')	('−')				(−)	6	0
3	Cardozo			(+)											1	0
3	Brandeis			(+)										(−)	2	0
1	McReynolds	(+)	−	−)										('−')	4	0
0	Byrnes								(−)	(−)					2	0
0	Vinson				−	−)	−	'−')					('−')		5	0
0	Sutherland			'−')											1	0
Division of votes:	+	9	7	7	7	6	5	5	3	3	3	3	4	0	109	
	−	0	1	2	2	3	4	4	5	5	4	4	5	8		
Number of inconsistencies per case:		0	0	0	1	0	0	0	0	0	0	0	0	0		1

$$CR = 1 - \frac{1}{84} = .988$$

FIG. 7. A Scalogram of Federal Search and Seizure Cases, 1937–1948

fully on the right to counsel cases and on the federal search and seizure cases because each of these sets of cases happens to be in a scalar relationship; and (2) Kort appears to have discovered a mathematical technique for approximating cumulative scales.[26] At least, the relating of Kort's method to scalogram analy-

[26] *Cf.* Robert N. Ford's discussion of "simple scaling" in M. W. Riley, J. W. Riley, and J. Toby, *Sociological Studies in Scale Analysis* (New Brunswick: Rutgers University Press,

Scale Scores	Respondent's Name	Weiss v. U.S., 308 U.S. 321 (1939)	Nardone v. U.S., 308 U.S. 338 (1939)	U.S. v. Di Re, 332 U.S. 581 (1948)	Nardone v. U.S., 302 U.S. 379 (1937)	McDonald v. U.S., 335 U.S. 451 (1948)	Johnson v. U.S., 333 U.S. 10 (1948)	Trupiano v. U.S., 334 U.S. 699 (1948)	Davis v. U.S., 328 U.S. 582 (1946)	Harris v. U.S., 331 U.S. 145 (1947)	Goldstein v. U.S., 316 U.S. 114 (1942)	Goldman v. U.S., 316 U.S. 129 (1942)	Zap v. U.S., 328 U.S. 624 (1946)	Scher v. U.S., 305 U.S. 251 (1938)	Total votes per justice	Total inconsistencies per justice
	Case:															
	Composite Values:	300.2	240.1	237.7	224.5	202.4	194.0	180.7	173.6	172.6	171.5	155.8	152.4	143.6		
	Position on Figure 7	1	2	4	3	5	6	7	10	12	8	9	11	13		
	Scale Position:	1	2	3	4	5	6	7	8	9	10	11	12	13		
12	Frankfurter	(+)	('+')	(+)		(+)	(+)	(+)	'+')	'+')	+)	+)	'+')		11	0
12	Murphy			(+)		(+)	(+)	('+')	+)	'+')	'+')	'+')	+)		9	0
12	Rutledge			(+)		(+)	(+)	(+)	'+')	+)			+)		7	0
11	Stone	(+)	(+)		(+)						+)	+)		(−)	6	0
9	Jackson			('+')		('+'	('+')	(+)	Y	'+')			Y		5	0
7	Douglas	(+)	(+)	(+)		('+')	(+)	(+)	('−')	(−)	(−)	(−)	('−')		11	0
5	Black	(+)	(+)	[−]	(+)	+	−	−)	(−)	(−)	(−)	(−)	(−)	(−)	13	1
4	Hughes	(+)	(+)		(+)									(−)	4	0
4	Butler	(+)	(+)		(+)									(−)	4	0
4	Roberts	('+')	(+)		('+')						('−')	('−')		(−)	6	0
4	Cardozo				(+)										1	0
4	Brandeis				(+)									(−)	2	0
3	Burton			(+)		'−')	−	−	(−)	(−)			(−)		7	0
3	Reed	(+)	Y	(+)		−)	−	−	(−)	(−)	(−)	(−)	(−)	(−)	11	0
1	McReynolds	(+)	−		−)									('−')	4	0
0	Byrnes										(−)	(−)			2	0
0	Vinson			−		−)	−	'−')		('−')					5	0
0	Sutherland				'−')										1	0
Division of votes:	+	9	7	7	7	6	5	5	3	4	3	3	3	0	109	
	−	0	1	2	2	3	4	4	4	5	5	5	4	8		
Number of inconsistencies per case:		0	0	1	0	0	0	0	0	0	0	0	0	0		1

$$CR = 1 - \frac{1}{84} = .988$$

FIG. 8. A Pseudo-Scale, According to Composite (Kort) values, of Federal Search and Seizure Cases, 1937–1948

1954), pp. 297–298. Ford shows that when the simple sum of correct responses is substituted for scale scores (in a study involving a small number of questions and a large number of respondents), the resulting ranks for 96 per cent of the respondents did not deviate by more than one rank from scale ranks derived from scale scores.

sis is sufficiently interesting to warrant further experimentation in which both methods are applied together to other sets of data.

V. GAME ANALYSIS

The judicial process is tailor-made for investigation by the theory of games. Whatever may be their obligations as officers of courts, attorneys frequently play the role of competing gamesmen, and the model of the two-person zero-sum game certainly can be applied to many trials. The two examples that I should like to describe briefly, however, involve the application of game theory to the analysis of the behavior of Supreme Court justices. I hope that I will be forgiven if I forego any attempt to explain game theory and its basic concepts, and simply describe the two games.[27]

The first of these I shall call the Hughberts Game. During the 1936 Term, the Court was divided between a three-justice liberal bloc and a four-justice conservative bloc, with Hughberts (Hughes and Roberts) in the middle. If we assume that, in the face of Roosevelt's attack upon the Court, the Chief Justice —with the support of Roberts—wished to maximize both his own authority within the Court and the degree of unanimity in the Court's decisions, while at the same time directing the Court to as liberal a course of decision as possible in order to forestall the possibility of the more drastic reforms proposed by the President, game theory can tell us how Hughberts should vote if he—I shall consider Hughes and Roberts to be a single player from now on—were to behave rationally in order to realize these objectives. A game must have a payoff which can be expressed in numerical terms, and for this purpose I have used the Shapley-Shubik empirical power index[28] in order to be able to compare the Court's actual voting behavior with the imputed utilities (*i.e.*, the payoff) postulated by the game model. Simply stated, the Shapley-Shubik index measures the extent to which each justice shared in the power of decision, which is defined as the probability of his having been pivotal in the winning coalition.

The left bloc and the right bloc are each defined as players in the game, which is three-person and zero-sum. Hughberts has a pure strategy, which in essence requires that he form a coalition with the Left when possible, that he form a coalition with the Right when splintering or non-participation makes it impossible for him to form a winning coalition with the Left, and that he always join the coalition of the Left and the Right when the other players do not choose to adopt conflicting strategies. In fact, the voting behavior of Hughes and Roberts conforms very closely to the prescriptions of the game model (Figure 9). In terms of the empirical payoff, the four-justice right bloc, the three-justice left bloc, and the two-justice center bloc are all approximately equal in power:

[27] For an extended discussion of the theory, written by mathemeticians for a social science audience, see R. Duncan Luce and Howard Raiffa, *Games and Decisions* (New York: Wiley, 1957).

[28] L. S. Shapley and Martin Shubik, "A Method for Evaluating the Distribution of Power in a Committee System," this REVIEW, Vol. 48 (September, 1954), pp. 791–792.

	The Left		Hughberts		The Right	
	Brandeis	.1312	Hughes	.1600	VanDevanter	.0957
	Cardozo	.1264	Roberts	.1536	Sutherland	.0864
	Stone	.1054			Butler	.0742
					McReynolds	.0672
Totals		.3630		.3136		.3235
Expected power:		.3333		.3333		.3333
Difference:		+.0297		−.0197		−.0098

It is easy to demonstrate that in a three-person simple majoritarian game, equality of power is imputed among the players. It is by no means a self-evident proposition, however, that among nine justices each casting a single and equal vote, two justices can be just as powerful as four justices.

I shall call the other example the Certiorari Game. Do Supreme Court justices combine into a bloc with the deliberate objective of forcing upon the rest of the Court the consideration of an issue which the bloc wants decided in a particular way? The data for the game consist of the decisions of the Supreme Court, both jurisdictional and on the merits, in Federal Employers' Liability Act evidentiary cases since 1942. The basic assumption is that a certiorari bloc was functioning throughout this period, although the number of justices affiliating with the bloc varied at different times and an antagonist player (Frankfurter) in opposition to the certiorari bloc entered the game (as such) only during the latter stages of the play. In order to simplify the discussion, let us confine our attention to the first period of the game, comprising the 1942–1948 Terms.

At that time, the certiorari bloc consisted of Murphy, Rutledge, Black, and Douglas. If we assume that the objective of the bloc was to maximize the number of decisions favorable to workmen's claims, game theory can prescribe how the bloc should behave rationally in order to accomplish this objective. Four justices are adequate to grant certiorari, but not (normally) to decide cases on the merits. It is assumed that, during this period, the remaining five justices had no fixed predisposition either towards or against the claimants. The only question in these cases is whether the trial court correctly evaluated the evidence; the cases turn, in other words, on questions of fact rather than law. Typically, they fall into two categories: (a) the trial court directs a judgment for the defendant railroad, on the ground that the evidence is insufficient for the case to go to a jury, or else the court directs a judgment for the defendant notwithstanding a jury verdict for the plaintiff; or (b) the trial judge enters a judgment for the plaintiff on the basis of a jury verdict. In either event, the decision of the trial court has been affirmed or reversed by a court of appeals, and either the plaintiff workman or the defendant railroad has petitioned the Supreme Court for certiorari. It is assumed that, since these cases turn only on the evaluation of evidence, there is an equal chance that any of the five uncom-

THE LEFT (3 votes)		HUGHBERTS (2 votes) +	HUGHBERTS (2 votes) −		THE RIGHT (4 votes)
	+	(3/9, 2/9, 4/9) [96] 2 (R) 1 (Bu, M) 1 (M) 1 (M)[St] 1 (Su)	(3/7, 0, 4/7) [0]	+	
	+	(3/5, 2/5, 0) [6] 1 [St, V]	(0, 1/3, 2/3) [4] 1 (H) 1 [St] 1 (R) 1 [Br, St]	−	
	−	(0, 1/3, 2/3) [5] 3 [St] 1 (Br) 1 (H, Br)[St]	(3/5, 2/5, 0) [8] 1 (M) 1 (V)[St]	+	
	−	(3/7, 0, 4/7) [0]	(3/9, 2/9, 4/9) [76] 2 (Bu, M) 1 (Bu) 1 (Br, R) 1 (M) 1 (M)[St]	−	

Fig. 9. Payoff Matrix for the Hughberts Game

Legend: The symbols + and − designate the players' strategies:
+ = voting for affirmance of the lower court's decision
− = voting for reversal of the lower court's decision

The imputations for partitioning of the payoff among the players, according to the intersection of strategies, are given within parentheses at the top of each cell.

The number of decisions falling within each cell is given in brackets. The number of decisions, in each cell, in which there were deviations from the blocs, are itemized. Justices who defected from their respective blocs are shown in parentheses, and those who failed to participate in particular decisions are shown in brackets, according to the following key:

Br = Brandeis	H = Hughes	M = McReynolds
C = Cardozo	R = Roberts	Bu = Butler
St = Stone		Su = Sutherland
		V = VanDevanter

(Mr. Justice Cardozo did not deviate from the voting position attributed to the left bloc in any of the 195 decisions of the 1936 Term.)

mitted justices will vote either for or against a claimant if the court of appeals has disagreed with the trial court. Therefore, since the certiorari bloc needs to pick up only one additional favorable vote on the merits, the chances of its doing so should be 31/32, for the only permutation of the five uncommitted members on which the bloc could lose would be for all five of the other justices to vote against the claimant. The certiorari bloc has a pure strategy: never to vote in favor of petitions filed by railroads, always to vote to grant certiorari in cases in which review is sought by workers *and* in which an appellate court has reversed a judgment in favor of the plaintiff, and always to vote for the petitioner on the merits. *If* the certiorari bloc follows its pure stratgy, the Court should decide 97 percent of the cases in favor of the claimants. If the bloc departs from its pure strategy, it can expect to win a smaller proportion of victories on the merits, because it has played irrationally.

As a matter of fact, the payoff to the certiorari bloc during this period was 92 percent (12 pro decisions and 1 con) in cases in which the bloc adhered to its pure strategy; of the 11 cases in which the bloc departed from its pure strategy by voting to grant certiorari for petitioners who had been two-time losers in the courts below, 8 were pro and 3 were con, for a payoff of only 73 percent. In later periods of the game, the bloc adhered much more closely to its pure strategy, and consequently enjoyed greater success. During the present period, the bloc consists of five justices, so the expected payoff is 100 percent. As a matter of fact, the bloc lost one of the fourteen cases decided on the merits during the 1956 and 1957 Terms, perhaps because the bloc, a little power drunk, became careless and granted certiorari in a case so frivolous that even the bloc members joined in the unanimous decision against the claimant.[29] An alternative explanation for this deviant decision might be that the certiorari bloc was not being irrational, but rather that it *deliberately* accepted jurisdiction with the expectation that the decision would go unanimously against the workman, for the public relations objective of countering criticism that it *always* favored workmen.[30]

VI. CONCLUSION

I hope that I may have succeeded in suggesting some of the kinds of hypotheses that may be worth looking into if we are willing to consider adding other strings to our bow, instead of limiting ourselves to the traditional workways in public law. In addition to the many political scientists who will doubtless continue to pursue the legal, historical and philosophical approaches to the study of public law, those who may have, or may develop, an interest in the quantitative approach to the study of judicial behavior will find a great deal of work awaiting their attention.

[29] Herdman v. Pennsylvania Railroad Co., 352 U.S. 518 (1957).

[30] See, *e.g.*, William H. DeParcq, "The Supreme Court and the Federal Employers' Liability Act, 1956–1957 Term," *Texas Law Review*, Vol. 36 (December, 1957) pp. 145–156; and Thomas Gibbs Gee, "A Dissenting Postscript or, Notes from Underground," *ibid.*, pp. 157–160.

[7]

Sophisticated Voting and Gate-Keeping in the Supreme Court

Gregory A. Caldeira
Ohio State University

John R. Wright
Ohio State University

Christopher J. W. Zorn
Emory University

"Sophisticated voting" has a solid theoretical foundation, but scholars have raised serious questions about its empirical importance in real-world institutions. The U.S. Supreme Court is one institution where sophisticated voting should be common, but, paradoxically, where scholarly consensus about its existence has yet to emerge. We develop and test a formal model of sophisticated voting on agenda setting in the Supreme Court. Using data on petitions for certiorari decided in October term 1982, we show that, above and beyond the usual forces in case selection, justices engage in sophisticated voting, defined as looking forward to the decision on the merits and acting with that potential outcome in mind, and do so in a wide range of circumstances. In particular, we present strong evidence for sophisticated behavior, ranging from votes to deny a case one prefers to reverse to votes to grant cases one prefers to affirm. More importantly, sophisticated voting makes a substantial difference in the size and content of the Court's plenary agenda.

1. Introduction

Votes cast by members of collegial bodies do not always faithfully represent their true preferences. Faced with three or more choices, voters may forsake a first choice that has little chance of winning in order to prevent a least favorite alternative from winning. Typically called "sophisticated" or "strategic" voting, this behavior has solid theoretical footing, and scholars have discovered

We appreciate the assistance of the staff at the Reading Room of the Library of Congress for our work on the papers of Earl Warren, William O. Douglas, William Brennan, and Thurgood Marshall; and the staff at the Mudd Library at Princeton, for the papers of Justice John Marshall Harlan, Jr. Saul Brenner, Lee Epstein, James Hardin, Charles Smith, Jeff Segal, and several anonymous reviewers also offered helpful comments. Zorn also thanks the John M. Olin Foundation for their support of this research. The Law and Social Science and Political Science Programs of the National Science Foundation supported the collection of some of the data used in this article. An earlier version of this article won the 1997 American Judicature Society Award of the Law and Courts Section of the American Political Science Association.

instances of it in legislatures and elections around the world (Abramson et al., 1992; Cain, 1978; Calvert and Fenno, 1994; Denzau, Riker, and Shepsle, 1985; Farquharson, 1969; Krehbiel, 1993; Krehbiel and Rivers, 1992; Riker, 1982, 1986; Volden, 1998).

Although most of the empirical research on sophisticated voting has dealt with legislatures or large electorates, sophisticated behavior is not unique to these institutions. The U.S. Supreme Court is one institution where sophisticated voting should be common, but, paradoxically, where scholarly consensus about its existence has yet to emerge (see Epstein and Knight, 1998; Spiller and Spitzer, 1996; but cf. Segal, 1997). We say paradoxically, because opportunities for strategic manipulation of the Court's plenary agenda are plentiful: the Court follows a sequenced, binary voting procedure for decisions on certiorari and the merits; the sifting of cases occurs out of sight, with no need to justify those decisions; cases are fungible; and decisions to grant plenary review usually presage the outcome on the merits. Thus the selection of cases is fertile soil for strategic manipulation, and the consequences for the Court's plenary agenda are potentially significant.

Our objective here is to investigate the role of the sophisticated behavior in setting the U.S. Supreme Court's agenda. Using data on petitions for certiorari decided in October Term 1982, we show that, above and beyond the usual forces in case selection, justices engage in sophisticated voting, defined as looking forward to the decision on the merits and acting with that potential outcome in mind, and do so in a wide range of circumstances. We present strong evidence for sophisticated behavior, ranging from votes to deny a case one prefers to reverse to votes to grant cases one prefers to affirm. Furthermore, sophisticated voting makes a substantial difference in the size and content of the Court's plenary agenda.

In Section 2 we describe sophisticated voting, weigh its theoretical and empirical importance, and evaluate previous research. In Section 3 we offer a model of sophisticated voting on the Court. Section 4 describes our data and addresses the central issue of measuring judicial preferences. We develop measures of the preferences of the justices, both individually and in the aggregate, which allow us to gauge strategic behavior. In Section 5 we consider sophisticated voting on certiorari at the individual level. By examining the interaction between the preferences of the individual justices and the balance of the Court, we demonstrate the influence of both ideological preferences and strategic concerns in voting on certiorari. In Section 6 we present evidence on the significance of sophisticated voting: a substantial number of cases qualified as "sophisticated" outcomes in which the Court denied certiorari because of forward-looking behavior by one or more of the justices.

2. Strategic Voting in Political Institutions

Political scientists typically characterize voters as "sophisticated" (or strategic) when they do not vote for their favorite alternative at one stage of a voting procedure in the hope of bringing about a more favorable outcome at a later stage. In contrast, voters are described as "sincere" when they always vote for their favorite alternative at each stage of the voting procedure (e.g., Farquharson, 1969). This terminology, though fairly standard, is somewhat unfortunate in that it fails to distinguish between voters who have rationally looked ahead in the voting procedure and attempted to anticipate future outcomes from those who have not.[1] Voters can be sophisticated, in the sense that they are forward looking, but nevertheless optimally vote for their favorite alternative at the first stage of a voting procedure. Voters who vote for their first choices, therefore, are not necessarily engaging in nonstrategic behavior. Austen-Smith (1987), for example, has shown that with endogenous and decentralized formation of the agenda, an "optimally constructed agenda" makes sophisticated and sincere voting observationally equivalent.

Terminological ambiguities notwithstanding, Riker (1986) and others have provided important examples of sophisticated voting in political institutions. Yet Krehbiel and Rivers (1990) raise serious doubts about the empirical significance of sophisticated voting in legislatures. One problem is that sophisticated voting requires a "precise agenda fixed in advance and known to all participants" (Farquharson, 1969). The sequence of votes in legislatures, however, is often fluid and not known to all members. A second problem lies in identifying the true preferences of legislators. Ordeshook and Palfrey (1988), for example, demonstrate the difficulty of finding sophisticated voting with incomplete information about preferences. If many recorded votes are sophisticated, then legislative voting records will not be a reliable guide to legislators' true preferences. A third problem is that legislative procedures permit legislators to avoid sophisticated votes that might otherwise create problems with constituents.

The issues Krehbiel and Rivers (1990) raise might make the study of sophisticated voting on the Court untenable. Yet agenda setting in the Court comes closer than does Congress to meeting the conditions of sophisticated voting. First, justices know with certainty the subsequent branches in the tree after certiorari. Although they may not know precisely which issues the Court will decide, they will have a general sense of the alternatives. Since the Court's agenda is essentially fixed, unlike the situation Austen-Smith (1987) describes, it does not present problems of observational equivalence between sophisticated and naive behavior. Second, the opprobrium associated with sophisticated votes on the merits does not attach to the Court's agenda, in part because justices need not explain their positions. Third, justices deal with the same issues and a small number of individuals year after year, so knowledge about preferences is both easier to obtain and more likely to be accurate. Moreover, as Calvert and Fenno (1994) argue, sophisticated voting is possible if the actors possess even probabilistic knowledge of the agenda and preferences.

Despite the possibilities for strategic manipulation of the Court's agenda, scholars remain divided over the existence and extent of such behavior. Schubert (1959) claims that during the mid-1940s, liberal justices chose to grant

1. Standard definitions of sophisticated and sincere voting appear in Ordeshook (1992:75), and discussion of the confusion surrounding these concepts can be found in Baum (1997:90–91). We define the concept explicitly for our purposes in the next section.

FELA petitions in which the lower court had decided against the worker, and in which the worker had a good chance of winning on the merits; and to deny certiorari in cases in which the lower court had favored the worker. Thus liberal justices engaged in sophisticated voting on FELA petitions. By contrast, Provine (1980) debunks the idea of strategic justices. During the Vinson and early Warren courts, conceptions of proper judicial behavior enforced jurisprudential criteria and "prevent[ed] the justices from exploiting possibilities for power-oriented voting on case selection" (Provine, 1980:172). Perry (1992) straddles the question of strategic behavior: the justices usually employ jurisprudential criteria; other times, ideological considerations come into play. Yet he also quotes justices and clerks who testify about various forms of strategic behavior.[2,3]

Palmer (1982) presents evidence for both policy-oriented and strategic behavior. Justices were more likely to vote for certiorari if they eventually voted to reverse on the merits—and if their side won on the merits (see also Brenner and Krol, 1989; Krol and Brenner, 1990). For cases decided on the merits during the Vinson Court, Boucher and Segal (1995:835) estimate the impact of a justice's policy preferences and the degree of support for his position within the Court on votes for or against certiorari: "[D]uring the ... Vinson Court a majority of the justices exhibited strategic voting behavior." Boucher and Segal claim evidence of aggressive grants but not of defensive denials.

The contradictions in previous work on sophisticated voting in the Court stem from several problems. First, prior work has lacked an adequate measure of judicial preferences; to detect sophisticated voting, we need to know where the justices stand initially. Second, previous studies have usually focused on cases decided on the merits rather than the full set of petitions. Selection bias plagues such samples; omitting cases never reviewed on the merits mitigates against finding evidence of sophisticated behavior. This omission is problematic for, as we shall see, much sophisticated voting involves denials of certiorari. Since

2. We have found many examples of "strategic recommendations" in memoranda from law clerks in the papers of Thurgood Marshall, John Marshall Harlan, Jr., and Lewis F. Powell. Consider a single example. Marshall's clerk raises strategic considerations in a memorandum on *Rust v. Sullivan* (89-1391) and *New York v. Sullivan* (89-1392):

> CA1 has ruled to the contrary of CA2 on a number of the claims. The lawyers are quite good, and the full range of potential arguments have been made. In the normal case, this would be a pretty clear grant. Here, though, I would deny. The rumor mill has it that SOC [Sandra Day O'Connor] has changed her vote in *Hodgson* and that the statute will be upheld in its entirety. If we can't win *Hodgson*, it's hard to imagine the abortion case we could win. This case has the First Amendment dimension, which might help us with AAS [Antonin Scalia] or AMK [Anthony M. Kennedy], but I doubt it. Because every abortion case on which cert is granted creates a new opportunity to overrule *Roe*, I would deny on defensive grounds. Tactical judgments aside, the case is a grant.

3. For state supreme courts, Hall (1992) finds persuasive evidence of the impact of electoral forces in judges' decisions in death penalty cases; liberal judges in such cases moderate their votes on the merits in order to minimize the chance of a future defeat at the polls.

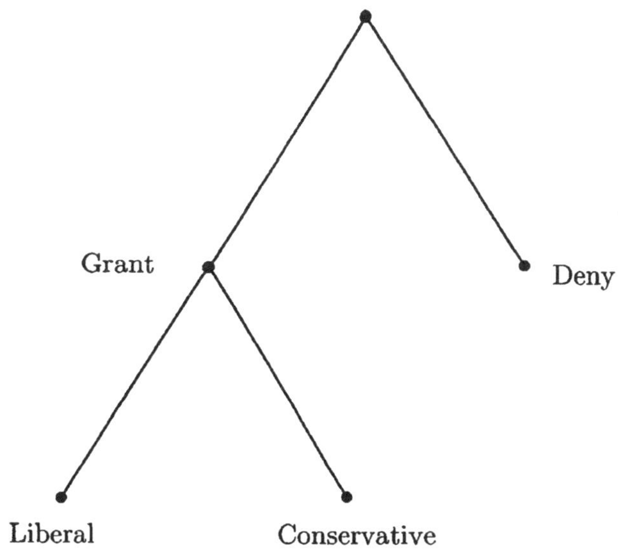

Figure 1. The Supreme Court's certiorari process.

most studies have included only cases given plenary review, we lack a complete model of voting on certiorari that includes strategic forces. Third, conceptual confusion characterizes much of this work; scholars have sometimes confused strategic and sincere behavior. We address these problems in the remainder of this article.

3. A Model of Sophisticated Voting on Certiorari

The Supreme Court follows a well-known binary procedure for decisions on certiorari and the merits. First, the Court decides whether to maintain or alter the status quo outcome established by the lower court, and second, for those outcomes it decides to alter, the Court establishes a new outcome to the right or the left of the status quo. This procedure is shown in Figure 1, where the Court's actions at the first stage are to deny (*d*) or to grant (*g*) certiorari, and the actions at the second stage are to decide the case in a liberal (*l*) or conservative (*c*) direction.[4]

We assume that each case on the Court's paid docket corresponds to a single dimension of the law, and that a point D on this dimension is the position of the status quo—the lower court's decision. Let L be the outcome when the Court grants certiorari and decides liberally on the merits and C be the

4. Strictly speaking, at the second stage justices must either affirm or reverse the lower court's decision. Affirming a conservatively decided case below, however, is tantamount to moving the outcome below in a more conservative direction; and affirming a case decided liberally below is tantamount to moving the outcome to the left. Similarly, reversing a case decided liberally (conservatively) below is equivalent to moving the outcome to the right (left).

outcome when the Court grants certiorari and decides conservatively. These three alternatives are ordered along a single ideological continuum, $L < D < C$.[5] We assume that the precise locations of L and C are determined exclusively by the fact patterns and legal possibilities of the case, and that justices have complete information about the locations of these potential outcomes prior to their decisions on certiorari.[6] Consequently, the justices may not craft opinions to locate outcomes at any point on the ideological line. The outcomes L, D, and C are instead exogenous, and the Court simply chooses among these alternatives.[7]

We assume that Supreme Court justices have single-peaked preference orderings over the outcomes L, C, and D, and we employ the notation $L \succ D \succ C$, for example, to denote the preference ordering L preferred to D preferred to C. A strategy for a justice is a pair of votes, one on certiorari and one on the merits. Given two alternatives at each stage, justices must choose from one of four possible strategies: (g, l), (g, c), (d, l), and (d, c), where g and d are the decisions on certiorari, and l and c are the decisions on the merits.

We say that justices employ *sophisticated* strategies when their optimal decision on certiorari depends on what they expect to happen on the merits (e.g., Farquharson, 1969). In other words, justices who use sophisticated strategies are forward looking, and they maximize their payoffs given their beliefs about outcomes at subsequent decision nodes. With sophisticated strategies, justices may—but will not necessarily—vote for their second preference on certiorari in order to lessen the likelihood of their least-preferred outcome on the merits. The sophisticated strategy for justices with preference, $L \succ D \succ C$, for example, is (d, l) instead of (g, l) when C is the anticipated outcome on the merits. In contrast, we say that justices employ *sincere* strategies when they vote for their most-preferred alternative on certiorari regardless of the likely outcome on the merits. Hence the sincere strategy for justices with $L \succ D \succ C$ is (g, l) even when C is the likely outcome on the merits. The certiorari decisions of justices who employ sincere strategies, therefore, can be predicted perfectly by knowledge of their preferences on the merits alone.

To specify the conditions under which justices vote for certiorari when using sophisticated strategies, let J represent a justice's ideal outcome on the ideological line containing L, D, and C; and define the justice's utilities for outcomes as $u(X) = -|J - X|$, where $X \in \{L, D, C\}$. We assume that justices are uncertain about the outcome on the merits, and so we let $p = \Pr(C)$ be a justice's belief that the outcome on the merits is conservative, and $1 - p$ be the

5. Since outcomes L and C establish new precedent, but D does not, we consider D to be a more moderate outcome.

6. As we explain below, however, we assume that justices are uncertain about which outcome will prevail on the merits.

7. If the justices could determine the locations of L and C without being constrained by the characteristics of the case or the issues decided in the lower court, the outcome on the merits would always be located at the ideal point of the median justice. In this situation, justices might bargain over the outcome on the merits simultaneously with the decision on certiorari, the median justice's wishes would always prevail, and four votes on certiorari could always be assured.

probability that the outcome is liberal. Justices employ sophisticated strategies when they maximize their payoffs given their beliefs about what will happen on the merits. The following proposition specifies when justices will vote to grant certiorari, given that they look ahead to the likely outcome on the merits.

Proposition (Sophisticated Voting). A justice will vote to grant certiorari if and only if

(a) $J > C$ and $p \geq \dfrac{D-L}{C-L}$.

(b) $D < J^* \leq J \leq C$ and $p \geq \dfrac{D-L}{C-L}$, where $J^* = \dfrac{C+L}{2} + \dfrac{D-L}{2p}$.

(c) $J < L$ and $p \leq \dfrac{D-L}{C-L}$.

(d) $L \leq J \leq J^{**} < D$ and $p \leq \dfrac{D-L}{C-L}$, where $J^{**} = \dfrac{p(C+L)-L-D}{2(p-1)}$.

Proof. We prove only (a) and (b); the proofs of (c) and (d) are analogous.

(a) $J > C$.

$$\begin{aligned} \text{EU (grant)} &= pu(C) + (1-p)u(L) \\ &= p(C-J) + (1-p)(L-J). \\ \text{EU (deny)} &= D - J. \end{aligned}$$

The justice votes to grant iff EU (grant) $\geq$ EU (deny), which implies

$$p(C-J) + (1-P)(L-J) \geq D - J.$$

Solving for p yields $p \geq \frac{D-L}{C-L}$.

(b) $J^* \leq J \leq C$

$$\begin{aligned} \text{EU (grant)} &= p(J-C) + (1-p)(L-J). \\ \text{EU (deny)} &= D - J. \end{aligned}$$

The justice votes to grant iff $p(J-C) + (1-p)(L-J) \geq D - J$.
Solving for p yields $p \geq \frac{D-L}{2J-C-L}$.
Cutpoint J^* is the smallest value of J such that this inequality holds, which occurs where EU (grant) = EU (deny), or equivalently,

$$p(2J^* - C - L) + L - J^* = D - J^*.$$

Solving for J^* yields $J^* = \frac{D-L}{2p} + \frac{C+L}{2}$.

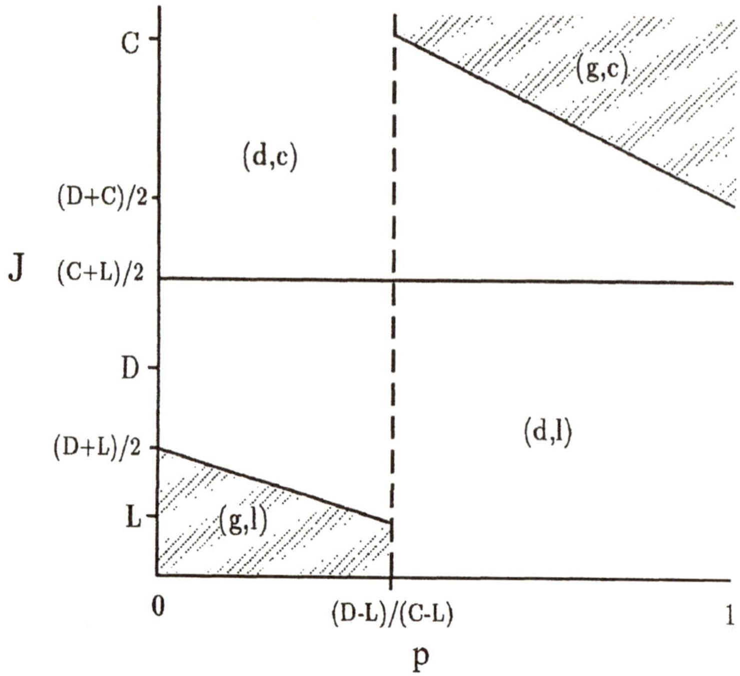

Figure 2. Certiorari voting under sophisticated behavior. Note: Shaded areas indicate ranges in which a vote for certiorari will occur. *J* is the position of the justice; *p* is the probability of a conservative outcome on the merits. See text for details.

We present this proposition graphically in Figure 2, where justices' ideal points, J, index the y-axis, and the probability of a conservative outcome, p, is on the x-axis. The sloped boundary lines in the northeast and southwest sections are given by the J^* and J^{**} equations, respectively. The strategies are indicated, as before, by (g, l), (g, c), (d, l), and (d, c). All strategies are sophisticated in Figure 2, because the conditions for their employment were derived under the assumption that justices maximize their payoffs given their beliefs about the outcome on the merits. With sophisticated strategies, justices may still vote to deny, their first choice, on certiorari. That is, justices with ideal points $J \in [(D + L)/2, (D + C)/2]$ may be forward looking and still always vote for their first choice, to deny; however, justices with $J > (D + C)/2$ or $J < (D + L)/2$ will sometimes vote to deny certiorari when it is their second choice. Justices who vote to grant certiorari under a sophisticated strategy cast what judicial scholars sometimes refer to as an "aggressive grant." Those who vote to deny when it is their second choice cast what is sometimes referred to as a "defensive denial."

Sincere voting, as defined earlier, implies that justices do not attempt to maximize their payoffs given their beliefs about what will happen on the merits. Instead, their decisions on certiorari will be driven completely by their own

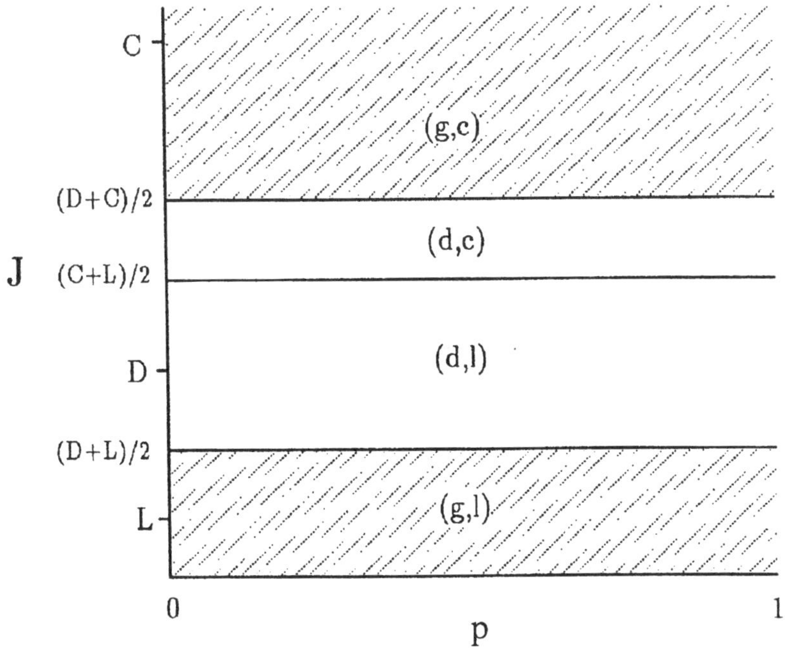

Figure 3. Certiorari voting under sincere behavior. Note: Shaded areas indicate ranges in which a vote for certiorari will occur. J is the position of the justice; p is the probability of a conservative outcome on the merits. See text for details.

preferences for outcomes on the merits. Figure 3 illustrates justices' strategies under sincere voting, where strategies are not conditional upon p, the expected outcome on the merits. In contrast to Figure 2, justices with preferences $L \succ D \succ C$ and $C \succ D \succ L$ always vote to grant cert.

Taken together, the results outlined and Figures 2 and 3 yield the following comparative statics regarding the differences between sophisticated and nonsophisticated judicial behavior on certiorari. For the sophisticated voting strategies in Figure 2, the following results are evident, where G is the likelihood of a vote to grant certiorari:

Hypothesis 1. If $p < \frac{D-L}{C-L}$, then $\partial G/\partial p < 0$, and $\partial G/\partial J < 0$.

Hypothesis 2. If $p > \frac{D-L}{C-L}$, then $\partial G/\partial p > 0$, and $\partial G/\partial J > 0$.

Under Hypothesis 1, for a liberal-leaning court, the probability of granting decreases as the likelihood of a conservative decision on the merits increases, and as the justice's ideology leans more conservatively. Conversely, for a conservative court (i.e., one with a high value of p), the likelihood of granting increases in both the justice's and the Court's conservatism. For the strategies in Figure 3, the following result is evident:

Hypothesis 3. $\partial G/\partial J$ is constant for all p.

That is, the likelihood of a sincere justice voting to grant certiorari does not depend in any way on the likely outcome should the case go to the merits. Instead, justices' votes on certiorari depend solely on their preferences over C, D, and L.

These hypotheses underscore our intuitive notions about sophisticated behavior. For example, on a conservative court with a case decided conservatively below, conservative justices, taking into account the likely outcome on the merits, will vote to grant certiorari and strengthen the lower court's decision. Conversely, liberals on a conservative court will vote to deny certiorari in order to prevent the court from affirming the lower court's decision, even though their first preference would be to grant and reverse the case in hopes of obtaining a more liberal outcome. This same logic obtains for cases decided liberally below. Generally, then, regardless of the direction of the lower court decision, when the ideology of the justice converges with the ideological predisposition of the Court on the merits, the justice will vote to grant certiorari; and when the ideological predispositions of the justice and the Court diverge, the justice will vote to deny cert.

Figure 2 and Hypotheses 1 and 2 suggest an empirical model for sophisticated voting of the form:

$$G \equiv \Pr(g) = f[\beta_{\mathrm{P}} p + \beta_{\mathrm{J}} J + \beta_{\mathrm{PJ}}(p \times J) + \beta_{\mathrm{X}}\mathbf{X}], \tag{1}$$

where G is the probability that a justice votes to grant certiorari, J is the justice's ideology, p is the ideological predisposition of the Court on the merits, $\mathbf{X}$ is a vector of exogenous control variables, and $\beta_{\mathrm{J}} = \partial G/\partial J$, $\beta_{\mathrm{P}} = \partial G/\partial p$, and $\beta_{\mathrm{PJ}} = \partial G/\partial(p \times J)$. The interaction term $p \times J$ accounts for the comparative static results in Hypotheses 1 and 2, where the effects $\partial G/\partial p$ and $\partial G/\partial J$ reverse direction at $p = (D - L)/(C - L)$. Empirically, this reversal implies that the coefficient for the interaction term should have a sign opposite that of the coefficients for p and J. Since sophisticated voting implies a reversal in the direction of $\partial G/\partial J$ over values of p, whereas sincere voting implies constancy of $\partial G/\partial J$ across p, the magnitude and direction of the interaction effect provide a test of the two types of voting.

Furthermore, given that $\partial G/\partial J$ changes direction at $p = (D - L)/(C - L)$, we can estimate $p = (D - L)/(C - L)$ by differentiating Equation (1) with respect to J and solving for p at the point where $\partial G/\partial J = 0$. This estimate of the cutting point provides another test of the null hypothesis of sincere voting against the hypothesis of sophisticated voting. Under the hypothesis of sophisticated voting, for observed values of p less than the estimated cutting point—that is, for liberal courts—increasing values of J should lead to lower probabilities of granting certiorari; for observed values of p greater than the estimated cutting point, increasing values of J should lead to higher probabilities of granting certiorari. In contrast, under the hypothesis of sincere voting, increasing values of J should exhibit identical effects on certiorari for values of p above and below the estimated cutting point.

4. Data, Conceptualization, and Measurement

Problematic to the empirical testing of sophisticated voting are measures of justices' preferences on the merits—the variable J in our theoretical analysis—and a measure of how the Court is likely to decide each case on the merits—the theoretical variable p. One approach to measurement followed by scholars in the past has been to use justices' votes on the merits as indicators of their preferences on the merits (e.g., Boucher and Segal, 1995; Brenner and Krol, 1989; Palmer, 1982). Unfortunately this approach has three serious drawbacks. First, it provides a measure of preferences on the merits only for cases granted certiorari. This necessarily introduces selection bias, for cases granted certiorari vary systematically from those denied (e.g., Caldeira and Wright, 1988). Second, using the votes on the merits as a measure of preferences introduces endogeneity, as the outcome on the merits may reflect sophisticated strategies on certiorari. And third, because preferences and actions are treated as equivalent, knowledge about preferences implies perfect knowledge about outcomes. Hence, this approach presumes that justices know with certainty how colleagues will vote on the merits, and this assumption is almost surely incorrect (see Calvert and Fenno, 1994).

Another measurement approach has been to derive justices' general ideological preferences from newspaper editorials and other published materials written prior to their confirmations (e.g., Segal and Cover, 1989). These measures have proven useful in a number of contexts (see, e.g., Epstein and Mershon, 1996), despite representing extremely broad measures of preferences. In order to establish justices' preferences on specific issues and particular cases, we seek a much finer-grained measure of preferences.[8]

We develop a measure of justices' preferences for outcomes on the merits of a given case based on their votes on the merits on similar, but different cases from the past. Across a broad range of issues, we compute their probable position on the merits for all paid cases in which the Court granted ($N = 144$) or denied ($N = 1{,}747$) certiorari during the 1982 term ($N = 1891$).[9] From Spaeth's *Supreme Court Judicial Database* (1997), we obtained the proportion of decisions on the merits in which each justice had voted in a conservative direction in each of 40 different issue areas between the term of the justice's appointment and the end of October term 1981. After generating these proportions for each issue for each justice (a total of 369 scores), we assigned to each petition in October term 1982 the scores for each justice, according to the issue addressed in the petition. Using our 40 issue areas, we were able

8. The measures employed by Epstein and Mershon, for example, are global, referring to preferences on civil liberties/civil rights or economic policies. In looking forward, however, justices need to know how colleagues will vote on specific issues, not on the general dimensions of economics or civil rights. The more specific our measure of preferences, the more leverage we have in estimating the likely positions of individual justices and the Court as a whole.

9. The 1982 Term is a good choice for at least two reasons: (1) Although conservatives usually held sway, liberals and moderates often had sufficient votes to grant cert and often coalesced for victories on the merits. (2) The data on conflict collected by the *NYU Law Review* for 1982 are unparalleled in quality, making our estimates crisper than would otherwise be the case.

to assign scores for each justice to 1114 of the 1891 cases (59%) on the paid docket.[10]

This procedure allows us to place each of the justices along an ideological continuum ranging from zero (no conservative votes on that issue in the past) to one (no previous liberal votes on that issue), and therefore corresponding to the variable J from our theoretical analysis. The distribution of justices' scores is approximately normal [$W' = 0.994$ (Shapiro and Francia, 1972)], with a mean of 0.48, a standard deviation of 0.25, and a slightly larger number of conservative than liberal preferences. This agrees with common knowledge of the Burger Court, which by 1982 leaned in a conservative direction, despite the presence of liberals Brennan and Marshall.

The analysis of sophisticated voting behavior also requires information about the likelihood that any given justice's preferred position will prevail on the merits. Thus we combine the ideological preferences of the different justices to obtain a measure of the likelihood that the Court as a whole will decide conservatively on the merits. For each justice in each case, we sum the ideological scores of the other eight justices and divide by eight, obtaining a measure of the average level of conservatism of the Court's other members. This yields a summary measure of the other justices' likely positions on a particular case, which can be interpreted as each justice's view of the expected probability of a conservative outcome on the merits. This measure corresponds to the variable p in the hypotheses of Section 3.

Diagnostics indicate the validity of our measures of ideological preference, both for the individual justices and for the Court as a whole. Our measure of J correlates strongly ($r = 0.89$, $p < .01$) with the scores used by Segal and Cover (1989), and it also exhibits substantial face validity, with Rehnquist and Burger scoring among the most conservative and Brennan and Marshall the most liberal.[11] Of importance, our measure of justices' voting predispositions on the merits avoids some of the problems of endogeneity endemic to other studies. Our measure of justices' preferences, although based on votes on the merits, is derived from votes across a variety of different courts and terms prior

10. These issues include the following areas of the law: *Miranda* and confessions, search and seizure, right to counsel, right to trial and juries, desegregation, reapportionment, immigration, sex discrimination, Native American rights, poverty law and benefits, torts against the United States, libel and slander, commercial speech, miscellaneous First Amendment cases, establishment and free exercise of religion, obscenity, miscellaneous due process cases, the takings clause, the Freedom of Information Act, abortion, attorney's fees, OSHA and consumer protection, federal regulation of transportation, federal regulation of utilities, federal regulation of communication, lawyers and admission to the bar, labor unions, antitrust and mergers, bankruptcy, personal injury and liability, pensions and benefits, state taxation, state regulation of business, federal securities regulation, environmental protection, zoning, intellectual property, general civil procedure, standing and access, and federal taxation.

11. In our model of voting, cases come from the lower courts in two types, liberal and conservative. Within these two types, there is a great deal of variation—for example, among cases decided in a conservative direction in the court below, some are more conservative than are others. Unfortunately it is impossible with a full term of data to devise a measure of where cases fall on the left-right continuum within issue areas.

to October Term 1982. Finally, to the extent votes on the merits are based on sincere preferences (e.g., Segal, 1997), aggregating those votes ought to provide the best empirical estimates of those preferences.

We also collected data on justices' certiorari votes, as well as an extensive set of control variables. For justices' votes on certiorari, we used Justice Brennan's docket books.[12] From *Records and Briefs of the Supreme Court*, we collected dissent in the lower court, disagreement between the lower courts, constitutional claims, nature of the issues, the United States as a petitioner, and the presence of amicus curiae briefs in support of or against certiorari. From the *New York University Supreme Court Project* (1984a, b), we ascertained whether the petitioner had alleged conflicts between or among lower courts, or between the lower court and the Supreme Court, and whether a square conflict between courts had occurred. We coded the ideological direction of the decision in the lower court below based on our reading of *United States Law Week* and of *Records and Briefs*. Following Spaeth (1997), we categorized the lower court's decision as liberal, conservative, or indeterminable.

5. Sophisticated Voting and Deciding to Decide

Our data are organized as a panel of 10,026 observations, with one observation for every justice for every cert petition during October Term 1982 (i.e., 1114×9). We analyze only 9321 of the 10,026, however, as data are missing on at least one variable for some observations. Each observation contains variables specific to justices and to cases. Our dependent variable is the vote on certiorari, coded 1 if the justice voted in favor of granting cert, and 0 otherwise. For our control variables, we code 1 if present, 0 if absent, and we expect positive signs in all cases.

We observe a vote for each case (indexed by i) and for each justice (indexed by j). For the model in Equation (2), where $\mathbf{X}_{ij}$ is a vector of explanatory variables, we expect heterogeneity over both i and j.

$$\Pr(\text{Grant})_{ij} = f(X_{ij}\beta). \tag{2}$$

For example, if a justice votes consistently from one case to the next, and this consistency is due to forces outside the model, the probability given in Equation (2) would covary across cases. Similarly, if justices influence each other's decisions in ways not captured by the independent variables, the probabilities in a particular case would covary across justices. We deal with this latter form of heterogeneity by treating each case as a separate observation and each justice's vote in that case as a separate measurement on that case.

Given the nature of our data, we adopt the method of generalized estimating equations (GEE) (Liang and Zeger, 1986a,b; see also Pendergast et al., 1996), an extension of the generalized linear models approach (e.g., McCullagh and Nelder, 1989) to time-series cross-sectional data. This approach has the ad-

12. None of the justices' docket books is a perfect record of voting in conference. On balance, Brennan's assiduity in record keeping recommends his docket books over Marshall's. On the similarity of the data across justices, see Maltzman and Wahlbeck (1996).

vantages of allowing for flexible dependence across repeated measures within a unit of analysis and of providing robust parameter estimates despite possible misspecification of that dependence. Here we treat each case as a single unit of analysis and each justice's vote within that case as a single observation. We allow the within-observation correlation matrix to be estimated without constraints—that is, we impose no particular form on the matrix of conditional interjustice correlations. This specification has two central advantages. First, it allows estimation to occur while taking account of the possibility of interjustice influence, thereby improving the efficiency of our estimates; and second, it provides an estimate of the extent of interjustice influence on certiorari voting through examination of the correlation matrix.[13]

Following our theoretical discussion in Section 3, the central variables in our test of sophisticated voting are the ideological preference of the justice on a given case, J, the ideological predisposition of the Court on the merits, p, and the interaction of the two. If justices employ sophisticated voting strategies, we expect that J and p will have direct negative impacts on the likelihood of voting for certiorari. This expectation follows because the direct effects of J and p can be interpreted only for a value of the interaction $p \times J = 0$. Since $p \times J = 0$ if and only if $J = 0$ or $p = 0$, the coefficients β_J and β_p must be interpreted in the context of a liberal Court [i.e., $p < (D - L)/(C - L)$]. Hence, on a liberal Court, the effect of increasing values of J (i.e., greater individual conservatism) and increasing values of p (i.e., more conservative, but still liberal-leaning Court; see Figure 2) should lead to lower probabilities of granting certiorari. Finally, given our expectation that the effects of J and p reverse direction at $p = (D - L)/(C - L)$, we anticipate the coefficient for the interaction term to be positive and greater in magnitude than either of the direct effects.

Results of the GEE estimation of our model of sophisticated voting appear in Table 1.[14] The model represents a substantial improvement in fit over the null model ($\chi^2 = 589.30$, $p < .001$),[15] and the results for the case-related

13. To check for other potential cases of interdependence in our data, we also estimated our model using heteroskedasticity-consistent standard errors (White, 1980). Results from that estimation confirm those we report here.

14. Separate analyses show the dramatic effects of selection bias. If, as many scholars have done in the past, we estimate our model in Table 1 only on cases decided on the merits, much of the evidence of strategic voting disappears. The effect of the Court's likely decision on the merits is essentially zero. A conservative justice is no more or less likely to vote for cert when the Court is liberal than when it is conservative. Yet a large (but insignificant) interaction implies that, as a justice becomes more liberal, the influence of the Court increases. The justice's score is marginally significant, suggesting that (a) when the Court is conservative, the more liberal is a justice the more likely he or she is to vote to deny; and (b) this effect disappears as the Court becomes more liberal. These results, in general, suggest strategic behavior by liberals but not by conservatives. To the extent that liberals were a minority in most cases, this makes sense; most cases in which the conservatives might have voted in a strategic fashion were probably denied and thus not included in the sample.

15. Because GEE models are estimated via quasi-maximum likelihood, the chi-square statistic reported here is not a standard likelihood-ratio test; it is, however, analogous to it.

Table 1. GEE Estimates for a Strategic Model of Certiorari Voting, October Term 1982

Variables	Coefficients
Constant	−1.690**
	(0.238)
U.S. as a petitioner	1.082**
	(0.121)
Lower court reversal	0.338**
	(0.074)
Alleged conflict	0.375**
	(0.096)
Actual conflict	1.221**
	(0.095)
Civil liberties issue	−0.071
	(0.089)
One amicus brief for certiorari	0.506**
	(0.120)
Two or three amicus briefs for certiorari	0.901**
	(0.173)
Four or more amicus briefs for certiorari	1.466**
	(0.196)
One or more amicus briefs against certiorari	0.656**
	(0.149)
Constitutional claim	0.020
	(0.082)
Dissent in lower court	0.152*
	(0.091)
Conservative lower court decision	−0.468**
	(0.077)
Justice's ideology (*J*)	−0.863**
	(0.406)
Ideological leaning of the court (*p*)	−1.776**
	(0.492)
Justice's ideology × ideological leaning of the court	3.124**
	(0.803)

$N = 9231$. Numbers in parentheses are standard errors One asterisk indicates $p < .05$, two indicates $p < .01$ (one tailed). See text for details.

independent variables generally conform to those in Caldeira and Wright (1988, 1990). Conflict, alleged and actual, increases the probability of a justice voting to grant certiorari, as do amicus briefs, reversal in the lower court, and the presence of the United States as a petitioner. In contrast, cases involving civil rights or liberties are no more or less likely to be granted certiorari than are other issues. Moreover, the relationship between the ideological direction of the lower court decision and voting to hear a case is negative, and, *ceteris paribus*, conservative cases are substantially less likely to be granted certiorari than liberal ones.

Turning to the indicators of strategic behavior, we note that all three are correctly signed and statistically significant at traditional levels of confidence. As we hypothesized, the coefficients for the justice's position on the merits (*J*)

Table 2. Simulated Probabilities of Voting for Certiorari, By Court and Justice Position and Lower Court Decision

Lower Court Decision	Justice's Conservatism (J)	Court's Conservatism (p)	Probability of Cert
Liberal	0.10	0.10	0.70
Liberal	0.10	0.90	0.26
Conservative	0.90	0.10	0.35
Conservative	0.90	0.90	0.67
Liberal	0.50	0.10	0.62
Liberal	0.50	0.90	0.55
Conservative	0.50	0.10	0.43
Conservative	0.50	0.90	0.37
Liberal	0.90	0.10	0.53
Liberal	0.90	0.90	0.82
Conservative	0.10	0.10	0.52
Conservative	0.10	0.90	0.13

Simulations are based on estimates in Table 1, with all other independent variables fixed at the same values as discussed in Figure 4. See text for details.

and the expected outcome on the merits (p) are negative, and the interaction term is positive. Consequently, when the Court is conservative on an issue, as a justice becomes more liberal, the net probability of voting to grant certiorari decreases. Conversely, when the Court is liberal, increasing liberalism of a justice increases the net probability of voting to grant certiorari. These results are strongly significant, even after controlling for ideology and the qualities of cases, and lend considerable support to the proposition that justices are sophisticated in their certiorari voting.

To provide a concrete interpretation of the combined effects of the coefficients in Table 1, we calculated predicted probabilities of voting to grant certiorari for various types of lower court decisions and different combinations of J and p. Our predictions, which appear in Table 2, are based on a non-U.S., non-civil rights, non-constitutional liberal case reversed without dissent in the lower court and brought to the Court with both an allegation of and actual conflict and one amicus brief in favor of granting certiorari. Such a case would be a strong contender for certiorari, but by no means an automatic grant. The results in Table 2 reinforce our conclusion that justices employ sophisticated voting strategies on certiorari. The effects of sophisticated voting emerge clearly: justices are much more likely to vote for certiorari when the Court is likely to decide in favor of their preferred outcome on the merits. In those instances where $J = p = .1$ or $J = p = .9$, the average predicted probability of certiorari is .68. However, in those instances where $J \neq p$ and $J \neq .5$, the average predicted probability of certiorari is only .32. For moderate justices, $J = .5$, the average predicted probability of certiorari is .48.

For an additional illustration of the net effects of the coefficients, we plot in Figure 4 the predicted probabilities of voting for cert as a continuous function of the ideology of the justice and that of the Court for the same benchmark

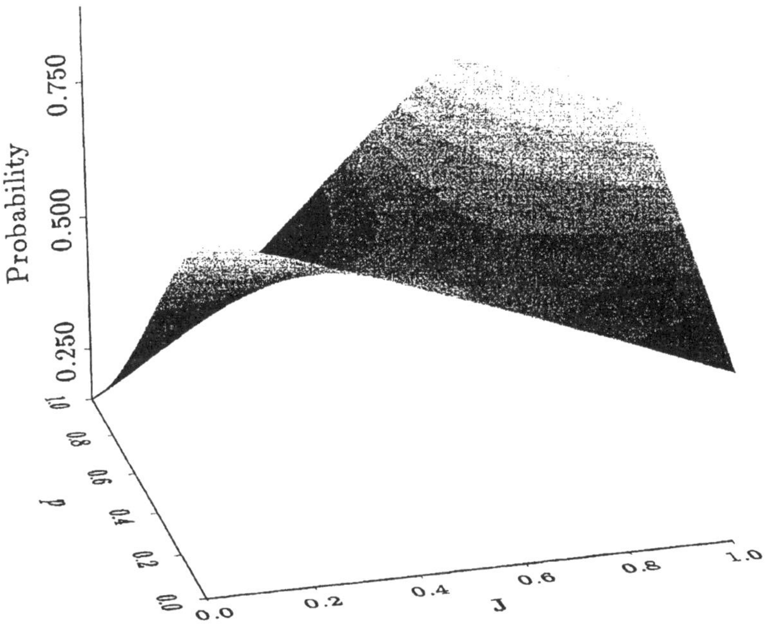

Figure 4. Predicted probabilities of voting for certiorari, by justices' and court's ideology. Note: Darker colors indicate smaller probabilities of voting for certiorari. See text for details.

case used in Table 2.[16] Consistent with Hypothesis 1, the probabilities for a conservative justice (i.e., justice's ideology = 1.0) decrease from 0.89 when the Court is very conservative to 0.45 when it is very liberal. The opposite is true for liberal justices: the probabilities of a vote for certiorari in that instance increase from 0.15 to 0.77 as the Court becomes more liberal. When the Court is conservative, a justice's probability of voting for certiorari declines from 0.89 to 0.15 with increasing liberalism, but on a liberal court, the probability of voting for cert increases from 0.46 to 0.77 with increasing liberalism.

Our null hypothesis of sincere voting states that justices' preferences for outcomes on the merits should affect their certiorari votes independently of the Court's likely decision on the merits. In other words, as illustrated graphically in Figure 3, the effect of J on granting certiorari should be constant across all values of p. The implication of this null hypothesis for model (1) and the estimation in Table 1 is that the coefficient of the interaction term should be

16. The equation used to generate the simulated probabilities for Figure 4 and Table 3 was

$$\Pr(\text{Cert}) = \Phi[0.747 - 0.863(J) - 1.776(p) + 3.124(p \times J)],$$

where 0.747 represents the sum (or "index") of the other variables.

zero. That is, there should be no differential effects of J dependent on p. However, given the strong statistical significance of the interaction coefficient in Table 1, we comfortably reject the null hypothesis of sincere voting.

As described in Section 3, a related test of sincere versus sophisticated voting involves estimating the cutting point $p = (D-L)/(C-L)$ and then estimating $\beta_J = \partial G/\partial J$ for values of p above and below the cutting point. Under the hypothesis of sincere voting, estimated values of β_J should be identical above and below the cutting point. In contrast, sophisticated voting predicts $\beta_J > 0$ for values of p above the cutting point, and $\beta_J < 0$ for values of p below the cutting point. We estimated the cutting point to be $p = .276$.[17] We then split the sample and used probit to estimate β_J in the two sets of observations. The results clearly recommend rejection of the null hypothesis. For $p > .276$ (i.e., a conservative Court), our estimated value of β_J was positive and statistically significant at a level of .01; for $p < .276$ (i.e., a liberal Court), our estimated value of β_J was negative and statistically significant at a level of .05.[18]

These findings provide solid support for the proposition that justices employ sophisticated strategies when voting on cert. In particular, we show a substantial relationship between not only a justice's own ideological position and his or her vote, but also between the positions of the other members of the Court and that vote. Our results are also robust: they hold despite controls for the effect of case quality, direction of the lower court decision, and interjustice influence at the certiorari stage. Furthermore, the nature of this relationship is consistent with expectations derived from a model of strategic behavior in which a justice considers the likely decision on the merits in his or her voting calculus. Our simulated probabilities show large changes in justice-specific probabilities of voting for cert depending on the ideological positions of the justices and that of the Court, indicating that such considerations are of substantive as well as statistical significance.

6. Consequences of Sophisticated Voting

Sophisticated voting is substantively important only when it affects outcomes. Thus we are ultimately interested in sophisticated *outcomes*—instances in which sophisticated voting by individual justices changes the content of the Court's plenary agenda. Undoubtedly some of the cases on the plenary agenda result from forward-looking votes for first choices. Observational equivalence precludes us from detecting such cases, however, because in those instances both sophisticated and naive justices opt for first choices when they vote to grant certiorari. Accordingly, we focus on cases in which justices look forward and vote to deny cert, their second choice, to prevent an unfavorable outcome. The likelihood of such outcomes depends critically on the distribution of justices'

17. The estimates in Table 1 are $Y = \Phi[\beta_0 + \cdots - 0.863(J) - 1.77(p) + 3.124(J \times p)]$. Thus we can find the point at which the function "turns over" by considering $\partial Y/\partial J = -0.863 + 3.124p$). Setting this to zero and solving, we find $p = .276$.

18. The estimated coefficients were 0.888 for the sample of conservative courts and -1.105 for the sample of liberal courts.

preferences. A court comprised of six liberal and three conservative justices, for example, would have enough votes to enact a liberal agenda no matter how the conservatives voted. For sophisticated voting to affect outcomes, then, certain distributional conditions for justices' preferences must be met.

To specify these conditions, we make several assumptions. First, we assume that justices are never indifferent between any two outcomes among L, D, and C. This restriction leaves us with six possible preference orderings, two of which can be eliminated given our previous assumptions that justices' preference orderings over the three outcomes are single peaked, with D between L and C.[19] Thus we have four possible preference orderings: $C \succ D \succ L$, $D \succ C \succ L$, $D \succ L \succ C$, and $L \succ D \succ C$. For convenience, we label justices as "liberals," "conservatives," or "moderates," depending on whether their first preference is L, C, or D, respectively. Finally, for notational simplicity, we denote the preference ordering $L \succ D \succ C$ by **L**; the ordering $C \succ D \succ L$ by **C**; and the orderings $D \succ L \succ C$ and $D \succ C \succ L$ by **DL** and **DC**, respectively. We let $N_{\mathbf{L}}$ be the number of justices having preference **L**, $N_{\mathbf{C}}$ be the number of justices having preference **C**, $N_{\mathbf{DL}}$ be the number of justices with preference **DL**, and $N_{\mathbf{DC}}$ be the number with preference **DC**.

With four possible preference orderings, several conditions must be met before strategic voting in the form of defensive denials by individual justices produces a sophisticated outcome. The necessary conditions for a sophisticated outcome are as follows:

(1) $N_{\mathbf{DL}} + N_{\mathbf{DC}} < 6$ (possibility of certiorari)

(2) a) $N_{\mathbf{L}} + N_{\mathbf{DL}} \geq 5$
or (majority on the merits)
b) $N_{\mathbf{C}} + N_{\mathbf{DC}} \geq 5$

(3) a) $N_{\mathbf{L}} < 4$ if (2a)
or (possibility of defensive denial)
b) $N_{\mathbf{C}} < 4$ if (2b)

The first condition simply ensures that certiorari is possible. Since all moderates have a straightforward strategy of voting to deny cert, $N_{\mathbf{DL}} + N_{\mathbf{DC}} < 6$ is necessary to ensure at least four potential votes for cert (Palmer, 1995; Schwartz, 1993). Condition (2) specifies that there will be a majority on the merits for reversing or affirming the lower court. This will be trivially satisfied since we assume justices are never indifferent. Finally, condition (3) ensures that neither liberals nor conservatives can dictate the outcome on certiorari, even if they are in the majority. If at least four justices were liberals, for example, and if the expected outcome on the merits was L, then defensive denials by conservatives could not affect the outcome on cert.

---

19. Preference orderings where D is last violate single-peakedness on a scale where D is the moderate outcome.

How often are these conditions satisfied? To obtain a theoretical estimate, we first computed the number of possible distributions of nine justices, given the four possible positions of **L**, **C**, **DC**, **DL**. One possible distribution, for example, might consist of nine justices with **L** orderings; another might be a court with four **L** and five **C** orderings; and still another with three **L**, four **DC**, and two **C** orderings. In total, there are 220 different configurations of the four preference orderings. We then counted the number of these distributions that satisfied conditions (1)–(3). We counted a total of 40 such configurations.[20]

If we assume each configuration is equally likely on any given case, the probability that the justices' preferences are distributed so as to produce a strategic outcome on a given case is $40/220 \cong .18$. Sophisticated outcomes will, of course, not occur on 18% of all of the cases brought before the Court. Many cases are not serious candidates for certiorari, and would be denied regardless of the policy preferences of the justices. Sophisticated voting arises because justices wish to deny cases the Court would otherwise grant, and thus the 18% applies to cases that ordinarily would be granted certiorari.

To make this interpretation more precise, we distinguish between a sophisticated plenary docket and an inclusive plenary docket. The inclusive plenary docket consists of all of those cases that would be granted when justices simply vote for their first preference on cert—regardless of whether they anticipated the outcome on the merits—and is unobserved, whereas the sophisticated docket is the observed docket that results from defensive denials and aggressive grants. If we let σ denote the size of the inclusive, unobserved docket, and **s** the size of the observed, sophisticated docket, then the relation between the two is $\mathbf{s} = \sigma - .18\sigma$. The sophisticated docket should be 18% smaller than the inclusive docket, assuming all configurations are equally likely.

Since our data contain 144 grants of certiorari (i.e., $\mathbf{s} = 144$), our theoretical prediction is that the size, σ, of the inclusive plenary docket should be $\sigma - .18\sigma = 144$, or $\sigma = 176$. Hence we predict 32 *sophisticated* outcomes. Empirically we identify a *sophisticated* outcome whenever (1) the Court denied certiorari to a case decided liberally (conservatively) below when, according to our estimated priors, we predict a conservative (liberal) majority on the merits and at least two justices voted for cert; or (2) the Court denied certiorari to a case decided liberally (conservatively) below when, according to our estimated priors, we predict a liberal (conservative) majority on the merits and at least two justices voted for cert.

20. The following 20 distributions satisfy conditions (1)–(3). Reversing the order of **C**, **DC**, **DL**, and **L** leads to another 20.

C	DC	DL	L	(cont.)	C	DC	DL	L	(cont.)	C	DC	DL	L
3	2	3	1		3	4	1	1		2	4	1	2
3	2	2	2		3	4	0	2		2	5	0	2
3	2	1	3		3	5	0	1		1	4	0	4
3	2	0	4		2	3	2	2		1	4	1	3
3	3	2	1		2	3	1	3		1	5	0	3
3	3	1	2		2	3	0	4		0	5	0	4
3	3	0	3		2	4	0	3					

Table 3. Sophisticated Outcomes on Certiorari, October term 1982

Term and Docket Number of Case	Ideological Outcome Below	Expected Vote on Merits, L–C	Justices Voting for Cert[a]	Type of Sophisticated Outcome[b]
82-281	Liberal	2–7	O,Bu,R	DD-R-L
82-964	Liberal	2–7	Bl,O,R	DD-R-L
82-1259	Liberal	2–7	Bl,O,R	DD-R-L
82-1510	Liberal	2–7	Bl,W,R	DD-R-L
81-1852	Liberal	4–4	S,W,R	DD-R-L
81-2240	Liberal	2–6	Bl,W,R	DD-R-L
82-22	Liberal	4–4	W,R	DD-R-L
82-274	Liberal	3–6	Bu,R	DD-R-L
82-446	Liberal	4–5	Bl,R	DD-R-L
82-1507	Liberal	4–4	W,R	DD-R-L
81-2275	Liberal	4–4	W,R	DD-R-L
81-2406	Liberal	4–4	W,R	DD-R-L
82-490	Conservative	8–1	Br,M	DD-R-C
82-787	Conservative	5–3	Br,S	DD-R-C
82-830	Conservative	5–4	M,Bl	DD-R-C
81-2344	Conservative	7–2	Br,Bl,W	DD-R-C
82-1585	Liberal	5–4	Br,W	DD-A-C
82-1586	Liberal	5–4	Br,W	DD-A-C

[a] O: O'Connor, Bu: Burger, Br: Brennan, Bl: Blackmun, R: Rehnquist, W: White, M: Marshall, S: Stevens

[b] DD-R-L refers to a "defensive denial" by liberals to prevent reversal of a case decided liberally below; DD-R-C, defensive denial by conservatives to prevent reversal of a case decided conservatively below; and DD-A-C, defensive denial by conservatives to prevent affirmation of a case decided liberally below.

Eighteen cases meet one of these criteria; these cases appear in Table 3. We emphasize that these cases are plausible, not definite instances of sophisticated outcomes, because we have no way of clearly identifying justices whose first preference is denial. We cannot establish with certainty, therefore, that the distribution of preferences on each case meets precisely all of our theoretical conditions. Nonetheless, the patterns of cases uncovered squares well with much of the conventional wisdom regarding the dynamics of the Burger Court. Most of the cases in Table 3 are defensive denials by liberals to prevent review and reversal of a case decided liberally below. Some, however, are defensive denials by conservatives to prevent a liberal majority from reviewing and reversing a case decided conservatively below, and two are defensive denials by conservatives to block aggressive grants by liberals.

At an individual level, a few of the positive votes for certiorari on these cases were cast by justices who generally are moderate. Frequently, however, these justices—for example, O'Connor, Blackmun, and Stevens—had estimated preferences on these cases that reflect conservative or liberal rather than moderate preferences. For example, Blackmun generally had conservative scores—.43, .19, .15, and .30—when he voted for certiorari on cases decided liberally below, but liberal priors when he voted for certiorari on cases decided conservatively below—.70 and .54. Only Justice White more frequently exhibited a moderate preference in 6 of the 10 instances in Table 3 for which he voted for certiorari. Perhaps in these instances Justice White was motivated more by jurisprudential considerations and less by ideological concerns.

7. Conclusion

Several of our results stand out. First, and foremost, we provide some of the first empirical evidence of Supreme Court justices behaving sophisticatedly across the board on agenda setting. We show that, whether liberal or conservative, in grants or denials, members of the Court act with an eye to the behavior of their fellow justices. This consistency is striking, and is at odds, in whole or in part, with a number of previous studies. By setting forth a formal model of the process, examining all of the Court's petitions for certiorari in a single term, and utilizing superior measures of both individual justices' and the Court's preferences, we believe that we have made significant improvements over earlier works on strategic behavior on agenda setting.

Second, and equally important, the sophisticated interactions we have uncovered have a substantial impact on the work of the Court. Theoretically, we identify a nontrivial difference between the Court's agenda under conditions of sincere and sophisticated behavior. Empirically, this difference is borne out in our identification of at least 18 omissions from the Court's plenary docket in October term 1982 to which we can trace defensive denials on certiorari. Thus sophisticated behavior in agenda setting has striking implications for the Court's decisions on the merits.

Third, our work has implications for the nature of Supreme Court decision-making more generally. Our finding that justices act in a sophisticated fashion in even the earliest stage of the Court's decisional process supports our contention that agenda setting is a prime locale for sophisticated action on the part of the justices. Even more important, sophisticated voting matters in the sense that the casting of sophisticated votes alters the ultimate outcome, which is, of course, precisely the point of doing so. We do not expect justices who act in a sophisticated fashion in setting the Court's agenda to abandon those strategies in favor of myopic preference seeking once the plenary agenda is set. A host of other behaviors—writing of majority opinions, opinion assignment, concurrences, and dissents—also provides opportunities for strategic interaction among the justices, something long recognized (e.g., Murphy, 1964) and more recently recalled (e.g., Epstein and Knight, 1998). For a number of reasons, it has been difficult to detect evidence of sophisticated voting in other political institutions. Not all decision-making bodies are equivalent from the perspective of sophisticated voting—the Supreme Court, with its mode of agenda setting, offers great opportunities; Congress, given its institutional rules, may not be so open to strategic manipulation.

To what extent may we generalize from our results for a single term? Over time, the Supreme Court varies enormously both in the ideological composition and balance of its membership and the nature of its caseload; and even the mechanics of agenda setting change, albeit at a slow pace. October term

1982 was, as we suggested in Section 4, a propitious term in which to detect sophisticated voting and its consequences. On lopsidedly liberal or conservative Courts—for example, October term 1992—we expect to find sophisticated voting making less of a difference in the shape of the plenary agenda. The dominant ideological coalition will in those situations "have the votes" to control both the composition of the agenda and the decision on the merits. Yet we would still expect to find many instances of sophisticated voting, as minority justices attempt—usually without success—to fend off unpleasant decisions on the merits. Just how often, and with what success, sophisticated voting occurs on agenda setting in the Court under various circumstances are important questions for future research. To answer these questions will require data on the Court's decision making on certiorari across a set of terms, issues, and compositions of the Court.

References

Abramson, Paul R., John H. Aldrich, Phil Paolino, and David W. Rohde. 1992. "'Sophisticated' Voting in the 1988 Presidential Primaries," 86 *American Political Science Review* 55–69.

Austen-Smith, David. 1987. "Sophisticated Sincerity: Voting Over Endogenous Agendas," 81 *American Political Science Review* 1323–1329.

Baum, Lawrence A. 1997. *The Puzzle of Judicial Behavior*. Ann Arbor: University of Michigan Press.

Boucher, Robert L., Jr., and Jeffrey A. Segal. 1995. "Supreme Court Justices as Strategic Decision-Makers: Aggressive Grants and Defensive Denials on the Vinson Court," 57 *Journal of Politics* 812–823.

Brenner, Saul, and John F. Krol. 1989. "Strategies in Certiorari Voting on the United States Supreme Court," 51 *Journal of Politics* 828–840.

Cain, Bruce E. 1978. "Strategic Voting in Britain," 22 *American Journal of Political Science* 639–655.

Caldeira, Gregory A., and John R. Wright. 1988. "Organized Interests and Agenda-Setting in the U.S. Supreme Court," 82 *American Political Science Review* 1109–1128.

———. 1990. "The Discuss List: Organized Interests and Agenda-Building in the Supreme Court," 24 *Law & Society Review* 807–836.

Calvert, Randall L., and Richard F. Fenno, Jr. 1994. "Strategy and Sophisticated Voting in the Senate," 56 *Journal of Politics* 349–376.

Denzau, Arthur, William Riker, and Kenneth Shepsle. 1985. "Farquharson and Fenno: Sophisticated Voting and Home Style," 79 *American Political Science Review* 1117–1134.

Epstein, Lee, and Jack Knight. 1998. *The Choices Justice Make*. Washington: CQ Press.

Epstein, Lee, and Carol Mershon. 1996. "Measuring Political Preferences," 40 *American Journal of Political Science* 261–294.

Farquharson, Robin. 1969. *Theory of Voting*. London: Hodge.

Hall, Melinda Gann. 1992. "Electoral Politics and Strategic Voting in State Supreme Courts," 54 *Journal of Politics* 427–446.

Krehbiel, Keith, and Douglas Rivers. 1990. "Sophisticated Voting in Congress: A Reconsideration," 52 *Journal of Politics* 548–578.

Krol, John F., and Saul Brenner. 1990. "Strategies in Certiorari Voting on the United States Supreme Court," 43 *Western Political Quarterly* 335–342.

Liang, Kung-Yee and Scott L. Zeger. 1986a. "Longitudinal Data Analysis for Discrete and Continuous Outcomes," 42 *Biometrics* 121–130.

———. 1986b. "Longitudinal Data Analysis Using Generalized Linear Models," 73 *Biometrika* 13–22.

Maltzman, Forrest, and Paul J. Wahlbeck. 1996. "Inside the Supreme Court: The Reliability of the Justices' Conference Records," 58 *Journal of Politics* 528–539.

McCullagh, P., and J. A. Nelder. 1989. *Generalized Linear Models*, 2nd ed. London: Chapman & Hall.

Murphy, Walter F. 1964. *Elements of Judicial Strategy*. Chicago: University of Chicago Press.

New York University Supreme Court Project. 1984a. "Appendices," 59 *New York University Law Review* 1403–1929.

———. 1984b. "Summaries of Cases Granted Certiorari during the 1982 Term," 59 *New York University Law Review* 823–1003.

Ordeshook, Peter C. 1992. *A Political Theory Primer*. New York: Routledge.

Ordeshook, Peter C., and Thomas R. Palfrey. 1988. "Agendas, Strategic Voting, and Signalling with Incomplete Information," 32 *American Journal of Political Science* 441–466.

Palmer, Barbara. 1995. "The Defensive Denial: Institutional Rules and Strategic Voting on the Supreme Court." Paper presented at the 1995 Meetings of the Midwest Political Science Association.

Palmer, Jan. 1982. "An Econometric Analysis of the U.S. Supreme Court's Certiorari Decisions," 39 *Public Choice* 387–398.

Pendergast, J. F., S. J. Gange, M. A. Newton, M. P. Lindstrom, and M. R. Fisher. 1996. "A Survey of Methods for Analyzing Clustered Binary Response Data," 64 *International Statistical Review* 89–118.

Perry, H. W., Jr. 1992. *Deciding to Decide: Agenda-Setting in the United States Supreme Court*. Cambridge: Harvard University Press.

Provine, Doris Marie. 1980. *Case Selection in the United States Supreme Court*. Chicago: University of Chicago Press.

Riker, William H. 1986. *The Art of Political Manipulation*. New Haven: Yale University Press.

Schubert, Glendon. 1962. "Policy Without Law: An Extension of the Certiorari Game," 14 *Stanford Law Review* 284–327.

Schwartz, Edward. 1993. "Information, Agendas, and the Rule of Four: Nonmajoritarian Certiorari Rules for the Supreme Court." Paper presented at the 1993 Meetings of the Midwest Political Science Association.

Segal, Jeffrey. 1997. "Separation-of-Powers Games in the Positive Theory of Congress and the Courts," 91 *American Political Science Review* 28–44.

Segal, Jeffrey A., and Albert J. Cover. 1989. "Ideological Values and the Votes of U.S. Supreme Court Justices," 83 *American Political Science Review* 557–566.

Shapiro, S. S., and R. S. Francia. 1972. "An Approximate Analysis of Variance Test for Normality," 67 *Journal of the American Statistical Association* 215–216.

Spaeth, Harold J. 1997. *The United States Supreme Court Judicial Database, 1953–1995*. Ann Arbor: Inter-University Consortium for Political and Social Research.

Spiller, Pablo T., and Matthew L. Spitzer. 1995. "Where Is the Sin in Sincere? Sophisticated Manipulation of Sincere Judicial Voters (With Applications to Other Voting Environments," 7 *Journal of Law, Economics, & Organization* 32–63.

Volden, Craig. 1998. "Sophisticated Voting in Supermajoritarian Settings," 60 *Journal of Politics* 149–173.

White, Halbert. 1980. "A Heteroscedasticity-Consistent Covariance Matrix and a Direct Test for Heteroscedasticity," 48 *Econometrica* 817–838.

[8]

Predicting Supreme Court Cases Probabilistically: The Search and Seizure Cases, 1962-1981

JEFFREY A. SEGAL
State University of New York at Stony Brook

The overwhelming concensus of Fourth Amendment scholars is that the Supreme Court's search and seizure cases are a mess. This article proposes that the confusion arises from the manner in which the cases were studied, not from the decisions themselves. A legal model with variables that measure the prior justification of the search, the nature of the intrusion, and a few mitigating circumstances is used to explain the Court's decisions on the reasonableness of a given search or seizure. The parameters are estimated through probit.

The results show that the search and seizure cases are much more ordered than had commonly been believed. Virtually all of the estimates are as expected. Additionally, the Court is shown to act more favorably toward the federal government than toward the states. Preliminary analysis suggests that the model has predictive as well as explanatory value.

Protections against unreasonable searches and seizures were deemed important enough by the nation's founding fathers to be included as the Fourth Amendment to our Constitution. The desire for such protection runs deep in both English and American democratic history. Few are not aware of William Pitt's assertion that:

> The poorest man in his cottage may bid defiance to all the force of the Crown. It may be frail—its roof may shake—the wind may blow through it—the storm may enter—but the King of England cannot enter; all his force dares not cross the threshold of the ruined tenement. (Landynski, 1966, p. 23)

Less well remembered is John Adams's recollection of the stirring speech of James Otis, Jr. against the writ of assistance, the colonial version of England's general warrant. The speech, Adams wrote, was the first in "the Chain of Causes and Effects" leading to independence (Landynski, 1966, p. 37). Today, the Fourth Amendment is "one of the laws most vital to our liberty" (Amsterdam, 1974, p. 377). It occupies a "place second to none in the Bill of Rights."[1]

Nevertheless, we are still not sure what makes a particular action by the government an unreasonable search or seizure within the meaning of the Fourth Amendment. According to Justice Frankfurter, "the course of true law pertaining to searches and seizures . . . has not run smooth."[2] Justice White, joined by Justice Burger, claims that the Court has ceased even "to strive for clarity and consistency of analysis."[3] Scholarly opinion agrees. LaFave has observed that "no area of law has more bedeviled the judiciary" (Amsterdam, p. 349). Dworkin (1973) simply states that the Fourth Amendment cases are "a mess" (p. 329). Amsterdam (1974) considers all of these comments to be "understatements" (p. 349).

The question of whether a given search or seizure violates the Fourth Amendment becomes even more important when one considers what happens to unconstitutionally obtained evidence. According to the Supreme Court, it may not be presented as evidence at a trial. This exclusionary rule means that, in the immortal words of Cardozo, "the criminal is to go free because the constable has blundered."[4]

Received: July 19, 1983
Revision received: December 1, 1983
Accepted for publication: February 13, 1984

I would like to thank Harold Spaeth, Alan Abramowitz, John Aldrich, Milton Lodge, and Daniel McGoldrick and the anonymous referees of this *Review* for their very helpful comments and criticisms. An earlier version of this article was presented at the Annual Meeting of the Midwest Political Science Association, Chicago, Illinois, 1983.

[1] *Harris* v. *United States,* 331 U.S. 145 (1947) (Frankfurter, J., dissenting).

[2] *Chapman* v. *United States,* 365 U.S. 610 (1961) (Frankfurter, J., concurring).

[3] *Coolidge* v. *New Hampshire,* 403 U.S. 443 (1971).

[4] *People* v. *Defore,* 242 N.Y. 13 (1926).

This article attempts to show that beneath the so-called mess of search and seizure decisions lies a coherent set of decisions. The Supreme Court has been more consistent in its decisions than either the Court or scholarly opinion would have us believe. These decisions can be successfully explained and predicted through the multivariate analysis of a legal model of the Court's decision making. The data are the 123 cases from 1962 until 1981 in which the Court decided the reasonableness of a search or seizure. The facts of each case, such as whether or not there was a warrant or probable cause, are the independent variables. The decision of the Court on the reasonableness of the search or seizure is the dependent variable. Probit is used to estimate the parameters.

A Legal Model of Supreme Court Decision Making

As Gibson (1978a) has shown, in order to understand judicial decision making, one must understand not only the attitudes of judges, but their role perceptions as well. Tate (1981) has identified background characteristics that directly affect roles and attitudes, and thus indirectly affect votes. All of this is very useful in trying to explain variance among judges or among courts, but when one tries to explain variance among decisions of a given judge or a given court, the roles and attitudes are stable; it is the facts of the cases that vary. Studies that try to explain variance in particular decisions are usually limited to sentencing studies (most recently, Croyle, 1983), where the dependent variable can be measured intervally.

Specification of the sentencing models almost universally is done within the context of legal or extralegal characteristics of the case (see Hagan, 1974). The legal model assumes decisions are based upon "standards set in constitution, statute, precedent or court rule" (Cook, 1977, p. 571). The most frequently used variables in these cases are severity of the crime and prior record. Extralegal models of sentencing deal with characteristics of the defendant that are legally irrelevant to the sentencing decision. More often than not, the key variable of interest is race. Hagan's exhaustive review concludes that "knowledge of extra-legal offender characteristics contributes little to our ability to predict judicial dispositions" (1974, p. 359). Nevertheless Gibson (1978b) has demonstrated that this may be true because these studies aggregate decisions by court rather than by judge. His own research gives evidence that although blacks in Fulton County receive higher sentences than whites, some judges sentence blacks more severely, whereas others sentence whites more severely.

Although findings suggest that lower court judges may not strictly follow statutory guidelines in sentencing, Supreme Court justices are probably even less constrained to follow the legal model. As Rohde and Spaeth (1976) point out, Supreme Court justices usually do not aspire to higher office, are not electorally accountable, and as an institution, are the court of last resort. Thus, they are relatively free to follow their personal policy preferences (1976, pp. 70-74). As Felix Frankfurter explained to President Roosevelt, "People have been taught to believe that when the Supreme Court speaks it is not they who speak but the Constitution, whereas, of course, in so many vital cases it is *they* who speak and *not* the Constitution" (Freedman, 1967, p. 383).

Thus it would certainly increase our knowledge of the Supreme Court if it could be demonstrated that a legal model based on "standards set in Constitution, statute, precedent or Court rule" (Cook, 1977, p. 571), could convincingly explain and predict Court decisions. Of course such a model is not necessarily inconsistent with policy preferences. Nevertheless, if these policy preferences parallel a legal decision structure, we may have some protection against judicial capriciousness (see, for example, Bickel, 1963).

Previous attempts to use fact models to explain and predict particular Supreme Court decisions have not been very successful. The best known of these is Kort's (1957) right-to-counsel study. Ad hoc estimation procedures, the use of more variables than cases, and the absence of any explicit theoretical justification for expecting the Court to behave as it had, were among the problems that plagued this pioneering effort (Fisher, 1958). Schubert (1959) attempted a reasonably precise replication of Kort's methodology and thus faced many of the same problems. Improvement was to come. Ulmer (1964) used an ad hoc formula but did manage to keep the number of variables less than the number of cases. Kort (1963) did the same by using factor analysis and then estimating the coefficients in his model through least squares regression. Ulmer (1969) used discriminant analysis to distinguish Frankfurter's civil liberties decisions by subject area, but his study was somewhat limited in that it could not tell us how Frankfurter would vote within double jeopardy, or search and seizure. Kort (1973) later demonstrated that discriminant analysis, which takes into account the dichotomous nature of the Supreme Court's decisions, is more appropriate than linear regression techniques.

Search and Seizure

In order to specify a decision-making model, I review briefly the Court's major search and seizure findings. The most basic requirements for a search to be reasonable are a warrant and probable cause. Probable cause is generally required whether there is[5] or is not a warrant.[6] Warrants require a finding of probable cause,[7] by a neutral and detached magistrate,[8] supported by oath or affirmation,[9] and particularly describing the place to be searched[10] and the things to be seized.[11]

For a search to be unreasonable, it generally must occur at a place where the accused has an "expectation of privacy."[12] The greatest expectation of privacy is in one's home. "At the very core (of the Fourth Amendment) stands the right of a man to retreat into his own home and there be free from unreasonable governmental intrusion."[13] Commercial premises are likewise given great protection. "The businessman, like the occupant of a residence, has a constitutional right to go about his business from unreasonable official entries."[14] Yet as Lafave (1978) notes, "commercial premises are not as private as residential premises" (vol. 1, p. 338). Still receiving protection, but in lesser amounts, are one's person[15] and one's car,[16] but these are nonetheless great compared to the protection one receives when the search takes place in an area in which he has no property interest,[17] such as the home of a third person. Further, the less intrusive an actual search is, the less the justification that is needed. For example, other things being equal, a frisk is more reasonable than a full search,[18] as is detentive questioning.[19]

Finally, because most searches that are brought before the court are in fact warrantless, we must consider exceptions to the warrant and probable-cause requirements. The first of these is the right to search incident to a lawful arrest. From 1950 through 1969, this included the right to search the person of the arrestee and the entire premises where the arrest occurred. This was limited in 1969 to include only the person and the area within his immediate control.[20] When a search occurs after, but not incident to, a lawful arrest, the Court has been split on the need for a warrant.[21] The end result has been that such searches are more reasonable than searches without a lawful arrest. An unlawful arrest cannot add to the reasonableness of a search, but it does not necessarily make the search any more unreasonable[22] unless it was dependent on that arrest.

A second mitigating factor concerns permission by those who have a property interest in the place to be searched, including the suspect,[23] a cohabitant,[24] and any participant to a wiretapped conversation.[25] Other mitigating circumstances include searches after hot pursuit,[26] searches at fixed or functional borders,[27] searches statutorily allowed pursuant to Congress's authority to regulate business,[28] and searches for evidence to be used solely in administrative[29] or grand jury hearings.[30] Seizures of objects in plain view are generally permitted.[31]

Thus the Court considers three categories of this information when deciding the reasonableness of a search. The first category involves the prior justification for the search, including the probable-cause and warrant requirements. Another category is the nature of the search itself: where the search took place, and the extent of the intrusion (i.e., a full search v. a stop-and-frisk or other limited intrusion). The Court also considers the exceptions to the probable-cause and warrant requirements. The more prior justification and the more exceptions associated with a search, the more reasonable it is. The more intrusive a search is, the less reasonable it is. Although cases often have idiosyncratic factors that affect the Court's decision, and the above factors do not determine the Court's resolution of any case, they should strongly predispose the Court toward finding the search reasonable or unreasonable.

Specification

The model will be specified using the above information about the reasonableness of the search, with one limit and one addition. The limit is that the value of all variables used must be known before the Court's decision is released. For exam-

[5]*United States* v. *Harris,* 403 U.S. 573 (1971).
[6]*Chambers* v. *Maroney,* 399 U.S. 42 (1970).
[7]*Aquilar* v. *Texas,* 378 U.S. 108 (1964).
[8]*Coolidge* v. *New Hampshire,* 403 U.S. 443 (1971).
[9]*Whiteley* v. *Warden,* 401 U.S. 560 (1971).
[10]*United States* v. *Ventrusca,* 380 U.S. 102 (1965).
[11]*Marron* v. *United States,* 275 U.S. 192 (1927).
[12]*Katz* v. *United States,* 389 U.S. 347 (1967).
[13]*Silverman* v. *United States,* 365 U.S. 505 (1961).
[14]See v. *City of Seattle,* 387 U.S. 54 (1967).
[15]*Davis* v. *Mississippi,* 394 U.S. 721 (1969).
[16]*Carroll* v. *United States,* 414 U.S. 132 (1925).
[17]*United States* v. *Calandra,* 414 U.S. 338 (1974).
[18]*Terry* v. *Ohio,* 392 U.S. 1 (1968).
[19]*United States* v. *Mendenhall,* 64 L.Ed. 497 (1980).
[20]*Chimel* v. *California,* 395 U.S. 752 (1969).
[21]*Chambers* v. *Maroney,* 399 U.S. 752 (1970).
[22]*Davis* v. *Mississippi,* 394 U.S. 721 (1969).
[23]*Schneckloth* v. *Bustamonte,* 412 U.S. 218 (1973).
[24]*Frazier* v. *Cupp,* 394 U.S. 731 (1969).
[25]On *Lee* v. *United States,* 343 U.S. 747 (1952).
[26]*Warden* v. *Hayden,* 387 U.S. 294 (1967).
[27]*United States* v. *Ramsey,* 431 U.S. 606 (1977).
[28]*Collonade Catering* v. *United States,* 397 U.S. 72 (1970).
[29]*Wyman* v. *James,* 400 U.S. 309 (1971).
[30]*United States* v. *Calandra,* 414 U.S. 338 (1974).
[31]*Coolidge* v. *New Hampshire,* 493 U.S. 443 (1971).

ple, the Supreme Court's decision on whether there was probable cause or whether an arrest was lawful cannot be used because, first, we do not know whether or not the Supreme Court's decision on probable cause precedes its decision on the reasonableness of the search. Thus we do not know whether the Court's decision on probable cause contributes to its decision on the reasonableness of the search or merely justifies that decision. Even if this were not a problem, the Supreme Court's decision on probable cause obviously cannot be used for prediction because its value is not known until the day the Court renders its decision. For probable cause and the lawfulness of an arrest, the lower court decisions are used as indicators. Further, while coding the lower court's subjective facts, each of its objective facts were compared to the Supreme Court's statement of facts. For the rare difference in interpretation of the facts as set out by the trial court, the lower court's interpretation was used, in order not to bias the results. Thus, all facts are as they are stated in the lower court decision.

Additionally, rather than assume, as Kort (1957) and others have, that changes in membership do not affect the Court's decisions, the model explicitly takes these changes into account. As the Court's membership changed with the Nixon and Ford appointees, one would quite reasonably expect the search and seizure decisions of the Court to have become more conservative even after controlling for the facts of the case (for example, see Wasby, 1976).

Dependent Variable

Reasonableness of the Search

The decision of the Court in a search or seizure case is coded 1 if the Court either found a search to be reasonable or allowed questionably obtained evidence to be used; if not, it is coded 0. Thus, the smaller or more negative the estimate for an independent variable, the more that variable leads to the finding of an unreasonable search. The larger the estimate for an independent variable, the more that variable leads to the finding of a reasonable search.

Independent Variables

Nature of the Intrusion

Home. When the search or seizure took place at the home of the defendant, the value is 1; otherwise it is 0. The estimate is predicted to be negative.

Business. When the search or seizure took place at the business of the defendant, the value is 1; otherwise it is 0. The estimate is predicted to be negative, but less negative than home.

Car. When the search took place in the car of the defendant, the value is 1; otherwise it is 0. The estimate is predicted to be negative, but less negative than business.

Person. When the search or seizure took place on the person of the defendant in public, the value is 1; otherwise it is 0. The estimate is predicted to be negative, but less negative than business.

When all of these variables are 0, the search occurred where the defendant had no property interest.[32]

Extent of the Intrusion

Search. A full search or seizure is 1; limited intrusions such as a stop and frisk or detentive questioning are 0. The estimate is predicted to be negative.

Prior Justification

Warrant. When a search or arrest took place after a warrant had been obtained, the value is 1; otherwise it is 0. The estimate is predicted to be positive.[33]

Probable Cause. The proportion of lower court judges finding probable cause. The estimate is predicted to be positive.

Arrest

Incident Lawful is the proportion of lower court judges finding that the search took place incident to a lawful arrest. The estimate is predicted to be positive.

After Lawful. The proportion of lower court judges finding that the search took place after but not incident to a lawful arrest. The estimate is predicted to be positive, but less than incident lawful.

Unlawful is the proportion of lower court judges finding that the search took place incident to or after an unlawful arrest. The estimate is predicted to be substantively and statistically insig-

[32]Although it is true that within each of these categories further categorization can take place, one is nevertheless faced with the task of constructing a model that is reasonably parsimonious. Some variance must be left to the error term. It is felt that no serious distortions have taken place.

[33]A *valid* warrant will almost certainly make a search reasonable, regardless of other factors. However, since we cannot know in advance whether a warrant is valid, only some warrants (and we don't know which) will make a search valid. Thus the existence of a warrant makes a search more likely to be reasonable.

nificant. When all of the Arrest variables are 0, the search took place without a prior arrest.

Exceptions. Because the probability of any of the following exceptions is quite small and there is no reason to believe that any one exception is more significant than another, an exceptions variable was created that takes on the value of the number of the following questions that can be answered positively; it can range from 0 to 6, but in fact ranged from 0 to 3.

- Was the search or seizure after hot pursuit?
- Was the search or seizure at a fixed or functional border?
- Was the search statutorily allowed pursuant to Congress's authority to regulate business?
- Was the evidence seized used solely for administrative or grand jury hearings?
- Was the seized evidence in plain view?
- Was permission for the search granted by either the defendant or a cohabitant?

The estimate is predicted to be positive.

Change takes on the value 0 during the Warren Court, 1 after Burger was appointed, 2 after Blackmun was appointed, 4 after Rehnquist and Powell were jointly appointed, and 5 after Stevens was appointed. The estimate is expected to be positive.[34]

Results

Because least squares regression is inappropriate when the dependent variable can only be measured dichotomously (Pindyk & Rubinfeld, 1976), the parameters were estimated for the variables specified above by probit, a maximum-likelihood estimation (MLE) technique. The MLEs represent the change in the cumulative normal probability function, which itself has a mean of 0 and a standard deviation of 1, that results from a one-unit change in the independent variable. The MLEs divided by the standard errors have a Z distribution and are thus amenable to classical hypothesis testing. (For those seeking further information, Aldrich and Cnudde (1975) provide an excellent summary.) The results are presented in Table 1.

[34]The operationalization of this variable is the result of the observed pattern of appointments to the Court. Had Carter received any appointments, a difference measure would have to have been used.

Table 1. Probit Estimates for Search and Seizure Decisions

Variable	MLE	S.E.	MLE/S.E.
Home	−2.31	.61	−3.78***
Business	−2.19	.64	−3.41***
Car	−2.02	.63	−3.21***
Person	−1.28	.54	−2.37**
Search	− .77	.44	−1.76*
Warrant	.95	.45	2.14*
Probable cause	− .32	.38	− .84
Incident lawful arrest	2.30	.81	2.84**
After lawful arrest	1.22	.50	2.47**
After unlawful arrest	− .57	.63	− .91
Exceptions	1.36	.35	3.91***
Change	.16	.07	2.26*
Constant	1.34		
Est R^2	.57		
$-2 \times$ LLR (X^2_{12})	56.68**		
Mean of dependent variable	.55		
% categorized correctly	76		
$n = 123$			

*Significant at .05.
**Significant at .01.
***Significant at .001.

As can be seen, the model does a good job of explaining the Court's decisions. Looking at the summary measures, we note that the overall significance of the model, as determined by -2×LLR, is significant at less than .01. The results clearly cannot be explained by chance alone. The estimated R^2 of .57 shows that the model fits rather well.

The mean of the dependent variable is .54; that is, the Supreme Court voted conservatively in 54% of its search and seizure cases. With no further information, one could predict the Court's decisions 54% of the time. By adding the independent variables, predictive accuracy has increased to 76%, a 48% reduction in error.

The parameter estimates are, with the exception of probable cause, as expected, including expectations about magnitude as well as direction. First we examine the variables that determine the nature of the intrusion, starting with where the search took place. It is quite clear that it is important to have a property interest in the area that was searched; overall, the court overturned only two of 12 searches in which the defendant did not have a property interest. The large estimates for the remaining place variables point this out. In comparisons among places in which the defendant has a property interest we see, as expected, that one's home gets the most protection. A search of one's home compared with a search where one does not have a property interests, results in the subtraction of 2.31 S.D. from the cumulative normal probability function when determining whether the search is reasonable. A search that had a probability of being upheld of .85 if it took place at the home of another (a fair guess for such a search) would have a probability of .10 of being upheld if the same search had taken place at the defendant's home.

Almost as high is the protection afforded when the search takes place at one's business. Compared to the same baseline (no property interest), 2.19 would be subtracted from the cumulative normal if an otherwise similar search took place at one's place of business. Also quite high, but again slightly lower, is the protection one gets in one's car. The search of one's car leads to a decrease of 2.02 S.D. from the cumulative normal. A search of one's person receives markedly less protection; 1.28 would be subtracted from the cumulative normal. A search that had a probability of being upheld of .85 if it took place where the defendant had no property interest (a search of a third person leading to discovery of the defendant's contraband, for example) would have a probability of being upheld of .41 if the search had instead been on the defendant's person.

The distinction between a "full search" and a "limited intrusion" is the second aspect of the nature of the search. Although 71% of the limited intrusions were upheld, only 53% of the full searches were sustained. A stop and frisk that has a probability of .70 of being upheld would as a full search have a probability of .40 of being upheld.

Against the factors that make a search more unreasonable must be weighed those factors that will make a search more reasonable. In terms of prior justification for a search, the two most important factors are having a warrant and probable cause. The existence of a warrant adds .95 to the cumulative probability function. Controlling for other variables shows that a search that had a probability of .5 of being reasonable without a warrant has a probability of being reasonable of .83 with a warrant.

The probable-cause variable did not fare as well. As discussed earlier, probable cause cannot be operationalized as the Supreme Court's decision on probable cause because its value is not known before the Court's opinion is released and, more important, because the Court's decision on probable cause is not clearly independent of its decision on the reasonableness of the search. As such, probable cause was operationalized as the lower court's decision on probable cause, which proved to be a not very reliable indicator. The estimate of -.32, although substantively small and statistically insignificant, suggests a negative relationship between a lower court finding of probable cause and the reasonableness of the search. The Supreme Court did, however, uphold 53% of the searches in which it did not find probable cause, as opposed to 65% of the searches in which it did. Probable cause is undoubtedly important; the trouble remains in trying to operationalize it.

Although probable cause and a warrant often help make an otherwise unreasonable search reasonable, searches can still be judged reasonable without them. The Supreme Court has taken note of several exceptions to the probable-cause and warrant requirements. The most important of these involves the right to search incident to an arrest. Table 1 shows clearly that when the lower court finds that a search took place incident to a lawful arrest, as compared to a search that was not preceded by an arrest, the Supreme Court will quite likely find the search to be reasonable. The cumulative normal probability function is increased by 2.30 S.D. A search that would have a probability of .50 of being upheld if there were no arrest would have a .99 probability of being upheld if incident to a lawful arrest. If the search were after, but not incident to, a lawful arrest, the probability would increase greatly but not quite as much. The parameter estimate of 1.22 would increase the probability of reasonableness from .50 to .89.

The value for an unlawful arrest was expected to be zero. An unlawful arrest certainly cannot justify an otherwise unreasonable search, but it also seems plausible that such an arrest should not make an otherwise reasonable search unreasonable. The estimate of –.57 is statistically insignificant, yet if this is the true value, it would have a moderate affect on the reasonableness of a search. A search that had a probability of .50 of being reasonable without an arrest has only a probability of .28 of being reasonable if preceded by an unlawful arrest.

The other exceptions were added together to form an exceptions variable. For each exception found in a case, 1.36 is added to the cumulative normal probability function. The typical effect is not much different from that of a search after a lawful arrest.

Finally, I have suggested that we must be concerned with at least one factor that does not directly affect the reasonableness of a search: change in the Court's membership. The change variable, which ranges from 0 to 5, is 0 during the Warren Court and increases by 1 for each Nixon and Ford appointee. The full difference between the Warren Court and the Burger Court after the appointment of Stevens is .80 (.16×5). A search that for the Warren Court had a probability of .38 of being upheld (they in fact upheld 38% of the searches before them) would have a probability of .69 of being upheld by the Burger Court. A search that for the Warren Court had a probability of being upheld of .50 would have a probability of .79 of being upheld by the pre-O'Connor Burger Court. It is interesting to note that a search with a warrant during the Warren Court would be almost as likely to be upheld as a similar search without a warrant by the pre-O'Connor Burger Court.

The United States as a Party to the Suit. Thus far only legal variables are considered in the model, those that relate directly to the reasonableness of the search, and one variable that measures changes in the Court's personnel, which is included not because it helps to gauge the reasonableness of a search, but because it helps to gauge the given Court's belief about the reasonableness of a search. It is possible, however, that the Court's decisions in search and seizure cases are concerned with more than the reasonableness of the search; there might be extralegal factors unrelated to the reasonableness of the search that nevertheless affect the Court's decisions.

Rokeach (1968) has argued that attitudes involve both an attitude toward an object (AO) and an attitude toward a situation (AS). Spaeth and Parker (1969) have shown this to have relevance to Supreme Court decisions. In the search and seizure cases the situation is obviously a search, a seizure, or both. The objects conducting the search are either state or federal officials. It therefore might be interesting to question whether the Court acts differently when the United States is a party to the suit.[35]

Much has been written claiming that the Supreme Court's responsiveness to the United States as a party is a vital factor in the Court's decision to grant certiorari (e.g., Tanenhaus et al., 1963). Does this favorable predisposition carry over to final decisions? Analysis by Spaeth and Teger (1982) shows the Court supporting the government 69.7% of the time in the 1966-1967 terms and 67.8% of the time in the 1969-1973 terms. Throughout these terms, only Douglas supported the federal government less than half of the time. The general support trend holds for criminal procedure cases. These and other studies showing support for the federal government as opposed to its adversaries are enlightening and might lead us to believe that in our search and seizure cases the Court may, on the whole, be predisposed to favor the government. But before we can use this information to help us explain specific Court decisions, we must have a point of comparison. In our population of search and seizure cases, those cases that do not involve the federal government do involve the state government. Our question is not whether the Supreme Court is more favorable to the United States than its adversaries; rather, we are concerned with whether the Supreme Court is more favorable to the federal government than it is to the states.

The model was rerun including a dummy that measured when the United States was a party to the suit. A comparison of the two models is presented in Table 2. Although the estimated R^2 barely improved and the percentage of cases categorized correctly did not improve, the overall fit of the model, as measured by $-2\times$LLR, represents a statistically significant improvement over the fit of the first model (see Aldrich, 1977). Furthermore, the point estimate of .59 is of moderate size and is statistically significant. A state search that had a probability of .50 of being upheld would have a probability of .72 of being upheld if it had been a federal case. What is so important about this finding is that it is the result *after* the facts of the case have been taken into account. The preference given to the United States does not

[35]Although other factors such as race or social class might have some influence, they do not seem to be salient for search and seizure decisions. This point is supported by Spaeth and Parker (1969), who found that Warren Court did not decide cases on the basis of whether or not the litigants were black. In addition, such information is contained neither in the Supreme Court's nor the lower court's statement of facts.

Table 2. Probit Estimates With and Without the United States as a Variable

	Without U.S.	With U.S.
Home	−2.31***	−2.12***
Business	−2.19***	−2.06***
Car	−2.02***	−1.86**
Person	−1.28**	−1.15*
Search	− .77*	− .91*
Warrant	.95*	.94*
Probable cause	− .32	− .29
Incident lawful arrest	2.30**	2.30**
After lawful arrest	1.22**	1.34**
Unlawful arrest	− .57	− .33
Exceptions	1.36***	1.23***
Change	.16*	.16*
U.S.	–	.59*
Summary Statistics with U.S.		
Constant	1.07	
Est R^2	.58	
−2 × LLR ($X^2{}_{13}$)	57.51**	
Mean of dependent variable	.55	
% categorized correctly	76	
n = 123		

*Significant at .05.
**Significant at .01.
***Significant at .001.

appear to be the result of federal searches being less severe than state searches.

The Residuals. The first model correctly categorized 76% of the Court's decisions. As Table 3 shows, the model predicted the Court's conservative decisions (81% correctly categorized) more accurately than its liberal decisions (67% categorized correctly). Table 4 shows what happens when the predictions are broken down by Court. The Warren Court's decisions were predicted with significantly greater accuracy: 86% to 70%. for the Warren Court, 12 of 15 conservative decisions were categorized correctly, as were 24 of 27 liberal decisions. The Burger Court's conservative decisions were predicted with the same degree of accuracy as the Warren Court's, but only 14 of the 28 liberal Burger Court decisions were correctly categorized.

Predicting from the Model: The 1981 Term. It is one thing to fit a line to previous behavior; it is quite another if that line fits future behavior as well. The original model was applied to the search and seizure decisions of the October 1981 term. This set involves seven different decisions over five different cases. (Two of the cases had two distinct decisions.) Five of the decisions were conservative, two were liberal. The model predicted all five of the conservative decisions correctly and one of the two liberal decisions. The incorrect prediction involved the admissibility of a voluntary confession made after an unlawful arrest. To the 5-4 majority, the confession could not be admitted because it was the result of an unlawful seizure. Although we are dealing with a limited population, that six of seven cases were predicted correctly suggests that the model has predictive as well as explanatory value.

Discussion

The parameter estimates are certainly interesting, but great care must be taken in interpreting them. Since dummy variables were used, it is important not to compare the magnitude of the coefficients without considering the baseline from which they were measured. For the prior justification variables, the arrest variables, and the exceptions variable, the baseline was zero. When prob-

Table 3. Predicted Decisions Compared with Actual Decisions[a]

Predicted	Actual		
	Conservative	Liberal	Total
Conservative	55 (81%)	17 (33%)	72
Liberal	13 (19%)	38 (67%)	51
Total	68	55	123

[a]76% of the decisions were predicted correctly.

able cause had the value zero, there was no probable cause; when the arrest variables all had the value zero, there was no arrest. Compare this to the search variable; when the search variable was zero, there was no search, but there still was some form of intrusion. If we were measuring this from a baseline of no intrusion the value would be very large, because if there were no intrusion, it would be extremely doubtful that the search could be unreasonable. Alternatively, consider the variables that measure where the search took place; they all take on the value zero when the search occurred where the defendant does not have a property interest. The value for *home* is not so large because one's home receives extraordinary amounts of protection, but, relatively speaking, because it receives much more protection than areas over which one has no property interest.

The above notwithstanding, the parameter estimates tell us quite a bit about the Supreme Court's search and seizure decisions. Although one's home seems to have more protection than one's business, which in turn has slightly more protection than one's car, the differences are not as substantial as one might have supposed. A search of a home that has a probability of .50 of being upheld would have a probability of .61 of being upheld if it instead were a search of a car. This factor certainly affects the reasonableness of the search, but compared to other factors that can intervene, it is far from determinative. Other points might seem to belabor the obvious—it is better to have a warrant than not to, full searches are inherently less reasonable than a stop and frisk —yet these points have not heretofore been demonstrated empirically.

It must be noted that, as in other areas of political inquiry, prediction will not work as well as retrodiction. The parameter estimates are derived so as best to fit the existing data set, not future ones. Also, the model is unable to predict what tomorrow's exceptions will be. The good faith exception, for example, may or may not dramatically change the Court's decision making. The model obviously cannot predict changes in doctrine. Finally, changes in the Court's membership can always have untold consequences. This fact should not, however, keep us from trying.

Conclusions

The results presented herein are very pleasing. It seems as if the model has taken one of the Court's most difficult areas, one characterized as "inconsistent," "bedeviling," and even "a mess"

Table 4. Predicted Decisions Compared with Actual Decisions, Controlling for Court

Predicted	Actual		
	Conservative	Liberal	Total
Warren Court[a]			
Conservative	12 (80%)	3 (11%)	15
Liberal	3 (20%)	24 (89%)	27
Total	15	27	42
Burger Court[b]			
Conservative	43 (81%)	14 (50%)	57
Liberal	10 (19%)	14 (50%)	24
Total	53	28	81

[a]86% of these cases were predicted correctly.
[b]70% of these cases were predicted correctly.

and found for the first time a clear and logical form. The legal model was quite satisfactory, yet evidence suggests that the Court is not immune from considering extralegal characteristics too.

Perhaps the reason for the bedevilment is that those who have been bedeviled have been too reliant on the case method as the means for analyzing these decisions. Such reliance seems reasonable enough. The opinion delivered in any given decision more often than not relies upon a single aspect of the case, for example, was there probable cause, or is a search several hours after a lawful arrest reasonable? Yet the decision itself is dependent upon many factors—presumably those mentioned above—that go largely undiscussed in the main body of the opinion. In a probable cause determination, it is all very well to know that probable cause was sufficiently established, but when it comes to understanding the decision itself, we must know where the search took place, the extent of the intrusion, and whether any exceptions were present, as well as the makeup of the Court.

References

Aldrich, J. Electoral choice in 1972: A test of some theorems of the spatial model of electoral competition. *Journal of Mathematical Sociology*, 1977, *5*, 215-237.

Aldrich, J., & Cnudde, C. Probing the bounds of conventional wisdom: A comparison of regression, probit and discriminant analysis. *American Journal of Political Science*, 1975, *19*, 571-608.

Amsterdam, A. G. Perspectives on the Fourth Amendment. *Minnesota Law Review*, 1974, *58*, 349-447.

Bickel, A. *The least dangerous branch: the Supreme Court at the bar of politics, U.S.A.* Indianapolis: Bobbs-Merrill, 1963.

Cook, B. B. Public opinion and federal judicial policy. *American Journal of Political Science*, 1977, *21*, 567-600.

Croyle, J. L. Measuring and explaining disparities in felony sentences: courtroom work group factors and race, sex and socioeconomic influences on sentence severity. *Political Behavior*, 1983, *5*, 135-153.

Dworkin, R. B. Fact style adjudication and the Fourth Amendment: the limits of lawyering. *Indiana Law Journal*, 1973, *48*, 329-368.

Fisher, F. M. The mathematical analysis of Supreme Court decisions and abuse of quantitative methods. *American Political Science Review*, 1958, *53*, 321-338.

Freedman, M. *Roosevelt and Frankfurter*. Boston: Little, Brown, 1967.

Gibson, J. L. Judges' role orientations, attitudes and decisions: an interactive model. *American Political Science Review*, 1978, *72*, 911-924. (a)

Gibson, J. L. Race as a determinant of criminal sentences: a methodological critique and a case study. *Law and Society Review*, 1978, *12*, 455-478. (b)

Hagan, J. Extra-legal attributes and criminal sentencing: an assessment of a sociological viewpoint. *Law and Society Review*, 1974, *8*, 337-363.

Kort, F. Predicting Supreme Court cases mathematically: analysis of the right to counsel cases. *American Political Science Review*, 1957, *57*, 1-12.

Kort, F. Content analysis of judicial opinions and rules of law. In G. Schubert (Ed.). *Judicial decision making*. Glencoe, Ill.: Free Press, 1963.

Kort, F. Regression analysis and discriminant analysis: An application of R. A. Fisher's theorem to data in political science. *American Political Science Review*, 1973, *67*, 555-559.

LaFave, W. *Search and seizure* (Vols. 1-3). St. Paul, Minn.: West, 1978.

Landynski, J. *Search and seizure and the Supreme Court*. Baltimore: Johns Hopkins University Press, 1966.

Pindyck, R. S., & Rubinfeld, D. L. *Econometric models and economic forecasts*. New York: McGraw-Hill, 1976.

Rohde, D., & Spaeth, H. *Supreme Court decision making*. San Francisco: W.H. Freeman, 1976.

Rokeach, M. *Beliefs, attitudes and values*. San Francisco: Jossey-Bass, 1968.

Schubert, G. *Quantitative analysis of judicial behavior*. Glencoe, Ill.: Free Press, 1954.

Spaeth, H. *Supreme Court policy making*. San Francisco: W.H. Freeman, 1979.

Spaeth, H., & Parker, D. Effects of attitude toward situation upon attitude toward object. *Journal of Psychology*, 1969, *73*, 173-182.

Spaeth, H., & Teger, S. Activism and restraint: a cloak for the justices' policy preferences. In S. C. Halpern & C. W. Lamb (Eds.). *Supreme Court activism and restraint*. Lexington, Mass.: Lexington, 1982.

Tanenhaus, J., Schick, M., Muraskin, M., & Rosen, D. *The Supreme Court's certiorari jurisdiction and cue theory*. In G. Schubert (Ed.). *Judicial decision making*. Glencoe, Ill.: Free Press, 1963.

Tate, C. N. Personal attribute models of the voting behavior of U.S. Supreme Court justices: Liberalism in civil liberties and economic decisions, 1946-1978. *American Political Science Review*, 1981, *75*, 355-367.

Ulmer, S. S. Discriminant analysis and an error criterion. In G. Schubert (Ed.). *Judicial behavior*. Chicago: Rand McNally, 1964.

Ulmer, S. S. The discriminant function and a theoretical context for its use in estimating the votes of judges. In J. Grossman & J. Tanenhaus (Eds.). *Frontiers of judicial research*. New York: John Wiley, 1969.

Wasby, S. L. *Continuity and change from the Warren Court to the Burger Court*. Pacific Palisades, Calif.: Goodyear, 1976.

[9]

VOTING BEHAVIOR ON THE UNITED STATES COURTS OF APPEALS, 1961–1964*

SHELDON GOLDMAN
University of Massachusetts

Voting behavior of public decision-makers has been of central concern for political scientists. For example, studies of legislatures (notably of Congress) have investigated such research problems as: (1) the extent to which voting on one issue is related to voting on other issues;[1] (2) the potency of party affiliation as an organizer of attitudes and a predictor of voting behavior;[2] and (3) the relationship of demographic characteristics to voting behavior.[3] These and related concerns have more recently occupied the attention of students of the judiciary whose focus has primarily been on the United States Supreme Court.[4] State courts of last resort have also provided a testing ground primarily for problems (2) and (3).[5]

* I am indebted to Professors Arthur E. Sutherland and Robert G. McCloskey of Harvard University and to Professor Joseph Tanenhaus of the University of Iowa for their suggestions and advice in the preparation of the larger study from which this paper is drawn. I am also grateful to the Woodrow Wilson Foundation for providing financial support for the research. Full responsibility for what follows, however, is mine.

[1] See, for example, Duncan MacRae, *Dimensions of Congressional Voting: A Statistical Study of the House of Representatives in the Eighty-First Congress* (Berkeley: University of California Press, 1958); David B. Truman, *The Congressional Party* (New York: Wiley & Sons, 1959); Charles H. Gray, "A Scale Analysis of the Voting Records of Senators Kennedy, Johnson, and Goldwater, 1957–1960," this REVIEW, 59 (1965), 615–621.

[2] Julius Turner, *Party and Constituency: Pressures on Congress* (Baltimore: John Hopkins Press, 1951); Malcolm E. Jewell, "Party Voting in American State Legislatures," this REVIEW, 49 (1955), 773–791; Frank J. Sorauf, *Party and Representation* (New York: Atherton Press, 1963); V. O. Key, Jr., *Politics, Parties, and Pressure Groups*, 5th ed. (New York: Crowell, 1965), pp. 677–689.

[3] Donald R. Matthews, *United States Senators and Their World* (Chapel Hill: University of North Carolina Press, 1960); Leroy N. Rieselbach, "The Demography of the Congressional Vote on Foreign Aid, 1939–1958," this REVIEW, 58 (1964), 577–588.

[4] C. Herman Pritchett, *The Roosevelt Court: A Study in Judicial Politics and Values, 1937–1947* (New York: Macmillan Co., 1948); Pritchett, *Civil Liberties and the Vinson Court* (Chicago: University of Chicago Press, 1954); S. Sidney Ulmer, "The Analysis of Behavior Patterns in the United States Supreme Court," *Journal of Politics*, 22 (1960), 629–653; Ulmer, "Toward a Theory of Sub-Group Formation in the United States Supreme Court," *Journal of Politics*, 27 (1965), 133–153; Joseph Tanenhaus, "Supreme Court Attitudes Toward Federal Administrative Agencies, 1947–1956—An Application of Social Science Methods to the Study of the Judicial Process," *Vanderbilt Law Review*, 14 (1961), 473–502; Glendon Schubert, *Quantitative Analysis of Judicial Behavior* (Glencoe: The Free Press, 1959); Schubert, "The 1960 Term of the Supreme Court: A Psychological Analysis," this REVIEW, 56 (1962), 90–108; Schubert, *The Judicial Mind: The Attitudes and Ideologies of Supreme Court Justices 1946–1963* (Evanston: Northwestern University Press, 1965); John R. Schmidhauser, "Judicial Behavior and the Sectional Crisis of 1837–1860," *Journal of Politics*, 23 (1961), 615–640; Schmidhauser, "*Stare Decisis*, Dissent, and the Backgrounds of the Justices of the Supreme Court of the United States," *University of Toronto Law Journal*, 14 (1962), 194–212. Glendon Schubert has traced the development of judicial behavior research in two articles: "Behavioral Research in Public Law," this REVIEW, 57 (1963), 433–445 and "From Public Law to Judicial Behavior," *Judicial Decision-Making*, Schubert (ed.) (New York: The Free Press of Glencoe, 1963), pp. 1–10. The latter work also contains an extensive bibliography of judicial behavior research on pp. 257–65. Also see Martin Shapiro, *Law and Politics in the Supreme Court* (New York: The Free Press of Glencoe, 1964), chap. 1.

[5] Schubert, *Quantitative Analysis*, pp. 129–42; S. Sidney Ulmer, "The Political Party Variable in the Michigan Supreme Court," *Journal of Public Law*, 11 (1962), 352–362; Stuart S. Nagel, "Judicial Characteristics and Judicial Decision-Making" (unpublished Ph.D. dissertation, Northwestern University, 1961) and the articles derived from that study, especially "Political Party Affiliation and Judges' Decisions," this REVIEW, 55 (1961), 843–850 and "Ethnic Affiliations and Judicial Propensities," *Journal of Politics*, 24 (1962), 94–110; James F. Herndon, "Relationships Between Partisanship and the Decisions of State Supreme Courts" (unpublished Ph.D.

However, the United States courts of appeals, second only to the Supreme Court in judicial importance, have been largely neglected.[6] This paper considers the above research problems with reference to the voting behavior on all eleven courts of appeals from July 1, 1961 through June 30, 1964.[7]

I. RESEARCH DESIGN

The voting behavior covered by this paper includes non-unanimous decisions and unanimous appeals court reversals of district court decisions.[8] Quantification of non-unanimous decisions has been amply justified by students of the judiciary;[9] however, some explanation should be made of the use of district court reversals.[10]

Only those unanimously decided reversals of district court decisions in which the district court judge's interpretation or application of the facts, precedents, principles, or statutes differed from that of an unanimous appellate court were considered. Such cases indicate that there are alternative paths to decision. The assumptions underlying the study of judicial voting behavior are, of course, that certain types of cases present the judges with reasonable judicial alternatives which can produce contrary results, and that a study of the dispositions of a relatively large number of such cases can reveal certain regularities in judicial voting behavior.[11]

The cases selected for study were assigned to one or more categories depending on the issues involved. Categories with small numbers of cases were either combined with others or discarded. In all, 2,055 cases which yielded 2,260 issues were utilized.[12]

For purposes of uncovering voting tendencies, a scoring system was devised which gave "high" numerical values to designated voting positions on the various issues. The issues and the voting behavior given high scores are presented in Table 1. With the exception of the "dissents" category and possibly "activism," the voting behavior outlined in Table 1 can be considered to be related to a politically "liberal" bent.[13]

---

dissertation, University of Michigan, 1963).

[6] Only a handful of studies of the courts of appeals have been conducted by political scientists. Among them are: Robert H. Salisbury, "The United States Court of Appeals for the Seventh Circuit, 1940–1950: A Study of Judicial Relationships" (unpublished Ph.D. dissertation, University of Illinois, 1955); Rondal Downing, "The U.S. Courts of Appeals and Employer Unfair Labor Practices Cases, 1936–1958" (mimeo, 1959); Alvin Dozeman, "A Study of Selected Aspects of Behavior of the Judges of the United States Court of Appeals for the Tenth Circuit" (unpublished Master's thesis, Michigan State University, 1960); Jack W. Peltason, *Fifty-Eight Lonely Men: Southern Federal Judges and School Desegregation* (New York: Harcourt, Brace, and World, 1961); Kenneth N. Vines, "The Role of the Circuit Courts of Appeal in the Federal Judicial Process: A Case Study," *Midwest Journal of Political Science*, 7 (1963), 305–320; Louis L. Loeb, "Judicial Blocs and Judicial Values in Four Selected United States Courts of Appeals, 1957–1960 Terms" (unpublished Ph.D. dissertation, American University, 1964); Loeb, "Judicial Blocs and Judicial Values in Civil Liberties Cases Decided by the Supreme Court and the United States Court of Appeals for the District of Columbia," *American University Law Review*, 14 (1965), 146 ff.; Marvin Schick, "The United States Court of Appeals for the Second Circuit: A Study of Judicial Behavior" (unpublished Ph.D. dissertation, New York University, 1965).

[7] The time period chosen conforms to the three fiscal years 1962, 1963, and 1964. The Administrative Office of the U.S. Courts bases its statistics on the cases decided or terminated during the fiscal year.

[8] The cases utilized are listed in Appendix A, pp. 274–339, of my "Politics, Judges, and the Administration of Justice: The Backgrounds, Recruitment, and Decisional Tendencies of the Judges on the United States Courts of Appeals, 1961–4" (unpublished Ph.D. dissertation, Harvard University, 1965; microfilm no. 65-9924, University Microfilms, Michigan). A detailed exposition of the methods and statistics used, their justification, and their limitations is presented there.

[9] See, for example, Pritchett, *Roosevelt Court*, *op. cit.*, p. xii; Pritchett, *Civil Liberties*, *op. cit.*, pp. 186–192; Schubert, *Quantitative Analysis*, *op. cit.*, chap. 1.

[10] Note that Vines, *op. cit.*, utilizes district court reversals.

[11] These assumptions are treated as hypotheses and are tested in Goldman, *op. cit.*, pp. 162–3, 175 n. 16, 192–6. The results lend support to the hypotheses.

[12] There were some non-unanimous decisions and unanimous reversals rendered during the time period studied which did not fit the categories and were not used. These cases, for the most part, involved patent and trademark issues and various commercial law cases (for example, cases involving disputing insurance companies).

[13] See Goldman, *op. cit.*, pp. 36–43 for a discussion of this point.

TABLE 1. VOTING POSITIONS ASSIGNED HIGH SCORES

Issue or Category	Voting Position
Criminal Law	For the claims of criminal defendants or prisoners
Civil Liberties	For malapportionment plaintiffs in reapportionment cases
	For Nego claims in cases involving school desegregation and voting
	For civil libertarian claims of aliens, conscientious objectors, and others
Government Regulation	For the governmental agency in regulation of business cases
Labor Cases	For the labor union and employees in labor-management and NLRB decisions
Private Economic	For the claims of the insured as opposed to the insurance company
	For the claims of the small business or subcontractor when opposed by large business or contractor
	Opposed to alleged anti-trust law violators
	For the tenant in landlord-tenant cases
	For the debtor or bankrupt
	For the buyer of goods as opposed to seller
	For the stockholder in stockholder suits
Fiscal Cases	For the government in tax, eminent domain, and other fiscal cases
Combined Injury	For the claims of injured employees
	For the injured or the fatally injured's estate
	For the injured in federal tort cases
Liberalism	All of the above voting positions for only the non-unanimously decided cases
Activism	For federal court jurisdiction
Dissents	Dissenting in non-unanimously decided cases

Unlike the United States Supreme Court or the highest state appellate courts, all judges on each of the eleven federal courts of appeals do not hear the same cases except on the few occasions when a court will sit *en banc*. Most cases are heard by three judge panels whose membership usually varies from case to case. The quantification-scoring system thus devised was results-oriented (i.e., oriented towards the disposition of the cases) and did not attempt to discern the intensity of the claims presented in the litigation. By examining the voting behavior of judges on a number of decisions involving choices which present the same general issues, it was thought to be possible to legitimately analyze statistically the judges' scores on the various issues even though the individual scores were based on different cases.[14] Although the different cases present different factual situations, the underlying stimuli of the policy alternatives, in terms of competing interests, are similar. By utilizing relatively large numbers of cases for the scores, the differences in the intensity of the claims should balance out.[15]

The quantification system assigned a high score, the numerical value of 2.0, to the voting positions indicated in Table 1; the value of 1.0 to a vote which in part adhered to those positions; and 0.0 to a vote which was contrary to them. The individual judge's score on each issue or category was determined by averaging the numerical values given to all of his votes for that issue. For example, if a judge voted on ten cases and his vote on seven of these favored the claims of the criminal defendant, while on the remaining three cases he opposed the criminal defendant's claims, the judge's score would be 1.4 on a continuum ranging from 0.0 to 2.0, thus indicating a relative bent towards favoring the claims of criminal defendants.[16]

[14] Note that Vines, *op. cit.*, and in "Federal District Judges and Race Relations Cases in the South," *Journal of Politics*, 26 (1964), 337–357 utilizes the disposition of racial relations cases by various judges on different courts deciding different cases which nevertheless contain the same general issue (i.e. Negro civil liberties).

[15] It might be argued that most or all of the Fifth Circuit cases we examined involving, for example, criminal, civil liberties, or labor issues, are inherently different from such cases raised in the Second or Ninth circuits. While this *may* be true for Negro civil liberties cases, the writer is unaware of any compelling evidence to lead one to suppose that it holds true for the other issues. In any event, the hypothesis that the underlying issues of the various cases subsumed within the categories differ on a geographical basis can only be tested by a content analysis of the cases themselves. It is relevant to note that students of the Supreme Court apparently reject this hypothesis and do not classify cases by their geographical origins.

[16] Alternatively, simple percentages could have been used. In the example above, the judge would

II. RATES OF DISSENSION AND REVERSALS

The cases utilized for the study were non-unanimous decisions and unanimous district court reversals. Table 2 presents the rates of dissension and unanimous district court reversals on the eleven courts of appeals for the period covered. It is clear, from Table 2, that outright decisional conflict on the appeals courts is the exception not the rule. It is also apparent that the rates of dissension vary considerably by circuit, with the District of Columbia, Second, and Fifth circuits having the largest percentages and numbers of split decisions.

TABLE 2. RATES OF DISSENSION AND UNANIMOUS DISTRICT COURT REVERSALS ON THE ELEVEN COURTS OF APPEALS

Circuit	Number of Split Decisions	Split Decisions as Percent of Total No. of Cases Decided*	Number of Unanimous District Court Reversals	Unanimous Reversals as Percent of Total No. of Cases**
D.C.	168	15.5%	100	13.1%
Second	140	11.5	115	13.4
Fifth	196	11.4	292	23.1
Third	67	9.4	83	17.0
Seventh	63	8.5	88	16.5
Fourth	41	5.9	123	24.8
Ninth	50	4.3	187	22.7
Tenth	23	3.6	70	15.8
Eighth	18	3.3	65	18.1
First	10	3.3	31	16.5
Sixth	20	2.8	105	20.7

* The total numbers of cases are listed in Table B-1 (total cases disposed of after hearing or submission), *Annual Report of the Director of the Administrative Office of the United States Courts* (Washington, D. C.: U. S. Government Printing Office), for fiscal years 1962, 1963, and 1964.

** *Ibid.*, for 1963 and 1964.

The rate of district court reversals by unanimous appeals courts involving the cases we utilized, also shown in Table 2, gives some indication of intracircuit conflict. The rates of unanimous reversals with the exception of the District of Columbia Circuit (whose rate of dissension is the highest) are larger than the rates of dissension. Differences among the circuits are apparent. The two southern circuits, the Fourth and Fifth, have the highest percentages of unanimous district court reversals. The Ninth and Sixth circuits follow with over 20 per cent of their cases consisting of unanimously decided district court reversals.

When the rates of dissension and unanimous reversals are combined, it is apparent that only a minority of each circuit's total number of cases decided are involved. Judicial consensus is apparently more typical than judicial conflict for the lower federal courts.[17] However, there are differences among the circuits. At one end, with the highest combined rates, are the Fifth, Fourth, Ninth, and District of Columbia circuits. At the other end, with the lowest combined rates, are the First and Tenth circuits. What accounts for these differences cannot be learned from these data. However, it is not unreasonable to assume that judicial strategy, bargaining, persuasion, and the like are at work in the process of fashioning a decision and that these are relevant variables.[18] Personality characteristics, judges' attitudes, as well as other variables (such as opinion-writing assignments) may be relevant.[19]

The diversity in the rates of dissension and unanimous district court reversals is considered in another context in Table 3, which shows the relative emphasis on the various issues by circuit. Table 3 presents the rank of each appeals court on each issue for the combined number of non-unanimous and unanimous reversals cases. The Fifth Circuit, for example, had the largest total number of cases utilized for our scores, hence its rank for the total number of cases was one. The District of Columbia Circuit had the second largest total number of cases utilized, hence its rank for the total number of cases was two. The differences between the rank for the total number of cases and each of the preceding categories suggest the relative amount of dissent and intracircuit conflict stimulated by that issue on the appeals courts.

be considered to have favored the claims of criminal defendants in 70% of the selected cases he handled. The method used in this study, however, seemed less cumbersome to work with. In addition, the continuum was considered to be an ordinal scale whereas the percentage implies an interval scale.

[17] Consensus on the United States Supreme Court (in terms of percentage of unanimous decisions) is markedly less. See Table 1 in Schubert, *The Judicial Mind*, *op. cit.*, p. 45.

[18] See Walter F. Murphy, *Elements of Judicial Strategy* (Chicago: University of Chicago Press, 1964), for examples concerning the United States Supreme Court.

[19] See, for example, Harold D. Lasswell, *Power and Personality* (New York: W. W. Norton & Co., 1948), pp. 61–88; Stuart S. Nagel, "Off-the-Bench Judicial Attitudes," ch. 2 in Schubert (ed.), *Judicial Decision-Making*, *op. cit.*; Robert J. Sickels, "The Illusion of Judicial Consensus: Zoning Decisions in the Maryland Court of Appeals," this REVIEW, 59 (1965), 100–104.

TABLE 3. RANK ORDER OF NUMBERS OF CASES USED FOR EACH APPEALS COURT TO DETERMINE SCORES FOR EACH ISSUE

Issue	Rank										
Circuit:	1st	2nd	3rd	4th	5th	6th	7th	8th	9th	10th	D.C.
Criminal Cases	11	3	7	5	2	9	6	10	4	8	1
Civil Liberties	11	3	8	2	1	7	6	10	5	9	4
Government Regulation	9	3	4	7	1	11	5.5	10	8	5.5	2
Labor Cases	11	1	7.5	7.5	3	6	4	9.5	5	9.5	2
Private Economic	11	3	4	10	1	8	6	9	2	5	7
Fiscal Cases	11	5	8	9.5	1	3.5	9.5	6	2	7	3.5
Combined Injury	11	2.5	4	5	1	7	6	8.5	8.5	10	2.5
Activism	11	2	3	4.5	1	8.5	6.5	6.5	4.5	10	8.5
Total Number of Cases	11	3	7	5	1	8	6	10	4	9	2

Table 3 tell us, for example, that the Fourth Circuit ranks second on civil liberties cases although it ranks fifth on the total number of cases. This would suggest that the Fourth Circuit, whose jurisdiction encompasses three southern and two border states, heard more civil liberties cases (notably, Negro civil rights cases) than any other circuit with the exception of the Fifth (whose jurisdiction covers only southern states). The table also suggests that during the period studied there was disagreement on civil liberties matters between the appeals court for the Fourth Circuit and its district courts as well as disagreement within the appeals court itself.[20] Table 3 further indicates that the Ninth Circuit ranks fourth for the total number of cases utilized yet ranks second on private economic and fiscal cases. The Third Circuit ranks seventh on the total number of cases yet has a rank of four for the government regulation, private economic, and combined injury categories. There are a number of other suggestive findings that need not be spelled out here. What is strongly suggested is that the *sources* of judicial conflict tend to differ among the circuits—perhaps not only a function of the personality-and-attitudes-of-the-judge variables but also of "constituency" variables manifested by differing numbers of types of cases brought to the various appeals courts.[21]

[20] Cf. Vines, "The Role of Circuit Courts of Appeal in the Federal Judicial Process," *op. cit.*

[21] It should be stressed that Table 3 is only a very rough approximation (based on the absolute number of cases) of the sources of judicial conflict. A more precise analysis would require the determination, for each issue, by circuit, of the percentage of the total number of cases which comprised non-unanimous and unanimous reversals cases. See Goldman, Table 25, *op. cit.*, p. 170.

TABLE 4. SPEARMAN RANK ORDER CORRELATIONS FOR ISSUE-CATEGORIES

	Criminal	Civil Lib.	Gov't. Reg.	Labor	Private Ec.	Fiscal	Injury	Activism	Dissents	Liberalism
Criminal		.61	.38	.44	.34	.16[a]	.38	.60	.06[a]	.54
Civil Lib.			.60	.50	.39	.17[a]	.55	.49	−.37	.72
Gov't. Reg.				.40[b]	.12[a]	−.08[a]	.42	.16[a]	−.29[a]	.47
Labor					.49	.12[a]	.47	.39	−.38	.46
Private Economic						.23[a]	.43	.49	−.12[a]	.61
Fiscal Cases							−.02[a]	.26[a]	−.04[a]	.18[a]
Combined Injury								.38	−.02[a]	.59
Activism									−.08[a]	.69
Dissents										−.10[a]

[a] Not statistically significant.

[b] Statistically significant between the .02 and .05 levels.

Note that unless otherwise indicated all the correlation coefficients are positive and are significant at least at the .01 level.

The differences among the appeals courts in terms of their rates of dissent and intracircuit conflict as well as the sources of conflict presented some difficulties in gathering case data for all the appeals judges. It was not possible to determine scores on all issues for all of the judges.[22] These are obvious difficulties in combining the eleven appeals courts for purposes of analysis. However, these difficulties, indicative of the institutional diversity of the courts, impose limitations but do not preclude analysis. Non-unanimous decisions and unanimous reversals were classified by the issues, and judges were given scores based upon their votes on the disposition of the claims of the litigants.

III. INTERRELATIONS OF ISSUES

The first research problem was the extent to which voting on one issue was related to voting on all other issues or categories. The concern was whether, for example, judges who had relatively high scores for civil liberties cases would have relatively high scores on the private economic cases, combined injury, or labor cases. Spearman rank order correlations were calculated and the correlation matrix is presented in Table 4.[23] All the correlations above +.3 or below −.3 were found to be statistically significant at least at the .05 level.

Table 4 suggests that there is a positive relationship among the following seven categories: criminal cases, civil liberties, labor cases, private economic cases, combined injury cases, activism, and "liberalism." The degree of association varies from .720 for the civil liberties and "liberalism" categories to .335 between criminal cases and private economic cases. The judges on the appeals courts, then, show a tendency either to support or oppose the claims of the following: the criminally prosecuted, the individual presenting a civil liberties claim against the actions of a governmental agency, the labor union or employee in controversies with management, the underdog claim in private economic cases, and the physically injured's claims. The judges who tend to support these claims will also tend to favor the application of federal law and standards as well as federal court jurisdiction when they are challenged. The data also tell us that judges with high scores on the "liberalism" category also tend to have high scores on the above categories. It seems reasonable to infer that the cases subsumed within these categories can be thought of in quasi-ideological politically "liberal" or "conservative" terms. However, three categories (government regulation, fiscal, and "dissents") require special mention because they were not found to be associated with all of the above seven categories.

The government regulation category is positively correlated with the "liberalism" category as well as the criminal cases, civil liberties, labor cases, and the combined injury categories. However, there appear to be no significant correlations with the private economic and activism categories (leaving aside, for the moment, the fiscal cases and "dissents" categories). This suggests that the policy alternatives contained within the government regulation category may be too complex and thus not amenable to direct quasi-ideological linkage with the other categories.[24]

The fiscal cases category is not associated with any of the other categories. The voting behavior of the judges in cases involving tax and other fiscal matters appears unrelated to the voting positions on any of the categories.[25]

Propensity to dissent was related only to civil liberties and labor cases, for which negative correlations were found. Those who had high scores on civil liberties and labor cases

[22] A minimum of five cases and typically ten cases were used to determine each judge's score for each category. It is relevant to note that the number of positions on the appeals courts varies from three on the First Circuit to nine on the Second, Fifth, Ninth, and District of Columbia circuits. These latter circuits also have the most judicial business. The results thus contain some distortion because of the large number of judges from the four largest circuits and the large number of cases which facilitated the collection of case data necessary to determine the scores. The maximum distortion was on the government regulation issue where 25 of the 38 judges with scores were from the four largest circuits.

[23] The Spearman rank correlation coefficient is described in detail by Sidney Siegel, *Nonparametric Statistics for the Behavioral Sciences* (New York: McGraw-Hill Book Co., 1956), pp. 202–213. The formula used to calculate the coefficients presented in Table 4 was one corrected for ties (found in Siegel, p. 207).

[24] Cf. Harold J. Spaeth, "Warren Court Attitudes Toward Business: The 'B' Scale," in *Judicial Decision-Making*, *op. cit.*, pp. 79–108; Tanenhaus, "Supreme Court Attitudes Toward Federal Administrative Agencies," *op. cit.*

[25] This finding bears some similarity to Schubert's finding in his article on "The 1960 Term of the Supreme Court," *op. cit.*, pp. 101–2, concerning the F scale (fiscal cases). Schubert noted that "the rankings of the justices on F is different from their rankings on either C [the civil liberties scale] or E [economic liberalism]." Also see Schubert, *The Judicial Mind*, *op. cit.*, pp. 150–155, and Table 27, p. 173.

TABLE 5. PARTY AFFILIATION AND MEDIAN SCORES BY ISSUE-CATEGORY

Issue	Democrats		Republicans		Difference in Medians	Significance Level
	Median	(N)	*Median*	(N)		
Criminal cases	1.67	(43)	1.71	(37)	0.04	n.s.*
Civil liberties	1.60	(23)	1.50	(24)	0.10	n.s.
Government regulation	1.265	(22)	1.125	(16)	0.14	n.s.
Labor cases	1.50	(29)	0.945	(24)	0.555	.0007
Private economic	1.20	(37)	0.93	(37)	0.27	.0009
Fiscal cases	0.91	(40)	0.80	(35)	0.11	.08
Combined injury	1.155	(34)	1.03	(26)	0.125	.05
Activism	1.33	(33)	1.23	(32)	0.10	.05
Liberalism	1.20	(41)	0.83	(37)	0.37	.003
Dissents	0.68	(41)	0.67	(37)	0.01	n.s.

* Not statistically significant at the .05 level.

tended to have low scores on the dissents category. Civil libertarians and those sympathetic to employees and labor unions, it would seem, tended to be in the majority when cases were decided non-unanimously.

In brief, while no perfect intercorrelations were uncovered, seven of the categories were shown to be positively related to each other. This provides some evidence of the existence of organized attitudes and the presence of what can be considered quasi-ideological voting behavior.[26]

IV. PARTY AFFILIATION AND JUDICIAL VOTING

The next research problem concerned the relationship of party affiliation to voting behavior. Examination of the scores of all the Democrats and Republicans on all the circuits yielded several statistically significant differences.[27] Table 5 reports the results and shows

[26] Note that another analysis reported in Goldman, *op. cit.*, pp. 179–197, uncovered the existence of voting blocs on all but the First, Sixth, and Eighth circuits. This finding tends to support the interpretation of the rank order correlation analysis in the above text.

[27] The Mann-Whitney U Test was used to determine whether there was a statistically significant difference in medians and distribution of the scores for each of the categories by the Democrats and Republicans. The U test is described in Siegel, *op. cit.*, pp. 116–127. Nonparametric inference statistics were used in this study because the cases utilized are only a sample of the decisions the appeals judges have made in the past and will make in the future. On the appropriateness of inferential statistics see Tanenhaus, "Supreme Court Attitudes Toward Federal Administrative Agencies," *op. cit.*, and also Tanenhaus and Albert Somit, *American Political Science: Profile of a Discipline* (New York: Atherton Press, 1964), pp. 144–149.

TABLE 6. MEDIAN SCORES BY ISSUE-CATEGORY FOR APPEALS JUDGES BY RELIGIOUS AFFILIATION

Issue	Catholic		Protestant		Jewish		Significance Level
	Median	(N)	*Median*	(N)	*Median*	(N)	
Criminal cases	1.655	(16)	1.69	(56)	1.55	(6)	n.s.
Civil liberties	1.60	(9)	1.48	(33)	1.625	(4)	n.s.
Government regulation	1.40	(9)	1.14	(26)	1.33	(3)	n.s.
Labor cases	1.50	(12)	1.115	(36)	1.365	(4)	n.s.
Private economic	1.18	(15)	1.00	(52)	1.10	(6)	n.s.
Fiscal cases	0.585	(16)	0.96	(53)	0.705	(4)	.04
Combined injury	1.30	(13)	1.11	(40)	1.055	(6)	n.s.
Activism	1.33	(15)	1.295	(42)	1.19	(6)	n.s.
Liberalism	1.00	(15)	1.00	(55)	0.86	(6)	n.s.
Dissents	0.61	(15)	0.68	(55)	0.485	(6)	n.s.

that the Democrats, as a group, had higher scores than the Republicans on the labor, private economic, injury, activism, and "liberalism" categories. There is a possibility that the Democrats, as a group, were more likely than the Republicans to favor the position of the federal government in fiscal matters (tax and eminent domain)—but this finding did not meet our criterion for statistical significance.

It is interesting to note that, in general, the Democrats appear relatively more "liberal" than Republicans in cases which involve what might be called "economic liberalism."[28] However, Democrats and Republicans appear equally "liberal" on the criminal and civil liberties categories. Perhaps the economic basis of American party politics is most relevant for our understanding of certain kinds of judicial behavior. As there is no strong relationship between civil-libertarian attitudes and party affiliation in the United States,[29] it may be that there are no major differences between Democratic and Republican judges on these matters. However, it must be observed that Democrats had higher scores on the "liberalism" category which included non-unanimously decided criminal and civil liberties cases. This leads us to suspect that on the really "important" cases that force the judges to stand up and be counted, the Democrats may have tended to vote more "liberally" than the Republicans.[30] However, it is also possible to argue that the higher scores of the Democrats on the "liberalism" category were the result of their voting on the other categories. On balance, the findings reported here emphasize that party affiliation as a background variable seems to best "explain" differences in voting behavior on issues primarily involving economic liberalism.[31]

V. DEMOGRAPHIC CHARACTERISTICS AND JUDICIAL VOTING

The possible nexus of demographic variables to judicial voting behavior was investigated. Religious affiliation was found to be unrelated to the voting behavior of the appeals judges on all but one of the categories.[32] Table 6 presents the results,[33] which suggest that Catholics were more prone than Protestants and perhaps Jews to oppose the position of the government in fiscal cases.[34]

When party affiliation was controlled, the median score of the Catholic judges was still significantly lower than the median score of the Protestant judges. If this relationship is not spurious and can be duplicated for other groups of judges, it will be of interest to discover what, if anything, in Catholic-American culture (or perhaps upper-class Catholic-American culture) may contribute to this behavior. Of course, one could assert that such behavior demonstrates the greater "liberality" of Catholic judges and then argue that the fiscal cases really pit Big Government against the underdog citizen or business. But if Catholic judges are more "liberal" than Protestant judges, why should their greater liberality be manifest (in our study) only in the fiscal cases?

No differences in voting behavior were found between lower-status Protestants (such as

[28] See Schubert's definition of "economic liberalism" in "The 1960 Term," *op. cit.*, p. 100, and *The Judicial Mind, op. cit.*, pp. 160–170.

[29] See Robert E. Lane, "Political Personality and Electoral Choice," this REVIEW, 49 (1955), 173–190; Samuel A. Stouffer, *Communism, Conformity, and Civil Liberties* (New York: Doubleday & Co., 1955); Herbert McClosky *et al.*, "Issue Conflict and Consensus Among Party Leaders and Followers," this REVIEW, 54 (1960), 406–427; Thomas A. Flinn and Frederick M. Wirt, "Local Party Leaders: Groups of Like Minded Men," *Midwest Journal of Political Science*, 9 (1965), 77–98. Flinn and Wirt as well as McClosky report that differences between Democratic and Republican party leaders on questions of civil liberties are not as prominent as differences on economic issues.

[30] Had there been more non-unanimously decided cases involving criminal law and civil liberties, we would have been able to test this hypothesis.

[31] See Goldman, *op. cit.*, chap. 7, for the findings concerning additional political variables tested for the study. On the relationship of party affiliation to the judicial behavior on other courts see Schubert, *Quantitative Analysis, op. cit.*, pp. 129–142; Ulmer, "The Political Party Variable in the Michigan Supreme Court," *op. cit.;* Herndon, *op. cit.;* Nagel, "Political Party Affiliation and Judges' Decisions," *op. cit.;* Don R. Bowen, "The Explanation of Judicial Voting Behavior from Sociological Characteristics of Judges" (unpublished Ph.D. dissertation, Yale University, 1965).

[32] These findings contradict those of Stuart Nagel's (for state supreme court justices) reported in "Ethnic Affiliations and Judicial Propensities," *op. cit.* Also see Bowen, *op. cit.*

[33] The test used to determine the statistical significance of the differences among the medians for each category was the Kruskal-Wallis one way analysis of variance by ranks. See Siegel, *op. cit.*, pp. 184–193 for a description of the test.

[34] The number of Jewish judges on the appeals courts is too small for us to draw reliable inferences from the data. The discussion of religious affiliation is therefore confined to a consideration of Catholic and Protestant judges.

Baptists, Lutherans, and Methodists) and higher-status Protestants (including Congregationalists, Episcopalians, Presbyterians, and Unitarians).[35]

Other demographic variables were tested and did not reveal any relationship to voting behavior either initially or when party was controlled. These background variables included: (1) place of birth (no differences in voting behavior among those born in communities with populations under 10,000, over 10,000 but under 50,000, and over 50,000); (2) occupations of the fathers of the judges (no differences in behavior between judges whose fathers had low-status occupations and those whose fathers had high-status occupations); (3) undergraduate and law schools attended (no differences among judges who were educated in Ivy League institutions, other private institutions, or public supported schools); (4) public legal (non-judicial) and/or elective office held any time prior to appointment; (5) federal district court experience; (6) bar association leadership; (7) occupation at time of appointment to the appeals court; (8) judges with more than five years of judicial experience; (9) American Bar Association ratings (judges who received the highest A.B.A. rating, "Exceptionally Well Qualified," did not display different voting behavior from those who received the lowest acceptable "Qualified" rating). Only one category, that of labor cases, was related to the age of the judge. Younger judges (under 60) were found to have had higher scores on the labor category than older judges (over 70) when party was held constant.

It would be easy to dismiss demographic variables other than party affiliation as irrelevant for voting behavior, but this would no doubt be incorrect. Such variables as religious affiliation and socio-economic background are known to be associated in the United States with party identification,[36] and surely judges are not immune to social and economic forces during the development of their political allegiances.[37] Furthermore, the possibility yet remains that demographic factors have played a part in shaping the hierarchy of values, the outlook, and philosophy of individual judges. Our investigation has only suggested that the demographic variables tested are not *directly* associated with judicial voting behavior.

VI. SUMMARY AND CONCLUSION

The eleven United States courts of appeals, as we have seen, differ in their rates of dissension and intracircuit conflict as well as the sources of judicial conflict. Presumably personality and "constituency" variables largely account for this. The institutional diversity of the appeals courts thus imposed limitations on data collection and analysis. Nevertheless, the study of judicial voting on the dispositions of selected cases and issues reported here revealed the following principal findings:

1. There appears to be some evidence of organized voting patterns by the judges on the United States courts of appeals. These voting patterns appear, to some extent, to involve "liberal" and "conservative" voting on issues involving political liberalism and economic liberalism.
2. Party affiliation was found to be associated with voting behavior, notably when the issues involved economic liberalism.
3. Other demographic variables such as religion, socio-economic origins, education, and age were found to be almost entirely unrelated directly to voting behavior.

These findings suggest that, for the cases examined, many of the policy choices of judges affiliated with the Democratic party tended to differ from those made by Republican affiliated judges. The data indicate that for some of the types of cases examined, it tends to make a difference (in terms of the disposition of cases) which political party does the appointing to the United States courts of appeals. Furthermore, it seems clear that just as for legislators, party is the principal characteristic associated with voting behavior. However, the correlation matrix presented in Table 4 suggests that more pervasive attitudinal structures may exist. On balance, the findings underscore the absence of a sharp ideological party cleavage in the United States but also give support to the contention that the center of gravity of the Democratic party is more "liberal" than that of the Republican party.

The findings lend support for the continuation of the political selection process involved in appeals court appointments.[38] It can be

[35] Cf. Nagel, *op. cit.*, *supra*, n. 32.

[36] See Angus Campbell *et al.*, *The American Voter* (New York: Wiley & Sons, 1960).

[37] Democratic administrations have appointed a greater percentage of Catholics to federal courts than have Republican administrations. There are also indications that Democratic appointees tend to have lower socio-economic origins than Republican appointees. See Goldman, *op. cit.*, chap. 3, and my "Characteristics of Eisenhower and Kennedy Appointees to the Lower Federal Courts," *Western Political Quarterly* 18 (1965), 755–763.

[38] The selection process concerning appointments to the U.S. courts of appeals is discussed in Goldman, "Politics, Judges, and the Administra-

argued that some degree of policy-making is inherent in the judges' role and that the ideal of party responsibility requires that the large bulk of presidential appointments should be in basic harmony with the values, if not the concrete goals, of the appointing administration. Our findings indicate that although party is the characteristic most strongly associated with voting, this association (when all of the business of the courts is considered) is too limited and imprecise for party affiliation to be consistently identified with specific judicial results by the appeals courts. The differences between Democrats and Republicans are matters of degree—enough to make party affiliation a significant variable, but not enough to create a judicial system so distorted as to resolve dogmatically and predictably even the slightest of legal doubts in favor of any particular class of litigants.

---

tion of Justice," *op. cit.*, chap. 4. Also see Harold Chase, "Federal Judges: The Appointing Process" (paper read before the Annual Meeting of the American Political Science Association, 1964) and Professor Chase's forthcoming study to be published by the Brookings Institution.

[10]

Judicial Policy-Making and Southern School Segregation

MICHEAL W. GILES

THOMAS G. WALKER

IN *Brown v. Board of Education* the United States Supreme Court set new constitutional standards in the field of race relations law by declaring that in public education the doctrine of "separate but equal" was no longer valid.[1] The effect of this decision was to establish a new national policy calling for massive desegregation throughout the country, and particularly in the Southern region. The primary responsibility for implementing the national policy at the local level was given to school authorities, who were to remain under the surveillance of the equity jurisdiction of the federal district courts.[2] The Supreme Court reasoned that because of their proximity to local conditions the district courts were best suited to accept the burden of judicial appraisal of school board actions. In subsequent years the Court periodically reaffirmed this position and conferred substantial powers on the district courts to facilitate the policy implementation process.[3]

The events which transpired in the South during the two decades following the *Brown* decision have been well chronicled in the pop-

[1] 347 U.S. 483 (1954).

[2] *Brown v. Board of Education,* 349 U.S. 294 (1955).

[3] See, for example, *Cooper v. Aaron,* 358 U.S. 1 (1958); *Swann v. Charlotte-Mecklenburg Board of Education,* 402 U.S. 1 (1971).

ular and academic press.[4] The partnership of school authorities and the district courts has been an uneasy one. Public school officials have not been eager to design or carry out plans intended to accomplish immediate and acceptable levels of desegregation. Faced with school authorities unwilling to comply voluntarily with the *Brown* mandate, district courts have had to confront the issue of applying to local situations the national policy set by the Supreme Court. Understandably the district courts have not relished altering local customs by judicial decree. As Court of Appeals Judge John Minor Wisdom noted, ". . . it is not surprising that in a conservative community a federal judge may feel he cannot jeopardize the respect due the court in all of his cases by appearing to be ahead and to the left of the Supreme Court and (the Court of Appeals) in cases involving civil rights. . . , which comprise only a small portion of his docket."[5]

The federal appellate courts have been far from explicit in directing instructions to the district tribunals. While the general constitutional policy is clear (i.e., racially defined dual school systems are in violation of the Equal Protection Clause of the Fourteenth Amendment), questions of defining racially segregated systems, approving remedies to alleviate public school segregation, designating timetables for adhering to court directives, and deciding when a school district is in full compliance are left to the initial discretion of the trial judge. Mandates from the Supreme Court and the various circuit courts provide a great deal of discretion and a wide range of choice. As Chief Justice Burger stated for an unanimous Court in *Swann v. Charlotte-Mecklenburg*, ". . . a district court has broad power to fashion a remedy that will assure a unitary school system."[6] In each instance in which a district judge confronts a school segregation case, he is called upon to forge legal policy. The degree of desegregation he enforces, the remedies he imposes, and the time period within which he demands compliance are clearly policy

[4] See, for example, J. W. Peltason, *Fifty-Eight Lonely Men* (Urbana: University of Illinois Press edition, 1971); Numan V. Bartley, *The Rise of Massive Resistance: Race and Politics in the South during the 1950s* (Baton Rouge: Louisiana State University Press, 1969); Benjamin Muse, *Ten Years of Prelude: The Story of Integration since the Supreme Court's 1954 Decision* (New York: Viking Press, 1964).

[5] "The Frictionmaking, Exacerbating Political Role of the Federal Courts," *Southwestern Law Journal*, 21 (Summer 1967), 419.

[6] 402 U.S. 1, 16 (1971).

decisions which can be made only upon a consideration of local circumstances and of the constitutional guarantees the judge is sworn to uphold. Not surprisingly, the great degree of discretion allowed a federal judge has resulted in a lack of uniformity in the judicial decisions reached.[7]

Attempting to understand and explain the policy choices of the Southern federal judges in race relations cases has been the objective of several studies.[8] Inevitably this body of research has focused upon the traditional segregationist political culture as the major factor behind the massive Southern resistance to the commands of *Brown*. Theoretically a judge is linked to the political culture in two basic ways. First, he is tied to the Southern ethos through his social background experiences. Several studies have demonstrated that federal district judges have deep roots in their home states.[9] Most have been born, raised, educated and have held public office in the state in which they serve. From the earliest age they have been ingrained with the Southern political culture, including its racially discriminatory tenets. While many Southern judges have modified or even rejected much of the regional culture as it applies to race relations, the residual impact of social background experiences cannot be ignored.[10] The racial attitudes developed by these judges through a lifetime cannot be expected to disappear with the acquisition of judicial robes.

The second linkages between the judge and the traditional South-

[7] Kenneth Vines, for example, reported that of 37 Southern district judges who were active in race relations litigation between 1954 and 1962 seven decided no cases in favor of Black petitioners and four others favored the Black litigant more than 90 percent of the time. See "Federal District Judges and Race Relations Cases in the South," *Journal of Politics*, 26 (May 1964), 337-357.

[8] The most notable of these are Peltason's *Fifty-Eight Lonely Men* and Vines' "Federal District Judges."

[9] Sheldon Goldman, "Characteristics of Eisenhower and Kennedy Appointees to the Lower Federal Courts," *Western Political Quarterly*, 28 (December 1965), 755-762; Sheldon Goldman, "Johnson and Nixon Appointees to the Lower Federal Courts," *Journal of Politics*, 34 (August 1972), 934-942; Vines, "Federal District Judges."

[10] The linkage between social background characteristics and judicial behavior is reasonably well established. See, for example, S. Sidney Ulmer, "Social Background as an Indicator to the Votes of Supreme Court Justices in Criminal Cases: 1947-1956 Terms," *American Journal of Political Science*, 17 (August 1973), 622-630; Stuart Nagel, "Political Party Affiliation and Judges' Decisions," *American Political Science Review*, 55 (December 1961), 843-850.

ern culture are the processes of public opinion and community pressure. When a Southern district judge moves to desegregate an educational institution or other public facility, he does so with the full knowledge that the policy he is initiating is directed at a generally hostile constituency. Judges, of course, are not immune from community evaluations of their performance. John R. Brown, Chief Judge of the Fifth Circuit, noted, "(L)ifetime tenure insulates judges from anxiety over worldly cares for body and home and family. But it does not protect them from the unconscious urge for the approbation of their fellow men . . ."[11] Judges do not live in the protected isolation of their federal courtrooms. As Jack Peltason explained, "He (the judge) must eventually leave his chambers and when he does he attends a Rotary lunch or stops off at the club to drink with men outraged by what they consider 'judicial tyranny' ".[12] Public opinion, like social background experiences, affects judges differently. Some are able to implement national policy with little regard for community attitudes. At the other extreme are those judges who believe that public sentiment should play an active role in judicial decision-making.[13]

While students of the Southern desegregation process have agreed on the importance of the regional political and social culture in understanding the policies imposed by district courts, there has been substantial methodological diversity. One methodological approach is represented by Peltason's classic research.[14] Through interviews with judges, community leaders, attorneys and litigants, and through searches of public records and newspaper files, Peltason was able to reconstruct the judicial policy-making process. The result of this research strategy was a thorough, insightful, descriptive account of the desegregation controversy. While studies of this type are valuable in their own right and even more worthwhile as catalysts for subsequent research efforts, they suffer from a failure to provide rigorous scientific verification of their conclusions.

A second methodological approach is represented by the work of

[11] "Hail to the Chief: Hutcheson, the Judge," *Texas Law Review*, 38 (December 1959), 145.

[12] *Fifty-Eight Lonely Men*, 9.

[13] See, for example, the views of federal judge Sidney Mize of Mississippi on this issue as quoted in Richard J. Richardson and Kenneth N. Vines, *The Politics of Federal Courts* (Boston: Little, Brown, and Company, 1970), 106.

[14] *Fifty-Eight Lonely Men*.

Kenneth Vines.[15] Vines essentially provided a quantitative, empirical test of several relationships suggested by Peltason. He examined the decision–making behavior of 37 Southern district judges who were active in race relations litigation. For each judge Vines calculated the percentage of decisions handed down which favored the Black litigant. Based upon the resulting percentage each judge was classified as an Integrationist, Moderate or Segregationist. Vines then attempted to explain these groupings by examining various community and judicial characteristics. This approach suffers from a methodological flaw, one particularly troublesome in doing research on district court judges. District courts are single judge tribunals hearing disputes which arise from a particular judicial district. Because multiple judges are not responding to identical case stimuli there is no satisfactory way to conduct valid comparisons. For example, Judge X, sitting in the Northern District of Texas, and Judge Y, sitting in the Southern District of Alabama, may have both decided 40 percent of their race relations cases in favor of Black litigants. But this does not mean that the two judges have identical, or even similar, propensities on civil rights matters. The nature of the cases arising from Judge X's district may be systematically different from those in Judge Y's jurisdiction. In short, there is simply no way to infer that if Judge Y had decided those cases actually heard by Judge X he would have done so at the same 40 percent pro-Black rate. The problem of comparing the behaviors of judges is a fundamental one which plagues all non-collegial court research.[16]

The study reported here is an attempt to contribute to our understanding of judicial policy-making in the desegregation controversy in three basic ways. First, the dependent variable employed in the present study will provide a meaningful measure of judicial desegregation policy which is more comparable across judges and judicial districts than desegregation measures used in previous studies. This will avoid several problems inherent in research on non-collegial courts. Second, we will examine desegregation policy as it existed when the nation entered the 1970s. Previous studies in the desegregation area have concentrated on the original attempts to implement

[15] "Federal District Judges."

[16] On this matter see Thomas G. Walker, "A Note Concerning Partisan Influences on Trial-Judge Decision Making," *Law and Society Review*, (May 1972), 645-649.

Supreme Court policy in the South. Yet there is considerable evidence to indicate that much of what we know about the first decade post-*Brown* may not be applicable in the second decade following that decision.[17] The Civil Rights Act of 1964, the Voting Rights Act of 1965, the activity of the Justice Department in behalf of Black litigants, and the emergence of the "New South" have made the situation in the 1970s much different from what it was in the years immediately following 1954. Third, we will present the results of a multivariate analysis of the impact of several sets of variables on the desegregation policies of Southern district judges. Included in this analysis are several variables repeatedly mentioned in the literature (but not previously subjected to rigorous empirical study), as well as additional variables examined here for the first time.

DATA

In this study we will examine the policy–making behavior of Southern federal judges in school segregation controversies in 1970. The desegregation of public schools provides an excellent subject for study because this category includes the most frequently heard and publicly sensitive of the race relations disputes. In 1954, Southern school systems were totally segregated by law, but by 1970 some level of desegregation was evident in every school system in the region.[18]

As the judiciary learned from painful experience the school segregation question was not one which could often be resolved by a single hearing or judicial decree. In most instances once a school district's desegregation efforts were challenged in court as being inadequate it marked only the beginning of long and continuous litigation lasting in some districts for more than a decade. In such circumstances the district judge having jurisdiction over the case maintained constant surveillance over the district to insure adequate compliance with constitutional standards.

The basic unit of analysis in the present study was the combination of a school district and its supervising judge. In order to gather the necessary data to conduct the designed research, we be-

[17] See Kenneth N. Vines, "Epilogue: 1970," in Peltason, *Fifty-Eight Lonely Men*, 255-267.

[18] Micheal W. Giles, "Percent Black and School District Size as Predictors of School Segregation," *Sociology of Education*, in press.

gan with the approximately 400 Southern school districts[19] listed by the U.S. Department of Health, Education and Welfare as being in compliance with court ordered desegregation in 1970.[20] Officials in each of these school districts were contacted and asked to supply information regarding the legal status of desegregation disputes in their districts in 1970. A total of 288 school districts responded and of these 151 provided complete information including verification that they were operating under active court supervision in 1970 and the name of the district judge involved.

The basic unit of analysis, therefore, became the 151 school district/supervising federal judge combinations. Of the 95 United States district judges serving the South in 1970, 42 (44 percent) were supervising at least one school district in the sample.

Dependent Variable

To measure the level of enforcement of desegregation an index of school segregation was computed for each of the 151 school districts. This index was adopted from Taeuber's index of residential segregation.[21] The index measures the amount of departure of each school in a school district from the racial balance for the entire district. The index varies from zero, signifying that each school in the district mirrors the racial balance of the district as a whole, to 1.00, indicating that a school district is totally segregated with no racial heterogeneity in any of its schools. The value that the index attains between these extremes may be interpreted as the percentage of

[19] For the purposes of this study the South is defined to include the states of Alabama, Arkansas, Florida, Georgia, Kentucky, Louisiana, Maryland, Mississippi, North Carolina, South Carolina, Tennessee, Texas, Virginia, and West Virginia.

[20] To receive federal education funds H.E.W. requires under Title VI of the Civil Rights Act of 1964 that a school district either comply with H.E.W. desegregation guidelines or have a desegregation plan accepted by a U.S. district court. In 1970, approximately 400 Southern school districts indicated their compliance with Title VI by means of court ordered desegregation. In some districts the order to desegregate was issued in 1969 or before. Thus, many of the 400 districts listed would not be under active supervision by a federal district judge in 1970.

[21] Karl E. Taeuber and Alma F. Taeuber, *Negroes in Cities* (Chicago: Aldine, 1965), 195-245. For a more complete explanation of the application of the Taeuber index to school districts see Micheal W. Giles "Measuring School Segregation," *Journal of Negro Education*, in press.

Black and/or White students who must be transferred in order to obtain district wide racial balance.[22] The information necessary to compute the index for each of the 151 districts was drawn from racial/ethnic surveys of the public schools conducted in 1970 by the U.S. Department of Health, Education and Welfare.[23]

The dependent variable, then, represents the degree of segregation remaining in the sampled Southern school districts in 1970. Because each of these districts was operating under court issued desegregation orders, the dependent variable also represents the amount of deviation from perfect racial balance which the supervising judge has allowed. This can be interpreted as the district judge's policy decision in implementing the *Brown* mandate at the local level. Operationalized in this manner, judicial policy-making is studied not in terms of the words the judge uses in his opinions but on the basis of the actual level of desegregation he enforces on the litigated school district.

The dependent variable improves upon previous research in two ways. First, it provides an exact measurement of desegregation levels within the litigated school districts. This procedure is superior to a simple "pro/con" measurement of a judge's decisions as employed in several previous studies. Second, the dependent variable is restricted to a single type of desegregation controversy, i.e., public schools. This allows a more accurate analysis than occurs when all race relations cases are grouped together (e.g., public accommodations, employment, juries, voting rights, etc.). These improvements, however, do not absolutely insure comparability across judges and judicial districts. Obviously there may be systematic differences in the conditions within the schools, as well as variation in local resistance to desegregation efforts; and these are factors which necessarily will be taken into account by the supervising judge. In order to compensate for this variation, the impact of school district and environmental variables will be included in the analysis presented below.

[22] For example, if the index value for a district was .60 this would indicate that either 60 percent of the Black students or 60 percent of the White students or some combination thereof would have to change schools in order to achieve racial balance.

[23] *Directory of Public Elementary and Secondary Schools in Selected Districts: Enrollment and Staff by Racial/Ethnic Group, Fall 1970* (Washington: U.S. Government Printing Office, 1971).

For the 151 sampled school districts the mean index of segregation was .3227, with a standard deviation of .2145. Individual school district segregation levels ranged from a low index score of .0111 to a high of .8640.[24]

Independent Variables

In order to explain the desegregation policies imposed by district judges in the sampled school districts we tested the impact of twelve independent variables which have been suggested as possible determinants of judicial behavior in this area of litigation. These independent variables can be classified into four categories: social background variables, environmental variables, community linkage variables and school district variables.

(1) *Social Background Variables.* As we noted in earlier sections of this paper, social background experiences which indicate a judge's degree of association with the traditional Southern culture may be related to how vigorously he enforces desegregation policy. In order to test this proposition we selected six judicial social background variables for analysis: birthplace, location of higher education, religious affiliation, political party identification, local political office held, and state political office held. These factors have been suggested by Peltason and others and have been empirically tested with varying success by Vines. We have generally followed the standard treatment of these variables in the literature in regard to the predicted association of each with desegregation policy. Judges who were expected to be less favorable toward massive desegrega-

[24] In order to validate the representativeness of the sample we compared the 151 school districts studied with the remaining H.E.W. listed school districts not included, as well as the 42 district judges appearing in the sample with the 53 Southern judges not studied. On the basis of both quantitative and qualitative comparisons, the differences were minimal. The sampled school districts had slightly larger pupil populations and slightly greater concentrations of Black students than the non-sampled districts. Of particular concern was the possibility that the sampled districts were unrepresentative in terms of existing segregation levels. This proved not to be the case, however. Both the sampled and non-sampled school districts had mean segregation index scores of .32. Similarly, the differences between the sampled and non-sampled judges were minimal. The only difference of consequence was that the sampled judges had slightly longer tenures than non-sampled judges, reflecting the fact that Southern school district litigation often involves disputes which have been pending before the same judge for several years.

tion were those who were born and educated in the South, were closely tied to (frequently racist) state and local politics, were aligned with the Democratic Party, and held membership in a fundamentalist Protestant faith. Judges without such ties to the traditional Southern culture were hypothesized to be more sympathetic to the desegregation policy established in *Brown*. Relatively complete social background information was collected from standard biographical sources for all of the 42 judges in the sample.

For purposes of analysis birthplace was coded "0" for judges born outside the South and "1" for those born within the region.[25] Judges receiving neither college nor law school training in the South were given a "0" on the education variable, while those attending *either* college or law school in the Southern region received a "1", and those who attended *both* a Southern college and law school were coded "2". Fundamentalist Protestant religion,[26] Democratic Party affiliation, local and state political offices held were similarly scored with the judge receiving a "1" if the variable was present and a "0" if it was not.

(2) *Environmental Variables.* In order to consider the impact of community opinion on desegregation policy, some measure needed to be devised to tap the local cultural ethos within a judge's jurisdiction. Given the importance in the literature placed on this variable, a study of Southern desegregation would be incomplete without including it. For this reason we examined the impact of two environmental variables. The first of these was the proportion of Blacks among the general population in the judge's district or division.[27] The literature has consistently indicated that the per-

25 In using dichotomized or ordinal variables in correlation and regression analysis we are following the lead of Ulmer, Tanenhaus, and others. See Ulmer, "Social Background as an Indicator"; Joseph Tanenhaus, et al., "The Supreme Court's Certiorari Jurisdiction: Cue Theory," in *Judicial Decision-Making*, ed. Glendon Schubert (New York: Free Press, 1963), 111-132; and Don Bowen, "The Explanation of Judicial Voting Behavior from Sociological Characteristics of Judges," (unpublished Ph.D. dissertation, Yale University, 1965).

26 Among the judges in our sample fundamentalist Protestants consisted of Southern Baptists and Methodists.

27 The basic unit of the federal court system is the judicial district which is comprised of one or more counties. In some instances a judicial district will be subdivided into divisions. Where a judge serves a district the environmental variable data are aggregated across all counties constituting the district. Similarly, if a judge serves a division of a district, the environmental variable data are aggregated across the counties comprising the division.

centage Black within a population is related to the racial climate.[28] The presumed linkage between percent Black and resistance to desegregation is through the social, economic or political threat perceived by Whites who reside in greater concentrations of Blacks. The greater the percent Black, the greater the perceived threat and the greater the resistance to school desegregation.[29] Indeed the level of Black concentration has previously been shown to influence district judge decision-making in race relations cases.[30] The second environmental variable was the percentage of total 1968 presidential election votes within the judicial district or division which were cast for George Wallace. The degree of support for the Wallace candidacy would appear to give a good indication of public attitudes toward desegregation. As Wallace support increases so too should a lack of community sympathy for court imposed segregation.

(3) *Community Linkage Variables.* If we assume a generally negative community climate toward court ordered integration in the South, it does not necessarily follow that all district judges will be similarly affected by this public sentiment. Some judges tend to be more vulnerable to public opinion than others. While there may be several plausible reasons for the differential impact of local sentiment, a particularly important one may be the strength of the judge's linkage to the community. For purposes of analysis we isolated two possible indicators of a judge's relationship with the community. First, a judge's linkage to local attitudes may be reflected in the number of associational memberships he holds within the community. Based upon information provided in standard biographical sources, each judge was given an organizational score equal to the number of civic and fraternal groups in which he listed membership (i.e., Elks, Lions, Chamber of Commerce, country clubs, etc.). There was a wide range of scores on this variable with several judges listing no organizational memberships and three listing ten or more. As the number of associational ties increases we

[28] For a summary discussion of this phenomenon see Hubert M. Blalock, Jr., *Toward a Theory of Minority Group Relations* (New York: John Wiley and Sons, 1967). For a study empirically linking percent Black at the aggregate level with individual level prejudice see F. G. Pettigrew, "Regional Variations in Anti-Negro Prejudice," *Journal of Abnormal and Social Psychology,* 59 (July 1959), 28-36.

[29] Hubert Blalock, "Per Cent Non-White and Discrimination in the South," *American Sociological Review,* 22 (December 1957), 618.

[30] Vines, "Federal District Judges."

would expect the district judge to pay more attention to community pressure. The second community linkage variable involved the location of the judge's court vis-a-vis the school district being desegregated. A judge's regular jurisdiction, be it an entire district or a division, generally encompasses several cities and counties and, therefore, several school districts. A judge, however, will usually hold his court in a single location within the judicial district, although he may occasionally hear cases throughout his jurisdiction. Judges are likely to live and develop associations in the area immediately surrounding the established locations of their courts. Therefore, we might expect that a judge would be more reluctant to impose activist desegregation policies on school districts which envelop the judge's court than if the schools are located in an outlying area. The pressure of the local community would appear more immediate and pertinent to the judge if it originated from his "home" area than if it came from a more remote portion of his jurisdiction. In order to test this variable, each school district/judge combination was coded "0" if the judge's court was not held within the litigated school district, and "1" if the locus of the court fell within the school district.

(4) *School District Variables.* In addition to judicial, environmental and community linkage variables, it was necessary to examine school district characteristics. It is reasonable to suspect that the nature of the school district under judicial surveillance will have an impact on the type of desegregation policy a judge orders. Some districts for perfectly understandable reasons may be more amenable to integration efforts than others. Two school system variables were used in the present study. The first was the percentage of students in the school district who were Black.[31] The influence of this variable theoretically is similar to that of percent Black among the general population. As the concentration of Blacks increases in the schools so, too, may White fear of the consequences of integration. Sending White students to fully integrated schools which have ten percent Black enrollment may be much easier to accomplish than ordering White children to attend integrated schools composed of 60 percent Black enrollment. Not only would we expect resistance to increase as Black enrollment increases, but also

[31] Thomas Dye, "Urban School Segregation: A Comparative Analysis," *Urban Affairs Quarterly*, 2 (December 1968), 141-163 and John Robey, "The Politics of School Desegregation," (unpublished thesis, University of Georgia, 1970).

as the percentage of Black students grows it may be more difficult to carry out desegregation for technical reasons. Using desegregation tools such as busing or altering attendance zones may be relatively easy when the goal is integrating the district's ten percent minority enrollment, but extremely difficult as minority enrollment approaches majority status. The second school district variable examined was the size of the educational system (measured in terms of total district enrollment). Recent studies have suggested that school district size may be related to segregation levels.[32] School district size is primarily a technical variable. The logistics of desegregation in a small district are simply less complex than in a large one. For this reason we would expect judges to tolerate somewhat higher levels of segregation in larger districts than in smaller ones.

Findings

In order to evaluate the explanatory power of our independent variables, we first tested the association of each with the levels of segregation which existed in the 151 school systems and then analyzed the combined impact of these variables.

Zero-Order Relationships

For the most part, our analysis of social background characteristics contributed little to an increased understanding of judicially imposed desegregation policy. The expectation that those judges most closely tied to the South would allow the highest levels of school segregation received little support. The relationships between two of the social background variables (birthplace and party identification) and level of school segregation are in the predicted direction, but fail to reach statistical significance. The level of segregation in school districts under the surveillance of judges born outside the South is only slightly lower than that allowed in districts supervised by judges of Southern origin. The utility of the birthplace variable, however, is severely restricted by its lack of variation. Only four of the 42 judges were born outside the South. Similarly, the correlation between party identification and school segregation is in the expected direction with Democrats approving higher levels

[32] James Palmer, "Mississippi School Districts: Factors in the Disestablishment of Dual Systems," Mississippi State Univerity Research Center Report No. 40, 1971.

of segregation than non-Democrats, but the relationship is quite weak. The analysis of three social background variables yielded unanticipated results. Although not statistically significant, holding a state or local political office and membership in a low status Protestant faith are negatively correlated with segregation. What makes this result particularly important is that Vines previously found the political office and religious affiliation variables to have a significant *positive* relationship with segregationist decisions.

TABLE 1

ZERO-ORDER CORRELATIONS (r) OF SOCIAL BACKGROUND, ENVIRONMENTAL, COMMUNITY LINKAGE, AND SCHOOL DISTRICT VARIABLES TO SEGREGATION IN 1970

Social Background Variables	
Birthplace	.022
Education	.160[a]
Religion	–.028
Political Party	.086
Local Political Office	–.026
State Political Office	–.032
Environmental Variables	
Percent Black	.095
Percent Wallace Vote	–.096
Community Linkage Variables	
Organizational Memberships	–.018
Court Location	.448[b]
School District Variables	
Percent Black Enrollment	.125
School District Size (in hundreds)	.537[b]

[a] $p < .05$
[b] $p < .01$

Among the background variables only the location of a judge's education is related to school segregation in the predicted direction and at a statistically significant level. The mean level of segregation allowed by the policies of judges who received non-South college *and* law school education is .233; for judges attending non-Southern schools for *either* college *or* law school the segregation level rises to .304; and the segregation index increases to .345 for judges obtaining *all* of their advanced education from institutions within the region. From these data we may conclude that the years spent by judges in non-Southern educational institutions expose them to national norms of race relations and mollify social attitudes acquired during the course of a Southern upbringing. This, of course, does not mean that Southern schools indoctrinate their students with racist attitudes; rather it indicates that Southern judges who attend only schools within the region receive less exposure to non-Southern views toward race.

The environmental variables fare little better than the social background characteristics in predicting desegregation policies. Black concentration within the judicial district or division is positively associated with segregation levels, but the relationship may easily be attributable to chance. The community's support for the 1968 Wallace candidacy, surprisingly, is negatively associated with the amount of school segregation tolerated by federal judges, albeit the association fails to reach conventional levels of statistical significance.

The lack of predictive ability provided by the environmental variables does not necessarily preclude the possibility that the analysis of community linkage may yield productive results. The first community linkage variable analyzed, the number of local organizational memberships held by the supervising judge, exhibited no relationship whatever to the level of segregation permitted. The court location variable, however, provided altogether different results. As hypothesized, a judge's policy will allow significantly higher levels of segregation if the court is located within the school district under supervision than it will if the school system is geographically divorced from the location of the court. This demonstrates that federal judges tend to be more vigilant in enforcing national desegregation standards in remote areas than when similar issues arise within the judge's immediate work/residence locale. This finding might lead one to speculate that while a judge may not generally be affected by hostile community pressures, such factors are relevant when a judge must desegregate his own community. This, however, is not the case. When we examined only those school district/judge combinations in which the court was located within the school system, the percent Black, Wallace vote and organization membership variables remained non-significant.[33]

There are three possible explanations for the significance of the

[33] These interaction hypotheses were tested by examining the contribution of each interaction term (i.e. location X percent Black; location X Wallace vote; and location X organizational memberships) to the regression equation in Table 2. None made a significant contribution.

court location variable. First, the court location variable may link the judge to environmental forces not included in the present study. Second, a judge's personal attitudes against massive social change may be greatly activated when he is desegregating his own community, whereas he is able to maintain greater detachment in litigation involving communities in which he has little personal stake. Finally, when faced with desegregating his own community a judge may be more concerned with public reaction than when dealing with an outlying area. Consequently, he may perceive a hostile environment—which may or may not exist.

School district variables provided additional insight into the desegregation policy process. While the percentage of Black enrollment in the school district was positively associated with segregation, the relationship failed to attain statistically meaningful levels. However, the size of the school district was substantially associated with the level of desegregation enforced by the supervising judge. As the size of the school district increases so too does the existing level of racial segregation within that education system.

The Combined Model

While the zero-order relationships tell us a great deal about possible determinants of court ordered desegregation policy, they do not provide a complete account of the explanatory power of the variables under analysis. First, zero-order relationships do not demonstrate the combined impact of the independent variables on Southern school segregation. And second, zero-order relationships fail to give adequate warning of the possible effects of inter-correlation among the independent variables. For example, two independent variables used in the present analysis, court location and school district size, are significantly correlated ($r = .575$). This should not be surprising because of the fact that most district courts are located in urban centers with large school systems. Therefore, the previously discussed relationship between court location and school segregation levels may simply be an artifact of the size of the school districts in which the courts are located. In order to deal with the question of spuriousness and assess the combined explanatory power of the independent variables, the data were examined using multiple regression. The results are presented in Table 2.

With one exception the results of this analysis are consistent with the zero-order correlations presented in Table 1. Percent Black

TABLE 2

PARTIAL REGRESSION COEFFICIENTS AND STANDARDIZED BETAS FOR SELECTED VARIABLES WITH SEGREGATION IN 1970

	b	Standardized Beta	F
School District Size (in hundreds)	.00048	.42000	26.861[b]
Percent Black Enrollment	.00251	.25914	14.923[b]
Court Location	.13949	.23861	8.936[b]
Education	.04946	.15490	5.273[a]
(Constant)	.05518		

$p < .05$ $R = .624$ $R^2 = .389$
$p < .01$

enrollment is not statistically significant in Table 1, but does make a significant contribution to the multiple regression. This inconsistency arises from the fact that Black enrollment and school district size are negatively correlated and, therefore, the size variable suppresses the zero-order correlation between Black enrollment and segregation. Apart from Black enrollment, none of the independent variables which had non-significant zero-order correlations with segregation make a significant contribution to the regression equation.

The combined efforts of school district size, Black enrollment, court location, and judicial education explain 39 percent of the variance in Southern school segregation. An examination of the standardized betas shows school district size to have the largest independent effect of any of these four variables. But even with the effects of size accounted for, court location remains significantly related to segregation levels. Indeed, court location, a previously unexplored variable, appears to have independent effect comparable to percent Black enrollment, a variable that has received considerable attention. Southern education, while making a significant contribution to the regression equation, is the least helpful of the four independent variables in explaining the desegregation policies of federal judges.

Although explained variance is the most common means for interpreting regression, the "dummy" variable structure of the court location variable permits another interpretation. The regression coefficient for court location is the difference between the mean segregation index scores for the dichotomized observations on this variable, adjusted for the effects of school district size, Black enrollment, and judicial education.[34] Thus, when the school district encompasses the location of the district court, the level of segregation averages 14 index points higher than when the court is not held within the school district boundaries. This means that in these school districts an average of 14 percent more of the Black and/or White students would need to be transferred to achieve racial balance than in those school districts geographically separated from the supervising judge.[35] Similarly, the adjusted average difference between judges who received college and law school training in the South and those who received both outside the region is ten index points.[36] These are not trivial differences from either a practical or statistical standpoint.

CONCLUSION

The purpose of this paper has been to examine judicial policymaking in Southern school segregation disputes with several specific objectives in mind. First, we desired to employ a measure of decision-making which provided a more accurate indicator of judicial race relations policy than had been used in previous studies. Second, we wanted to study court ordered desegregation policy as it was implemented in the second decade post-*Brown* in order to search for possible differences with earlier periods in the desegration effort. Third, we hoped to examine the impact of several categories of independent variables on judicial desegregation policy—

[34] See William Mendenhall, *The Design and Analysis of Experiments* (Belmont, California: Wadsworth Publishing Company, 1968), 58.

[35] The unadjusted mean segregation index for those school districts having the district court located within their boundaries is .543; whereas, those school districts separated from the court retaining jurisdiction have an unadjusted mean of .281. Clearly a good deal of this raw difference is attributable to size differences between the two groups of school districts.

[36] This figure is derived by multiplying the regression coefficient for education (.04946) by the "2" code for those judges receiving all of their advanced education in the South. The education variable most properly should be broken down into two "dummy" variables—one measuring the difference between its "0" and "1" categories and one to measure the difference between its "1" and "2" categories. The present procedure is simpler, but does not give misleading results. The difference between the unadjusted means of categories "O" and "2" is .112. Since education has low correlations with school district size, Black enrollment, and court location, it is not surprising that the adjusted differences differ little from the unadjusted.

some of these variables being replicated from previous studies and others being analyzed systematically for the first time. And finally, we wanted to provide a multivariate analysis which would be capable of explaining meaningful amounts of variance in Southern school segregation.

A number of conclusions may be drawn from the data analyzed in the present study, especially when considered in light of previous research. First, the influence of judicial social background characteristics, which were found to be significantly related to district court race relations decisions by Vines, was minimal on the desegregation policies examined here. This may well be due to the fact that by 1970 a new generation of federal judges was staffing the Southern courts. Of the judges in our sample, a full two-thirds took office after the period studied by Vines and almost 80 percent were appointed after the original publication of Peltason's study. Apart from the education variable, none of the social background factors were found to be significantly related to school desegregation levels.

Second, the environmental factors examined in the present study demonstrated no substantial relationship with school district segregation. This again is in conflict with studies conducted during the years immediately following *Brown* which generally linked the district's racial climate and public attitudes to race relations decisions of local federal judges.

Third, the community linkage variables yielded mixed results. The number of organizational ties which the judge had with his community showed no relationship to the degree of school desegregation imposed. Once again much of the literature on Southern school integration efforts would predict otherwise. The linkage variable which does have a demonstrated impact is court location. Judges tend to allow substantially more segregation in their own communities than when implementing desegregation policy in other areas. What makes this variable particularly intriguing is that its influence occurs independent of environmental factors or the number of community associational memberships held by the judge. The differential application of law indeed appears to be worthy of more extensive analysis than we are able to provide here.

Finally, the school district variables yielded the greatest amount of explained variance. Both the Black concentration within the schools and the size of the school district were significantly related to the level of segregation allowed by district court orders. The

Black enrollment variable may suggest the continuing impact of public resistance to desegregation. On the other hand, the combined importance of Black enrollment and school district size may well signify a substantial change from the original round of Southern desegregation efforts. Emphasis appears to have shifted from intense battles over the principle of integration to a judicial analysis of conditions within the schools. The prominence of these variables indicates that desegregation may be in the process of becoming a more technical procedure. The primary question (both legally and behaviorally) may now focus on how much desegregation can be practically ordered by the judge given extant school district characteristics, rather than whether integration should occur at all. This interpretation is consistent with the tone of Supreme Court desegregation precedents handed down in the late 1960s and early 1970s.[37] The evolution of the desegregation process may be following the same pattern as exhibited in the reapportionment cases—that is, an intensely political question gradually eroding into technical applications of Supreme Court established national legal policy. The history of desegregation, however, has been a much more lengthy and painful one.

[37] See, for example, *Green v. County School Board,* 391 U.S. 430 (1968); *Monroe v. Board of Commissioners,* 391 U.S. 450 (1968); *Alexander v. Holmes County Board of Education,* 396 U.S. 19 (1969); *Davis v. Board of School Commissioners,* 402 U.S. 33 (1971); and *Keyes v. School District No. 1,* 413 U.S. 189 (1973).

[11]

CIVIC VIRTUE AND THE FEMININE VOICE IN CONSTITUTIONAL ADJUDICATION

*Suzanna Sherry**

> A woman's writing is always feminine; it cannot help being feminine; at its best it is most feminine; the only difficulty lies in defining what we mean by feminine.[1]

WHAT is true of women's writing is also true of women's jurisprudence. This article contends that modern men and women, in general, have distinctly different perspectives on the world and that, while the masculine vision parallels pluralist liberal theory, the feminine vision is more closely aligned with classical republican theory, represented in its various forms by Aristotle, Machiavelli, and Jefferson. A feminine jurisprudence, evident, for example, in the decisions of Justice O'Connor, might thus be quite unlike any other contemporary jurisprudence. Emergence of a feminine jurisprudence might therefore influence whether academic calls for new (or rather recycled) jurisprudential theories based upon our classical republican tradition will ultimately have little impact or will usher in a paradigm shift in moral, political, and constitutional theory.

American political and jurisprudential theory has long repudiated its classical republican origins in favor of a highly pluralist liberal vision. Contemporary constitutional interpretation is thus grounded on a thoroughly individualist liberal philosophy. Modern historians, however, have recently refocused attention on the less individualist republican spirit animating the Revolution. This has led a number of constitutional scholars to advocate a return to the nation's early republican values in interpretation of the Constitution. In light of the liberal underpinnings of the last 200 years of

---

* Associate Professor of Law, University of Minnesota. A.B. 1976, Middlebury College; J.D. 1979, University of Chicago. I would like to thank Laura J. Cooper, Richard T. Eldridge, Daniel A. Farber, Geoffrey R. Stone, Gerald Torres, and G. Edward White for their helpful comments on earlier drafts of this article, and Theodore J. May for his invaluable research assistance.

[1] Virginia Woolf.

American jurisprudence and the depth of the original transformation from a republican to a liberal ideology, these scholars might be engaged in a futile exercise. This article suggests, however, that modern liberalism is a characteristically masculine response to the failure of Jeffersonian republicanism. Because the masculine perspective has been the dominant—and virtually the sole—influence on the legal and political structure, that structure is bound to reflect a more masculine or liberal emphasis on individualism over community. A feminine jurisprudence, instead of rejecting the communitarian and virtue-based framework of Jeffersonian republicanism, might embrace and adapt it for modern society.

A full description of a feminine jurisprudence requires an examination of the modern liberal jurisprudence to which the feminine paradigm offers such a contrast. The article will first describe and differentiate the classical tradition from its modern counterpart, and briefly set out the transition from the former to the latter in the American context. It will then identify the characteristically modern framework of the three dominant contemporary schools of jurisprudence: conservatism, liberalism, and radicalism. Finally, the article will draw on feminist work in psychological and literary theory to sketch out the basic feminine alternative to the modern paradigm, and examine Justice O'Connor's opinions both to suggest the operation of a feminine paradigm and to sketch its possible contours in a jurisprudential or constitutional context.

I. Two Paradigms

Let us imagine two contrasting (and somewhat idealized) paradigms of political and moral philosophy.[2] The "modern" paradigm is individualist. The underlying theme of this atomistic vision is autonomy and separation. Individuals are seen as distinct units:

[2] As I am using the term, a paradigm is that underlying belief structure common to all practitioners in a given discipline. See T. Kuhn, The Structure of Scientific Revolutions 10-11 (1962). A paradigm limits what can be perceived as a problem or solution and blinds those who work within it to alternative paradigms. Id. See S. Fish, Is There A Text In This Class? The Authority of Interpretive Communities 270-74 (1980); Tushnet, Truth, Justice, and the American Way: An Interpretation of Public Law Scholarship in the Seventies, 57 Tex. L. Rev. 1307, 1346 (1979). Recent studies on expert decisionmaking processes suggest, moreover, that paradigms become so internalized that they are unrecognized even by astute experts trying to describe their own thought processes. See, e.g., Johnson, What Kind of Expert Should A System Be?, 8 J. Med. & Philos. 77 (1983).

the individualist paradigm denies the possibility of intersubjective conceptions of self.[3] Thus, relationships among individuals, including the communities they form, are secondary. As Michael Sandel describes it: "[W]hat separates us is in some important sense prior to what connects us—epistemologically prior as well as morally prior. We are distinct individuals first, and *then* we form relationships and engage in co-operative arrangements with others; hence the priority of plurality over unity."[4]

The modern response to this basic human separateness can, in the context of epistemological and moral theory, take either of two forms. The more common is adoption of an essentially pluralistic and non-teleological view of human nature. This view holds that there is no unitary end toward which humans aspire, no transcendent concept of the good life. "[T]he variety and heterogeneity of human goods is such that their pursuit cannot be reconciled in any single moral order . . . ."[5]

If there is no human *telos* and no unitary moral order, the mechanism for mediating among competing individual interests must necessarily be abstract and universalizable, for it must be applicable to myriad individuals in unforeseeable circumstances. It cannot be contextual, for a contextual resolution of different interests presupposes an identifiable hierarchy of human values (e.g., one's rights "as a person" are more important than one's rights "as a woman").[6] Belief in such a hierarchy—or at least the utilization of

---

[3] Sandel defines intersubjective conceptions of self as those which "allow that in certain moral circumstances, the relevant description of self may embrace more than a single, individuated human being." M. Sandel, Liberalism and the Limits of Justice 62 (1982). The depth of the modern paradigm's rejection of this concept is illustrated by Charles Fried's comment that it is too "obscure" even to comprehend. Fried, Book Review, 96 Harv. L. Rev. 960, 966-67 (1983) (reviewing M. Sandel, supra).

[4] M. Sandel, supra note 3, at 133; accord D. Richards, The Moral Criticism of Law 51 (1977).

[5] A. MacIntyre, After Virtue: A Study in Moral Theory 133 (1981) (describing, but not advocating, modern liberal theory).

[6] For example, if all persons have a right to equal treatment, it might mean that women are entitled to no special dispensations as a result of their capacity to become pregnant: pregnancy may be excluded from an employer's medical or disability plans because both men and women then have the same medical coverage. See General Electric Co. v. Gilbert, 429 U.S. 125, 134-35 (1976); Geduldig v. Aiello, 417 U.S. 484, 496-97 n.20 (1974). On the other hand, if gender (a more specific quality than personhood) is relevant, women may be entitled to greater medical coverage because of their capacity to become pregnant. See 42 U.S.C. § 2000e(k) (1982); Kay, Models of Equality, 1985 U. Ill. L. Rev. 39 (1985). Liberalism has a hard time resolving disputes at this level.

such a hierarchy to resolve differences within a society[7]—is incompatible with the pluralistic basis of the modern tradition. Moreover, a concern with context is also incompatible with the atomistic perspective of modernism: "[I]f individuals are distinct and not essentially connected with one another, then morality can be expected to concern itself not with the particularity of relationships among people, but with abstractly characterizable features of interactions among individuals whose natures are taken as given."[8]

The modern paradigm must therefore encompass a system of abstract rules that recognizes both the priority of the individual and the likelihood that diversity will engender dispute. The modern political tradition has supplied just such a system. The concept of individual rights contains all the features required by an individualist political philosophy. Rights are abstract and universal, and are expected to resolve disputes without attending to the concrete attributes of the particular individuals involved. A rights-based theory does not require a unitary human *telos*, but instead allows each individual to develop and progress toward realization of his own values. Rights are the perfect mediating mechanism for a collection of individuals whose aims are essentially in conflict.

The alternative modern response to the separateness of individuals is to seek an abstract mediating principle at the level of describing human nature itself: to identify and justify abstract, transcendent human values. These values are epistemologically rational in that they are derived by intellectual means alone, and they are characteristically modern insofar as they are intentionally divorced from the contexts in which humans live. This transcendental method of avoiding contextual decisionmaking can derive its description of human nature from an abstract idealization of a

---

[7] See, e.g., B. Ackerman, Social Justice in the Liberal State 10-12 (1980); A. MacIntyre, supra note 5, at 11, 235-37; M. Sandel, supra note 3; Dworkin, Liberalism, *in* Public and Private Morality 113, 142 (S. Hampshire ed. 1978).

[8] Scheman, Individualism and the Objects of Psychology, *in* Discovering Reality: Feminist Perspectives on Epistemology, Metaphysics, Methodology, and Philosophy of Science 225, 237 (S. Harding & M. Hintikka eds. 1983).

universal human *telos*,[9] from a contractarianism rationally deduced from humanity in the state of nature,[10] or from thin air.[11]

The modern paradigm thus reflects an infrastructure of independent, autonomous individuals, tied together by nothing more than the necessity of society. The particular characteristics of those individuals are irrelevant;[12] and thus the modern tradition has had to develop a transcendental approach to conflicts between individuals, focusing on the abstract rights of each rather than on the relationship between them.

The "classical" paradigm stands in radical contrast to the modern perspective. The central theme is connection rather than autonomy. The classical paradigm recognizes an intersubjective vision of self, insofar as "selves must be beings that exist in communities," and self-knowledge is a communal project.[13] Relationships among individuals are more important than the discrete, abstract individuals themselves. Thomas Jefferson, one of the last adherents of the classical paradigm,[14] described perfectly the contrast between the modern focus on individuals and the classical emphasis on relations among individuals:

---

[9] Modern philosophers fitting this description are rare: Alasdair MacIntyre is the best example. See A. MacIntyre, supra note 5. MacIntyre and Aristotle, from whom the former derives much of his philosophy, are in a peculiar position vis-a-vis the modern/classical dichotomy. Insofar as identifying a human *telos* represents a virtue-based, non-individualist philosophy, they illustrate the classical paradigm. However, as the text suggests, their adoption of *transcendent* human *teloi* translates easily into the modern paradigm of abstraction. Thus Aristotle, the father of the classical perspective, provides the seeds of both the modern masculine paradigm (insofar as it is abstract) and the feminine paradigm (insofar as it is teleological). The masculine paradigm abandons Aristotle's teleology, and the feminine paradigm abandons his transcendence.

[10] John Rawls may be thought to fit in this category (although his rights theories are also compatible with the more Dworkinian method of avoiding contextuality). See Kronman, Alexander Bickel's Philosophy of Prudence, 94 Yale L.J. 1567, 1600-01 (1985) (associating Rawls with Rousseau).

[11] See, e.g., R. Unger, Passion (1984).

[12] The modern paradigm views individuals as fungible "ciphers." See Reynolds v. Sims, 377 U.S. 533, 623 (1963) (Harlan, J., dissenting).

[13] See R. Eldridge, The Situation of the Self: Waywardness, Self-Knowledge, Value, and Community in Wordsworth's Poetry (unpublished manuscript, copy on file with Virginia Law Review Association).

[14] See infra notes 21-54 and accompanying text. Jefferson's library contained an extensive collection of works by both Aristotle and Machiavelli, the two seminal thinkers of the classical tradition as I am describing it. See E. Sowerby, Catalogue of the Library of Thomas Jefferson (1983).

> Self-interest, or rather self-love, or *egoism*, has been more plausibly substituted as the basis of morality. But I consider our relations with others as constituting the boundaries of morality. With ourselves we stand on the ground of identity, not of relation, which last, requiring two subjects, excludes self-love confined to a single one. To ourselves, in strict language, we can owe no duties, obligation requiring also two parties. Self-love, therefore, is no part of morality.[15]

The classical tradition "entails the affirmation that *homo* is naturally a citizen and most fully himself when living in a *vivere civile*."[16]

Moreover, because humans are perceived fundamentally as members of a unitary community, it is possible to construct a shared *telos*. The community chooses and shapes its own aspirations from among competing visions of the good life, not by a mechanism of mediation, nor by abstract philosophizing, but by a conscious selection and ordering of values. The enduring values thus chosen are the product neither of mere interest calculus nor of rational thought divorced from reality, but rather an artistic or creative weaving of rational thought, intuition, and tradition. The classical paradigm is thus teleological, both in the generic sense of being goal-based and in the more specialized Aristotelian sense of envisioning a human end. This is not to suggest an Aristotelian *telos* that transcends history and society. It is instead to suggest an immanent *telos*: one defined in the context of the historically bound community that aspires to it.[17] The *telos* provides a context in which disputes can be resolved in individual cases, and there is less need to resort to a doctrine of abstract rights.

The modern and classical traditions thus exhibit three characteristic differences. First, modernism is atomistic where classicalism is holistic. In the modern paradigm, society is a collection of individuals; in the classical view, individuals are bits of society.

---

[15] Letter to Thomas Law, June 13, 1814, *in* The Complete Jefferson 1032 (S. Padover ed. 1943).

[16] Pocock, Virtues, Rights, and Manners: A Model for Historians of Political Thought, 9 Pol. Theory, Aug., 1981, at 353, 355.

[17] See supra note 9. For an elaboration of this difference between transcendent and immanent *teloi*, see R. Eldridge, supra note 13; cf. Kronman, supra note 10 (advocating, following Bickel, a contextual, experiential, or immanent moral/political system in contrast to a modern notion of a universal and abstract rationally-derived system).

Second, modernism is *either* pluralistic and thus necessarily non-teleological *or* transcendently teleological, while classicalism is unitarily but contextually (immanently) teleological. To describe fully a classical moral or political philosophy one must identify an immanent human *telos*; to describe a modern philosophy is to deny that such a *telos* exists. Third, modernism is abstract and therefore rule-based where classicalism is contextual. A theory of rights is only necessary—indeed only coherent—in the modern paradigm.[18]

A form of the classical paradigm dominated the political and moral theories of the Greek philosophers, culminating in the Aristotelian tradition. Aristotelian and Christian theories, both envisioning organic communities of virtue,[19] constituted the reigning paradigm for nearly two thousand years. The classical focus on human virtue and human community, however, failed to sustain a changing world, and self-interest captured the human imagination. The Enlightenment marked a paradigm shift, the beginnings of what became the modern individualist tradition.[20] Although the classical paradigm underlay one final post-Enlightenment experiment, the American Revolution, that flirtation with classical republican political thought also died, and Locke's Enlightenment liberalism—the political theory of the modern paradigm—ultimately formed the ideological basis of the American republic. The transformation of American ideology from classical republicanism to modern liberalism illustrates the failure of the classical tradition. That failure rests on a fundamentally pessimistic perception of human nature and a sadly alienated perception of self. From man as a virtuous (or at least perfectable) *zoon poli-*

[18] MacIntyre describes the differences between the classical and modern traditions in similar fashion. See A. MacIntyre, supra note 5, at 146-47, 223-34; see also Oakeshott, The Rule of Law, *in* On History and Other Essays 125 (1983) (describing similar differences between "teleocratic" and "rule of law" societies).

[19] A number of scholars have compared Christianity, especially early Christianity, to the modern liberal tradition, identifying the former as closer to what I am describing as the classical paradigm. See J. Elshtain, Public Man, Private Woman: Women in Social and Political Thought 56-79 (1981); N. Noddings, Caring: A Feminine Approach to Ethics and Moral Education (1984) (relying heavily on Martin Buber); see also Cover, Foreword: Nomos and Narrative, 97 Harv. L. Rev. 4, 12-14 (1983) (identifying Judeo-Christian norms as "paideic" or communitarian). There are, of course, major differences between the two theories, and highly divergent variations within each tradition, but all are easily described, in contrast to the modern paradigm, as virtue-based and anti-individualist.

[20] See A. MacIntyre, supra note 5.

tikon, the modern paradigm moves to man as incorrigibly selfish and inevitably singular.

II. The Demise Of The Classical Paradigm In American History: From Revolution To Ratification

In the last two decades there has been a "remarkable historiographic upheaval"[21] over the ideological origins of the American Revolution. Once thought to be thoroughly individualist in its outlook, the Revolution has been reinterpreted by contemporary historians "not as a Lockean effort to protect property from taxation and regulation but as a Machiavellian effort to preserve the young republic's 'virtue' from the corrupt and corrupting forces of English politics."[22] These historians thus find the origins of American revolutionary ideology in classical republicanism, primarily as envi-

---

[21] D. Winch, Adam Smith's Politics: An Essay in Historiographic Revision 29 (1978).

[22] J. Diggins, The Lost Soul of American Politics: Virtue, Self-Interest, and the Foundations of Liberalism 9-10 (1984). The most influential of these revisionist republican works include B. Bailyn, The Ideological Origins of the American Revolution (1967); J. Pocock, The Machiavellian Moment: Florentine Political Thought and the Atlantic Republican Tradition (1975); G. Wood, The Creation of the American Republic 1776-1787 (1969). The older, Lockean tradition is admirably represented by L. Hartz, The Liberal Tradition in America (1955). According to this interpretation, the founding fathers wholeheartedly endorsed the paradigm of the Enlightenment, rejecting classical notions of virtue and *polis*. Hartz confidently describes "the national acceptance of the Lockean creed, ultimately enshrined in the Constitution." Id. at 9.

There is a backlash against the republican revisionists. Both John Diggins and Isaac Kramnick dispute Pocock's description of the American Revolution as essentially Machiavellian. Kramnick merely finds the total rejection of any Lockean influence unpalatable. Kramnick, Republican Revisionism Revisited, 87 Am. Hist. Rev. 629 (1982). In his view, the American experience represented part of the ongoing paradigm shift initiated by the Enlightenment: English and American radicals "knew their Aristotle, their Machiavelli, and their Montesquieu. But they also knew their Locke." Id. at 664.

Diggins seems to deny that classical republicanism had *any* influence on the American revolutionaries, describing his most recent book as a "corrective to the pretensions of American virtue." J. Diggins, supra, at 15. He admits, however, that the rhetoric of the Revolution was republican and that the question of virtue as a foundation for the state was at least debated. See, e.g., id at 24, 31. Moreover, most of his counter-republican illustrations center on the Constitutional era rather than the earlier revolutionary era and thus do not disprove the thesis that the original American paradigm was republican and became liberal only later. See, e.g., id. at 68, 77, 85-86, 97-98.

Diggins, unlike most modern historians, puts little faith in political rhetoric as illuminating ideology or reasons for action. See id. at 347-58; cf. Appleby, What is Still American in the Political Philosophy of Thomas Jefferson?, 39 Wm. & M. Q., 3d ser., 287, 308 (1982) (denying that Jeffersonians were classical republicans, but admitting that Pocock and others "are surely correct to insist that civic humanism shaped the terms of political debate in the early national period").

sioned by Machiavelli. Within a short time, however, that ideology began to undergo a major transformation. Perhaps as early as 1787, or as late as the aftermath of the Civil War,[23] classical republicanism faded from the American political consciousness, to be replaced by the liberalism of Locke and Madison.

The contrast between the republican Revolution and the liberal Constitution is stark. Republicanism, unlike liberalism, exalts the good of the whole over the good of its individual members. Where liberalism finds the primary purpose of government to be promotion of the diverse goods of its individual citizens, republicanism finds its primary purpose to be definition of community values and creation of the public and private virtue necessary for societal achievement of those values. The framing of the Constitution completed an ideological transformation from "the perhaps naive Jeffersonian faith in the capacity of the individual for self-development and self-restraint [to] the more generally accepted realism and consecration of self-interest which we associate with Alexander Hamilton."[24] The remainder of this section will describe that transformation.[25]

---

[23] See, e.g., G. Wood, supra note 22, at 606 (1787 and the adoption of the Constitution signaled "the end of classical politics"); L. Banning, The Jeffersonian Persuasion: Evolution of A Party Ideology (1978) (liberalism triumphed no earlier than the end of the War of 1812); R. Ketcham, Presidents Above Party: The First American Presidency, 1789-1829 (1984) (classical politics ended with rise of Jacksonian democracy); D. Howe, The Political Culture of the American Whigs 301-05 (1979) (republican or Whig values lasted until after Civil War); Ross, The Liberal Tradition Revisited and the Republican Tradition Addressed, *in* New Directions in American Intellectual History 116, 122-29 (J. Higham & P. Conkin eds. 1979) (republicanism lingered through 1880's); J. Pocock, supra note 22, at 526-45 (classical influence and awareness of the "Machiavellian moment" continues to present day); cf. M. Horwitz, The Transformation of American Law, 1780-1860, at 253 (1977) ("Law, once conceived of as . . . a paramount expression of the moral sense of the community, had come [by 1850] to be thought of as facilitative of individual desires . . . .").

[24] Katz, Thomas Jefferson and the Right To Property in Revolutionary America, 19 J.L. & Econ. 467, 487 (1976).

[25] The description of this transformation is of necessity generalized and somewhat simplistic. The framers, whether liberal or republican, were neither as monolithic nor as fundamentally antithetical as this description supposes. For an excellent discussion of the different strands of American republicanism, see Kelley, Ideology and Political Culture From Jefferson to Nixon, 82 Am. Hist. Rev. 531, 536-39 (1977). What I hope to create, however, is a heightened sense of three essential disputes: (1) whether society was an organic whole or a collection of individuals; (2) whether man was irretrievably self-interested or potentially virtuous and community-minded; and (3) whether the function of government was to define and safeguard the common good or protect individual liberties. I rely primarily on the work of historians and do not pretend to be making a new contribution in describing these con-

Three themes dominated the thought of the neoclassical American republicans: the good of the commonwealth as a whole, the subordination of individual interests through the promotion of civic virtue, and citizen participation in a deliberative, value-selective form of government.[26] These three themes were derived from classical republicanism and were the focus of the American revolutionaries and their English predecessors, the "country" party of Bolingbroke and Burgh.[27] Commonwealth, virtue, and an ordered system of values are, moreover, integrally and necessarily related to one another. The good of the commonwealth requires that citizens subordinate their private interests, and the fostering of civic virtue is the mechanism by which they may be expected to do so. Neither private virtue nor public good, however, can be defined in a vacuum: in the republican vision, a primary function of government is to order values and to define virtue, and thereby educate its citizenry to be virtuous.[28]

The republicans conceived of society in organic terms, viewing it

---

flicts or their ultimate resolution. Quotations from Adams, Jefferson, Madison, and the like are therefore used solely for their illustrative value, not their probative value.

[26] See Katz, supra note 24; J. Pocock, supra note 22, at 506-52; G. Wood, supra note 22, at 46-70, 91-124.

Several other aspects of republican thought must be distinguished as not relevant to the thesis of this article. First, a republican form of government meant (and still means) rule by the people rather than by a monarchy. See, e.g., The Federalist No. 39, at 250-51 (J. Madison) (J. Cooke ed. 1961) ("we may define a republic to be . . . a government which derives all its powers directly or indirectly from . . . the people"). This feature of republican theory, of course, not only survived but became the centerpiece of the liberal Constitution. Adherence to the republican concept of popular representation thus did not undergo any significant transformation. Second, even early Revolutionary thinkers had difficulty with the elitist, anti-egalitarian features of classical republicanism. Thus, the egalitarianism that creates such a dilemma for modern liberalism, see sources cited at infra note 119, was present from the beginning; again, no serious transformation was necessary. Finally, republicanism has also been associated with a bias against modern commerce and industry. Joyce Appleby notes that modern historians have "turned the Jeffersonians into nostalgic men fighting a rearguard action against the forces of modernity." Appleby, Commercial Farming and the "Agrarian Myth" in the Early Republic, 68 J. Am. Hist. 833, 835 (1982); see Horne, Bourgeois Virtue, Property and Moral Philosophy in America, 1750-1800, 4 Hist. Pol. Thought 317 (1983). The agrarian, anti-commercial aspect of republicanism is largely irrelevant to this article, except insofar as it suggests that republicanism is handicapped by its adulation of the past.

[27] See L. Banning, supra note 23, at 21-69; J. Pocock, supra note 22, at 406-22, 462-505; Murrin, The Great Inversion, or Court versus Country: A Comparison of the Revolution Settlements in England (1688-1721) and America (1776-1816), *in* Three British Revolutions: 1641, 1688, 1776, at 368 (J. Pocock ed. 1980).

[28] See Sunstein, Interest Groups in American Public Law, 38 Stan. L. Rev. 29, 36 (1985).

as an independent entity distinct from its members.[29] The common good was thus distinct from and paramount to the good of individuals. Thomas Paine identified this corporate vision of society with the definition of republicanism itself: "[T]he word *republic* means the *public good*, or the good of the whole, in contradistinction to the . . . good . . . of one man."[30] Samuel Adams, like Aristotle, metaphorically compared the body politic to the body human.[31] Thomas Jefferson placed societal needs above individual interest: "I [am] convinced [man] has no natural right in opposition to his social duties."[32]

In the early years of the Revolution, individual liberty was presumed to be synonymous with public liberty.[33] For classical republicans, individual fulfillment came from "sharing in a collective autonomy, a collective freedom and glory."[34] Another aspect of the classical vision of man as but a part of a larger whole was the notion of defining people by their social roles or functions.[35] This notion was echoed by the American republicans in their vision of the differing virtue, and thus the differing functions, of the "few" and the "many": the republicans envisioned a natural aristocracy.[36]

The classical design for virtue in government was thus a passion for the public good. The American revolutionaries recognized, however, that such a scheme of government could work only where individual citizens were imbued with a civic virtue that required subordination of private interest to public good.[37] Thomas Jefferson, as noted earlier, opposed virtue to self-interest: "Self-love . . . is

---

[29] See L. Banning, supra note 23, at 47; G. Wood, supra note 22, at 53-65.

[30] Paine, Dissertations on Government, etc. (1786), *in* 1 The Complete Writings of Thomas Paine 372-73 (P. Foner ed. 1945).

[31] See S. Adams, "Candidus," Feb. 3, 1776, *in* 3 Writings of Samuel Adams 266 (H. Cushing ed. 1906); 3 The Life and Works of John Adams 478-79 (C. Adams ed. 1865).

[32] Letter to Danbury Baptists, Jan. 1, 1802, *in* 8 The Writings of Thomas Jefferson 113 (H. Washington ed. 1864).

[33] G. Wood, supra note 22, at 63; Katz, supra note 24, at 482.

[34] H. Pitkin, Fortune Is a Woman: Gender and Politics in the Thought of Niccolo Machiavelli 81 (1984); see id. at 80-105.

[35] See A. MacIntyre, supra note 5, at 114-22.

[36] See J. Pocock, supra note 22, at 515-17 (describing the republican conception of a "natural aristocracy" of the few, which would be discerned by the many democratically).

[37] L. Banning, supra note 23, at 107; see J. Diggins, supra note 22, at 10, 12; H. Storing, What the Anti-Federalists Were For 15-23 (1981); G. Wood, supra note 22, at 53-54; Howe, Republican Thought and the Political Violence of the 1790s, *in* National Unity on Trial, 1781-1816, at 73, 81 (E. Ferguson ed. 1970).

no part of morality. Indeed it is exactly its counterpart. It is the sole antagonist of virtue, leading us constantly by our propensities to self-gratification in violation of our moral duties to others."[38] John Adams described the relationship between public and private good:

> Public virtue cannot exist in a nation without private, and public virtue is the only foundation of republics. There must be a positive passion for the public good, the public interest, honor, power, and glory, established in the minds of the people, or there can be no republican government, nor any real liberty; and this public passion must be superior to all private passions. Men must be ready, they must pride themselves, and be happy to sacrifice their private pleasures, passions, and interests, nay, their private friendships and dearest connections, when they stand in competition with the rights of society.[39]

The early republicans thus placed their faith in the virtue of the populace. A republic was made and maintained by the character and spirit of its people.[40] Jefferson wrote repeatedly that man was innately moral.[41]

If private virtue was to ensure public good, however, the function of government was to choose both the public good and the private virtue that supported it, "to select the values that ought to control public and private life."[42] Although apparently little dis-

---

[38] Letter to Thomas Law, supra note 15, at 1032-33.

[39] Letter to Mercy Warren, April 16, 1776, *in* The Selected Writings of John and John Quincy Adams 57-58 (A. Koch & W. Peden eds. 1946).

[40] See G. Wood, supra note 22, at 52-53; Katz, supra note 24, at 482; see also Jefferson, Notes on the State of Virginia, Query XIX, at 225 (1803) ("It is the manners and spirit of a people which preserve a republic . . . ."); Jefferson, Letter to Elbridge Gerry, March 29, 1801, *in* 8 Writings of Thomas Jefferson 40, 43 (P. Ford ed. 1897) ("the steady character of our countrymen is a rock to which we may safely moor").

[41] The best example is a letter to his nephew written in 1787:

> Man was destined for society. His morality therefore was to be formed to this object. He was endowed with a sense of right and wrong merely relative to this. This sense is as much a part of his nature, as the sense of hearing, seeing, feeling . . . . It is given to all human beings in a stronger or weaker degree . . . . It may be strengthened by exercise, as may any particular limb of the body.

Letter to Peter Carr, Aug. 10, 1787, *in* 12 The Papers of Thomas Jefferson 14 (J. Boyd ed. 1955); see Letter to John Adams, Oct. 14, 1816, *in* 15 The Writings of Thomas Jefferson 73, 76 (A. Lipscomb & A. Bergh eds. 1903); Letter to Thomas Law, supra note 15, at 1032.

[42] Sunstein, supra note 28, at 31 (quotation from unedited manuscript at 5); see also Michelman, Politics and Values or What's Wrong With Rationality Review, 13 Creighton L. Rev. 487, 509 (1985) (in Rousseauean republican vision "values are an intended *outcome* of

cussed, the anti-pluralist nature of republicanism follows inevitably from its anti-individualism. Only where the object of government is to promote individual goods and interests can diverse, idiosyncratic value systems be accommodated. In the unitary community envisioned by classical republicans, both public good and private virtue must be defined by the commonwealth as a whole. Individual liberty may mean the right to pursue private goods; public liberty must mean the right to participate in defining public good. Thus, an important object of republican government is the structuring of a shared *telos*, a common value system for citizens and their community.[43]

This notion of community values was so closely tied to the notion of virtue itself that it was rarely made explicit. There are, however, some indications in republican writings that a primary end of government was to select the values that would promote a virtuous citizenry. The chief object of government, according to one anti-federalist, should be the "the attainment of virtue, and happiness among ourselves."[44] The anti-federalist insistence that only a small, homogeneous republic could succeed also suggests the anti-pluralist foundation of republicanism.[45] Wisdom and judgment in both the populace and its representatives was seen as a necessary prerequisite to good government.[46] Without these qualities, no nation could be expected to structure its values. The American Senate, "the repositor[y] of classical republican honor and wisdom,"[47] served the same deliberative function. Moreover,

---

politics; they are public as well as private in origin, originating in political engagement and dialogue as well as in private experience").

[43] Diggins suggests that American republicanism failed in part because its sponsors lacked such a moral vision or *telos*. J. Diggins, supra note 22, at 31.

[44] "Brutus," Jan. 3, 1788, *in* The Anti-Federalist 145, 146 (H. Storing ed., abridgement by M. Dry, 1985).

[45] See infra note 52 and accompanying text.

[46] J. Diggins, supra note 22, at 26-28.

[47] G. Wood, supra note 22, at 209; see H. Storing, supra note 37, at 61 (discussing federalist responses to anti-federalist criticisms of separation of powers: "The sole intention of [the separation] is to produce wise and mature deliberation."); G. Wood, supra note 22, at 208-20. Although this is not, of course, the only function the republicans envisioned for the Senate, even the property-protecting function of the upper house is a far cry from its function as envisioned by the liberal federalists:

> The remedy for this inconveniency [the disproportionate strength of the legislature] is, to divide the legislature into different branches; and to render them by different modes of election, and different principles of action, as little connected with each

the people's participation in the process of selecting values for the community might itself foster individual virtue. A belief in an ordered system of values was thus both a corollary to and an outcome of a reliance on individual virtue.

The notion of common good maintained by a virtuous citizenry was, however, beset by contradictions. Republicanism held that true liberty could only be maintained by the security of property. Yet property would beget wealth, which, when concentrated in the hands of the few, would be destructive of virtue and freedom. Republicanism's predicament lay between the promotion of collective liberty through a system of private property and fear of the corrupting influences of luxury.[48] In locating the authority of government in the governed, republicanism created another dilemma: what would move an uncoerced citizenry to obey?[49] "The republican conundrum was thus how to change the flow of authority from top-down to bottom-up; the republican solution was that obedience must be internalized."[50] Yet the doctrine of civic virtue provided only a partial answer. Jefferson, for example, in advocating pursuit of the virtuous life, never confronted the potential conflict between individual and societal definitions of virtue.[51]

The new republicans also faced a problem unique to America. Republics had always been small, and republicanism assumed that only in small communities could there develop a homogeneity of interest and passion for the public good. The American revolutionaries had to reconcile this republican ideal with the seemingly unlimited geography of the American continent.[52] Finally, Americans were wholly ambivalent about their own nature: did their rusticity and distance from England make them "natural republicans," or

---

> other, as the nature of their common functions, and their common dependence on the society, will admit.

The Federalist No. 51, at 350 (A. Hamilton or J. Madison) (J. Cooke ed. 1961).

[48] See G. Wood, supra note 22, at 64-65; Katz, supra note 24. For attempted reconciliations of this tension, see J. Pocock, supra note 22, at 533-39; Katz, supra note 24.

[49] See G. Wood, supra note 22, at 66-67; Katz, supra note 24, at 482.

[50] Katz, supra note 24, at 482.

[51] J. Diggins, supra note 22, at 41-42.

[52] For the classic formulation of this small republic theory, see C. Montesquieu, The Spirit of the Laws 20-22, 40-48 (Paris 1748) (T. Nugent trans. 1949). For other discussions of this theory, see L. Banning, supra note 23, at 107; J. Diggins, supra note 22, at 48-49, 65; G. Wood, supra note 22, at 473, 502-05; Howe, supra note 37, at 84.

was their virtue in jeopardy from within?[53] Despite these recognized problems, there seemed little doubt in 1776 that America would be a republic, and all those committed to republicanism shared essentially the theory of government described above.[54]

By the time of the Constitutional Convention of 1787, that picture of virtually unanimous enthusiasm for classical republican politics had changed drastically. The central factor in the crisis was republicanism's utter dependence "upon a virtuous citizenry."[55] Republicanism was totally dependent on civic virtue to obligate citizens to the public good.[56] In the years of the Articles of Confederation, the founders began to reject the ideals of republicanism because of a perceived licentiousness and lack of virtue among the people. At least as early as 1782, Hamilton attacked the notion of republican virtue: "We may preach till we are tired of the theme . . . ."[57] Virtue, he warned in 1788, would become an appendage of wealth—only the wealthy, being more learned and of better moral character than the poor, would maintain virtuous practices.[58] Man was selfish, and any hope for public interests would have to come from private interests.[59]

Hamilton, Madison, and others began to see human motivations, rather than an education in virtue, as the means by which to control politics and society. The fear of popular corruption, and the construction of government mechanisms to combat it, runs throughout *The Federalist* and other contemporaneous writings.[60] During the ratification debates, both the federalists and the antifederalists defended their position as the one better able to combat

[53] See G. Wood, supra note 22, at 123.

[54] Id. at 60, 91-93.

[55] J. Diggins, supra note 22, at 24.

[56] G. Wood, supra note 22, at 92.

[57] The Continentalist No. 6, July 4, 1782 *in* 3 The Papers of Alexander Hamilton 103 (H. Syrett & J. Cooke eds. 1962).

[58] Hamilton, Address before the New York Ratifying Convention of Poughkeepsie, New York, June 21, 1788, *in* 5 The Papers of Alexander Hamilton 36, 42-43 (H. Syrett & J. Cooke eds. 1962). Hamilton's notion that wealth would promote virtue shows how far the nation's ideology had changed from the original fear of wealth as corruptive.

[59] See G. Stourzh, Alexander Hamilton and the Idea of Republican Government 70-71 (1970).

[60] See, e.g., The Federalist No. 10 (J. Madison); The Federalist No. 15, at 96 (A. Hamilton) (J. Cooke ed. 1961) ("Why has government been instituted at all? Because the passions of men will not conform to the dictates of reason and justice, without constraint."); L. Banning, supra note 23, at 89-91; J. Diggins, supra note 22, at 87-98.

and control "the natural lust of power so inherent in man."[61]

Even so staunch a republican as John Adams at times lost faith in the people:

> One is . . . astonished at the reflection of Machiavel, 'Such was the spirit of patriotism amongst them in those days, that they cheerfully gave up their private interests for the public good,' when every page of his history shows, that the public good was sacrificed everyday, by all parties, to their private interests, friendships, enmities.[62]

Thomas Jefferson, the patron saint of American republicanism, may have experienced a similar disillusionment. As early as 1776, he expressed doubts about the security of a classical republic: "The fantastical idea of virtue and the public good being a sufficient security to the state . . . I assure you was never mine."[63] At least one reading of his philosophy suggests that by the time of his presidency, he had thoroughly assimilated Madisonian liberalism.[64]

The federalists therefore hoped to create a republican government that did not require virtuous citizens for its sustenance.[65] Assuming that man would not be virtuous, they sought to change human conduct even though human nature was fixed.[66] John Adams, for example, was intent on exploiting "talent and control[ling] power through the Christian sin of pride, utilizing the

---

[61] George Mason of Virginia, *in* 3 The Debates in the Several State Conventions on the Adoption of the Federal Constitution as Recommended by the General Convention at Philadelphia, in 1787, at 32 (J. Elliot 2d ed. 1836); see Kenyon, Men of Little Faith: The Anti-Federalists on the Nature of Representative Government, *in* National Unity on Trial, 1781-1816, at 11, 20-21, 33-35 (E. Ferguson ed. 1970).

[62] John Adams, 2 A Defense of the Constitutions of Government of the United States of America 109 (1787-88).

[63] Thomas Jefferson to Edmund Pendleton, Aug. 26, 1776, *in* The Portable Thomas Jefferson 357 (M. Peterson ed. 1975); see also Letter to Dupont de Nemours, April 24, 1816, *in* 14 The Writings of Thomas Jefferson 487 (A. Lipscomb & A. Bergh eds. 1903) ("[T]he human character . . . requires in general constant and immediate control, to prevent its being biased from right by the seductions of self-love.").

[64] See L. Banning, supra note 23, at 89; Katz, supra note 24, at 487; cf. Appleby, supra note 22, at 289-91 (Jefferson's infatuation with Montesquieu's theories was waning by 1790); Grampp, A Reexamination of Jeffersonian Economics, *in* National Unity on Trial, 1781-1816, at 209 (E. Ferguson ed. 1970) (Jefferson's economic theories also changed).

[65] See The Federalist No. 51, at 351-52 (A. Hamilton or J. Madison) (J. Cooke ed. 1961); L. Banning, supra note 23, at 99, 107; J. Diggins, supra note 22, at 6; D. Epstein, The Political Theory of The Federalist 45 (1984); J. Pocock, supra note 22, at 522-23; G. Wood, supra note 22, at 432, 473, 502-05, 535-47, 559-60; Katz, supra note 24, at 487.

[66] G. Wood, supra note 22, at 475.

love of praise as a surrogate for reason and virtue."[67] Adams abandoned the concept of virtue as a *cause* of a republic and a "well-ordered constitution," instead seeing virtue as an *effect* of good government.[68] A well ordered constitution required a balance of powers to check the tendency toward tyranny and corruption; an unvirtuous citizenry could not be relied upon to do so.

Madison turned the large size of the new republic to his advantage by arguing that the size would prevent the formation of factions and thus protect the government from corruption.[69] Madison was convinced that factions were due to the "unequal distribution of property," which gave rise to "unfriendly passions" and "violent conflicts."[70] Because this was the "natural" condition of man, the Republic could be preserved only by the "machinery of government."[71] If character would not save the Experiment, structure would; if not virtue, operation. In an age of empiricism, the founders measured their ideal of a virtuous citizen against the citizens of their time. The incongruence of ideal and reality led to a government based on a deeply pessimistic view of human nature as irretrievably self-interested.[72]

In abandoning virtue as the basis of good government, the framers also shifted the purpose of government from perfecting human virtue to promoting individual desires. Despairing of the nobility of human nature, the founders constructed a constitutional structure designed to withstand and cater to its baser aspects.[73] The purpose

---

[67] J. Diggins, supra note 22, at 71.

[68] Id. at 70-71.

[69] See The Federalist No. 10 (J. Madison); Sunstein, supra note 28.

[70] The Federalist No. 10 at 59 (J. Madison) (J. Cooke ed. 1961).

[71] J. Diggins, supra note 22, at 53 (citing Federalist No. 51).

[72] Gordon Wood's description of the depth of the transformation cannot be improved upon:

> [The Lockean] image of a social contract formed by isolated and hostile individuals was now the only contractual metaphor that comprehended American social reality. . . .
>
> . . . .
>
> . . . The Constitution represented both the climax and the finale of the American Enlightenment, both the fulfillment and the end of the belief that the endless variety and perplexity of society could be reduced to a simple and harmonious system. By attempting to formulate a theory of politics that would represent reality as it was, the Americans of 1787 shattered the classical Whig world of 1776.

G. Wood, supra note 22, at 601-02, 606.

[73] As stated by one commentator: "Between Machiavelli and Locke lies the dilemma of American politics. Classical political philosophy aims to discipline man's desires and raise

of government was to protect private aims and interests.[74] The "principal task of modern [l]egislation" was not the enobling of the human spirit but "[t]he regulation of these various and interfering interests."[75]

At best, this theory of government exalts the isolated individual over the member of a community by shifting the function of government from promoting or perfecting human nature to protecting the exercise of individual human nature. Both Madison and the later Jefferson put this private, self-directed individual ahead of the community. "Justice," wrote Madison, "is the end of government. It is the end of civil society."[76] Madison's conception of justice meant "the protection of each man's faculties,"[77] and thus rejected as a governmental function the deliberately selective *perfecting* of those faculties.[78]

A more cynical interpretation of *The Federalist* and of the Constitution it defends finds not even this regard for individual faculties, but rather an almost Hobbesian view of human existence as "nasty, brutish and short."[79] Despite all the rhetoric in *The Federalist* about justice, the Constitution is defended primarily on its ability to secure safety and prosperity. Jay introduced the first fourteen papers as addressing the need to provide for "the preservation of peace and tranquility . . . against dangers from *foreign arms and influence*, [and against] dangers of the *like kind* arising from domestic causes."[80] Papers three through ten accordingly ad-

---

him far above his vulgar wants; liberalism promises to realize desires and satisfy wants. The first is more noble, the second more attainable." J. Diggins, supra note 22, at 16.

[74] There is some debate about whether man's private interests were primarily economic or political. See generally D. Epstein, supra note 65. In either case, the interests were self-centered, not altruistic, and thus inconsistent with republican virtue.

[75] The Federalist No. 10, at 59 (J. Madison) (J. Cooke ed. 1961).

[76] The Federalist No. 51, at 352 (J. Madison or A. Hamilton) (J. Cooke ed. 1961).

[77] D. Epstein, supra note 65, at 86.

[78] See id. at 79, 84-85, 162-63. Despite his thesis that Madison and the federalists also sought to protect the good of the commonwealth, Epstein acknowledges that promoting individual faculties was Madison's "more fundamental end." Id. at 163. Jefferson's belief that the end of government was the promotion of individual capacities is more difficult to document by reference to specific passages, but one author has concluded that "Jefferson wanted government to offer protection to the personal realm where men might freely exercise their faculties." Appleby, supra note 22, at 293. How much Jefferson actually changed his views is open to some debate.

[79] T. Hobbes, Leviathan 97 (1952) (reprinted from 1651 ed.).

[80] The Federalist No.3, at 13-14 (J. Jay) (J. Cooke ed. 1961).

dress the propensity of the proposed union to safeguard against these dangers, and eleven through thirteen address the economic advantages of union. In number fourteen, Madison summarized the benefits of a union in language that again stresses security at the expense of civilization:

> We have seen the necessity of the union, as our bulwark against foreign danger, as the conservator of peace among ourselves, as the guardian of our commerce and other common interests, as the only substitute for those military establishments which have subverted the liberties of the old world; and as the proper antidote for the diseases of faction, which have proved fatal to other popular governments, and of which alarming symptoms have been betrayed by our own.[81]

Protection of individual rights, when discussed in any but the most rhetorical terms, is left to the states.[82] Human potential and human aspirations to higher values are left untouched. Even the authors of *The Federalist* implicitly admitted that this is a sad "reflection on human nature."[83]

Based on the "psychology of temptation and the politics of suspicion,"[84] the Constitution of 1787, and especially the Bill of Rights of 1789, represent a triumph of modern liberalism over classical republicanism.[85] Individualism had become the founda-

---

[81] The Federalist No. 14, at 83 (J. Madison) (J. Cooke ed. 1961). To complete the triad, Hamilton also described the objects of government similarly:

> The Principal purposes to be answered by Union are these—The common defence of the members—the preservation of the public peace as well against internal convulsions as external attacks—the regulation of commerce with other nations and between the States—the superintendence of our intercourse, political and commercial, with foreign countries.

The Federalist No. 23, at 146-47 (A. Hamilton) (J. Cooke ed. 1961).

[82] See The Federalist No. 17, at 105-06 (A. Hamilton) (J. Cooke ed. 1961) (identifying "the administration of private justice" as one of the reasons that state governments command greater popular affection and loyalty than will the federal government).

[83] The Federalist No. 51, at 349 (A. Hamilton or J. Madison) (J. Cooke ed. 1961).

[84] J. Diggins, supra note 22, at 74.

[85] For a discussion of the liberal nature of the Constitution, see, e.g., G. Wood, supra note 22, at 430-564. But see infra note 149 (suggesting different interpretation of the Constitution). For detailed discussions of the liberal origins of parts of the first and fifth amendments, see Note, The Origins and Original Significance of the Just Compensation Clause of the Fifth Amendment, 94 Yale L.J. 694, 704-05 (1984); Note, Reinterpreting the Religion Clauses: Constitutional Construction and Conceptions of The Self, 97 Harv. L. Rev. 1468, 1471-72, 1475-85 (1984) [hereinafter cited as Note, Reinterpreting the Religion Clauses]; see also Walters v. National Ass'n of Radiation Survivors, 53 U.S.L.W. 4947, 4965 n.18 (U.S.

tion of the Republic,[86] whereas in 1776 it was anathema to it. Because the ancient republics had died, and because it appeared that this new republic might also succumb to corruption, Americans adopted the individualism of Locke over the Republic of Machiavelli and Harrington.[87]

This early American partiality to an individualist ideology foreshadowed a jurisprudential tradition that has lasted almost two centuries. Individual autonomy serves as the underlying paradigm for virtually the entire modern American jurisprudential tradition. The next section of this article attempts to demonstrate that the three major schools of contemporary American jurisprudence, although they differ on virtually everything else, share this common paradigm.[88]

1985) (Stevens, J., dissenting) ("[A]ll of the checks and balances [of the Constitution] are consistent with the interest in protecting individual liberty from the possible misuse of power by a transient unrestrained majority.").

[86] Madison wrote that it might be "unfavorable to liberty" if each individual were to become "insignificant . . . in his own eyes." National Gazette, Dec. 19, 1791, *in* 14 The Papers of James Madision 170 (R. Rutland, T. Mason, et. al. eds. 1983).

[87] At least one interpretation suggests that the classical paradigm was once again briefly and unsuccessfully revived in the anti-federalist triumph of 1800. See L. Banning, supra note 23, at 273-302. On both sides of the Atlantic, the classical paradigm survived underground—in literature—for a time after its political demise. See generally R. Ferguson, Law & Letters in American Culture 96-195 (1984) (reviewing the strains in American literature during the early 1800's.); R. Eldridge, supra note 13.

[88] What follows in the text is necessarily a highly simplified description of the three schools of jurisprudence. I have, however, tried to retain the essence of each school. For an insightful elaboration upon liberalism and radicalism, as described in the text, see Shiffrin, Liberalism, Radicalism, and Legal Scholarship, 30 UCLA L. Rev. 1103 (1983). I am identifying Robert Nozick as the prime example of the third, neo-conservative school, which is not included in Shiffrin's analysis.

At least one political philosopher has drawn paradigm lines quite differently. In his introduction to a collection of essays on Nozick's theories, Jeffrey Paul identifies Rawls' "distributivist liberalism" as the "current ideological paradigm" and suggests that Nozick's vision of the minimal state is "a wholly new conceptual paradigm." Reading Nozick: Essays on Anarchy, State, and Utopia 2 (J. Paul ed. 1981). My thesis is that Nozick and Rawls share the deeper underlying paradigm of autonomy, which cannot be perceived absent the illumination of a contrasting, classical paradigm. Anthony Kronman also has noticed the common grounding of the otherwise different schools of jurisprudence; he notes that Bruce Ackerman, Roberto Unger, and Richard Posner all adhere to "some independent scheme of values based only upon reason and a few elementary propositions regarding the nature of the human species." Kronman, supra note 10, at 1572.

III. The Jurisprudence Of The Modern Paradigm: From Nozick To Unger

A. *Conservative Jurisprudence: Nozick*

Robert Nozick's minimal state is an archetypal example of the consequences of an individualistic philosophy. He identifies as his "root idea" the fact that "there are different individuals with separate lives," and asserts that all valid moral and political philosophy must "reflect the fact of our separate existences."[89] The minimal state is merely a method of allowing each individual to reach the highest form of individuality:

> The minimal state treats us as inviolate individuals . . .; it treats us as persons having individual rights with the dignity this constitutes. . . . [This treatment] allows us, individually or with whom we choose, to choose our life and to realize our ends and our conception of ourselves, insofar as we can, aided by the voluntary cooperation of other individuals possessing the same dignity. How *dare* any state or group of individuals do more. Or less.[90]

Nozick denies entirely the validity of any doctrine that recognizes connection or community as a separate and valuable principle:

> But why may not one violate persons for the greater social good? Individually, we each sometimes choose to undergo some pain or sacrifice for a greater benefit or to avoid a greater harm . . . . In each case, some cost is borne for the sake of the overall social good. . . . But there is no *social entity* with a good that undergoes some sacrifice for its own good. There are only individual people, different individual people, with their own individual lives. Using one of these people for the benefit of others, uses him and benefits others. Nothing more.[91]

Nozick thus perfectly illustrates the first tension between the mod-

---

[89] R. Nozick, Anarchy, State, and Utopia 33 (1974); see Nagel, Libertarianism Without Foundations, *in* Reading Nozick: Essays on Anarchy, State, and Utopia, 191, 193 (J. Paul ed. 1981).

[90] R. Nozick, supra note 89, at 333-34.

[91] Id. at 32-33. This rejection of the concept of a social entity, distinct from the individuals who make it up, is not limited to Nozick; at least one of his severest critics belittles the idea of a social entity while affirming the necessity of balancing harms and benefits. See Nagel, supra note 89, at 197; see also J. Rawls, A Theory of Justice 264 (1971) (using individualistic concepts to develop a concept of community).

ern and classical traditions: his minimalist state is based on a wholly atomistic philosophy, with no room for collectivity.

This preference for individualism and its concomitant need for mediating devices is also embodied in the contemporary law and economics movement: "The economist rejects absolutes: what is good is what the individual prefers; a good society is one that maximizes freedom of choice. The economists' values speak to the question of *how* society should be organized in order to satisfy individual desires, whatever they may be."[92]

B. Liberal Jurisprudence: Rawls and Dworkin

The essence of the myriad traditions that make up modern liberalism is also atomistic. That liberal political philosophy takes autonomy as an underlying principle is almost a truism.[93] Ronald Dworkin has recognized that liberal theories, including both his own and that of Rawls, are what he calls "rights-based", as opposed to "goal-based."[94] As he explains the distinction, rights-based theories[95] "place the individual at the center," while goal-

[92] Meyers, An Introduction to Environmental Thought: Some Sources and Some Criticisms, 50 Ind. L.J. 426, 452 (1975).

[93] For statements in general support of the proposition, see, e.g., J. Elshtain, supra note 19, at 14-16; M. Sandel, supra note 3, at 11; R. Unger, Knowledge & Politics 21-22 (1975); Dworkin, supra note 7, at 259-65; Eisenstein, The Sexual Politics of the New Right: Understanding the "Crisis of Liberalism" for the 1980s, *in* Feminist Theory: A Critique of Ideology 77, 79 (N. Keohane, M. Rosaldo, & B. Gelpi eds. 1982) [hereinafter cited as Feminist Theory]; Johnson, Do You Sincerely Want To Be Radical?, 36 Stan. L. Rev. 247, 256 (1984); Klare, Judicial Deradicalization of The Wagner Act and the Origins of Modern Legal Consciousness 1937-1941, 62 Minn. L. Rev. 265, 276 & n.36 (1978); Nagel, supra note 89; Richards, Human Rights and Moral Ideals: An Essay on the Moral Theory of Liberalism, 5 Soc. Theory & Prac. 461, 465 (1980); Shiffrin, supra note 88, at 1145 & n.144; Tushnet, Following the Rules Laid Down: A Critique of Interpretivism and Neutral Principles, 96 Harv. L. Rev. 781, 783-85 (1983); Note, Reinterpreting the Religion Clauses, supra note 85, at 1471. But see F. Schauer, Free Speech: A Philosophical Enquiry 47-48 (1982)(noting that much of liberal doctrine emphasizes "the interests of society at large rather than. . .the interests of the individual). Isaiah Berlin drew an illuminating distinction between autonomy and heteronomy, or dependence on the external world, suggesting that the former, although not exclusive, is the "essence" of mankind. I. Berlin, Two Concepts of Liberty 21-22 (1958); accord, Tushnet, An Essay on Rights, 62 Tex. L. Rev. 1363, 1392 (1984).

[94] See Dworkin, supra note 7, at 168-77, 204-05; M. Sandel, supra note 3, at 66, 138.

[95] Dworkin also identifies another type of individualist theory as "duty-based". The main difference between the two is that a rights-based theory focuses on the individual's independence of choice, while a duty-based theory is concerned with the individual's adherence to a moral standard. Both, unlike goal-based theories, are centered on the individual, and the two differ only in whether the emphasis is on individual conformity or individual indepen-

based theories are more concerned with community well-being than with individual welfare.[96] Although Dworkin admits that this classification is rather crude, it serves to highlight the difference between the individualistic modern paradigm and the communitarian classical paradigm.

The connection between liberalism and an atomistic conception of self goes much deeper than the difference between rights-based and goal-based theories of justice. The very primacy of justice in the liberal political philosophy is itself a manifestation of liberals' concern for individual values over fraternal values.[97] Michael Sandel's telling critique of John Rawls' theory of justice illustrates how an obsession with justice is only necessary in an ethos in which individuals are seen as separate and in conflict.[98] Rawls, like Dworkin, builds his entire jurisprudence around an individualistic conception of human nature.[99] He rejects utilitarianism because it "does not take seriously the distinction between persons,"[100] and devises a "veil of ignorance" to ensure that those who would agree

---

dence. Dworkin, supra note 7, at 171-72. Modern duty-based theories are comparatively rare. They might be characterized as a less mature version of either a rights-based or a goal-based theory. See infra notes 202-209 and accompanying text.

[96] Dworkin, supra note 7, at 172.

[97] As described by Michael Sandel:

> 'Deontological liberalism' is above all a theory about justice, and in particular about the primacy of justice among moral and political ideals. Its core thesis can be stated as follows: society, being composed of a plurality of persons, each with his own aims, interests, and conceptions of the good, is best arranged when it is governed by principles that do not *themselves* presuppose any particular conception of the good . . . .

See M. Sandel, supra note 3, at 1. Although Sandel offers a persuasive critique of Rawls' deontological individualism, his own project is less successful because he fails to adequately integrate community and intersubjectivity into his political theory. See Sagoff, Book Review: The Limits of Justice, 92 Yale L.J. 1065, 1080 (1983) (reviewing M. Sandel, supra note 3).

[98] Sandel contrasts Rawls' well-ordered society, with its emphasis on distributive justice, with the family, in which altruism and concern for others obviate the need for a developed theory of justice; he suggests that enforcing "justice" in a family situation is in fact destructive. M. Sandel, supra note 3, at 33; see Hardwig, Should Women Think in Terms of Rights?, 94 Ethics 441, 447 (1984); Olsen, The Family and the Market: A Study of Ideology and Legal Reform, 96 Harv. L. Rev. 1497 (1983).

[99] See, e.g., J. Rawls, supra note 91, at 251-57, 264; M. Sandel, supra note 3, at 10-11, 51-52, 61-64, 133, 148-49 (1982); Nagel, Rawls on Justice, *in* Reading Rawls: Critical Studies of A Theory of Justice 1, 9-10 (N. Daniels ed. 1974).

[100] J. Rawls, supra note 91, at 27.

to the basic terms of his contractarian system of justice remain uninfluenced by social constraints.[101]

Moreover, one of the constraints of Rawls' "original position" (the blind state of nature from which he derives the contractual terms of justice) is that the participants are mutually disinterested, without reason to further the interests of others.[102] The depth of Rawls' attachment to this individuated conception of the self may be seen in his characterization of benevolence as a "second-order" notion. Determined to incorporate only widely shared propositions into his original position, Rawls assumes with little argument that benevolence, or concern for the interests of others, is not sufficiently embedded in human nature to find a place in the original position.[103] The modern paradigm exalts a devotion to one's own interests; a contemporary version of the classical paradigm, on the other hand, might consider benevolence a widely shared human trait.

Dworkin denies, although not very convincingly, that his version of liberalism adopts an atomistic or individualistic view of human nature.[104] Rawls does not deny that his theory is individualistic but argues that it is not incompatible with communitarian ideals.[105] The main premise of his argument for community is that only through union with others can an individual become complete.[106] Even this premise, however, is a weak endorsement of communitarian values because, as Sandel has noted, it presupposes distinct individuals with different needs and interests as the measuring unit.[107] Moreover, Rawls' premise that individuals "are to deliber-

---

[101] See Scanlon, Rawls' Theory of Justice, *in* Reading Rawls: Critical Studies of A Theory of Justice 169, 171 (N. Daniels ed. 1974). Scanlon himself notes that an individualistic conception of persons "may not be absolute," nor is the conception itself "formed outside of or independent of particular social and historical circumstances." Id. at 178. This admission, coupled with Scanlon's suggestion that despite the conception's contextual nature, it is "uncontroversial" in this "era and civilization," illustrates the pervasiveness of the modern paradigm. See id.

[102] See J. Rawls, supra note 91, at 127-29.

[103] Id. at 191. Rawls dismisses concern for the interests of others as "extensive ties of natural sentiment." Id. at 129. Sandel criticizes Rawls' relegation of benevolence to "second-order" status. M. Sandel, supra note 3, at 171.

[104] Dworkin, supra note 7, at 142.

[105] See Rawls, Fairness to Goodness, 84 Philos. Rev. 536 (1975).

[106] See J. Rawls, supra note 91, at 523; M. Sandel, supra note 3, at 61.

[107] See supra note 4 and accompanying text.

ate as if they prefer more rather than less primary goods,"[108] already incorporates an unconnected view of human nature, in which self-interest is paramount to altruism.

At base, liberal moral theory is individualistic largely because it excludes any intersubjective conceptions of self;[109] without an intersubjective self, the contours of the conflict between individual and community are antecedently determined. Although modern liberalism may recognize the necessity of connection, it emphasizes individualism to such an extent that wherever the two conflict—as they are bound to do[110]—it is the modern and not the classical paradigm that prevails.[111] The depth of contemporary adherence to the atomism of the modern paradigm may be illustrated by Edwin Baker's comment that "most people in the post-Enlightenment world" will accept the basic Rawlsian premise of autonomy.[112]

In addition to a decidedly individualist bias, liberal jurisprudence exhibits two other traits characteristic of the modern paradigm: liberalism epitomizes an abstract, rule-based theory, and liberalism is a highly pluralistic philosophy. In a world of self-interested individuals, abstract rules or principles are a necessary alternative to such contextual moral notions as virtue.[113] Dworkin's own notion of rights as "trump" is characteristic of liberal theories: in the game of life, we must find fair rules to play by.[114] The central idea of the liberal perspective is that of entitlement: "distinct individuals have interests that they are entitled to protect if they

---

[108] Rawls, supra note 105, at 543.

[109] See supra note 3.

[110] See, e.g., Brest, The Fundamental Rights Controversy: The Essential Contradictions of Normative Constitutional Scholarship, 90 Yale L. J. 1063 (1981); Kennedy, The Structure of Blackstone's Commentaries, 28 Buff. L. Rev. 205, 211-12 (1979); Shapiro, Fathers and Sons: The Court, the Commentators, and the Search for Values, *in* The Burger Court: The Counter-Revolution That Wasn't 218, 223-33 (V. Blasi ed. 1983).

[111] For example, while Rawls defines rights as the absence of restrictions and sets a minimal subsistence level for all members of society, he does not allow certain morally irrelevant factors, such as intelligence, luck, or a certain amount of economic good fortune, to count as "restrictions." As long as the worst off groups are better off in an absolute sense with these restrictions than they would be without them, his distributivist principles have been satisfied. See J. Rawls, supra note 91, at 75-78, 204, 224-26, 277-78. His theory of justice thus places "absolute well-being" above "relative share," see D. Richards, supra note 4, at 48, emphasizing the individualist rather than relational cast of his theory.

[112] Baker, Sandel on Rawls, 133 U. Pa. L. Rev. 895, 924 (1985).

[113] See supra notes 6-8 and accompanying text.

[114] Dworkin, supra note 7, at xi.

so wish."[115] The scope of individual entitlement, of course, varies with each theory. Dworkin, among many others, finds a right to "equality."[116] The basic Rawlsian right is "fairness"—which takes some six hundred pages to define. Still other theories list various individual liberties as rights. Each of these definitions of rights or entitlements, however, shares the common feature of abstractness. Once the entitlement is defined and the neutral principles specified, it remains only to follow the rules laid down.

The classical perspective, because it is less constrained by the fascination for "distinctness," can encompass a broader notion of what we owe to others as extensions of ourselves. Virtues, unlike rights, can be defined contextually. It may, for example, be virtuous to abort a child whose life will be filled with physical pain, and less virtuous to abort a child simply because he or she is of the "wrong" gender. Liberalism recognizes only that the woman has a right to an abortion (or that the fetus has a right to life), regardless of the circumstances. The notion of compassion further illustrates the difference between a right and a virtue because what constitutes compassion depends on the circumstances. Compassion may sometimes be a virtue; being the object of compassion can never be a right.[117]

Liberalism is also a quintessentially pluralistic philosophy. With no human *telos* against which to measure different theories of rights, liberalism has no hierarchy of values. A liberal state is therefore required to remain neutral toward its citizens' diverse and competing definitions of the good life.[118] Liberalism thus be-

---

[115] Id. at 176.

[116] Id. at 272-78.

[117] Judith Jarvis Thomson draws a similar distinction between rights (with their correlative duties) and moral virtues, or "oughts." See Thomson, A Defense of Abortion, 1 Phil. & Pub. Aff. 47, 60-62 (1971).

[118] See, e.g., B. Ackerman, supra note 7, at 10-12; A. MacIntyre, supra note 5, at 11, 235-37; M. Sandel, supra note 3; Dworkin, supra note 7; Heller, The Importance of Normative Decisionmaking, 1976 Wis. L. Rev. 385, 475; Tushnet, Darkness on the Edge of Town: The Contributions of John Hart Ely to Constitutional Theory, 89 Yale L.J. 1037-38 (1980). Although David A.J. Richards argues that liberals are free to criticize others' moral choices, he admits that the state must remain neutral: criticism is acceptable, penalties are not. Richards, supra note 93. Robin West has developed an intriguing theory of "pragmatic liberalism," which is committed to an evolving but non-neutral definition of the good life. West, Liberalism Rediscovered: A Pragmatic Definition of the Liberal Vision, 46 U. Pitt. L. Rev. 673 (1985). Whether or not it is a viable approach, it is definitely not a liberal approach.

comes mired in such endless conflicts as those between negative and positive rights, and between liberty and equality.[119]

C. Radical Jurisprudence: CLS and Unger

It is more difficult to see how the Conference on Critical Legal Studies (CLS) embodies the individualist paradigm. One might read that movement's ideology to reject the modern paradigm of autonomy in favor of the communitarian paradigm suggested here. Shiffrin notes that "democratic radicals" (his encompassing nomenclature for the critical legal scholars) criticize liberalism for being "excessively individualistic."[120] Roberto Unger explicitly denounces the liberal dichotomy between individual and society and seeks to reconcile the two under the ideal of sympathy.[121] Mark Tushnet has offered a powerful critique of the liberal theory of rights.[122] On closer examination, however, even the critical legal scholars vacillate between endorsement of a communitarian perspective and mere tinkering with the liberal perspective. Moreover, despite their desire to expose the underlying contextuality of the abstract propositions of liberalism, they exhibit a characteristically modern tendency toward abstraction.[123] Finally, the contrast be-

---

[119] See, e.g., Dworkin, supra note 7, at 123; Nagel, supra note 89.

[120] Shiffrin, supra note 88, at 1109.

[121] R. Unger, supra note 93, at 191-235. For examples of attempts to perform this reconciliation in a specific legal context, see, e.g., Sax, Takings, Private Property and Public Rights, 81 Yale L. J. 149 (1971); Note, Reinterpreting the Religion Clauses, supra note 85.

[122] Tushnet, An Essay on Rights, supra note 93; see Kennedy, Critical Labor Law Theory: A Comment, 4 Indus. Rel. L. J. 503 (1981).

[123] See Cole, Getting There: Reflections on Trashing From Feminist Jurisprudence and Critical Theory, 8 Harv. Women's L.J. 59, 65 (1985) ("by building abstraction upon abstraction, the trashers approach the kinds of formalism and idealism that they set out to critique"). The following exchange provides a delightful illustration of the masculine abstraction of radical scholarship:

> Morris: It's a very crude kind of historicism he's peddling, surely? And bad aesthetics.
> Hilary: This is all very fascinating, I'm sure, but could we discuss something a little more practical? Like what the four of us are going to do in the immediate future?
> Desiree: It's no use, Hilary. Don't you hear the sound of men talking?
> Morris: (to Philip) The paradigms of fiction are essentially the same whatever the medium. Words or images, it makes no difference at the structural level.
> Desiree: 'The structural level,' 'paradigms.' How they love those abstract words. 'Historicism'!

D. Lodge, Changing Places 250-51 (1975). Astute readers might ask why this article itself contains an abundance of references to paradigms and structures. As Carol Gilligan has

tween the classical paradigm and the critical legal scholars is most marked in the absence of any teleological underpinnings to modern radical scholarship.

Roberto Unger perhaps best exemplifies the radical effort to recognize and resolve the tension between autonomy and heteronomy.[124] Unger's attempted synthesis of individual and community captures the spirit of the conflict inherent in any attempt to reintegrate the classical tradition into the modern paradigm. Although he is fundamentally unable to suggest a realistic method for achieving this synthesis,[125] his discussion of the liberal failure to credit the relational aspect of the self indentifies liberalism with the modern perspective.

Even Unger, however, is unable to overcome the peculiarly modern attachment to a strong notion of individualism and autonomy. He warns of the consequences of too strong a commitment to connection: "The relational view threatens our ability to identify individuals or mankind. Because everything is ultimately connected with everything else, there would be no place to set the boundaries of individual or species nature."[126] He continues that theme in his more recent book:

> We present to one another both an unlimited need and an unlimited danger, and the very resources by which we attempt to satisfy the former aggravate the latter . . . .
>
> . . . Each of [our] ventures into a life of longing for other people

---

noted, women's fluency in the masculine voice "must correlate with educational attainment in society." DuBois, Dunlap, Gilligan, MacKinnon, & Menkel-Meadow, Feminist Discourse, Moral Values, and the Law—A Conversation, 34 Buff. L. Rev., 11, 59 (1985) (Gilligan) [hereinafter cited as DuBois].

[124] See Hutchinson & Monahan, The "Rights" Stuff: Roberto Unger and Beyond, 62 Tex. L. Rev. 1477 (1984) (suggesting that Unger provides a coherent and elaborate formulation).

[125] Unger appears to suggest, irrationally, that the community needs to be both limited in number and encompassing of all humanity. R. Unger, supra note 93, at 221. He also labels the ideal of sympathy—by which the reconciliation of self and community is achieved—as a "dreamt-of circumstance," id. at 217, perhaps suggesting that he recognizes the apparent impossibility of achieving such a reconciliation absent a new paradigm to illuminate the way. Other critical legal scholars also appear to recognize the current hopelessness of their utopian vision. See, e.g., Kelman, Trashing, 36 Stan. L. Rev. 293, 296 n.11 (1984); Kennedy, supra note 110, at 212-13.

[126] R. Unger, supra note 93, at 194. In another passage he seems equally despairing of the consequences of too much emphasis on either half of the dichotomy: "It is the experience of the conflict between the hope that one might think for oneself and the need to be understood or, to rephrase it in a stronger and negative form, between the fear of enslavement and the fear of madness." Id. at 215.

threatens to create a craven dependence and to submerge our individual selves under group identities and social roles.[127]

Other critical legal scholars appear equally unable to confront the classical paradigm of connection without real terror. Duncan Kennedy, for example, has suggested that "at the same time that it forms and protects us, *the universe of others . . . threatens us with annihilation* and urges upon us forms of fusion that are quite plainly bad rather than good."[128]

The radical position on the notion of individual rights is similarly ambivalent. Trashing liberalism and its attendant theory of rights is a favorite CLS pastime, but it "appears to be directed more at exposing the injustice of contemporary social relations than at denigrating the core idea of human rights."[129] Tushnet, for example, devotes a large portion of his critique of rights theory to demonstrating the potential for misuse of "rights-talk."[130] Peter Gabel has attempted to justify and transform the concept of rights for the achievement of radical ends.[131] Unger's own program contains a revised vision of rights as they would exist in his reconstituted society.[132] Although one motif of the Conference on Critical Legal Studies is the identification of the inevitable contextuality of our world, the amplification of this theme leads CLS into variations on modern rights theory.

The ultimate failure of the radical project confirms the final difference between the modern and classical paradigms. Radical jurisprudence attempts to reconcile the individual and community

---

[127] R. Unger, Passion: An Essay on Personality 20 (1984).

[128] Kennedy, supra note 110, at 212 (emphasis added); see Baker, supra note 112, at 897 (criticizing Sandel's notion of the group subject because it "could provide the basis for a dangerous and unwarranted notion of group or community rights"); Gordon, New Developments in Legal Theory, *in* The Politics of Law: A Progressive Critique 281, 288 (D. Kairys ed. 1982) ("one of the most threatening aspects of social existence [is] the danger posed by other people"); cf. Hutchinson & Monahan, supra note 124, at 1499 & n.105 (decrying Unger's optimism that a reconstituted society would choose the "right" values: "This optimistic leap of faith . . . has little basis in history.").

[129] Hutchinson & Monahan, supra note 124, at 1487; see id. at 1482-89. The CLS position on rights is not only ambivalent, it is often unintelligible. See, e.g., Gabel & Kennedy, Roll Over Beethoven, 36 Stan. L. Rev. 1, 37-41 (1984).

[130] Tushnet, An Essay in Rights, supra note 93, at 1386-94.

[131] Gabel, The Phenomenology of Rights-Consciousness and the Pact of the Withdrawn Selves, 62 Tex. L. Rev. 1563 (1984).

[132] See, e.g., Unger, The Critical Legal Studies Movement, 96 Harv. L. Rev. 563, 597-602, 611-15 (1983).

without any sense of what it is to be a member of a human community. The critical legal scholars, in their haste to deconstruct the world, have neglected to construct a human *telos*. Alasdair MacIntyre suggests that what the modern world lacks is a normative description of human aspiration: the Enlightenment, in rejecting Aristotelian teleology, destroyed the context of moral philosophy. Without such a context, post-Enlightenment moral theories were doomed to failure from the outset.[133] John Diggins ascribes the failure of American republicanism to the same lack: "Ultimately the idea of virtue had no determinative content, no transcendent quality that stood over and against the objective world of power and interests, no moral vision that inspired the individual to identify with values higher than his own interests."[134]

Radical jurisprudence is in this regard no different. Despite its claim of being a new paradigm, it is ultimately little more than a rejection of the old one: it is substantively empty because it has no teleological content. The reason for adopting a critical or radical approach, Tushnet has suggested, is because such a stance "is defined as the party in opposition to what exists."[135] The Conference on Critical Legal Studies seem to be, as one author has described the modernist movement in art, "less an argument *for* a particular style than a reaction *against* the traditional modes . . . ."[136]

Unger's work is again instructive because his is the most ambitious attempt to construct a post-modern paradigm by reintegrating the classical paradigm. After criticizing the liberal ideology, he attempts to construct a positive description of its successor.[137] He begins by sketching out the "social consciousness"[138] and outward manifestations of an unliberal state but concludes that such a survey "fails to supply a standard by which to judge the merits of the contending views and ideals."[139] He thus recognizes that, without a definition of the transcendent quality of humanity, no at-

---

[133] See A. MacIntyre, supra note 5 at 49-59.

[134] J. Diggins, supra note 22, at 31.

[135] Tushnet, An Essay on Rights, supra note 93, at 1398.

[136] Boyle, Modernist Social Theory: Roberto Unger's *Passion*, 98 Harv. L. Rev. 1066, 1077 (1985).

[137] See R. Unger, supra note 93, at 174.

[138] He uses "social consciousness" to mean something very like what Kuhn calls a paradigm: "The concept of social consciousness refers to a widely shared way of conceiving society and its relation to nature and to individuals." Id. at 148.

[139] Id. at 181.

tempt to revive the notion of man as part of a community can succeed.

When he tries to define such a transcendent quality, however, his attachment to modern individualism defeats the project from the outset. His explication suffers from two fundamental theoretical problems, which serve to turn his attempt at a positive description into yet another negative one.

First, he defines the universal quality of humanity as that of "a predicament rather than that of a substance."[140] What characterizes a human *telos* seems to be, for Unger, not the striving for a particular goal but the necessity of struggle in and of itself. In a later work, *Passion*, he makes this explicit: virtue consists in "context-smashing," or going beyond social context, and the human *telos* is context-transcendance itself.[141] It does not seem to matter where we go, just that we keep moving. There is thus no substantive content to his teleology.[142]

Second, he subscribes to the modern notion that a description of human nature is factual while any specification of a human *telos* is normative. The major project of *Passion* is to justify the discredited leap of faith from fact to value,[143] and to show that normative values can be derived from factual premises. What Diggins and MacIntyre appear to recognize, which Unger does not, is that a

---

[140] Id. at 195-96.

[141] See R. Unger, supra note 127, at 88-89. To say that Unger makes anything "explicit" may be to accord his work both more and less credit than it is due. What he says is that the Christian-romantic ethic is "corrigible" to the extent that it incorporates and reconciles a notion of empowerment. Id. at 69-76. He then states:

> Philosophy conceived in this spirit is simply context-smashing . . . . If someone were to ask us why we want to live in the present in this way, we should answer: first, because this is the kind of being we really are and, second, because by living in this fashion we empower ourselves individually and collectively.

Id. at 88-89.

[142] In this, Unger echoes the liberal emphasis on process as the most important human or jurisprudential value. See, e.g., J. Ely, Democracy and Distrust (1980); Tribe, Ways Not to Think About Plastic Trees: New Foundations for Environmental Law, 83 Yale L.J. 1315, 1338 (1974). Again, the radical scholars often criticize the liberal reliance on process but seem ultimately to endorse process over substance themselves.

[143] The most explicit declaration of Unger's underlying adherence to the dichotomy between facts about human nature and prescriptions about human conduct lies in frequent references to attributing normative force or normative consequences to conceptions of human nature or identity. This disjunction between a conception and its implications strongly suggests that he believes the former to be "fact" and the latter "value." See, e.g., R. Unger, supra note 127, at 3, 21, 40-41, 43, 78.

description of human nature must also be normative insofar as it presupposes "the existence of reasons for human action that are not contingent upon any desires or purposes that men actually have but are intrinsically authoritative."[144] In other words, what MacIntyre calls "untutored human nature" cannot be understood except in the context of the normative "human-nature-as-it-could-be-if-it-realised-its-*telos*."[145]

The urge to ground a prescriptive theory of human ends in concrete human *fact* is an instance of the second, rarer form of modernism's rejection of immanent *telos*: there must be an abstract quality out there somewhere, called "human nature," to which we can anchor our normative schemes: "The temptation to place the moral foundations of society in a pre-existing state of nature reflects the powerful wish to give one's favored scheme of values a precision and unconditional legitimacy that put it safely beyond the realm of political controversy."[146] A contextual paradigm recognizes that normative schemes, embedded in society and social roles, are all there are.

IV. Reviving The Classical Paradigm

There has recently been a resurgence of interest in the classical paradigm. In addition to the critical legal scholars, who do not explicitly identify their project with either Aristotelianism or republicanism, scholars in a number of disciplines are evidencing renewed interest in the classical paradigm. The best known modern Aristotelian is Alasdair MacIntyre, who argues quite cogently that a return to a morality grounded on a human *telos* and human virtues is the only solution to modern dilemmas.[147] Modern Jeffersonians abound and come in every imaginable political variety.[148]

---

[144] J. Diggins, supra note 22, at 31.

[145] A. MacIntyre, supra note 5, at 51.

[146] Kronman, supra note 10, at 1603.

[147] A. MacIntyre, supra note 5; see P. Foot, Virtues and Vices and Other Essays in Moral Philosophy (1978); I. Murdoch, The Sovereignty of Good (1971). It is interesting that of these most prominent modern classicists, one is explicitly Christian in outlook, see supra note 19, and two are women, see infra note 166.

[148] See R. Bernstein, Beyond Objectivism and Relativism: Science, Hermeneutics, and Praxis (1983); F. Dallmayr, Polis and Praxis: Exercises in Contemporary Political Theory (1984); Sunstein, supra note 28. Diggins characterizes the scholarship as an effort to "rescue America from liberalism." J. Diggins, supra note 22, at 19. Justice Powell, the only native Virginian on the Supreme Court, has explicitly adopted a Jeffersonian view of the historical

The most common theme of the new republicans is to suggest that our republican heritage is embodied in the Constitution and should be relevant to modern interpretations of that document.[149]

The renewed interest in the classical paradigm raises two important questions. The first, not dealt with in this article, seeks the causes for this resurgence of a long-dormant philosophy. The second concerns the future of classical theory. A political or moral philosophy based on virtue and community has failed at least once and perhaps as many as four times.[150] What is the likelihood that modern Aristotelianism will ultimately prove more persuasive than its predecessor or that the current variations on republicanism, unlike the Jeffersonian vision, may realistically be implemented?[151] Classical republicanism has always been identified as a backward-looking tradition;[152] is there any way to make it more forward-

---

circumstances surrounding the framing of the Constitution, arguing that promoting the general welfare was a primary motivation for the Constitution. See EEOC v. Wyoming, 103 S. Ct. 1054, 1075 (1983) (Powell, J., dissenting). What is particularly interesting, in light of the thesis of this article, is that Justice O'Connor was the only other justice to join his opinion.

[149] Cass Sunstein, for example, suggests that Madisonian liberalism seeks safeguards against the "naked preferences" of individuals and powerful interest groups. Sunstein, supra note 28, at 82; see Sunstein, Naked Preferences and the Constitution, 84 Colum. L. Rev. 1689 (1984). David Epstein's careful exigesis of *The Federalist* attempts to demonstrate that its authors were concerned not only with private rights but also with the public good as an end of government. See D. Epstein, supra note 65. Similarly, Jonathan Macey has suggested that the Constitution was designed to be "public-regarding" in the sense that it was designed to favor the interests of the polity over the desires of special-interest groups. Like the framers, however, Macey relies on the structure of the Constitution, rather than on human virtue, to achieve this object; he explicitly eschews any reliance on virtue. See Macey, Promoting Public-Regarding Legislation Through Statutory Interpretation: An Interest-Group Model, 86 Colum. L. Rev. 223 (1986).

[150] The Enlightenment constitutes the first, undisputed transition from the classical to the modern paradigm. Various interpretations of American history suggest that the drafting of the Constitution in 1787 and the fading of the anti-federalists of the early nineteenth century constitute two more failures of the classical paradigm. See supra notes 21-87 and accompanying text. Finally, a number of scholars have suggested that the critical legal studies movement has failed in its attempt to integrate the classical paradigm. See, e.g., Johnson, supra note 93, at 261-62, 285; Leff, Book Review, 29 Stan. L. Rev. 879 (1977); Shiffrin, supra note 88, at 1110 & n.33, 1179-87.

[151] John Diggins, for example, deplores Lockean liberalism but rejects the possibility of a revival of republicanism based on what he sees as a non-existent Jeffersonian heritage, advocating instead a Calvinist approach. See J. Diggins, supra note 22; Wood, Hellfire Politics, New York Review of Books, Feb. 28, 1985, at 29. Mark Tushnet suggests that regardless of the framers' ideology, "it is unclear that the republican tradition is readily available to us." Tushnet, Anti-Formalism in Recent Constitutional Theory, 83 Mich. L. Rev. 1502, 1540 (1985).

[152] See, e.g., Berthoff, Independence and Attachment, Virtue and Interest: From Republi-

looking and thus more viable? In particular, this article addresses the question whether a republican-inspired interpretation of the United States Constitution is either possible or distinct from current interpretations.

It is tempting to ascribe the death of virtue to an inevitable human progression, both personal and political.[153] Such a thesis may be bolstered by traditional theories of individual moral development, which suggest that individuals progress from a morality of self-centeredness through a morality of other-centeredness to a fully mature morality based on abstract, universal principles.[154] There is a striking parallel between the modern paradigm of political philosophy and such a mature individual morality. Lawrence Kohlberg describes the mature or "postconventional" stage in stunningly individualistic and abstract (i.e., modern) terms:

> To count as postconventional, . . . terms [like "rights"] must be used in a way that makes it clear that they have a foundation for a rational or moral *individual who has not yet committed himself to any group or society or its morality.*[155][The value] perspective [is that] of a rational individual aware of values and *rights prior to social attachments* and contracts.[156] [At this stage, the] [p]rinciples are universal principles of justice . . . .[157]

Perhaps the similarity between the modern paradigm and Kohlberg's highest stage of moral development is best captured in his description of the postconventional stage as embodying a "prior-to-society" individual perspective.[158]

The classical tradition, on the other hand, is marked by the "other-centeredness" characteristic of the middle stages of development. The similarity is illustrated by the quotation from Jeffer-

---

can Citizen to Free Enterpriser, 1787-1837, *in* Uprooted Americans: Essays to Honor Oscar Handlin 97, 101-102 (R. Bushman ed. 1979); Kramnick, supra note 22, at 631; Murrin, supra note 27, at 406. Cass Sunstein also suggests—and then attempts to refute—that republicanism might be too "romantic and outmoded" for the modern world. See Sunstein, supra note 28, at 76, 82.

[153] See, e.g., R. Unger, supra note 93, at 244-53.

[154] See Kohlberg, Moral Stages and Moralization: The Cognitive-Developmental Approach, *in* Moral Development and Behavior: Theory, Research, and Social Issues 31 (T. Lickona ed. 1976).

[155] Id. at 37 (emphasis added).

[156] Id. at 35 (emphasis added).

[157] Id.

[158] Id. at 33.

son cited earlier: "Self-interest, or rather self-love, or *egoism*, has been more plausibly substituted as the basis of morality. But I consider our relations with others as constituting the boundaries of morality."[159] Kohlberg describes the middle stage of maturity (the "conventional" level) as marked by "see[ing] things from the point of view of shared relationships between two or more individuals."[160] He also describes this level repeatedly in terms of subordination of individual interests to societal needs:

> [The identifying characteristics of the conventional stage are] (1) concern about social approval; (2) concern about loyalty to persons, groups, and authority; and (3) concern about the welfare of others and society . . . . What fundamentally defines and unifies the characteristics of the conventional level is its *social perspective*, a shared viewpoint of the participants in a relationship or a group. The conventional individual subordinates the needs of the single individual to the viewpoint and needs of the group or the shared relationship.[161]

Jefferson's rejection of self-interest in favor of a morality based on others might be viewed as a transition from the earliest (selfish) stages of morality to the middle stages. The transition from the other-centeredness of republicanism to the abstraction of liberalism thus might be seen to represent a transition to the highest stages. Under this theory, the rejection of the classical paradigm simply represents a maturing process, and attempts to revive it will ultimately fail unless some radically new factor is present.

Newer theories of moral development suggest, however, that the modern and classical paradigms do not simply mirror *consecutive* stages of moral development, but instead reflect a *continuing* human tension at both the personal and political levels.[162] If the tension between autonomy and heteronomy is newly resolvable every generation, and individual resolution of the tension largely determines what that generation's dominant philosophy will be, are we likely to resolve the tension any differently than earlier gen-

[159] Letter to Thomas Law, supra note 15, at 1032.

[160] Kohlberg, supra note 154, at 38.

[161] Id. at 33-36; see also id. at 34-35 (table of six moral stages).

[162] See N. Chodorow, The Reproduction of Mothering: Psychoanalysis and the Sociology of Gender (1978); D. Dinnerstein, The Mermaid and the Minotaur: Sexual Arrangements and the Human Malaise (1976); C. Gilligan, In A Different Voice: Psychological Theory and Women's Development (1982).

erations? To avoid the Scylla of liberalism's overemphasis on autonomy and the Charybdis of the neoclassical tendency to romanticize the community and subsume the individual, we must reconcile the modern and classical traditions, not simply replace the former with the latter.[163] None of the authors discussed so far offers a means by which that reconciliation can take place without, as Drucilla Cornell puts it, "having to jump over our own shadow."[164]

Recent feminist scholarship on differences between men and women, however, has far-reaching implications for the modern par-

[163] The ideal of reconciliation highlights another problem with the critical legal studies movement. CLS literature — from the law review articles to *The Lizard* — rejects any notion of conciliation, leaving instead an impression of confrontation. In criticizing the established order, these scholars seem to deny that there is any good in the world: a favorite deconstructionist exercise is to demonstrate how judicial responses we *thought* were benevolent were in fact counterproductive. See, e.g., Freeman, Legitimizing Racial Discrimination Through Antidiscrimination Law: A Critical Review of Supreme Court Doctrine, 62 Minn. L. Rev. 1049 (1978); Klare, Critical Theory and Labor Relations Law, *in* The Politics of Law: A Progressive Critique 65 (D. Kairys ed. 1982); Trubek, Complexity and Contradiction in the Legal Order: Balbus and the Challenge of Critical Social Thought About Law, 11 Law & Soc'y Rev. 529 (1977); Tushnet, A Marxist Analysis of American Law, 1 Marxist Persp. 96 (1978); cf. Hutchinson, From Cultural Construction to Historical Deconstruction, 94 Yale L. J. 209 (1984) (CLS response to the failure of liberalism is nihilism). The radical response to the existence of the dichotomy—and to the current dominance of individuality—is to disintegrate one's opponents and their viewpoints. The response described here, and ascribed to a feminine perspective, is to integrate the paradigms. Thus, the injection of a feminine viewpoint might significantly alter the style, and perhaps the underlying objective, of even the Conference on Critical Legal Studies. Reconciliation seems to be vital: one consequence of modern failures to reconcile self and community may be the rise of the law and economics movement. See Heller, The Importance of Normative Decisionmaking: The Limitations of Legal Economics as a Basis for a Liberal Jurisprudence—As Illustrated By the Regulation of Vacation Home Development, 1976 Wis. L. Rev. 385, 468-502.

It is not so surprising that even a radical movement excludes the feminine paradigm. Past radical groups have treated women little better than their liberal or conservative counterparts. See generally H. Eisenstein, Contemporary Feminist Thought 126 (1983) (women within the New Left treated as inferiors, servants, and sexual objects); S. Evans, Personal Politics: The Roots of Women's Liberation in the Civil Rights Movement and the New Left 76-87, 111-12, 176-79 (1979) (women viewed in accordance with traditional sex roles in civil rights projects and Students for a Democratic Society); A. Jaggar & P. Struhl, Feminist Frameworks 10-11 (1978) (male militants at Columbia attempted to impose domestic tasks on female militants). CLS appears to be no different. See Johnson, supra note 93, at 281 n. 89 (suggesting CLS is as white-male-dominated as the faculty of Yale Law School); cf. Schlegel, Notes Toward an Intimate, Opinionated, and Affectionate History of the Conference on Critical Legal Studies, 36 Stan. L. Rev. 391 (1984) (in discussing almost two dozen major figures in CLS, Schlegel mentions one woman, in passing, on the penultimate page of his article).

[164] Cornell, Toward a Modern/Postmodern Reconstruction of Ethics, 133 U. Pa. L. Rev. 291, 314 (1985).

adigm and its potential for shadow jumping. The new scholarship suggests that men and women, by and large, develop strikingly different conceptions of self and thus of the world. The next section of this article describes what might be called a feminine perspective and suggests that the feminine perspective strongly resembles the classical paradigm while the masculine perspective strongly resembles the modern paradigm. Although all of us have some mix of the two paradigms in our own world-view, and some men are more classical and some women more modern, the classical perspective may be more dominant in women:

> This is not to say that there is a monolithic "women's viewpoint" any more than there is a monolithic "men's viewpoint." Plainly there is not. Rather, it is to suggest that women's life experiences still differ sufficiently from men's that a diverse group of women would bring a somewhat different set of perceptions and insights . . . than would a similarly diverse group of men.[165]

If the modern paradigm is an inevitable result of male domination of the public sphere, the influx of large numbers of women into that sphere might radically alter the chances of re-integrating the classical paradigm or at least change the likely balance of the resolution of the tension between the two paradigms.[166]

---

[165] Williams, The Equality Crisis: Some Reflections on Culture, Courts, and Feminism, Women's Rts. L. Rep. 175, 175 n.2 (1982). Williams appears to limit the effect of different "life experiences" to "certain issues," id., presumably those especially affecting women. For a refutation of this latter argument, see infra notes 169-70 and accompanying text.

[166] See Olsen, Statutory Rape: A Feminist Critique of Rights Analysis, 63 Tex. L. Rev. 387, 400-01 n.64 (1984) (suggesting that "legal liberalism" is a result of male dominance). Two of the best modern attempts at reconciling the paradigms are made by women. See Cornell, supra note 164; West, supra note 118. Drucilla Cornell reconciles them under the theory of "dialogism," and Robin West under the theory of "pragmatic liberalism," but both represent a conscious attempt to integrate self and community, to achieve, in Cornell's words, a theory of a "decentered subject, relational at its core . . . [but which] does not dissolve the self totally in an all-encompassing community." Cornell, supra note 164, at 299. The men writing in the area tend simply to deconstruct the liberal paradigm or resurrect the classical paradigm but do not integrate the two. See, e.g., A. MacIntyre, supra note 5; M. Sandel, supra note 3; R. Unger, supra note 93. But see Shiffrin, supra note 88, at 1111-12, 1192-1215 (synthesizing the two schools under the rubric of "eclectic liberalism"). Many simply despair of the possibility of reconciliation. See, e.g., Brest, supra note 110, at 1108; Johnson, supra note 93, at 257; Tushnet, Following the Rules Laid Down, supra note 93. It is delightfully ironic that in the same article in which Brest expresses pessimism that this fundamental tension between self and other can ever be resolved, he also asks, in the context of identifying judges as their law clerks' "adopted fathers," "[w]ho knows how our world might appear if one could honestly add 'or mothers'?" Brest, supra note 110, at 1106

V. Women's Perspective: Recapturing the Jeffersonian Moment

A. *Introduction*

New studies in a variety of academic disciplines suggest that women in fact may have a unique perspective, a world-view that differs in significant respects from that of men. Feminist scholars in such diverse fields as philosophy, history, sociology, art, and anthropology have identified peculiarly feminine perspectives in those disciplines.[167] Recent work in psychology and in literary theory is particularly illuminating. Psychological studies suggest that women's moral development and concept of self may differ from those of men. Feminist literary theory suggests that women's writing differs from men's in ways that reflect a radically different perspective. Despite the independence of the research and the differences in both topics of investigation and terms of description, the feminine perspective identified in each of these fields is, at its core, a single, common approach. That approach is captured in the tension between women's primary concern with intimacy or connection and men's primary focus on separation or autonomy.[168]

---

n.230. Perhaps he would not be so certain the tension is unresolvable if "or mothers" could honestly be added.

[167] See R. Morgan, The Anatomy of Freedom: Feminism, Physics and Global Politics (1982); N. Noddings, supra note 19; E. Showalter, A Literature of Their Own (1977); P. Spacks, The Female Imagination (1975); Blecki, Feminist Literary Criticism: An Introduction, *in* Feminist Literary Criticism: A Symposium 1 (K. Bordan & F. Rinn eds. 1974); Harding & Hintikka, Introduction, *in* Discovering Reality: Feminist Perspectives on Epistemology, Metaphysics, Methodology, and Philosophy of Science ix (S. Harding & M. Hintikka eds. 1983); O'Brien, Feminist Theory and Dialectical Logic, *in* Feminist Theory: A Critique of Ideology 99 (N. Keohane, M. Rosaldo, & B. Gelpi eds. 1982); Garfunkel, The Improvised Self: Sex Differences in Artistic Identity (Dissertation, Dep't of Psych. & Soc. Rel., Harv. Univ., 1984); Goodman, Women's Studies: The Debate Continues, N.Y. Times Magazine, Apr. 22, 1984, at 39; Kolbert, Scientifc Ideas: Women's vs. Men's, N.Y. Times, Oct. 17, 1985, at C1, col. 1; Goleman, Psychology Is Revising Its View of Women, N.Y. Times, Mar. 20, 1984, at C1, col. 1.

[168] The most persuasive explanation for the differences between men and women is based on differences between boys' and girls' development of an ego or sense of self. Ego development occurs while the child is still quite young and is therefore significantly influenced by the child's primary caretaker. Because, in general, girls are raised by a primary caretaker of the same gender and boys are raised by a primary caretaker of the opposite gender, girls reaffirm their early attachments while boys repudiate them. Thus, women come to see themselves as fundamentally connected and men see themselves as fundamentally detached. See N. Chodorow, supra note 162, at 166-68; C. Gilligan, supra note 162, at 5-23. Other explanations for the differences between men and women include the socialization process,

This difference between men and women may influence the manner in which they think about, write about, and practice their disciplines. Thus, it is probable that women's unique perspective on law and jurisprudence, as a function of their different world-view, extends well beyond areas traditionally seen as affecting women,[169] and in fact encompasses all legal issues. Just as women's writing on all subjects—not just on intimacy, domesticity, or women's place in society—reflects a different cast, women's views on the law in general may provide insights and approaches that are less natural to, and therefore less available to, male lawyers and judges.

This different approach to the law makes women a potentially innovative force in the legal community. Because women have been excluded from the mainstream of legal authority and legal change, the legal system, like moral, political, and philosophical discourse, has become "a set of cultural and symbolic forms that view human experience from the distorted and one-sided perspective of a single gender."[170] This is not to suggest merely that the legal structure

---

the mother's varying reaction to sons and daughters, and biological differences. See, e.g., E. Erikson, Identity, Youth and Crisis (1968); E. Janeway, Man's World, Woman's Place: A Study in Social Mythology (1971); J. Miller, Toward a New Psychology of Women (1976); Flax, The Conflict Between Nurturance and Autonomy in Mother-Daughter Relationships and Within Feminism, Fem. Stud., June 1978, at 171.

[169] It long has been recognized that women may make unique contributions to specific areas of law because personal experience in those areas gives them a distinct perspective on the legal rules and underlying policy considerations. Until recently, female educators and practitioners alike generally have been channeled into a few limited areas of law, primarily areas such as family law, trusts and estates, and discrimination law. See, e.g., Fossum, Women Law Professors, 1980 Am. Bar Found. Research J. 903, 911-13; White, Women in the Law, 65 Mich. L. Rev. 1051, 1063 (1967). One limitation of the view that women make "unique contributions" to certain areas of the law is that it relies on the premise that one cannot fully understand an aspect of the law unless one has personally experienced it. Thus, only members of minority groups can teach discrimination law, only women can teach rape law, and so on. If this is followed through to its logical conclusion, all law teachers will ultimately become specialists in unalterable areas, depending not only on gender but also on ethnic, social, and economic backgrounds. For example, black students at Harvard Law School boycotted a course on race discrimination because it was taught by Jack Greenberg, a white lawyer with extensive civil rights litigation experience. See N.Y. Times, Aug. 9, 1982, at A9, col. 1. This is socially unwise, educationally unsound, and may well be constitutionally defective.

[170] O'Brien, supra note 167, at 99. As early as 1946, Justice Douglas noted that:

> The truth is that the two sexes are not fungible; a community made up exclusively of one is different from a community composed of both; the subtle interplay of influence one on the other is among the imponderables . . . . [A] flavor, a distinct quality is lost if either sex is excluded.

ignores or minimizes significant gender differences,[171] but rather that because women have been excluded from shaping our legal structure in general, that structure reflects a distorted view of the tension between autonomy and connection and between the individual and society.

What sort of distortion has the masculine paradigm introduced into our legal system? Feminist scholars identify three primary dichotomies between men's and women's thinking: while women emphasize connection, subjectivity, and responsibility, men emphasize autonomy, objectivity, and rights. Although the parallels between the feminine perspective and classical paradigm, or between the masculine perspective and modern paradigm, are not precisely congruent, the similarities are too strong to ignore.

Recall the introductory description of the characteristic differences between the classical and modern paradigms. The contrast between women's emphasis on connections among individuals, and men's on individual autonomy, is almost exactly parallel to that between classical holism and modern atomism. Women's preference for a subjective approach, and men's for an objective approach, recall the dichotomy between contextuality and abstraction. Finally, the male emphasis on rights matches the modern paradigm's reliance on an abstract, rule-based method for mediating between competing interests in a pluralist society; the feminine ethic of caring and responsibility suggests instead the classical tendency to define human existence in terms of relationships to others and to favor contextual societal values and individual virtues. The remainder of this section explores these similarities in detail.

A brief caveat is in order. First, I am not contending that gender-based differences are universal, only that they are likely enough that the historical exclusion of women from the shaping of

---

Ballard v. United States, 329 U.S. 187, 193-94 (1946).

[171] The Supreme Court's treatment of pregnancy-based classifications illustrates the tendency to treat women as if they were men. See General Elec. Co. v. Gibert, 429 U.S. 125 (1976); Geduldig v. Aiello, 417 U.S. 484 (1974); see also Wildman, The Legitimation of Sex Discrimination: A Critical Response to Supreme Court Jurisprudence, 63 Or. L. Rev. 265, 280-84, 301-04 (1984) (discussing the Supreme Court's inability to view reproductive freedom cases as essentially sexual discrimination cases). It is equally fallacious, however, to assume that legal recognition of gender differences is the solution. Doctrinal recognition of generalized gender differences is dangerous because it both perpetuates those differences and adopts an unfairly universal approach to a contextual problem. See Law, Rethinking Sex and the Constitution, 132 U. Pa. L. Rev. 955, 968 (1984); Wildman, supra.

the legal system has had a profound impact, which cannot be reversed—or, to a large extent, even recognized—until women begin to participate in that enterprise. Second, I am not limiting my analysis to a feminist perspective: feminists have a particular political agenda that may or may not be shared by all women (and is shared by some men). Rather, this is an analysis of a feminine perspective that encompasses aspects of personality and relationship to the world that have nothing to do with one's political preferences.[172] Finally, I am not suggesting that the feminine perspective

[172] For examples of authors suggesting the existence of a femin*ist* perspective rather than a femin*ine* perspective, see, e.g., H. Eisenstein, supra note 163 (alternates between the two); J. Elshtain, supra note 19, at 221 (discussing the political prescriptions of radical feminist discourse); MacKinnon, Feminism, Marxism, Method and the State: Toward A Feminist Jurisprudence, 8 Signs: J. Women in Culture & Soc'y 635 (1983) (describing the liberal state as the embodiment of male interest and suggesting a feminist theory of state); Polan, Toward A Theory of Law and Patriarchy, *in* The Politics of Law: A Progressive Critique 294 (D. Kairys ed. 1982) (suggesting a marxist-feminist approach to law).

The few legal scholars who have suggested the existence of a femin*ine* jurisprudence fall into three categories. First, a number of authors have made the suggestion, with little or no elaboration on the potential content or effect of a feminine jurisprudence. See, e.g., Fox, Goodbye to Gameplaying, Juris Dr., Jan. 1978, at 37; Pearson & Sachs, Barristers and Gentlemen: A Critical Look at Sexism in the Legal Profession, 43 Mod. L. Rev. 400, 413 (1980); Williams, supra note 165, at 175 n.2. Second, there are those who believe that a feminine perspective is either derived from, or useful for, resolving "women's issues." See, e.g., Cole, Strategies of Difference: Litigating For Women's Rights In a Man's World, 2 J.L. & Inequality 33, 51-52 (1984); DuBois, supra note 123, at 13-15 (Dunlap); Freedman, Sex Equality, Sex Differences, and the Supreme Court, 92 Yale L.J. 913, 965-68 (1983); cf. Karst, Woman's Constitution, 1984 Duke L.J. 447, 460-61, 480, 485 (a feminine perspective can be used for this and more). This argument suffers from an overly narrow focus. See supra note 169. In particular, a focus on women's perspective as "the voice of the victim" suggests that the perspective is limited merely to remedying gender inequality (broadly conceived). See, e.g., DuBois, supra note 123, at 27-74 (MacKinnon).

Third, two authors have attempted the project I address in the text, but with a more limited scope. Carrie Menkel-Meadow has sketched out the difference a women's perspective makes in pedagogical technique and in the procedural form of the legal system, but she has not extended the analysis to jurisprudential matters. See DuBois, supra note 123, at 50-59 (Menkel-Meadow); Menkel-Meadow, Portia, In a Different Voice: Speculations on a Woman's Lawyering Process, 1 Berkeley Women's L.J. 39 (1985); Menkel-Meadow, Women in Law?: A Review of Cynthia Fuchs Epstein's *Women in Law*, 1983 Am. Bar Found. Research J. 189, 192. Menkel-Meadow, Women as Law Teachers: Toward the Feminization of Legal Education, *in* Humanistic Education in Law: Essays on the Application of a Humanistic Perspective to Law Teaching, Monograph III at 16 (1981) (Project for the Study and Application of Humanistic Education in Law: Columbia Univ. School of Law).

Kenneth Karst also has described potential feminine innovations in constitutional law but has limited himself to innovations "within the range of permissible judicial interpretation of the Constitution as we know it." Karst, supra, at 480. His article also focuses only on differences in moral perception, rather than on the wholly different paradigm I am suggesting

is any better than the masculine perspective, just that it is different. The incorporation of a new perspective need not imply a hierarchical ranking; I am arguing merely that the law has been distorted by its one-sided focus and that the feminine perspective described here represents a move toward correcting that distortion.[173] In particular, the feminine perspective is a natural reflection of the classical paradigm, and its integration is likely to remove the particular distortions of modern liberalism.

B. Connection and Automomy

Like the classical paradigm, the feminine perspective views individuals primarily as interconnected members of a community. Nancy Chodorow and Carol Gilligan, in groundbreaking studies on the development of self and morality, have concluded that women tend to have a more intersubjective sense of self than men and that the feminine perspective is therefore more other-directed.[174] Other studies tend to confirm this finding.[175] The essential difference between the male and female perspectives mirrors the fundamental difference between the modern and classical paradigms: "[t]he basic feminine sense of self is connected to the world, the

---

here. A more fundamental problem with Karst's analysis is that he seems to equate the feminine paradigm with liberal (or perhaps somewhat radical) political ideology. See, e.g., id. at 495 & n.185. In doing so, he defeats his own purpose, for he all but suggests that the feminine paradigm was operating (albeit unconsciously) in the Warren era. See, e.g., id. at 497-99; DuBois, supra note 123, at 14-15, 69 (Dunlap, DuBois). Finally, Karst is correct to disclaim the ability of a male to explore a feminine paradigm, see, e.g., Karst, supra, at 447-48; his own masculine emphasis on autonomy manifests itself sporadically throughout the article. See, e.g., id. at 477 (identifying the dilemmas of autonomy, but assuming that autonomy is something to strive for despite its dilemmas); id. at 479 (describing autonomy as "threatening" to women, rather than as unnecessary or simply outside their emotional ken).

[173] As Carol Gilligan notes, the discourse about the two perspectives in the context of jurisprudence "is no longer either simply about justice or simply about caring, it is about bringing them together to transform the domain." DuBois, supra note 123, at 45; see id. at 60-61 (Gilligan).

[174] See N. Chodorow, supra note 162; C. Gilligan, supra note 162. See also DuBois, supra note 123, at 47-48 (Gilligan) (in one study, five percent of men and 60% of women tended to focus on the feminine rather than the masculine perspective).

[175] For example, even at a very young age, female children tend to be more dependent on and reluctant to leave their mothers. See Goldberg & Lewis, Play Behavior in the Year-Old Infant: Early Sex Difference, 40 Child Dev. 21 (1969); Messer & Lewis, Social Class and Sex Differences in the Attachment and Play Behavior of the Year-Old Infant, 18 Merrill-Palmer Q. Behav. & Dev. 295 (1972).

basic masculine sense of self is separate."[176] Women thus tend to see others as extensions of themselves rather than as outsiders or competitors.[177]

Gilligan suggests that Kohlberg's description of a morally mature person—a "rational individual aware of values and rights prior to social contracts" who adopts "universal principles of justice," including "respect for the dignity of human beings as individual persons"[178]—instead describes a masculine morality.[179] That masculine perspective embodies the individualism inherent in the modern paradigm. The parallel between the classical paradigm and feminine morality, by contrast, is clearly illustrated by Gilligan's quotation of a typical female response to a moral dilemma:

> By yourself, there is little sense to things. It is like the sound of one hand clapping, the sound of one man or one woman, there is something lacking. *It is the collective that is important to me*, and that collective is based on certain guiding principles, one of which is that *everybody belongs to it*, and that you all come from it. You have to love someone else, because while you may not like them, you are inseparable from them. In a way, it is like loving your right hand. *They are part of you; that other person is part of that giant collection of people that you are connected to.*[180]

Women's emphasis on connection also suggests that the cliche that women are more cooperative and less competitive than men may have some basis in fact. Historically, women have tended to

---

[176] N. Chodorow, supra note 162, at 169; see Chodorow, Family Structure and Feminine Personality, *in* Woman, Culture and Society 43, 44 (M. Rosaldo & L. Lamphere eds. 1974) (feminine personality defines itself in relation and connection to other people more than does masculine personality); Douvan, New Sources of Conflict in Females at Adolescence and Early Adulthood, *in* Feminine Personality and Conflict 31, 38 (1970); Garai & Scheinfeld, Sex Differences in Mental and Behavioral Traits, 77 Genetic Psych. Monographs 169, 270 (1968); C. Gilligan, supra note 162, at 8 ("femininity is defined through attachment"). But see E. Maccoby & C. Jacklin, The Psychology of Sex Differences 142-50 (1974).

[177] Psychologists use the term "fluid ego boundaries" to suggest what I am calling an intersubjective sense of self. For theories that women's ego boundaries are more fluid (and thus that their conceptions of self are more intersubjective), see N. Chodorow, supra note 162, at 67-99, 169; J. Miller, supra note 168, at 71-73; Carlson, Sex Differences in Ego Functioning: Exploratory Studies of Agency and Communion, 37 J. Consulting & Clinical Psych. 267, 270-71 (1971); Gutmann, Women and the Conception of Ego Strength, 11 Merrill-Palmer Q. Behav. & Dev. 229 (1965); Scheman, supra note 8, at 238-39.

[178] Kohlberg, supra note 154, at 34-35 (describing the post-conventional level).

[179] See C. Gilligan, supra note 162, at 18-22.

[180] Id. at 160 (some emphasis in original, some added).

achieve their goals communally; from quilting bees to consciousness-raising sessions, women have banded together rather than striving individually.[181] There are analogous differences between the organization and ideology underlying women's traditional dominion, the family, and men's traditional arena, the marketplace: as Frances Olsen notes, the market is based on an individualist ethic and the family on an altruistic ethic.[182]

Some of the most intriguing evidence of a feminine perspective comes from the field of literary criticism, where feminist critics are discovering characteristic differences in both style and substance between male and female authors. In seeking to identify this "uniquely female literary consciousness,"[183] they are discovering indications of a similar tension between autonomy and connection. Male writers typically portray individuals as existing prior to and divorced from society. The male metaphor, and the male travail, is individualist.[184] In contrast, women writers are less apt to focus on purely individual heroism. Unlike the archtypal masculine "coming of age" novel, the developing feminine counterpart describes women's maturation in the context of a group of women, the definition of one "self" from among many "selves":

> For the woman writer, "the group" is a kind of interior quest, a portrait of the artist as several different young selves—contrasting,

---

[181] See, e.g., N. Auerbach, Communities of Women: An Idea in Fiction (1978); S. Evans, supra note 163, at 214-15 (small groups became the primary structure of women's liberation); G. Lerner, The Majority Finds Its Past: Placing Women in History 43, 121 (1979); Heilbrun, A Response To *Writing and Sexual Difference*, *in* Writing and Sexual Difference 291, 292 (E. Abel ed. 1982). Women's preference for cooperation over competition may explain early findings that women feared success. Sassen, Success Anxiety in Women: A Constructivist Interpretation of Its Source and Significance, 50 Harv. Educ. Rev. 13 (1980).

[182] Olsen, The Family and the Market: A Study of Ideology and Legal Reform, 96 Harv. L. Rev. 1497, 1505 (1983); see also M. Sandel, supra note 3, at 33 (family life governed by the principle of justice differs in kind from family life governed by spontaneous affection). The universality of separate spheres for men and women is reflected in the distinction between the public political world and the private world of household or family made in all but the simplest society. See J. Elshtain, supra note 19, at 6, 14.

[183] Showalter, Introduction, *in* The New Feminist Criticism: Essays on Women, Literature, and Theory 6 (E. Showalter ed. 1985); see Showalter, Feminist Criticism in the Wilderness *in* The New Feminist Criticism: Essays on Women, Literature, and Theory 243 (E. Showalter ed. 1985).

[184] See S. Gilbert & S. Gubar, The Madwoman in the Attic: The Woman Writer and the Nineteenth Century Literary Imagination 67 (1979); Baym, Melodramas of Beset Manhood: How Theories of American Fiction Exclude Women Authors, *in* The New Feminist Criticism: Essays on Women, Literature, and Theory 63, 71 (E. Showalter ed. 1985).

> perhaps warring, images that are ghosts of her adult destiny. She exorcises them by giving each self her own life. The group portrait thus releases the "other" woman within the mature writer—all those women she chose not to be when she grew up.[185]

Feminist literary critics are also beginning to identify some characteristically feminine styles, which also suggest an intersubjective perspective. For example, women writers more frequently use a technique of rotating a novel's perspective from one character to another.[186] This technique is often criticized by male critics,[187] and it may be that women authors are more receptive to the technique because they are better able to perceive not only the relations among characters but also those between themselves and the characters they create. They almost literally "become" their characters (male and female) for the same reason that their intersubjective perspective keeps them from fully separating themselves from others. Males, on the other hand, with their emphasis on autonomy, see the technique as a violation of the ideal of separation.

C. *Contextuality and Abstraction*

Scholarship in literature and psychology also suggests that women are more contextual and men more abstract. Piaget, for example, found that girls playing children's games tend to treat the rules of the game as less fixed and more flexible than do boys and that girls are more likely to stop a game altogether—thus preserving friendships—if a dispute arises. For boys, development and application of fixed, abstract rules is almost as important as the object of the game itself.[188] Again, Kohlberg's description of moral development (i.e., the development of the masculine perspective) stresses a progression from context-bound judgments to abstract moral principles.[189] Women, on the other hand, in responding to moral dilemmas, tend instead to look to circumstances rather than to abstractions: the right moral response depends on the context.[190]

---

[185] Gould, Life After Radcliffe, N.Y. Times Book Review, Sept. 23, 1984, at 9.

[186] See, e.g., Mellown, Character and Themes in the Novels of Jean Rhys, *in* Contemporary Women Novelists: A Collection of Critical Essays 118, 130 (P. Spacks ed. 1977).

[187] Id.

[188] See J. Piaget, The Moral Judgment of The Child 82 (1965); see also Lever, Sex Differences in the Games Children Play, 23 Social Probs. 478 (1976) (similar findings).

[189] See Kohlberg, supra note 154.

[190] See C. Gilligan, supra note 162, at 38.

This concept of feminine reliance on context is borne out in some empirical experiments. For example, the greater familiarity of even young boys with universal principles is well illustrated by a simple experiment in which boys and girls were shown pictures of everyday objects and asked to group related objects:

> [B]oys tend to bracket together objects (or pictures of objects) whose intrinsic characteristics are similar, whereas girls weight more heavily the functional and relational characteristics of the entities to be compared. For instance, boys frequently bracketed together such entities as a truck, a car, and an ambulance, while girls bracketed such entities as a doctor, a hospital bed, and an ambulance.[191]

The boys focused on the abstraction of "locomotion," seeing the objects as independent units, while the girls emphasized instead the concrete relationships among objects.[192] Other studies confirm that males of all ages are better able to separate discrete objects from their backgrounds and relationships than are females. Males are said to be less field-dependent; that is, they have a greater "ability to overcome the influence of an embedding context."[193]

Moreover, current controversies in philosophy tend to break down along gender lines. Despite exceptions, male philosophers often endorse more abstract and less contextual theories. For example, mainstream discussions of virtue tend to assume that virtues are abstract qualities. Committing murder under dangerous circumstances, though a criminal act, may still constitute an instance of the virtue of courage. Philippa Foot, on the other hand, suggests that virtues are contextual, not abstract: the virtue of courage is exhibited only under circumstances where the act itself can be considered courageous.[194]

Some of the most sophisticated attempts to develop "concrete universals"—a notion of essences (*teloi*) located in space and

[191] Hintikka & Hintikka, How Can Language Be Sexist? *in* Discovering Reality: Feminist Perspectives on Epistemology, Metaphysics, Methodology, and Philosophy of Science 139, 145 (S. Harding & M. Hintikka eds. 1983) (footnote omitted).

[192] Id. at 145-46; see Maccoby, Sex Differences in Intellectual Functioning, *in* The Development of Sex Differences 25-55 (E. Maccoby ed. 1966).

[193] J. Sherman, On the Psychology of Women: A Survey of Empirical Studies 21 (1971); see Witkin & Goodenough, Field Dependence and Interpersonal Behavior, 84 Psychological Bull. 661, 662 (1977) (explaining concept of field dependence).

[194] See P. Foot, supra note 147, at 15-17.

time[195] and thus reconciling context with the notion of a human *telos*—have been written by women.[196] Iris Murdoch, for example, deplores the loss of a human *telos*, but denies that her (or anyone's) moral theories can be used "as a formula which can be illuminatingly introduced into any and every moral act."[197] She explicitly argues that moral concepts are necessarily "concrete universals."[198] That women are disproportionately represented among modern philosophers seeking both a contextual and a teleological moral theory suggests that, for whatever reason, the reconciliation of the modern and classical paradigms is more natural to women.

Literary criticism also recognizes the difference between the abstraction of men and the concreteness of women. One critic has suggested, for example, that George Eliot's *Mill on the Floss* illustrates the tension between the male notion of universal maxims and the female unwillingness to differentiate the universal from its particular applications.[199] Women's writing has also been charac-

---

195 See Gould, The Woman Question: Philosophy of Liberation and the Liberation of Philosophy, *in* Women and Philosophy: Toward a Theory of Liberation 5 (C. Gould & M. Wartofsky eds. 1976). Gould defines the concept of concrete universality by contrasting it with abstract universality. Within the abstract conception, universals are only those things common to all humans and so are fixed and unchanging. Id. at 9, 27. The concrete universal, by contrast, is the totality or all common and all different characteristics of a class. Id. at 26. The concrete universal, therefore, is not a fixed essence, but "develops in time . . . [and is] concretely located in history and society." Id. at 27.

196 Philippa Foot attempts to construct a contextual theory of virtue. See P. Foot, supra note 147. Iris Murdoch rejects the modern concept of identity as dependent upon impersonal reality, and tries to construct a contextually teleological moral theory based on morality as "an individual . . . making a specialized personal *use* of a concept." I. Murdoch, supra note 147, at 25. Robin West describes "pragmatic liberalism" as essentially requiring a contextual teleology: pragmatic liberalism is "committed to a *naturalistic* and *evolving* conception of the good life," as opposed to either a "moralistic and static" conception or "indiscriminate preference maximization." West, supra note 118, at 674, 682. Drucilla Cornell attempts to revive the Hegelian concept of "geist" to reconcile universality and context. Cornell, supra note 164, at 359-372. Whether these attempts are characterized as revivals or as reformations of the classical paradigm, they all reject the modern paradigm.

197 I. Murdoch, supra note 147, at 42-43; see Gould, supra note 195, at 5 (describing the philosophic approach of concrete universality and suggesting that it can be used to analyze the position of women).

198 I. Murdoch, supra note 147, at 29.

199 Jacobus, The Question of Language: Men of Maxims and *The Mill on the Floss*, *in* Writing and Sexual Difference 37, 42 (E. Abel ed. 1982). Jacobus contrasts Eliot's remark, in her novel, that "the man of maxims is the popular representative of the minds that are guided in their moral judgment solely by general rules," with the view of the central character, Maggie Tulliver—" 'to lace ourselves up in formulas is to ignore the special circum-

terized (and criticized) as less linear and unified and more fluid than men's;[200] this again suggests a focus on context rather than on abstract rules of progression. Even feminine literary criticism is more contextual: Elaine Showalter has suggested that one characteristic of feminist criticism is the rejection of (masculine) objective, non-experiential critical theories.[201]

D. Responsibility and Rights

Until recently, the archetypal developmental continuum of individual moral sensibility was believed to be an orderly progression from self-centeredness through other-centeredness to the development of logical, independent, universal principles—rights—that depend neither on one's own needs nor on what others believe is right.[202] Although this progression mirrors male moral development, it fails to reflect the moral growth pattern of women.[203]

Gender-based differences in moral structure, long seen as evidence of women's moral immaturity,[204] may in fact be evidence of a feminine morality that differs in its emphasis from that of males. In her study of moral development, Carol Gilligan found that women tend to view a moral problem as "a problem of care and responsibility in relationships rather than as one of rights and rules."[205] When faced with the moral dilemma of whether a man should steal a drug he cannot afford to save his dying wife, Gilligan found that, while men struggle with the conflicting rights of the parties, women focus on the druggist's "moral obligation to show compassion,"[206] "not on the conflict of rights but on the failure of response."[207] Although men and women may agree that the man ought to steal the drug, men justify it in terms of a resolution be-

---

stances that mark the individual lot.' " Id. (quoting G. Eliot, Mill on the Floss 628 (A. Byatt ed. 1979)).

[200] Gardiner, On Female Identity and Writing By Women, *in* Writing and Sexual Difference 177, 185 (E. Abel ed. 1982); Jacobus, supra note 199, at 39-40.

[201] Showalter, Feminist Criticism in the Wilderness, supra note 183, at 244.

[202] See L. Kohlberg, The Philosophy of Moral Development (1981); Kohlberg, supra note 154.

[203] See C. Gilligan, supra note 162, at 18-22.

[204] See L. Kohlberg, supra note 202; N. Noddings, supra note 19, at 42; J. Sherman, supra note 193, at 101-02.

[205] C. Gilligan, supra note 162, at 73.

[206] Id. at 54 (quoting a subject of Gilligan's study).

[207] Id.

tween conflicting rights of husband and druggist, and women in terms of the need for more compassion by the druggist in the face of the husband's compassion for his wife.[208] Whether personal or political,[209] the moral structure of "mature" males reflects a paradigm of independent rights, while that of females emphasizes relational responsibilities.

Gilligan's work suggests that moral development from the conventional level may take either of two directions: progression toward a contextual moral theory (expanding on Aristotelian notions of what is right or good but placing human *teloi* in context) *or* progression toward an abstract moral theory (emphasizing rights as a form of trump). Recognition of alternative routes of moral development may shed new light on the failure of Jeffersonian republicanism and the ultimate triumph of liberalism. The classical paradigm, especially in its republican form, may be an example of the conventional level on the verge of its masculine successor. The republican vision represented an incomplete or immature ideology, but its maturation might have taken either of two paths: development of a mature virtue-based ideology or rejection of virtue in favor of rights. The former reflects a feminine vision, the latter a masculine perspective. Because the feminine paradigm has been conspiciously absent from the shaping of moral or political traditions, the development of the nation's ideology has paralleled individual moral development in the male pattern, not the female pattern.[210]

---

[208] See, e.g., id. at 29.

[209] The two types of morality—personal and political—are intimately connected: "every moral vision is ultimately and irreducibly a political vision: a vision (or understanding or experience) of the world and of our place, as fundamentally social beings, in that world." Perry, Freedom of Expression: An Essay on Theory and Doctrine, 78 Nw. U.L. Rev. 1137, 1149 (1984).

[210] Anthony Kronman has described an analogous bifurcated path out of the Hobbesian state of nature. He suggests that parties in a state of nature, wishing to enter into contracts that neither they nor any third party has the pure strength to enforce, must develop mechanisms to provide security of performance. Three of his potential mechanisms presume that the parties' interests are unalterably opposed to one another and thus rely on such hostile devices as taking hostages. These mechanisms are quintessentially masculine. The final mechanism he describes as "union": the parties "reduce the risk of opportunism by taking steps to increase the likelihood that each will see his own self-interest as being internally connected to the welfare of the other." This last mechanism is fundamentally feminine. Although Kronman suggests that all four mechanisms still survive in our post-nature law of contracts, the very numerical imbalance between masculine and feminine mechanisms illus-

VI. Toward a Feminine Jurisprudence: The Feminine Perspective of Justice O'Connor

The preceding argument suggests that the Constitution, especially in light of subsequent interpretations in the liberal tradition, is a quintessentially masculine document. Calls for a more classical interpretation are unlikely to succeed as long as the interpreters are exclusively male. But the interepreters are no longer exclusively male. Justice O'Connor's four years on the Supreme Court provide an excellent opportunity to test the thesis that a feminine perspective might result in a feminine jurisprudence and to sketch the contours of one version of that jurisprudence. If the thesis is correct, O'Connor's jurisprudence should differ in characteristically feminine or classical ways from the jurisprudence of her brethren. The remainder of this article will explore the feminine aspects of her jurisprudence. In particular, it will focus on differences between Justices O'Connor and Rehnquist: because they are otherwise ideologically similar, and because they so often vote together,[211] their disagreements are significant. This pattern of disagreement is highly suggestive of the operation of a uniquely feminine perspective.[212]

A. *Community Values*

Despite the fundamental dichotomy between a jurisprudence of rights and a jurisprudence of community, there is one type of case in which the two will intersect to yield the same result. Both individualists and communitarians may be expected to protest infringement of individual rights that protect against diminution of

trates the prevalence of the masculine paradigm. See Kronman, Contract Law and the State of Nature, 1 J.L. Econ & Organization 5 (1985).

[211] During the 1981 term, O'Connor and Rehnquist voted together in 81.6% of the Court's full-opinion decisions; in 1982-1983 they voted together in 85.7% of the Court's full-opinion decisions; and in 1983-1984 they voted together in 91.9% of the Court's full-opinion decisions. In the 1981 and 1983 terms, only Brennan and Marshall voted together more often, and in the 1982 term no two justices did so. See The Supreme Court, 1981 Term, 96 Harv. L. Rev. 62, 305 (1982); The Supreme Court, 1982 Term, 97 Harv. L. Rev. 70, 296 (1983); The Supreme Court, 1983 Term, 98 Harv. L. Rev. 87, 308 (1984).

[212] This data cannot be quantified or proven scientifically and is thus open to criticism that it is possible to find indications of a feminine perspective in the writings of *any* Justice. These indications are, however, so prevalent in O'Connor's jurisprudence, and so characteristic of her disagreements with her brethren, that I doubt whether an analysis of any other Justice's work would yield such a consistently suggestive pattern.

or exclusion from community membership. Two issues frequently before the Supreme Court exhibit this intersection. In establishment clause cases, government endorsement of religion might be deemed to devalue the community status of non-believers. In discrimination cases, a demand for equal treatment can be viewed as a demand to be treated as an equal member of the community. The common thread in these cases is that the rights at issue belong to individuals as members of communities rather than as autonomous units. While most constitutional and statutory rights protect the individual *against* the community, anti-establishment and anti-discrimination values safeguard the individual's right to *belong* to the community. It is therefore highly suggestive that O'Connor frequently disagrees with Rehnquist (and often with Chief Justice Burger as well) in such cases.

1. *Establishment Clause Cases*

In three major establishment clause cases, Justice O'Connor joined the majority in striking down state statutes while Justice Rehnquist dissented.[213] In several other cases, the two justices disagreed at least in part.[214] This pattern of disagreement suggests that O'Connor does not fully share Rehnquist's hostility to individual rights. O'Connor's explanation of her position on the establishment clause is not, however, fully congruent with established liberal doctrine on the protection of individual rights. She relies instead on a strikingly unique vision of the harms that the establishment clause is intended to prevent. That vision fits the feminine paradigm to the extent that it derives its force from a preference for notions of community over notions of individual rights.

---

[213] See Thornton v. Caldor, Inc., 105 S. Ct. 2914 (1985); Wallace v. Jaffree, 105 S. Ct. 2479 (1985); Larkin v. Grendel's Den, Inc., 459 U.S. 116 (1982).

[214] See Aguilar v. Felton, 105 S. Ct. 3232 (1985) (both justices dissent from majority invalidation of parochial school aid program, but on different grounds); Grand Rapids School Dist. v. Ball, 105 S. Ct. 3216 (1985) (majority invalidates two programs providing public aid to parochial schools: Rehnquist would uphold both programs, but O'Connor only one); Lynch v. Donnelly, 465 U.S. 668 (1984) (both join majority in upholding public display of creche, but O'Connor concurs separately to "clarify" her view of the appropriate test); Larson v. Valente, 456 U.S. 228 (1982) (majority invalidates reporting regulations applicable to some religious organizations but not others: neither O'Connor nor Rehnquist would grant standing, but only Rehnquist joins White's dissent on the merits).

Justice O'Connor first described her own views of the establishment clause in *Lynch v. Donnelly.*[215] In that case, the Court upheld, against an establishment clause challenge, the inclusion of a creche in a municipality's annual Christmas display. Justice O'Connor joined the majority opinion but also wrote separately "to suggest a clarification of [the Court's] Establishment Clause doctrine."[216] She read the precedents to establish a rule forbidding "government endorsement or disapproval of religion."[217] Her explanation for that rule reveals her reliance on the values of community rather than individual rights: "Endorsement sends a message to nonadherents that they are outsiders, not full members of the political community, and an accompanying message to adherents that they are insiders, favored members of the political community. Disapproval sends the opposite message."[218]

This theory came to fruition a year later in *Wallace v. Jaffree.*[219] In *Lynch*, O'Connor had found no message of exclusion from community in the decision to erect a creche. In *Wallace*, she found that Alabama's school prayer statute did communicate such a message. She therefore joined the "liberal" majority in voting, over strong dissents by Burger, White, and Rehnquist, to invalidate the statute. She did not, however, join Stevens' majority opinion, which held that, under the three-prong test developed in *Lemon v. Kurtzman*,[220] the statute was fatally flawed by its religious purpose. She relied instead on the test she had fashioned in *Lynch*. In light of the controversy surrounding the statute's enactment, she held that an "objective observer" would necessarily conclude that both the intended and received message of the statute was endorsement of religious activity. Elaborating on the importance of community membership, O'Connor suggested that diminution of that membership, as well as exclusion from the community, violates the establishment clause: "the religious liberty protected by the Establishment Clause is infringed when the government makes adherence to religion relevant to a person's standing in the politi-

[215] 465 U.S. 668 (1984).
[216] Id. at 687 (O'Connor, J., concurring).
[217] Id.at 688
[218] Id.
[219] 105 S. Ct. 2479 (1985).
[220] 403 U.S. 602 (1971).

cal community."[221]

A theory that characterizes the evil of government endorsement of religion as a detriment to one's membership in the community, rather than as a violation of one's individual rights, goes a long way toward explaining the pattern of disagreement between O'Connor and her fellow conservatives. Although she often joins the conservative contingent in denying protection to ordinary individual rights—those that inhere solely in the individual—she is less willing to permit violations of what might be termed intersubjective individual rights. Government endorsement of religion deprives individuals of what O'Connor views as a value qualitatively different from most ordinary individual rights: full membership in the community. This very anomalous sort of right derives its force not from the independence of individuals but from their mutual interdependence.

2. *Discrimination Cases*

Although it is not surprising that Justice O'Connor is more receptive to claims of gender discrimination than is Justice Rehnquist,[222] it is more difficult to explain her greater willingness to remedy the effects of race discrimination and discrimination against aliens.[223] Moreover, in several cases that defy easy charac-

---

[221] *Wallace*, 105 S. Ct. at 2497 (O'Connor, J., concurring).

[222] See, e.g., Arizona Governing Comm. v. Norris, 463 U.S. 1073 (1983) (O'Connor finds paying lower retirement benefits to women violates Title VII; Rehnquist does not); Newport News Shipbuilding & Dry Dock Co. v. EEOC, 462 U.S. 669 (1983) (O'Connor finds failure to cover medical expenses of employees' pregnant spouses, when all other medical costs of spouses are covered, violates Title VII; Rehnquist does not); Mississippi Univ. for Women v. Hogan, 458 U.S. 718 (1982) (O'Connor finds exclusion of men from state nursing school violates equal protection clause; Rehnquist does not); North Haven Bd. of Educ. v. Bell, 456 U.S. 512 (1982) (O'Connor finds employment discrimination within the scope of Title IX's prohibition against gender discrimination by institutions receiving federal funds; Rehnquist does not); Zipes v. TWA, 455 U.S. 385 (1982) (both agree with majority that filing charges with the EEOC is an equitable, not a jurisdictional, prerequisite to bringing a suit under Title VII, but only Burger and Rehnquist join Powell's separate concurrence to stress the necessity of timely charges for any award of retroactive seniority). But see Grove City College v. Bell, 465 U.S. 555 (1984) (both agree that Title IX is limited to narrow program receiving federal funds); Ford Motor Co. v. EEOC, 458 U.S. 219 (1982) (both agree that, in a gender discrimination case under Title VII, an offer of reinstatement, even without an offer of retroactive seniority, tolls an employer's backpay liability).

[223] On race discrimination, see, e.g., Firefighters Local Union No. 1784 v. Stotts, 467 U.S. 561 (1984) (in case limiting scope of affirmative action in employment, O'Connor writes separately to stress the narrowness of the Court's holding); Guardians Ass'n v. Civil Serv.

terization, the difference between her position and that of Justice Rehnquist seems to lie in her reluctance to accept conduct that condemns groups or individuals to outsider status. Although her reasoning in this area is less clearly articulated than in her establishment clause jurisprudence, an examination of several cases illustrates the underlying framework of an emphasis on community. That framework indicates that her greater sympathy for the victims of race or alienage discrimination is part of a consistent pattern of protection of the value of full membership in communities.

Two companion cases involving apportionment illustrate Justice O'Connor's views on discrimination. Apportionment cases involve one of the most fundamental aspects of community membership, the right to participate in the shaping of the community's values

---

Comm'n, 463 U.S. 582 (1983) (under Title VI, O'Connor would allow greater relief to victims of discrimination than would Rehnquist; she also notes that she might construe Title VI to prohibit non-intentional discrimination were the issue not foreclosed by precedent); Bob Jones Univ. v. United States, 461 U.S. 574 (1983) (O'Connor joins majority upholding IRS regulation making discriminatory schools ineligible for tax-exempt status; Rehnquist dissents); Kolender v. Lawson, 461 U.S. 352 (1983) (O'Connor finds "stop-and-identify" statute unconstitutionally vague, noting danger of discriminatory enforcement against particular groups; Rehnquist dissents); NAACP v. Claiborne Hardware Co., 458 U.S. 886 (1982) (O'Connor joins majority finding NAACP-sponsored boycott of white merchants protected by first amendment and therefore not subject to action for damages; Rehnquist concurs in result only, without opinion); Rogers v. Lodge, 458 U.S. 613 (1982) (O'Connor joins majority affirming district court's finding that at-large election district maintained for racially discriminatory purpose; Rehnquist dissents); Hathorn v. Lovorn, 457 U.S. 255 (1982) (O'Connor finds that state court asked to implement change in state voting laws must first determine whether pre-clearance by attorney general is necessary under Voting Rights Act; Rehnquist finds that state courts have no role in enforcing the Voting Rights Act); Blanding v. DuBose, 454 U.S. 393 (1982) (O'Connor joins per curiam opinion construing Voting Rights Act to require perfect compliance with detailed procedures; Rehnquist concurs, but writes separately to lament the "unreasonably burdensome and unrealistic control" over state and local governments given to the federal government under the Act.); Canaday v. Lumberton City Bd. of Educ., 454 U.S. 957 (1981) (O'Connor joins majority in granting injunction against annexation pending Voting Rights Act clearance; Rehnquist dissents); Board of Educ. v. Davis, 454 U.S. 904 (1981) (Court denies certiorari in school desegregation case; Rehnquist dissents).

On discrimination against aliens, see, e.g., Sure-Tan, Inc. v. NLRB, 467 U.S. 883 (1984) (O'Connor holds that employer commits unfair labor practice by reporting illegal alien to INS in retaliation for participation in union activities; Rehnquist dissents on ground that illegal aliens are not "employees" within the meaning of the NLRA); Bernal v. Fainter, 467 U.S. 216 (1984) (O'Connor joins majority in invalidating restriction of notary public status to citizens; Rehnquist dissents); Toll v. Moreno, 458 U.S. 1 (1982) (O'Connor would allow in-state tuition discrimination against some aliens; Rehnquist would allow it against all aliens).

through the electoral process. In *Brown v. Thomson*,[224] the Court upheld Wyoming's apportionment scheme for its house of representatives despite a maximum deviation of eighty-nine percent from population equality between counties. Justice Powell's opinion relied heavily on the fact that the plaintiffs were challenging only the representation granted to the state's least populous county. Under the apportionment formula provided by the Wyoming legislature, Niobrara County would not have been entitled to any representation in the Wyoming house. The legislative scheme, however, guaranteed each county at least one representative. Plaintiffs challenged Niobrara County's mathematically undeserved single representative on the ground that it diluted the votes of residents of more populous counties. O'Connor, Rehnquist, Burger, and Stevens joined Powell's opinion while Brennan, White, Marshall, and Blackmun dissented.

In *Karcher V. Daggett*,[225] decided the same day, the Court invalidated a New Jersey congressional apportionment scheme with a maximum deviation of 0.6984%. Justice Brennan's majority opinion held that the state failed to meet its burden of showing that "the population deviations in its plan were necessary to achieve some legitimate state objective."[226] O'Connor again joined the majority, along with Marshall, Blackmun, and Stevens; Burger, White, Powell, and Rehnquist dissented. Thus, Rehnquist, Burger, and Powell would have upheld imperfect apportionment schemes in both cases and Brennan, Marshall, and Blackmun would have invalidated both plans. The discrepancy in White's voting pattern apparently rested on the size of the numerical deviation, and Stevens explained his vote in *Karcher* as a vote against deliberate political gerrymandering.[227] What seems irreconcilable at first glance is O'Connor's approval of the large deviation in *Brown* and her condemnation of the small deviation in *Karcher*.

O'Connor explained her apparently inconsistent votes in a concurrence in *Brown*.[228] After an initial bow both to equality as a guiding ideal and to a need for flexibility, she relied on two aspects

---

[224] 462 U.S. 835 (1983).
[225] 462 U.S. 725 (1983).
[226] Id. at 740.
[227] Id. at 744 (Stevens, J., concurring).
[228] 462 U.S. at 848 (O'Connor, J., concurring). Stevens joined her concurrence in *Brown*, although she did not join his in *Karcher*.

of the Wyoming scheme to justify treating it more favorably than the New Jersey scheme. First, while New Jersey failed to demonstrate that its deviations were necessary to any non-discriminatory purpose, O'Connor had "no doubt that the population deviation resulting from the provision of one representative to Niobrara County is the product of the consistent and nondiscriminatory application of Wyoming's longstanding policy of preserving county boundaries."[229] Second, emphasizing that even this policy would not justify a statewide maximum deviation of eighty-nine percent,[230] O'Connor noted that the relevant deviation in the case was not the eighty-nine percent "when the State of Wyoming is viewed as a whole, but the additional deviation from equality produced by the allocation of one representative to Niobrara County."[231]

Both votes are consistent with classical republican ideals. In *Karcher*, O'Connor voted to uphold the principle of "one person, one vote," thus preserving to each citizen an undiluted voice in the electoral process. In *Brown*, however, that republican principle collided with another classical ideal. O'Connor's reliance on the importance of preserving county boundaries, a justification rejected by the liberal dissenters,[232] echoes a theme discussed in the next section: the notion of the community itself as an independent entity with interests to be protected. O'Connor was willing to protect individuals' access to community membership and participation only to the point at which it conflicted with ensuring the viability of a certain type of community. The priority of the community's interests, at the cost of diminishing the value of membership for some of its members, recalls the republican demand that individuals subordinate their selfish desires to the needs of the collective. O'Connor's emphasis on the fact that the additional deviation in this case was quite small suggests both a limit to the sacrifices that communities may demand of their members and a feminine tendency to examine apportionment questions in context rather than in the abstract.[233]

Another case involving neither race nor gender discrimination

---

[229] Id. at 849.
[230] Id. at 850.
[231] Id. at 849
[232] See id. at 853-55 (Brennan, J., dissenting).
[233] See supra notes 188-201 and accompanying text; infra notes 269-306 and accompanying text.

helps to elucidate the boundaries of O'Connor's view of the relationship between community values and discrimination. In *United Brotherhood of Carpenters & Joiners v. Scott*,[234] union members assaulted and severely injured nonunion employees. The victims sued under 42 U.S.C. § 1985(3), alleging a conspiracy to violate their civil rights. White's majority opinion held that the plaintiffs stated no cause of action. The claim of conspiracy to violate the victim's first amendment rights of association with other nonunion employees failed because it involved neither state action nor an attempt to influence state action. The majority then relied upon established precedent to hold that a section 1985(3) claim of conspiracy to deprive plaintiffs of equal protection of the laws does not require state action, but does require a class-based animus. The majority concluded that a bias against others because of their economic views or status did not constitute the requisite "class-based animus."

Unsurprisingly, the decision evoked an angry dissent from the liberals. Blackmun authored the dissent, which was joined by Brennan, Marshall, *and O'Connor*. Blackmun prefaced his lengthy and thorough historical examination of the legislative intent in enacting section 1985(3) with a telling description of how the problem ought to be framed:

> The Ku Klux Klan Act was the Reconstruction Congress' response to politically motivated mob violence in the postbellum South designed to intimidate persons in the exercise of their legal rights. . . . Today, in a classic case of mob violence intended to intimidate persons from exercising their legal rights, the Court holds that the Ku Klux Klan Act provides no protection.[235]

This characterization of the issue helps explain why an otherwise politically conservative Justice O'Connor might join the dissent. Mob violence aimed at intimidating persons from exercising legal rights—whether against blacks in the postbellum South or against the non-union employees in *Scott*—is a time-tested method of keeping outsiders on the outside. The majority's division of class-based animus into biases based on race, on political status, and on economic status, each subject to different rules under section

[234] 463 U.S. 824 (1983).
[235] Id. at 839-40 (Blackmun, J., dissenting).

1985(3), overlooks the fundamental similarity of all instances of mob violence inspired by a desire to keep members of another class from sharing in the benefits adhering to membership in the conspirators' own group.

A final case, *Zobel v. Williams*,[236] serves to highlight the unique status of the feminine perspective in modern jurisprudence. That case involved a challenge to an Alaska statute that distributed a state budget surplus to state residents in varying amounts depending on their length of residency. Burger, in an opinion joined by all the justices except Rehnquist and O'Connor, found the scheme invalid under the equal protection clause. Rehnquist, the sole dissenter, would have upheld the statute. O'Connor concurred in the judgment only: she found the statute valid under the equal protection clause but invalid as a violation of the right to travel protected by the privileges and immunities clause.

Alaska attempted to justify its distribution scheme as a way to reward residents for their past contributions to the state. Using only a rational basis test to strike down the statute, the majority found this objective illegitimate. O'Connor disagreed:

> I respectfully suggest . . . that the Court misdirects its criticism when it labels Alaska's objective illegitimate. A desire to compensate citizens for their prior contributions is neither inherently invidious nor irrational. Under some circumstances, the objective may be wholly reasonable. Even a generalized desire to reward citizens for past endurance, particularly in a State where years of hardship only recently have produced prosperity, is not innately improper.[237]

In a footnote, she suggested community volunteer work and contributions to the state's ecology as examples of the types of benefits to the community that it might be rational to reward.[238] Reiterating the legitimacy of rewarding past service to the community, O'Connor stated that she "would recognize them as valid goals and inquire only whether their implementation infringed any constitutionally protected interest."[239] She ultimately found such an infringement of the right to travel and therefore joined the majority

[236] 457 U.S. 55 (1982).

[237] Id. at 72 (O'Connor, J., concurring) (footnote omitted).

[238] Id. at 72 n.1.

[239] Id.

in holding the statute invalid.

O'Connor's opinion in *Zobel* is illuminating in a number of respects. Her refusal to find an equal protection violation in a case *not* involving a "discrete and insular minority"—a group with outsider status—is consistent with the feminine jurisprudential rejection of individual rights except where they implicate community membership. Her reliance on the right to travel suggests protection of the right to join a community: she notes that "[s]tripped to its essentials, the plan denie[d] non-Alaskans settling in the state the same privileges afforded longer term residents."[240] Most important, O'Connor, unlike most of the Court, is willing to allow communities to discriminate among members on the basis of their past willingness to suppress their own selfish desires for the benefit of the community. A republican community may—indeed must—reward individual virtue. An egalitarian community of autonomous individuals may not.[241]

3. *A Community Perspective*

A communitarian feminine jurisprudence is manifested in a variety of other O'Connor opinions. In several cases, she seems to treat the community as a discrete and important juridical entity. In *Allen v. Wright*,[242] parents of black public schoolchildren sought standing to challenge IRS procedures that were allegedly ineffective in preventing discriminatory private schools from illegally obtaining tax exempt status. The plaintiffs alleged that the availability of tax-exempt status for discriminatory private schools made it more difficult to integrate the public schools their children attended. O'Connor's majority opinion rejected this argument and several others, and found that the plaintiffs lacked standing. In attempting to base their standing to sue on the effect of the tax exemptions on public schools, the plaintiffs relied heavily on *Coit v. Green*.[243] In *Coit*, the district court allowed parents of black public school students to challenge the IRS grant of tax exemptions to

[240] Id. at 73.

[241] Contrast O'Connor with Baker's description of Rawlsian liberalism: "people in the original position, not knowing if they themselves would be virtuous, would not choose rules that aim at rewarding virtue." Baker, supra note 112, at 913.

[242] 104 S. Ct. 3315 (1984).

[243] 404 U.S. 997 (1971) (mem.).

racially discriminatory private schools.[244] The Supreme Court affirmed summarily. In *Allen*, O'Connor sought to distinguish *Coit* by focusing in part on the size of the affected community: she noted that "the suit in *Coit* was limited to the public schools of one State,"[245] in contrast to the *Allen* complaint, "which aims at nationwide relief."[246] As Brennan pointed out in dissent, the size of the community is irrelevant to standing but instead "relates solely to the scope of a properly certified class."[247] O'Connor's use of the distinction is therefore novel. It perhaps suggests an underlying perception that small, homogenous, cohesive communities are the appropriate targets of judicial relief.

Communities are not only independent juridical entities, but, in Justice O'Connor's view, they are often entitled to more favorable treatment than individuals. In *Block v. North Dakota*,[248] O'Connor was the sole dissenter from the Court's application of a general statute of limitations to bar a state's suit to quiet title. Her opinion stressed that the state should not be subject to the statute of limitations applicable to ordinary individuals because the state holds land "in trust for the public."[249] In *Idaho v. Oregon*,[250] she would have held ordinary rules limiting equitable remedies similarly inapplicable to a state's suit to protect its fishing rights.[251] Finally, in *Jefferson County Phamaceutical Association v. Abbott Laboratories*,[252] she would have held the sale of phamaceutical products to state and local government-operated hospitals (for resale in competition with private pharmacies) exempt from the Robinson-Patman Act. [253] She seemed again to rely on a notion that government institutions are unique because of their status vis-a-vis their citizens: she found the exemption appropriate because "[s]tate and local governments have developed programs for providing services to

[244] Green v. Connally, 330 F. Supp. 1150 (D.D.C. 1971), summarily aff'd sub nom. Coit v. Green, 404 U.S. 997 (1971).

[245] *Allen*, 104 S. Ct. at 3332.

[246] Id. at 3333.

[247] Id. at 3340 n.9 (Brennan, J., dissenting).

[248] 461 U.S. 273 (1983).

[249] Id. at 295 (O'Connor, J., dissenting).

[250] 462 U.S. 1017 (1983).

[251] See id. at 1032-38 (O'Connor, J., dissenting).

[252] 460 U.S. 150 (1983).

[253] See id. at 189 (O'Connor, J., dissenting).

the public . . . based on the . . . assumption [that they are exempt]."[254]

O'Connor is particularly unlikely to take a typical conservative approach—and thus particularly likely to disagree with Rehnquist—in cases implicating participation in the processes of government. On issues as diverse as restrictions on the broadcast media,[255] exemptions to the Freedom of Information Act,[256] interpretation of the Voting Rights Act,[257] and rewards to citizens for community service,[258] she has disagreed with Rehnquist (and often with the liberals as well) on the explicit or implicit ground that his position undermines the right or duty of citizens to participate in government. Inexplicable under ordinary conservative political theory, her position may reflect both an emphasis on membership in the community and a view that shaping the values of the community through governmental processes is one important function of community members.

O'Connor also is more likely to find and stress the "public purpose" of various governmental actions. In *Merrion v. Jicarilla Apache Tribe*,[259] she agreed with a liberal majority that the Indian tribe's taxing power derived from the tribe's general power to "control economic activities within its jurisdiction, and to defray the cost of providing governmental services;"[260] she rejected the conservative dissent's argument that it derived merely from the power to exclude non-Indians from reservation lands.[261] In a contracts clause case, *Energy Reserves Corp. v. Kansas Power & Light Co.*,[262] she joined a portion of a liberal majority opinion rejected by the conservative concurrences; the controversial section concluded that even if there had been an impairment of contract, there was a sufficient public purpose to uphold the governmental action.[263] She also wrote a unanimous opinion in a takings case, *Hawaii Housing Authority v. Midkiff*,[264] that can only be explained from a commu-

---

[254] Id. at 188 (O'Connor, J., dissenting).
[255] See FCC v. League of Women Voters, 104 S. Ct. 3106 (1984).
[256] See FBI v. Abramson, 456 U.S. 615 (1982).
[257] See cases cited supra note 223.
[258] See Zobel v. Williams, 457 U.S. 55 (1982).
[259] 455 U.S. 130 (1982).
[260] Id. at 137.
[261] See id. at 160 (Stevens, J., dissenting).
[262] 459 U.S. 400 (1983).
[263] See id. at 416-17.
[264] 104 S. Ct. 2321 (1984). For further discussion of this aspect of this case, see Sherry,

nitarian perspective, essentially approving land redistribution for its own sake.

Finally, describing O'Connor as a communitarian is as explanatory as the "conservative" label when it comes to her obvious hostility to the rights of criminal defendants. Not only does she constitute part of the core conservative majority in most criminal procedure cases, she occasionally construes the fourth and fifth amendments even more narrowly than some of her conservative brethren. In *Segura v. United States*,[265] she was the only justice to join Burger's characterization of the fourth amendment as primarily precluding unreasonable, rather than warrantless, seizures. In *Pillsbury Co. v. Conboy*,[266] only she and Stevens dissented from a holding that an individual could not be required to testify as to the content of his own grand jury testimony at a civil deposition without further grant of immunity. In *Colorado v. Nunez*,[267] a case in which certiorari was dismissed as improvidently granted, she joined White's concurring opinion reaching the merits of the fourth amendment question and construing that amendment to afford very narrow protection.[268] If the community is more important than individual rights, it is quite predictable that Justice O'Connor would be a strong law and order proponent: she will protect the community from crime even at the expense of the individual rights of criminal defendants.

B. *Virtue in Context*

The emerging jurisprudence of Justice O'Connor also exhibits a characteristically feminine perspective in its emphasis on contex-

Issue Manipulation by the Burger Court: Saving the Community from Itself, 70 Minn. L. Rev. 611 (1986).

[265] 104 S. Ct. 3380 (1984).

[266] 459 U.S. 248 (1983).

[267] 465 U.S 324 (1984).

[268] See id. at 326-27; see also New York v. Quarles, 467 U.S. 649 (1984) (O'Connor concurs in part and dissents in part; agrees that nontestimonial evidence derived from informal interrogation is admissable and states that she would agree with the Court's public safety exception to *Miranda* rule for oral statements if the Court were writing on a clean slate); Anderson v. Fuller, 455 U.S. 1028 (1982) (joining Burger dissent from denial of certiorari where court of appeals concluded that there was insufficient evidence of intention in a felony-murder conviction). But see Welsh v. Wisconsin, 466 U.S. 740 (1984) (O'Connor joins majority holding that a warrantless nighttime entry into defendant's home to arrest him for a non-jailable civil traffic offense violated the fourth amendment).

tual decisionmaking and its focus on the virtues of the decisionmaker rather than the rights of those about whom decisions are made. These two notions seem intertwined in the legal context insofar as the rejection of rigid, bright-line rules often undermines the protection of individual rights and thus leaves a gap in the theory of decisionmaking. The feminine focus on the virtue of connection—which, at least in the criminal context, often translates as compassion or mercy—fills that gap.

O'Connor often rejects bright-line rules and occasionally makes explicit her preference for contextual determinations. *Wilson v. Garcia*[269] involved the question of the appropriate statute of limitations for actions under 42 U.S.C. § 1983. Established doctrine under 42 U.S.C. § 1988 directs courts to look to state law for the appropriate limitations period, and courts accordingly have applied the limitations period applicable to the state cause of action most closely analogous to the section 1983 claim. This led courts to apply varying limitation periods to claims under section 1983, depending on the characterization of plaintiff's particular claim.[270] With O'Connor as the sole dissenter, the Court in *Wilson* decided that all section 1983 actions should be characterized as personal injury actions for purposes of determining the appropriate statute of limitation. Stevens' majority opinion rested primarily on a need for a uniform rule. O'Connor argued instead for the application of "individualized statutues of limitation."[271] She noted that the diversity of claims under section 1983, " 'ranging from simple police brutality to school desegregation cases,' "[272] made the Court's "single inflexible analogy" inappropriate.[273] She pejoratively characterized the majority's demand for uniformity as a mere " 'desire for symmetry of abstract legal principles.' "[274] Finally, she pointed out the new rule would not ensure uniformity: "The Court's new analogy lacks any magical power to conjure uniformity where diversity

---

[269] 105 S. Ct. 1938 (1985).

[270] See id. at 1946 & nn.32-33 (recognizing problem and citing cases).

[271] Id. at 1950 (O'Connor, J., dissenting).

[272] Id. at 1951 (quoting Note, Choice of Law Under Section 1983, 37 U. Chi. L. Rev. 494, 504 (1970)).

[273] Id.

[274] Id. at 1953 (quoting Mishkin, The Variousness of "Federal Law": Competence and Discretion in the Choice of National and State Rules for Decision, 105 U. Pa. L. Rev. 797, 813 (1957)).

is the natural order."[275]

O'Connor's strong dislike of bright-line rules is particularly evident in a labor case, *Charles D. Bonanno Linen Service v. NLRB*.[276] The sole issue in the case was whether a bargaining impasse justified an employer's withdrawal from a multiemployer bargaining unit. The majority adopted a uniform rule prohibiting withdrawal under those circumstances, and Burger's dissent (in which Rehnquist joined) advocated a uniform rule permitting withdrawal. O'Connor dissented separately to argue that the answer should depend on an examination of "the circumstances surrounding and following an impasse."[277] Similarly, in *United States v. Mechanik*,[278] Justice Rehnquist's majority opinion adopted a per se rule that subsequent conviction by a petit jury makes certain constitutional violations in the grand jury harmless error. O'Connor's concurrence rejected both the majority's rule and the presumption of the existence of prejudice from grand jury violations. She instead would direct courts to examine, in each case, whether "the violation substantially influenced the grand jury's decision to indict, or if there is grave doubt as to whether it had such effect." [279] Thus, even where she agrees with Rehnquist's result, she will sometimes file a separate opinion to record that the basis for her decision is the particular circumstances of the case.[280] She

[275] Id.; see Chardon v. Soto, 462 U.S. 650 (1983) (O'Connor joins majority in applying local rule, not uniform federal rule, pertaining to effect of denial of class certification on statute of limitations); DelCostello v. International Bhd. of Teamsters, 462 U.S. 151 (1983) (O'Connor dissents from application of uniform federal statute of limitations to an employee's combined suit against employer for breach of collective bargaining agreement and against union for breach of its duty of fair representation). O'Connor frequently disagrees with Rehnquist on statute of limitations issues, although not always in any particular pattern. See, e.g., County of Oneida v. Oneida Indian Nation, 105 S. Ct. 1245 (1985) (Rehnquist joins Steven's dissent; O'Connor does not); Honda Motor Co. v. Coons, 105 S. Ct. 808 (1985) (Rehnquist dissents from denial of certiorari; O'Connor does not); Simmons v. Sea-Land Serv. Inc., 459 U.S. 931 (1982) (White and O'Connor dissent from denial of certiorari; Rehnquist does not).

[276] 454 U.S. 404 (1982).

[277] Id. at 427 (O'Connor, J., dissenting); see Shepard v. NLRB, 459 U.S. 344 (1983) (Rehnquist writes majority opinion affirming NLRB refusal to award "complete relief" for violations of NLRB prohibition against "hot cargo" agreements; O'Connor alone dissents and would require NLRB to determine whether requested relief was necessary under the circumstances to effectuate the prohibition).

[278] 54 U.S.L.W. 4167 (U.S. Feb. 25, 1986).

[279] Id. at 4170.

[280] See, e.g., United States v. Boyle, 105 S. Ct. 687 (1985); Toll v. Moreno, 458 U.S. 1

also often writes separately to note that the Court's decision does not foreclose individual determinations to the contrary on remand or under other circumstances.[281]

O'Connor further elaborated her requirement of individualized decisionmaking in a criminal case that saw her aligned with the liberal majority against the conservative contingent. In *Eddings v. Oklahoma*,[282] she joined the majority holding that the eighth amendment requires an individualized consideration of mitigating circumstances in capital cases. The Court thus invalidated a state law that, as interpreted by the state courts, precluded the consideration of family background and personal history. The Chief Justice dissented, joined by White, Rehnquist, and Blackmun. O'Connor wrote a separate concurrence to explain the need for "extraordinary measures to ensure . . . that the sentence was not imposed out of whim, passion, prejudice, or mistake."[283] Those safeguards, in effect, ensure that the punishment is tailored to individual desert.

Individualized decisionmaking does not always lead O'Connor to a decision in favor of the individual. In *Mennonite Board of Missions v. Adams*,[284] she dissented (with Powell and Rehnquist) from the majority's finding that failure to observe a uniform requirement of notice by mail before property could be sold for taxes constituted a violation of due process. While the majority invalidated the sale because it failed to conform to the applicable rule, O'Connor would have held the notice sufficient under the particular circumstances of the case.

O'Connor's requirement of contextual decisionmaking apparently applies not only to the end result of a case but also to the Supreme Court's consideration of the applicable legal test. *Bearden v. Georgia*,[285] raised the question whether a court could

---

(1982).

281 See, e.g., Walters v. National Ass'n of Radiation Survivors, 105 S. Ct. 3180 (1985); United States v. Locke, 105 S. Ct. 1785 (1985); Ohio v. Kovacs, 105 S. Ct. 705 (1985); General Bldg. Contractors Ass'n v. Pennsylvania, 458 U.S. 375 (1982); Smith v. Phillips, 455 U.S. 209 (1982).

282 455 U.S. 104 (1982).

283 Id. at 118 (O'Connor, J., concurring).

284 462 U.S. 791 (1983).

285 461 U.S. 660 (1983). O'Connor's invalidation of the automatic revocation of probation is also an example of her compassionate view of punishment in general. See infra notes 295-301 and accompanying text.

revoke the probation of an indigent who failed to pay a fine and restitution. O'Connor's majority opinion held that where the probationer fails to pay through no fault of his own, a court must first determine whether there are any alternatives to imprisonment before revoking probation. Earlier cases involving imprisonment of indigent defendants had rested exclusively on equal protection grounds,[286] and the parties in *Bearden* consequently focused on whether strict scrutiny or rational basis was the appropriate standard of review.[287] O'Connor rejected this formulaic approach and decided the legal issue itself by reference to the circumstances:

> Whether analyzed in terms of equal protection or due process, the issue cannot be resolved by resort to easy slogans or pigeonhole analysis, but rather requires a careful inquiry into such factors as "the nature of the individual interest affected, the extent to which it is affected, the rationality of the connection between legislative means and purpose, [and] the existence of alternative means for effectuating the purpose."[288]

O'Connor thus seems to reject the rigid, abstract decisionmaking process that characterizes modern equal protection law.

One prerequisite for individualized decisionmaking is a modicum of procedural protections to ensure accurate assessment of individual circumstances. Thus, although O'Connor is unwilling to enforce the rights of criminal defendants where those rights are peripheral to the truthfinding function of the criminal justice system,[289] she jealously guards other sorts of procedural protections. She has joined majority opinions, over Rehnquist dissents, in cases holding that indigent defendants are guaranteed *effective* assistance of counsel on first appeal,[290] that a state must provide an indigent defendant with a psychiatric expert if the defendant makes a preliminary showing that sanity is likely to be a significant factor at trial,[291] and that technical procedural rules cannot bar a defendant from obtaining the protection of an instruction that cautions the jury not to draw an adverse inference from the defendant's failure

---

[286] See Tate v. Short, 401 U.S. 395 (1971); Williams v. Illinois, 399 U.S. 235 (1970).
[287] *Bearden*, 461 U.S. at 665.
[288] Id. at 666-67 (footnote omitted) (quoting Williams v. Illinois, 399 U.S. 235, 260 (1970) (Harlan, J., concurring)).
[289] See supra notes 265-68 and accompanying text.
[290] See Evitts v. Lucey, 105 S. Ct. 830 (1985).
[291] See Ake v. Oklahoma, 105 S. Ct. 1087 (1985).

to testify.[292] Full consideration of factual and legal circumstances is conducive to individualized decisionmaking, and O'Connor therefore is generally hostile to procedural "technicalities," whether they preclude consideration of issues favorable to the state or the criminal defendant.[293] Outside the criminal context, she again favors greater procedural protections than the conservative label would predict.[294]

Another general exception to O'Connor's adoption of the conservative, law-and-order position is the area of punishment in general and capital punishment in particular. An examination of her opinions in this area suggest three characteristically feminine aspects. First, punishment decisions are a quintessential example of her call for individualized decisionmaking, leading her to eschew hard and fast rules condemning individuals to death.[295] Second, leniency toward convicted criminals suggests that she may allow the virtue of mercy or compassion to alter the formal rules of the criminal justice system.[296] Third, she tends to focus on the responsibil-

---

[292] See James v. Kentucky, 466 U.S. 341 (1984); see also Carter v. Kentucky, 450 U.S. 288 (1981) (establishing right to such instruction).

[293] Compare New York v. Quarles, 467 U.S. 649, 660 (1984) (O'Connor, J., concurring) (suggesting that she might be willing to alter *Miranda* requirements) with Boag v. MacDougal, 454 U.S. 364 (1982) (joining majority that liberally construes an indigent prisoner's pro se complaint and therefore reverses its dismissal).

[294] See, e.g., Cleveland Bd. of Educ. v. Loudermill, 105 S. Ct. 1487 (1985); Gregory v. Town of Pittsfield, 105 S. Ct. 1380 (1985) (O'Connor dissenting from denial of certiorari).

[295] See, e.g., Enmund v. Florida, 458 U.S. 782, 827-31 (1983) (O'Connor, joined by Rehnquist, dissents from majority opinion invalidating death penalty in felony-murder conviction for lack of intent, but agrees that case should be remanded for a new sentencing hearing because court failed to consider individual mitigating circumstances); Eddings v. Oklahoma, 455 U.S. 104 (1982) (O'Conner concurs to emphasize need for individualized consideration of mitigating circumstances).

[296] See, e.g., Arizona v. Rumsey, 467 U.S. 203 (1984) (O'Connor's majority opinion held that sentencing procedure in a capital case is equivalent to trial on the merits of imposing the death penalty, and the double jeopardy clause prohibits death sentence on remand after life sentence was set aside); Ralston v. Robinson, 454 U.S. 201 (1981) (O'Connor joins Steven's dissent from majority holding that a juvenile sentence could be converted into an adult sentence, which would result in more severe confinement conditions); see also Brown v. Chaney, 105 S. Ct. 601 (1984) (Burger, White, and Rehnquist, but not O'Connor, dissent from denial of certiorari where lower court had vacated death sentence). O'Connor also declined to join Rehnquist's dissent in Caldwell v. Mississippi, 105 S. Ct. 2633 (1985), discussed infra. Although she did not comment on specific portions of his opinion, and it is therefore impossible to describe exactly her views on compassion and mercy, it is at least plausible to suggest that she would not subscribe to the following (paradigmatically male) comment in Rehnquist's opinion:

> Despite the Court's rhetorical references to the need for "reliable" sentencing deci-

ity and virtue of the decisionmaker rather than on the rights of the defendant.[297]

O'Connor's concurring opinion in *Caldwell v. Mississippi*[298] illuminates her focus on the responsibility of the decisionmaker rather than the rights of the defendant. *Caldwell* was a challenge to a death sentence imposed after the prosecutor told the jury:

> [Y]our decision [to impose the death sentence] is not the final decision . . . Your job is reviewable . . . [Defense counsel is] insinuating that your decision is the final decision and they're gonna take Bobby Caldwell out in front of this Courthouse in moments and string him up and that is terribly, terribly unfair. For they know, as I know, and as Judge Baker has told you, that the decision you make is automatically reviewable by the Supreme Court. Automatically[.][299]

Marshall's majority opinion vacating the sentence focused on the likelihood that such an instruction would create unreliability and bias against the defendant. In a typically male or modern or liberal characterization of the constitutional flaw in the prosecutor's statement, Marshall concluded that:

> The "delegation" of sentencing responsibility that the prosecutor here encouraged would thus not simply postpone *the defendant's right to a fair determination of the appropriateness of his death; rather it would deprive him of that right*, for an appellate court, unlike a capital sentencing jury, is wholly ill-suited to evaluate the appropriateness of death in the first instance.[300]

O'Connor joined most of the majority opinion and concurred in the result, but she wrote separately primarily to clarify that she did not interprete *California v. Ramos*[301] to preclude giving accu-

---

> sions rendered by jurors that comprehend their "awesome responsibility," I do not understand the Court to believe that emotions in favor of mercy must play a part in the ultimate decision of a capital sentencing jury. Indeed, much of our Eighth Amendment jurisprudence has been concerned with eliminating emotion from sentencing decisions.

Id. at 2650.

[297] See, e.g., Caldwell v. Mississippi, 105 S. Ct. 2633 (1985) (discussed infra notes 298-302 and accompanying text).

[298] Id.

[299] Id. at 2637-38.

[300] Id. at 2640 (emphasis added).

[301] 463 U.S. 992 (1983).

rate and non-misleading information about appellate review to a sentencing jury. The flavor of her opinion, however, is entirely different from that of Marshall's. Where Marshall rests on the statement's detrimental effect on the defendant, O'Connor's brief opinion instead emphasizes the detrimental effect on the jury's sense of its own awesome responsibility:

> In my view, the prosecutor's remarks were impermissible because they were inaccurate and misleading in a manner that diminished the jury's sense of responsibility.
>
> . . . .
>
> In telling the jurors, "your decision is not the final decision . . . [y]our job is reviewable," the prosecutor sought to minimize the sentencing jury's role . . . .
>
> . . . .
>
> Although the subsequent remarks of the prosecutor to which Justice Rehnquist refers in his dissent . . . may have helped to restore the jurors' sense of the importance of their role, I agree with the Court that they failed to correct the impression that the appellate court would be free to reverse the death sentence if it disagreed with the jury's conclusion that death was appropriate.[302]

This analysis seems to focus on the jury's action for its own sake, rather than simply because of its likely effect on the defendant. Responsible decisionmaking may be a virtue in and of itself, regardless of its probable consequences. Moreover, responsible decisionmaking is a relational virtue in that it reflects the jury's relationship to the defendant: the jury is in a position to be merciful, just, and compassionate toward him, and not simply in a position to enforce (or refrain from violating) his rights. A view of the sentencing decision as implicating the jury's duty to act in a just manner is paradigmatically feminine.

This contrast between rights and obligations, between rule-based demands and aspirational virtues, is also apparent in the ways that O'Connor and Rehnquist view the special role of lawyers in our society. In *Zauderer v. Office of Disciplinary Counsel,*[303] O'Connor, joined by Rehnquist and Burger, dissented from the majority holding that a state cannot bar nonmisleading but unsolicited legal advice. In *Supreme Court of New Hampshire v.*

---

[302] 105 S. Ct. at 2646-47 (O'Connor, J., concurring).
[303] 105 S. Ct. 2265 (1985).

Piper,[304] however, O'Connor joined a majority holding that, over a Rehnquist dissent, invalidated residency requirements for membership in the bar. Thus, each would have allowed the state to create special rules for lawyers—not applicable to the general public—in at least some contexts. The two cases considered together contrast O'Connor's view of lawyers as special in virtue of their greater responsibility with Rehnquist's view of lawyers as special in view of the nature of their craft.

In *Zauderer*, O'Connor found free, unsolicited legal advice qualitatively different from the advertisements or free products of other business, and consequently more regulable. She based this conclusion on the greater obligations of lawyers toward society:

> In my view, state regulation of professional advice in advertisements is qualitatively different from regulation of claims concerning commercial goods and merchandise, and is entitled to greater deference than the majority's analysis would permit. . . . The States understandably require more of attorneys than of others engaged in commerce. Lawyers are *professionals*, and as such they have greater obligations. As Justice Frankfurter once observed, "[f]rom a profession charged with [constitutional] responsibilities, there must be exacted . . . qualities of truth-speaking, of a high sense of honor, of granite discretion." The legal profession has in the past been distinguished and well served by a code of ethics which imposes certain standards beyond those prevailing in the marketplace and by a duty to place professional responsibility above pecuniary gain.[305]

This passage provides a stark contrast to Rehnquist's *Piper* dissent, in which he explicitly refused to subscribe to a virtue-based theory of the difference between lawyers and others:

> My belief that the practice of law differs from other trades and businesses for Art. IV, § 2 purposes is not based on some notion that law is for some reason a superior profession. The reason that the practice of law should be treated differently is that law is one occupation that does not readily translate across state lines. Certain aspects of legal practice are distinctly and intentionally *nonnational*.[306]

---

[304] 105 S. Ct. 1272 (1985).
[305] *Zauderer*, 105 S. Ct. at 2295-96 (citations omitted).
[306] *Piper*, 105 S. Ct. at 1282-83 (footnote omitted).

In several contexts, then, O'Connor seems more willing to integrate rights and responsibilities and to command that people act not only fairly but also virtuously.

Conclusion: A Second Look at Community and Context

In light of the revolutionary effect women's personality differences might have on jurisprudence, it is unsurprising to find that Justice O'Connor approaches legal issues from a different perspective than that of her male colleagues. Her voting record, however, puts her squarely in the conservative camp on most issues. This nexus between a feminine voice and a conservative voice may seem troubling to many. As an intellectual exercise, perhaps, it is useful to isolate the feminine influence, but it does not seem to change results. The current trend on the Court, with O'Connor's enthusiastic participation, is away from the liberal results of the Warren Court. In particular, the Court seems to be adopting an approach of "aggressive majoritarianism," fostering community and consensus at the expense of individual rights.[307] Had Justice Stewart been replaced by a male ideological soulmate of Justice Rehnquist, a similar result likely would have been achieved. The contexts in which O'Connor reaches a less politically conservative result than Rehnquist are few and well-defined; her impact is noticeable, but not notable. So why does it matter that she draws her jurisprudence from her femininity rather than her politics?

There are three significant differences. First, regardless of the *content* of a feminine perspective, recognition of its existence and its different voice might itself change the outcome of some cases. Where political or intellectual diversity is a legal issue, whether one treats men and women as fundamentally similar or fundamentally different may have a significant effect. Two recent examples are *Roberts v. United States Jaycees*[308] and *Steele v. FCC*.[309] In *Roberts*, the Court held that the first amendment did not protect the Jaycees' policy of excluding women from full membership. The appellate court had sustained the Jaycees' argument that admission of women would infringe the organization's first amendment

---

[307] See Sherry, supra note 264; Stone, O.T. 1983 and the Era of Aggressive Majoritarianism: A Court in Transition, 19 Ga. L. Rev. 15 (1984).

[308] 104 S. Ct. 3244 (1984).

[309] 770 F.2d 1192 (D.C. Cir. 1985).

rights by changing the content of the group's message. The Supreme Court explicitly rejected this argument on the ground that it rested "solely on unsupported generalizations about the relative interests and perspectives of men and women."[310] Similarly, in *Steele*, the FCC sought to support its policy of preferentially granting broadcast licenses to women on the ground that female ownership and management would increase programming diversity. The Court of Appeals for the District of Columbia rejected that argument, again explicitly rejecting any notion of a feminine perspective:

> [I]t simply is not reasonable to expect that granting preferences to women will increase programming diversity. Women transcend ethnic, religious, and other cultural barriers. In their social and political opinions and beliefs, for example, women in fact appear to be just as divided among themselves as are men. Therefore it is not reasonable to expect that a women would manifest a distinctly "female" editorial viewpoint.[311]

Thus, recognition of a feminine perspective— regardless of its content—might alter the decisions of male judges.

Second, an even more significant difference lies in the potential for development of a feminine jurisprudence. The Court's move toward aggressive majoritarianism is only one translation of a communitarian philosophy or a perspective of connection. If, as Unger has suggested, liberalism corrupts consensus (thus undermining community),[312] one response is to reconstruct the authority of consensus by fiat. Enforced homogeneity, however, although it may inject consensus and community into the jurisprudential paradigm, is not the only—nor the most sophisticated—conception of community.[313] It represents what Claire Dalton has called a "cor-

---

[310] *Roberts*, 104 S. Ct. at 3255. O'Connor concurred only in the judgment, suggesting that even if admission of women would change the content of the organization's message, she would find the conduct unprotected as primarily commercial association. She was thus unwilling to accept the majority's blithe assumption that admission of women would have no effect on the content of the Jaycees' expression. See id. at 3257-58.

[311] *Steele*, 770 F.2d at 1199. Judge Patricia Wald dissented, finding the FCC hypothesis of diversity reasonable. This suggests that women are more likely to accept the idea of a feminine perspective.

[312] R. Unger, Law In Modern Society 169 (1976).

[313] See R. Dworkin, supra note 94, at 134-37.

rupting form" of community, stressing a community of sameness rather than a community of diversity.[314]

Feminine jurisprudence is in its infancy, both in terms of application by judges and its elaboration by scholars and teachers. Like all moral, legal, and political theories, it needs time to develop. As Michael Perry has noted, the American legal self-image, like the American religious self-image, is one of evolution:

> Our religious self-understanding has generally involved a commitment—though not necessarily a fully conscious commitment—to the notion of moral evolution, because in the main we have avoided the pretense that our current understanding of the moral universe . . . was perfect and complete. Rather, we know that we are fallible and that we must struggle incessantly to achieve a better—a broader and deeper understanding. We also know that we are frail and that our frailty necessitates an ongoing struggle to bring our collective (political) practice into ever closer harmony with our evolving, deepening moral understanding.[315]

The moral and jurisprudential theories sketched out in this article have not had the time, or the give and take of serious scholarship, to develop. This article is itself only a very tentative first step: once the paradigm has been exposed, the hard work of constructing a feminine jurisprudence (and refining its content through evolution) lies ahead.

Finally, recognition of Justice O'Connor's unique perspective, and the unique perspective of women in general, might aid us in ameliorating the distortions of an overly individualist liberal paradigm. Insufficient attention to connection promotes naked self-interest at the expense of altruism, impoverishes our self-perception, and stunts our capacity for growth. Merely communicating a feminine emphasis on connection may be enlightening: "Teaching is not always a matter of either arguing or providing evidence. . . . It

---

[314] C. Dalton, Remarks on Personhood 7 (Jan. 5, 1985) (paper presented at meeting of Jurisprudence Section, AALS 1985 Annual Meeting).

[315] M. Perry, The Constitution, the Courts, and Human Rights 99 (1982) (footnotes omitted). See also B. Pascal, Thoughts on Religion and Philosophy 243 (I. Taylor trans. 1894) ("Those whom we term the Ancients, were in fact novices in everything, and formed, properly speaking, the infancy of Humanity; and, as we have added to their knowledge the experience of succeeding ages, it is in ourselves we must find that antiquity we so reverence in others.").

is sometimes rather a matter of imparting a way of looking at things."[316]

[316] Eldridge, On Knowing How to Live: Coleridge's "Frost At Midnight," 7 Philos. & Lit. 213, 227 (1983).

[12]

What Do Judges and Justices Maximize? (The Same Thing Everybody Else Does)

Richard A. Posner*

This article presents a positive economic theory of the behavior of appellate judges and Justices. The essay argues that the effort to insulate judges from significant economic incentives, through devices such as life tenure and stringent conflict of interest rules, has not rendered judicial behavior immune to economic analysis. Drawing on analogies to the managers of non-profit enterprises, to those who vote in political elections, and to theatrical spectators, the essay models the judicial utility function in terms that allows judges to be seen as ordinary people responding rationally to ordinary incentives. This model provides a theoretical alternative to the common view of judges as Prometheans or saints, and it suggests new ways of looking at such practical issues as the design of the judicial compensation system.

I. Introduction

This article proposes a new, positive economic theory of judicial behavior. My focus is on the "ordinary" appellate judge with secure tenure (for example, a federal court of appeals judge or U.S. Supreme

* Judge, United States Court of Appeals for the Seventh Circuit; Senior Lecturer, University of Chicago Law School. Earlier versions of this article were delivered at a conference on economic analysis of law sponsored by the George Mason University School of Law, on January 28, 1993, and at the annual meeting of the American Law and Economics Association, on April 30, 1993. I thank the participants in both conferences, plus Gary Becker, Douglas Baird, Harold Demsetz, Frank Easterbrook, David Friedman, Henry Hansmann, Lawrence Lessig, Nelson Lund, Martha Nussbaum, Mark Ramseyer, Eric Rasmusen, and Michael Trebilcock, for many helpful comments, and Benjamin Aller for valuable research assistance.

Court Justice), as distinct from judicial "titans," real or imagined, on whom most of the previous literature explicitly or implicitly focuses. Analogizing judges to the managers of nonprofit enterprises, to voters in political elections, and to spectators at theatrical performances, I present a simple model in which judicial utility is a function mainly of income, leisure, and judicial voting. I show how this model can be used to explain various judicial behaviors (ranging from stare decisis to what I call "go-along voting"), to make falsifiable predictions concerning judicial effort, and to provide a framework both for evaluating changes in judicial compensation and rules of conduct and for comparing judicial with legislative behavior. Although my principal interest is in the economic theory of judicial behavior (with some borrowings from "law and literature" in Part V), the approach may have value for the solution of practical problems of judicial administration, as well as some relevance to the economic analysis of other occupations in which nonpecuniary income is a large part of total compensation.

The motivation for the article should be plain. At the heart of economic analysis of law is a mystery that is also an embarrassment: how to explain judicial behavior in economic terms, when almost the whole thrust of the rules governing compensation and other terms and conditions of judicial employment is to divorce judicial action from incentives—to take away the carrots and sticks, the different benefits and costs associated with different behaviors, that determine human action in an economic model. Since the judges are the central actors in the drama of the common law and play lead roles in statutory and constitutional law as well, the failure thus far to explain their actions in economic terms mocks the claim of economic analysis to explain the salient features, institutional as well as doctrinal, of the law in general and the common law and other judge-made law in particular. The economic analyst has a model of how criminals and contract parties, injurers and accident victims, parents and spouses—even legislators, and executive officials such as prosecutors—act, but falters when asked to produce a model of how judges act.

Instead of trying to explain directly why judges adopt one judicial philosophy or another, or decide a particular case one way or another, or follow or don't follow precedent, I shall concentrate on the antecedent question: Are judges rational? Or have the elaborate efforts made to strip them of incentives placed their behavior beyond the reach of rational-choice models? I shall argue that judges *are* rational and specifically that they can fruitfully be viewed as composites of three types of rational maximizer: the manager of a nonprofit enterprise, the voter, and the theatrical spectator. I bring in a fourth type, the player of games for fun, to explain the ruled quality of most judicial decision-making without having to assume that judges are unusually selfless or self-disciplined. Although none of these types is easy to model in rational-maximizer terms, enough progress has been or can be made in fitting them to the economic model to provide a framework for understanding judicial behavior as rational too. This framework makes it possible to consider in a new light not only the question of judicial rationality but also more practical issues such as limits on judicial moonlighting, the difference between dictum and holding, trends in judicial conflict-of-interest rules, the effect of higher judicial salaries, the tension between judges and law professors, and whether judges are hard-working and conscientious.

My approach downplays the "power trip" aspect of judging, the focus of most of the few previous efforts to model the judicial utility function. In fact, I assume that trying to change the world plays no role in that function. Not that judges are indifferent to power; they enjoy, I shall argue, the power that goes with deciding cases. But only a small minority, whom I shall largely ignore, have a visionary or crusading bent.[1] We know that the framers of the Constitution attempted to design a government that could be operated by moral and intellectual mediocrities, a characterization of officialdom from which not even federal judges are exempt. The inclusion in the design of such rules or institutions as life tenure for judges suggests that the framers believed that judges could not be counted on to behave with consistent courage, although some of course have behaved so.[2] Politics, personal friendships, ideology, and pure serendipity play too large a role in the

---

[1] Hence the common criticism of the Supreme Court in the Burger years as lacking any "vision" or sense of mission. This is true of most courts most of the time, but is not necessarily a good criticism.

[2] Notably the federal judges who supervised public school desegregation in the South after *Brown v Board of Education*.

appointment of federal judges to warrant treating the judiciary as a collection of genius-saints miraculously immune to the tug of self-interest.[3] By treating judges and Justices as ordinary people,[4] my approach makes them fit subjects for economic analysis; for economists have no theories of genius.[5] It is fortunate for economic analysis, therefore, that most law is made not by the tiny handful of great judges but by the great mass of ordinary ones, although I shall consider briefly in Part VI the extension of my analysis to extraordinary judges. Because there are so many ordinary judges, and because anti-intellectualism runs deep in the American soul, there is even a cult of ordinariness in judging. Exceptionally able judges arouse suspicion of having an "agenda," that is, of wanting to be something more than just corks bobbing on the waves of litigation or umpires calling balls and strikes.

My focus is on federal appellate judges: not only because I am one and know this group of judges best,[6] but also because efforts to strip away incentives have progressed furthest with this group. Article III of the Constitution erects such a high hurdle to removing a federal judge from office that pretty much the only thing that will get him removed is criminal activity. A federal judge can be lazy, lack judicial temperament, mistreat his staff, berate without reason the lawyers who appear

---

[3] We are beginning, at last, to get a glimpse, from judges, of some of the unvarnished realities of a judicial career. Besides Richard A. Posner, *The Problems of Jurisprudence* (Harvard, 1990), see Frank H. Easterbrook, *What's So Special about Judges?* 61 U Colo L Rev 773 (1990), and Patricia M. Wald, *Some Real-Life Observations about Judging*, 26 Ind L Rev 173 (1992).

[4] "Most judges, even Supreme Court Justices, have been plucked from well deserved intellectual obscurity." Charles W. Collier, *The Use and Abuse of Humanistic Theory in Law: Reexamining the Assumptions of Interdisciplinary Legal Scholarship*, 41 Duke L J 191, 221 (1991). From political obscurity as well, one might add.

[5] But see Daniel L. Rubenson and Mark A. Runco, *The Psychoeconomic Approach to Creativity*, 10 New Ideas in Psychology 131 (1992), for a stab at one.

[6] In so saying I do not mean to suggest that judges have privileged access to the judicial utility function. A utility function is not a psychological or phenomenological concept but a device for generating hypotheses. I doubt that *any* judge subjectively experiences his work in the way modeled in this article. I know I do not.

before him, be reprimanded for ethical lapses, verge on or even slide into senility, be continually reversed for elementary legal mistakes, hold under advisement for years cases that could be decided perfectly well in days or weeks, leak confidential information to the press, pursue a nakedly political agenda, and misbehave in other ways that might get even a tenured civil servant or university professor fired; he will retain his office. His pay cannot be lowered, either—and neither can the pay of a good judge be raised. All judges of the same rank are paid exactly the same, and so the carrot is withdrawn along with the stick. Another reason there is no carrot is that a judge is, of course, forbidden to accept bribes from litigants, to pocket filing fees or other fees levied on litigants, or to collect royalties from people who cite his opinions. He gets a fixed salary, period.

Well, there is a small carrot. Supreme Court Justices are often appointed from the ranks of federal court of appeals judges,[7] and although the probability of such an appointment is low for any particular judge even if he or she is one of the relatively few who are talked about for such a promotion, it figures in the thinking of some judges. But the impact of a particular decision on the prospects for promotion is normally very slight. Some decisions have no impact at all on those prospects and in the case of almost all the remaining decisions the impact is unpredictable—the decision may offend as many influential people as it pleases.

Promotion to jobs outside the judiciary is discouraged by the structure of judicial compensation, which is heavily backloaded.[8] The pension is extraordinarily generous (one's final salary, for life, including annual cost-of-living increases), but there is no vesting until age 65,

---

7 Indeed, at present seven of the nine Justices—Blackmun, Stevens, Scalia, Kennedy, Souter, Thomas, and Ginsburg—are former federal court of appeals judges, though Souter was one for only a few months and Thomas for only a year and a half. Historically the percentage has been lower.

8 The incentive effects of different methods of compensating employees and other agents are the subject of an extensive economic literature, pertinently illustrated by Edward Lazear and Sherwin Rosen, *The Economics of Compensation of Government Officials*, in Robert W. Hartman and Arnold R. Weber, eds, *The Rewards of Public Service: Compensating Top Federal Officials* 101 (Brookings, 1980), and by Ronald N. Johnson and Gary D. Libecap, *Agency Growth, Salaries and the Protected Bureaucrat*, 27 Econ Inquiry 431 (1989). On the effect of the backloading of compensation on the turnover

so anyone who quits sooner gives up a large expected benefit. The attractive pension arrangements are important for inducing judges of advanced age to retire. Article III presumably outlaws mandatory retirement for Article III judges, and makes it very difficult to force judges to retire even for cause. So here a carrot must do all the work.

The compensation and tenure structure for federal district judges is the same as that for appellate judges except that the salary is slightly lower and they have greater prospects for promotion,[9] although for the

---

of federal civil servants, see Richard A. Ippolito, *Why Federal Workers Don't Quit*, 22 J Human Resources 281 (1987) ("Ippolito, *Why Federal Workers Don't Quit*"). I shall take for granted the compensation and tenure regime of federal judges.

[9] Mark A. Cohen, *The Motives of Judges: Empirical Evidence from Antitrust Sentencing*, 12 Intl Rev L & Econ 13 (1992), presents some empirical evidence that desire for promotion affects the behavior of district judges. Another article by Cohen provides additional empirical evidence for a district-judge utility function that contains such arguments as desire to exercise discretion, aversion to heavy workloads, and desire for promotion to the court of appeals. Mark A. Cohen, *Explaining Judicial Behavior or What's "Unconstitutional" about the Sentencing Commission?*, 7 J L Econ & Org 183 (1991) ("Cohen, *Explaining Judicial Behavior*"). Other papers that analyze judicial behavior in utility-maximizing terms are Robert D. Cooter, *The Objectives of Private and Public Judges*, 41 Public Choice 107 (1983) ("Cooter, *Objectives*"); Jeffrey N. Gordon, *Corporations, Markets, and Courts*, 91 Colum L Rev 1931, 1967–71 (1991); Richard S. Higgins and Paul H. Rubin, *Judicial Discretion*, 9 J Legal Stud 129 (1980) ("Higgins and Rubin, *Judicial Discretion*"); Thomas J. Miceli and Metin M. Cosgel, *Reputation and Judicial Decision-Making* (forthcoming in J Econ Behavior & Org); Erin O'Hara, *Implicit Collusion or Social Constraint: Toward a Game Theoretic Analysis of Stare Decisis* (unpublished manuscript, Clemson University Departments of Legal Studies and of Economics) ("O'Hara, *Implicit Collusion*"); Bruce H. Kobayashi and John R. Lott, Jr., *Judicial Reputation and the Efficiency of the Common Law* (unpublished manuscript, 1993) (George Mason University School of Law) ("Kobayashi and Lott, *Judicial Reputation*"). Kobayashi and Lott point out that a judge who wanted to maximize citations to his decisions would have an incentive to upset existing precedents—and to replace them not only with his own decisions but with his own *inefficient* decisions, because, other things being equal, inefficient decisions are likely to generate more litigation, hence more occasions for citing the judge's decisions. Such a judge, however, belongs more to the "Promethean" than to the "ordinary" category, and it is the latter on which I focus. I leave aside the question whether a true Promethean would be likely to be a simple citation maximizer.

most part only to the court of appeals. More important in keeping them in line is the fact that a district judge presides more or less continuously at trials and other proceedings in open court in which he is required to make rulings and talk to lawyers and jurors. If he isn't on the ball this soon becomes known and he gets a bad reputation in the legal community. Appellate judges, in contrast, are largely shielded from direct evaluations of their work. They never have to make rulings in open court, or indeed open their mouth in court. Provided they can pick competent law clerks, they will be able to churn out, regardless of their own efforts or ability, professionally competent opinions—and opinions are virtually their only public product and hence virtually the only basis upon which the legal profession, or the rest of the world, can evaluate them. It is the unique insulation of federal appellate judges from accountability that makes their behavior such a challenge to the economic analysis of law, and more broadly to the universalist claims of the economic theory of human behavior.

II. THE NONPROFIT ANALOGY

The natural starting point for discussing the behavior of federal judges might seem to be the behavior of other government bureaucrats, an area in which there is a growing literature in political science and in economics.[10] Although I shall cite this literature in places, I do not think that the conventional bureaucrat provides the most fertile analogy. The judge has more secure tenure and is largely free from control by superiors and from legislative oversight. Three other analogies are more promising. One is to managing a nonprofit enterprise, the second is to voting in political elections, and the third is to watching a play or movie.

The theory of nonprofit enterprise that we owe to Henry Hansmann[11] posits that the nonprofit form is likely to be the preferred

[10] See, for just a few examples of this literature, William A. Niskanen, *Bureaucracy and Representative Government* (Aldine, Atherton, 1971); Randall L. Calvert, Matthew D. McCubbins, and Barry R. Weingast, *A Theory of Political Control and Agency Discretion*, 33 Am J Pol Sci 588 (1989); Mark Bagnoli and Michael McKee, *Controlling the Game: Political Sponsors and Bureaus*, 7 J L Econ & Org 229 (1991).

[11] Henry B. Hansmann, *The Role of Nonprofit Enterprise*, 89 Yale L J 835 (1980); see also Henry B. Hansmann, *Ownership of the Firm*, 4 J L Econ & Org 267

means of providing a service when the buyers cannot observe the enterprise's output. If you want to help the starving people of Somalia, and to this end you make a contract with a food distributor to provide X amount of soybeans to those people, you will find it very difficult to determine whether the distributor has done this. He is more likely to do it if he is forbidden to pocket the residual income (after paying all expenses)[12]—in other words the profit—from the distribution. For then the benefit to him of cheating on the contract is reduced.

The nonprofit form does not solve, but merely alleviates somewhat, the problem of the disloyal agent. The nonprofit provider has less incentive to be efficient than a profit-maximizing provider would have, because cost savings do not accrue to him as profit. We therefore expect more slack in a nonprofit enterprise and also more transforming of profits into salary or other employee perquisites, a normal consequence of constraining monetary profits.[13] Why don't *all* the profits get transformed into salary or perks? First, beyond a point perhaps soon reached, the utility conferred by a perk may be only a small fraction of its cost. Second, people will not donate to a nonprofit organization whose employees are known to have astronomical salaries or to overindulge in perks—as the United Way recently discovered to its sorrow. Third, a form of enterprise that constrains profit-making may attract as employees people less preoccupied with money-making than the comparable employees of profit-making enterprises. They may be more risk averse and hence more willing to trade money income for job

(1988). The economic literature on nonprofit enterprise is further illustrated by Burton A. Weisbrod, *The Nonprofit Economy* (1988) ("Weisbrod, *Nonprofit Economy*"); Edwin G. West, *Nonprofit Organizations: Revised Theory and New Evidence*, 63 Public Choice 165 (1989) ("West, *Nonprofit Organizations*"); David Easley and Maureen O'Hara, *The Economic Role of the Nonprofit Firm*, 14 Bell J Econ 531 (1983).

[12] A big loophole, of course: those expenses include his salary!

[13] This has long been a staple observation in the literature on the regulation of public utilities. See, for example, Armen A. Alchian and Reuben A. Kessel, *Competition, Monopoly, and the Pursuit of Money*, in *Aspects of Labor Economics* 157 (National Bureau of Economic Research, 1962); Richard A. Posner, *Economic Analysis of Law* 350, 653 (Little, Brown, 4th ed 1992) ("Posner, *Economic Analysis of Law*"). "Slack" is perhaps better viewed as leisure, a perquisite, than as something separate from perquisites; that is in fact the approach I shall take.

security, or their utility functions may be dominated by nonpecuniary sources of utility. In either event, given their preferences (or "character") they are not as likely to try to squeeze the last penny of pecuniary advantage from their situation. I do not put much weight on this point, however, in view of the empirical evidence against it.[14]

The parallel between the nonprofit enterprise and the federal courts, as distinct from public enterprises staffed by officials of more uncertain tenure, should be apparent. The public would find it difficult, should it attempt to hire judicial services from a private organization, to determine the extent to which its contractor was producing "justice." True, there is a good deal of private judging, particularly but, especially with the recent emergence of "rent-a-judge" and mediation services offered by law firms, not only in the form of arbitration. But the arbitrator or other private judge is hired by the parties to a dispute to resolve that dispute rather than to produce the full range of judicial services. The full range includes rulemaking through the issuance of opinions that interpret common law principles, statutes, rules and regulations, and constitutional provisions; the provision of a stand-by dispute-resolution service for people who can't agree on a neutral arbiter; and the interposition of a neutral body between the state and the citizen. The arbitrator's or other private judge's more circumscribed output is more readily observable than the output of a "full service" public judicial system.[15] The incentive effect of conditioning the private judge's compensation on satisfying a market demand may therefore enable the slack associated with the nonprofit counterpart service to be avoided at reasonable cost. Hence in some areas of dispute resolution private judging can compete effectively with public judging even

---

[14] Summarized in West, *Nonprofit Organizations* at 168–69 (cited in note 11).

[15] Well, not entirely. The absence of an opinion (commercial arbitrators, as the theory predicts, generally do not issue opinions, though labor arbitrators generally do) makes it more difficult to evaluate the quality of a judge's work. A related point is that arbitrators are understood to exercise broad discretion, and, as I shall note shortly, discretionary judgments are more difficult to evaluate than "ruled" ones. On the difficulty of evaluating judicial performance, see John Paul Ryan, *Evaluating Judicial Performance: Problems of Measurement and Politics*, in Philip L. Dubois, ed, *The Analysis of Judicial Reform* 121 (Lexington, 1982).

though the latter is subsidized.[16] The coexistence of profit and non-profit firms is common in other industries as well, despite the tax advantages that the nonprofits enjoy.[17]

Since the output of a full-service judiciary cannot readily be evaluated, a rational public is reluctant to buy that output from a profit-making enterprise, which would be tempted to grab for big profits by skimping on the costs of the service. Nor can the public easily delegate the evaluative function to the legislative or executive branches; they are not trustworthy or easily monitored agents either. No doubt the Justice Department could evaluate judicial performance by neutral criteria, but it would have an incentive to use political criteria as well, and if it fired or demoted judges allegedly for professional incompetence the public would find it difficult to evaluate the evaluation.

Nor is hiring competitive judicial firms the answer, quite apart from the problem of maintaining consistency of legal doctrines and rulings that would be created by a competitive judiciary. Competition doesn't work well when none of the customers for an industry's product or service can make even a rough determination of the quality of the output offered by the competing firms and warranties or equivalent guarantees are infeasible. Unable to rely on the market or on incentive compensation, the public forbids the judges to take monetary profits from judging not only by accepting bribes or being paid out of court fees, fines, or other revenues generated by the judicial process but also through such indirect means as sitting on a case in which a relative, or a company in which the judge owns stock, is a party. As the discretionary power of the judiciary increases, we can expect the rules on conflict of interest to become more stringent, for the more discretion judges exercise, the more difficult it is to determine the quality of judicial output.

Because the judiciary has been placed on a nonprofit basis, we should expect that judges on average do not work as hard as lawyers of comparable age and ability. I believe that this is true, at least of appel-

---

16 On the economics of arbitration, and of private judging generally, see William M. Landes and Richard A. Posner, *Adjudication as a Private Good,* 8 J Legal Stud 235 (1979); Cooter, *Objectives* (cited in note 9).

17 See, for example, Weisbrod, *Nonprofit Economy* ch 8 (cited in note 11).

late judges.[18] The enormous caseload increases of recent decades have been accommodated mainly by expansions in staff, though judges do I think work harder today than they did thirty or forty years ago. It is not surprising that judicial "moonlighting" is strictly limited, presumably so that judges cannot easily transform judicial leisure into cash income—which by increasing the value of that leisure would induce rational judges to do less judicial work.

The fact that through incentives and selection the structure of judicial compensation makes judges less likely to work hard than their peers in private practice should not be regarded as *necessarily* a deplorable consequence of the judiciary's nonprofit form of organization. Since leisure is a form of income, an increase in leisure should reduce the amount of pecuniary income demanded by judges of a given quality. Hence by not forcing judges to work too hard—probably a futile undertaking anyway—the judiciary's nonprofit structure enables competent people to be attracted to judging at lower wages than would otherwise be necessary. The offset is highly imperfect, because the greater leisure of the low-paid judge means that more judges must be hired in order to get the work done. Nevertheless the leisure, or slack, that results from the nonprofit organization of the judiciary is not a pure cost to the system.

That slack can be limited, moreover, by careful screening of judicial candidates. Especially if behavior has a habitual component, a person known to be a hard worker in his present job may be a good bet to continue working hard even after the incentives that may initially

18 Compare the finding that members of Congress who have announced that they are retiring vote less in their last term of office—the penalty for shirking is less. John R. Lott, Jr., *Political Cheating*, 52 Public Choice 169, 179–82 (1987). As an aspect of my taking the structure of judicial compensation and tenure for granted, I shall not inquire why Congress as it were "permits" judges not to work too hard, by increasing the number of judges and their staffs in order to meet increases in workload. But it is apparent that Article III limits the power of Congress to force judges and their staffs to work harder than they want to work. The judges can always allow court queues to grow, thus shifting the costs of a heavier workload from their own shoulders to those of litigants and the public generally. As should be plain from the discussion in the text below of incentive compensation for judges, it would be infeasible to try to overcome this problem by fixing output quotas for judges, unless quality of judging is disregarded.

have induced him to work hard are removed. In fact the screening of candidates for federal judicial appointment is elaborate (just as—and for a similar reason—premarital search is more protracted the more difficult it is to get a divorce), and most judges are appointed at an age at which their work habits have had many years to become firmly fixed. Perhaps that is one reason why persons under 40 are rarely appointed to federal judgeships. It is true that academic tenure is usually awarded at a younger age, but since academic salaries are not fixed or outside earnings effectively constrained, and there is more than one academic employer, academics retain monetary incentives to work hard.

Nonprofit organizations are not constrained to pay all employees of the same rank the same compensation. Nor for that matter is the federal judiciary. Secretaries and other support personnel can receive quality raises and bonuses, and there is even a cash prize (the $15,000 Devitt Award) for federal judges, though only one is awarded each year. Nevertheless, if we set the prize to one side, federal judges of the same rank (and apart from the Supreme Court Justices all Article III judges are in one of just two ranks—district judge or circuit judge) are all paid the same regardless of their productivity, stature, etc.—even regardless of their years of service.[19] The difference in treatment between judicial and support personnel reflects the fact that the former have much more discretionary power, which ultimately is what makes judicial output so difficult to value. To recognize differences in the quality or value of that output would resurrect the problem that gave rise to the nonprofit organization of the judiciary in the first place. The judge who spent less time per case so that he could grind out more cases faster for higher pay would be like a profit-making judiciary that minimized its costs in order to pocket a larger profit. Suppose a judge who increased his output by 1 percent received an extra $5,000 a year. His monetary incentive would be to reduce the time he spent on each case by 1 percent, so that he could decide 1 percent more cases in the same amount of time. For then, assuming that he was not working more intensively (and why should he be?), the $5,000 bonus would represent

[19] Except that the older a judge is, the greater the expected value of his pension. This is a big exception to the uniformity of judicial salaries, but it is not something over which the individual judge has any control.

a pure profit, made possible by the difficulty encountered by the "buyers" of his decisions in evaluating their quality.

III. SOME ELEMENTS OF THE JUDICIAL UTILITY FUNCTION

I said that I do not think federal appellate judges work as hard as comparable lawyers in private practice. Most of them, however, work quite hard—often at an age when their counterparts in private practice have retired and are living in Scottsdale or La Jolla. They must be deriving utility from the work of being a judge, and not just from the status of being a judge, which they could retain while doing very little and sometimes—when they have reached retirement age—nothing. Their utility function must in short contain something besides money income (from their judicial salary) and leisure. Let us consider some possibilities, with particular reference to components of utility that can be affected by judicial effort.

Popularity. Cooter suggests that public judges "seek prestige" among "the lawyers and litigants who bring cases before the judges." They do this, he believes, "by ignoring [the] effects [of their decisions] upon parties other th[a]n the disputants."[20] What he calls prestige sounds more like popularity. No matter; he is correct that many federal appellate judges, although they are in no way dependent upon the goodwill of the bar (unlike their counterparts in elected state judiciaries), are sensitive to their popularity with members of the bar, especially if, as is common, many of their friends are drawn from the bar. People like to be liked. Few judges, however, care whether they are popular with the litigants themselves. How could they be? Virtually every decision produces a happy winner and an unhappy loser. Judges' desire to be popular with lawyers may express itself in reluctance to impose sanctions upon or even to criticize lawyers who perform below reasonable professional standards, but I believe not otherwise.

Prestige. In a sense distinct from popularity on the one hand and deference (outward shows of respect, discussed later) on the other, prestige is unquestionably an element of the judicial utility function. The thirst for prestige is manifested primarily in opposition to any large increase in the number of judges, at least high-level judges, and to extending the title "judge" to lower-level judicial personnel, such as

20 Cooter, *Objectives* at 129 (cited in note 9).

magistrates and bankruptcy referees (now called "magistrate judges" and "bankruptcy judges," to the dismay of many Article III judges). Judges normally reluctant to ascribe base motives to their group have been vocal in insisting that a substantial increase in the number of judges would, by diluting judicial prestige, increase the difficulties of recruitment.[21] Apart from opposing an increase in the number of judges or a dilution of the title "judge," there is little an individual judge can do to enhance his prestige as a judge. That prestige inheres in the whole judiciary. Free-rider problems make it unlikely that any one judge will exert himself strenuously to raise the prestige of all. But it would be a mistake to regard prestige as entirely a group asset. A manifestly incompetent judge or one who engages in scandalous or disreputable behavior will lose prestige even if he retains his judgeship.

Public interest. I exclude from the judicial utility function the desire to promote or maximize the public interest. Its inclusion would be inconsistent with an approach that treats judges as "ordinary" human beings. Although views concerning the public interest undoubtedly affect judicial preferences, just as they affect voter preferences (more on this shortly), they do so, I assume, only insofar as decisions expressing those views enhance the judge's utility.

Avoiding reversal. Judges don't like to be reversed (I speak from experience), but aversion to reversal does not figure largely in the judicial utility function. It is nonexistent in the case of Supreme Court Justices, and fairly unimportant in the case of court of appeals judges because reversals of appellate decisions by the Supreme Court have become rare[22] and most reflect differences in judicial philosophy or legal policy rather than mistake or incompetence by the appellate

---

[21] See, for example, Gordon Bermant, et al, *Imposing a Moratorium on the Number of Federal Judges: Analysis of Arguments and Implications* (Federal Judicial Center, 1993).

[22] Not because the Court is affirming a higher percentage of decisions, but because the interaction of a growing lower-court caseload with a relatively fixed Supreme Court decisional capacity has resulted in the Court's accepting for review a declining fraction of lower-court decisions. Of more than a thousand majority opinions that I have written for the Seventh Circuit, the Supreme Court has granted certiorari in only about ten. I believe that this is a representative percentage.

judges.[23] Hence they are not perceived as criticism. Higgins and Rubin found that reversal rates do not affect district judges' chances of promotion.[24]

Reputation. As my reference to criticism implies, a potentially significant element in the judicial utility function is reputation, both with other judges, especially ones on the same court—one's colleagues (and here reputation merges with popularity)—and with the legal profession at large. Reputation is a function of effort, but, for the judge of ordinary abilities, only of a minimum level of effort. Effort beyond that level may actually make a judge unpopular among his colleagues, and this in two ways: first, by making him seem a rate breaker, show off, or know it all. Employers like a Stakhanovite; fellow employees do not. Second, a busy, active, forceful judge can impose costs on his colleagues by writing many separate opinions to which they have to respond, by criticizing their work, and by making arguments that they have difficulty answering. Thus concern with reputation does not explain why judges don't always retire at the earliest opportunity, which would be financially the wisest course. Some do, but many do not.

I am speaking, as throughout most of this article, of the ordinary judge. For the extraordinary judge, as we shall see, reputation may be a dominating objective and may be highly correlated with effort.

IV. Voting as a Source of Judicial Utility

Voting and Related Maximands. The elements of the judicial utility function canvassed in the preceding section are, I believe, less important for the average federal appellate judge than the one I want to high-

---

Congress sometimes "overrules" judicial decisions. I don't think most judges care a fig about (and often they don't even know about) legislative "overruling," which they are apt to regard as the consequence of politics rather than as any form of criticism.

[23] The remarkable fact that the Supreme Court had not reversed a single one of the 400 majority decisions that Judge Robert Bork had written or joined at the time of his nomination to the Supreme Court was deemed irrelevant in a report commissioned and relied on by Senator Biden, the Chairman of the Senate Judiciary Committee. *Response Prepared to White House Analysis of Judge Bork's Record: Statement of Committee Consultants,* reprinted in 9 Cardozo L Rev 219, 238–42 (1987).

[24] Higgins and Rubin, *Judicial Discretion* (cited in note 9).

light in this section, which is best understood by analogy to voting in political elections.[25] Although voting is not compulsory in this country, vast numbers of people vote in elections in which the likelihood that their vote will affect the result of the election is vanishingly close to zero. This suggests that voting is a valued consumption activity of many people. Well, judges are constantly voting. A federal appellate judge votes several hundred times a year. And although his votes are frequently "wasted" because the case would have been decided the same way without him (he was not the swing vote), they have more impact than the votes of ordinary electors. A judge's vote sometimes decides the outcome of a case, and the outcome of a case is usually important to at least a few people, and in the case of some court of appeals cases and many Supreme Court cases to many—even millions of—people. So if voting in elections is a source of utility, we should not be surprised that voting in cases is a source of utility.

An alternative explanation for electoral voting is that people do it out of a sense of duty, and activity so motivated is different from ordinary consumption.[26] No doubt many do vote out of duty. But the pure consumption element is important, perhaps especially for judges. A federal judgeship remains a coveted job, and most judges enjoy their work. They are not reluctant conscripts of conscience.

---

[25] The analogy is used for a different purpose—to explain with the aid of Arrow's impossibility theorem the difficulty of a court's achieving consistency across decisions—in Frank H. Easterbrook, *Ways of Criticizing the Court*, 95 Harv L Rev 802, 823–31 (1982).

[26] Amartya Sen, *Rational Fools: A Critique of the Behavioural Foundations of Economic Theory*, in Amartya Sen, *Choice, Welfare and Measurement* 84, 97 (MIT, 1982). Elsewhere, however, Sen has described voting, much in the spirit of the present analysis, as being guided by a desire to record one's true preference. Amartya Sen, *Collective Choice and Social Welfare* 195–196 (Elsevier Science, 1970). The duty and consumption explanations for voting are merged in William H. Riker and Peter C. Ordeschook, *A Theory of the Calculus of Voting*, 62 Am Pol Sci Rev 25, 28 (1968)—an article representative of the large economic literature on the rationality of voting. For other examples of that literature, see R. D. Tollison and T. D. Willett, *Some Simple Economics of Voting and Not Voting*, 16 Public Choice 59 (1973); Thomas Schwartz, *Your Vote Counts on Account of the Way It Is Counted: An Institutional Solution to the Paradox of Not Voting*, 54 Public Choice 101 (1987);

Another source of judicial utility must be mentioned at this juncture. It is the deference that judges receive from lawyers and from the public generally.[27] This deference, like that accorded wealthy people, is of the shallowest kind: as soon as the judge loses office, as soon as the wealthy person loses money, the deference ceases.[28] Sensitive people realize this, but it does not eliminate the pleasure that everyone derives from being treated in a respectful manner. The republican simplicity of manners—the "I'm no better than the next guy" deportment—that most American judges affect is intended to be admired rather than to be taken seriously.

The deference is not separate from the voting, however, and therefore need not be assigned a separate place in the judicial utility function. Judges receive deference because they have power. They don't in fact have much power (Supreme Court Justices are an important exception, and the petty tyranny of some trial judges is a well-known fact), and they're not in fact much deferred to (with the same exception). But such deference as they do receive comes from their being, like wealthy people, more powerful than most people, not from being—like athletes, popular entertainers, and a few heroes, saints, and scientists—admired. Most judges are quickly forgotten when they leave office.

The pure utility of voting, when one's vote is highly unlikely to have any effect, is different from the "power trip" aspect of voting. Most economic analyses of judicial behavior have been concerned with

---

Garey C. Durden and Patricia Gaynor, *The Rational Behavior Theory of Voting Participation: Evidence from the 1970 and 1982 Elections*, 53 Public Choice 231 (1987), and—of particular relevance to my analysis—Geoffrey Brennan and Loren Lomasky, *The Impartial Spectator Goes to Washington: Toward a Smithian Theory of Electoral Behavior*, 1 Econ & Philosophy 189 (1985) ("Brennan and Lomasky, *The Impartial Spectator*").

27 Lawyers, like other sellers of services, are, in contrast to judges, deference givers rather than deference receivers. I suspect, therefore, that a much higher percentage of practicing lawyers than of judges are ex-salesmen.

28 Well, not entirely. Retired judges (even judges who have resigned to pursue a career in practice) usually retain the title "judge," and the title commands some deference even when separated from the office.

judges' power[29]—not as a source of deference or as the garnish on voting, as I am using it here, but as a source of satisfaction, or even of exhilaration, akin to that experienced by creative people. Artists make works of art that sometimes change sensibility; judges make decisions that sometimes change social or business practices. Artists impose their aesthetic vision on society; judges impose their political vision on society. They do this mainly through the precedential force of their decisions, since a single decision rarely (not never) has a big impact. Economic analysis of precedent emphasizes the tradeoff between the loss of power that results from judges' following their predecessors' decisions rather than innovating, on the one hand, and, on the other, the loss of power that results if, by refusing to follow their predecessors' decision and thus weakening the practice of decision according to precedent, they reduce the likelihood that their successors will follow their decisions.[30] My theory abstracts from these issues (though I shall suggest an alternative theory of stare decisis, it does not depend on influence maximizing). It thus is applicable to judges, I believe the majority, even on the Supreme Court, who have no great interest in changing (or resisting change in) law or society although they do obtain satisfaction from casting votes that are not merely symbolic expressions, but count.

---

[29] For a notable example, see Rafael Gely and Pablo T. Spiller, *A Rational Choice Theory of Supreme Court Statutory Decisions with Applications to the* State Farm *and* Grove City *Cases*, 6 J L Econ & Org 263 (1990); see also Eugenia Froedge Toma, *Congressional Influence and the Supreme Court: The Budget as a Signaling Device*, 20 J Legal Stud 131 (1991).

[30] See, for example, Lewis A. Kornhauser, *Modeling Collegial Courts I: Path Dependence*, 12 Intl Rev L & Econ 169 (1992); Lewis A. Kornhauser, *Modeling Collegial Courts II: Legal Doctrine*, 8 J L Econ & Org 441 (1992); Posner, *Economic Analysis of Law* 534–36, 541–42 (cited in note 13). There is a serious free-rider problem, since one judge's flouting precedent will be unlikely to damage the practice seriously. But the problem can be held in check, at least to some extent, by the highest court in the jurisdiction. The members of that court are few enough to be concerned about the impact of their behavior with respect to precedent on the survival of the practice of decision according to precedent in their jurisdiction. Id at 542. We might expect, therefore, that a comparison of the different state supreme courts (which differ in size) would show that the smaller the court, the less frequently it overrules its previous decisions.

For the handful of judges who today still write their own opinions, and for some who do not, there is additional utility, akin to that which a literary or scholarly author obtains, from being a published author. There is also the intrinsic pleasure of writing, for those who like to write, and of exercising and displaying analytical prowess or other intellectual gifts, for those who have them and want to use them. But I ignore these and other additional sources of satisfaction in the work of a judge as adding little of analytical significance to voting. Also, they are not important to most judges, who are happy to cede opinion-writing to eager law clerks, believing (consistent with my analysis) that the core judicial function is deciding, that is, voting, rather than articulating the grounds of decision.

Implications. The relatively modest, completely invariant salary, coupled with (indeed, in part a function of, as we have seen) the utility conferred by voting and by the deference which the judicial voting power brings in its train, explains how judges are motivated to vote and also why they do not sell their votes in some crude sense. Although it does not explain why they vote in a nonrandom manner, the analogy to political voting helps explain this. People who vote in elections the outcomes of which they cannot influence nevertheless do not vote randomly. The utility is not in the act of voting but in voting for someone or something. It is related to the utility that people derive from speaking their mind about some subject, even though nothing will be changed thereby.

Since judges derive power, as well as the pure consumption value of voting, from judicial activity, and power is no less when it is exercised randomly—indeed, arbitrary power is especially feared, so perhaps is especially powerful—we might expect judges to vote *less* responsibly than the ordinary voter. Of course if most judges voted randomly, the whole caboodle of judges would be got rid of eventually. But random voting by a single judge would not endanger that judge's tenure, so standard free-rider analysis would predict a lot of random judicial voting. Yet this is rare. As I have been emphasizing, for judges as for ordinary citizens voting has a consumption value that is independent of its instrumental, power-exercising value (which as I have said is negligible for the ordinary citizen—yet he votes); and this consumption value depends on choosing whom to vote for. Moreover, the cost of nonrandom voting to judges sitting in panels, as all appellate judges do almost all the time, is very low. Even in a three-judge panel, provided that at least one judge has a strong opinion on the proper outcome of the case, or even that a law clerk of one judge has a strong opinion on the matter, the other judges, if not terribly interested in the case, can simply cast their vote with the "opinionated" judge. This will not be random behavior and will incidentally be leisure-serving. If both indifferent judges vote against the opinionated one, he may write a fierce dissent that will either make them look bad or require them to invest time in revising the majority opinion to blunt the points made by him. Notice that if one indifferent judge decides to go along with the opinionated one, the other indifferent one is likely to go along as well—otherwise he will be forcing himself to write a dissenting opinion, at least given the current norm of explaining a dissenting vote rather than voting without explanation.

"Going-along" voting is only one example of the influence of leisure-seeking on judicial behavior. Another—once leisure is defined for these purposes, as it should be, as an aversion to any sort of "hassle," as well as to sheer hard work—is the insistence by judges that their decisions are coerced by "the law" and hence that the judge shouldn't be blamed by the losing party or anyone else distressed by the outcome. (Call this the theory of power without responsibility.)

A third example of the operation of leisure in the judicial utility function is the strong norm of equality in appellate-court assignments. Judges of the same court hear the same number of cases and generally are assigned the same number of decisions to write.[31] Any effort by one judge to hear more than his proportional share of cases or snag more than his proportional share of writing assignments is not only rebuffed but resented.

A fourth example is the distinction between "holding" and "dictum"—the latter being anything in a judicial opinion which is not essential to the outcome. Dicta, unlike holdings, are not considered to be binding on judges of the same or a subordinate court in subsequent decisions. This principle can be rationalized in various ways, but leisure-seeking is an important and neglected element of the complete

[31] In the latter regard, however, the Supreme Court is more flexible than the courts of appeals.

explanation. Because dictum is nonbinding, a judge can, without thereby mortgaging his future votes, join an opinion by one of his colleagues that contains much with which he disagrees. In exchange, other judges will join his opinions even though they disagree with much in them. This "live and let live" attitude made possible by the difference in authority between holding and dictum reduces the amount of effort that judges need invest either in their own opinions (to meet objections by other judges to dicta) or in the opinions of their colleagues (to purge those opinions of objectionable dicta).

A fifth example, though another for which there are alternative explanations, is the multitude of devices, most judge-invented, for ducking issues presented by the parties to appeals: the issue is moot or unripe, or calls for an "advisory opinion," or presents a nonjusticiable political question, or the party pressing it lacks standing, or the appeal was filed a day late, or the appellant had failed to exhaust some administrative or judicial remedy. These devices enable the judges to reduce their work, as well as to avoid the hassle involved in wrestling with difficult, politically sensitive issues. The former consequence (reducing work) is probably the less important, and this for two reasons. First, screening all appeals to identify the handful that can be denied without reaching the merits is itself a time-consuming, demanding task. (But of course without such screening the number of cases might soar. Imagine if every potential litigant were entitled to obtain an advisory opinion from a court!) Second, the more expeditious dispatch of judicial business enabled by limiting the number of cases reviewable on the merits may, by reducing court queues (which are a cost of using the courts), increase the demand for judicial services. The analogy is to building a new highway, which by reducing highway congestion will induce an increase in traffic.

My approach may help explain why judges adhere to stare decisis but not rigidly. If they adhered rigidly, they would not be voting as often, because voting implies discretion; if there is no felt choice, there is no pleasure in choosing. (That may be why so many district judges held the federal sentencing guidelines unconstitutional.[32] They believed that the guidelines would turn criminal sentencing, formerly an area of almost unlimited district-judge discretion, into a process of

[32] Cohen, *Explaining Judicial Behavior* at 183–86 (cited in note 9).

mechanical computation.) Yet if judges considered every case afresh they would, if conscientious, have to work much harder in each case; deciding a case conscientiously without reading the previous decisions is like writing a good article without doing any research to discover what has already been written on the subject. They would also lose the protection from criticism and attack that comes from being able to blame an unpopular decision on someone else (that is, on earlier judges). And there might be more litigated cases, because of the greater uncertainty of legal rights and duties in a system not stabilized by stare decisis. The last two points—more hassle and more uncertainty—may be more important than the first—more work—because following precedent requires research. On the other hand, uncertainty can make for more work, too, by generating more litigated cases.

"Going-along" voting and "live and let live" opinion-joining are practices related to but distinct from vote trading ("logrolling"). They are distinct because they are leisure-serving rather than power-maximizing. It is therefore understandable why vote trading by judges is condemned, and is in fact rare, while the other practices, which are common, are condoned or ignored. Legislators have a different utility function from judges, in part because they face reelection. Power and influence are more important to them than to judges, and therefore they engage in logrolling.[33] Here then is an economic reason to suppose, contrary to the extreme claims of some legal realists and critical legal scholars, that judges are not just legislators in robes. This analysis also predicts, however, that vote trading may occur among elected judges.

Admittedly, both "going along" voting and "live and let live" opinion-joining can be explained alternatively as devices for increasing judicial productivity, for by saving time they enable judges to decide more cases in the same amount of time as well as to reallocate time from work to leisure. And such policies as flexible deference to precedent and forbearance to decide premature cases may have strong public-interest justifications.[34] A task for future research is to disentangle

---

[33] Barry R. Weingast, *The Political Institutions of Representative Government: Legislatures,* 145 J Institutional & Theoretical Econ 693 (1989).

[34] See, for example, William M. Landes and Richard A. Posner, *The Economics of Anticipatory Adjudication* (unpublished manuscript, 1993) (University of Chicago Law School).

self-interest from other motivations for judicial doctrines and practices.

V. THE JUDGE AS SPECTATOR AND AS GAMESTER

A difficult question remains—that of the judge's motivation, when all monetary punishments and rewards have been stripped away and a choice between work and leisure is not in the offing, to vote for one side rather than another, or to vote for one interpretation of a statute or legal doctrine rather than another, or to adopt one judicial philosophy (such as "conservative," "liberal," "activist," or "restrained") rather than another. The traditional objection to the secret ballot—that it promotes, or at least protects, irresponsible voting—has carried the day with respect to voting by judges. Every judicial vote is public,[35] although sometimes a judge will tell his friends that he joined an opinion with which he disagreed because he didn't think the issue important enough to warrant a dissenting opinion. The public character of judicial voting facilitates criticism, which can be expected to have a greater effect on behavior when ordinarily more powerful incentives, such as money, are not in play. Yet most judges in fact are relatively insensitive to criticism other than by other judges, believing conveniently that most of it is motivated by political disagreement, envy, ignorance (willful or otherwise) of the conditions under which judges work, and self-promotion. Moreover, public comment on judicial decisions other than by the Supreme Court is rare. Only a tiny fraction of the tens of thousands of other appellate opinions published each year receive any sort of critical attention that might get back to the judge and alter his future behavior.

Choices of the kind that face a judge who must vote in a case—choices that cannot be made on the basis of wanting to increase one's pecuniary income, leisure, fame, or other forms of utility—are common in other areas of living. They are for example the choices we make when watching dramatic or cinematic performances. Athletic contests are different, mainly because of the built-in "bias" in favor, normally, of the "home" team, a bias that makes the judicial analogy

[35] Not a universal feature of judging: Mark Ramseyer tells me that in Japan, when lower-court judges sitting in three-judge panels decide cases, the votes are not made public and dissents are never written.

strained. The bias is highly relevant to state court adjudication, however, and can help explain not only the federal diversity jurisdiction but also the exclusive federal jurisdiction over many types of case that pit a state resident against federal taxpayers.

The audience for a play or movie is detached, having no tangible stake in the outcome of whatever struggle is being depicted on stage or screen. Yet ordinarily it is induced to "choose" one side or the other. Usually the choice is manipulated by the author—he "tells" us as it were to side with the hero against the villain. But in dramatic works of deep ambiguity, which often are highly popular among intellectuals on that account, such as *Hamlet,* or *Measure for Measure,* or *Pygmalion,* the choice offered to the spectator is a real one, because the author either has not resolved in his own mind the central tension in the situation dramatized or has not been able (or desired) to communicate the resolution clearly. This explains the popularity of revisionist interpretations of literature, such as arguing that the real hero of *Paradise Lost* is Satan. The spectator, or, in the last example, the reader (but a "live" performance provides a closer analogy to the judicial process, though today many cases are submitted for decision without any oral argument or other hearing—much as when a play is read rather than performed), has to weigh the evidence and come to a decision. The position of the judge is similar.[36] If spectators get consumption value out of such choices, it is not surprising that judges do.

Spectators make choices about the meaning of a play or movie by bringing to bear their personal experiences and any specialized cultural competence that they may have by virtue of study of or immersion in the type of drama that they are watching, and often by discussing their reactions with friends who may have a similar competence. The judge brings to bear on his spectatorial function not only a range of

---

[36] The analogy between the judge and the literary reader or spectator is developed, though for a different purpose, in Martha C. Nussbaum, *Equity and Mercy* (forthcoming in Philosophy and Public Affairs). On the dramaturgical character of trials, see Milner S. Ball, *The Play's the Thing: An Unscientific Reflection on Courts under the Rubric of Theater,* 28 Stan L Rev 81 (1975), and on the forensic character of drama, see Kathy Eden, *Poetic and Legal Fiction in the Aristotelian Tradition* 176–83 (Princeton, 1986). There has been some economic analysis of the arts, but I have found none that bears on the issues in this article.

personal and political preferences, but also a specialized cultural competence—his knowledge of and experience in "the law." And if he is an appellate judge he will often discuss with his professional colleagues the proper outcome of the contest before making up his mind.

Of course not every case has the rich ambiguities of *Hamlet*. Many cases involve puzzles soluble with the technical tools of legal analysis—here the judge is like the reader of a detective story. The jury as factfinder performs a similar function. It is a different kind of spectatorship from the one I am stressing here, that of the appellate judge asked to decide not where truth lies but which party has the better case. But in either case the choice, like that of the theater audience, is a disinterested one; the judge's or jury's income is not affected by it. A further point is that the less informed the tribunal is, the more "dramatic" the trial must be to hold the "audience's" attention. It is not surprising that Anglo-American trials, historically dominated by juries, are far more dramatic than Continental trials, historically dominated by professional judges.

The voting and spectatorship analogies to judicial decision-making are similar. This is most easily seen by comparing applause to voting—for in a large audience the clapping of a single spectator contributes little more to the overall decibel level than a single vote in an election contributes to the outcome. The voter is the spectator[37] in a contest between candidates, much as the reader or viewer of *Antigone* is the spectator of a contest between Antigone and Creon. It is no surprise that voter turnout is higher, the more publicized and the closer an election is,[38] just as the audience for a heavily advertised, highly dramatic play is likely to be larger than the audience for a meagerly advertised, undramatic play.

Why has the spectatorship analogy to judging been overlooked?[39] One reason is the piety in which the public discussion of judges is

---

37 Brennan and Lomasky, *The Impartial Spectator* at 189 (cited in note 26).

38 John H. Aldrich, *Rational Choice and Turnout*, 37 Am J Pol Sci 246, 266–68 (1993); Gary W. Cox and Michael C. Munger, *Closeness, Expenditures, and Turnout in the 1982 U.S. House Elections*, 83 Am Pol Sci Rev 217 (1989).

39 Well, not completely. See Yosal Rogat, *The Judge as Spectator*, 31 U Chi L Rev 213 (1964). Rogat's article is a criticism of Justice Holmes for having been *too* detached, too much an observer of rather than a participant in life

usually clothed. The analogy seems to give judging a frivolous air. But serious engagement with the arts as reader or viewer is not a frivolous activity; nor is "play" (contrasted with work) incompatible with adherence to rules. A chess player would reduce rather than enhance the pleasure he received from playing the game if he violated its rules, and so would the theatergoer who refused to enter into the lives of the characters on the stage, on the ground that they were not real people; and likewise the judge who violates the rules of the judicial game. Sports fans, theater fans, movie fans, and opera fans often develop a degree of connoisseurship which enhances their pleasure. In other words, they learn the rules (broadly understood) of the game they are watching, and respond in accordance with those rules. It is the same with judges, but with the important difference that some of the rules of the judicial game are uncertain and contested.

A second reason why the spectatorship analogy to judging has been overlooked is the domination of analyses of judicial behavior by legal academics. The academic is a spectator too, but he is a spectator not of the little drama that the judge witnesses—the trial or other contest that the judge resolves—but of the judge's opinion. He usually does not attend oral argument or even read the briefs in the cases that he discusses. Naturally, therefore, he tends to ascribe more importance to the opinion, to its reasoning, its rhetoric, etc. than to the decision itself. Yet these are secondary factors for most judges. For the judge, as for Hamlet, "the play's the thing."[40] When judges got busy, the first thing to be delegated was opinion writing; yet even today it would be considered a scandal if judges delegated the hearing of testimony or argument (though there is in fact some delegation of these functions to magistrates and masters).

The analogy to spectatorship can help us see how judicial outcomes reflect both the judges' preferences going in *and* the quality of the briefing and argument in particular cases. It can also help us understand the function of confirmation hearings in enabling legislators to

---

(like his friends Henry Adams and Henry James)—in short an insufficiently empathetic spectator.

[40] Compare Joseph Bensman and Robert Lilienfeld, *Craft and Consciousness: Occupational Technique and the Development of World Images* 19–22 (Wiley, 1973).

ascertain a judicial candidate's policy preferences, since those preferences can be expected to guide or at least influence a judge's decisions. We might also expect that "ideologues" would be appointed to judgeships at an earlier age on average than other candidates. Not only may it be difficult to determine the trajectory of the nonidealogue's views save by a process of inference from behavior over a long career, but to the extent that an ideologue is inherently more predictable there is less worry that if appointed young he will have a long time to change his views.[41]

Contrary to appearances, this analysis does not justify complacency about judicial performance. To eliminate by means of rules governing conflicts of interest all personal stakes from the judge's decision-making increases the weight (by reducing the cost) of ethical considerations, including the ethical duty to follow legal rules, but at the same time, as with the nonprofit enterprise, it reduces the penalty for careless, erratic, inattentive, or willful decision-making. The problem is deeper. We can see it by returning to the analogy between political and judicial voting, and by examining more critically than before the analogy between judicial and theatrical spectatorship. Most political campaigners appeal primarily, though not exclusively, to the voter's self-interest.[42] The judge, in contrast, like the theatrical spectator, is asked to cast a disinterested vote. It is easy to see why the spectator's vote is likely to be disinterested; what has he—being powerless—to gain by refusing to play the spectator's game? But a judge has some power. Supposing that the conflict of interest rules are effective in insulating his decision from any consequences for his personal or family wealth, one can still imagine a host of inappropriate considerations that might enter into his utility function: personal dislike of a lawyer or litigant in the case, gratitude to the appointing authorities, desire for advancement, irritation with or even a desire to undermine a judicial

---

41 Compare John R. Lott, Jr. and W. Robert Reed, *Shirking and Sorting in a Political Market with Finite-Lived Politicians,* 61 Public Choice 75, 87–88, 91 n 26 (1989).

42 Brennan and Lomasky, *The Impartial Spectator* at 189 (cited in note 26), emphasize the element of disinterest in political voting. They follow Adam Smith's *Theory of Moral Sentiments* in arguing that disinterested actions are likely where the cost of such actions to the actor is low.

colleague or subordinate, willingness to trade votes, desire to be on good terms with colleagues, not wanting to disagree with people one likes or respects, fear for personal safety, fear of ridicule, reluctance to offend one's spouse or close friends, and racial or class solidarity. These are common factors in the decisions of everyday life—why not in the decisions of judges, unless we ascribe to them a utility function different from that of the ordinary person, which would be inconsistent with treating them as ordinary persons?

Such factors do influence judicial decisions, but less often than the suspicious layman might suppose. The reason is not that judges have different utility functions from other people but that the utility they derive from judging would be reduced by more than they would gain from giving way to the temptations that I have listed. It is the same reason that many people do not cheat at games even when they are sure they can get away with cheating. The pleasure of judging is bound up with compliance with certain self-limiting rules that define the "game" of judging. It is a source of satisfaction to a judge to vote *for* the litigant who irritates him, the lawyer who fails to exhibit proper deference to him, the side that represents a different social class from his own; for it is by doing such things that you know that you are playing the judge role, not some other role, and judges for the most part are people who want to be—judges. This is consistent with most judges' not wanting to work too hard, for working as hard as a lawyer in private practice is not one of the rules of the judicial game. It is also consistent with judges' often voting their policy preferences and strong personal convictions. For in our system the line between law and policy, the judging game and the legislating game, is blurred. Many cases cannot be decided by reasoning from conventional legal materials. Such cases require the judge to exercise a legislative judgment, although a more confined one than a "real" legislator would be authorized to exercise.[43]

The analogy to playing games is worth pursuing a bit. Rules are not always irksome restraints. They are often constitutive. It is difficult to write a sonnet, because the sonnet is a genre with rigid rules; but without the rules, there would be no sonnets, and this would be a loss

[43] The legislative function of the judge is one reason that a judge is not permitted to use random methods, such as coin flipping, for deciding even cases that are truly indeterminate from a conventionally "legal" standpoint.

not only for the reader but for the sonneteer. And similarly with a game,[44] for example chess. If you decided that your bishops should be allowed to make the same moves as your queen, or that some of your pieces should be allowed to make moves off the chessboard, you would no longer be playing the game of chess. It is true that people sometimes cheat at games when they think they can get away with it. But that is because the pleasure of the game is not the only argument in their utility function. A person might cheat at tennis (this is very common in fact) because he saw an advantage from winning, but if at all reflective he would realize that his pleasure from playing the game itself was diminished, that he was trading off that pleasure against another source of utility. The judicial "game" has rules that lawyers learn in law school and then in practice or teaching, and both self-selection and the careful screening of federal judicial candidates help to assure that most lawyers who become federal judges will be lawyers who enjoy this particular game. They are therefore likely to adhere, more or less, to the rules limiting the materials and considerations that enter into their decisions.[45] The rules, it should be noted, are not the rules of substantive law, to which the community is subject but to which judges in their judicial capacity relate differently, as law givers and law appliers; they are the institutional rules of judging, to which only judges are subject. These rules, as I have said, are not altogether clear or uniform, especially in application; they are probably less clear and uniform, at least

---

[44] For pertinent discussions of games, see Bernard Suits, *What Is a Game?*, 34 Philosophy of Science 148 (1967); Arthur Allen Leff, *Law and*, 87 Yale L J 989, 998–1003 (1978); Johan Huizinga, *Homo Ludens: A Study of the Play-Element in Culture* chapters 1, 4 (Roy, 1950); and especially Thomas Morawetz, *The Concept of a Practice*, 24 Philosophical Studies 209 (1973). I emphasize that the notion of "game" that I am using here is unrelated to that used in game theory. Game theory is concerned with strategic behavior; I am not. For my purposes, solitaire is a good example of a game, but it is not a game in game-theory terms because it does not involve an interaction between persons.

[45] This is related to Wittgenstein's important point that rules bind because they are accepted—rather than being accepted because they bind. Nothing *in* a rule imposes an obligation to follow it. The decision to obey comes from outside, from force or socialization or, I am arguing, from the fact that the rule is constitutive of a pleasurable activity. Compare Sabina Lovibond, *Realism and Imagination in Ethics* 55–57 (U Minnesota, 1983).

in the United States, than the substantive law. Some judges play by "activist" rules, more by rules of "restraint" because those rules are more congenial to the legal profession's self-image; and judges, like game players, sometimes bend or break the rules for the sake of other values, such violations being in fact rather common because detection and sanctioning are difficult. Nevertheless most judicial decisions do have a "ruled" quality, and the analogy to games helps to show how this property of decisions is consistent with utility maximization and how therefore it does not presuppose—what would be contrary to the assumptions of my analysis—heroic self-abnegation on the part of the judges.

Another aspect of rules makes it reasonable to expect most judges to abide by the rules of the judicial game. In creating games, as in creating art, people create a reality in which they can find temporary refuge from, by imaginative transformation of, the sinister realities of ordinary life, the realities of hatred, disease, crime, betrayal, war and so forth. The judicial game has aspects of this refuge and transformation. Its raw materials are the ugly realities of life, but they are transformed in the judicial game to intellectual disputes over rights and duties, claims and proofs, presumptions and rebuttals, jurisdiction and competencies. And that is a comfort; it spares the judge who inflicts or upholds the death penalty from having to think of himself as a killer. But to get this comfort the judge must play by the rules of the judicial game, because the rules constitute the game.

Elected judges play the judge game too, and legislators play a related game called statesmanship or public service. But unlike life-tenured federal judges, these players face higher costs (and obtain no greater benefits) from abiding by the rules of the game and therefore break them more often. Not always, which is why many and indeed most decisions by nonelected judges have a ruled quality and why much legislation has a genuine public-spirited character—not necessarily because the voters are public spirited but because legislators derive satisfactions from acting in the public interest that may outweigh the costs when those costs are small.

VI. A VERY SIMPLE FORMAL MODEL OF THE JUDICIAL UTILITY FUNCTION

The implications of the analysis for concrete problems in judicial administration—such as the selection of judges and the structure of judicial compensation—can be further explored with the help of a simple formal model. The model is also helpful in distinguishing between the question whether judicial behavior is consistent with rationality (which I hope I have succeeded in showing it is) and the more difficult question whether judicial behavior is in fact rational; for the fact that judges with secure tenure nevertheless do some work can hardly be considered a robust demonstration of the applicability of the rational approach to human behavior to judges.

Consider, then, the following judicial utility function, in which effort is proxied by time:[46]

$$U = U(t_j, t_l, I, R, O) \qquad (1)$$

t_j is the number of hours per day that the judge devotes to judging, t_l is the time he devotes to leisure[47] (here defined as all activities other than judging, so that $t_j + t_l = 24$), I is pecuniary income, initially limited to judicial salary, R is reputation, and O represents the other sources of judicial utility discussed in this article besides that of judicial voting itself—popularity, prestige, and avoiding reversal. R, O, and (especially) I can be assumed to be invariant to t_j above a low threshold,[48] and let us assume that the average judge is well above it. On these assumptions, the judge will allocate his time between leisure and judging so that the last hour devoted to judging yields him the same utility (from judicial voting) as the last hour devoted to leisure, since otherwise he could increase his total utility by reallocating time from the less to the more valuable activity.

---

46 A richer model would consider energy or intensity as an additional choice variable, along with time, as in Gary S. Becker, *A Treatise on the Family* 64–79 (Harvard, enlarged ed 1991). I shall come back to this point.

47 Leisure need not be consumed off the premises, as it were. Loafing on the job is a form of leisure in my model.

48 Presumably a judge who refused to do any work at all would be impeached and removed, making $I=0$.

In this first cut at a model of judicial utility, income[49] is assumed to have no effect on the utility of judging and of leisure. But it might have an effect. Economists ordinarily assume that an increase in income will result in an increase in the utility of leisure relative to work because of the diminishing marginal utility of money. This is because work is assumed to generate no utility apart from that derived from the income which it produces. But if work (here, judging) produces nonpecuniary utility, just like leisure, it is not obvious that an increase in income will cause a reallocation of time from work to leisure. Indeed, "fun" work like judging might be considered a form of leisure.[50] Hence a more discriminating analysis of the effect of income on leisure is necessary.

A higher income will affect leisure in two potentially offsetting ways. The first is by reducing the time devoted to household production.[51] This will free up time for other activities, not only pleasurable leisure activities but also judging, itself a source of utility in my model. The value of leisure is reduced when a higher income enables a person to avoid the chores that he needed "leisure" (that is, time free from his market employment) to perform, so there is substitution for these leisure activities. Second, a higher income increases the utility generated by pleasurable leisure activities, such as travel, by enabling a higher quality of those activities to be bought. A trip to the South Seas is more fun than sitting in a rocking chair on the back porch. Of course, increased *quality* of leisure need not translate into increased *time* devoted to leisure; an alternative would be the substitution of an expensive for an inexpensive vacation of the same length of time. But I assume that people who have more money to spend on leisure activities

[49] I am speaking of course of pecuniary income.

[50] Another example of "productive consumption" would be the business lunch. Gary S. Becker, *A Theory of the Allocation of Time*, 75 Econ J 493, 504 (1965). Economic analysis of the nonpecuniary amenities or disamenities of work goes back to Adam Smith's discussion of the compensating wage differential for dangerous or dirty work. The modern literature on the psychic benefits of work is illustrated by Robert E. B. Lucas, *Hedonic Wage Equations and Psychic Wages in the Returns to Schooling*, 67 Am Econ Rev 549 (1977).

[51] Remember that, in the model, leisure includes all nonjudging activities. An increase in income will enable the purchase of additional labor-saving appliances and the hiring of additional household help.

will increase the time devoted to, as well as the quality of, those activities.

I would expect the effect of a higher income in increasing the demand for leisure time to predominate in the case of an increase in the income of a person whose present income is high enough to have enabled him to eliminate most of his household chores. I therefore predict that a higher judicial salary is likely to reduce the amount of work done by existing judges. But the qualification "existing judges" is important. By increasing the field of selection and specifically by attracting judges who set a higher value on income, and hence on work, relative to leisure, an increase in judicial salary may enable a harder-working class of judges to be recruited. Also, by reducing turnover, especially of the judges with the best private-sector opportunities (who are probably on average the best judges), the higher salary may conduce to a more experienced, higher-quality judiciary. But the possible cost in reduced effort should not be ignored—though here we must bear in mind that time and effort are not synonyms. If effort or energy is limited and leisure requires less effort than judging, a reallocation of time from judging to leisure activities may actually increase the effort that the judge devotes to judging and hence the quality of his judicial output. This is the economic interpretation of Brandeis' famous dictum, in explaining why he took a month's vacation every summer: "I can do twelve months' work in eleven months but not in twelve months."

Let me further complicate the analysis by allowing the judge to obtain some income from moonlighting. The opportunities for such income have been greatly curtailed recently[52]—judges no longer can accept payment for speeches or articles, and their income from teaching has been capped at a modest percentage (approximately 15 percent) of their judicial salaries. Book royalties are not limited, however—so one predicts that judges will give fewer speeches and write more books.

The effect of curtailing nonjudicial income can be modeled by partitioning judges' income into a fixed and a variable component, the

---

52 Title VI of the Ethics Reform Act of 1989, 5 USC app 7 §§ 501–505, effective January 1, 1991. See also Regulations of the Judicial Conference of the United States under Title VI of the Ethics Reform Act of 1989 concerning Outside Earned Income, Honoraria, and Outside Employment.

second representing moonlighting income. With this refinement, and ignoring the arguments in the judicial function (other than judicial income) that are not likely to be significantly responsive to changes in the amount of time invested in judging, the judicial utility function can be rewritten as

$$U = U(I_f, I_v(t_v), t_j, t_l) \tag{2}$$

I has been divided into a fixed and variable component. The former is the judge's judicial salary. The latter is his moonlighting income, and depends on the time he allots to moonlighting (t_v). So $I = I_f + I_v(t_v)$, where $t_j + t_l + t_v = 24$. In considering how much time to allocate to judging, the rational judge will consider not only the negative impact on his leisure but also the negative impact on his nonjudicial income. That impact will be less, the fewer lawful opportunities the judge has to obtain such income. Hence we can expect that the curtailment of judicial moonlighting has increased both the judicial effort of the existing judges (save for the book writers!) and their leisure, since the opportunity to moonlight makes leisure more costly. The prediction with respect to leisure is more confidently made. Moonlighting income at time $t+1$ may be a positive function of judicial effort at time t, so curtailing opportunities for moonlighting income may reduce the return to judicial effort and, as a result, the amount of that effort. Therefore a cautious prediction is that the curtailment of moonlighting income, coupled with the increase in judicial salaries,[53] has increased judges' consumption of leisure. This is an empirically testable prediction,[54] at least if the extra consumption of leisure is at the expense of judicial work as well as of moonlighting; and if the prediction is confirmed empirically this would be some evidence that judges behave in accordance with the rational model of human behavior.

I want to say more about the selection of judges because the formal model is again helpful. A person will accept a judgeship if his net expected utility from it is positive, which is to say if that utility exceeds

---

[53] The recent curtailment of judicial moonlighting was coupled with a substantial judicial pay raise (nominally 25 percent, effectively almost 40 percent), also as of January 1, 1991.

[54] For example, a lengthening of court queues unexplained by any other factor (including moonlighting) would be evidence that judges were increasing their consumption of leisure.

the utility that he obtains in his present employment (in the practice of law, let us assume) plus the cost (other than the forgone income from practice) of becoming a judge, for example the inconvenience, exasperation, and loss of privacy entailed in filling out elaborate forms and undergoing a searching investigation by the FBI and possibly a severe grilling by the Senate Judiciary Committee. Formally, then, the condition for accepting a judgeship is that

$$U_J(t_j, t_l, I_J, R_J, P_J) - U_L(t_L, I_L) - C > 0 \qquad (3)$$

where U_J is the utility from being a judge, I_J is the judicial salary, P_J is the prestige of being a judge, U_L is the utility of practicing law, t_L is the time a lawyer spends working, C is the cost of becoming a judge, and the other terms are either as before or self-explanatory. Lawyers are assumed to have no leisure—more realistically, l_J should be viewed as the contribution to the judge's utility of the additional leisure that a judge has compared to a practicing lawyer. The other arguments in the judicial utility function (that is, the components of O other than prestige) have been dropped as not particularly helpful to the analysis of judicial selection. The utility terms should be translated into present values to be comparable to C, but I omit this detail.

Certain points are obvious enough. The more costly it is to become a judge and the lower the judicial income is relative to income in practice, the less likely a lawyer is to accept a judgeship. Hence the fact that federal judges of the same rank are paid the same no matter where they live, even though the cost of living and the salaries of lawyers vary widely across the country, enlarges the field of selection in low-cost versus high-cost areas. And the more a lawyer values leisure, prestige, and judging versus lawyering, the more likely he will be to accept a judgeship. A slightly subtler point is that if in order to enlarge the field of selection steps are taken to increase judicial prestige by limiting the growth in the number of judges, the amount of leisure that a judge can enjoy without imperiling his reputation will fall and as a result the field of selection may not, on balance, be enlarged. However, although the number of candidates may be the same (or even smaller), there will be a shift in the composition of the group away from leisure-loving judges, with the result that limiting the growth of the number of judges may not reduce judicial output.

More formally, let *EU* be the net expected utility of being a judge. It is therefore equal to the left-hand side of inequality (3). If *S* is the set of candidates for judicial appointment, $S = S(EU)$, and is larger the greater the expected utility of being a judge. So far as relevant here, *EU* is a positive function of P_J (judicial prestige) and of t_l (the time devoted to leisure). Let *n* be the number of judges. Both P_J and t_l are affected by *n*, but in opposite directions. An increase in the number of judges increases judges' leisure by reducing the average judicial workload ($d_{tl}/dn > 0$), but reduces the prestige of judges ($dP_J/dn < 0$). If these effects of an increase in *n* are perfectly offsetting, so that *EU* is unchanged, the field of selection will not be enlarged. But the composition of the field will be altered in favor of judges who attach greater weight to prestige and less to leisure. As long as prestige is not positively correlated with leisure-loving, the net effect will be an increase in the propensity of judges to work. This analysis has policy relevance in view of recent calls to limit the number of federal judges. And the analysis is empirically testable because if it is correct we should observe that, other things being equal, judicial output increases less than proportionately to an increase in the number of judges.

Although my focus is on the ordinary judge, there have been of course some extraordinary judges; let us consider whether this is consistent with the model. One does not expect large quality differences between employees paid the same wage in the same job by the same employer. Such a wage would either overpay the lower-quality employees or underpay the higher-quality ones (it could of course do both), and in the latter event the higher-quality employees would leave, unless their skills were not transferable to another employer. One possibility is that the judicial wage has been set at a level that is compensatory for the extraordinary judge but overpays the ordinary one; then we would expect queuing for the job by the ordinary candidates—and there is in fact queuing for federal judgeships.[55] Another possibility, however, is that while the wage is the same for the ordinary and the

---

[55] There is also very little turnover among federal judges, which might seem to be additional evidence that they are overpaid. However, the heavily back-loaded character of federal judicial compensation provides an alternative explanation for the low turnover of federal judges. Compare Ippolito, *Why Federal Workers Don't Quit* at 281 (cited in note 8).

extraordinary judge, the full income (U) is as high or higher for the latter, because R_J in his judicial utility function is higher than R_J in the judicial utility function of the ordinary judge. (The more talented judge is more likely to obtain a greater reputation.) The higher R_J in the left-most term of inequality (3) might offset the higher I_L in the next term, with the result that U_J might exceed U_L by the same amount as in the case of the ordinary judge. This is a further illustration of the importance of nonpecuniary income in the compensation structure of judges.

Along similar lines it has been argued that an increase in judicial salaries could actually reduce the quality of the judiciary, by diluting the effect of low judicial salaries in screening out candidates who do not anticipate large nonpecuniary gains as a result of being able to develop a reputation for being a superior judge.[56] Moreover, an increase in judicial salaries could, by making a judgeship a richer patronage plum, increase the role of political as distinct from merit considerations in the selection of judges. These are only partial effects, however. An increase in judicial salaries will also make it easier to attract candidates who have good incomes in the private practice of law, or in law teaching or other law-related activities, and these lawyers are probably on average the abler candidates. Putting these points together, we can speculate that an increase in salaries will increase the quality of the judiciary but reduce the variance in that quality.

Should we expect systematic behavioral differences between ordinary and extraordinary judges? I conjecture that the function relating judicial work to judicial ability is U-shaped. Very weak judges must work hard to reach the threshold above which judicial prestige does not vary greatly with output; very strong judges have an incentive to work hard because hard work can be expected to have a multiplicative rather than merely an additive effect on ability.

It might seem that strong judges would be less likely than weak ones to adhere to precedent because they would not want to feel themselves bound by the decisions of previous judges who were on average weaker than they. But this is not clear, and not only because these strong judges want the precedents *they* create to be followed. If aban-

[56] Paul E. Greenberg and James A. Haley, *The Role of the Compensation Structure in Enhancing Judicial Quality*, 15 J Legal Stud 417 (1986).

donment or erosion of stare decisis increased judicial workloads, which we recall is plausible although not certain, more judges would be appointed, and the influence of each judge would be diluted.[57] Moreover, we should recall the earlier point that judges, strong as well as weak, enjoy playing the judicial "game," a game that has certain rules of which one (in the Anglo-American legal system) is that judges should give great although not controlling weight to precedents as authorities. Two of the strongest judges in our history, Oliver Wendell Holmes and Learned Hand, were quite deferential toward precedents.

Inequality (3) can be used to predict differences between court of appeals judges and Supreme Court Justices. Since I_J, $U_j(t_j)$, and especially P_J are substantially higher for the latter than for the former, we expect, and observe, that there is more vigorous "campaigning" for Supreme Court appointments and that refusal to accept appointment to the Court is rare. Moreover, Supreme Court Justices are less likely to resign to pursue other careers than lower-court judges are (even after correcting for differences in age). Although they have better opportunities (that is, a higher I_L), their loss in voting power and in prestige would be very great. And because $U_J(t_j)$ (the utility of time devoted to judging) is much greater for Supreme Court Justices than for court of appeals judges (since a Supreme Court vote has a much greater expected outcome), while $U_L(t_l)$ (the utility of time devoted to leisure) presumably is the same, we can expect Supreme Court Justices on average to work harder than court of appeals judges, especially with the same limitations having been placed on their moonlighting activities.[58]

[57] O'Hara, *Implicit Collusion* at 14 (cited in note 9).

[58] This is analogous to the phenomenon noted earlier that people are more likely to vote in closely contested elections for high offices such as the Presidency than in one-sided elections for unimportant offices. A partially offsetting factor is that since there are more Supreme Court Justices than the number of judges on most lower-court panels (for example, in the federal courts of appeals the vast majority of cases are heard and decided by panels of only three judges), a Supreme Court Justice is less likely to be the swing vote, hence less likely to make a difference in the outcome of the case. This is probably a minor factor, especially since the greater controversiality of Supreme Court cases results in a much higher fraction of decisions that are decided by a single vote than in the courts of appeals, where dissents are relatively infrequent. Cutting the other way is that "going along" voting is less common in the Supreme Court.

The prediction that Supreme Court Justices work harder than other judges is plausible only if allowance is made for differences in age and workload between them and other judges. Supreme Court Justices are older on average than court of appeals judges (implying that they have a lower energy level and hence a diminished capacity for hard work), and have (possibly as a concomitant) a lighter workload, in major part because their jurisdiction is discretionary, which enables them to limit their workload. If greater age and lighter workload are assumed to cancel out—the average Justice works fewer hours but his hours are divided among fewer cases—we are left with a simple prediction that the average Supreme Court Justice does work harder per case than the average court of appeals judge does. If, however, as seems plausible, judicial effort has a diminishing effect on the satisfactions from judicial voting, a reduction in workload will reduce total judicial effort rather than merely redistribute it among fewer cases, and then we might expect the Justices to work less hard than the court of appeals judges do, even on a per-case basis. If as I believe the average Justice does work somewhat harder than the average court of appeals judge, this implies that the diminishing marginal utility of judicial effort is offset by the higher average utility resulting from the greater power and case selectivity of the Supreme Court compared with the courts of appeals.

A further difference in workload is that Supreme Court cases tend to be more sensitive and controversial than cases (even the same cases) in the lower courts. So we can expect the Justices, in order to reduce the element of hassle in their work, to be particularly adept at using decision-avoidance doctrines, such as mootness, ripeness, political question, and absence of a real case or controversy, to avoid having to decide the merits of such cases.

VII. CONCLUSION

Judges are rational, and they pursue instrumental and consumption goals of the same general kind and in the same general way that private persons do. That has been the main thesis of this article. The article does not explain the content of judicial doctrines, and it may seem to undermine the theory that the common law and other areas of judge-made law are on the whole efficiency-enhancing[59] by disparaging the ability and the will of judges to conceive and impose so singular and ambitious a vision. Actually it supports that theory by showing that the conditions of judicial employment enable and induce judges to vote their personal convictions and policy preferences—or in a word their values.

Reference to the legislative function of the judiciary and to the rules of the judicial game further contributes to dissolving the tension between the analysis of the judicial utility function in this article and the efficiency theory of the common law. When a really new case arises, the rules of the judicial game require the judge to act the part of a legislator and therefore vote his values, although the rules do not require and may even forbid him to acknowledge that this is what he is doing. Efficiency – not necessarily by that name – is an important social value that judges, given their limited remedial powers and the value pluralism of our society, can promote in a reasonably effective, consistent, objective, and hassle-free fashion. One therefore expects it to be influential in judicial decisionmaking when judges are called upon to exercise a legislative function. The decision of a really new case establishes a precedent for future guidance. At this point the rules of the judicial game require the judges to follow the precedent rather than to decide each future case from the ground up. Hence the subsequent cases may not bear any visible imprint of economic thinking, but they will be efficient decisions if the precedent, reflecting the judges' legislative activity, was based implicitly or explicitly on a desire to enhance efficiency. Law can thus be efficient even if only a small minority of cases concern themselves with efficiency. Since the judges have a larger legislative role in common law than statutory cases, we expect common law rules to be on average more efficient than statutory ones.

But this is a side issue. The value of the approach taken in this article is that it demystifies judges at the same time that it domesticates them for economic analysis, and that it both explains the principal features of judicial behavior and generates a number of empirically testable predictions. I have focused on the federal judiciary but the approach can and should be extended to elected judges, to Continental

---

59 See, for example, Posner, *Economic Analysis of Law* part 2 (cited in note 13). But see Koyayashi and Lott, *Judicial Reputation* (cited in note 9).

European judges, to jurors, and to legislators. For example, my analysis predicts that judges elected for a term work harder than appointed judges and also that they are less inclined to follow precedent because they are more responsive to the current balance of political power, hence less "independent." Through the testing of these predictions and those suggested earlier in the article, we can move toward the goal of a theoretically sophisticated and empirically validated understanding of the basic institution of our legal system.

[13]

Strategic Policy Considerations and Voting Fluidity on the Burger Court

FORREST MALTZMAN and PAUL J. WAHLBECK *George Washington University*

Justices are strategic actors. This is particularly evident when they change their votes between the original conference on the merits and the Court's announcement of the final decision. We predict that such voting fluidity may be influenced by strategic policy considerations, justices' uncertainty over issues involved in a case, the chief justice's interest in protecting his prerogatives, and other institutional pressures. To test our hypotheses, we explore the occurrence of fluidity on the Burger Court (1969–85). Using logistic regression, we show that justices' decisions to change their votes stem primarily from strategic policy considerations. In limited instances, the decision to switch can be attributed to either uncertainty or institutional pressures. Our findings suggest that the decision of a justice to join an opinion results from more than his or her initial policy preferences; final votes are influenced as well by the politics of opinion writing.

Justices, unlike computers, do not react automatically or always "stay put"....

—Chief Justice Warren Burger,
letter to Justice William O. Douglas,
July 27, 1972

As Chief Justice Burger suggests, Supreme Court justices change their votes. They may reconsider the vote they cast at the initial conference on the merits at any time before the Court's final decision is announced. Justice William Brennan, for example, once told Justice Potter Stewart, "I voted the other way at conference but you've convinced me" (Brennan 1969). What prompts a justice to change positions? Murphy (1964) suggests that the answer rests, at least in part, in the strategic interaction among justices. After all, the key resource that policy-minded justices have at their disposal is their vote and opinion—and these can be used as bargaining chips to affect the content of the Court's opinion. It thus seems likely that justices might switch their votes in response to draft opinions as they attempt to obtain final Court opinions consistent with their views.

The nature of this strategic interaction is frequently seen in exchanges over opinion passages. Justices often ask the opinion author to address their concerns by modifying the draft opinion through the addition of a phrase or the deletion of a few sentences. These requests are frequently presented as a condition for joining the opinion. Justices tacitly threaten to withhold support if the changes are not made; indeed, they may refrain from joining the opinion and may instead write or join a concurring or dissenting opinion. At times, justices are more blunt. After asking Justice Hugo Black to make two additions to his majority opinion, Justice Potter Stewart threatened to join John Harlan's dissent: "At the risk of seeming unreasonably stubborn, I am still unwilling to join your opinion so long as it contains the view expressed in the phrase 'over a long period of time' in the 6th line on page 12. Perhaps I had better wait to see John Harlan's separate opinion" (Stewart 1969). Ultimately, Black altered the draft opinion, and Stewart switched from the position he first expressed at conference and joined Black's opinion.

Even though Chief Justice Burger and most judicial scholars recognize that justices alter their votes, our understanding of why and when they switch positions is still limited. Indeed, since the first discussion of justices' strategic behavior by Murphy (1964), very little empirical work has been done to examine the nature of this strategic interaction (Epstein and Knight 1995). In this paper, we articulate and test a comprehensive model of why justices do not always "stay put." We argue that justices' decisions to alter their votes are potentially shaped by three factors: strategic policy considerations, uncertainty about the legal issues involved in a case, and institutional pressures and considerations inherent in the Court.

VOTING FLUIDITY

Fluidity is not the norm on the Court, but neither is it rare: During the 1946–75 period, a justice was likely to switch his or her vote from affirm to reverse or from reverse to affirm 7.3% of the time (Dorff and Brenner 1992).[1] Nevertheless, over half of Supreme Court cases decided during the six terms covered in Brenner (1980) had at least one instance of fluidity. Following the landmark work by Howard (1968), several studies have attempted to examine and explain empirically the occurrence of fluidity (Brenner 1980, 1982; Dorff and Brenner 1992; Hagle and Spaeth 1991). The explanations these authors offer have focused primarily on the attributes of individual justices and case characteristics, such as a justice's freshman status, the size of the majority coalition, and the salience of the case. We build upon previous analyses of voting fluidity in three respects.

First, we examine the relationship between strategic policy considerations and changing votes. In spite of the

---

Forrest Maltzman and Paul J. Wahlbeck are assistant professors of Political Science, George Washington University, Washington D.C. 20052.

An earlier version of this paper was presented at the 1995 annual meeting of the Midwest Political Science Association. The authors gratefully acknowledge the comments and advice of Sarah Binder, Saul Brenner, Lee Epstein, Jim Levobic, Lee Sigelman. Elliot Slotnick, Harold Spaeth, Jim Spriggs, and Jack Wright. We also appreciate the research assistance provided by Mary DeCamp. The authors also thank Justice William Brennan for access to his personal papers. Financial support for this project was provided for by the George Washington University Junior Scholar Incentive Program and the University Facilitating Fund.

[1] During the 1946–55 period, a justice changed his vote from affirm to reverse (or vice versa) 9% of the time (Brenner 1980), and during the 1956–67 period, 10% of the time (Brenner 1982).

insight that voting fluidity provides judicial scholars in investigating the strategic interaction among justices, most studies do not explore the role of policy considerations. The only study that has tested that role (Hagle and Spaeth 1991) finds a significant bivariate relationship between the occurrence of fluidity and the juxtaposition of the author's and the voting justice's ideology. Other studies investigate other ideologically related hypotheses, such as whether fluidity is less prevalent among outcome-oriented, liberal justices or in cases with liberal outcomes (Dorff and Brenner 1992), but they do not address whether justices change positions because they are ideologically closer to the opposing writer than to the writer assigned the opinion for their original positions.

Second, with a single exception (Dorff and Brenner 1992), previous analyses of fluidity have not attempted to test a multivariate model. Instead, they have used bivariate analysis to isolate factors related to the frequency of voting fluidity, such as justices' length of experience on the Court. By examining the effect of one factor at a time, most previous work has not disentangled the effects of the multiple influences on fluidity. Multivariate controls allow us to assess the independent influence of numerous factors potentially affecting justices' votes. Conclusions drawn from previous bivariate analyses may not hold when multivariate controls are in place.

Third, we expand the scope of previous research to include all cases decided during the Burger Court (1969–85) and all instances in which a justice voted on the initial decision either to affirm or reverse.[2] Previous studies have tended to focus solely on either the tendency of justices to switch into the minority or on their propensity to join the majority. Although Brenner (1980, 1982) did assess the frequency of both types of fluidity, no study has yet developed a comprehensive model of fluidity. For example, although Dorff and Brenner (1992) use a multivariate model, their analysis is based on a limited data set assessing only the votes of justices who initially sided with the minority. In contrast, Hagle and Spaeth (1991) limit their analysis to justices originally voting with the majority; and Brenner, Hagle, and Spaeth (1989) look solely at fluidity that changes the outcome of a decision. All of these studies present important instances of fluidity, but none captures the complete range of fluidity that can occur. Collectively, therefore, they provide only a partial account of the politics of Court decision making. By building on these earlier important works, we hope to develop a more complete model of the politics of fluidity and to expand our understanding of Court dynamics.

FLUIDITY AND THE DELIBERATIVE PROCESS

Voting fluidity on the Supreme Court presents a paradox to judicial scholars. Although Chief Justice Burger asserts that justices do not act "automatically," the dominant explanations of judicial behavior virtually lead us to expect justices to do so. At the very least, vote switching seems inconsistent with dominant explanations of Court behavior (Howard 1968). The attitudinal model of Court decision making suggests that preferences alone account for the behavior of Supreme Court justices (Segal and Spaeth 1993, 65).[3] Indeed, attitudinalists view justices as "'naive' decision makers who always vote their unconstrained attitudes" (Epstein and Knight 1995, 2). They argue that justices make decisions exclusively on the basis of their fixed preference concerning the case outcome, and the Court's written opinions are therefore just "post-hoc rationalizations" of their earlier decision on the merits, cloaking their true motivations (Frank [1930] 1970, Schubert 1965, Segal and Spaeth 1993). If this is an accurate depiction of judicial decision making, reevaluation of a justice's position and subsequent vote change as a result of the Court's deliberation and circulation of draft opinions is an anomaly. If justices have a clear set of policy preferences or attitudes that they apply in reaching the decision on the merits, what explains vote change?

In this article, we suggest a more nuanced role for the influence of policy preferences on justices' votes. In particular, we suggest that justices' votes may change while they are considering a case because of the context of the decision-making process. At least three elements of that process are likely to convince justices to alter previously held positions. First, their preferences are not always firm on every issue. Such uncertainty leaves them open to the persuasion of their fellow justices during the decision-making process. Second, the dynamics of the coalition-building process—in which opinions are drafted and amended—can often entirely reshape the nature of the Court's ruling and reasoning, thereby making the outcome more or less attractive to the justices. Third, institutional considerations may encourage justices to change their votes for reasons that are independent of their policy concerns. We elaborate each of these competing influences below.

Consider first the effects of justices' uncertainty about the legal and political issues raised in a new case. Justices may not have strong policy preferences about every issue that comes before the Court, and the policy implications of the case may not be apparent until the majority opinion is drafted. As a result, we might expect a justice who does not have fixed views on a given issue to switch his or her vote during deliberation of the case, perhaps after being persuaded by a fellow justice

[2] Previous studies of Court fluidity have focused on fluidity during the Vinson and Warren Courts and the early years of the Burger Court. The opportunity to study fluidity during the entire Burger Court has only recently been provided by the release of Justice Thurgood Marshall's and Justice William Brennan's papers.

[3] While the attitudinal model may be the most prominent model of Supreme Court decision making, other scholars have maintained that preferences alone do not account for the actions of Supreme Court justices. For example, the decision to grant certiorari depends in part upon non–attitudinal factors, such as the interests of the solicitor general (Tanenhaus et al. 1963) or the need to correct errors made by lower courts (Provine 1980, Songer 1979, Ulmer 1984). Likewise, the chief justice's assignment of cases depends in part upon organizational demands upon the Court (Maltzman and Wahlbeck 1996a). Court decisions on the merits are also influenced by legal precedent (George and Epstein 1992), party resources (Songer and Sheehan 1992; but see Sheehan, Mishler, and Songer 1992), and attorney experience (McGuire 1995).

(Howard 1968, Murphy 1964). Murphy explains that "judges can be persuaded to change their minds about specific cases as well as about broad public policies, and intellectual persuasion can play an important role in such shifts" (1964, 44). The importance of persuasion is reflected in a memo from Justice Harlan to Justice Black about his decision to change his vote in *Detroit and Toledo Shore Line* v. *United Transportation Union* (1969). Harlan wrote Black, "As one of those whose Conference vote was to reverse this case, I am persuaded by your opinion that affirmance is the proper result" (Harlan 1969). Preferences, in short, may be endogenous to the decision-making process. Rather than acting on sincerely held preferences brought to the bench, justices' views about particular cases may be susceptible to influence during the process of deliberation.

Although a decision to change a vote may reflect an evolution of thinking after the initial conference vote, we suspect that an important source of fluidity may be the nature of the opinion drafts that are circulated. Justices and members of the legal community care about more than the decision to reverse or affirm: they care about the legal rules articulated in the opinions. After all, these legal rules not only affect the litigants in a specific case, but also establish guidelines or referents that will affect similarly situated parties (Spriggs 1996, Wahlbeck 1994). The Court's opinions can therefore be seen as broad policy statements. What these opinions say, of course, depends upon both the policy views of the opinion author and the composition of the coalition expected to sign the opinion. Thus, fluidity in a justice's vote is likely to reflect a response to the opinion circulated after the conference on the merits.

Take, for example, *Wardius* v. *Oregon* (1973). In this case, Justice Brennan's docket books reveal that Justice Rehnquist initially voted with the minority. Nevertheless, on March 14, 1973, he circulated an explanatory note: "I voted to affirm in this case at Conference, but before writing a dissent to Thurgood's proposed opinion I think I will wait to see if anything narrower ... is written" (Rehnquist 1973). On June 4, Justice Marshall circulated a new draft with a cover letter stating that "since the Court appears hopelessly splintered on the disposition of petitioner's contentions concerning the state's exclusionary rule, I have decided that it may be best to leave this question for another day" (Marshall 1973). On June 6, Marshall's decision to limit the breadth of his opinion was rewarded when Rehnquist joined his opinion to reverse. Rehnquist's vote in this case clearly reflected something other than a desire to affirm the decision of the lower court. Instead, Rehnquist was willing to abandon his preferred outcome in order to ensure that the majority opinion was narrowly drawn. Thus, Rehnquist changed his vote once the opinion as crafted by Marshall more closely reflected his preferred policy outcome. Changes in draft opinions may yield changes in justices' votes.

Beyond such strategic interactions among opinion authors and their coalitions, institutional considerations might also be at play in leading justices to change their votes. As members of a nine-justice bench, Supreme Court justices are potentially susceptible to a variety of pressures beyond policy preferences. First, the visibility of each justice's vote exerts unique pressures on the Court. Justices on the Court, like individuals in all institutions, may feel uncomfortable remaining outside the dominant group. As a result, justices may change their votes from the minority to the majority because of small-group influences that are independent of policy preferences. Second, justices may feel constrained by concerns about the effects of the Court's decisions. This constraint is potentially enhanced by producing a unanimous opinion from the bench (Johnson and Canon 1984).

In sum, preferences alone—independent of the process of reaching decisions on the Court—cannot explain why justices change their votes. Indeed, according to Howard (1968), such voting fluidity suggests the need to refine the attitudinal model: "If a vote or an opinion has changed in response to a multiplicity of intracourt influences before its public exposure, how reliable is that vote or opinion as an indicator of attitude, ideology, or if one pleases, predilection?" (p. 44). In our view, a model of voting fluidity must take into account both policy preferences and these "intracourt influences."

EXPLAINING FLUIDITY

Fluidity stems from the strategic interaction among justices. We therefore expect justices to switch to the opinion that best represents their policy preferences and we expect this relationship to hold even after subjecting it to controls for issue uncertainty, the chief justice's interest in leading the Court, and other institutional considerations. We address each of these in turn.

Policy Considerations

The strategic model portrays justices as responding to the positions articulated by other justices. As a result, we expect justices to sign the opinion that is closest to their own policy preferences (Epstein and Mershon 1993, Rohde and Spaeth 1976, Segal and Spaeth 1993). Previous findings on voting fluidity are consistent with this expectation. For example, Hagle and Spaeth (1991) show that nearly 75% of the time when a justice switches from the majority to the minority, s/he is ideologically closer to the marginal justice in dissent than to any member who sides with the majority (p. 122). Similarly, Brenner and Spaeth (1989) and Brenner, Hagle, and Spaeth (1989) show that minimum winning coalitions are most likely to break up when the marginal justice in the majority is closer to the dissenters than to any member of the majority. In these instances, the marginal justice is likely to switch and undermine the initial majority's victory.

The extent to which a particular opinion reflects a justice's policy preferences depends upon three factors. First, the views of the authors writing majority and dissenting opinions are important. After all, as Justice William Brennan once wrote to Chief Justice Burger, "[My] votes are tentative depending upon what is written pro and con" (Brennan 1971). Because the justices who write opinions have a disproportionate capacity to shape the final opinion (Murphy 1964), the following hypothesis seems reasonable:

HYPOTHESIS 1: *The closer a justice is ideologically to the person writing the opinion for his or her conference coalition as compared to the author of the opposing opinion, the less likely the justice is to switch.*

Second, the ideological composition of the original coalition may influence a justice's final vote on a case. Although authors clearly have a significant influence over a particular opinion, the justices who make up a coalition can also substantively affect the opinion they expect to sign (Epstein and Knight 1995, Murphy 1964, Schwartz 1996). Authoring justices frequently respond to the concerns articulated by other potential coalition members by adopting their suggestions. Justice Stewart, for example, once reported to the conference that he "restructured this opinion somewhat, in an effort to meet the difficulties expressed" by other justices (Stewart 1970). Thus, as justices attempt to retain a majority, the views they articulate in an opinion may be moderated by a desire to appease another justice. This leads us to expect the following:

HYPOTHESIS 2: *The closer a justice is ideologically to the original coalition as compared to the opposing coalition, the less likely the justice is to switch.*

Third, the size of the initial coalitions is likely to be important. If the initial majority coalition is a minimum winning coalition, authors on both sides will recognize the fragility of their coalitions and thus be particularly responsive to the concerns of those justices forming the original coalition. Until the opinion commands a "Court" of five justices, the author has an incentive to accommodate other justices to reach a majority (Biskupic 1995, Riker 1962). This leads to the following hypothesis:

HYPOTHESIS 3: *A justice is less likely to switch votes if the initial majority coalition was a minimum winning one.*

Uncertainty

There are, of course, alternative explanations to account for a justice's decision to switch his or her vote. A plausible hypothesis is that the justice did not fully understand the issues involved in a particular case when casting the initial vote. Indeed, in his ground-breaking study of fluidity on the Court, Howard (1968) suggests uncertainty as a factor that could account for such voting fluidity: "Shifting perspectives appear to have been a function of additional thought and homework, by a clerk or a justice, into issues that were only partially perceived at first because of inadequate argument, briefs, or time" (p. 47). This is supported by statements of justices indicating how they reached results contrary to their original positions—"mature reflection" or "research and labor" convinced them to change votes (Harlan 1970, Marshall 1969).

A justice's uncertainty should vary with both the case and the justice. When a case is particularly complex and thus raises multiple legal issues, the likelihood that a justice will understand all aspects of the case at the time of the initial vote is low. Justice William Douglas suggested this to the conference in *Dandridge* v. *Williams* (1969):

> I voted to reverse. As you will recall, the decision by the three-judge court was on the Equal Protection Clause that I think did not sustain the Court's position. . . . I have now concluded that the case was rightly decided below, not for the constitutional reason but because of the federal statute and the Supremacy Clause. I am, therefore, changing my vote to affirm (Douglas 1969).

Thus, we hypothesize the following:

HYPOTHESIS 4: *The more complex the case, the more likely a justice is to switch.*

Conversely, a justice's level of certainty will be highest when the case is highly salient. In these cases, the justice's positions will be relatively fixed, and the likelihood that new information will alter a justice's opinion is relatively low (Brenner and Palmer 1988). Consistent with this finding are Brenner's (1980, 1982) and Hagle and Spaeth's (1991) findings that fluidity is not more likely in a case that is particularly salient. We expect little fluidity in highly salient cases, but justices may be more willing to acquiesce to a contrary opinion in cases that are not seen as important. In fact, Dorff and Brenner (1992) show that justices are more likely to switch from the minority to the majority if the case is not salient. This leads us to expect the following:

HYPOTHESIS 5: *The more salient the case, the less likely a justice is to switch.*

Uncertainty is also likely to reflect a justice's judicial experiences and personal expertise. The longer a justice has served on the Court, the more likely he or she is to understand all of the relevant issues when casting the initial vote on merits. In contrast, "it is not uncommon for a new justice to undergo a period of adjustment . . . before his voting behavior stabilizes into observable, not to mention predictable, patterns" (Howard 1968, 45). Consistent with this claim, Dorff and Brenner (1992) find that freshmen justices are more likely to switch than are their senior colleagues (but see Hagle and Spaeth 1991). Conversely, a justice's relative expertise in an issue area will also likely affect the propensity to switch. Presumably, justices with substantive expertise in a particular area are more likely to cast an informed vote at the initial conference than are their colleagues who have only a passing familiarity with a particular type of case. These expectations lead to two further hypotheses:

HYPOTHESIS 6: *Freshmen are more likely to switch than are more senior justices.*

HYPOTHESIS 7: *Policy experts are less likely to switch than are justices with less expertise in an issue area.*

Institutional Considerations

The chief justice is in a unique institutional position. Unlike other justices on the Court, the chief justice has the prerogative to assign the Court's opinion when s/he is in the majority. This prerogative is one of the chief's most important sources of power (Maltzman and Wahlbeck 1996a, Murphy 1964, Rohde 1972, Rohde and Spaeth 1976, Segal and Spaeth 1993, Slotnick 1979). For this reason, it may be in the chief justice's strategic interest to switch from the minority to the majority after conference. Although judicial scholars have not studied the frequency of such strategic behavior, anecdotal evidence from the justices' papers and chronicles of Court politics have suggested that Chief Justice Burger frequently engaged in such behavior (Woodward and Armstrong 1979). For example, in an unpublished opinion, Justice Douglas accused Burger of trying to control the opinion assignment by altering his vote in *Roe* v. *Wade*:

> The Chief Justice represented the minority view in the Conference and forcefully urged his viewpoint on the issue. . . . Hence traditionally the senior Justice in the majority—who in this case was not myself—should have made the assignment of the opinion . . . . The cases were, however, assigned by the Chief Justice (Douglas 1972a).[4]

In addition to changing his or her vote to control the assignment, the chief may feel additional institutional pressures to vote with the majority. As the leader of the Court, s/he may seek to present the Court as unified and himself or herself as the leader. As a result, we might expect the chief to subordinate his or her policy preferences and switch to side with the majority. Regardless of why the chief moves from the minority to the majority, there is good reason to propose the following:

HYPOTHESIS 8a: *The chief justice is more likely than other members to switch from the minority to the majority.*

Conversely, the chief justice will want to retain control of the opinion and will rarely switch from the majority to the minority:

HYPOTHESIS 8b: *The chief justice is less likely than other justices to switch from the majority to the minority.*

The power of the chief to assign the majority opinion is not the only institutional feature of the Court. For two additional reasons, the nature of the initial voting coalitions might increase the probability that justices will switch their votes. First, Supreme Court scholars have maintained that the impact of Court decisions is enhanced when the Court rules overwhelmingly, sending a clear signal to lower court judges and other implementers (Howard 1968, Johnson and Canon 1984, Murphy 1964). As a result, Howard (1968) argues that minority coalition justices frequently alter their votes because of their loyalty to the Court as an institution. The size of the voting coalitions may affect justices' desire to change their votes for unconscious reasons as well. Indeed, social psychologists have maintained that an individual's perception of the appropriate conclusion is most likely to change when he or she is one of few dissenters (Asch 1951, 1952; Hare 1976). The influence of the majority is particularly intense in small groups (Hare 1976). Brenner and Dorff (1992) argue that this is why justices are more likely to switch from dissenting to concurring than from concurring to dissenting. This leads to a final set of hypotheses consistent with these expectations:

HYPOTHESIS 9a: *Justices who vote in the conference minority are more likely to switch than justices who are members of the conference majority.*

HYPOTHESIS 9b: *Justices who dissent are more likely to switch to the majority opinion if relatively few justices are dissenting.*

HYPOTHESIS 9c: *If the Court is unanimous on the initial conference vote, justices will be less likely to switch.*

DATA AND METHODS

Our analysis is based upon cases decided by the Burger Court (1969–85 October terms).[5] By comparing the initial conference vote of each justice to his final vote, we were able to identify instances of fluidity. To determine the conference vote of each justice, we relied upon the docket books of Justice William Brennan. These docket books provide a highly reliable record of how each justice voted in conference, especially when the vote supported either affirmation or reversal (Maltzman and Wahlbeck 1996b). To determine the final vote of each justice, we used Spaeth (1994a).

If a justice voted to affirm at the initial conference on the merits and eventually supported reversal in the final decision or, alternatively, initially voted to reverse but ultimately affirmed the lower court, we coded the justice's action as fluid.[6] If the justice voted either to affirm or reverse initially as well as in the final decision, we portrayed the justice's vote as stable. If a justice voted for an outcome other than to reverse or affirm (for example, to "dismiss as improvidently granted" or vacate) at either vote, the justice's pair of votes was excluded from the analysis. During the Burger Court, there were 18,411 pairs of individual votes. Of these, 2,899 (15.7%) were excluded from our analysis because of a vote for a position other than to affirm or reverse or

[4] Based on an examination of the justices' conference vote, some might question Justice Douglas's assertion that he was not the senior associate justice in *Roe*. In fact, at least according to his records, he was the most senior justice in the coalition that favored striking down the abortion laws. In a letter to Chief Justice Burger, he explained why he was not the senior associate justice: "The reason Bill Brennan, not I, represented the consensus at the first Conference on the Abortion Cases was that I thought at the time that the cases—at least Georgia's—could be disposed of on Equal Protection grounds—a theory that did not hold up on further study" (Douglas 1972b).

[5] We limited our analysis to cases that were orally argued before the Court and in which the Court released a signed opinion. We omitted per curiam decisions, memorandum decisions, and decrees. We also excluded those cases in which no clear majority existed at the initial conference because there was a tied decision or because a majority of the Court voted for an outcome other than to reverse or to affirm. The docket sheets for the 57 cases missing from Brennan's records are also excluded. Finally, we excluded those cases that did not fit into one of the 12 substantive issue areas that Spaeth (1994a) identified. (See footnote 8.)

[6] We limited our analysis to those instances in which a justice initially voted to affirm or reverse because in these instances the docket books of the justices are most reliable (Maltzman and Wahlbeck 1996b). If we included in our analysis votes that were neither to affirm nor to reverse, what would appear to be fluidity could indeed simply reflect docket-book coding errors.

because the majority supported such a position. Another 53 vote pairs were omitted because the conference vote was tied.[7] Because our dependent variable is dichotomous (identifying whether a justice changed his or her vote after the original conference on the merits), we used a logistic regression model (Aldrich and Nelson 1984, King 1989). The hypotheses suggest that a justice's decision to switch depends upon a series of justice- and case-specific variables.

Next, we describe how we constructed the independent variables necessary to test the hypotheses of voting fluidity.

Justice-Specific Attributes

Author Distance. To assess the ideological distance between a justice and the authors of the majority and minority opinions, we calculated an issue-specific ideological score for the compatibility between each justice and both the majority opinion author and the dissent author closest to the justice in question. To determine this score, we used twelve substantive value groups identified by Spaeth (1994a).[8] For each of these groups, we calculated the percentage of cases in which each justice voted for the liberal outcome (Epstein et al. 1994, Table 6-1). We calculated author distance by subtracting the difference between each justice and the author on the other side of the case from the distance between each justice and the author on the side the justice initially supported.[9] When a justice was closer to the opposing writer than to the justice writing the opinion for the side a justice initially supported, our measure produces a positive value. If the writers were equidistant from a justice, the author distance is zero. If a justice was closer to the writer for the side s/he initially supported than to the opposition writer, the measure is negative. Hypothesis 1 leads us to expect fluidity to be positively related to author distance.

Coalition Placement. To determine a justice's position in relation to the coalitions that formed at the initial conference, we compared each justice's issue-based ideological rank with the mean rank for both the minority and majority coalition that formed at this conference.[10] We gave a justice a placement score of +1 if his or her ideological rank was either at the initial coalition's mean or was located between that mean and the rank most closely associated with the outcome supported by the conference coalition, that is, one for liberal outcomes and nine for conservative outcomes.[11] If a justice's rank was located between the mean member of the two coalitions that initially formed, the justice's position was coded as 0. If a justice's rank was located between the opposition coalition mean and the rank identified with the outcome supported by that coalition, we coded the justice's placement as −1.[12] Hypothesis 2 leads us to expect a negative correlation between fluidity and coalition placement.

Freshman. Any justice who had served less than two full years when the oral argument was heard was coded as 1. All others were coded as 0.[13] Hypothesis 6 leads us to expect a positive correlation between freshman status and fluidity.

Expertise. To measure whether a justice had substantive policy expertise, we calculated an issue-specific opinion ratio (OR) for each justice.[14] The OR is based on the total number of majority opinions, dissents, and concurrences written by each justice during his or her entire tenure on the Supreme Court.[15] More specifically, the OR is the number of cases in which a justice wrote an opinion, dissent, or concurrence, divided by the number

---

[7] Although we excluded votes that were neither to affirm nor to reverse from our dependent variable, several of our independent variables are based upon the size and makeup of the coalitions that formed on the initial merits vote, i.e., minimum winning coalitions. Excluding votes other than affirm and reverse from the calculation of those independent variables would obviously create a tremendous amount of measurement error. A justice's vote to dismiss a case does not mean that the other justices were unaware of how this justice would have voted if the Court had opted to decide the case. Justices frequently voice more than one preference at the conference. A justice might say, for example, that s/he favors dismissal, but would also support an affirmation of the lower court decision. While we could have omitted the entire case if this problem arose, this would raise questions about the generalizability of the findings. In 492 cases during the Burger Court, a justice voted for an outcome that was neither to reverse nor to affirm. To keep these cases in our analysis, we opted to substitute a justice's final vote for any initial vote that was for an outcome other than to reverse or to affirm.

[8] Spaeth (1994a) identifies 13 value groups. His 13th group consists of miscellaneous cases. Because of the ambiguous nature of this value area, we dropped these cases from our analysis.

[9] If a case was unanimously decided, no justice served as a referent for the opposition author. To solve this problem, we created an opposition author referent score. This score is the polar opposite of the outcome that was reached. If the Court unanimously voted for a conservative outcome, the opposition author ideology score was treated as 100% liberal. Conversely, if the Court voted unanimously for a liberal outcome, the opposition-author ideology score was treated as 0% liberal. This method is similar to Hagle and Spaeth's (1991, 122) treatment of unanimous cases.

[10] This procedure is analogous to a Wilcoxon rank-sum test that determines whether the median of two groups is similar. We used it to develop an indication of the coalition's ideological composition. On the basis of each justice's liberal support score, we assigned a rank of 1 to 9 to each justice on each of the 12 issue areas (Spaeth 1994a). We then summed the ranks of justices in each coalition and divided by the number of justices.

[11] We derived the ideological direction of the case outcome from Spaeth (1994a).

[12] If a case was unanimously decided, we created an opposition coalition referent score. This score is the polar opposite of the opinion that was reached. If the Court unanimously voted for a liberal outcome at its initial vote, justices who were more liberal than the mean of all justices were given a +1 placement score. Justices who were more conservative than the mean were given a 0 placement score. No justice was given a −1 score on a unanimous case. A similar coding scheme was employed for unanimous cases with a conservative outcome.

[13] To calculate each justice's length of tenure, we compared the oral argument date and the anniversary of the justice's Senate confirmation (Epstein et al. 1994, Table 4-12).

[14] Each justice was given a unique opinion ratio for each of 133 narrow issue areas that Spaeth (1994a) identifies. To select the 133 issues, we relied upon the 263 issue categories that Spaeth names and then grouped those issues that Spaeth reports as being related. For example, the five specific issue areas that Spaeth identifies as related to federal transportation regulation (railroad, boat, truck, pipeline, and airline) are grouped together.

[15] For justices Black and Douglas, we used the total number of opinions written since 1953 because this variable was generated from Spaeth (1994a), whose data begins in 1953.

of like cases that had reached the Court since that justice's appointment. Since the OR takes into account all opinions written by each justice over his or her Supreme Court career, it is insensitive both to a justice's ideological position relative to colleagues and to the chief justice's assignment decisions. If a justice's OR was more than 1.65 standard deviations above the mean OR for the justices serving when a case was heard, we considered the justice a specialist in that issue area.[16] If a justice was a specialist in an issue area relevant to a particular case up for assignment, that justice was coded as 1. Others were coded as 0. Hypothesis 7 leads us to expect a negative relationship between expertise and fluidity.

Chief Justice. To see whether the chief justice acts differently from other members of the Court, we created two additional dummy variables. The first is a dummy variable to designate the chief. The second variable designates the chief justice when s/he initially voted with the minority. Because the chief has a strategic interest in changing a minority vote to a majority vote, we call this variable *Strategic Chief*. Hypothesis 8a suggests a positive correlation between the chief's being in the minority (*Strategic Chief*) and switching his final vote. Hypothesis 8b suggests a negative correlation between the chief and fluidity in other circumstances.

Minority Coalition Member. If a justice was a member of the minority coalition at the conference on the merits, this variable was coded as 1; otherwise it was coded as 0. Hypothesis 9a leads us to expect a positive relationship between conference minority voters and fluidity.

Case-Specific Attributes

Minimum Winning Coalition (MWC). If a case was decided at conference by a margin of one vote or less, it was coded as 1; otherwise it was coded as 0. Hypothesis 3 suggests that when a case is decided by a minimum winning coalition, justices will be less likely to switch.

Case Complexity. We anticipate that a justice will be more likely to switch in cases that raise complex legal issues than in simpler cases. Although numerous measures of case complexity exist, no one measure fully captures the concept of complexity. Thus, we measured case complexity by factor analyzing three indicators and then used each case's factor scores as a measure of complexity. The joint variance, we argue, best captures case complexity. The first measure was the number of issues raised by a case.[17] The second was the number of legal provisions relevant to a case.[18] The third was the number of opinions released in a case.[19] Factor analysis of these three indicators produced a single factor with an eigenvalue of greater than 1. Since we presume that complex cases raise more issues, pertain to more legal provisions, and result in more opinions than do simpler cases, Hypothesis 4 leads us to expect our factor scores to be positively related to voting fluidity.

Case Salience. Hypothesis 5 predicts that a justice will make a more informed decision at the initial conference if the case is highly salient. Thus, fluidity should be rare in salient cases. As an indicator of case salience, we used the Epstein et al. (1994, Table 2-10) list of landmark cases. If a case was included on the list, it was coded as 1; otherwise it was coded as 0.

Dissent. To test the hypothesis that a justice who initially votes with the minority will be more likely to join the majority if relatively few justices initially voted to dissent (Hypothesis 9b), we created a dissent-size variable. If a justice was the only dissenter, this variable was 4. If two justices voted to dissent, the variable was 3; if three justices dissented it was 2; and if four justices dissented it was 1. We reversed the direction of our dissent count because all justices who voted with the majority were given a 0 for their dissent count. Our expectation is that our dissent variable will be positively correlated with a justice's decision to switch his or her vote.

Unanimity. If every participating member of the Court initially voted with the majority, it was coded as 1; otherwise it was coded as 0. Hypothesis 9c suggests that a justice is unlikely to switch to the minority if the Court was initially unanimous. Thus, we expect a negative coefficient.

FINDINGS

Table 1 provides an overview of our dependent variable. The table shows how frequently each of the 13 justices who served on the Burger Court changed his or her vote after the initial conference. During the Burger Court, at least one justice changed positions in 36.6% of the cases, while individual justices switched their votes 7.5% of the time. The table also shows that there was considerable variation by type of vote and across members. Whereas the average justice who voted with the minority at the initial conference changed his or her vote 18.1% of the time, a justice who initially voted with the majority was likely to switch 4.6% of the time. Justice Black switched 14.9% of the time and Justice Marshall 10.7%, but Justice Stevens switched only 5.8% of the time.

Table 2 presents the estimated coefficients and significance levels for a maximum likelihood logit model

[16] The decision to use 1.65 standard deviations should result in a 5% likelihood that a justice will specialize in an issue area. During the natural court that began with Sandra Day O'Connor's appointment, for example, 31 of the 133 issue areas (23.3%) had no specialist, while 71 areas (53.4%) had a solitary specialist. In 28 areas (21.1%), two justices were specialists, and three areas (23%) had three specialists.

[17] We relied here upon Spaeth's (1994a) case classification system. Spaeth classifies each case by 263 issues. The variable we employed is a count of the number of issues that Spaeth identifies for each case. During the Burger Court, this count ranged from one to three.

[18] This number is a count of the legal provision variable in the Spaeth (1994a) data set. For the cases included in our analysis, the count ranges from one to six.

[19] The number of opinions was derived from Spaeth (1994a). Specifically, we counted for each case the number of justices who wrote a majority, concurring, or dissenting opinion. If a joint opinion, joint dissent, or joint concurrence was written, we assume that only one additional opinion, dissent, or concurrence was written. The maximum number of opinions that any case had during the Burger Court was seven.

TABLE 1. Frequency of Vote Changes (Fluidity), by Conference Status and Justice

	Percent Fluidity When in		
Justice	Conference Majority	Conference Minority	Overall Percent Fluidity
Black	11.5%	24.4%	14.9%
Blackmun	4.0	20.5	6.7
Brennan	5.1	15.7	8.5
Burger	4.3	17.8	6.3
Douglas	8.2	11.4	9.6
Harlan	5.4	27.3	8.6
Marshall	7.6	18.2	10.7
O'Connor	5.6	13.6	6.8
Powell	3.9	20.5	6.2
Rehnquist	3.3	23.4	8.9
Stevens	4.4	10.4	5.8
Stewart	3.8	18.2	6.5
White	3.3	22.5	6.2
AVERAGE	4.6	18.1	7.5

Note: This table shows how frequently each of the 13 justices who served on the Burger Court changed his or her vote after the initial conference. This is calculated by dividing the number of cases in which the justice changed votes by the justice's total number of conference votes in the majority coalition, the minority coalition, and overall.

TABLE 2. Logistic Regression of Vote Fluidity (model 1)

Variable	Coefficient	Standard Error
Policy		
Author distance (Hypothesis 1)	0.061***	0.002
Coalition placement (Hypothesis 2)	−0.459***	0.054
Minimum winning coalition (Hypothesis 3)	−0.337**	0.113
Uncertainty		
Case complexity (Hypothesis 4)	0.112***	0.036
Landmark (Hypothesis 5)	0.071	0.155
Freshman (Hypothesis 6)	0.266*	0.132
Expert (Hypothesis 7)	−0.152	0.113
Institutional		
Chief Justice	−0.089	0.154
Strategic Chief (Hypothesis 8)	0.166	0.275
Minority coalition member (Hypothesis 9a)	0.913***	0.185
Dissenters (Hypothesis 9b)	0.382***	0.070
Unanimity (Hypothesis 9c)	−0.143	0.130
Constant	−3.030***	0.067
Number of cases	15,459	
−2 × Log likelihood ratio	5271.491***	
Reduction of error	24.700	
Percent correctly classified	94.300	
Pseudo-R^2	36.200	

*significant at .05 (one-tailed test)
**significant at .01 (one-tailed test)
***significant at .001 (one-tailed test)

predicting whether a justice would switch votes. The statistically significant chi-square test of the log-likelihood ratio allows us to reject the null hypothesis that each of our independent variables, except the constant, is equal to 0. The pseudo-R^2 (36.2) demonstrates that the model explains the variance in fluidity moderately well. The model correctly classifies 94.3% (14,582) of the cases. Compared with predicting that a justice would never switch, the proportional reduction in error associated with the model is 24.7%.

We find strong support for the expectation that fluidity is a function of strategic policy calculations (Table 2). All three measures of a justice's ideological placement are statistically significant. The coefficient of the author-distance variable suggests that justices are more likely to switch if they are ideologically distant from the writer of the opinion to which they initially committed and ideologically proximate to the opposition writer. These findings provide empirical support for Hypothesis 1. The effect of the coalition placement score is also suggestive of the effects of policy preferences. The closer justices are to the opposition coalition, and the farther they are from their own coalition, the more likely they are to switch. This is consistent with Hypothesis 2. If the initial majority coalition is a minimum winning coalition, this also affects the likelihood of fluidity. Justices are less likely to switch if the original coalition was of minimum winning size. This suggests that in crafting opinions with the initial support of a minimum winning coalition, both majority and dissenting opinion writers are likely to attend to the preferences of their initial supporting coalition in order to hold it together.

To illustrate the substantive effect of the statistically significant independent variables reported in Table 2, we ran several simulations of the likelihood that a justice would switch. We held all significant independent variables constant except one, and the results in Table 3 show how each independent variable affects the likelihood that a justice would change his vote after the initial merits conference.[20]

The importance of such policy calculations is illus-

[20] The benchmark probability is the likelihood of a vote change when the value of each variable is set at its mean or, in the case of a dichotomous variable, at the mode. By setting the values of our independent variables at various levels and then changing them one at a time, it is possible to observe the effect of each variable. For example, to simulate the probability of a justice changing his or her vote when s/he is closer to the writer of the opinion s/he initially supported than to the nearest justice writing on behalf of the other side ("closer to ally"), we set the author distance score at −96.8. This score would occur if a justice were perfectly aligned with the author s/he initially supported and if the nearest opposition writer were on the opposite end of the ideological spectrum. The simulation for the justice who is initially "closer to opponent" is calculated by reversing the placement of the authors. For the "closer to opponent" simulation, the author distance score is set at 85.5. The simulated probability of the "equidistant" justice is based upon an author distance score of 0. The simulated probabilities for coalition placement, number of dissenters, conference minority, and freshman justices are calculated for the categories specified in the table. For the simulated probability for the most complex cases, the complexity score is set at one standard deviation above the mean. Thus, the factor value for the "hard" complex case simulation is set at 0.97. This is compared to the "easy" case simulation where we set the complexity score at the minimum observed factor value of −0.98. This is about one standard deviation below the mean.

TABLE 3. Simulated Probability of Vote Change

Characteristics	Probability
Benchmark	.018
Author distance	
Closer to ally	.000
Equidistant	.046
Closer to opponent	.898
Coalition placement	
Far side of initial coalition	.013
Between coalitions	.021
Far side of opposite coalition	.033
Minimum winning coalition	.013
Case complexity	
Easy	.016
Hard	.020
Freshman Justice	.023
Dissenters	
3 Justices	.077
1 Justice	.152
Minority coalition member	.044

trated in these results. Whereas the justice who is equidistant between the authors switches 4.6% of the time, a justice with ideological views similar to those of the justice authoring the opinion within the original coalition is likely to change his or her vote 0.01% of the time. The likelihood of fluidity is 89.8% if the justice is ideologically proximate to the writer of the opposing opinion and distant from the writer authoring the opinion for the vote the justice initially cast. Similar patterns appear for the coalition placement score. Justices who are farther from the opposing coalition than from their initial coalition's mean ideological score are likely to switch 1.3% of the time. Conversely, justices who are on the far side of the opposing coalition's ideological mean are likely to switch 3.3% of the time. If the initial majority coalition is a minimum winning coalition, however, the probability of switching drops from the 1.8% benchmark to 1.3%.

In contrast, the model provides mixed support for the uncertainty hypotheses, no support for our expectation about the influence of the institutional factors unique to the chief justice, but strong support for our expectation about the general influence of institutional factors. Hypotheses 4–7 (predicting the effects of case complexity, case salience, justice experience, and justice expertise) suggest that varying degrees of uncertainty across cases and justices might affect voting fluidity. The results provide su'port for only two of these hypotheses. As indicate' ı Table 2, our measure of case complexity is significantly related to justices' decisions to switch votes. The likelihood that a justice will be fluid in a complex case is 25% greater than the likelihood of changing in an easy case. This outcome provides support for Hypothesis 4.

Contrary to Hypothesis 5, justices are not less likely to switch in salient cases.[21] We suspect that this is true because in salient cases opinion authors discourage fluidity by making an extra effort to accommodate each justice who is inclined to support their position. Epstein and Knight's (1995, 34) finding that in important cases opinion authors circulate more draft opinions is consistent with such an explanation. Consistent with Hypothesis 6, freshmen justices are significantly more likely to switch than are their more senior colleagues, as reflected in Table 2. Whereas the benchmark justice switched 1.8% of the time, the freshman justice switched 2.3% of the time (see Table 3). Contrary to Hypothesis 7, however, experts were just as likely as their colleagues to switch their votes. Although it is contrary to our hypothesis, this finding is understandable. Substantive experts are likely to be concerned with an opinion's content. Thus, experts may be just as willing as their less experienced colleagues to use their votes as leverage to encourage various opinion authors to write legal rules consistent with their preferences. This may lead them to change their votes even though their original votes were based upon a clear understanding of the law.

The statistical insignificance of the chief justice and strategic chief coefficients indicates that, contrary to Hypothesis 8, Chief Justice Burger did not act differently than did his colleagues. There is no evidence that Burger routinely changed his vote from the minority to the majority in order to control the opinion assignment. Although it is conceivable that the chief did switch his vote to control the assignment on a few salient cases, there is no general pattern to that effect.[22]

Institutional considerations also appear to have a powerful influence on justices decisions to switch votes. Justices who initially sided with the minority were more likely to switch their votes than those who sided with the majority (Hypothesis 9a). Compared to the benchmark, a justice was more than twice as likely to change positions when he or she was in the conference minority. The model supports Hypothesis 9b; for justices initially siding with the minority, the likelihood of joining the majority increased as the size of the minority coalition shrank. The simulated probabilities illustrate these dynamics. A justice who was one of three members of the minority had a 7.6% chance of switching. For a lone dissenter, however, the likelihood of switching more than doubled, to 15.2%. The negative but statistically insignificant unanimity coefficient in our model, however, does not support Hypothesis 9c.

Previous attempts to identify the causes of fluidity have focused on votes that altered the initial outcome, on justices who initially voted with the majority, or on

[21] Nevertheless, some might suspect that salience explains fluidity only in combination with ideological distance. To test this, we reran the model so that salience interacted with both the writer and coalition placement variables. Both of these variables were insignificant, and all the variables that were significant in Table 1 retained their significance.

[22] One might argue that we have minimized the effect of the chief justice switching to the majority by exclusively examining conference votes to affirm or reverse. Conventional wisdom suggests that Burger, more frequently than any other justice, passed at conference. By not expressing a position at conference, Burger remained flexible and could join the majority and thus assign the majority opinion. According to Brennan's record of Burger's conference votes, he passed in 3.1% of the 2,065 cases in which he participated. This was the highest pass rate on the Court; Hugo Black's rate of 1.7% was the next highest. Burger's pass rate was significantly higher than those of all other justices taken together.

justices who initially voted with the minority. Implicit in these studies is the idea that different sets of factors lead a justice to switch in different directions, thus requiring that directions of fluidity be modeled separately. For instance, if ideology led a justice to engage in conformity voting (changing a vote from the minority to the majority), and uncertainty led a justice to engage in counter-conformity voting (changing a vote from the majority to the minority), the development of a general model would not make sense.

After we developed a general model of vote change that encompasses the full range of fluidity, we estimated a second model to test whether the influence of the factors we identified is conditional on the direction of fluidity (Table 4). This model includes all the variables used in the first model, which then interact with a dummy variable to signify whether a justice initially voted with the minority. The first model's variables interaction with a minority dummy variable enables us to test whether these variables have significantly different effects on conformity and counterconformity voting.[23]

The results suggest that the effects of most of the variables are not conditional on the direction of fluidity. Nevertheless, the model does suggest that there are significant differences between the processes for switching from majority and minority opinions. Two of the three policy variables (author distance and minimum winning coalition) are statistically significant and in the predicted direction. Members of the minority are even more likely than members of the majority to switch if they are ideologically closer to the opposing author than to the author of the opinion with which they initially sided. They are also slightly less likely to change their votes if there is a minimum winning coalition. In general, these results suggest that strategic policy considerations are magnified for justices who are in the minority, but the significance of uncertainty is diminished. This is demonstrated by the statistically significant and negative case complexity variable. We suspect that this results from the fact that justices who initially cast a minority vote may hold more intense convictions than the average majority justice and thus are less susceptible to the persuasion of their colleagues.

TABLE 4. Logistic Regression of Vote Fluidity (model 2)

Variable	Coefficient	Standard Error
Policy		
Author distance (Hypothesis 1)	0.053***	0.002
Coalition placement (Hypothesis 2)	−0.553***	0.070
Minimum winning coalition (Hypothesis 3)	−0.189	0.132
Uncertainty		
Case complexity (Hypothesis 4)	0.203***	0.042
Landmark (Hypothesis 5)	0.119	0.187
Freshman (Hypothesis 6)	0.344*	0.165
Expert (Hypothesis 7)	−0.102	0.148
Institutional		
Chief Justice	−0.056	0.151
Strategic chief (Hypothesis 8)	0.064	0.287
Minority coalition member (Hypothesis 9a)	1.324***	0.276
Dissenters (Hypothesis 9b)	0.225**	0.095
Unanimity (Hypothesis 9c)	−0.074	0.129
Minority coalition		
Author distance × minority coalition	0.018***	0.004
Coalition placement × minority coalition	0.117	0.113
MWC × minority coalition	−0.562*	0.245
Case complexity × minority coalition	−0.241**	0.078
Landmark × minority coalition	−0.069	0.332
Freshman × minority coalition	−0.243	0.275
Expert × minority coalition	−0.111	0.233
Constant	−2.999***	.072
Number of cases	15,459	
−2 × Log likelihood ratio	5,224.733***	
Reduction of error	26.500	
Percent correctly classified	94.500	
Pseudo-R^2	36.700	

*significant at .05 (one-tailed test)
**significant at .01 (one-tailed test)
***significant at .001 (one-tailed test)

CONCLUSION

Although fluidity on the Supreme Court is relatively rare, our findings suggest that it occurs in a predictable fashion. Whether joining the majority or defecting to the minority after an initial vote on the merits, the probability that a justice will switch is captured by a multivariate model of fluidity. While legal uncertainty might also make justices' initial conference votes more tenuous, our results suggest that voting fluidity is more likely to be conditional on policy and institutional considerations. Calculations about preferred policy outcomes and institutional motivations seem to lead justices to review their initial positions and occasionally to join the opposite coalition.

While strategic policy considerations affect justices in both the majority and minority, it is clear that these considerations play a more important role for justices who initially cast dissenting votes. A justice who initially dissented is more likely to change his or her vote if the conditions are ripe than is a justice in the majority. We suspect that the greater emphasis that minority justices place on these considerations stems from the fact that the majority opinion author has little incentive to be responsive to the suggestions of a dissenter. Since the

[23] Because our institutional variables (unanimity and number of dissenters) already take into account whether a justice is part of the minority at the initial merits conference, we are unable to repeat these two variables. The strategic chief variable also takes into consideration whether the chief initially voted with the minority. Thus, we do not repeat this variable in our second model.

majority opinion becomes the law of the land, justices who wish to shape the law have an incentive to be part of the majority. Consistent with this theory is the fact that justices who initially voted with the majority switched only 4.6% of the time, and justices who initially dissented switched 18.1% of the time (see Table 1).

These results shed light on the dynamic nature of coalition building within the Court. Although Murphy's (1964) classic study argues that decision making on the Court is a dynamic process in which justices bargain over preferred outcomes, judicial scholars often attribute judicial behavior to factors exogenous to the decision-making process. But our model suggests that fluidity is, at least in part, a response to the initial set of opinions and coalitions that emerges after the first conference. First, the content of the opinion and the position of its author are important: Justices who find themselves ideologically closer to the opposing coalition, for example, are more likely to switch than those who ideologies differ significantly. Second, the size of the initial coalition is also important. When defecting to the minority is likely to leave a justice isolated in the minority, s/he is less likely to defect; when joining the majority means escaping a small minority, however, a justice is likely to switch votes. Modeling fluidity to include switching both into and out of the majority thus gives us a broader perspective on the dynamics of coalition building on the Court.

Although this study makes clear that justices are willing to change their votes because of their policy preferences and their strategic calculations, it is important to note that changing a vote is probably the most drastic action a justice can take. Writing a concurrence or making a simple suggestion to an opinion author are strategic actions that are probably more common than is changing votes. Nevertheless, our understanding of these activities is based on only anecdotal evidence. Supreme Court scholars have made few attempts to study systematically the nonvoting activities in which justices engage. Of course, opinion authors themselves are also likely to act strategically. It seems reasonable to expect that under some conditions opinion authors would be willing to accommodate their colleagues, and in other instances they would be likely to use their position to implement their own goals. To develop a richer understanding of judicial behavior than the attitudinal model affords, a more thorough explanation of the coalition-building and opinion-writing processes is needed.

Over the past twenty years, scholars of the Court have articulated and refined an "attitudinal model" that has had a tremendous amount of explanatory power. As a result, few scholars have attempted to test empirically the model of strategic interaction that Murphy articulated in 1964. Recently, students of the Court have proposed building upon the attitudinal model by recognizing the kinds of strategic calculations that Murphy suggested dominate on the Court (Epstein and Knight 1995). Our findings provide strong support for moving the study of judicial politics beyond the attitudinal model.

REFERENCES

Aldrich, John H., and Forrest D. Nelson. 1984. *Linear Probability, Logit, and Probit Models*. Beverly Hills, CA: Sage Publications.

Asch, Solomon E. 1951. "Effects of Group Pressure upon the Modification and Distortion of Judgments." In *Groups, Leadership, and Men*, ed. Harold Steere Guetzkow. Pittsburgh: Carnegie.

Asch, Solomon E. 1952. *Social Psychology*. New York: Prentice-Hall.

Biskupic, Joan. 1995. "As Deadline Nears, Court Leaders Pin Hopes on 'Holding 5.' " *Washington Post*. 7 June 1995.

Brennan, William J. 1969. Memorandum to Potter Stewart, November 4, 1969. Available in Justice William J. Brennan's papers, Box 205. Washington, DC: Library of Congress.

Brennan, William J. 1971. Memorandum to Warren Burger, March 8, 1971. Available in Justice William J. Brennan's papers, Box 239. Washington, DC: Library of Congress.

Brenner, Saul. 1980. "Fluidity on the United States Supreme Court: A Reexamination." *American Journal of Political Science* 24 (August): 526–35.

Brenner, Saul. 1982. "Fluidity on the Supreme Court: 1956–1967." *American Journal of Political Science* 26 (May):388–90.

Brenner, Saul, and Robert H. Dorff. 1992. "The Attitudinal Model and Fluidity Voting on the United States Supreme Court." *Journal of Theoretical Politics* 4 (2):195–205.

Brenner, Saul, Timothy M. Hagle, and Harold J. Spaeth. 1989. "The Defection of the Marginal Justice on the Warren Court." *Western Political Quarterly* 42 (September):409–25.

Brenner, Saul, Timothy M. Hagle, and Harold J. Spaeth. 1990. "Increasing the Size of Minimum Winning Original Coalitions on the Warren Court." *Polity* 23 (Winter):309–18.

Brenner, Saul, and Jan Palmer. 1988. "The Time Taken to Write Opinions as a Determinant of Opinion Assignments." *Judicature* 88 (October–November):179–84.

Brenner, Saul, and Harold J. Spaeth. 1988. "Majority Opinion Assignments and the Maintenance of the Original Coalition on the Warren Court." *American Journal of Political Science* 32 (February):72–81.

Burger, Warren E. 1972. Memorandum to William O. Douglas, July 27. Available in Justice William O. Douglas's papers. Washington, DC: Library of Congress.

Detroit and Toledo Shore Line v. *United Transportation Union*. 1969. 396 U.S. 142.

Dorff, Robert H., and Saul Brenner. 1992. "Conformity Voting on the United States Supreme Court." *Journal of Politics* 54 (August):762–75.

Douglas, William O. 1969. Memorandum to the Conference, December 31, 1969. Available in Justice William J. Brennan's papers, Box 211. Washington, DC: Library of Congress.

Douglas, William O. 1972a. Dissent in *Roe* v. *Wade* (Draft). Available in Justice William O. Douglas's papers. Washington, DC: Library of Congress.

Douglas, William O. 1972b. Memorandum to Chief Justice Burger, August 7, 1972. Available in Justice William O. Douglas's papers. Washington, DC: Library of Congress.

Epstein, Lee and Jack Knight. 1995. "Documenting Strategic Interaction on the U.S. Supreme Court." Presented at the annual meeting of the American Political Science Association, Chicago, IL.

Epstein, Lee, and Carol Mershon. 1993. "The Formation of Opinion Coalitions on the U.S. Supreme Court." Presented at the annual meeting of the Midwest Political Science Association, Chicago, IL.

Epstein, Lee, Jeffrey A. Segal, Harold J. Spaeth, and Thomas G. Walker. 1994. *The Supreme Court Compendium: Data, Decisions and Developments*. Washington DC: Congressional Quarterly Press.

Frank, Jerome. [1930] 1970. *Law and the Modern Mind*. Reprint. Gloucester, MA: Peter Smith.

George, Tracey E., and Lee Epstein. 1992. "On the Nature of Supreme Court Decision Making." *American Political Science Review* 86 (June):323–37.

Hagle, Timothy M., and Harold J. Spaeth. 1991. "Voting Fluidity and the Attitudinal Model of Supreme Court Decision Making." *Western Political Quarterly* 44 (March):119–28.

Hare, A. Paul. 1976. *Handbook of Small Group Research*. 2nd ed. New York: Free Press.

Harlan, John M. 1969. Memorandum to Hugo Black, November 28, 1969. Available in Justice William J. Brennan's papers, Box 205. Washington, DC: Library of Congress.

Harlan, John M. 1970. Memorandum to Hugo Black, February 24, 1970. Available in Justice William J. Brennan's papers, Box 217. Washington, DC: Library of Congress.

Howard, J. Woodford, Jr. 1968. "On the Fluidity of Judicial Choice." *American Political Science Review* 62 (March):43–56.

Johnson, Charles A., and Bradley C. Canon. 1984. *Judicial Policies: Implementation and Impact*. Washington, DC: Congressional Quarterly Press.

King, Gary. 1989. *Unifying Political Methodology: The Likelihood Theory of Statistical Inference*. New York: Cambridge University Press.

Maltzman, Forrest, and Paul J. Wahlbeck. 1996a. "May It Please the Chief? Opinion Assignments in the Rehnquist Court." *American Journal of Political Science* 40 (May):421–33.

Maltzman, Forrest, and Paul J. Wahlbeck. 1996b. "Inside the U.S. Supreme Court: The Reliability of Conference Data." *Journal of Politics* 58 (May):528–39.

Marshall, Thurgood. 1969. Memorandum to the Conference, December 10, 1969. Available in Justice William J. Brennan's papers, Box 206. Washington, DC: Library of Congress.

Marshall, Thurgood. 1973. Memorandum to the Conference, June 4, 1973. Available in Justice William J. Brennan's papers, Box 303. Washington, DC: Library of Congress.

McGuire, Kevin T. 1995. "Repeat Players in the Supreme Court: The Role of Experienced Lawyers in Litigation Success." *Journal of Politics* 57 (February):187–96.

Murphy, Walter. 1964. *Elements of Judicial Strategy*. Chicago: University of Chicago Press.

Provine, Doris Marie. 1980. *Case Selection in the United States Supreme Court*. Chicago: University of Chicago Press.

Rehnquist, William. 1973. Memorandum to the Chief Justice, March 14, 1973. Available in Justice William J. Brennan's papers, Box 303. Washington, DC: Library of Congress.

Riker, William H. 1962. *The Theory of Political Coalitions*. New Haven, CT: Yale University Press.

Roe v. *Wade*. 1973. 410 U.S. 113.

Rohde, David W. 1972. "Policy Goals, Strategic Choice and Majority Opinion Assignments in the U.S. Supreme Court." *Midwest Journal of Political Science* 16 (November):652–82.

Rohde, David W., and Harold J. Spaeth. 1976. *Supreme Court Decision Making*. San Francisco: Freeman.

Schwartz, Bernard. 1996. *Decision: How the Supreme Court Decides Cases*. New York: Oxford University Press.

Schubert, Glendon. 1965. *The Judicial Mind*. New York: Free Press.

Segal, Jeffrey A., and Harold J. Spaeth. 1993. *The Supreme Court and the Attitudinal Model*. New York: Cambridge University Press.

Sheehan, Reginald S., William Mishler, and Donald R. Songer. 1992. "Ideology, Status, and the Differential Success of Direct Parties before the Supreme Court." *American Political Science Review* 86 (June):464–71.

Songer, Donald R., and Reginald S. Sheehan. 1992. "Who Wins on Appeal? Upperdogs and Underdogs in the United States Courts of Appeals." *American Journal of Political Science* 36 (February):235–58.

Slotnick, Elliot. 1979. "Who Speaks for the Court? Majority Opinion Assignments from Taft to Burger." *American Journal of Political Science* 23 (February):60–77.

Songer, Donald. 1979. "Concern for Policy Outputs as a Cue for Supreme Court Decisions on Certiorari." *Journal of Politics* 41 (November):1185–94.

Spaeth, Harold J. 1994a. *United States Supreme Court Judicial Database, 1953–1992 Terms*. 5th release. Ann Arbor, MI: Inter-University Consortium for Political and Social Research.

Spaeth, Harold J. 1994b. "The Breakup of the Original Vote Coalition on the Vinson Court: Is the Conference Vote on the Merits Really the Final Vote?" Presented at the annual meeting of the Southern Political Science Association, Atlanta.

Spriggs, James F., II. N.d. "The Supreme Court and Federal Administrative Agencies: A Resource-Based Theory and Analysis of Judicial Impact." *American Journal of Political Science*. Forthcoming.

Stewart, Potter. 1969. Memorandum to Hugo Black, December 2, 1969. Available in William J. Brennan's papers, Box 205. Washington, DC: Library of Congress.

Stewart, Potter. 1970. Memorandum to the Conference, April 23, 1970. Available in William J. Brennan's papers, Box 217. Washington, DC: Library of Congress.

Tanenhaus, Joseph, Marvin Schick, Matthew Muraskin, and Daniel Rosen. 1963. "The Supreme Court's Certiorari Jurisdiction: Cue Theory." In *Judicial Decision Making*, ed. Glendon Schubert. New York: Free Press.

Ulmer, S. Sidney. 1984. "The Supreme Court's Certiorari Decisions: Conflict as a Predictive Value." *American Political Science Review* 78 (December):901–11.

Wahlbeck, Paul J. 1994. "The Life of the Law: Judicial Politics and Legal Change." Presented at the annual meeting of the Midwest Political Science Association, Chicago.

Wardius v. *Oregon*. 1973. 412 U.S. 470.

Woodward, Bob, and Scott Armstrong. 1979. *The Brethren: Inside the Supreme Court*. New York: Simon and Schuster.

Part III
Constraints on Judicial Power

[14]

LOWER COURT CHECKS ON SUPREME COURT POWER

WALTER F. MURPHY
Princeton University

Practicing politicians as well as students of politics have long recognized the check on presidential power imposed by the federal administrative machinery. High policy must be interpreted; it can sometimes be changed or even frustrated by the bureaucrats who apply laws and executive orders. Officials down the line have interests, loyalties, and ambitions which go beyond and often clash with the allegiance accorded a given tenant of the White House. Each bureaucrat has his own ideas about proper public policy, particularly in his field of special competence. If a career civil servant, he may identify only partially, if at all, the good of the governmental service, not to say the good of the public, with the ends sought by the Administration. And if he owes his appointment or promotion to other sources than the merit system, he may find a positive conflict between his loyalties to the President and to other politicians or political groups.

This conflict can occur at all administrative levels.[1] Cabinet members may make up the President's official family, but some of them are at times his chief rivals for power within his own political party, or, more often, representatives of those rivals. Or the department heads may be so split with sibling political rivalry among themselves that common loyalty to their nominal leader may be subordinated to other values. An observer has lately written: "The conditions which a system of fragmented power sets for the success and the survival of a Cabinet officer encourage him to consolidate his own nexus of power and compel him to operate with a degree of independence from the President."[2]

Internal friction or drag is thus an inherent part of the executive process, a factor to be weighed in choosing among policy alternatives, much the same as congressional, or judicial, or pressure group resistance. Less obviously, but not necessarily less significantly, a similar bureaucratic factor must be reckoned with in the execution of Supreme Court decisions. Except in disputes between states or the rare litigation involving diplomats, the Supreme Court usually does not render either the initial or the final decision in a case. If it reverses a

[1] Clinton Rossiter has remarked: "Were the Presidents of the last fifty years to be polled on this question, all but one or two, I am sure, would agree that the 'natural obstinacy' of the average bureau chief or commissioner or colonel was second only to the 'ingrained suspicions' of the average congressman as a check on the President's ability to do either good or evil." *The American Presidency* (New York, 1956), pp. 40–41. For more detailed discussions of the problems involved here, consult David Truman, *The Governmental Process* (New York, 1951), chs. 13–14, and works cited. For an analogy in prison administration, see Gresham Sykes, *The Society of Captives* (Princeton: Princeton University Press, 1958), pp. 53–58. Even the Soviet system has similar problems of "family relationships" in administrative management: Barrington Moore, *Terror and Progress USSR* (Cambridge: Harvard University Press, 1954).

[2] Richard F. Fenno, Jr., "President-Cabinet Relations: A Pattern and a Case Study," this REVIEW, Vol. 52 (1958), pp. 388, 404. (Italics in original omitted.)

state decision, the Court remands the case to state courts for disposition "not inconsistent with this opinion"; and it frequently gives only slightly more precise directions in overruling federal tribunals. The Supreme Court typically formulates general policy. Lower courts apply that policy, and working in its interstices, inferior judges may materially modify the High Court's determinations.[3]

I

As might be expected, state judges have a wider field in which to operate. Two technical rules help to enlarge their area of discretion. The first, already mentioned, is the vague criteria which the Supreme Court imposes when it overturns a state decision. Second, the Supreme Court will review only those state cases which were based on a substantial federal question. The Court has reiterated time and again its practice of not reviewing state decisions which have sufficient independent grounding in state law so that a reversal of the determinations of federal issues would not affect the final outcome of the case. Whether this doctrine is one of administrative convenience or is a constitutional limitation has been questioned,[4] but as long as it is followed a state appellate judge who is a skillful opinion writer can, when so minded, do much to prevent Supreme Court review, even of federal questions.

Considering the perennial friction between state and national interests and outlooks, the different elements weighed in the appointment of state and federal judges, their allegiances (former if not current) to opposing political parties or to separate levels of party hierarchy, the different ambitions of the judges, and their varying conceptions of the role of the judiciary in a federal and democratic system, the wonder is that occasions of open conflict are the exception rather than the rule. Perhaps the use of the vague remand prescription acts as a psychological safety valve in allowing some of the pressure of resentment against reversal to be siphoned off in construing Supreme Court instructions.[5]

[3] Much lower court leeway is created by the fact that since Supreme Court opinions often represent a compromise among divergent approaches and views of individual Justices, there are sometimes multiple threads running through an official opinion which are inconsistent with the dominant pattern of thought. Even where a judge wishes to hew strictly to the High Court's line he may be left in doubt as to what was dogma and what was dicta. Alpheus T. Mason's *Harlan Fiske Stone: Pillar of the Law* (New York: The Viking Press, 1956) is studded with examples of opinion compromises. See especially the intra-Court memoranda and draft opinions in Home Building and Loan Association v. Blaisdell, 290 U. S. 398 (1934), and Colgate v. Harvey, 296 U. S. 404 (1935), found at pp. 360–365 and pp. 399–402 of Mason's book.

[4] Note, "Evasion of Supreme Court Mandates in Cases Remanded to State Courts since 1941," *Harvard L. Rev.*, Vol. 67, p. 1251 (1954); Note, "Supreme Court Disposition of State Decisions Involving Non-Federal Questions," *Yale L. J.*, Vol. 49, p. 1463 (1940). In keeping with his controversial constitutional theories, W. W. Crosskey disputes the basic concept of dual jurisdiction. *Politics and the Constitution* (Chicago: University of Chicago Press, 1953), especially ch. 25. For a full explanation of the contrary view, read the dissenting opinion of Mr. Justice Frankfurter in Irvin v. Dowd, 3 L. ed. 2d 900 (1959).

[5] For historical accounts of state court defiance of Supreme Court decisions, see Charles

An additional safety valve is criticism of Supreme Court decisions, a practice in which judges who have been reversed engage only slightly less bitterly than disappointed litigants. The most serious recent verbal attack came when the 1958 Conference of State Chief Justices issued a sharp accusation that Justices of the Supreme Court were usurping state judicial power by confusing their own policy views with constitutional commands.[6] The Conference chose to launch this attack at the strategic moment when congressional assaults against the Supreme Court had reached a climax.

Both these devices permit exercise of power as well as escape of pressure. Criticism may persuade the Court of the error of its ways, or help convince Congress of a need for remedial legislation. The interpreting authority may even be stretched to accomplish a *de facto* overturning of Supreme Court decisions. A study published in 1954 reported that in eleven terms, some 46 Supreme Court reversals of state decisions required additional litigation. "In slightly less than half of these cases the party successful in the Supreme Court was unsuccessful in the state court following the remand."[7] This study also indicated that, with one exception,[8] the evasion had been accomplished by interpretation rather than by defiance. For example, when the High Court ruled in 1952 that Oklahoma's loyalty oath violated due process in not distinguishing between knowing and innocent membership in proscribed organizations,[9] the Oklahoma court in which the case had begun read *scienter* into the state statute and sustained the judicially amended version.[10]

The line between evasion and defiance is always difficult to draw, and when in 1954 the Supreme Court declared Jim Crow legally dead,[11] the attitude of many segregationist state judges shifted perceptibly. Yet the manner in which Southern judicial resistance has been expressed is significant. These judges have criticized the *School Segregation* decisions on and off the bench; they were among the leaders of the movement in the 1958 Conference of State Chief Justices to reprimand the Supreme Court.[12] They have given moral support and, one may guess, perhaps legal advice to Southern political leaders. But when

Warren, "Federal and State Court Interference," *Harvard L. Rev.*, Vol. 43, p. 345 (1930); and Note, "Interposition v. Judicial Power," *Race Rel. L. Rep.*, Vol. 1, p. 465 (1956).

[6] *Resolutions Adopted at the Tenth Annual Meeting of the Conference of Chief Justices* (Chicago: Council of State Governments, mimeo., 1958).

[7] Note, *Harvard L. Rev.*, cited above, note 4.

[8] Ashcraft v. Tennessee, 322 U. S. 143 (1944); 327 U. S. 274 (1946). The intervening Tennessee decisions are unreported.

[9] Wieman v. Updegraff, 344 U. S. 183 (1952).

[10] The lower court decision is unreported. The details can be found in the follow-up case of the same title, 301 P. 2d 1003 (Sup. Ct. of Okla., 1956).

[11] Brown v. Board, 347 U. S. 483 (1954); 349 U. S. 294 (1955).

[12] Chief Judge Frederick W. Brune of Maryland, chairman of the Chief Justices' committee which prepared the critical report, has officially denied that any attack on the School Cases was intended. (*New York Times*, January 8, 1959, 30:1.) There can be no doubt, however, that the Supreme Court's racial decisions had a great deal to do with the attitude of the state judges. See the speech of Charles Alvin Jones, Chief Justice of Pennsylvania, reported in *Harvard L. Record,* October 23, 1958.

pressed, no state supreme court has yet failed to concede that the School Segregation cases are the law of the land and binding on lower courts.[13] Resistance of state supreme courts (and, though not universally, of state lower courts[14]) has taken three specific forms: (1) refusing to expand the school decision to other areas;[15] (2) upholding the constitutionality of state efforts to evade compliance;[16] and (3), in line with the state chief justices' censure, balking at Supreme Court decisions in related areas of race and of federal-state relations.[17]

Two recent cases illustrate a combination of these resistance methods. The School Segregation decisions of 1954 seemed to spell final victory for a Negro named Virgil Hawkins who for over five years had been seeking admission to the University of Florida law school. A week after *Brown* v. *Board*, the Supreme Court sent the *Hawkins* case back to the Florida supreme court for reconsideration in light of the public school decisions.[18] The Florida high court did reconsider and declared: "We deem it to be our inescapable duty to abide by this decision of the United States Supreme Court interpreting the federal constitution."[19] A majority of the state justices, however, felt that "sound judicial discretion" required them to withhold issuance of a mandamus requiring immediate admission, in order to determine the effects of integration at the university.

Disappointed at this further delay, Hawkins took his case back to the Supreme Court, which entered a new order stating that the factors it had spelled out as allowing delay in desegregating grammar and high schools did not apply at the professional school level.[20] Once again the case went back to the Florida supreme court, and once again that tribunal, via three opinions for the majority and two for the dissenters, interpreted its way out of ordering Hawkins's

[13] McKinney v. Blankenship, 282 S.W. 2d 691 (Sup. Ct. of Texas, 1955); Constantian v. Anson County, 93 S.E. 2d 163 (Sup. Ct. of No. Car., 1956); Florida ex rel. Hawkins v. Board, 83 So. 2d 20 (Sup. Ct. of Fla., 1955); Roy v. Brittain, 297 S.W. 2d 72 (Sup. Ct. of Tenn., 1956).

[14] The extreme example is that of the Birmingham, Alabama, judge who not only refused to follow the Supreme Court's racial decisions but also declared the Fourteenth Amendment unconstitutional. (*New York Times*, March 23, 1957, 14:4–5.) Perhaps the most vindictive remarks from the bench about the Supreme Court in its current crisis were made by the Alabama judge whose decision regarding voluntariness of a confession had been reversed in Fikes v. Alabama, 352 U. S. 191 (1957): "The opinion is the voice of the Supreme Court of the United States, but the hand is the hand of the NAACP. The opinion of the majority of the Court speaks the truth neither as to the facts nor as to the law. The opinion offends and is repugnant to judicial sensibilities." Quoted in 103 *Cong. Rec.* 4012 (85th Cong., 1st Sess., March 19, 1957).

[15] Bissell v. Commonwealth, 100 S.E. 2d 1 (Sup. Ct. of Appeals of Va., 1957); North Carolina v. Cooke, 193 S.E. 2d 846 (Sup. Ct. of No. Car., 1958); State v. Clyburn, 101 S.E. 2d 295 (Sup. Ct. of No. Car., 1958).

[16] Joyner v. Board, 92 S.E. 2d 795 (Sup. Ct. of No. Car., 1956); Defabio v. Fairfax County, 100 S.E. 2d 760 (Sup. Ct. of Appeals of Va., 1957).

[17] Williams v. Georgia, 88 S.E. 2d 376 (Sup. Ct. of Ga., 1955); Naim v. Naim, 90 S.E. 2d 849 (Sup. Ct. of Appeals of Va., 1956).

[18] Florida ex rel. Hawkins v. Board, 347 U.S. 971 (1954).

[19] 83 So. 2d 20, 23 (1955).

[20] 350 U. S. 413 (1956).

immediate admission. The majority expressed a belief, based on the report of a special commissioner, that violence would be the result of even limited integration of the law school. The opinion added, "we cannot assume that the Supreme Court intended to deprive the highest court of an independent sovereign state of one of its traditional powers, that is, the right to exercise a sound judicial discretion as to the date of the issuance of its process in order to prevent a serious public mischief."[21]

In *Williams* v. *Georgia*, the Georgia supreme court handled a different type of racial issue with considerably more bluntness. A Negro, convicted of murder in a state court, managed to obtain review by the United States Supreme Court. In arguing the case, the state attorney conceded that Negroes had been excluded from the jury panel and therefore that the defendant had been denied a fair trial. The state attorney contended, however, that since the defense had not challenged the method of jury selection within the time limits set by Georgia law, no substantial federal question was presented. The Supreme Court found that a real constitutional issue was involved, but declined to exercise its jurisdiction. The majority of the Justices stated that they could not imagine that the "courts of Georgia would allow this man to go to his death as the result of a conviction secured from a jury which the State admits was unconstitutionally impaneled."[22] Instead of reversing the Georgia supreme court, the federal Supreme Court simply remanded the case for further consideration.

The Georgia supreme court disposed of the remand by a three paragraph opinion whose resistance can be gauged from the declaration in the opening paragraph: "we will not supinely surrender sovereign powers of this State." Speaking for all seven justices, the Georgia chief justice erroneously held that the United States Supreme Court had found itself without jurisdiction, and on that finding reaffirmed the conviction.[23] The Negro was electrocuted.[24]

II

There are both similarities and differences between the political relations of state courts and lower federal courts to the Supreme Court. Formal state-federal competition is absent, but it is often replaced by a local-national clash which can be almost equally as abrasive. This, in turn, is affected by the varying considerations in appointment of lower and Supreme Court judges. The Executive Department chooses district and, to a lesser extent, circuit judges in close cooperation with senators and national committeemen from the President's party and occasionally with congressmen from the state or states involved. Even a senator from the opposition party may enter the bargaining process. It would not be much of an exaggeration to say, as President Taft

[21] 93 So. 2d 354, 358 (1957).

[22] 349 U. S. 375, 391 (1955).

[23] *Supra* note 17.

[24] After the second decision of the Georgia supreme court, the U. S. Supreme Court denied certiorari, 350 U. S. 950 (1956).

once did, that at least as regards district judges, the President's power is largely one of veto rather than of full scale appointment.[25]

At the Supreme Court level there are still many political restrictions on the appointing power, but the President can weigh these competing values on a national rather than on a local scale. Even if Eisenhower's judicial probation-promotion policy remains in effect, High Court members are likely to be different types of men from those usually selected for the lower bench.

When the normal friction between trial and appellate judge is added to these other factors, a substantial reservoir of potential conflict has been built up. On the other hand, several forces act to soften this strife. First, and this bond unites federal with state judges as well as the three levels of federal judges with each other, they are all participants in the cult of the robe. They share the same holy mysteries and dispense the same sacred doctrine. No matter how fierce their inter-court rivalries, common possession of this magic sets judges apart from the rest of men and gives them interests and outlooks as *judges.* Second, district, circuit, and Supreme Court judges are all *federal* officials, in a sense joint competitors, whether they like it or not, with state judges for power.

The concept of an independent judiciary, which can increase the number of collisions between state and national tribunals, is balanced within the national system by appellate court supervision which, if it does not prevent conflict, does help keep that conflict from coming out into the open. A state judge owes his appointment to local political groups and can be removed, if at all, only by state action. Federal district and circuit judges are made even more independent by their life tenure, but their inferior position in the hierarchical chain of national authority subjects them to more strict Supreme Court surveillance. Under its power as supervisor of the administration of federal justice, the Supreme Court can set more exacting standards for lower courts of the United States than for state tribunals.

This makes federal court defiance less likely than state, but district and circuit judges are not mere pawns in the judicial game. They sometimes lash out in caustic criticism too. In 1958, for example, the Court of Appeals for the Ninth Circuit reversed the conviction of a pair of communist leaders on the basis of the Supreme Court's narrow interpretations of the Smith Act in *Yates* v. *United States.*[26] Judge Chambers remarked tartly that the court would have upheld the validity of the convictions on the basis of past practice had not the Supreme Court changed the law. "One may as well recognize that the Yates decision leaves the Smith Act, as to any further prosecutions under it, a virtual shambles—unless the American Communist Party should witlessly set out to reconstitute itself again with a new 'organization'."[27]

The reactions of a number of lower federal judges to the state chief justices'

[25] Quoted in George H. Haynes, *The Senate of the United States: Its History and Practice* (Boston, 1938), II, 722.

[26] 354 U. S. 298 (1957).

[27] Fujimoto v. United States, 251 F. 2d 342, 342 (1958). The other two circuit judges specifically disassociated themselves from these comments on the Yates case.

censure of the Supreme Court were no more subtle. The *U. S. News and World Report* polled all district and circuit judges, asking if they agreed or disagreed with the report of the state chief justices. Only 128 of 351 answered: 59 of them expressed approval, 50 disapproval, and 19 voiced no opinion.[28]

Another channel of criticism, more discreet but also more directly pointed toward securing remedial congressional action, is the Judicial Conference,[29] either at the national or circuit level. The Judicial Conference of the United States several times in recent years has endorsed bills to reverse Supreme Court decisions allowing relatively liberal opportunities for state prisoners to seek *habeas corpus* in federal courts.[30] But it was the Judicial Conference for the District of Columbia Circuit which struck one of the harshest blows with this weapon.

At the close of its 1956 term the Supreme Court had, in *Mallory* v. *United States*,[31] extended the application of its libertarian decision in the earlier *McNabb* case.[32] *McNabb* had ruled that confessions secured as a result of questioning during a prolonged period of delay between arrest and arraignment could not be used as evidence in a federal court. While the delay in *McNabb* had been several days, in *Mallory* less than eight hours had elapsed between arrest and confession. Nevertheless, the Court held that even this shorter period fell within the prohibition against "unnecessary delay" in arraignment imposed by Rule 5(a) of the Federal Rules of Criminal Procedure. Frankfurter's unanimous opinion conceded that "circumstances may justify a brief delay," but the police must "arraign the arrested person as quickly as possible so that he may be advised of his rights and so that the issue of probable cause may be promptly determined."[33] The Federal Rules were declared to allow "arresting officers little more leeway than the interval between arrest and the ordinary administrative steps required to bring a suspect before the nearest available magistrate."[34]

[28] October 24, 1958, pp. 36–37.

[29] 28 U. S. C. §331 provides that every year the Chief Justice of the United States shall call a meeting of the chief judges of each circuit, the chief judge of the Court of Claims, and a district judge from each circuit. This conference is directed to make a survey of the business of the courts of the United States and to submit to Congress a report including any suggestions for improvements. 28 U. S. C. §333 establishes similar rules for a judicial conference in each circuit. See Judge John J. Parker, "The Integration of the Federal Judiciary," *Harv. L. Rev.*, Vol. 56, p. 563 (1943).

[30] *Annual Report of the Proceedings of the Judicial Conference of the United States* (Washington, 1958), p. 28. Earlier recommendations are summarized in *House Report No. 1293 on H.R. 8361*, 85th Cong., 2d Sess. This report lists and discusses the various Supreme Court rulings which would have been modified by the proposed bill. The bill did not pass the 85th Congress, and in 1959 the Judicial Conference shifted its position, endorsing instead a proposal which would have modified lower court *habeas corpus* procedure while leaving intact the substance of Supreme Court decisions in this area. (*New York Times*, April 29, 1959, 18:6–7.)

[31] 354 U. S. 449 (1957).

[32] 318 U. S. 332 (1943).

[33] 354 U. S. 449, 454 (1957).

[34] *Ibid.*, at 453.

This decision, resulting as it did in the freeing of a chronic criminal who had just been found guilty of a brutal rape, stirred up a hornet's nest in Congress[35] as well as more tactfully expressed displeasure among lower court judges. At its next meeting, the Judicial Conference for the District of Columbia Circuit, the circuit in which *Mallory* had originated, endorsed pending legislation which would have rewritten Rule 5(a) so as to erase the *McNabb-Mallory* holdings.[36]

District Judge Alexander Holtzoff, the trial judge in the *Mallory* case and a Department of Justice careerist years before, was even sharper than the Judicial Conference in his opposition to the Supreme Court decision. In reply to a letter from a Senate subcommittee, the judge, who had acted as secretary to the advisory committee which had assisted the Court in drafting the Federal Rules, supplied some of the pertinent legislative history of Rule 5(a). He reported that the advisory committee had considered adding a subsection to Rule 5 to the effect that confessions obtained during an "unnecessary delay" between arrest and arraignment should be inadmissible. The committee, however, had rejected this proposal because it felt that such exclusions would punish the public more than delinquent police officials.[37] In similar oral testimony before another Senate subcommittee, Judge Holtzoff was deferential to the Supreme Court, but no less firm in his conviction that the Court had erred in *Mallory*. He reminded the Senators that *Mallory* was based not on constitutional but only on statutory interpretation. While such interpretation was within the power of the High Court, "it is equally within the power of the Congress to change this principle by legislation."[38]

The later handling of the *Mallory* decision, without new legislation, provides a classic example of the power of inferior judges to reshape legal doctrine expounded by the Supreme Court. By means of explaining, limiting, and distinguishing, the district and circuit judges in the District of Columbia have been able to permit the use in evidence of a high percentage of confessions secured during delays in arraignment.[39]

[35] A number of bills to reverse the Mallory decision were introduced in the 85th Congress. H.R. 11477 passed both the House and Senate, but in somewhat different forms. The conference report was agreed to by the House, but was defeated in the Senate minutes before final adjournment when Senator Carroll (D., Colo.) raised a point of order which Vice President Nixon sustained.

[36] *Washington Post & Times Herald*, May 9, 1958.

[37] Letter of Judge Alexander Holtzoff to General Counsel of the Senate Subcommittee on Improvements in the Federal Criminal Code, January 21, 1958.

[38] Senate Subcommittee on Constitutional Rights, *Hearings on Confessions and Police Detention*, 85th Cong., 1st Sess. (March 7, 11, 1958), p. 4.

[39] Senate *Hearings*, *supra* note 38, contain a collection of 13 lower court decisions, many of them otherwise unreported, interpreting *Mallory*. For other opinions applying or avoiding that case, read: United States v. White, 153 F. Supp. 809 (1957); United States v. Valente, 155 F. Supp. 577 (1957); United States v. Hodges, 156 F. Supp. 313 (1957); United States v. Armpriester, 156 F. Supp. 134 (1957); Mullican v. United States, 252 F. 2d 398 (1958); Smith v. United States, 254 F. 2d 751 (1958); Edwards v. United States, 256 F. 2d 707 (1958); Washington v. United States, 258 F. 2d 696 (1958).

Confessions were ruled admissible in 16 of these 21 cases.

Retired Associate Justice Stanley Reed, recalled to temporary duty on the Court of Appeals, and District Judge Holtzoff played prominent parts in this process. In *Porter* v. *United States*,[40] Reed, who had dissented from *McNabb*, shifted emphasis from the accused's right to be promptly arraigned to the accused's right not to be inflicted with the "serious stigma" of arraignment until the police had made "some pertinent and definitive inquiry." In this manner Reed was able to sustain admission of statements made during a 17-hour interval between arrest and arraignment.

Holtzoff continued his respectful resistance by closely limiting the value of *Mallory* as a binding precedent to the specific facts of the case. In overruling objections to a confession obtained during a short period of questioning (less than 45 minutes) before arraignment, Holtzoff stated: "An opinion of a court is not to be treated and read as an essay in determining the rule of law to be evolved therefrom . . . . The process is limited to collating not the statements in the various decisions and opinions, but the precise rulings."[41] On this basis, he concluded:

> While there are some statements in the opinion of the Court that are somewhat broader than the precise holding, the actual rule that can be deduced from the [Mallory] case in the light of the facts there involved, is that a period from 2:30 P.M. until 10:00 P.M.,—about seven and one-half hours,—is too long an interval and constitutes an unreasonable delay in bringing a prisoner before a committing magistrate.[42]

In this opinion Holtzoff brought out the underlying difference here between the lower courts and the Supreme Court. *Mallory* and its predecessors were concerned with the rights of the individual. If the Court was engaging in a balancing process, its thumb was on the side of the defendant's rights. Holtzoff and many of his colleagues in the District of Columbia circuit preferred to see the judicial thumb, if not off the scales, at least shifted to the side of the general public. Where the Supreme Court had been viewing the conflict as between a defendant's constitutional rights and police administration, the lower courts saw the clash as between an individual's rights to technical procedures and the public's right to basic protections.

> Every member of the community has a constitutional right to be protected in the safety of his person and his property. The victim of the crime must not become a forgotten man. His rights are much greater than those of the criminal. When the criminal law ceases to protect the public, it has failed of its purpose.[43]

The Supreme Court had spoken in *Mallory*, and while its opinion obviously did not set precise or very narrow limitations on lower court discretion, it did impose broad restrictions on the number and kinds of decisional alternatives open to federal judges. On the other hand, many problems come before lower courts on which the Supreme Court has not yet passed judgment. In deciding such cases, these tribunals can do, once removed, what the Supreme Court it-

[40] 258 F. 2d 685 (1958).
[41] United States v. Heideman and Brennan, 21 F.R.D. 335, 337 (1958).
[42] *Ibid.*, 338.
[43] *Ibid.*, 340.

self occasionally does in an analogous situation. For the High Court's question "What would the Founding Fathers or Congress have willed had they foreseen the case at bar?" the lower courts can substitute "What would the Supreme Court have visualized the Framers or Congress as willing had the Supreme Court foreseen this case?" This kind of speculation comes close to giving oneself a blank check.

Further complications enter when judges sense shifts in Supreme Court policy. Two schools of thought tell lower courts how to handle such problems. One, represented by the late Jerome Frank, feels that "when a lower court perceives a pronounced new doctrinal trend in Supreme Court decisions, it is its duty, cautiously to be sure, to follow not to resist it."[44] In a footnote to this statement, Frank added: "To use mouth-filling words, cautious extrapolation is in order."

Judge John J. Parker provided one of the most dramatic occasions of an inferior court's declining to follow an explicit Supreme Court precedent. In 1940, in the *Gobitis*[45] case, the High Court had with only one dissenting vote sustained the authority of Pennsylvania to compel children of Jehovah's Witnesses attending public schools to salute the flag, despite First Amendment and First Commandment scruples. Just two years later a case with almost identical facts arose in West Virginia, but, in the teeth of *Gobitis*, Judge Parker held the regulation invalid. This was not defiance. Parker noted that three of the *Gobitis* majority had confessed error[46] and that two others had retired, leaving the flag salute supporters a minority of three. "Under such circumstances and believing, as we do, that the flag salute here required is violative of religious liberty when required of persons holding the religious views of plaintiffs, we feel that we would be recreant to our duty as judges, if through a blind following of a decision which the Supreme Court itself has thus impaired as an authority, we should deny protection to rights which we regard as among the most sacred of those protected by constitutional guarantees."[47]

But prediction is a risky enterprise, and while Parker's nose-counting turned out to be correct, other guesses, however informed, can be and have been wrong.[48] This is the reasoning behind the views of the more conservative school

[44] Perkins v. Endicott Johnson, 128 F. 2d 208, 218 (1942). The Supreme Court affirmed this decision, 317 U. S. 501 (1943).

[45] Minersville School District v. Gobitis, 310 U. S. 586 (1940).

[46] Jones v. Opelika, 316 U. S. 584, 623–624 (1942).

[47] Barnette v. West Virginia, 47 F. Supp. 251, 253 (1942). It is worth noting that it had been Parker's strict adherence to Supreme Court precedent in an anti-labor case some fifteen years earlier which had alienated organized labor and helped defeat Senate confirmation of his nomination to the Supreme Court. The case was United Mine Workers v. Red Jacket Consolidated Coal & Coke Co., 18 F. 2d 839 (1927). For details see Subcommittee of the Senate Committee on the Judiciary, *Hearings on the Confirmation of Hon. John J. Parker*, 71st Cong., 2d Sess. (April 5, 1930).

[48] In Gardella v. Chandler, 172 F. 2d 402 (1949), Judge Frank thought that the Supreme Court had turned into an "impotent zombi" its 1922 decision (Federal Baseball Club v. National League, 259 U. S. 200) that professional baseball was beyond the scope of congressional regulatory power, and consequently outside the reach of the

of thought which holds that inferior judges should follow doubtful precedents until the Supreme Court specifically voids them.[49] As Chief Judge Calvert Magruder of the First Circuit has recently said: "We should always express a respectful deference to controlling decisions of the Supreme Court, and do our best to follow them. We should leave it to the Supreme Court to overrule its own cases." In keeping with this philosophy Judge Magruder called Parker's decision in the second flag case "an unseemly thing."[50]

Magruder was taking an instrumental rather than an ideological position, however. He admitted that when a new situation arises a lower court has two choices: either to concentrate on previous Supreme Court opinions and milk available dicta for possible guidance, or to strike out afresh and give its own opinion of what the law should be. And Magruder confessed that he himself had used both methods. He conceded further that on one occasion where he was using the second method "it was necessary to deal somewhat roughly, though very respectfully," with an explicit Supreme Court decision which he thought "shaky."[51]

Perhaps the most significant portion of Judge Magruder's address was his open acknowledgment that lower court jurists, although mindful of their obligation to the Supreme Court, were sometimes simply unwilling to follow the Justices in their interpretation of the law. As an example the judge cited a 1957 decision of his court limiting the definition of a seaman under the Jones Act.

Sherman Act. In 1953, however, the Supreme Court continued baseball's anti-trust immunity, though not affirming all that the earlier case had implied. Toolson v. New York Yankees, 346 U. S. 356. Even more to the point was the slap the Court administered in Spector Motor Service v. McLaughlin, 323 U. S. 101 (1944). A majority of the Court of Appeals for the Second Circuit (including Judge Frank) had detected a "new doctrinal trend" of the Supreme Court regarding state taxation of interstate commerce, and invalidated a Connecticut tax. In reversing this decision, the majority opinion, written by Justice Frankfurter, rebuked the lower court for its over-hasty anticipation.

[49] As Judge Chase of the Second Circuit said, dissenting from one of Jerome Frank's opinions: " . . . we should not be astute in seeking to anticipate that the court which has the power to do so will change that decision. To do so would not only be an unwarranted attempt to usurp the authority of that court but would make its task in general much more difficult. . . . [U]ntil, and unless, we are advised by competent authority that it is no longer the law we should continue to abide by it." Gardella v. Chandler, 172 F. 2d 402, 405 (1949). *Cf.* the opinion for the Court of Appeals for the Seventh Circuit in Aetna Portland Cement v. FTC, 157 F. 2d 533 (1946).

Learned Hand apparently took a middle position between his brethren on the Second Circuit. "I agree that one should not wait for formal retraction in the face of changes plainly foreshadowed. . . . Nor is it desirable for a lower court to embrace the exhilarating opportunity of anticipating a doctrine which may be in the womb of time, but whose birth is distant; on the contrary I conceive that the measure of its duty is to divine, as best it can, what would be the event of an appeal in the case before it." Dis. op. in Spector Motor Service v. Walsh, 139 F. 2d 809, 823 (1944).

[50] "The Trials and Tribulations of an Intermediate Appellate Court," *Cornell L. Q.* Vol. 44, pp. 1, 4 (1958).

[51] *Ibid.*, p. 7. The Supreme Court case in question was Bull v. United States, 295 U. S. 247 (1935).

The Supreme Court had summarily reversed the Court of Appeals, but, Magruder frankly stated, were the issue to come up once more, "I am afraid that we shall again 'stick our necks out' and say, as a matter of law, that the man is not a seaman, thereby courting another probable reversal by the Supreme Court."[52]

The power of prediction evidently confers considerable latitude on its user. He may be discerning what he believes the future does hold, what he hopes the future will hold, or what he judges the future should hold. Such guessing can influence the Supreme Court, or Congress, and it can also embarrass both by creating not just one but, by the time certiorari is granted and the case heard on review, a whole series of *faits accomplis*. On the other hand, refusal to accord official recognition to changing doctrine can also confer power. Disavowal of authority may be used to conceal or at least to give good form to serious disagreement with Supreme Court policy. In South Carolina, District Judge George Bell Timmerman, Sr., father of the governor, twice after 1954 insisted on applying the rule of *Plessy* v. *Ferguson*[53] to bus segregation, asserting that the school cases had only involved education and not transportation. "One's education and personality," Timmerman said disdainfully, "is not developed on a city bus."[54]

The authority to make findings of fact gives trial judges extensive power which appellate tribunals can only partially control.[54a] And in the *School Segregation Cases*, the Supreme Court broadened the scope of this inherent authority by specifically directing the exercise of the widest sort of judicial

[52] *Loc. cit.*, p. 10. The case referred to was Grimes v. Raymond Concrete Pile Co., 245 F. 2d 437 (1957); reversed, 356 U. S. 252 (1958).

[53] 163 U. S. 537 (1896).

[54] Flemming v. South Carolina Gas & Electric Co., 128 F. Supp. 469, 470 (1955). After the Court of Appeals reversed Timmerman, 224 F. 2d 752 (1955), he tried to salvage something by ruling that if not currently law, at least *Plessy* had been law at the time the bus dispute had begun. 1 *Race Rel. L. Rep.* 679 (1956). This, too, was reversed, 239 F. 2d 277 (1956). See also Timmerman's bitter statements dissenting in Bryan v. Austin, 148 F. Supp. 563 (1957).

Not to be outdone by Timmerman's *bon mot* about buses and personality, Judge Walter Hoffman of the U. S. District Court for Eastern Virginia, in throwing out a suit against segregated rest rooms in a state courthouse, remarked: "The underlying reasons for the rejection of the 'separate but equal' doctrine would not appear to be applicable to toilet facilities. . . . " Dawley v. Norfolk, 159 F. Supp. 642, 648 (1958). In spite of this sardonic piece of humor, Hoffman has rigidly followed the letter and spirit of Brown v. Board.

[54a] See especially Jerome Frank, *Courts on Trial: Myth and Reality in American Justice* (Princeton: Princeton University Press, 1950). The Supreme Court, however, has not always felt itself bound by lower court findings of fact. The older cases on this point are collected in Annotations at 49 L. ed. 546 and 58 L. ed. 1245. Among the more recent decisions asserting the right of the Court to review and reevaluate facts as well as law are: Truax v. Corrigan, 257 U. S. 312 (1921); Norris v. Alabama, 294 U. S. 587 (1934); United States v. Appalachian Power Co., 311 U. S. 377 (1940); Smith v. Allwright, 321 U. S. 649 (1944); Craig v. Harney, 331 U. S. 367 (1947); Niemotko v. Maryland, 340 U. S. 268 (1951); Feiner v. New York, 340 U. S. 315 (1951); Kern-Limerick v. Scurlock, 347 U. S. 110 (1954); Michel v. Louisiana, 350 U. S. 91 (1955); Konigsberg v. State Bar, 353 U. S. 252 (1957).

discretion, guided only by the flexible formula "with all deliberate speed." This is obviously a grant of vast power, and the high bench has relied on the Courts of Appeals to supervise its exercise. At this writing, after four years of lower court administration of school segregation problems, the Supreme Court has consented to full-scale review of only one such decision,[55] and there it affirmed the Court of Appeals.

Such a policy constitutes a manifestation of faith as well as an invitation for assumption of power. And occasionally a judge will seize the full implications of this invitation. Flying directly in the face of the desegregation ruling, and even after one reversal by the Court of Appeals, District Judge William H. Atwell declined to order Dallas, Texas, to set a date for integration because this would cause "civil wrongs." Lest his own feelings be mistaken, Atwell declared: "I believe that it will be seen that the [Supreme] Court based its decision on no law but rather on what the Court regarded as more authoritative, modern psychological knowledge . . . . It will be recalled that in 1952, Mr. Justice Frankfurter said it was not competent to take judicial notice of 'Claims of social scientists.' "[56]

As a retired jurist called back for temporary service, Judge Atwell may have felt a wider margin of freedom than his more active brethren, but the significant fact remains that 48 months after the Supreme Court's implementation decision neither of the two Southern communities in which the original school cases began had yet been required to admit a single Negro child to a hitherto white school.[57] Indeed, although there had been several court orders for a "prompt start" on plans for eventual segregation, when the school year closed in June, 1959, the only two Deep Southern states to have even token public school integration in some localities were North Carolina and Virginia.

This is not to deny that most federal judges are trying their best to carry out desegregation in a sincere and workable manner, but even the most imaginative member of the realist school of jurisprudence could hardly conceive of a more fertile field for free play of judicial predilections, conscious and sub-conscious. As a reaction against this freedom and its resultant responsibility, there is

[55] Cooper v. Aaron, 3 L. ed. 2d 5 (1958).

[56] Bell v. Rippy, 146 F. Supp. 485, 486 (1956). The earlier decision is reported at 133 F. Supp. 811 (1955), and the reversal, *sub nom.* Brown v. Rippy, at 233 F. 2d 796 (1956). This second decision, of course, was also reversed, *sub nom.* Borders v. Rippy, 247 F. 2d 268 (1957), but this did not end the matter. Atwell immediately went to the opposite extreme and ordered Dallas schools integrated in the middle of the academic year. 2 *Race Rel. L. Rep.* 985 (1957). This decision was also reversed by the Court of Appeals, 250 F. 2d 690 (1957).

[57] In the case which originated in Prince Edward County, Virginia, the district judge in 1958 set 1965 as the date for compliance, 164 F. Supp. 786 (1958). The Court of Appeals reversed, and ordered admission of qualified Negro students to hitherto white schools in September 1959, 266 F. 2d 507 (1959). The county replied in June, 1959 by refusing to appropriate money for continued operation of public schools. For a discussion of various private school plans, consult Walter F. Murphy, "Private Schools with Public Funds?", *Journal of Politics*, Vol. 20 (1958), p. 635; for current developments see the *Southern School News* (Nashville, Tenn., monthly).

evidence of a growing resentment among lower court judges in Southern and border states, a feeling that they have been left to engage in a violent emotional battle against prevailing white mores while the Justices in Washington refuse to stoop to such conflict by primly denying certiorari in segregation cases.

It is possible that the Court of Appeals for the Eighth Circuit in the August 1958 phase of the Little Rock campaign was trying to force the Supreme Court's hand when it took the somewhat unusual step of staying its own order to preserve the *status quo.*[58] If the case had not been immediately reviewed by the Supreme Court, the stay would have allowed Central High School to transfer its Negro students and to reopen as a segregated institution. This would have been an immense victory for Governor Faubus's obstructionist tactics.

If the Court of Appeals was trying to compel the High Bench to reiterate its principles and re-enter the fight, the circuit judges succeeded wonderfully well. Both the opinion of the Chief Justice and Frankfurter's concurrence spelled out the Court's constitutional authority and interpretation, as well as its policy intentions, in a far more powerful form than had either of the two previous school decisions.[59]

III

The lower courts can and do check the Supreme Court, but the Supreme Court can act to counter lower court power. While it cannot fire and hire new personnel as the President can sometimes do, the Court can review and reverse inferior judges. This is important beyond any effect on a particular case. Judges, no more than other men, enjoy the prospect of public correction and reprimand. The Supreme Court can put added bite to this psychological whip by sarcasm and scathing criticism of its own. Alternatively, the Court may resort to more diplomatic means as it did in *Williams* v. *Georgia.*[60] But the limitations on such efforts at peaceful coexistence were clearly spelled out when the Georgia supreme court not only refused to review Williams' conviction but also declined to recognize any federal jurisdiction.

In a more subtle fashion, the Supreme Court may nip evasions by means of gratuitous legal advice, a method which almost touches the tabu against advisory opinions. Thus after the final Florida decision in the *Hawkins* litigation, the United State Supreme Court denied certiorari; it added the notation, however, that this denial was not intended to prejudice the right of Hawkins to take his case to a federal district court.[61] The NAACP got the hint and won a compromise victory in a relatively short time.[62]

[58] Cooper v. Aaron, 257 F. 2d 33 (1958).

[59] Cooper v. Aaron, *supra* note 55.

[60] *Supra* note 22. Compare the similar conciliatory efforts in Deen v. Hickman, 3 L. ed. 2d 28 (1958).

[61] Florida ex rel Hawkins v. Board, 355 U. S. 839 (1957).

[62] Even this victory is significant for the thesis of this article. The federal district court first refused to allow Hawkins to introduce any evidence. The Court of Appeals reversed, Hawkins v. Board, 253 F. 2d 752 (1958). The final result of nine years of litigation was an injunction forbidding the University to deny entrance to its *graduate* schools because of

Similarly, in its September 1958 Little Rock opinion the Court managed to warn federal courts and state officials, as well as potential plaintiffs, that it would not look with favor on projected private school plans. This was accomplished by means of a general statement: "the prohibitions of the Fourteenth Amendment extend to all action of the State denying equal protection of the laws; whatever the agency of the State taking the action, or whatever the guise in which it is taken."[63] Even more meaningful were two of the citations appended to the last clause. These referred to decisions of Courts of Appeals which had prohibited states from allowing ostensibly private agencies to carry out discrimination forbidden to state governments.[64]

When confronted with systematic evasion the Supreme Court could, as a last resort, invoke its inherent power to punish for contempt in order to coerce either state or federal judges. But this is as unlikely to be used as is the impeachment and removal power of Congress. More probably, the Court would do as it did in the second restrictive covenant cases[65] and what it indicated it would do in its Little Rock opinion: cast all technicalities aside and bring the full weight of its constitutional authority to bear on the substantive issues in the dispute. Or, if the case had originated in a federal court, it might act as it did in 1958 and make the final determination of the problems itself.[66] Faced with such countermeasures, lower courts would no doubt retreat in an effort both to save face and to salvage as much as possible, realizing that the battle could be continued in the administrative and legislative processes much more easily if a final showdown in the judicial process were avoided.

In such a fashion this aspect of judicial decision-making comes full circle. The Supreme Court must take into account the reaction of inferior judges, and lower courts must attempt to divine the counter-reaction of the Supreme Court. Meanwhile, both must keep a wary eye on public opinion and maneuverings within the other branches of government to ascertain how these will affect the policy concerned. Judges have not solved the dilemmas caused by this feedback process, nor have administrators. And if power can be checked only by power, it may be healthy for the continued existence of limited government if neither judicial nor administrative officers ever fully resolve these conflicts.

---

race. The district court, however, refused to order Hawkins's admission, 162 F. Supp. 851 (1958).

[63] Cooper v. Aaron, *supra* note 55, at 16. (Citations omitted.)

[64] Derrington v. Plummer, 240 F. 2d 922 (1956); Department of Conservation v. Tate, 231 F. 2d 615 (1956).

[65] Barrows v. Jackson, 346 U. S. 249 (1953).

[66] Yates v. United States, 356 U. S. 363 (1958).

[15]

Judicial Partisanship and Obedience to Legal Doctrine: Whistleblowing on the Federal Courts of Appeals

Frank B. Cross† **and Emerson H. Tiller**††

In traditional legal analysis, scholars take for granted the effect of Supreme Court doctrine. Lower courts are presumed to adhere to the self-enforcing principle of stare decisis and to apply the doctrines of higher courts to the particular facts of the underlying case.[1] Precedent reputedly controls lower-court decisions.[2] Whether such obedience to legal doctrine occurs as routinely as this analysis suggests, however, has not been adequately addressed in the legal literature. Indeed, there are few empirical studies by legal scholars bearing on the matter at all.[3] In this Essay, we go to the heart of the issue and

---

† Professor of Business Regulation and the Law, University of Texas at Austin.

†† Assistant Professor of Business, Politics and the Law, University of Texas at Austin. We thank Charles Cameron and participants at the 1997 Conference on the Scientific Study of Judicial Politics for helpful comments.

1. The Supreme Court has declared that stare decisis "is a basic self-governing principle within the Judicial Branch." Patterson v. McLean Credit Union, 491 U.S. 164, 172 (1989).

2. *See* Kathleen M. Sullivan, *The Supreme Court—1991 Term, Foreword: The Justices of Rules and Standards*, 106 HARV. L. REV. 22, 64-65 (1992) (reporting the traditional position that "[c]ourts are to stick to law, judgment, and reason in making their decisions and should leave politics, will, and value choice to others"). Archibald Cox refers to the "discipline of legal reasoning" as a means of "minimiz[ing] the danger of writing [Justices'] personal values and preferences" into their opinions. ARCHIBALD COX, THE COURT AND THE CONSTITUTION 70 (1987). David Shapiro contends that requiring judges to give reasons for their opinions serves "a vital function in constraining the judiciary's exercise of power." David L. Shapiro, *In Defense of Judicial Candor*, 100 HARV. L. REV. 731, 737 (1987). Chief Judge Harry Edwards of the D.C. Circuit Court of Appeals states that "it is the law—and not the personal politics of individual judges—that controls judicial decision-making in most cases resolved by the court of appeals." Harry T. Edwards, *Public Misperceptions Concerning the "Politics" of Judging: Dispelling Some Myths About the D.C. Circuit*, 56 U. COLO. L. REV. 619, 620 (1985).

3. See sources cited *infra* Section II.B for legal scholarship discussing judicial obedience to doctrine in the context of administrative law. For studies on obedience within the judiciary, consider Richard L. Pacelle, Jr. & Lawrence Baum, *Supreme Court Authority in the Judiciary*, 20 AM. POL. Q. 169 (1992), which concludes through a study of cases remanded by the Supreme Court that lower courts tend to

ask the following question: If judges have personal or partisan policy preferences, why would they follow established legal doctrine when it conflicts with those preferences? While there is undoubtedly more than one valid explanation for principled adherence to legal doctrine, we suggest that the prospect of a "whistleblower" on the court—that is, the presence of a judge whose policy preferences differ from the majority's and who will expose the majority's manipulation or disregard of the applicable legal doctrine (if such manipulation or disregard were needed to reach the majority's preferred outcome)—is a significant determinant of whether judges will perform their designated role as principled legal decisionmakers. We do more than merely propose this theory; we test it empirically and find substantial support for our claim.

To be sure, legal doctrine endorsed by the Supreme Court plays a critical role in the decisionmaking of federal jurists, and it would be an overstatement to claim that most judges casually disregard doctrine when it stands in the way of reaching their desired policy outcome. Nonetheless, much of the scholarship simply assumes the sincere application of legal doctrine without considering the possibility that it may at times be nothing more than a convenient rationalization for political decisionmaking.[4] Indeed, many legal scholars explicitly discard the proposition that judges disregard legal doctrine in favor of partisan or ideological policymaking, or ignore the proposition with silent disdain, even in the face of reputable empirical studies in political science demonstrating the existence of such subversions of legal precedent and doctrine.[5]

The traditional position has been challenged by legal realists, critical legal scholars, and political scientists, who are all highly skeptical of the practical importance of legal doctrine. They contend, and empirically demonstrate, that judges often decide cases according to their political proclivities and use

recognize high-court authority; and Donald R. Songer et al., *The Hierarchy of Justice: Testing a Principal-Agent Model of Supreme Court-Circuit Court Interactions*, 38 AM. J. POL. SCI. 673 (1994), which reaches mixed conclusions regarding the effect of Supreme Court precedent on circuit court behavior.

4. *But see* Richard J. Pierce, Jr., *Two Problems in Administrative Law: Political Polarity on the District of Columbia Circuit and Judicial Deterrence of Agency Rulemaking*, 1988 DUKE L.J. 300, 303-07 (surveying a set of administrative law cases in the D.C. Circuit and concluding that the decisions are best explained by the policy predilections of individual judges and by whether a majority of the judges on a panel were appointed by a Republican or a Democratic president).

5. *See* H.W. PERRY, JR., DECIDING TO DECIDE: AGENDA SETTING IN THE UNITED STATES SUPREME COURT 4 (1991) (reporting that legal scholars "ignore with impunity" the empirical research on political decisionmaking by judges); Daniel B. Rodriguez, *The Positive Political Dimensions of Regulatory Reform*, 72 WASH. U. L.Q. 1, 4 (1994) (discussing the reluctance of legal scholars to consider the empirical findings of political scientists). The assumption of the importance of doctrine in judicial decisions is so strong that some commentators have criticized the Supreme Court for paying *too much* attention to precedent in its decisions. *See, e.g.*, Frank H. Easterbrook, *Stability and Reliability in Judicial Decisions*, 73 CORNELL L. REV. 422, 426-27 (1988) (criticizing reliance on precedent in statutory interpretation); William N. Eskridge, Jr., *Overruling Statutory Precedents*, 76 GEO. L.J. 1361 (1988) (same).

precedent, if at all, as an ex post facto justification for their decisions.[6] This scholarship challenges the presumption that judges follow the law out of a sense of responsibility or role orientation. While the Supreme Court can theoretically play a disciplining role by enforcing adherence to doctrine on appeal, the Court's limited resources may preclude effective control.[7] According to the attitudinal model, lower-court obedience to legal doctrine has little practical effect in determining judicial decisions.[8]

Just as practitioners of the traditional position have ignored political variables, those in the other camp (legal realists, critical legal scholars, and political scientists) have paid little heed to the role legal doctrine might play in judicial decisionmaking.[9] Indeed, many of their claims of political decisionmaking fail to incorporate any legal variables.[10] For the most part, these scholars stand steadfast in the belief that the explanatory value of legal

6. Among the most prominent presentations of this position is JEFFREY A. SEGAL & HAROLD J. SPAETH, THE SUPREME COURT AND THE ATTITUDINAL MODEL (1993), in which the authors claim that virtually all Supreme Court decisions are determined by the Justices' politics rather than the law. *See id.* at 72-73. The authors present considerable empirical evidence to this effect, showing that Justices' votes can be predicted based on their political attitudes as revealed in prior decisions. *See id.* at 255. As for decisions relying on precedent, the authors claim that "opinions containing such rules merely rationalize decisions; they are not the causes of them." *Id.* at 66. Such rationalization comes rather easily, as precedents are typically available on both sides of any case. *See, e.g.*, Allan C. Hutchinson & Patrick J. Monahan, *Law, Politics, and the Critical Legal Scholars: The Unfolding Drama of American Legal Thought*, 36 STAN. L. REV. 199, 206 (1984) (presenting the Critical Legal Studies view that "[l]egal doctrine can be manipulated to justify an almost infinite spectrum of possible outcomes").

7. *See, e.g.*, Peter L. Strauss, *One Hundred Fifty Cases per Year: Some Implications of the Supreme Court's Limited Resources for Judicial Review of Agency Action*, 87 COLUM. L. REV. 1093, 1095 (1987) (observing that "the Court's awareness [of] how infrequently it is able to review lower court decisions has led it to be tolerant, even approving, of lower court and party indiscipline in relation to existing law"). Several rational choice models of judicial review of agency decisionmaking have incorporated the notion that actors have limited resources and the derivative proposition that this creates discretion for agencies and lower courts. *See* Pablo T. Spiller, *Agency Discretion Under Judicial Review*, 16 MATHEMATICAL & COMPUTER MODELING 185 (1992) (modeling the role of decision costs in creating discretion for agencies); Pablo T. Spiller & Emerson H. Tiller, *Decision Costs and the Strategic Design of Administrative Process and Judicial Review*, 26 J. LEGAL STUD. 347 (1997) (discussing the ability of Congress to manipulate the resources of agencies and courts for purposes of achieving policies desired by Congress); Emerson H. Tiller, *Controlling Policy by Controlling Process*, 14 J.L. ECON. & ORG. 114 (1998) (modeling the ability of a court to manipulate agency resources to achieve a policy desired by the court); Joseph L. Smith & Emerson H. Tiller, The Strategy of Judging: Evidence from Administrative Law (1997) (unpublished manuscript, on file with the *Yale Law Journal*) (testing empirically models of strategic choice by circuit courts); Emerson H. Tiller & Pablo T. Spiller, Strategic Instruments: Politics and Decision Costs in Administrative and Judicial Process (1997) (unpublished manuscript, on file with the *Yale Law Journal*) (modeling the ability of agencies and courts strategically to select grounds upon which to base a decision in order to impose costs upon reviewing actors).

8. A leading political scientist and lawyer claims that the "evidence overwhelmingly supports the attitudinal model and, equally overwhelmingly, fails to support the legal model as an explanation of why the justices decide their cases as they do." Harold J. Spaeth, *The Attitudinal Model*, *in* CONTEMPLATING COURTS 296, 296 (Lee Epstein ed., 1995). He emphasizes that "the mere fact that a court cites precedent provides no evidence that precedent actually determines the outcome of the case." *Id.* at 302.

9. Perry suggests that political scientists show a "lack of appreciation of the nature of the courts, the law, and the legal system." PERRY, *supra* note 5, at 3.

10. *See* Donald R. Songer & Susan Haire, *Integrating Alternative Approaches to the Study of Judicial Voting: Obscenity Cases in the U.S. Courts of Appeals*, 36 AM. J. POL. SCI. 963, 967 (1992) (reporting that "scholars in the empirical tradition have given little systematic attention to the potential effect of variables that might reflect the traditional model").

variables is at best not capable of being tested or, as is more likely, nonexistent.[11]

The battle over the significance of doctrine has persisted without truly being joined. Traditional legal scholars have assiduously guarded their disciplinary turf against outsiders as have those promoting the more cynical explanations of judicial decisionmaking. In this Essay, we fuse the various judicial decisionmaking models of political scientists and legal scholars to explain and demonstrate empirically under what conditions appellate court judges do obey the legal doctrines the Supreme Court has set out. We examine this proposition in the context of administrative law, where the Supreme Court has laid down a reputedly path-breaking legal doctrine governing judicial review of administrative agencies. We ask whether, and under what conditions, appellate courts adhere to this command.

I. A THEORY OF COMPLIANCE WITH DOCTRINE

Once the Supreme Court sets forth doctrines, lower courts may comply or disobey. If lower courts comply, they may do so for a number of reasons: (1) compliance with doctrine enables the lower courts to effect their political preferences;[12] (2) the lower courts are dutifully performing their roles as sincere jurists, applying the principles in an ideologically (or politically) neutral manner;[13] or (3) the lower courts fear exposure of any noncompliance and consequent reversal. Lower courts may disobey because (4) they wish to effect their political preferences;[14] or (5) they mean to apply doctrine dutifully but are influenced to apply the rules in a way that achieves their political

11. Segal and Spaeth complain that the legal model cannot be objectively operationalized in an empirical study. *See* SEGAL & SPAETH, *supra* note 6, at 33-34. They have recently sought to test the legal model by examining whether Supreme Court Justices followed precedents from which they initially dissented. *See* Jeffrey A. Segal & Harold J. Spaeth, *The Influence of* Stare Decisis *on the Votes of United States Supreme Court Justices*, 40 AM. J. POL. SCI. 971 (1996). While they found that dissenters continued to dissent, notwithstanding the creation of the original precedent, *see id.* at 971, this finding hardly disproves the legal model. That model does not dictate that Justices must follow a precedent they believe to be contrary to the Constitution.

12. In this circumstance, the legal and political models are mutually reinforcing.

13. This is the conventional legal model. For a discussion, see Frank B. Cross, *Political Science and the New Legal Realism: A Case of Unfortunate Interdisciplinary Ignorance*, 92 NW. U. L. REV. 251, 255-63 (1997).

14. *See* William N. Eskridge, Jr., *Overriding Supreme Court Statutory Interpretation Decisions*, 101 YALE L.J. 331 (1991) (discussing how the Supreme Court's statutory interpretation decisions are restrained by the risk of being overridden by subsequent legislation); McNollgast, *Politics and the Courts: A Positive Theory of Judicial Doctrine and the Rule of Law*, 68 S. CAL. L. REV. 1631, 1643-44 (1995) (claiming that lower courts restrain their rulings so as to avoid higher-court reversal). *But cf.* Pablo T. Spiller & Emerson H. Tiller, *Invitations To Override: Congressional Reversals of Supreme Court Decisions*, 16 INT'L REV. L. & ECON. 503 (1996) (illustrating how the Supreme Court may prod Congress into reversing one of its decisions to maximize the Court's doctrinal and policy preferences).

preferences.[15] Each of these five modes may operate at different times and under different circumstances.[16]

Our first theoretical proposition is simple: Judges are more likely to obey legal doctrine when such doctrine supports the partisan or ideological policy preferences of the court majority. In those cases in which doctrine does not support the partisan or ideological policy preferences of the court majority, we expect somewhat more disobedience. Our second theoretical proposition is that courts are more likely to comply with doctrine (rather than to decide based solely on their political preferences) when the judicial panel is politically or ideologically divided. This results from the presence of a minority position on the panel that creates an opportunity for whistleblowing—a minority member with doctrine on her side and the ability, through a dissent, to expose disobedient decisionmaking by the majority. The minority member may threaten to highlight the disobedience externally to a higher court or to Congress, producing exposure and possible reversal.[17] Alternatively, the minority may expose the subconscious disobedience internally, causing the majority to acknowledge its disregard or unintentional manipulation of doctrine. Consequently, in the presence of such a whistleblower, the majority must sometimes capitulate and keep its decision within the confines of doctrine.

We apply our analysis to the federal courts of appeals.[18] These courts are

15. Even the behavioralist political scientists who maintain that judges are acting politically do not necessarily claim that these actions are consciously disobedient to legal doctrine. *See* C.K. Rowland, *The Federal District Courts*, *in* THE AMERICAN COURTS: A CRITICAL ASSESSMENT 61, 79 (John B. Gates & Charles A. Johnson eds., 1991) (observing that judges of different ideologies "will often see similar evidence differently, remember evidence that fits their relevant mental constructs more vividly and accurately than evidence that does not, and interpret ambiguous information in ways consistent with their schematic predilections"); *see also* Scott C. Idleman, *A Prudential Theory of Judicial Candor*, 73 TEX. L. REV. 1307, 1318-19 (1995) (indicating that "[m]any omissions of candor, after all, are not conscious ploys on the part of judges, but rather the product of either less-than-thorough or genuinely self-deceptive analysis").

16. It is also possible that a lower court tried to apply the doctrine dutifully but misunderstood that doctrine as it was intended by the Supreme Court. We do not consider this a disobedience of doctrine in our analysis.

17. For an example of a case in which a minority judge (Democrat) chided the majority (Republicans) for not following doctrine, see *Engine Manufacturers Ass'n v. EPA*, 88 F.3d 1075 (D.C. Cir. 1996), which involved an industry association's challenge to an EPA rule where a Republican panel majority vacated one section of the regulation. The lone Democrat dissented, arguing that the *Chevron* doctrine, *see* Chevron U.S.A. Inc. v. Natural Resources Defense Council, Inc., 467 U.S. 837 (1984), should have required approval of the entire rule. For the role of dissent more generally, consider a recent study on search-and-seizure cases suggesting that dissents are driven in part by the ideological preferences of judges. *See* Steven R. Van Winkle, Dissent as a Signal: Evidence from the U.S. Courts of Appeals (1997) (unpublished manuscript, on file with the *Yale Law Journal*) (finding dissents more likely to occur on a circuit court panel when the dissenter was of the same ideological position as the full circuit majority, thus suggesting a political whistleblowing effect).

18. The approach taken here is consistent with the recent law and positive political theory movement, which has addressed questions of constitutional law, federalism, administrative law, statutory interpretation, and judicial expansion through rational choice and institutional theory. *See, e.g.*, Jenna Bednar & William N. Eskridge, Jr., *Steadying the Court's "Unsteady Path": A Theory of Judicial Enforcement of Federalism*, 68 S. CAL. L. REV. 1447 (1995) (analyzing the variance in Supreme Court federalism decisions through the insights of positive political theory); Linda R. Cohen & Matthew L. Spitzer, *Judicial Deference to*

organized such that three-judge panels are randomly selected to hear appeals from lower federal district courts or federal regulatory agencies. After these panels make their decisions, the outcome may be appealed to the full circuit sitting en banc or to the Supreme Court. Figure 1 illustrates the likelihood that the panel follows established doctrine given the alignment of preferences within the judicial panel (measured by either party affiliation of the judges or some other independent measure of judicial preferences) and the consistency

---

Agency Action: A Rational Choice Theory and an Empirical Test, 69 S. CAL. L. REV. 431 (1996) (using insights of positive political theory to predict when the Supreme Court will manipulate administrative law); William N. Eskridge, Jr. & John Ferejohn, *The Article I, Section 7 Game*, 80 GEO. L.J. 523 (1992) (analyzing Article I, Section 7 of the U.S. Constitution through the lens of positive political theory as a "sequential game" consisting of interactions among the branches based on their individual preferences); William N. Eskridge, Jr. & John Ferejohn, *Making the Deal Stick: Enforcing the Ordinal Constitutional Structure of Lawmaking in the Modern Regulatory State*, 8 J.L. ECON & ORG. 165 (1992) (applying game-theoretical work in positive political theory to find a more systematic basis for evaluating Supreme Court constitutional decisions regarding the lawmaking functions of agencies); John M. de Figueiredo & Emerson H. Tiller, *Congressional Control of the Courts: A Theoretical and Empirical Analysis of Expansion of the Federal Judiciary*, 39 J.L. & ECON. 435 (1996) (using positive political theory to explain the expansion of the federal judiciary as a product of unified government); Rafael Gely & Pablo T. Spiller, *A Rational Choice Theory of Supreme Court Statutory Decisions with Applications to the* State Farm *and* Grove City *Cases*, 6 J.L. ECON. & ORG. 263, 265 (1990) (using positive political theory models to illustrate that "[t]he ability of other political actors . . . to reverse the Supreme Court . . . is what constrains the scope and power of the Court"); Matthew D. McCubbins et al., *Administrative Procedures as Instruments of Political Control*, 3 J.L. ECON. & ORG. 243 (1987) (using positive political theory to examine how interest groups monitor agency compliance with congressional directives); Matthew D. McCubbins et al., *Structure and Process, Politics and Policy: Administrative Arrangements and the Political Control of Agencies*, 75 VA. L. REV. 431 (1989) (same); McNollgast, *Legislative Intent: The Use of Positive Political Theory in Statutory Interpretation*, LAW & CONTEMP. PROBS., Winter 1994, at 3 (proposing the use of positive political theory as a descriptive model of the legislative process to clarify statutory intent); McNollgast, *supra* note 14, at 1631 (using positive political theory to explain adherence to doctrine and court packing); McNollgast, *Positive Canons: The Role of Legislative Bargains in Statutory Interpretation*, 80 GEO L.J. 705 (1992) (advocating the use of positive political theory to attain a clearer understanding of statutory intent); Terry M. Moe, *Political Institutions: The Neglected Side of the Story*, J.L. ECON. & ORG., Special Issue 1990, at 213, 230 (using institutional theory to explain how administrative procedure is traded for substance in a way that "public agencies will tend to be structured in part by their enemies—who want them to fail"); Daniel B. Rodriguez, *Management, Control, and the Dilemmas of Presidential Leadership in the Modern Administrative State*, 43 DUKE L.J. 1180 (1994) (considering the role of the President in regulatory reform through an analysis informed by positive political theory); Pablo T. Spiller & Rafael Gely, *Congressional Control or Judicial Independence: The Determinants of U.S. Supreme Court Labor-Relations Decisions, 1949-1988*, 23 RAND J. ECON. 463 (1992) (using positive political theory to analyze the conditions under which the Supreme Court may impose its policy preferences on the Constitution without risking being overruled by constitutional amendment); Pablo T. Spiller & Matthew L. Spitzer, *Judicial Choice of Legal Doctrines*, 8 J.L. ECON. & ORG. 8 (1992) (using positive political theory to suggest why the Supreme Court will use constitutional rather than statutory interpretation in a strategic game with Congress). For some comments on and criticisms of these various approaches, see Linda R. Cohen, *Politics and the Courts: A Comment on McNollgast*, 68 S. CAL. L. REV. 1685 (1995); Murray J. Horn & Kenneth A. Shepsle, *Commentary on "Administrative Arrangements and the Political Control of Agencies": Administrative Process and Organizational Form as Legislative Responses to Agency Costs*, 75 VA. L. REV. 499 (1989); Jack Knight, *Positive Models and Normative Theory: A Comment on Eskridge and Ferejohn*, 8 J.L. ECON. & ORG. 190 (1992); Glen O. Robinson, *Commentary on Administrative Arrangements and the Political Control of Agencies: Political Uses of Structure and Process*, 75 VA. L. REV. 483 (1989); Daniel B. Rodriguez, *The Administrative State and the Original Understanding: Comments on Eskridge and Ferejohn*, 8 J.L. ECON. & ORG. 197 (1992); Peter L. Strauss & Andrew R. Rutten, *The Game of Politics and Law: A Response to Eskridge and Ferejohn*, 8 J.L. ECON. & ORG. 205 (1992); and Emerson H. Tiller, *Putting Politics into the Positive Political Theory of Federalism: A Comment on Bednar and Eskridge*, 68 S. CAL. L. REV. 1493 (1995).

of these preferences with the outcome dictated by adhering to doctrine. The alignment numbers (3-0 and 2-1) do not necessarily indicate the actual voting of the judges (since compromises may be made among the panel members); the numbers indicate only the underlying policy preference alignments of the panel members.

FIGURE 1. LIKELIHOOD THAT DOCTRINE IS FOLLOWED GIVEN THE JUDICIAL PANEL'S POLICY ALIGNMENTS

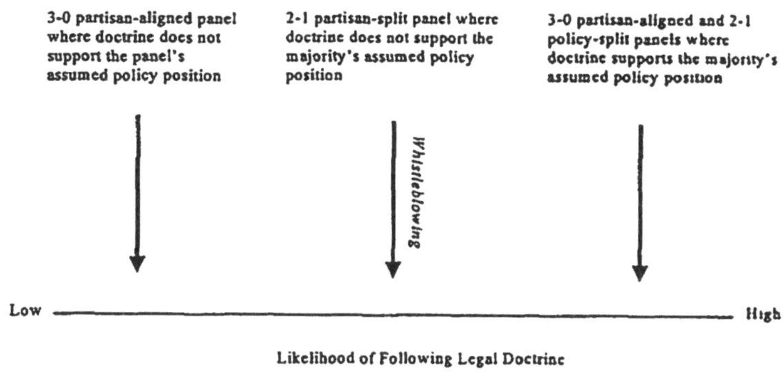

Figure 1 suggests that if the policy favored by the majority of the members on the panel would be accomplished through adherence to the applicable legal doctrine—that is, when there is convergence between sincere application of the doctrine and the policy preferences of the majority—then that panel will be more likely to follow the doctrine than if convergence did not exist. In such a case, legal doctrine is not a constraint upon the pursuance of policy goals; instead, it helps to legitimize the policy outcome of the unified panel. In contrast, if the three members of the panel are unified in their policy preferences and if they would not benefit from sincere application of the doctrine—that is, there is no convergence between the majority's policy preferences and the sincere application of doctrine—then they would be more likely to ignore doctrine. If the members of the panel are divided two-to-one in their policy preferences, however, and if the minority member's policy preferences converge with the application of doctrine while the majority's preferences do not, the minority member could act as a whistleblower, forcing the majority to follow the doctrine more often than if all three members were unified against application of the doctrine. In this sense, doctrine does matter because it is a real constraint upon the court majority's ability to pursue policy goals.

II. JUDICIAL OBEDIENCE TO THE *CHEVRON* DOCTRINE: APPLYING THE THEORY TO ADMINISTRATIVE LAW

The Supreme Court in *Chevron U.S.A. Inc. v. Natural Resources Defense Council, Inc.*,[19] seemingly commanded lower courts to grant considerable deference to federal administrative agency interpretations of statutes. The decision was of great import for administrative law and also offers an ideal test case for determining whether Supreme Court doctrine has a material effect in restraining the decisions of lower courts. One can examine lower-court decisionmaking in the wake of *Chevron* and observe whether the lower court is granting deference neutrally, as per doctrine, or is manipulating the deference doctrine to achieve politically desirable outcomes. We employ *Chevron* cases to test our theories of judicial decisionmaking. First, however, some background on *Chevron* and its interpretation is necessary.

A. *The Terms of* Chevron

Chevron arose from a creative statutory interpretation by the Environmental Protection Agency (EPA) that modified the definition of a pollution source to enhance the efficiency of control measures. The rule was challenged by environmentalists and struck down by the D.C. Circuit,[20] which found the EPA's interpretation of the statute contrary to congressional intent. The Supreme Court, however, reversed the D.C. Circuit and, in the process, set forth what has become known as the *Chevron* doctrine of deference to agency statutory interpretations.

On its face, *Chevron* analysis provides for a two-step inquiry. First, a judge must determine if "Congress has directly spoken to the precise question at issue."[21] If so, the agency must adhere to the unambiguous legislative command, and a court may reverse a contrary agency interpretation. In *Chevron* itself, the Court found the statutory language ambiguous and the legislative history silent.[22] If the congressional directive is ambiguous, a court is to move on to the second analytical step—whether the agency's interpretation of ambiguity is reasonable.[23] This reasonableness standard has been analogized to the purportedly deferential arbitrary-and-capricious standard of review.[24]

19. 467 U.S. 837 (1984).

20. *See* Natural Resources Defense Council, Inc. v. Gorsuch, 685 F.2d 718 (D.C. Cir. 1982), *rev'd sub nom.* Chevron U.S.A. Inc. v. Natural Resources Defense Council, Inc., 467 U.S. 837 (1984).

21. *Chevron*, 467 U.S. at 842.

22. *See id.* at 862.

23. *See id.* at 843-44. Reasonableness in the *Chevron* case was found in part because of the agency's need to reconcile "conflicting policies." *Id.* at 865.

24. *See* Laurence H. Silberman, Chevron—*The Intersection of Law & Policy*, 58 GEO. WASH. L. REV. 821, 827 (1990); *see also* 5 U.S.C. § 706 (1994).

While the general thrust of *Chevron* is deference to administrative agency interpretations, the opinion did not command mechanistic deference. A lower court can refuse to defer because the agency interpretation is contrary to the plain meaning of the statute (step one) or because the interpretation is unreasonable (step two).[25] A court striking down a rule on these grounds can claim to be obedient to doctrine. Thus obedience to doctrine cannot be measured strictly by the amount of deference given to agencies. Nonetheless, legal commentators considered *Chevron* to represent "a watershed administrative law ruling that would encourage reviewing courts to defer to agency interpretations and policy directions."[26] The decision reputedly made "fundamental alterations . . . in our constitutional conception of the administrative state,"[27] "revolutionized judicial review of agency statutory interpretation,"[28] represents "one of the most important decisions in the history of administrative law,"[29] and constitutes (because *Chevron* is considered by some to be the counter-*Marbury v. Madison*[30] for the administrative state) "a pillar in administrative law for many years to come."[31] In short, most thought that *Chevron* would result in greater deference by the judiciary to administrative agency decisions.

Many commentators criticized the Supreme Court's approach. Some emphasized the judicial province over saying what the law is and objected to the Court's abandonment of this authority.[32] This effect may disrupt the Constitution's separation of powers, unduly weakening the judicial check and transferring excessive control to the President[33] or to the bureaucracy

25. *See Chevron*, 467 U.S. at 842-43.

26. Peter H. Schuck & E. Donald Elliott, *To the* Chevron *Station: An Empirical Study of Federal Administrative Law*, 1990 DUKE L.J. 984, 991; *see also* Sidney A. Shapiro & Richard E. Levy, *Judicial Incentives and Indeterminacy in Substantive Review of Administrative Decisions*, 44 DUKE L.J. 1051, 1051 (1995) (reporting that "[a]dministrative law scholars, whether they agreed or disagreed with the Court's standards, assumed that [*Chevron* and *Motor Vehicle Manufacturers Ass'n v. State Farm Mutual Automobile Insurance Co.*, 463 U.S. 29 (1983)] were landmark decisions that signaled a turning point in the substantive review of agency decisions").

27. Cynthia R. Farina, *Statutory Interpretation and the Balance of Power in the Administrative State*, 89 COLUM. L. REV. 452, 456 (1989).

28. Mark Seidenfeld, *A Syncopated* Chevron*: Emphasizing Reasoned Decisionmaking in Reviewing Agency Interpretations of Statutes*, 73 TEX. L. REV. 83, 84 (1994).

29. 1 KENNETH CULP DAVIS & RICHARD J. PIERCE, JR., ADMINISTRATIVE LAW TREATISE § 3.2, at 110 (3d ed. 1994).

30. 5 U.S. (1 Cranch) 137 (1803).

31. Cass R. Sunstein, *Law and Administration After* Chevron, 90 COLUM. L. REV. 2071, 2075 (1990).

32. *See, e.g.*, Cornell W. Clayton, *Separate Branches—Separate Politics: Judicial Enforcement of Congressional Intent*, 109 POL. SCI. Q. 843, 871 (1994-1995) (arguing that the *Chevron* approach "should cause great concern for those committed to the rule of law"); *see also* Michael Herz, *Deference Running Riot: Separating Interpretation and Lawmaking Under* Chevron, 6 ADMIN. L.J. AM. U. 187, 189 (1992) (noting that "[i]ts detractors portray *Chevron* as . . . abandon[ing] to administrative agencies the judicial authority and obligation to 'say what the law is'").

33. *See, e.g.*, Farina, *supra* note 27, at 498 (claiming that if "Congress chooses to delegate regulatory authority to agencies, part of the price of delegation may be that the court, not the agency, must hold the power to say what the statute means"); Abner S. Greene, *Checks and Balances in an Era of Presidential Lawmaking*, 61 U. CHI. L. REV. 123, 123 (1994) (explaining that when the President executes a law that is "vague or silent on a key issue . . . the resulting rule—from either rulemaking or adjudication—is a

itself.[34] One critic questioned the basis for deference in political theory, suggesting that judicial restraint could lead to the maintenance of policies contrary to the public interest.[35] Other commentators, however, have defended *Chevron*, arguing that courts should restrain themselves from intervening in fundamentally political decisions made by more accountable administrative agencies.[36] An active approach to judicial review "allows judges to rely on their personal politics to decide statutory issues."[37] Additionally, commentators have argued, courts should defer to the greater experience and expertise of agencies regarding the statutes they administer.[38]

Regardless of the merits of *Chevron*, its two-step procedure creates a loophole through which disobedient courts may advance their policy preferences at the expense of sincere application of doctrine. A court that dislikes the outcome of an agency decision can declare that the interpretation is contrary to plain statutory meaning and still claim obedience to doctrine.[39] This loophole enables a lower court to "transform *Chevron* from a deference doctrine to a doctrine of antideference."[40] Indeed, the two-step test can be a recipe for disobedience, simultaneously providing a command of deference and showing lower courts how to evade it.[41]

---

policy choice in much the same way that statutes are policy choices").

34. *See* Theodore J. Lowi, *Two Roads to Serfdom: Liberalism, Conservatism and Administrative Power*, 36 AM. U. L. REV. 295, 296 (1987).

35. *See* Seidenfeld, *supra* note 28, at 104-11.

36. *See, e.g.*, Maureen B. Callahan, *Must Federal Courts Defer to Agency Interpretations of Statutes?: A New Doctrinal Basis for* Chevron U.S.A. v. Natural Resources Defense Council, 1991 WIS. L. REV. 1275, 1289; Richard J. Pierce, Jr., *Political Control Versus Impermissible Bias in Agency Decisionmaking: Lessons from* Chevron *and* Mistretta, 57 U. CHI. L. REV. 481, 484-87 (1990).

37. Seidenfeld, *supra* note 28, at 116.

38. *See* Stephen Breyer, *Judicial Review of Questions of Law and Policy*, 38 ADMIN. L. REV. 363 (1986); John P. Dwyer, *The Pathology of Symbolic Legislation*, 17 ECOLOGY L.Q. 233, 311 (1990); Daniel B. Rodriguez, *The Positive Political Dimensions of Regulatory Reform*, 72 WASH. U. L.Q. 1, 122 (1994); Antonin Scalia, *Judicial Deference to Administrative Interpretations of Law*, 1989 DUKE L.J. 511, 519.

39. From our sample of cases, consider *American Petroleum Institute v. EPA*, 52 F.3d 1113 (D.C. Cir. 1995), in which the majority decided not to engage in *Chevron* deference but instead used *Chevron* as authority for not deferring. In that case, petitioners, a group of petroleum manufacturers and refiners, challenged an EPA rule in which the EPA had broadly interpreted its power under various environmental statutes to mandate the use of renewable oxygenates in its regulations for the reformulated gasoline program under the Clean Air Act, 42 U.S.C. §§ 7401-7671 (1994). The three-judge panel, all Republican appointees, ruled against the EPA and held for the petroleum trade associations. *See American Petroleum Inst.*, 52 F.3d at 1115. Relying on the "plain meaning" of the statute, the panel stated that the statute was quite clear about what the EPA could consider in promulgating the rule and that the EPA had overstepped the boundaries of the statute. The panel made this finding in spite of statutory language stating that the agency could consider impacts on cost, energy requirements, and other health and environmental impacts and that the EPA had the authority to promulgate such regulations as are necessary for it to carry out its functions under the Act. *See* 42 U.S.C. §§ 7545(k)(1), 7601(a)(1). Moreover, the statute did not explicitly limit those regulations to implementing emission or other particular standards. *See* 42 U.S.C. § 7545(k)(1). The panel, nonetheless, chose against deference, stating that "step one" of the *Chevron* test dictated the outcome. *American Petroleum Inst.*, 52 F.3d at 1119.

40. Thomas W. Merrill, *Judicial Deference to Executive Precedent*, 101 YALE L.J. 969, 992 (1992).

41. *See* Shapiro & Levy, *supra* note 26, at 1069-70 (claiming that the *Chevron* doctrine is indeterminate and allows for an open-ended interpretation of its meaning by lower courts).

When examining an individual opinion striking down a rule, it can be difficult to identify disobedience. The opinion will justify its nondeference through reference to statutory language, legislative history, and doctrine itself. While one may disagree with the rationale and even question its sincerity, it is impossible to demonstrate conclusively that any particular opinion's rationale for nondeference is insincere or disobedient. Nevertheless, the opinion may be disobedient, as conclusive demonstrations of sincerity are also lacking. By looking at a pattern of cases, we strive to test for disobedience.

B. *The Political Investigation of* Chevron

The legal model implies that *Chevron* established a neutral principle commanding appellate courts to defer to administrative statutory interpretations and assumes that the courts will adhere faithfully to this command. The initial approach in legal scholarship to *Chevron* tracked this model and analyzed *Chevron* in terms of legal process values. Such analysis, though sensitive to the practical political consequences of *Chevron* deference, generally ignored the prospect that the courts might manipulate *Chevron* for political effect. Indeed, both critics and defenders assumed that *Chevron* would have significant effects on judicial behavior, as the legal model predicted. A leading defender of judicial deference suggested that *Chevron* had "transformed dramatically the approach taken by courts in reviewing agency interpretations of statutory provisions."[42] Few authors considered the possibility that the doctrinal principles of *Chevron* might have little real world impact,[43] though one commentator recently suggested that a new "hypertextualism" in judicial statutory interpretation has undermined the deference that the *Chevron* Court intended.[44]

While legal research has typically ignored the politics of doctrinal evolution, *Chevron* has been something of an exception to the rule. At least two significant empirical studies have considered the role of *Chevron* in appellate decisionmaking.[45] These studies have explicitly acknowledged the claims of legal realism and political science regarding judicial decisionmaking.

42. Richard J. Pierce, Jr., Chevron *and Its Aftermath: Judicial Review of Agency Interpretations of Statutory Provisions*, 41 VAND. L. REV. 301, 302 (1988). Pierce has subsequently suggested that the effect of *Chevron* has dissipated somewhat over time. *See* Richard J. Pierce, Jr., *Legislative Reform of Judicial Review of Agency Actions*, 44 DUKE L.J. 1110, 1112 (1995) [hereinafter Pierce, *Legislative Reform*]. Nonetheless, he believes that the "*Chevron* test has largely realized its potential at the circuit court level." Richard J. Pierce, Jr., *The Supreme Court's New Hypertextualism: An Invitation to Cacophony and Incoherence in the Administrative State*, 95 COLUM. L. REV. 749, 749 (1995).

43. For a rare exception, see Russell L. Weaver, *Some Realism About* Chevron, 58 MO. L. REV. 129, 130 (1993).

44. Pierce, *Legislative Reform*, *supra* note 42, at 1123. Pierce focused this criticism on the Supreme Court's, rather than the appellate courts', application of *Chevron*.

45. A third study considered the Supreme Court's use of its *Chevron* precedent. *See* Merrill, *supra* note 40.

The first major *Chevron* study was performed by Peter Schuck and Donald Elliott.[46] The authors studied several aspects of the decision, including its effect on appellate court decisionmaking. They hypothesized that "[i]f the Court meant what it said in *Chevron* and its progeny, and if reviewing courts took its words seriously, one would expect the distribution of outcomes in agency cases to reflect the effects of *Chevron*."[47] Specifically, "one would expect the courts to affirm more frequently and to remand less frequently."[48] Schuck and Elliot tested for the relative rate of affirmances immediately after *Chevron*. As realists, the authors were at least somewhat doubtful of this effect.[49]

Schuck and Elliott found that in the immediate wake of *Chevron*, appellate court remands and reversals declined, and the proportion of those remands and reversals grounded in substantive interpretation of the law declined even more pronouncedly.[50] This result, they claimed, contradicted the prediction of the law skeptics and suggested that *Chevron* had a distinct effect on lower-court decisions. These post-*Chevron* results were statistically significant.

Schuck and Elliott examined similar appellate results occurring three years later and found that affirmance rates had begun to creep back down toward (but not as low as) pre-*Chevron* levels.[51] They tentatively attributed the change to the Supreme Court's becoming slightly less deferential to agency constructions. While one can imagine a variety of reasons for this result, the authors suggested "the tantalizing hypothesis that over a large number of cases the results of judicial review may be far more sensitive to subtle changes in legal doctrine than we had anticipated."[52] This study, therefore, offers some support for the legal model of judicial decisionmaking that considers appellate judges to be responsive to changes in doctrine.

Linda Cohen and Matthew Spitzer undertook the second major empirical *Chevron* study in tandem with a major theoretical analysis, again informed somewhat by legal realism.[53] While acknowledging that Schuck and Elliott were "almost certainly correct" in claiming a *Chevron*-effect on appellate courts,[54] they made rather trenchant criticisms of Schuck and Elliott's

46. *See* Schuck & Elliott, *supra* note 26.

47. *Id.* at 1026.

48. *Id.*

49. The authors note that strong law skeptics would claim that "doctrinal changes such as *Chevron* should not affect the pattern of results reached in subsequent cases by lower courts, provided that the judges' personal and political predilections remain essentially unchanged during the period under study." *Id.* at 1029.

50. *See id.* at 1030, 1033.

51. *See i*ᵈ at 1038.

52. *Id.* Schuck and Elliott conceded, however, that the results may be attributable to "the passage of time, other changes in legal doctrine, the changing composition of the judiciary, or some other confounding factor." *Id.*

53. *See* Linda R. Cohen & Matthew L. Spitzer, *Solving the* Chevron *Puzzle*, LAW & CONTEMP. PROBS., Spring 1994, at 65.

54. *Id.* at 90.

approach. First, they observed that Schuck and Elliott considered the rates of substantive statutory remands, but not reversals or affirmances, and did not even "indicate how many statutory constructions were upheld."[55] Second, they noted that changes in results may have had nothing to do with the judiciary itself but may have reflected an adjustment by administrative agencies or their challengers.[56]

Cohen and Spitzer also considered the overall rate at which appellate courts upheld agency interpretations and found "a slight increase in the appellate affirm rate in the mid-1980s," though the increase was somewhat smaller than that found by Schuck and Elliott.[57] They also considered contemporaneous Supreme Court certiorari and merits decisions involving judicial review of administrative decisions. This review led to a rational choice conclusion that the (conservative) Supreme Court slowly but steadily approved a higher level of judicial agency supervision as the appellate courts became relatively more conservative.[58] They implied that the Supreme Court rather precisely titrates the amount of deference due agencies (given the political circumstances) and that the appellate courts respond. In short, Cohen and Spitzer argued that appellate courts are responsive to the Supreme Court's doctrinal decisions, though their analysis was grounded more in political science than in the traditional legal model.

The Cohen-Spitzer study, as well as the Schuck-Elliott study, have been cited as evidence that *Chevron* "marked a major change in administrative law."[59] The studies, however, were recently reviewed and reanalyzed by Sidney Shapiro and Richard Levy.[60] Their data suggest that *Chevron* had relatively little effect upon appellate court decisions, as the affirmance rate between 1988 and 1990 was actually lower than the rate before *Chevron*.[61] *Chevron*'s doctrinal indeterminacy, Shapiro and Levy argue, has empowered appellate courts to render essentially political, outcome-oriented decisions.[62] Thus, ironically, an analysis of two studies generally concluding that appellate courts respond to Supreme Court doctrine (though for different reasons) led to the conclusion that appellate courts do not so respond. Plainly, the consequences of the Supreme Court's *Chevron* holding remain uncertain.

Our research builds upon this existing body of empirical work in the hopes of clarifying the issue. We limit our analysis to statutory interpretation of cases

55. *Id.* at 91.
56. *See id.*
57. *Id.* at 103. One problem recognized by the authors was that their database "included all administrative decisions, rather than just those that addressed statutory interpretation cases." *Id.*
58. *See id.* at 105.
59. Seidenfeld, *supra* note 28, at 84 n.5.
60. *See* Shapiro & Levy, *supra* note 26, at 1070-71.
61. *See id.* This conclusion is somewhat uncertain, as it depends on comparing data from the Schuck-Elliott study with data from the Cohen-Spitzer study, even though the two studies used somewhat different sources of data.
62. *See id.* at 1053.

explicitly invoking *Chevron*, rather than looking at all administrative law opinions. We also consider the political orientations of the judges and match them with outcomes, focusing less on the overall frequency of deference and more on the patterns of applying that deference by ideological outcome.

III. An Empirical Examination

We reviewed all opinions from the D.C. Circuit Court of Appeals between 1991 and 1995 that cited *Chevron*—according to Shepard's Citations, over two hundred in all. Cases that cited *Chevron* for something other than the deference principle were excluded. Each case was then coded for, among other things, (1) whether the court gave deference to the agency statutory interpretation; (2) whether the court upheld or reversed the agency policy;[63] (3) the direction of the policy outcome (liberal vs. conservative) from the agency; and (4) the partisan makeup of the court panel (Democrats vs. Republicans).

With respect to policy direction, our coding tracked practices relatively common in the political science literature.[64] If an industry group was challenging a federal regulation, then the agency position was coded as liberal. If nongovernmental public interest organizations or individual plaintiffs challenged the agency position, we coded the agency position as conservative, unless the organization or individual was clearly conservative in orientation, in which case we coded the agency position as liberal. Cases without any clear political content were winnowed from the database, leaving about 170 decisions coded. If the court reversed the agency in favor of a liberal challenger, we coded the case outcome as liberal; if the court reversed the agency in favor of a conservative challenger, we coded the outcome as conservative.

With respect to coding the preferences of the reviewing court panel, each judge was assigned a political party affiliation according to the President who appointed the judge. We assumed that, in general, Democratic appointees are more liberal and Republicans more conservative in policy orientation. During the time period under consideration, the D.C. Circuit was dominated by Republican appointees, although a significant number of Democratic appointees were present. Each panel therefore had a majority (2-1 or 3-0) of either Republican or Democratic judges. This coding enabled us to test whether the partisanship of the judicial panel influenced the political outcomes of litigation and the degree to which *Chevron* deference affected this association.

63. This coding required some subjective judgment, as administrative law cases commonly raise a variety of discrete issues. If the court upheld the challenge to agency action in any substantial part and granted the challenger a significant measure of the relief sought, the case was coded as upholding the challenge. In a handful of cases where the court deferred on statutory interpretation, yet reversed on other grounds, the case was coded as upholding the challenge.

64. *See* Cross, *supra* note 13, at 290-91.

A simple comparison of judicial party affiliation and political decisions reveals a fairly profound partisan effect. Table 1 displays the political results of cases according to the makeup of the deciding panel of judges. Each cell contains the absolute number of cases.

TABLE 1. POLITICS AND JUDICIAL OUTCOMES

	REPUBLICAN MAJORITY	DEMOCRATIC MAJORITY	TOTALS
CONSERVATIVE CASE OUTCOME	62	13	75
LIBERAL CASE OUTCOME	52	28	80
TOTALS	114	41	155

Thus, a panel consisting of a majority of Republicans rendered a conservative decision 54% of the time (62 of 114), while a panel consisting of a majority of Democrats rendered a liberal decision 68% of the time (28 of 41). The presence of some "liberal" decisions by conservative courts and "conservative" decisions by liberal courts may be a function of a combination of factors. It may be a misspecification problem—politics lie upon a continuum, and some policies may be too conservative for a given "conservative" court or too liberal for a "liberal" court. Or, our coding of agency decisions by nature of the litigant challenging the agency may misidentify some litigants' political affiliations. Alternatively, the mismatch may indicate that doctrine is having a significant effect in constraining all-out partisan decisionmaking. Nonetheless, these simple results suggest that there is a significant political determinant to judicial decisionmaking, at least in *Chevron* review.

Our theory suggests that whether deference is granted (that is, whether the *Chevron* doctrine is being adhered to) is dependent upon the convergence between the partisan policy preferences of the panel's majority and the outcome resulting from the application of *Chevron*. Put differently, the court panel is more likely to follow *Chevron* when the agency has issued a policy consistent with the panel's assumed policy preferences (liberal for Democrats and conservative for Republicans) than when there is no such alignment between the court's policy preferences and the agency policy. To bear out this relationship and to sort out the effects of several other variables that may affect the likelihood that a court will defer to an agency, we ran a statistical test. Using logistic regression techniques, we specified the equation as follows:

$$\text{DEFERENCE} = \text{INTERCEPT} + B_1\text{POLICY CONVERGENCE} + B_2\text{UNIFIED PANEL} + B_3\text{MAJORITY PARTY} + B_4\text{YEAR} + u_t.$$

POLICY CONVERGENCE is both the political variable and the main variable of interest. It indicates whether there is alignment between the assumed preferences of the panel's majority (as measured by the political party affiliation of the majority of members on the panel) and the policy outcome of the agency (as measured by the litigants challenging the agency). We postulate that deference is more likely when the assumed partisan preferences of the panel's majority favor the agency outcome (Republicans favoring conservative agency outcomes and Democrats favoring liberal agency outcomes).

We also include a variable to indicate whether the reviewing panel members were from the same political party (UNIFIED PANEL). Our theory suggests that a politically unified panel, that is 3-0 Republican or 3-0 Democrat, is more likely to disregard the constraints of doctrines that do not support the court's policy preferences when there is no policy convergence. When there is no whistleblower on a panel, that is the panel is politically unified, judges will see doctrine as less of an obstacle to political decisionmaking.

Next, we include a variable for the political party of the majority of the members on the panel (MAJORITY PARTY). It is possible that judges of one party (for a variety of reasons, both political and sincere) are more true to legal doctrine than the judges of the other.[65] Finally, we include the variable YEAR, which represents the actual year in which a particular case was decided, the first year being set at zero. This is intended to capture the possibility that the *Chevron* doctrine has grown weaker over time.

The results are set out in Table 2.

TABLE 2. RESULTS OF LOGIT

INDEPENDENT VARIABLES	COEFFICIENT	(STANDARD ERROR)
INTERCEPT	−140.246	(261.8195)
POLICY CONVERGENCE	1.4655^{***}	(0.4233)
UNIFIED PANEL	-0.7179^{*}	(0.4228)
MAJORITY PARTY	−0.3364	(0.4525)
YEAR	1.0706	(0.1313)

$^{*}p \le 0.1$; $^{**}p \le 0.05$; $^{***}p \le 0.01$
Chi-square is 19.605 with 4 DF ($p = 0.0006$)

65. We also include this variable to offset any bias to measuring POLICY CONVERGENCE that may result from the presence of a large number of Republican panels in the sample.

As predicted, the effect of POLICY CONVERGENCE is properly signed and highly significant. The results indicate that when the agency's policy outcome is consistent with the policy preferences of the panel's majority, the court is more likely to defer than if there is no such convergence. We calculate the impact of this variable to be 31%—that is, the panel is 31% more likely to defer (that is, follow doctrine) when its policy preferences are consistent with the agency's policies than when they are not.[66] The results also indicate that whether the panel was politically divided (2-1) or united (3-0) had an effect on whether the panel deferred to the agency, although the significance of these results is somewhat less ($p = 0.09$). We calculated the impact of this variable to be 17%—that is, it is 17% less likely that the court will defer when it is unified than when it is split 2-1. Neither the political party of the panel majority (MAJORITY PARTY) nor the year in which the decision was made (YEAR) proved significant. In other words, neither Democrats nor Republicans appeared any more or less committed to doctrine than judges of the other party. Likewise, the passing of time did not appear to diminish or strengthen the effects of *Chevron*.

While the above results suggest that a division among panel members does affect whether doctrine will be followed (as indicated by the marginal significance of the UNIFIED PANEL variable), they do not necessarily establish that the presence of a whistleblower is the mechanism. It is possible that 2-1 majorities whose policy preferences are consistent with those of the agencies nonetheless decide, with some regularity, to capitulate to the minority member. Recall that our whistleblower theory postulates that there should be an effect when a 2-1 majority is in conflict (in terms of its partisan policy preferences) with the agency over policy outcomes, rather than when the 2-1 majority is in agreement with the agency's policy choice.

To examine the whistleblower hypothesis further, we segregated the data by whether there was a politically unified panel (3-0 Republican and 3-0 Democratic majorities) or politically divided panel (2-1 Republican-to-Democrat majorities and vice versa). We then separated the data with respect to deference (our measure for judicial obedience) and whether there was policy convergence between the deciding court panel and the agency. The data are presented in Table 3.

66. The impact is computed by subtracting the probability of deference when POLICY CONVERGENCE equals 0 from the probability of deference when the variable equals 1. *See generally* TIM FUTING LIAO, INTERPRETING PROBABILITY MODELS: LOGIT, PROBIT, AND OTHER GENERALIZED LINEAR MODELS (Sage Univ. Papers Series, Quantitative Applications in the Social Sciences No. 07-101, 1994).

TABLE 3. POLITICS, LEGAL DOCTRINES, AND JUDICIAL DECISIONMAKING

	UNIFIED PANEL		DIVIDED PANEL		TOTALS	
	POLICY CONVERGE	NO POLICY CONVERGE	POLICY CONVERGE	NO POLICY CONVERGE[67]	POLICY CONVERGE	NO POLICY CONVERGE
DEFERENCE	10	7	37	47	47	54
NO DEFERENCE	4	14	7	29	11	43
TOTALS	14	21	44	76	58	97

Consider first the politically unified panels. In the 21 cases where it appeared to be to the unified panels' policy advantage to disobey *Chevron*, the panels did so two-thirds of the time. In other words, unified panels deferred to the agency only 33% (7 of 21) of the time when the policy outcomes that would have resulted from adhering to doctrine appeared inconsistent with the panel's political preferences. In the 14 cases in which it appeared to be to the advantage of the unified panels to obey *Chevron*, the panels did so 71% (10 of 14) of the time.

Now consider the divided panels. Of the cases in which it was to the panels' advantage to obey *Chevron*, they did so 84% (37 of 44) of the time. This is not surprising, as doctrine in such cases poses no conflict for the majority. Now consider the 76 cases involving the whistleblower scenario, in which it appeared to be to the advantage of the majority not to defer. These panels continued to obey the doctrine 62% (47 of 76) of the time. Compare this rate of obedience to that of unified panels whose policy preferences seemed inconsistent with the application of the *Chevron* doctrine (33%). In short, the presence of a whistleblower makes it almost twice as likely that doctrine will be followed when doctrine works against the partisan policy preferences of the court majority. These results are consistent with our theory as illustrated in Figure 2.

To determine whether this whistleblower effect was statistically significant, we ran a chi-square test. In running the test, we considered the subset of cases in which application of the doctrine appeared to work against the majority's policy preferences (essentially those cases for which the agency policy and the panel majority's policy preferences were not aligned). The test indicated, at a significance level of 0.05, that obedience to legal doctrine was not independent of the presence of a whistleblower. In other words, the data indicate that the presence of a whistleblower improves the chances that the court will apply the applicable legal doctrine.[68]

67. This column indicates the whistleblowing scenario.

68. For purposes of symmetry, we also tested cases in which it was in the policy interest of the split-panel majority to apply doctrine (that is, policy convergence existed). We looked at the inverse of the whistleblower situation in particular—that is, we wanted to know if the presence of a divided panel (regardless of policy convergence between the agency and the court) meant there would be a significant change in the level of *Chevron* deference. This would suggest that majorities merely capitulate on occasion

FIGURE 2. RATE THAT CHEVRON DOCTRINE WAS FOLLOWED

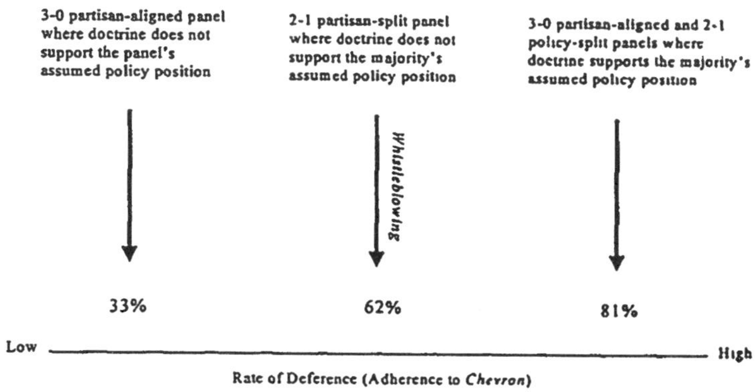

IV. DISCUSSION

The data raise an intriguing question about decisions to grant deference: Why does panel composition matter so dramatically? Circuit court decisions, of course, are decided by majority vote. Consequently, a 2-1 majority has every bit as much power to effect their partisan inclinations as does a 3-0 majority. Yet in practice, a 3-0 majority will be far more driven by partisanship than a 2-1 majority. While the number of 3-0 Democrat panels is too small to provide convincing results, the results on the Republican side are dramatic. The presence of a single Democrat on a panel appears to have had a distinct political moderating effect on the two Republicans. Republican majorities still decided along partisan lines in a material subset of cases, but the subset was clearly smaller than for politically unified panels.

The most likely explanation for the doctrine's impact on politically divided panels is the whistleblower effect. The presence of a politically opposed minority representative means that there is someone on the panel who can identify the majority's disobedience to doctrine. A traditional rational choice model might suggest that whistleblowing increases the risk of reversal by a higher court or by Congress and that the possibility it might occur thus dissuades judges from disobeying doctrine. On this theory, a minority judge's stormy dissent enhances higher courts' external monitoring of judicial decisions

to minorities, not that the threat of exposure causes majorities to defy *Chevron*. A chi-square test suggested that our whistleblower theory remained intact. There was no significant difference ($p = 0.36$) between a divided panel and a unified panel in following doctrine when the application of *Chevron* would appear to advance policy interests of the majority.

by exposing the partisan biases of a majority that has ignored the dictates of doctrine.[69]

While the increased possibility of reversal as a risk of whistleblowing may well explain some decisions, there are reasons to suspect that the risk of reversal is not always a threat to panel majorities. First, the Supreme Court can review only a small fraction of the cases decided by circuit courts.[70] Congress likewise has a considerable agenda of issues more pressing than reversing typical statutory interpretation by a circuit court. Second, during the entire time period of our study, the Supreme Court was majority Republican and relatively conservative. Hence, if Supreme Court reversal was a risk, it should have been a risk primarily for majority Democrat panels. One would not expect much concern from Republican judges rendering conservative holdings. Yet Republican panels often deferred to liberal agency interpretations. The risk of reversal should be greater for Democrat panels, yet the evidence presented in Table 1 demonstrates that such panels were, if anything, more partisan than Republican panels.

If the risk of reversal cannot explain doctrinal adherence in divided panels, the dynamics of panels themselves are likely to explain whistleblowing. The minority member in such panels may simply force the majority to acknowledge its subconscious disobedience to doctrine and therefore to mend its ways. The collegiality and collaborative decisionmaking of multi-judge panels could largely explain such a result.[71] This theory is consistent with a recent study of the federal district courts, which found that judges are committed to the neutral operation of the legal model of decisionmaking but that the operation of that model is influenced and biased by differing evaluations of evidence and argument.[72] Judges employ "cognitive shortcuts to process imperfect information" under the legal model, and these shortcuts produce apparently political results.[73] In short, on multi-judge panels, the minority judge can serve as a whistleblower by revealing these biasing cognitive shortcuts. Once the majority can no longer readily rationalize its decision under the legal model, it will frequently concede to the commands of that model.

69. *See* ROBERT A. CARP & RONALD STIDHAM, THE FEDERAL COURTS 179-82 (2d ed. 1991) (suggesting that individual judges can influence the panel majority by threatening to go public with a dissent).

70. *See* Richard S. Higgins & Paul H. Rubin, *Judicial Discretion*, 9 J. LEGAL STUD. 129, 137 (1980) (concluding based on a study "that, if constraints operate on judges, these constraints must come from sources other than possibilities of reversal"); Strauss, *supra* note 7, at 1096 (noting the Supreme Court's limited power of supervision).

71. Two political scientists who generally subscribe to an attitudinal model of decisionmaking acknowledge that most judges "can be swayed by an articulate and well-reasoned argument from a colleague with a differing opinion." CARP & STIDHAM, *supra* note 69, at 176.

72. *See* C.K. ROWLAND & ROBERT A. CARP, POLITICS AND JUDGMENT IN FEDERAL DISTRICT COURTS (1996).

73. *Id.* at 171.

There remain two other explanations for why judges sometimes grant deference to agency interpretations contrary to their politics. Consider first a split panel with two Republicans and one Democrat. With only two Republicans on the panel, an issue might be a higher priority to one of the Republicans than to the other, and the less interested judge would be more likely to defer to the agency than if both other judges were Republicans who favored nondeference. Yet this does not seem to be a politically logical explanation, even given the possibility of judicial logrolling. One would expect the Republican who did not care about the issue to defer to the Republican who did care about the issue, in anticipation of complementary deference when their roles were reversed. The judge generally has more to gain from deferring to a colleague than from deferring to an agency.

A second alternative explanation is the presence of a moderate Republican judge who generally sides with Democrats when given the chance. Examination of individual decisions, however, does not support this theory. Of all the cases in which a majority Republican panel granted deference to a liberal agency interpretation, no specific Republican judge showed up on even half of the panels. Moreover, the Republican who appeared most frequently on this set of panels was Judge David Sentelle, who has a reputation for staunch conservatism.[74] The presence of nonideological deference decisions by majority Republican panels cannot be attributed to a closet liberal on the circuit.

V. CONCLUSION

Partisanship clearly affects how appellate courts review agency discretion. In our study of administrative law decisions by the D.C. Circuit, we have found that panels controlled by Republicans were more likely to defer to conservative agency decisions (that is, to follow the *Chevron* doctrine) than were the panels controlled by Democrats. Similarly, Democrat-controlled panels were more likely to defer to liberal agency decisions than were those controlled by Republicans. Nonetheless, legal doctrine appears to play an important role in the partisan struggle over policy. Minority judges can use doctrine to corral the partisan ambitions of a court majority whose policy preferences would best be accomplished by neglecting the dictates of doctrine. The minority member acts as a whistleblower, ready to expose any cheating by the majority. In our study, we found that the presence of a

74. Judge Sentelle became well known when, shortly after lunching with Senators Jesse Helms and Lauch Faircloth of North Carolina, he replaced Whitewater special prosecutor Robert Fiske with the presumably more aggressive Kenneth Starr. *See* Sara Fritz, *Starr Mixes Ambition, Judicious Style*, L.A. TIMES, Jan. 27, 1996, at A1. The press has described Sentelle as one of the "most conservative members" of the D.C. Circuit. *E.g.*, Nancy Lewis, *Conviction of Drug Gang Leader Upheld*, WASH. POST, Apr. 29, 1995, at A18.

whistleblower—that is, a minority member with *Chevron* deference favoring the minority member's political preference—significantly increases the chances that the court majority will follow doctrine. While a partisan split panel does not negate all partisan influences on *Chevron* review, it clearly moderates such influences and makes doctrine more likely to be followed.

[16]

Overriding Supreme Court Statutory Interpretation Decisions

William N. Eskridge, Jr.†

CONTENTS

---

† Professor of Law, Georgetown University Law Center. I am very grateful to Jim Brudney, Ted Eisenberg, Dan Farber, John Ferejohn, Owen Fiss, Phil Frickey, Larry Fullerton, Keith Krehbiel, Bob Katzmann, Rick Pildes, Dick Posner, Steve Shiffrin, Matt Spitzer, Barry Weingast, and participants in a faculty workshop at the Cornell Law School for comments on an earlier draft of this Article. I am equally grateful to Bob Pitofsky and Judy Areen, who as deans at Georgetown provided me with several summers' worth of research grants and extra research assistants to enable me to do the necessary empirical work for this project. Special thanks to my research assistants Amy Birnbaum, Kathleen Blanchard, Dixon Osburn, Bob Schoshinski, Jami Silverman, Ken Smurzynski, and Stuart Weichsel. Your work was excellent.

This project would not have been possible if Wendy Williams, Steve Goldberg, and Peter Byrne had not rescued me from professional oblivion in 1987. This article is for you.

As if to debunk the conventional wisdom, the 101st Congress busied itself with efforts to override numerous Supreme Court decisions construing federal statutes.[1] Successful legislation overrode eight recent opinions interpreting federal statutes.[2] Overturning an older decision, another law for the first time rejected a Supreme Court interpretation discriminating against bisexuals, gay men, and lesbians.[3] Even abortive override efforts in the 101st Congress

1. This Article will use the term "override" to mean any time Congress reacts consciously to, and modifies a statutory interpretation decision. A congressional "override" includes a statute that: (1) completely overrules the holding of a statutory interpretation decision, just as a subsequent Court would overrule an unsatisfactory precedent; (2) modifies the result of a decision in some material way, such that the same case would have been decided differently; or (3) modifies the consequences of the decision, such that the same case would have been decided in the same way but subsequent cases would be decided differently. With only a few exceptions, this Article will not use the term "override" to include statutes for which the legislative history—mainly committee reports and hearings—does not reveal a legislative focus on judicial decisions.

2. Pennsylvania Dep't of Pub. Welfare v. Davenport, 495 U.S. 552 (1990); Public Employees Retirement Sys. v. Betts, 492 U.S. 158 (1989); Dellmuth v. Muth, 491 U.S. 223 (1989); Finley v. United States, 490 U.S. 545 (1989); Coit Indep. Joint Venture v. Federal Sav. & Loan, 489 U.S. 561 (1989); United States v. Fausto, 484 U.S. 439 (1988); Gwaltney of Smithfield, Ltd. v. Chesapeake Bay Found., Inc., 484 U.S. 49 (1987); Secretary of Interior v. California, 464 U.S. 312 (1984). Appendix I lists the statutes overriding these decisions.

3. The Immigration Act of 1990, Pub. L. No. 101-649, § 601, 104 Stat. 4978, 5067 (1990), rewrote the exclusion provisions of the Immigration and Nationality Act, in part to override Boutilier v. INS, 387 U.S. 118 (1967), which had interpreted the Act to exclude bisexuals, gay men, and lesbians from the United States.

illustrated Congress' attention to the Court's statutory interpretation cases. Most prominent among the unsuccessful override efforts was the vetoed Civil Rights Act of 1990, which would have overturned nine recent decisions narrowly construing Title VII of the Civil Rights Act of 1964 and related statutes. A similar Civil Rights Act of 1991, however, was enacted into law by the 102d Congress.[4]

Congress' attention to the Court's statutory decisions raises issues that are critically important to statutory interpretation scholarship. Specifically, Congress' recent override activity presents scholars with an opportunity to revisit longstanding academic debates about (1) congressional awareness of, and responsiveness to, Supreme Court decisions in general; (2) political theories that realistically describe both the legislative process and the interaction between the Court and Congress; and (3) the ramifications of the first two debates for the theory and practice of statutory interpretation.

Three obstacles thus far have hindered academic debate on these topics. First, and most important, existing scholarship has not yielded much reliable data about when and how often Congress overrides the Court. Even the leading empirical studies by political scientists are, on the whole, disappointingly incomplete. Second, theoretical literature on the legislative process is divided into opposing viewpoints that fail to recognize alternative approaches. One side views the political process as dominated by rent-seeking interest groups, while the other sees politics as deliberation about the common good. Without a

4. The proposed Civil Rights Act of 1990 would have overturned Independent Fed'n of Flight Attendants v. Zipes, 491 U.S. 754 (1989); Patterson v. McLean Credit Union, 491 U.S. 164 (1989); Lorance v. AT&T Technologies Inc., 490 U.S. 900 (1989); Martin v. Wilks, 490 U.S. 754 (1989); Wards Cove Packing Co. v. Atonio, 490 U.S. 642 (1989); Price Waterhouse v. Hopkins, 490 U.S. 228 (1989); Crawford Fitting Co. v. J.T. Gibbons, Inc., 482 U.S. 437 (1987); Library of Congress v. Shaw, 478 U.S. 310 (1986); Evans v. Jeff D., 475 U.S. 717 (1986). Identical bills were introduced in both chambers to override these cases. S. 2104, 101st Cong., 2d Sess. (1990), and H.R. 4000, 101st Cong., 2d Sess. (1990). Congress passed the override bill as amended. The President vetoed the bill, and his veto was sustained by a 66-34 vote in the Senate. 136 CONG. REC. S16,589 (daily ed. Oct. 24, 1990). The Civil Rights Act of 1991, which passed Congress in November 1991 and was signed by President Bush on November 21, *see* Andrew Rosenthal, *Reaffirming Commitment, Bush Signs Rights Bill*, N.Y. TIMES, Nov. 22, 1991, at A1, overrides these nine decisions, as well as EEOC v. Arabian American Oil Co., 111 S. Ct. 1227 (1991); West Virginia Univ. Hospitals, Inc. v. Casey, 111 S. Ct. 1138 (1991); and Marek v. Chesney, 473 U.S. 1 (1985).

Also in 1990, the House Judiciary Committee reported a crime control bill that would have overridden at least nine interpretations of the federal habeas corpus statute: Sawyer v. Smith, 110 S. Ct. 2822 (1990); Saffle v. Parks, 494 U.S. 484 (1990); Butler v. McKellan, 494 U.S. 407 (1990); Penry v. Lynaugh, 492 U.S. 302 (1989); Teague v. Lane, 489 U.S. 288 (1989) (plurality opinion); Murray v. Carrier, 477 U.S. 478 (1986); United States v. Frady, 456 U.S. 152 (1982); Engle v. Isaac, 456 U.S. 107 (1982); and Fay v. Noia, 372 U.S. 391 (1963). *See* H.R. REP. NO. 681(I), 101st Cong., 2d Sess. 123-35 (1990), *reprinted in* 1990 U.S.C.C.A.N. 6472, 6528-41. The habeas corpus title of the bill was amended on the floor of the House and, as amended, was dropped in conference with the Senate. Title XI of the proposed Crime Control Act of 1991, H.R. 3371, 102d Cong., 1st Sess. (1991), which passed the House in October 1991, would override some of these decisions.

Also in 1990, the Senate passed a bill that would have overridden the celebrated case of Chevron, U.S.A. Inc. v. Natural Resources Defense Council, Inc., 467 U.S. 837 (1984) (interpreting Clean Air Act to permit companies to balance out pollution levels within large "bubble"). *See* S. REP. NO. 228, 101st Cong., 2d Sess. 24 (1990), *reprinted in* 1990 U.S.C.C.A.N. 3385, 3410. This provision was dropped in conference with the House.

consensus, or even dialogue between the competing camps, political science scholarship is not as helpful to legal scholarship as it might be. Third, legal theories touching on the political process do not represent the most up-to-date political science data and theory. Hence, even if reliable empirical data and useful theoretical consensus existed, they would not necessarily inform legal discourse.

Based on more comprehensive empirical evidence documenting congressional responses to the Court's statutory interpretation decisions, this Article presents a revised view of the legislative process and the interaction between the Court, Congress, and the President. It further discusses the implications that this revised discourse has for the theory and practice of statutory interpretation. Part I and the appendices to this Article report the results of an empirical survey of congressional overrides of Supreme Court—as well as lower court—interpretations of federal statutes. It concludes that Congress and its committees are aware of the Court's statutory decisions, devote significant efforts toward analyzing their policy implications, and override those decisions with a frequency heretofore unreported. Congressional overrides are most likely when a Supreme Court interpretation reveals an ideologically fragmented Court, relies on the text's plain meaning and ignores legislative signals, and/or rejects positions taken by federal, state, or local governments.

The Article then uses the empirical data and case studies to develop a theoretical model that deepens our understanding of the interaction between the Court, Congress, and the President. Part II develops the model by drawing insights from competing distributive and deliberative theories of legislation. The model posits that a dynamic game exists between the Court, the relevant congressional committees, Congress, and the President. In this game, ultimate statutory policy is set through a sequential process by which each player—including the Court—tries to impose its policy preferences. The game is a dynamic one because each player is responsive to the preferences of other players *and* because the preferences of the players change as information is generated and distributed in the game.

Part III applies the data and the sequential game model to rethink legal issues of statutory interpretation. Descriptively, a central theme is that the Court's statutory interpretation decisions are more responsive to the expectations of the current Congress than to those of the enacting Congress. But the Court is also responsive to its own institutional and personal preferences—especially its preference for coherence and predictability in the law. This descriptive analysis provides new insights into several otherwise puzzling doctrines of statutory interpretation, including the Court's invocation of special stare decisis for statutory precedents, its willingness to find meaning in legislative inaction, and its reliance on subsequent legislative history.

Normatively, this Article analyzes the Court's traditional role as an important player contributing to the operation of the pluralist political process. The

Court facilitates the operation of pluralism over time by updating statutes to reach new situations, to reflect new values, and to accommodate the current preferences of governing political forces. Current critics, however, believe that the Court should not pay attention to current legislative preferences in statutory interpretation and instead should attend only to statutory text or original intent. This Article argues that the Court's traditional practice survives this objection but is more vulnerable to another objection: that the Court's practice fails to give sufficient attention to interests and perspectives that are unrepresented in our pluralist political system.

I. Congressional Overrides of the Supreme Court's Statutory Interpretation Decisions, 1967-90

A number of empirical studies have focused on congressional responses to the Supreme Court's statutory decisions.[5] They conclude that the Court's decisions sometimes generate override bills but that these are few in number. For several reasons, these studies are not as useful as they might be. They take an unsystematic or fragmented approach to statutory overrides and, as a result, do not generate a complete sample. They also either ignore unsuccessful overrides or fail to analyze them systematically. Finally, because of the first two problems, these studies have failed to generate reliable conclusions about the conditions that will provoke an override.

These prior studies have only reinforced assumptions that Congress is generally ignorant of and unresponsive to the Court's statutory decisions.[6] However, since 1975, each Congress has overridden (on average) about a dozen

---

5. The main studies are Beth M. Henschen, *Statutory Interpretations of the Supreme Court: Congressional Response*, 11 AM. POL. Q. 441 (1983) (legislative responses, including codifications, to Court's labor and antitrust decisions, 1950-72); Beth M. Henschen & Edward I. Sidlow, *The Supreme Court and the Congressional Agenda-Setting Process*, 5 J.L. & POL. 685 (1989) (same); Thomas R. Marshall, *Policymaking and the Modern Court: When Do Supreme Court Rulings Prevail?*, 42 W. POL. Q. 493 (1989); Harvey P. Stumpf, *Congressional Response to Supreme Court Rulings: The Interaction of Law and Politics*, 14 J. PUB. L. 377 (1965); Note, *Congressional Reversals of Supreme Court Decisions: 1945-1957*, 71 HARV. L. REV. 1324 (1958) (21 instances of congressional reversal of Supreme Court decisions, 1945-57) [hereinafter Note, *Congressional Reversals*]; Note, *The Continuing Colloquy: Congress and the Finality of the Supreme Court*, 8 J.L. & POL. (forthcoming 1992) (122 statutes that have overturned or modified Supreme Court constitutional, common law, and statutory decisions, 1804-1990); Michael E. Solimine & James L. Walker, The Next Word: Congressional Responses to Supreme Court Statutory Decisions (1991) (unpublished paper on file with the author) (51 congressional responses to Supreme Court's decisions, 1970-88).

This list does not include articles and books that are more casually empirical, anecdotal, or episodic than the standard citations provided above. Some of these articles are most useful, however. *See, e.g.*, Carol F. Lee, *The Political Safeguards of Federalism? Congressional Responses to Supreme Court Decisions on State and Local Liability*, 20 URB. L. 301 (1988) (legislative response to decisions impairing state and local interests); Abner J. Mikva & Jeff Bleich, *When Congress Overrules the Court*, 79 CAL. L. REV. 729 (1991) (comparing congressional overrides of the Court during New Deal and during Reagan Administration).

6. Judge Abner J. Mikva of the D.C. Circuit Court of Appeals, a former member of the House of Representatives, claims in Abner J. Mikva, *How Well Does Congress Support and Defend the Constitution?*, 61 N.C. L. REV. 587, 609 (1983), that "most Supreme Court decisions never come to the attention of Congress." *See also* HARRY WELLINGTON, INTERPRETING THE CONSTITUTION: THE SUPREME COURT AND THE PROCESS OF ADJUDICATION 11 (1990).

of the Court's statutory decisions.[7] The current study also shows that Congress monitors the Court's statutory decisions with great care, reflected in the fact that after 1975 almost half of the Court's statutory interpretation decisions per year have been or will be the specific focus of congressional hearings.

This part presents the methodology and results of my empirical study.[8] It provides a more complete listing of congressional overrides, explores the failure stories more systematically, and suggests conditions for successful overrides. It provides the empirical context for a richer and more reliable academic discussion of the interaction between the Court, Congress, and the President in statutory interpretation.

A. *Congressional Override Legislation, 1967-90*

Previous studies have been faced with what might be an intractable problem. Given the enormous amount of material (thousands of pages of statutes and millions of pages of recorded legislative history) and the failure of the written record to reflect the complete legislative process, we may never have a complete list of all statutes overriding Supreme Court decisions. We can do better than existing lists, however, which for the most part have been compiled through a very casually empirical process.[9]

The *United States Code Congressional and Administrative News (U.S.C.C.A.N.)* collects the main committee reports and other materials for most of the public laws enacted by Congress in any given year. Committee reports, including conference committee reports, routinely discuss judicial decisions affected by proposed statutory provisions.[10] My research assistants and I searched the reports printed in the *U.S.C.C.A.N.* for the period 1967 to 1990, noting every time a report said a proposed statutory provision "overruled," "modified," or (in some cases) "clarified" a federal judicial interpretation of a federal statute. I then correlated these references to provisions in the enacted public law, weeding out references to provisions that ultimately were not

---

7. This study does not include statutes codifying or accepting the Court's statutory interpretation decisions, statutes responding to the Court's common law or constitutional decisions, or statutes overriding the Court's decisions without evidence that Congress was specifically responding to the Court. Each Congress responded to several Supreme Court decisions in these categories, and including these responses would generate 15-20 override statutes per Congress.

8. The three appendices and the methodological statement at the end of this Article explain this in more detail.

9. *See, e.g.*, Note, *Congressional Reversals*, *supra* note 5, at 1324 n.3 (researcher compiled congressional overrides through "[i]nterviews with members of the Harvard Law School community and a search of written materials" such as the *Congressional Quarterly Almanac* and law review articles); *cf.* Solimine & Walker, *supra* note 5 (relying mainly on the *Congressional Quarterly Almanac* and anecdotal evidence). The best methodology is found in Henschen & Sidlow, *supra* note 5, at 692 n.30 (examining legislative hearings to pinpoint override bills), although that study is limited to labor and antitrust overrides and to the period 1950-72.

10. For elaborate and detailed bills, such as omnibus tax bills, budget reconciliation bills, and recodifications (such as for bankruptcy and criminal codes), the committee report usually contains, for each section, a statement of existing law, reasons for changing the existing law, and the proposed changes.

enacted or that did not substantially override a decision.[11] I supplemented this method with a more selective search of committee reports reproduced in microfiche by the Congressional Information Service, with an examination of hearings conducted by the House and Senate Judiciary Committees (for part of this period), and with the consultation of secondary sources.

Appendix I lists the Supreme Court and other federal court statutory interpretations that have been the subject of overrides during this period.[12] Table 1 records the number of statutes in each Congress that contained override provisions; the number of Supreme Court statutory interpretation decisions overridden in each Congress, also broken down into recent (ten years or less between decision and override) and older decisions; and the number of lower federal court decisions overridden in each Congress.[13] Appendix I lists these decisions by name.[14]

11. This method has some gaps. Not all public laws generate committee reports, not all committee reports are reproduced in *U.S.C.C.A.N.* (which also edits the reports), and not all overrides of judicial decisions are reported in committee reports.

12. This study incorporates overrides of lower federal court decisions to add perspective. A broader sample should provide a more reliable picture of changes in congressional responsiveness over time. Further, including lower court decisions gives a better idea of the great variety of subject areas covered by override bills. Finally, the broader sample will be a corrective for the conclusion, discussed in text accompanying *infra* notes 14-15, that Congress is aware of—and overrides many—Supreme Court decisions. The same cannot be said for lower court decisions; Congress tends not to be aware of them and overrides a much smaller percentage of them.

13. Lower federal court decisions include decisions by federal district courts, circuit courts of appeals, magistrates, military tribunals, and specialized federal courts (such as the Tax Court).

14. Table 1 raises an important "counting" problem. A statute overriding a leading Supreme Court or lower court decision also overrides cases following that leading decision. Counting each of the later or collateral decisions, in addition to the leading decision, would inflate artificially the number of overrides. Also, those later cases would prove too difficult to track down. This study seeks to avoid double counting. Therefore, Table 1 treats a series of Supreme Court or lower court decisions standing for the same statutory interpretation as *one* "Supreme Court Decision Overridden" or one "Lower Court Decision Overridden." On the other hand, Table 1 counts each of two Supreme Court interpretations overridden by a statute when the cases stand for two different propositions or when the cases interpret different statutes or provisions. In borderline cases, the study relied on the treatment in the committee reports: were the two decisions treated as independent, or was one considered a derivative of the other?

TABLE 1. *Congressional Overrides of Federal Statutory Decisions (1967-90)*

CONGRESS	OVERRIDE STATUTES	TOTAL DECISIONS OVERRIDDEN	SUPREME COURT DECISIONS OVERRIDDEN			LOWER COURT DECISIONS OVERRIDDEN
			TOTAL	≤10 YRS.	>10 YRS.	
101st (1989-90)	15	27	9	8	1	18
100th (1987-88)	24	39	12	9	3	27
99th (1985-86)	25	45	18	14	4	27
98th (1983-84)	16	44	15	11	4	29
97th (1981-82)	17	24	8	6	2	16
96th (1979-80)	20	31	8	5	3	23
95th (1977-78)	14	43	19	11	8	24
94th (1975-76)	17	34	12	10	2	22
93d (1973-74)	10	14	7	6	1	7
92d (1971-72)	7	12	8	4	4	4
91st (1969-70)	8	15	2	2	0	13
90th (1967-68)	14	16	6	6	0	10
TOTAL	187	344	124*	92*	32	220

* The 124 Supreme Court decisions overridden include three decisions overridden in more than one Congress. Altogether, only 121 different decisions were overridden during this period, and only 89 recent (less than or equal to 10 years old) decisions were overridden.

As Table 1 suggests, Congress frequently overrides or modifies statutory decisions by lower federal courts as well as those by the Supreme Court. Where earlier studies have found only three or four Supreme Court decisions overridden by each Congress, this study finds an average of ten per Congress. While some of the difference results from the more thorough count in this study, most of it is explained by a change in Congress' responsiveness over time. The 94th Congress was a turning point. The four Congresses from 1967-74 generated an average of six Supreme Court overrides per Congress, not many more than the numbers uncovered in prior studies. In contrast, the eight Congresses from 1975-90, beginning with the 94th, generated an average of twelve Supreme Court overrides per Congress. When we consider the overrides involving the decisions of all federal courts, the difference is even more dramatic. The 90th through 93d Congresses (1967-74) generated an average of fourteen lower court overrides per Congress, while the 94th through 101st Congresses (1975-90) generated an average of thirty-five lower court overrides per Congress, two-and-one-half times the number for the previous period.

The substantial increase in congressional overrides for lower court decisions reflects a number of obvious developments. First, those years have seen a geometric increase in the number of lower federal court opinions to which Congress might respond. Second, Congress has passed more omnibus statutes, such as reconciliation statutes, statutory reform efforts, and recodifications. Finally, organized interest groups have proliferated, producing more monitoring of judicial decisions that are then brought to Congress' attention. The latter two reasons also probably play a role in the increase in congressional overrides of the Supreme Court's statutory decisions.[15]

Perhaps the most interesting (and heretofore unappreciated) variable associated with the increased override activity is the growth of congressional committee staff. As part of the legislative reform process in the early 1970's, the staffs of the House and Senate standing committees doubled between 1970 and 1975. Between 1973 and 1975 alone, the House committee staffs increased by two-thirds, and the Senate committee staffs increased by one-third.[16] The numbers are almost as explosive for the judiciary and labor committees, the main committees generating congressional overrides.[17] Staff size in House and Senate committees continued to rise through 1979 and then stabilized (for the House) or declined (for the Senate) in the 1980's. A similarly dramatic increase in the sizes of Members' personal staffs and of the staffs of congressional support agencies also occurred in the first half of the 1970's.[18]

Because staffs are essential to monitoring judicial decisions (often through interest group communications), organizing congressional hearings (a virtual prerequisite for an override), and drafting committee reports and statutes, the dramatic increases in staff levels enable Congress to respond to statutory decisions by the federal judiciary more often. Therefore, it should not be surprising that the leaps in committee staff numbers closely match the burst in congressional override activity. The explosion in staff in the period 1973-75 coincides with the increase in congressional override activity in the period 1975-76. The peak of override activity in the period 1977-78 roughly parallels the peak in committee staff increases at that time. Moreover, the plateau in override activity in the 1980's tracks the leveling off of committee staff.

Although the increased size of committee staffs (especially in the judiciary and labor committees) correlates well with the increased override activity, it is not clear that staff size is the cause—and not the effect—of override activity. The traditional explanation for the surge in congressional staff numbers during

15. The first reason (increased number of decisions) does not apply to the Supreme Court. For purposes of comparison, during the entire period of this study, the Supreme Court issued about 80 statutory interpretation decisions each year.

16. NORMAN J. ORNSTEIN ET AL., VITAL STATISTICS ON CONGRESS, 1989-90, at 136 tbl. 5-5 (1990).

17. The House Judiciary Committee staff went from 27 in 1960, to 35 in 1970, to 69 in 1975, to 80 in 1979, and then stabilized at between 75 and 81 in the 1980's. The House Education and Labor Committee staff went from 25 in 1960, to 77 in 1970, to 114 in 1975, and then stabilized at between 119 and 127 in the period since 1975. *Id.* at 137 tbl. 5-6.

The Senate Judiciary Committee staff went from 137 in 1960, to 190 in 1970, to 251 in 1975, to 223 in 1979, and then fell back to between 134 and 141 during the 1980's. The Senate Labor and Human Resources Committee staff grew from 28 in 1960, to 69 in 1970, to 150 in 1975, to 155 in 1979, and then fell back to between 119 and 127 in the 1980's. *Id.* at 138 tbl. 5-7.

18. House Members' personal staffs jumped from 4055 in 1967 to 6939 in 1976, and then increased only incrementally in the 1980's. Senators' personal staffs jumped from 1749 in 1967 to 3251 in 1976, with slow increases after that. *Id.* at 132 tbl. 5-2; *see also id.* at 133 fig. 5-1 (graphic display of dramatic leaps in member and committee staff sizes).

the 1970's emphasizes internal congressional changes.[19] New Democratic Members of Congress in the early 1970's demanded a greater diffusion of power, which placed more authority in subcommittees. The proliferation of subcommittees, and thus of independent power centers, required more staff in the House. The Senate experienced some committee staff increase, but also greatly expanded Members' personal staffs in 1975.[20] This traditional explanation suggests that the increased override activity stemmed from changes internal to Congress.

Another explanation, however, is that congressional staff size—and override activity—increased as a response to divided government.[21] A Democratic Congress has strong incentives to monitor statutory implementation by a Republican Presidency, and increased monitoring requires an augmented staff. Confronted with a Republican Supreme Court after 1971 (four Nixon appointees and later one Ford appointee in place) and an increasingly Republican judiciary in general, the Democratic Congress in the 1970's had an incentive to monitor judicial decisions more carefully than it had in the 1960's. This partisan incentive might have rendered the Democratic leadership in Congress more receptive to demands by Democrats for more power, more subcommittees, and more staff.

This divided-government explanation correlates with some of the data. The boom in congressional overrides started in 1975-78, when enlarged Democratic majorities in Congress (and, after 1976, a Democratic President) became more aggressive in scrutinizing the work of Republican judges. Override activity fell off from 1979-82, as the lower courts were operating with more Democratic appointees.[22] This evidence would support the suggestion that both the staff increases in key committees and the increased override activity resulted from a Democratic Congress' distrust of a Republican judiciary.

This suggestion is not supported by data from the 1980's, however. For example, between 1983 and 1987, override activity sharply increased from the 1979-82 dip, even though the Senate was in Republican hands and a Republican President could exercise a viable veto threat. And congressional override activity has not increased noticeably since 1987, even though the federal judiciary has received even larger numbers of Republican appointees and the Senate has returned to Democratic hands. The evidence from the 1980's correlates very well with the suggestion that staff size has exercised an indepen-

19. *See* LEROY N. RIESELBACK, CONGRESSIONAL REFORM IN THE SEVENTIES (1977); STEVEN S. SMITH & CHRISTOPHER DEERING, COMMITTEES IN CONGRESS 194-98 (1984); Lawrence C. Dodd & Bruce I. Oppenheimer, *The House in Transition*, *in* CONGRESS RECONSIDERED 27-32 (Lawrence C. Dodd & Bruce I. Oppenheimer eds., 1st ed. 1977).

20. *See* ORNSTEIN ET AL., *supra* note 16, at 126.

21. This point was suggested to me by Matt Spitzer.

22. In 1979-82, override activity fell significantly from its 1977-78 "high." By then President Carter had appointed more than half of the federal judiciary (albeit no Supreme Court Justices).

dent influence on the level of congressional overrides. Just as staff size reached a plateau in the 1980's, so did override activity.

B. *Congressional Monitoring of Supreme Court Statutory Decisions (Judiciary Committees), 1979-87*

A second difficulty with previous surveys is their inattention to proposed overrides.[23] This is an important feature of the overall picture, in part because an examination of the proposed, but unsuccessful, overrides yields a richer vision of congressional monitoring of the Court's statutory decisions. Is Congress actively aware of the Court's decisions? How does it become aware? For what decisions are serious but unsuccessful override efforts mounted? Why do some efforts fail, while others succeed? The failure stories provide a data base with which the success stories may be compared, giving us clues about the types of overrides likely to pass and the ones more likely to fail.

My study of failed overrides is based on a sampling, rather than a comprehensive search, methodology.[24] About half of the Supreme Court's statutory interpretation decisions in any given Term deal with issues within the jurisdiction of the House and Senate Judiciary Committees.[25] I examined the hearings of these committees during the 96th through 100th Congresses (1979-88), searching for analysis and criticism of specific Supreme Court statutory decisions. Appendix II lists those Supreme Court cases examined in either House or Senate Judiciary Committee hearing during this period. Where applicable, Appendix II also lists the override bill(s) associated with each decision and indicates the fate of each bill. Table 2 presents the data as collected in Appendix II, but correlated with the five Congresses studied.

23. The only study that attempts to consider proposed overrides is Henschen & Sidlow, *supra* note 5, which is dated (1950-72) and limited to labor and antitrust issues.

24. The approach is dictated by limited human resources. The best way to learn about failed override efforts would probably involve examination of all of the committee hearings for this period. These hearings are collected in the Library of Congress' legislative section in the Jefferson Building. But there are literally thousands of volumes of such hearings for the period in question. Although I found committee hearings fascinating literature, reading them all would take years to do. Life is short, and so I made the decision to limit my research to all the House and Senate Judiciary Committee hearings from 1979 to 1988.

25. Specifically, these issues include general administrative process and freedom of information, immigration, bankruptcy, the antitrust laws, substantive criminal law, federal jurisdiction, federal tort and contract liability, habeas corpus, patent law, copyright and trademark law, and civil rights law. These areas usually constitute the main areas at issue in 40 or more of the Court's statutory decisions each year (see Table 3), about half of the 80 or so statutory decisions the Court hands down annually. Note that there is significant overlap with the jurisdiction of at least one other committee: The labor committees in both the House and Senate share jurisdiction with the judiciary committees for issues of job discrimination under Title VII.

TABLE 2. *Judiciary Committee Scrutiny of Supreme Court Statutory Decisions (1979-88)*

CONGRESS	DECISIONS SCRUTINIZED: TOTAL	WITHIN 5 YRS.	WITHIN 5-10 YRS.	OVER 10 YRS.	DECISIONS OVERRIDDEN AS A PERCENTAGE OF ALL CONGRESSIONAL OVERRIDES
100th (1987-88)	52	23	13	16	58% (7/12)
99th (1985-86)	55	27	15	13	39% (7/18)
98th (1983-84)	44	21	15	8	60% (9/15)
97th (1981-82)	65	38	9	18	63% (5/8)
96th (1979-80)	46	15	14	17	50% (4/8)

As Table 2 suggests, more than half of the congressional overrides involved statutory subjects within the jurisdiction of the House and Senate Judiciary Committees. The overrides that have received the most popular and legal attention very often involve statutory policy within these committees' jurisdiction.[26]

Appendix II and the data underlying Table 2 show that a substantial number of Supreme Court decisions, especially recent ones, were the focus of one or more House and Senate Judiciary Committee hearings in each Congress.[27] Table 3 takes a seven-year period of the Court's decisions (1977 through 1983 Terms), records how many decisions were the focus of House and Senate Judiciary Committee hearings, and determines what percentage of each Terms's decisions within the committees' jurisdiction were scrutinized. This seven-year period was used because it begins the ten-year period covered by the study of House and Senate Judiciary Committee hearings (see Table 2).

TABLE 3. *Judiciary Committee Scrutiny of Supreme Court Statutory Decisions (1977-1983 Terms)*

COURT TERM	DECISIONS WITHIN COMMITTEE JURISDICTION	DECISIONS SCRUTINIZED	PERCENTAGE SCRUTINIZED
1977 Term	39	18	47%
1978 Term	32	14	44%
1979 Term	43	21	49%
1980 Term	35	12	35%
1981 Term	40	12	30%
1982 Term	43	15	35%
1983 Term	43	13	30%

26. This is especially true of the 101st Congress. About half of the enacted overrides originated with the House or Senate Judiciary Committees, as did the two spectacular failures—the proposed Civil Rights Act of 1990, S. 2104, 101st Cong., 2d Sess. (1990), and the habeas provisions of the Crime Control Act of 1990, H.R. REP. NO. 681(I), 101st Cong., 2d Sess. 122-36 (1990) (deleted in conference), *reprinted in* 1990 U.S.C.C.A.N. 6472, 6527-41.

27. Note that Table 2 counts several decisions more than once, because they were the focus of hearings in more than one Congress. Hence, the total number of different decisions scrutinized in this period is not the sum of the decisions scrutinized in each Congress.

Table 3 shows that the Judiciary Committees actively hold hearings to evaluate Supreme Court statutory decisions within their jurisdiction. Although as of 1988 the committees had scrutinized only a third of the decisions from the 1980 through 1983 Terms, in a few years the percentage of decisions from that period will probably approach the forty percent or higher figures of earlier Terms.[28] This finding itself is striking.

Additionally, House and Senate Judiciary Committee members and staff seem to be aware of decisions besides those for which hearings are held. The House and Senate Judiciary Committees' knowledge of judicial developments is not unusual when compared with that of other committees, especially the labor committees (Education and Labor in the House, Human Services in the Senate) and the tax committees (Ways and Means in the House, Finance in the Senate). Contrast this data, which shows significant legislative interest in Supreme Court statutory decisions, with Dr. Robert Katzmann's empirical work, which suggests that committee member and staff awareness of lower court statutory interpretations is much more selective than their awareness of Supreme Court interpretations.[29]

Tables 1 through 3 and this Article's underlying research suggest that the Supreme Court's statutory decisions are accessible to Congress. Moreover, this research indicates that key staff members become aware of any significant Supreme Court decision affecting issues within their committee's jurisdiction, but not necessarily every significant lower court decision. Almost half of the Court's decisions are examined over time in "oversight" hearings—committee members, other relevant officials, and representatives of private groups discuss the policies adopted in those decisions. But less than a fifth of the decisions seriously examined by the relevant committees are actually overridden by Congress.

C. *Supreme Court Decisions Most Likely To Be Overridden by Congress*

A final difficulty with previous studies is their failure to explain convincingly the circumstances under which Congress will override Supreme Court statutory decisions. The rest of this part will make empirical and comparative

28. This is because the "Decisions Scrutinized" column is cumulative. As the committees examine more decisions each year, they add to the total from prior years.

29. Dr. Robert Katzmann conducted a survey of congressional staff awareness of 15 significant statutory opinions of the D.C. Circuit in 1989. He found the staff unaware of 12 of the 15 decisions, including the four cases within the jurisdiction of the well informed House Subcommittee on Courts, Civil Liberties, and the Administration of Justice. Dr. Katzmann found that "staffs tend to be aware of cases when those cases are so-called major cases, that is, those cases in which the Supreme Court has resolved the matters, or cases in which the losing party, for example, an interest group or trade organization, seeks some sort of relief through the legislative process. Otherwise, the staff member is dependent upon what he or she might glean from the summaries offered by a reporting service if he or she has the time or inclination to peruse them." *Proceedings of the Forty-Ninth Judicial Conference of the District of Columbia Circuit*, 124 F.R.D. 241, 323-24 (1988) (remarks of Robert Katzmann).

observations about the characteristics of Supreme Court decisions that render them most likely to be overridden. Part II will then utilize political science theory to develop a model of congressional overrides.

Appendix III compiles some simple information about the 121 Supreme Court statutory decisions overridden in the last twelve Congresses. From the list in Appendix III, Table 4 characterizes the areas of law with the most override activity.[30]

TABLE 4. *Subject Matter of Statutes Overriding Supreme Court Statutory Interpretation Decisions (1967-90)*

SUBJECT MATTER	NUMBER OF OVERRIDES	PERCENTAGE OF TOTAL
Criminal Law	18	15%
Antitrust	11	9%
Civil Rights	11	9%
Bankruptcy	10	8%
Federal Jurisdiction & Procedure	9	7%
Environmental Law	9	7%
Income Tax	8	7%
Copyright, Trademark & Patent Law	8	7%
Intergov'tl Relations & Federalism	6	5%
Longshoremen & Shipping	6	5%
Federal Torts/Contracts	4	3%
Armed Services & Veterans Affairs	4	3%
Immigration	4	3%
Gov't Employment	3	3%
Freedom of Information	2	2%
Admiralty (Ports)	2	2%
Common Carriers	1	1%
Traditional Labor Law	1	1%
ERISA	1	1%
Banking Regulation	1	1%
Stockyards	1	1%
Social Welfare	1	1%
TOTAL	121	101%

Table 4 demonstrates that the House and Senate Judiciary Committees have jurisdiction over most override efforts. The judiciary committees have primary or exclusive jurisdiction over 54% of the total overrides in this period (criminal law; federal jurisdiction and procedure; antitrust; bankruptcy; copyright, trademark, and patent law; federal torts/contracts; immigration; and freedom of information) and secondary or shared jurisdiction over another 17% of the

30. My methodology for characterizing decisions usually follows the United States Code: civil rights decisions were overridden by changes to title 42; criminal law, title 18; federal jurisdiction and procedure, title 28; bankruptcy, title 11; income tax, title 26; antitrust, title 15; copyright, trademark, and patent law, titles 17, 15, and 35, respectively; armed services and veterans affairs, title 38; longshoremen and admiralty, title 33; immigration law, title 8; environmental law, titles 7, 16 & 42; United States government workers, selected parts of title 5; federal torts and contracts, selected parts of titles 28 and 41, respectively; freedom of information, title 5; labor law and ERISA, title 29; banking regulation, title 12; and stockyards, title 7. The main departure from this methodology is the category of intergovernmental (federal/state) relations, where the statutory overrides occurred in various parts of the United States Code. *See generally* Lee, *supra* note 5 (in-depth analysis of congressional overrides of decisions affecting state and local governments).

overrides (civil rights in education and the workplace, intergovernmental relations, government employment). The labor committees have primary or exclusive jurisdiction over 13% of the overrides (civil rights in education and the workplace, government employment, traditional labor law, and ERISA). The public works committees and tax committees are also important sources of overrides, with primary jurisdiction over 7% (environmental law) and 7% (income tax) of total overrides, respectively. Altogether, almost nine out of ten overrides are generated from these four committees.

Table 4 also suggests the relative subject matter of override activity. Although statutory overrides of Supreme Court civil rights decisions have received the most publicity, there has been much more override activity for criminal law in this period, and just about as much activity for bankruptcy, federal jurisdiction and procedure, and antitrust law.[31] Given their low visibility in the political system, it may be surprising that cases involving criminal law, bankruptcy, and federal jurisdiction and procedure have generated so many overrides. The significant activity is the result of ambitious codification and reform efforts by judiciary subcommittees responsible for each of those areas of law. In contrast, there has been a surprising lack of overrides in securities law, given the intense public interest and litigation in this area.[32]

When Congress chose to override the Court, it usually did so with relative speed. Almost half of the Supreme Court cases in the study were overridden within two years of their decision (ten were overridden the year they were decided), two-thirds were overridden within five years, and three-fourths within ten years (see Appendix III).[33] To explore more fully the interaction between the Court and Congress, the remainder of this section will focus on the eighty-nine cases overridden within ten years of their decision (see Table 1).[34] Tables 5 through 7 present data describing the division of the Court in these eighty-nine overridden cases, the political characterization, if any, of the Court's division, the mode of reasoning underlying the Court's interpretation, and the nature of the losers in overridden cases (the parties who are likely to petition Congress for an override).

31. The enactment of the Civil Rights Act of 1991, which overrides 12 Supreme Court decisions (most of which interpret civil rights statutes), make the civil rights category the leading override area for the period 1967-92.

32. Labor law also produced fewer overrides than expected, but this is probably due to the current limits of "traditional labor law" (mainly, the National Labor Relations Act). If "labor law" included discrimination in the workplace, federal employee and civil service issues, federal regulation of state employees, and pension (ERISA) issues, then Table 4 would list more than ten overrides.

33. Most of the cases that were overridden after a relatively long delay involved recodification statutes (especially the Bankruptcy Act of 1978), reconciliation statutes (often overturning old tax decisions), and other omnibus acts covering a number of related issues in one statute.

34. Although 10 years is an arbitrary figure, it is a useful cutoff point for analyzing short-term congressional responses to the Court. Most of the decisions overridden more than 10 years after they were decided were the subject of omnibus reconciliation or recodification bills (see Appendix I) in which the override was not the main focus of the legislation.

Table 5 reports the voting splits among the Justices, to provide information on the divisions within the Court for decisions overridden soon after they were handed down.[35] Table 5 also indicates whether the Court split along identifiable ideological lines in these decisions.[36]

TABLE 5. *Voting and Political Divisions in Supreme Court Decisions Overridden by Congress Within Ten Years of the Court's Decision (1967-90)*

VOTING SPLITS	NUMBER OF OVERRIDES	PERCENTAGE OF TOTAL
4-4 or Memorandum Decisions	6	7%
5-4 Decisions	14	16%
6-3 Decisions	30	34%
7-2 Decisions	15	17%
8-1 Decisions	12	13%
9-0 Decisions	12	13%
TOTAL	89	100%

POLITICAL SPLITS	NUMBER OF OVERRIDES	PERCENTAGE OF TOTAL
Conservative/Liberal	34	38%
Liberal/Conservative	18	20%
No Clean Division	37	42%
TOTAL	89	100%

Table 5 suggests that overridden statutory decisions usually involved issues producing a fragmented, ideologically divided Court. A majority of the overridden decisions involved a 4-4, 5-4, or 6-3 division on the Court, and three-fifths of the decisions reflected an ideological split (usually with Justices Brennan and Marshall opposing Justice (or later Chief Justice) Rehnquist). The tendency for Congress to override identifiably "conservative" Supreme Court decisions significantly more often than identifiably "liberal" opinions is a very recent

35. In determining splits, the study counts concurring Justices as part of the majority even when they did not join the majority opinion. The study counts Justices concurring in part and dissenting in part based on how they voted on the issue for which Congress overrode the Court. Finally, as Table 5 reflects, the study attempts to place decisions with fewer than nine total votes in the most similar category used for full Court decisions. For example, the study places 8-0 decisions (where only eight Justices voted) in the 9-0 decision category.

36. The study follows the standard liberal/conservative characterizations. The usual clue to an ideological split is that consistently liberal Justices were on one side and consistently conservative Justices on the other. The consistently liberal Justices for this study include Chief Justice Warren and Justices Douglas, Brennan, Fortas, Marshall, and (for the 1980's) Blackmun and Stevens. The consistently conservative Justices include Chief Justices Burger and Rehnquist, and Justices Rehnquist, Powell (for the 1970's), O'Connor, Scalia, and Kennedy. I considered Justices Harlan, Stewart, and White to be moderates. Thus, if a Supreme Court opinion in the 1980's finds Chief Justice Burger and Justice Rehnquist in the majority with Justices Brennan and Marshall dissenting, I would identify the opinion as "conservative," while I would categorize a decision with Justice Rehnquist joining Justices Brennan and Marshall in dissent as "no split."

phenomenon, attributable entirely to events of the 1980's.[37] In the last five years covered by the study (1986-90), congressional overrides of identifiably "liberal" Supreme Court statutory decisions all but vanished (three of thirty-eight). Almost half of the overrides (sixteen of thirty-eight) reversed identifiably "conservative" decisions, although a similar number (nineteen of thirty-eight) of the overridden decisions could not be characterized ideologically (see Appendix III).

Table 6 reports the various modes of reasoning underlying the Court's holdings in the overridden decisions, in an attempt to identify those most likely to produce an interpretation that Congress would later reject.[38]

TABLE 6. *The Primary Reasoning in Supreme Court Decisions Overridden by Congress within Ten Years of the Court's Decision (1967-90)*

PRIMARY REASONING	NUMBER OF DECISIONS	PERCENT OF TOTAL
Plain Meaning	23.5	26%
Legislative History	19.0	21%
Canons	16.0	18%
Statutory Precedents	13.5	15%
Purpose & Policy	6.5	7%
Common Law & Constitutional Law	3.5	4%
No Opinion	7.0	8%
TOTAL	89.0	99%

37. Of the 39 Supreme Court decisions of the 1980's that Congress overrode (as of January 1991), 17 were conservative decisions, 16 reflected no clean division, and only 6 were liberal decisions (see Appendix III).

38. The main methodological difficulty involved identifying the Court's *primary* reasoning, for the Court almost never relies on just one reason. *See* William N. Eskridge, Jr. & Philip P. Frickey, *Statutory Interpretation as Practical Reasoning*, 42 STAN. L. REV. 321 (1990) (demonstrating lack of one identifiable reason behind various Court decisions). To determine the Court's primary reasoning, I considered three factors: (1) explicit statements by the Court (for example, if the Court declared that the text was clear and not trumped by the loser's legislative history arguments, the study identified the primary reasoning as plain meaning); (2) the placement and length of the Court's analysis (for example, if the Court began its analysis with a canon of statutory construction and then demonstrated that no other argument offset it, the study identified the primary reasoning as reliance on canons of construction); and (3) the persuasiveness of the Court's analysis and the Court's own apparent confidence in its opinion (if the Court's legislative history argument was subordinate to, but more convincing than, what appeared to be a makeweight textual argument, the study identified the primary reasoning as legislative history). For about a fourth of the Court's decisions, I felt that there was no "primary" reasoning, and in these cases I identified the two main candidates, considering each as one-half of the Court's reasoning for counting purposes.

As set forth in greater detail in the methodological statement preceding the appendices, *infra* text accompanying notes 304-10, the modes of reasoning included: (1) "plain meaning," where the Court relies on the probable meaning of the "plain" text, construed according to standard dictionaries, rules of grammar and syntax, and the overall statutory structure; (2) "legislative history," where the Court relies on the history of the statute before Congress enacted it; (3) "statutory precedents," where the court relies on prior Supreme Court decisions construing the statute or related statutes; (4) "canons," where the Court relies on canons of construction, usually expressed as presumptions or clear statement rules; (5) "purpose and policy," where the Court relies on purpose of the statute and other policy arguments; and (6) "common law and constitutional law," where the Court relies on common law or constitutional decisions to fill gaps in statutory policy.

The most interesting feature revealed by Table 6 is that Congress is much more likely to override "plain meaning" decisions than any other type of Supreme Court statutory decision. When decisions dominated by canons of statutory construction are added to the total of plain meaning decisions, about half of the overrides fall within this category. In contrast, Congress rarely appears to override those interpretations grounded on statutory "purpose."

In an effort to identify the groups that are likely to petition Congress for an override, Table 7 characterizes the groups who "lost" in decisions that later were overridden by Congress.[39]

TABLE 7. *"Losing" Groups in Supreme Court Decisions Overridden by Congress within Ten Years of the Court's Decisions (1967-90)*

"Losing" Groups	Number of Decisions	Percent of Total
United States & U.S. Departments	22	25%
Organized Business	16	18%
Diffuse Citizenry	10	11%
State & Local Governments	9	10%
Organized Workers	7	8%
Environmentalists	6	7%
Women	4	4%
Disabled	4	4%
Criminal Defendants & Suspects	2	2%
Racial Minorities	2	2%
Noncitizens	2	2%
Veterans Groups	1	1%
The Poor	1	1%
Religious Groups	1	1%
Unclear	2	2%
Total	89	98%

Table 7 suggests that the big "winners" among the "losers"—the groups most likely to persuade Congress to override an adverse Supreme Court decision—are federal, state, and local governments, which together have procured more than one-third (35%) of the overrides of recent decisions. Another 26% were obtained by organized business and labor groups. Less than one-eighth (11%) of the overrides reversed losses for groups that include most Americans—litigants, appellants, consumers, government tort victims, Freedom of Information Act petitioners, and antitrust plaintiffs. These groups are identified as "diffuse citizenry," that is, groups that include, or potentially include, most or all Americans.

39. *See* methodological statement preceding the appendices, *infra* text accompanying notes 304-12, for an explanation of what or whom I am including in each group listing.

The data presented in Tables 5 through 7 suggest that the typical congressional override will focus on Supreme Court decisions that adjudicate issues producing an ideologically divided vote on the Court and that harm the interests of federal, state, or local governments, or of well-organized interest groups. This is useful information, but does not answer the question: How does the typical overridden Supreme Court decision compare with the typical Supreme Court decision that is *not* overridden? In other words, Tables 5 through 7, standing alone, are of limited utility because they do not compare overriden decisions with decisions that Congress allowed to stand. To facilitate such comparisons, Tables 8 and 9 draw upon the sample (profiled in Table 3 above) of Supreme Court statutory decisions from the 1977 through 1983 Terms.

Table 8 compares the voting splits, ideological divisions, and primary reasoning of three sets of decisions from those Terms: (1) decisions never examined by the House and Senate Judiciary Committees, (2) decisions examined but not overridden, and (3) decisions from those Terms that were within the Judiciary Committees' jurisdiction and were overridden.[40]

40. Although the third group (decisions overridden from the 1977 through 1983 Terms) is small (18 decisions), its overall percentages roughly match those for all of the overrides in Tables 5 and 6. This finding provides some confidence that the sample is representative.

TABLE 8. *Comparison of Overridden Supreme Court Decisions with Supreme Court Decisions within Judiciary Committee Jurisdiction But Not Overridden (1978-84)*

VOTING SPLIT	TOTAL DECISIONS	DECISIONS NOT SCRUTINIZED	DECISIONS SCRUTINIZED: TOTAL	DECISIONS SCRUTINIZED: OVERRIDDEN	DECISIONS SCRUTINIZED: NOT OVERRIDDEN
9-0 Decisions	85	61 (72%)	24 (28%)	1 (1%)	23 (27%)
8-1 Decisions	33	22 (67%)	11 (33%)	3 (9%)	8 (24%)
7-2 Decisions	36	20 (56%)	16 (45%)	1 (3%)	15 (42%)
6-3 Decisions	65	38 (58%)	27 (41%)	6 (9%)	21 (32%)
5-4 Decisions	56	29 (52%)	27 (48%)	7 (12%)	20 (36%)
TOTAL	275	170 (62%)	105 (38%)	18 (7%)	87 (32%)
POLITICAL DIVISIONS					
Conservative/Liberal	83	49 (59%)	34 (41%)	8 (10%)	26 (31%)
Liberal/Conservative	58	31 (55%)	27 (46%)	7 (12%)	20 (35%)
No Clear Division	134	90 (67%)	44 (33%)	3 (2%)	41 (31%)
TOTAL	275	170 (62%)	105 (38%)	18 (7%)	87 (32%)
PRIMARY REASONING					
Plain Meaning	48.5	29.5 (61%)	19.0 (40%)	6.5 (14%)	12.5 (26%)
Legislative History	42.5	20.5 (48%)	22.0 (52%)	3.0 (7%)	19.0 (45%)
Precedent	104.5	67.0 (64%)	37.5 (36%)	4.0 (4%)	33.5 (32%)
Canons	26.0	15.0 (57%)	11.0 (43%)	3.0 (12%)	8.0 (31%)
Purpose & Policy	37.0	28.5 (77%)	8.5 (23%)	0.5 (1%)	8.0 (22%)
Common Law & Other	16.5	9.5 (58%)	7.0 (42%)	1.0 (6%)	6.0 (36%)
TOTAL	275.0	170.0 (62%)	105.0 (38%)	18.0 (7%)	87.0 (32%)

Table 8 generates several interesting observations. First, decisions subject to judiciary committee scrutiny were much more likely to have a dissenting opinion and to reflect a close division on the Court; this was particularly true of decisions that were ultimately overridden.[41] Not surprisingly, issues that generate division in the Court are the ones most likely to generate serious congressional scrutiny.

Second, decisions that were overridden were much more likely to have had an ideologically identifiable split on the Court than either decisions not scrutinized or decisions scrutinized but not overridden.[42] For the period in question

41. Specifically, 72% of the 9-0 decisions were not examined by the judiciary committees, but only 52% of the 5-4 decisions were not examined. Putting it another way, 72% of the overridden decisions (13 of 18) reflected 6-3 or 5-4 votes, while only 47% of the examined-but-not-overridden decisions (41 of 87) reflected such votes, and only 39% of the unscrutinized decisions (67 of 170) reflected such votes.

42. Specifically, overridden decisions make up only 2% of the "No Clear Division" decisions, in contrast to the 10% and 12% these decisions constitute in the other two categories. Putting it another way, only 15% (3 of 18) of the overridden decisions reflected "No Clear Division," while 47% (41 of 87) and

(1977-84), the Court as a whole was moderately conservative, and all three groups of decisions reflect that (hence, more identifiably conservative decisions in each category). If Table 8 included data from the late 1980's, when overrides of identifiably liberal decisions all but dried up,[43] the overridden decisions category would probably overrepresent "conservative" decisions, when compared to the other categories.

Third, decisions that were overridden were more likely to have relied on a statute's plain meaning or the canons of construction than either decisions not scrutinized or decision scrutinized but not overridden.[44] Interestingly, decisions scrutinized but not overridden tended to have more legislative history reasoning than the other two categories, while purpose and policy reasoning was greatly overrepresented in the unscrutinized decisions category.

The most dramatic and instructive contrast between the different categories of decisions is revealed in Table 9, which identifies the "losing" groups by category (only for decisions in the 1977 through 1983 Terms).[45]

TABLE 9. *Comparison of "Losing" Groups in Overridden Decisions with "Losing" Groups in Decisions Within Judiciary Committee Jurisdiction, but Not Overridden (1978-84)*

			Decisions Scrutinized		
"Losing Group"	Total Decisions	Decisions Not Scrutinized	Total	Overridden	Not Overridden
Diffuse Citizenry	77	53 (68%)	24 (32%)	1 (1%)	23 (31%)
Organized Business	54	30 (55%)	24 (45%)	1 (2%)	23 (43%)
Criminal Defendants & Suspects	34	24 (71%)	10 (29%)	1 (3%)	9 (27%)
State & Local Gov'ts	34	16 (48%)	18 (53%)	3 (9%)	15 (44%)
United States & U.S. Dep'ts	24	15 (62%)	9 (38%)	5 (20%)	4 (18%)
Racial Minorities	20	17 (85%)	3 (15%)	1 (5%)	2 (10%)
The Poor	7	5 (71%)	2 (29%)	0 (0%)	2 (29%)
Organized Workers	6	3 (50%)	3 (50%)	2 (33%)	1 (17%)
Noncitizens	5	2 (40%)	3 (60%)	1 (20%)	2 (40%)
Environmentalists	4	1 (25%)	3 (75%)	0 (0%)	3 (75%)
Women	2	0 (0%)	2 (100%)	2 (100%)	0 (0%)
Foreign States	1	1 (100%)	0 (0%)	0 (0%)	0 (0%)
Disabled	1	0 (0%)	1 (100%)	1 (100%)	0 (0%)
Not Clear	6	3 (50%)	3 (50%)	0 (0%)	3 (50%)
Total	275	170 (62%)	105 (38%)	18 (7%)	87 (32%)

53% (90 of 170) of the scrutinized-but-not-overridden and unscrutinized decisions, respectively, reflected "No Clear Division."

43. *See supra* text accompanying note 37.

44. Specifically, these are the highest percentages for the "Decisions Overridden" column, next to the lowest for the "Decisions Scrutinized but Not Overridden" column, and middling for the "Decisions Not Scrutinized" column. Justice Stevens recently made this observation in West Virginia Univ. Hosp., Inc. v. Casey, 111 S. Ct. 1138, 1153-58 (1991) (Stevens, J., dissenting).

45. *See* methodologic.' ---tement preceding the appendices, *infra* text accompanying notes 304-12, for an explanation of what or whom I am including in each group listing.

Table 9 strongly supports the suggestion from Table 7 that federal, state, and local governments are unusually successful in having their Supreme Court losses reversed by Congress.[46] Table 9 also contributes an additional insight: State and local governments are *more* likely than the United States to have their losses scrutinized by Congress, but then much *less* likely to have the losses actually overridden.

Although the numbers are too small to draw strong conclusions, Table 9 suggests that big business (like state and local governments) fares much better at obtaining judiciary committee scrutiny of decisions it loses than it is at obtaining actual overrides. In contrast, organized worker groups (not only unions, but retired persons and federal employees) fare particularly well in overturning adverse decisions. Conversely, diffuse random groups (such as victims of state constitutional violations or federal torts) fare poorly; and criminal defendants and suspects, as well as the poor, have had virtually no success in obtaining overrides. Further, middle class women fare comparatively well when their collective interests are harmed by a statutory decision.

This data provides some basis for generalizing about which Supreme Court statutory decisions stand the best chance of being overridden in the 1990's.[47] (1) They will likely be split decisions in which political ideology provides a basis for the split. (2) For now, conservative Court decisions relying on plain meaning of the statutory text and/or the canons of statutory construction are most likely to be overturned, subject to qualifications to be introduced in the next part of the Article. (3) The most important variables seem to be the identity of the party who lost the case and the identity of the party whose interests the Court's interpretation harms in the long run (often the same). If the ruling harms the federal government's interests, an override is particularly likely. Women, the disabled, state and local governments, environmentalists, and organized workers are also relatively able to command Congress' support for an override, while consumers, litigants, nonbusiness and less wealthy taxpayers, and the poor are much less likely to muster such support.

To illustrate the importance of "who loses the case," consider the following contrast. The Supreme Court's decision in *General Electric Co. v. Gilbert*,[48] interpreting Title VII of the Civil Rights Act of 1964 to permit employment discrimination based upon pregnancy, presented a classic case for an override.

46. Specifically, 21% of the United States' losses and 9% of the losses for state and local governments were overridden by Congress—much higher figures than those for organized private groups, including big business (2%) and minorities (5%). Putting it another way, 44% (8 of 18) of the "Decisions Overridden" category were ones where federal, state, and local governments lost Supreme Court cases, compared with 22% in the "Decisions Scrutinized But Not Overridden" category (19 or 87) and 17% in the "Decisions Not Scrutinized" category (31 of 170).

47. Caveat: Prediction about the Court/Congress interaction in the 1990's based upon data from the 1980's is risky, so the following conclusions should be discounted appropriately. Also, while each of the three generalizations is true for a majority of the overrides studied (Tables 5-9), a majority of the overrides will not necessarily fit the overall picture painted by *all three* generalizations together.

48. 429 U.S. 125 (1976).

The Court was split (6-3); the split was along ideological lines (conservative over liberal) for which neither Congress nor the President had much sympathy; the decision relied on plain meaning and constitutional precedent; and the decision represented a public defeat for organized women's groups, unions, and the Equal Employment Opportunity Commission. Although employer and insurance groups supported the decision, Congress promptly overrode it. A few years later, in *American Tobacco Co. v. Patterson*,[49] the Court interpreted Title VII to protect post-1964 seniority systems that had a discriminatory impact upon African Americans. Although the Court was even more closely divided (5-4) along ideological lines than it was in *Gilbert*, the *American Tobacco* issue did not even generate override hearings.[50] The critical difference between *Gilbert* and *American Tobacco* lies in the relative clout of the losing groups. The combined efforts of women's groups, unions, and the federal government effected a prompt reversal of *Gilbert* over employer group objections, while African Americans standing alone could not muster sufficient interest to generate hearings on the issues decided in *American Tobacco*.

II. Modeling the Interaction Between the Court, Congress, and the President in Statutory Interpretation

Even the best empirical data is of only limited use without a theoretical framework. Despite the multiplicity of theoretical works analyzing the legislative process, most prior studies of congressional overrides have failed to draw on this literature to help explain and predict overrides. In an effort to remedy this shortcoming, this part will survey the political theories of the legislative process, including the role of interest groups and committees. The section will attempt to synthesize political science and legal scholarship to produce a model that reflects the complexity of the process yet remains capable of generating some useful predictions. It will conclude with a dynamic model of the interaction between the Court, Congress, and the President in statutory interpretation cases. One of the contributions of this Article will be to highlight, through formal and historical analysis, the important (but often unappreciated) role of the President in the override process, especially during periods of divided government.

49. 456 U.S. 63 (1982).

50. Even though the labor committees of the next Congress held extensive oversight hearings on Title VII, it appears that *American Tobacco* was never even mentioned. *See Oversight Hearings on the Federal Enforcement of Equal Employment Opportunity Laws: Hearings Before the Subcomm. on Employment Opportunities of the House Comm. on Education and Labor*, 98th Cong., 1st Sess. (1983); *Oversight of the EEOC, 1983: Hearings Before the Senate Comm. on Labor and Human Resources*, 98th Cong., 1st Sess. (1983); *see also Civil Rights Act of 1984: Joint Hearings on S. 2568 Before the Subcomm. on Education, Arts and Humanities and the Subcomm. on the Handicapped of the Senate Comm. on Labor and Human Resources*, 98th Cong., 2d Sess. (1984).

Oversimplifying somewhat, one might identify two theoretical traditions for describing the legislative process.[51] The first, the deliberative tradition,[52] conceives of the legislature as deliberating to improve the general welfare or common good. This tradition assumes that legislators are public-regarding—they "desire to participate in formulation of good public policy."[53] Thus, they fairly arbitrate interest group conflicts, correct market failures, and promote worthy public values in the political community. According to this view, the legislature itself is organized to facilitate the discovery and implementation of good public policy, through the creation of specialized committees. The relationship between the legislature and the other branches of government, including the judiciary, is one of cooperation. Congress sets public-seeking national policy, and the judiciary and the executive implement it.

The cogency of such an optimistic view of the legislative process has steadily eroded, as scholars have shown the process to be frequently private regarding and "rent seeking" (distributing benefits to a group without normative justification).[54] A different "distributive" tradition (often characterized as "public choice" theory) has emerged in political science over the last twenty-five years.[55] This tradition has replaced "a romantic and illusory set of notions about the workings of governments"[56] with more "realistic"—or, perhaps,

51. *See generally* WILLIAM N. ESKRIDGE, JR. & PHILIP P. FRICKEY, CASES AND MATERIALS ON LEGISLATION: STATUTES AND THE CREATION OF PUBLIC POLICY 1-93 (1988).

52. The classics in this tradition are ARTHUR F. BENTLEY, THE PROCESS OF GOVERNMENT (1908); WILFRED E. BINKLEY & MALCOLM MOOS, A GRAMMAR OF AMERICAN POLITICS (1949); ROBERT A. DAHL, A PREFACE TO DEMOCRATIC THEORY (1956). These works set forth a vision of pluralist legislative process in which most viewpoints are represented and legislators solve collective action problems. *See also* ARTHUR C. PIGOU, THE ECONOMICS OF WELFARE (4th ed. 1962). This "optimistic pluralism" has been the dominant legal theory for most of the century and was canonized in HENRY H. HART & ALBERT SACKS, THE LEGAL PROCESS: BASIC PROBLEMS IN THE MAKING AND APPLICATION OF LAW (tentative ed. 1958).

More recent deliberative theories of the legislative process are RICHARD F. FENNO, CONGRESSMEN IN COMMITTEES (1973); STEVEN KELMAN, MAKING PUBLIC POLICY: A HOPEFUL VIEW OF AMERICAN GOVERNMENT (1987); JOHN W. KINGDON, AGENDAS, ALTERNATIVES, AND PUBLIC POLICIES (1984); ARTHUR MAASS, CONGRESS AND THE COMMON GOOD (1980).

53. KELMAN, *supra* note 52, at 261.

54. *See* ELMER E. SCHATTSCHNEIDER, POLITICS, PRESSURES AND THE TARIFF: A STUDY OF FREE PRIVATE ENTERPRISE IN PRESSURE POLITICS, AS SHOWN IN THE 1929-1930 REVISION OF THE TARIFF (1935).

55. *See* JAMES M. BUCHANAN & GORDON TULLOCK, THE CALCULUS OF CONSENT: LOGICAL FOUNDATIONS OF CONSTITUTIONAL DEMOCRACY (1962); ANTHONY DOWNS, AN ECONOMIC THEORY OF DEMOCRACY (1957); MORRIS P. FIORINA, CONGRESS: KEYSTONE OF THE WASHINGTON ESTABLISHMENT (1977); DAVID R. MAYHEW, CONGRESS: THE ELECTORAL CONNECTION (1974); WILLIAM A. NISKANEN, BUREAUCRACY AND REPRESENTATIVE GOVERNMENT (1971); MANCUR OLSON, THE LOGIC OF COLLECTIVE ACTION (1965); KENNETH A. SHEPSLE, THE GIANT JIGSAW PUZZLE (1978); Sam Peltzman, *Toward a More General Theory of Regulation*, 19 J.L. & ECON. 211 (1976); George J. Stigler, *The Theory of Economic Regulation*, 2 BELL J. ECON. & MGMT. SCI. 3 (1971).

More recent works of significance include BRUCE CAIN ET AL., THE PERSONAL VOTE: CONSTITUENCY SERVICE AND ELECTORAL INDEPENDENCE (1987); MICHAEL T. HAYES, LOBBYISTS AND LEGISLATORS: A THEORY OF THE POLITICAL PROCESS (1981); WILLIAM H. RIKER, LIBERALISM AGAINST POPULISM (1982); TOWARDS A THEORY OF THE RENT-SEEKING SOCIETY (James Buchanan et al. eds., 1980); *see also* DENNIS C. MUELLER, PUBLIC CHOICE II, at 307-47 (1989) (survey).

56. James M. Buchanan, *Politics Without Romance: A Sketch of Positive Public Choice Theory and Its Normative Implications*, *in* THE THEORY OF PUBLIC CHOICE II, at 11 (James M. Buchanan & Robert D. Tollison eds., 1984).

cynical—views. The distributive tradition views legislation as the distribution of benefits to well-organized interest groups, typically at the expense of (and not in pursuit of) the general welfare.[57] Legislation is, in this view, an economic transaction, in which groups "purchase" governmental benefits from legislators. On the demand side, wealthy established interests are best represented, while the interests of broad categories of the citizenry (consumers, the poor, etc.) are underrepresented.[58] On the supply side, distributive theory assumes that legislators "are single-minded seekers of reelection,"[59] a goal furthered by pandering to well-organized groups (who may provide money and support) at the expense of the general public (which is often ignorant of the costs it bears).[60] The bottom line, some distributive theorists declare, is too much legislation for the benefit of small, established groups, and too little legislation pursuing the more diffuse goal of the general welfare.[61]

Because it lends itself to an analysis that claims some predictive value, distributive theory has attracted the attention of many law professors.[62] But just as distributive theory has attracted increased attention, both political scientists and their counterparts in law have come to realize its limitations.[63]

---

57. In addition to the sources in *supra* note 55, see Gary S. Becker, *Public Policies, Pressure Groups, and Dead Weight Costs*, 28 J. PUB. ECON. 329 (1985) [hereinafter, Becker, *Pubic Policies*]; Gary S. Becker, *A Theory of Competition Among Pressure Groups for Political Influence*, 98 Q.J. ECON. 371 (1983).

58. *See* OLSON, *supra* note 55, as elaborated in MANCUR OLSON, THE RISE AND DECLINE OF NATIONS: ECONOMIC GROWTH, STAGFLATION, AND SOCIAL RIGIDITIES (1982); SCHATTSCHNEIDER, *supra* note 54, as elaborated in ELMER E. SCHATTSCHNEIDER, THE SEMI-SOVEREIGN PEOPLE 35 (1960) ("The flaw in the pluralist heaven is that the heavenly chorus sings with a strong upper-class accent . . . ."); *see also* John Ferejohn, *Congress and Redistribution, in* MAKING ECONOMIC POLICY IN CONGRESS 131 (Allen Schick, ed., 1983). The best empirical study of interest groups is more restrained in its pessimism. *See* KAY L. SCHLOZMAN & JOHN T. TIERNEY, ORGANIZED INTERESTS AND AMERICAN DEMOCRACY (1986).

59. FIORINA, *supra* note 55, agrees that legislators' motivations are more complicated but makes this simplifying assumption in order to work out his powerful analytical model; *see also* MAYHEW, *supra* note 55, at 5, 16-17 ("focus on the reelection goal" as most realistic perspective on legislative process).

60. *See generally* FIORINA, *supra* note 55; MAYHEW, *supra* note 55.

61. *See* HAYES, *supra* note 55; OLSON, *supra* note 55.

62. *See, e.g.*, Bruce Ackerman, *Beyond* Carolene Products, 98 HARV. L. REV. 713 (1985); Richard L. Doernberg & Fred S. McChesney, *On the Accelerating Rate & Decreasing Durability of Tax Reform*, 71 MINN. L. REV. 913 (1987); William N. Eskridge, Jr., *Politics Without Romance: Implications of Public Choice Theory for Statutory Interpretation*, 74 VA. L. REV. 275 (1988); Daniel A. Farber & Philip P. Frickey, *Is* Carolene Products *Dead? Reflections on Affirmative Action and the Dynamics of Civil Rights Legislation*, 79 CALIF. L. REV. 685 (1991); Jonathan R. Macey, *Promoting Public-Regarding Legislation Through Statutory Interpretation: An Interest Group Model*, 86 COLUM. L. REV. 223 (1986); Fred S. McChesney, *Regulation, Taxes, and Political Extortion, in* REGULATION AND THE REAGAN ERA: POLITICS, BUREAUCRACY, AND THE PUBLIC INTEREST 223 (Roger E. Meiners & Bruce Yandle eds., 1989); Richard A. Posner, *Economics, Politics, and the Reading of Statutes and the Constitution*, 49 U. CHI. L. REV. 263 (1982); Jonathan Turley, *Transnational Discrimination and the Economics of Extraterritorial Regulation*, 70 B.U. L. REV. 339 (1990).

63. *See, e.g.*, DANIEL A. FARBER & PHILIP P. FRICKEY, LAW AND PUBLIC CHOICE: A CRITICAL INTRODUCTION (1990); ROBERT A. KATZMANN, INSTITUTIONAL DISABILITY: THE SAGA OF TRANSPORTATION POLICY FOR THE DISABLED (1986); Herbert Hovenkamp, *Legislation, Well-Being, and Public Choice*, 57 U. CHI. L. REV. 63 (1990); Mark Kelman, *On Democracy-Bashing: A Skeptical Look at the Theoretical & "Empirical" Practice of the Public Choice Movement*, 74 VA. L. REV. 199 (1988); Jerry L. Mashaw, *The Economics of Politics and the Understanding of Public Law*, 65 CHI.-KENT L. REV. 123 (1989); Daniel Shaviro, *Beyond Public Choice and Public Interest: A Study of the Legislative Process as Illustrated by Tax Legislation in the 1980s*, 139 U. PA. L. REV. 1 (1990).

Empirical studies of the legislative process do not bear out many of the predictions of distributive theory. For instance, a raw distributive theory does not explain such important statutes as the Civil Rights Act of 1964,[64] the deregulation movement of the 1970's and 1980's,[65] the evolution of environmental statutes,[66] and even such public choice chestnuts as tariff and tax legislation.[67]

There is some truth in both the deliberative and the distributive theories. Distributive theories highlight the role that self-interested groups outside Congress play in affecting the legislative process, while deliberative theories remind us of the importance of the internal processes and the public accountability of legislators. Distributive and deliberative theories might be viewed as complementary, rather than competing. They also share a common problem. Both theories, as traditionally articulated, view "interest"—whether private (distributive) or public (deliberative)—as predefined and *exogenous* to the political process.[68] A more realistic view of the political process views interests (both of groups and of legislators) as *endogenous* to the political process, that is, as shaped by that process.[69]

To conceptualize the lawmaking process, this part draws upon this idea of endogenous interests and expands upon recent work on information theory.[70] Because information theory emphasizes the internal dynamics of Congress in the production of public policy, it is linked to the deliberative tradition. Information theorists argue that Congress is structured to deal with uncertainty about the effect of various policy choices on shared goals and objectives. Congress tries to resolve this uncertainty by delegating information-gathering and deliberating activities to subgroups. Once it is better informed about the consequences of various choices, Congress is better able to set policy. A particularly signifi-

---

64. *See* CHARLES WHALEN & BARBARA WHALEN, THE LONGEST DEBATE: A LEGISLATIVE HISTORY OF THE CIVIL RIGHTS ACT (1985).

65. *See* KINGDON, *supra* note 52.

66. *See* BRUCE ACKERMAN & WILLIAM T. HASSLER, CLEAN COAL/DIRTY AIR (1979); E. Donald Elliott et al., *Toward a Theory of Statutory Evolution: The Federalization of Environmental Law*, 1 J.L. ECON. & ORGANIZATION 313 (1985).

67. *See* RAYMOND A. BAUER ET AL., AMERICAN BUSINESS AND PUBLIC POLICY (1963) (discussing trade legislation); JEFFREY H. BIRNBAUM & ALAN S. MURRAY, SHOWDOWN AT GUCCI GULCH: LAWMAKERS, LOBBYISTS, AND THE UNLIKELY TRIUMPH OF TAX REFORM (1987).

68. *See generally* William N. Eskridge, Jr. & Gary Peller, *The New Public Law Movement: Moderation as a Postmodern Cultural Form*, 89 MICH. L. REV. 707, 747-50 (1991).

69. "Interest" here has three different meanings: (1) interest as a group's or legislator's ultimate goals and objectives; (2) interest as a group's or legislator's belief that a certain measure will contribute to those goals and objectives; and (3) interest as a group's or legislator's willingness to trade off some goals and objectives for others. All of these meanings are endogenous to the political process, although the first meaning is usually more stable over time than are the other two.

70. *See generally* KEITH KREHBIEL, INFORMATION AND LEGISLATIVE ORGANIZATION (1991); Thomas W. Gilligan & Keith Krehbiel, *Organization of Informative Committees by a Rational Legislature*, 34 AM. J. POL. SCI. 531 (1990); Thomas W. Gilligan & Keith Krehbiel, *Collective Choice Without Procedural Commitment*, *in* MODELS OF STRATEGIC CHOICE IN POLITICS 295 (Peter L. Ordeshook ed., 1989). For an interesting twist on the role of information in politics, see Michael A. Fitts, *Can Ignorance Be Bliss? Imperfect Information as a Positive Influence in Political Institutions*, 88 MICH. L. REV. 917 (1990).

cant intellectual contribution of information theory is its fluid definition of the public interest as the consensus that emerges at the end of the information-gathering and deliberating process.

This contribution of information theory provides a lesson for the distributive tradition. Heretofore, the distributive viewpoint has suggested that information is merely an expression of an interest group's position and has no independent role in the political process beyond posturing and manipulation. While information is manipulated in the political process, it does place limits on political discourse and contributes to a political dynamic that tangibly affects interest group activity. Like Congress, groups are uncertain about their interests and about how best to achieve them. Groups seek to reduce uncertainty by obtaining relevant information about the consequences of various policies. This information not only helps them to define their preferences, but also allows them to judge whether they can persuade others, perhaps because a particular policy is good for all, or many, sides. In turn, groups respond to, and are often transformed by, information generated by other groups and legislators.

The present study of congressional overrides offers an excellent opportunity to attempt to synthesize the distributive and deliberative traditions, using the insights suggested by information theory. The opportunity is possible because an override story is often a story over time, in which the power of information to influence the behavior of both groups and Congress is most readily apparent. Consider the following example, drawn from this study's collection of overrides.

The Immigration and Nationality Act of 1952 provided that "[a]liens afflicted with psychopathic personality, epilepsy, or a mental defect" were to be excluded from entry into the United States.[71] The exclusion was originally urged upon Congress by the Public Health Service (PHS) to prevent at least some gay men and lesbians from entering the United States. Reflecting then "modern" views within the medical community, the PHS considered homosexuality a disease, and urged that it be included as a medical basis for exclusion. Congress acquiesced to the PHS's "psychopathic personality" euphemism. No one objected to the provision, in part because the victims—gay men and lesbians—were afraid even to identify themselves, much less to organize politically to oppose such legislation. In *Boutilier v. INS*,[72] the Supreme Court interpreted "psychopathic personality" to mean "homosexuality," even though the medical consensus on this issue had significantly eroded and the excluded alien in the case was actually bisexual, not homosexual.[73] No effort was made to override *Boutilier* because no interest groups opposed the decision.

---

71. Immigration and Nationality Act of 1952, § 212(a)(4), 66 Stat. 163, 182 (repealed 1990).

72. 387 U.S. 118 (1967).

73. *See* William N. Eskridge, Jr., *Gadamer/Statutory Interpretation*, 90 COLUM. L. REV. 609, 654 (1990) (providing fuller analysis of this decision).

Much changed in the next decade. New circumstances transformed views on these issues. Especially after the Stonewall Riot in 1969, gay men and lesbians became politically active and sought to dismantle legal disabilities based upon sexual orientation. Through activism and the spread of information about the actual lives of homosexuals and the irrelevance of their sexual preference to their abilities and capacities, gay and lesbian groups in the 1970's persuaded the leading medical organizations to remove homosexuality from the category of disease.[74] This shift was the result of a major struggle within the psychiatric community, recognizing the cogency of long-neglected studies showing sexual preference to be unrelated to mental illness and rejecting the earlier medical consensus that homosexuality is an illness. Reflecting the outcome of this debate within the profession and an emerging literature rebutting earlier medical stereotypes about homosexuality, the PHS (an agency staffed by medical personnel) in 1979 abandoned its original position and announced that it no longer considered homosexuality a medically excludable condition and that homosexuality should no longer operate to exclude gay men and lesbians.[75] Unmoved, the Immigration and Naturalization Service (INS) publicly disagreed with the PHS in the early 1980's but carried on its own internal debate, which resulted in its substantial failure to enforce the exclusion.[76]

In the 1980's, liberal Democrats in Congress repeatedly introduced legislation to override *Boutilier*.[77] Abandoned by the medical community, the PHS, and even the INS (which must have found the exclusion ridiculous to administer), and under sharp attack from the then-organized gay and lesbian community, *Boutilier* no longer enjoyed much support. Efforts to override it gathered momentum in Congress in the late 1980's, as two Members of the House declared themselves to be openly gay, and public sympathy for gay men and lesbians was further spurred by the AIDS epidemic. *Boutilier* was finally overridden in 1990 by bipartisan agreement and without much fuss.[78]

This override story allows information theory to identify interconnections between the distributive and deliberative perspectives on legislation. As the distributive perspective suggests, Congress will generally not override Supreme Court statutory decisions unless a politically salient group presses for an override and unless other relevant groups, especially government officials and

---

74. RONALD BAYER, HOMOSEXUALITY AND AMERICAN PSYCHIATRY: THE POLITICS OF DIAGNOSIS 101-78 (1981).

75. Memorandum from Julius B. Richmond, Surgeon General and Assistant Secretary for Health, to Dr. William H. Foege, Director of the Center for Disease Control, and Dr. George I. Lythcott, Administrator of the HSA (Aug. 2, 1979) (on file with author).

76. The INS announced that it would exclude gay men and lesbians only if they made unsolicited declarations of sexual preference to an INS agent. 62 Interpreter Releases 166-67 (INS 1985).

77. *See, e.g.*, S. 2210, 96th Cong., 2d Sess. (1980) (sponsored by Sen. Cranston); H.R. 6303, 96th Cong., 2d Sess. (1980) (Rep. Beilenson and 28 cosponsors by May 20); H.R. 3524, 97th Cong., 1st Sess. (1981) (Rep. Dixon and 29 cosponsors by Oct. 28); S. 1086, 98th Cong., 1st Sess. (1983) (Sen. Cranston).

78. Immigration Act of 1990, Pub. L. No. 649, § 601, 104 Stat. 4978, 5067.

political party leaders, acquiesce in the override.[79] But, contrary to distributive theory as traditionally articulated, interests of relevant groups change over time in response to new information, new arguments, and new frameworks of thought.

In the 1950's and 1960's, the configuration of interests made an override of *Boutilier* inconceivable, but the later outpouring of pro-gay and lesbian information and theory after the Stonewall Riot transformed the relevant private interests. First, gay men and lesbians "came out" in greater numbers and made their interests politically salient. Second, leading professional groups revised their views about homosexuality in response to demands by the gay and lesbian community and to accumulated evidence inconsistent with the old views. Third, government officials changed their positions in response both to new information and to pressure brought upon them by the first two changes.

As the deliberative perspective suggests, Congress will generally not override a Supreme Court decision without painstaking deliberation over whether the decision undermines its policies and whether alternative approaches are desirable. This deliberation usually generates both House and Senate committee hearings. Hearings and informal contacts provide Congress with more information about the consequences of the Supreme Court's decisions and about the alternatives from which Congress might choose. The *Boutilier* issue was the subject of hearings throughout the 1980's, and the hearings reflected the waning appeal of the statutory precedent and the increasingly undesirable policy it represented. Deliberation over time transformed legislative views about what the "public interest" demanded.

Starting with this information-based synthesis of the distributive and deliberative features of politics, the remainder of this part will develop a model of congressional overrides, using *Boutilier* and other case examples from the study. The model is developed in three stages: first, an exploration of the importance of interest groups (broadly defined to include ideological and governmental groups); then, a discussion of the critical role of congressional committees; and, finally, the development of a formal model describing the dynamic interaction between the Supreme Court, Congress, and the President in statutory interpretation cases.

A. *The Importance of Interest Groups*

The central importance of interest groups best illustrates the distributive features of the legislative override process.[80] Interest groups are important

79. Recall the contrast at the end of Part I between Congress' reaction to *Gilbert* (a prompt override in response to pressure) and its nonreaction to *American Tobacco* (acquiescence because of interest group opposition).

80. The main sources for the discussion that follows are HAYES, *supra* note 55; OLSON, *supra* note 55; SCHATTSCHNEIDER, *supra* note 54; SCHLOZMAN & TIERNEY, *supra* note 58; Becker, *Public Policies*, *supra* note 57; *see also* FARBER & FRICKEY, *supra* note 63, at 21-37, for an excellent critical synthesis of

because they bring issues to the attention of Congress, and because they are capable of maintaining issues on the national agenda and blocking legislative initiatives. The distributive possibilities arise in part because interest groups form selectively. Not all potential "interests" form organized groups, and groups have varying arrays of resources and influence. Generally, groups are most likely to be politically salient (i.e., "organized") if they have: (1) a small, cohesive set of members; (2) significant resources or power; and/or (3) a preexisting organizational apparatus to unite them for purposes beyond lobbying and legislation.[81] If some interests are well organized and others are not, there is a risk that organized interests will reap a disproportionate share of government benefits.

Recent political science scholarship suggests that this account has some validity, but contains caveats reflecting the informational features of interest groups.[82] An important caveat is that "interest" needs to be understood as a complex phenomenon—not simply as wealth maximization. Instead, "interest" inevitably reflects an ideological component, an appeal to a group's concept of a good society. Many politically salient interest groups are primarily driven by ideology, including civil rights groups such as the ACLU and NAACP, environmental organizations, free enterprise study institutes, consumer welfare watchdogs, and even political parties.[83] Indeed, in the modern administrative state, the state and groups within the state (such as agencies) are interest groups, and the way in which they define their interests (literally, the "public interest") is intrinsically ideological.[84] Even traditional private economic interest groups go through ideological processes as they decide which issues to stress, allies to seek, and arguments to make. One reason for this process is that an interest group cannot obtain what it wants without persuading other actors—political parties, experts, and legislators and their staff—that it has good reasons supporting the desired legislation.

---

this literature.

81. *See* OLSON, *supra* note 55.

82. This discussion is based upon FARBER & FRICKEY, *supra* note 63, at 21-37; INTEREST GROUP POLITICS 1-69, 162-82 (Allan J. Cigler & Burdett A. Loomis eds., 2d ed. 1986); SCHLOZMAN & TIERNEY, *supra* note 58; Elliott et al., *supra* note 66, at 313; Joseph P. Kalt & Mark A. Zupan, *Capture and Ideology in the Economic Theory of Politics*, 74 AM. ECON. REV. 279 (1984); William H. Panning, *Formal Models of Legislative Processes*, *in* HANDBOOK OF LEGISLATIVE RESEARCH 669 (Gerhard Loewenberg et al. eds., 1985).

83. *See* JEFFREY M. BERRY, LOBBYING FOR THE PEOPLE: THE POLITICAL BEHAVIOR OF PUBLIC INTEREST GROUPS (1977); ANDREW S. MCFARLAND, PUBLIC INTEREST LOBBIES (1976); SCHLOZMAN & TIERNEY, *supra* note 58, at 28-35; Jeffrey M. Berry, *On the Origins of Public Interest Groups*, 10 J. POL. 392 (1978); Michael A. Fitts, *The Vices of Virtue: A Political Party Perspective on Civic Virtue Reforms of the Legislative Process*, 136 U. PA. L. REV. 1567 (1988); John M. Hansen, *The Political Economy of Group Membership*, 79 AM. POL. SCI. REV. 79 (1985); V. Kerry Smith, *A Theoretical Analysis of the "Green Lobby,"* 79 AM. POL. SCI. REV. 132 (1985); David Vogel, *The Public Interest Movement and the American Reform Tradition*, 95 POL. SCI. Q. 607 (1980).

84. *See* W.M. Crain & Robert E. McCormick, *Regulators as an Interest Group*, *in* THE THEORY OF PUBLIC CHOICE II, *supra* note 56, at 287.

The case studies and data in my survey of congressional overrides provide evidence supporting the following synthetic view of interest groups in the legislative process. First, interest groups form around shared perspectives, based upon both economic and ideological considerations, in different mixes for different groups. Groups are most likely to organize when they are small, cohesive, and sociopolitically privileged. Diffusion, heterogeneity, and political marginalization render groups less likely to become organized, but sometimes potentially more powerful if organized. Second, interest groups have goals, proposals, and priorities that are determined by both internal and external political processes. Hence, those goals, proposals, and priorities are subject to change as groups acquire new information and feedback from the political process. Third, interest groups cannot secure their distributive goals (benefits for themselves) without providing reliable information to other actors in the legislative process. On any given issue, several groups are potential competitors; to prevail, a group usually must persuade other groups to acquiesce, since intense interest group opposition is fatal to most initiatives. Thus, even an economically driven (traditional) interest group must provide persuasive information and arguments to more ideologically driven groups—including relevant agencies, political parties, the media, and experts—to assure either their neutrality or support.

1. *The Agenda-Setting Role of Interest Groups*

Interest groups regularly bring judicial decisions to the attention of Congress and are usually the impetus behind congressional focus on Supreme Court statutory decisions. If no organized interest is (or perceives itself to be) harmed by a recent Supreme Court decision, the decision will probably not provoke a congressional hearing, much less an override. It is for this reason that there were no congressional hearings on the *Boutilier* issue until gay men and lesbians became an organized political force, with important legislative allies, in the 1980's. While many observers criticized *Boutilier*,[85] the decision's validity did not command legislative deliberation until a newly salient group pressed its significance. Contrast the long congressional inattention to *Boutilier* with Congress' immediate attention to controversial civil rights decisions of the 1988 Term.[86] Those statutory cases moved immediately onto the legislative agenda because a rainbow of middle class civil rights groups, as well as the Democratic Party, considered them important.

This phenomenon helps explain why there are relatively few hearings and overrides to protect the interests of criminal defendants and suspects (see Tables

85. *See, e.g.*, Maurice Roberts, *Sex and the Immigration Laws*, 14 SAN DIEGO L. REV. 9 (1976-77); Thomas R. Byrne, Jr. & Francis M. Mulligan, Note, *"Psychopathic Personality" and "Sexual Deviation": Theoretical Terms or Legal Catch-Alls—Analysis of the Status of the Homosexual Alien*, 40 TEMPLE L.Q. 328 (1967).

86. *See supra* note 4.

7 and 9). The Supreme Court on average decides between three and seven statutory cases per Term involving the rules of habeas corpus for state and federal prisoners, substantive federal criminal law, and rules of federal criminal procedure. The cases won by state and federal governments, which leave criminal convictions intact, rarely generate even a judiciary committee hearing.[87] In contrast, cases lost by state and federal governments, which overturn convictions, readily command judiciary committee hearings and often lead to overrides.[88] In the period of this study, Congress overrode eighteen Supreme Court interpretations of federal criminal statutes;[89] fifteen of the eighteen overrode interpretations adverse to state and federal law enforcement.[90] The reason for this asymmetry is that state and federal law enforcement officials are powerful interests that can command congressional attention, while criminal defendants and suspects are more diffuse, marginalized, and less sympathetic groups.

Much the same story could be told for other relatively diffuse or marginalized groups. Supreme Court decisions hurting the economic interests of consumers, welfare and medicaid beneficiaries, alcoholics, migrant workers, inner-city youth, and the working poor rarely generate legislative interest. These groups are not well organized, and advocacy groups that might represent them tend to reflect an upper-middle-class bias and often lack sufficient resources to pursue many initiatives. In contrast, as suggested in Tables 7 and 9, organized groups are very effective in getting their statutory issues before Congress. The most successful groups are federal, state, and local governments; big

87. Exceptions to this generalization are issues that tend to affect businesses, such as civil RICO liability, *see Hearings, infra* note 103; well-to-do citizens, such as wiretapping; and organized groups, such as the gun lobby.

88. For example, the judiciary committee hearings on habeas corpus in my study (1979-88) focused in large part on cutting back the remedy. *See Habeas Corpus Reform: Hearings on S. 238 Before the Senate Comm. on the Judiciary*, 99th Cong., 1st Sess. (1985); *Comprehensive Crime Control Act of 1983: Hearings on S. 829 and H.R. 2151 Before the Subcomm. on Criminal Law of the Senate Comm. on the Judiciary*, 98th Cong., 1st Sess. (1983); *The Habeas Corpus Reform Act of 1982: Hearings on S. 2216 Before the Senate Comm. on the Judiciary*, 97th Cong., 2d Sess. (1982); *Habeas Corpus Procedures Amendments Act of 1981: Hearings on S. 653 Before the Subcomm. on Courts of the Senate Comm. on the Judiciary*, 97th Cong., 1st Sess. (1981).

89. *See infra* Appendix I for the overrides of Carpenter v. United States, 484 U.S. 19 (1987); McNally v. United States, 483 U.S. 350 (1987); California v. Cabazon Band of Mission Indians, 480 U.S. 202 (1987); United States v. Baggot, 463 U.S. 476 (1983); United States v. Sells Eng'g Inc., 463 U.S. 418 (1983); Dickerson v. New Banner Inst., Inc., 460 U.S. 103 (1983); Williams v. United States, 458 U.S. 279 (1982); Busic v. United States, 446 U.S. 398 (1980); United States v. New York Tel. Co., 434 U.S. 159 (1977); United States v. Park, 421 U.S. 658 (1975); United States v. Maze, 414 U.S. 395 (1974); United States v. United States Dist. Court, 407 U.S. 297 (1972); Alderman v. United States, 394 U.S. 165 (1969); United States v. Guest, 383 U.S. 745, 754-55 (1966) (adverse dictum); United States v. Seeger, 380 U.S. 163 (1965); Reilly v. Pinkus, 338 U.S. 269 (1949); Williams v. United States, 327 U.S. 711, 715 (1946) (dictum); Caminetti v. United States, 242 U.S. 470 (1917).

90. The three overrides protecting the rights of criminal defendants and suspects all involved issues of interest to mainstream, middle class America. See the overrides of United States v. New York Tel. Co., 434 U.S. 159 (1977), where the ACLU and allied groups procured legislation to protect against wiretap abuse, Dickerson v. New Banner Inst., Inc., 460 U.S. 103 (1983), in which the gun lobby prevailed, and Caminetti v. United States, 242 U.S. 470 (1917), in which Congress updated the Mann Act's prohibition to permit greater sexual liberties between consenting adults.

business (routinely represented by the Business Roundtable and the Chamber of Commerce); specific industries (represented by trade associations); unions (the AFL-CIO and individual unions); women (NOW and other groups); the disabled; and environmentalists (Sierra Club and others).

A group's ability to place an issue on the legislative agenda does not ensure that the group will do so. There are many reasons endogenous to the political process why a group might not press a statutory issue that it lost in court. For example, a group may not believe it can prevail on the issue and does not want to deplete valuable political capital or credibility by pressing frivolous positions. After losing an important issue of Title VII interpretation in *American Tobacco v. Patterson* in 1982, civil rights groups did not press for an override,[91] probably because they did not have the votes for an override that benefitted only African-American workers and/or because they did not want to expend political capital to seek relief for an issue that pitted their interests against those of labor unions, which were often political allies in civil rights battles in Congress. In contrast, civil rights groups did press for an override of *Wards Cove Baking Co. v. Atonio*[92] and other 1989 decisions cutting back on Title VII, for several reasons: the cumulative effect of those decisions was felt to be devastating to the overall enforcement of Title VII; the decisions hurt middle class women and minorities as well as working class minorities (the only victims of *American Tobacco*), hence offering opportunities for coalition-building; and there were excellent arguments that the Court was "setting back the clock" in civil rights by retreating from twenty years of more liberal interpretations of Title VII.

2. *Persistence of Issues on the Legislative Agenda*

Interest groups also provide the "push" to keep issues on the legislative agenda. This has both distributive and deliberative features. On the one hand, a determined interest group can press Congress to "stick with" an issue, and organized group activity is essential to keeping an issue on the legislative agenda over time. In the present study, there is not a single congressional override that did not have strong support outside of Congress. Moreover, almost all of the overrides had support from both private interest groups and government groups.

On the other hand, legislative deliberation over time gives the interest group an opportunity to build up a coalition supporting its policy proposal, to educate Congress about the issue and its proposal, and to persuade legislators that its position is justified. Thus, the persistence of the *Boutilier* issue in hearings throughout the 1980's reflected both the gay and lesbian community's com-

91. There were several Title VII oversight hearings during the year after *American Tobacco*, *see supra* note 50, yet no civil rights group even mentioned the case.

92. 490 U.S. 642 (1989).

mitment to obtaining a benefit for its members and its effort to demonstrate the irrationality of the antihomosexual policy. Similarly, the persistence of civil rights issues on the national agenda, culminating in the Civil Rights Act of 1991, was due in part to a coalition of African-American, women's, and labor groups.

Consider another example. The Supreme Court in *Stencel Aero Engineering Corp. v. United States*[93] held the United States immune from indemnity claims by government contractors sued in tort for defects in products they sold to the United States. Although this statutory decision is hardly one of the more important ones (in either doctrinal or policy terms) of the last several decades, it stimulated more House and Senate Judiciary Committee hearings than any other Supreme Court decision in the period studied. Indeed, there were hearings on the indemnity issue in every Congress from 1979 to 1988.[94] The hearing record suggests the evolution of this issue: Stencel was a big employer in the district of a Member of Congress who introduced the first override bill, presumably as a favor to an important business in his community.[95] That alone would have generated enough hearings for one or two Congresses, but probably not many more. The issue persisted on the legislative agenda, however, not only because it was being "pushed" by the industry trade group and the ABA's Public Contracts Section, but also because it raised an important policy problem: The proliferation of products liability lawsuits against government suppliers, who were prevented from impleading the United States due to the doctrine of sovereign immunity, financially threatened many such companies and raised doubts about their willingness to continue selling to the government. The contractors won the support of allied groups and legislators but met powerful

93. 431 U.S. 666 (1977).

94. For hearings on bills to override *Stencel* and the later, related case of Lockheed Aircraft Corp. v. United States, 460 U.S. 190 (1983), see *Federal Procurement Liability Reform Act of 1987: Hearing on H.R. 2378 Before the Subcomm. on Administrative Law and Governmental Relations of the House Comm. on the Judiciary*, 100th Cong., 1st Sess. (1987); *Fair Allocation of Governmental Fault Act: Hearing on H.R. 1623 Before the Subcomm. on Administrative Law and Governmental Operations of the House Comm. on the Judiciary*, 99th Cong., 1st Sess. (1985); *Indemnification of Government Contractors: Hearing on S. 1254 Before the Senate Comm. on the Judiciary*, 99th Cong., 1st Sess. (1985); *Government Contractors' Liability and Indemnification Act: Hearings on H.R. 4083 and H.R. 4199 Before the Subcomm. on Administrative Law and Governmental Relations of the House Comm. on the Judiciary*, 98th Cong., 2d Sess. (1984) [hereinafter 1984 *House* Stencel *Hearings*]; *Indemnification of Government Contractors: Hearings Before the Subcomm. on Administrative Practice and Procedure of the Senate Comm. on the Judiciary*, 98th Cong., 1st Sess. (1983). For exploratory hearings which occurred before a bill was proposed, see *Indemnification of Government Contractors: Hearings Before the Subcomm. on Agency Administration of the Senate Comm. on the Judiciary*, 97th Cong., 2d Sess. (1982). For older hearings on bills merely to override *Stencel*, see *Government Contractors Product Liability Act: Hearing on H.R. 1504 Before the Subcomm. on Administrative Law and Governmental Relations of the House Comm. on the Judiciary*, 97th Cong., 1st Sess. (1981) [hereinafter 1981 *House* Stencel *Hearings*]; *Government Contractors Product Liability Act: Hearings on H.R. 5351 Before the Subcomm. on Administrative Law and Governmental Relations of the House Comm. on the Judiciary*, 96th Cong., 2d Sess. (1980) [hereinafter 1980 *House* Stencel *Hearings*].

95. Representative Gudger of North Carolina introduced H.R. 5351, 96th Cong., 1st Sess. (1979), soon after the *Stencel* decision in 1977. He also introduced H.R. 5358, a private bill for relief to Stencel. *See* 1980 *House* Stencel *Hearings*, *supra* note 94 (reproducing both bills).

economic counterarguments from the Departments of Justice and Defense.[96] After ten years of deliberation on the issue, it was the Supreme Court, and not Congress, that bailed out the government contractors by giving them a federal "defense" that could be invoked in state law products liability actions.[97]

3. *Critical Nature of Interest Group Opposition*

Appendix II suggests that the vast majority of override issues that reach the legislative agenda do not result in legislation. Most Supreme Court decisions scrutinized by congressional hearings are in no danger of being overridden. Just as some interest groups bring issues onto the legislative agenda, other interest groups simultaneously try to ensure that no proposal is actually enacted. Congress is unlikely to pass legislation on an issue that produces a "conflictual" demand pattern, where important interest groups differ sharply over what should be done. Legislation is more likely, however, when a "consensual" demand pattern exists, that is, all the main groups acquiesce in the legislation.[98] Information theory, of course, suggests that demand patterns can change over time. If an originally conflictual demand pattern changes to a more consensual one (through compromise and/or new information), an override is much more likely.

Contrast the override efforts for *Boutilier* and *Stencel*. Bills to override the former had the support of groups with relatively little monetary or voting clout, but *Boutilier* was ultimately overridden in 1990 because no salient group supported the decision. This process required two decades of public education on the nature of homosexuality and on the numbers of individuals in our society who are homosexual. The demand pattern shifted on this issue. Conversely, despite impressive interest group support, *Stencel* was never overridden by Congress because the conflictual demand pattern persisted. The Departments of Defense and Justice and consumer groups opposed the legislation intensely and were never persuaded to support it.

Another example of this latter phenomenon is the legislative reaction to *Illinois Brick Co. v. Illinois*,[99] in which the Supreme Court held that "indirect purchasers" of a product had no standing to sue under the antitrust laws. Because it was perceived as retreating from vigorous enforcement of the antitrust laws and as denying important groups (such as the states) access to treble damage recoveries, *Illinois Brick* yielded a firestorm of protest and

---

96. For the best articulation of the suppliers' arguments, see *1981 House* Stencel *Hearings*, *supra* note 94. For the government's counter-arguments, see 1984 *House* Stencel *Hearings*, *supra* note 94.

97. *See* Boyle v. United Technologies Corp., 487 U.S. 500 (1988). The dissent noted that Congress had been debating that very issue for a decade and had afforded the contractors no relief. *Id.* at 515-16 & n.1 (Brennan, J., dissenting).

98. The above analysis is taken from HAYES, *supra* note 55, at 93-126. *See also* Michael T. Hayes, *The Semi-Sovereign Pressure Groups: A Critique of Current Theory and an Alternative Typology*, 40 J. POL. 134 (1978).

99. 431 U.S. 720 (1977).

generated a decade of congressional hearings.[100] Although the override effort had strong support from the Department of Justice, the states, consumers' groups, unions, and women's groups, it failed in large part due to the intense opposition of the Business Roundtable, the Chamber of Commerce, and other business groups. This opposition was effective, not because these interest groups were invincible (they were routed in the 1978 override of *Gilbert*, for example), but because their support for the *Illinois Brick* decision was backed by powerful data and economic analysis.[101]

The most important statutory interpretation issues of the last thirty years have produced the most conflict, with important interests and cogent arguments supporting both sides of the case. The Court's most dramatic policymaking decisions have remained untouched by Congress because interested groups are often intensely opposed and proffer powerful but contradictory analytical arguments on how to resolve such issues. This phenomenon is evident on issues such as affirmative action in employment, the home video and audio recording of copyrighted works,[102] the application of criminal racketeering laws to garden variety commercial disputes,[103] and contribution in antitrust cases.[104]

---

100. *See The Antitrust Improvements Act of 1986 (*Illinois Brick*): Hearing Before the Senate Comm. on the Judiciary*, 99th Cong., 2d Sess. (1986) [hereinafter *1986 Senate* Illinois Brick *Hearing*]; *Antitrust Fairness Amendments of 1983 and Oversight of Corporate Interlocks: Hearings Before the Subcomm. on Monopolies and Commercial Law of the House Comm. on the Judiciary*, 98th Cong., 2d Sess. (1984) [hereinafter *1984 House* Illinois Brick *Hearings*]; *Taxpayer Antitrust Enforcement Act of 1983 (*Illinois Brick*): Hearings on S. 915 Before the Senate Comm. on the Judiciary*, 98th Cong., 1st & 2d Sess. (1983-84); *Restoring Effective Enforcement of the Anti-Trust Laws: Hearings on H.R. 2050 Before the Subcomm. on Monopolies and Commercial Law of the House Comm. on the Judiciary*, 96th Cong., 1st Sess. (1979) [hereinafter 1979 *House* Illinois Brick *Hearings*]; *Antitrust Equal Enforcement Act of 1979: Hearings On S. 1468 Before the Subcomm. on Antitrust, Monopoly, and Business Rights of the Senate Comm. on the Judiciary*, 96th Cong., 1st Sess. (1979) [hereinafter *1979 Senate* Illinois Brick *Hearings*].

101. *See, e.g.*, 1979 *Senate* Illinois Brick *Hearings*, *supra* note 100, at 174-89 (statement of Professors Richard Posner and William Landes, arguing that override would retard vigorous antitrust enforcement).

102. Dozens of bills were introduced in anticipation of and in response to Sony Corp. of America v. Universal City Studios, Inc., 464 U.S. 417 (1984), in which the Court called upon Congress to enact responsive legislation, but the motion picture industry and other groups were able to head off override bills. *See, e.g.*, *Home Video Recording: Hearing Before the Senate Comm. on the Judiciary*, 99th Cong., 2d Sess. (1986); *Home Audio Recording Act: Hearings Before the Subcomm. on Patents, Copyrights and Trademarks of The Senate Comm. on the Judiciary*, 99th Cong., 1st & 2d Sess. (1985-86); *Video and Audio Home Taping: Hearing on S. 31 Before the Subcomm. on Patents, Copyrights, and Trademarks of the Senate Comm. on the Judiciary*, 98th Cong., 1st Sess. (1983); *Copyright Office/Copyright Royalty Tribunal: Hearing Before the Subcomm. on Courts, Civil Liberties, and the Administration of Justice of the House Comm. on the Judiciary*, 98th Cong., 1st Sess. (1983); *Home Recording of Copyrighted Works: Hearings Before the Subcomm. on Courts, Civil Liberties, and the Administration of Justice of the House Comm. on the Judiciary*, 97th Cong., 2d Sess. (1982); *Copyright Infringements (Audio and Video Recorders): Hearings on S. 1758 Before the Senate Comm. on the Judiciary*, 97th Cong., 1st & 2d Sess. (1981-82).

103. The Department of Justice and the National Association of Attorneys General, for example, opposed the business community's efforts to override Sedima, S.P.R.L. v. Imrex Co., Inc., 473 U.S. 479 (1985). *See, e.g.*, *RICO Reform: Hearings Before the Subcomm. on Criminal Justice of the House Comm. on the Judiciary*, 100th Cong., 1st & 2d Sess. (1987-88); *Proposed RICO Reform Legislation: Hearings on S. 1758 Before the Senate Comm. on the Judiciary*, 100th Cong., 1st Sess. (1987); *RICO Reform: Hearings Before the Subcomm. on Criminal Justice of the House Comm. on the Judiciary*, 99th Cong., 1st & 2d Sess. (1985-86); *Oversight on Civil RICO Suits: Hearings Before the Senate Comm. on the Judiciary*, 99th Cong., 1st Sess. (1985). Indeed, in the 99th Congress, overwhelming business support propelled the *Sedima* override through the House, 132 CONG. REC. H9377 (daily ed. Oct. 7, 1986), but the Department

In the last twenty-four years, there have been only a handful of overrides in which Congress acted against the strong opposition of an important interest group, and the overrides in those cases required a herculean effort.[105]

This same difficulty confronted the civil rights community's effort to override *Wards Cove*. Notwithstanding support from the Democratic Party, all of the leading civil rights groups, many unions, and consumer groups, the proposed Civil Rights Act of 1990 failed in the 101st Congress primarily because big business and the Republican Party were able to raise opposing policy concerns, such as the possibility of excessive damages and litigation and of employers' setting quotas for minority hiring. Essentially the same legislation became law in the 102d Congress because both big business (in early 1991) and the Republican White House (in October 1991) signaled their willingness to acquiesce in a massive override in return for damage caps and anti-quota reassurances in the legislation.

B. *The Critical Role of Committees*

The deliberative features of the legislative override process are at first blush most apparent in the critical role played by committees.[106] A difficulty inherent to the legislative process is that policy must be made under conditions of uncertainty. Is the "problem" identified by the groups petitioning Congress really an important social or economic problem not adequately handled by

---

of Justice stopped the bill on the floor of the Senate. 132 CONG. REC. S16,704 (daily ed. Oct. 16, 1986).

104. Although the leading business groups and the Department of Justice strongly favored overriding the Court's decision in Texas Industries, Inc. v. Radcliff Materials, Inc., 451 U.S. 630 (1981), and the Court's opinion itself called for a legislative response, the opposition of consumer groups and antitrust attorneys killed override efforts. *See, e.g.*, *The Antitrust Remedies Improvement Act and the Intellectual Property Reform Act of 1987: Hearings on S. 1407 and S. 635 Before the Subcomm. on Antitrust, Monopolies and Business Rights of the Senate Comm. on the Judiciary*, 100th Cong., 1st & 2d Sess. (1987-88); *Individual Treble Damage Liability: Hearing on S. 1300 Before the Senate Comm. on the Judiciary*, 99th Cong., 1st Sess. (1985); *Antitrust Damage Allocation: Hearings Before the Subcomm. on Monopolies and Commercial Law of the House Comm. on the Judiciary*, 97th Cong., 1st & 2d Sess. (1981-82); *The Antitrust Equal Enforcement Act: Hearings Before the Senate Comm. on the Judiciary*, 97th Cong., 1st & 2d Sess. (1981-82).

105. *See, e.g.*, the overrides reported in Appendix I for Grove City College v. Bell, 465 U.S. 555 (1984) (override intensely opposed by Department of Justice and unsuccessfully vetoed by President); NLRB v. Bildisco & Bildisco, 465 U.S. 513 (1984) (override intensely opposed by Business Roundtable and other business groups); City of Mobile v. Bolden, 446 U.S. 55 (1980) (override opposed by Department of Justice).

106. *See* JOSEPH COOPER, CONGRESS AND ITS COMMITTEES: A HISTORICAL APPROACH TO THE ROLE OF COMMITTEES IN THE LEGISLATIVE PROCESS (1988); *see also* JOSEPH COOPER, THE ORIGINS OF THE STANDING COMMITTEES AND THE DEVELOPMENT OF THE MODERN HOUSE (1970); RICHARD F. FENNO, JR., CONGRESSMEN IN COMMITTEES (1973); KREHBIEL, *supra* note 70; DAVID E. PRICE, WHO MAKES THE LAWS? CREATIVITY AND POWER IN SENATE COMMITTEES (1972); STEVEN SMITH & CHRISTOPHER J. DEERING, COMMITTEES IN CONGRESS (1984); Gilligan & Krehbiel, *supra* note 70; Thomas W. Gilligan & Keith Krehbiel, *Asymmetric Information & Legislative Rules with a Heterogeneous Committee*, 33 AM. J. POL. SCI. 459 (1989); Keith Krehbiel, *Are Congressional Committees Composed of Preference Outliers?*, 84 AM. POL. SCI. REV. 149 (1990); Keith Krehbiel, *Why Are Congressional Committees Powerful?*, 81 AM. POL. SCI. REV. 929 (1987); David E. Price, *Congressional Committees in the Policy Process*, *in* CONGRESS RECONSIDERED (Laurence C. Dodd & Bruce I. Oppenheimer eds., 3d ed. 1985).

existing laws and institutions? If so, what policy alternatives exist? What are the costs and benefits of each? Congressional practice had been to deal with this uncertainty through deliberation and information gathering. Congress early on realized that it could not make informed decisions on the many issues it faced if it confronted and debated all the issues on the floor. Hence, Congress established specialized committees to gather information about problems brought to the legislature, to identify alternative policies, and to make recommendations based upon deliberation of the different perspectives.

This traditional, deliberative understanding of the role of committees has been questioned from a distributive perspective.[107] These scholars argue that the committee selection process is skewed in favor of "preference outliers," that is, Members of Congress whose preferences do not reflect the chamber norm. Thus, if farm state legislators want to sit on the House Agriculture Committee, union supporters choose the House Education and Labor Committee, and military boosters opt for the House Armed Services Committee, all of those committees may consist of legislators whose preferences are much more pro-farmer, pro-union, and pro-military than the preferences of the chamber as a whole. Under this view, committees become means by which government benefits are distributed to interest groups. If the committee is stacked in favor of client groups, the chamber as a whole defers to the committee, and if the committee uses its "gatekeeping" power to set the legislative agenda on issues within its jurisdiction, then interest groups can use their influence to obtain more benefits than the chamber as a whole would desire. This leads to an effective "capture" of the legislative process, as well as of the committees, by the relevant groups.[108]

The distributive perspective reveals a fascinating feature of the committee process, one supported by anecdotal evidence. It is subject to both analytical and empirical doubt, however.[109] Why would a majoritarian chamber tolerate a committee selection process that yielded outlier committees? Why would the chamber defer to such a committee? Distributive theorists respond by emphasizing intensity of preferences. Each legislator is willing to tolerate nonmajoritarian decisions on issues not of great concern for her constituents (and her reelection) in return for satisfaction of her own outlier preferences on issues of great and

107. *See* SHEPSLE, *supra* note 55; Kenneth A. Shepsle & Barry R. Weingast, *The Institutional Foundations of Committee Power*, 81 AM. POL. SCI. REV. 85 (1987); *see also* Gilligan & Krehbiel, *supra* note 106; Barry R. Weingast & Mark J. Moran, *Bureaucratic Discretion or Congressional Control? Regulatory Policymaking by the Federal Trade Commission*, 91 J. POL. ECON. 765 (1983); Barry R. Weingast & William J. Marshall, *The Industrial Organization of Congress*, 96 J. POL. ECON. 132 (1988).

108. This is related to the "cozy triangle" literature on the capture of both relevant committees and agencies by regulated interests. *See generally* RANDALL B. RIPLEY & GRACE A. FRANKLIN, CONGRESS, THE BUREAUCRACY, AND PUBLIC POLICY 9-12, 55-66 (3d ed. 1984) (occasions and techniques for interaction between Congress and the bureaucracy).

109. The main skeptic is Keith Krehbiel, whose recent book criticizes the evidence developed in SHEPSLE, *supra* note 55, and presents an informational perspective on the committee process. KREHBIEL, *supra* note 70.

intense concern to her constituents.[110] Information theory suggests that this is not in fact what happens: Committees are not populated by preference outliers, and to the extent that outliers do gravitate to certain committees, they are typically met by outliers in precisely the opposite direction.[111] Information theory also suggests that committees do not tend to be "captured" by one set of interests, for otherwise Congress would have insufficient reason to rely on their judgments.

The data and case studies generated by this survey suggest a synthetic view of congressional committees. First, most committees are not dominated by preference outliers. Among the committees most relevant to statutory interpretation issues, the tax committees, banking committees, environmental policy committees, and committees in charge of admiralty law are not now, and probably have not traditionally been, dominated by preference outliers.[112] On some issues at some points in time, the judiciary committees have been preference outliers (left of the chamber median),[113] and the labor committees have been preference outliers for the entire period of this study (left of the chamber median).[114] Second, even if a committee consists of preference outliers on at least some issues, the committee is usually constrained by the preferences of the full chamber, which are not easily evaded. This constraint means that the committee will not normally report a bill that it believes will be defeated on

110. Weingast & Moran, *supra* note 107, at 771-72.

111. See KREHBIEL, *supra* note 70. For example, just as Democrats who strongly favor civil rights might desire to be on the Judiciary Committees to press the interests of an important constituency, Republicans who favor business interests might want to be on the same committees, for precisely the same reason. Both may be preference outliers, but they will tend to cancel out one another.

112. *See id.* at 129 tbl. 4.6 (deviations of various House committees from House median).

113. Krehbiel argues that for the period 1985-86, the House Judiciary Committee was not much of a preference outlier, though it was to the left of the House median. *Id.* His observation seems borne out by the Committee's performance on the Civil Rights Act of 1990. The Judiciary Committee voted for a favorable report on the bill by a 25 to 12 vote, *see* Transcript of Judiciary Committee Mark-Up (on file with author), which resembles the favorable vote of 272 to 154 in the House as a whole. *See* 136 CONG. REC. H6769 (daily ed. Aug. 3, 1990). At the beginning of this study, however, the House Judiciary Committee was a preference outlier (to the left of the chamber median) on civil rights issues. The Committee in 1969 was chaired by the liberal Emanuel Celler and consisted of 15 liberal Democrats, 5 liberal, Eastern Republicans, and 4 Midwestern Republicans who were liberal on civil rights, a total of 24 pro-civil rights votes, against five Southern Democrats (opposed to civil rights) and six conservative Republicans (neutral or reluctant). *See* 1969 CONG. Q. ALMANAC 66 (listing committee members); WHALEN & WHALEN, *supra* note 64. This was much more liberal than the House as a whole.

The Senate Judiciary Committee today may be at or near the chamber median. By my count, the 1990 Senate Judiciary Committee had average 1988 ADA scores (ratings given by Americans for Democratic Action for "liberal" decisions, with the most liberal rating equaling 100%) of 74% for its Democratic majority and 15% for its Republican minority, about the same as the chamber medians of 72% (Democrats) and 19% (Republicans). *See* ALMANAC OF AMERICAN POLITICS 1990. At the beginning of this study, the Senate Judiciary Committee, chaired by the conservative Senator Eastland and populated with a number of other Southern Democrats, was probably to the right of the Senate median.

114. KREHBIEL, *supra* note 70, at 128-29 tbl. 4.6 (finding 1985-86 House Education and Labor Committee significantly left of chamber median). By my count, the 1990 Senate Labor and Human Resources Committee had cumulative ADA scores of 88% support for its Democratic members and 26% for its Republican members, significantly to the left of the chamber medians of 72% (Democrats) and 19% (Republicans). *See* ALMANAC OF AMERICAN POLITICS 1990 (listing committee members and ADA scores).

the chamber floor. Hence, it will either report bills that it believes meet the chamber's preferences, or it will try to change those preferences through information and persuasion. Third, an outlying committee has some power to delay or kill proposals that the chamber would adopt. To be sure, committees occasionally report bills that they oppose in response to demand by the chamber, and the chamber can and will bypass a committee that is bottling up legislation. But most measures are not salient enough for the chamber even to know what its preferences are. Committees can delay or raise the costs of enacting legislation on salient issues and hence discourage legislation at the margin, while in some instances committees can exercise their strategic power (particularly during conference committee) to kill or dilute legislation they do not like.

This theory emphasizes three committee roles in congressional overrides: screening out most override proposals; providing a forum for developing override proposals that will satisfy the chamber median and avoid most interest group conflict; and serving as a policy center that generates arguments and information for shaping, and perhaps changing, the chamber's own initial preferences.

The primary role of congressional committees is to serve as devices to screen out the vast majority of policy proposals submitted to Congress. Committees will kill override legislation for three reasons. First, the committee can discourage an override proposal that the chamber might prefer (the outlier phenomenon). Although this is not nearly as regular an occurrence as distributive theory would suggest, it occasionally affects the prospects of override proposals. For example, the outlier phenomenon was probably the reason there was never a serious legislative effort to override *Griggs v. Duke Power Co.*,[115] in which the Supreme Court interpreted Title VII of the Civil Rights Act to permit disparate impact lawsuits. *Griggs* harmed big business, which saw itself faced with Title VII lawsuits simply for having "bad numbers," and in 1971-72 a majority in Congress probably did not agree with the sweeping reconceptualization of Title VII in *Griggs*.[116] However, the Labor Committees in both chambers were significantly to the left of their chamber medians and probably preferred *Griggs* to any bill their chambers would have passed. Hence, no committee-generated bill contained a *Griggs* provision, and both committees

115. 401 U.S. 424 (1971).

116. *See* HUGH D. GRAHAM, THE CIVIL RIGHTS ERA: ORIGINS AND DEVELOPMENT OF NATIONAL POLICY, 1960-1972 at 388-91 (1990). Note also that the House in 1971 voted to override judicial interpretations of 42 U.S.C. § 1981 (1988) which hurt the interests of private employers, and a majority of Senators on the floor were prepared to do the same in 1972. *See infra* text accompanying note 188. Essentially the same coalition would have opposed *Griggs*, which, if anything, was a more serious threat to employer interests.

inserted language in their reports for the 1972 amendments to Title VII that strongly approved of *Griggs*.[117]

Second, a much more common phenomenon is a committee's refusal to report an override that it likes but that it believes the chamber will reject. This was probably the case with the efforts to override *Illinois Brick*. Both the Senate and House Judiciary Committees favored an override of the decision in 1979-80, and the Senate Committee reported a bill, which died on the Senate Calendar. Although the Judiciary Committees in both chambers continued to hold hearings on *Illinois Brick* after 1980, the House Judiciary Committee, which strongly favored overriding the decision, never reported an override bill. The probable reason was that it saw virtually no chance for enactment, especially after the pro-business Republicans gained control of the Senate in 1981.[118] Conversely, the Senate Judiciary Committee during the period of Republican control (1981-87) often failed to report override bills that it believed would fail on the floor of the Senate or be killed in the Democratic-controlled House Judiciary Committee.[119]

A final reason a committee will kill an override proposal, especially one that it likes, is its judgment that the proposal is not "ripe" for the chamber's consideration. Committees and subcommittees see their role as building a record for the chamber's consideration of proposed legislation, informing the chamber of the various arguments and interest alignments, and working out a compromise or consensus on the issue. This explains the reluctance of a sympathetic subcommittee of the House Judiciary Committee to report a *Boutilier* override in the early- and mid-1980's. The subcommittee contented itself with building a record against the case without pressing for legislation favoring a controversial group (gay men and lesbians). Finally, the subcommittee acted in the 100th Congress and included the *Boutilier* override in a bill which generally rewrote the bases for exclusion. That bill got through Committee to the full House, which was unable (for agenda and time pressure reasons) to consider it.[120]

---

117. *See* H.R. REP. NO. 238, 92d Cong., 1st Sess. 21-22 (1971), *reprinted in* 1972 U.S.C.C.A.N. 2137, 2156-67; S. REP. NO. 415, 92d Cong., 1st Sess. 14 (1971).

118. Rep. Rodino (D-N.J.), Chair of the House Judiciary Committee, poignantly noted in the 1984 House hearings that he and his staff had worked on overriding *Illinois Brick* for eight years. 1984 *House* Illinois Brick *Hearings*, *supra* note 100, at 27. The hearings carry with them a sense of "just going through the motions," given the disinclination of Senator Hatch (R-Utah), the Chair of the Senate subcommittee, to permit a bill to get to the Senate. *See* 1986 *Senate* Illinois Brick *Hearings*, *supra* note 100, at 1.

119. *See, e.g.*, *The Habeas Corpus Reform Act of 1982: Hearing on S. 2216 Before the Senate Comm. on the Judiciary*, 97th Cong., 2d Sess. (1982) (habeas corpus reform bill, overriding Fay v. Noia, 372 U.S. 391 (1963) and other cases); *Affirmative Action and Equal Protection: Hearings Before the Subcomm. on the Constitution of the Senate Comm. on the Judiciary*, 97th Cong., 1st Sess. (1981) (override bill for United Steelworkers v. Weber, 443 U.S. 193 (1979), approving voluntary affirmative action under Title VII); *Municipal Liability Under 42 U.S.C. 1983: Hearings on S. 584, S. 585, and S. 990 Before the Subcomm. on the Constitution of the Senate Comm. on the Judiciary*, 97th Cong., 1st Sess. (1981) (override bill for various decisions imposing "excessive" § 1983 liability on municipalities).

120. The subcommittee held hearings on H.R. 1119 on June 23, 1987. *See Exclusion and Deportation of Aliens: Hearing on H.R. 1119 Before the Subcomm. on Immigration, Refugees and International Law of the House Comm. on the Judiciary*, 100th Cong., 1st Sess. (1987). It reported a clean bill, H.R. 4427,

The *Boutilier* override was then included, without much fuss, in the immigration reform law passed in the 101st Congress.

C. *A Model of the Court/Congress/President Interaction in Statutory Interpretation*

This Article's discussion of general theories of the legislative process, interest groups, and committees lays the foundation for a realistic and theoretically robust model of the interaction between the Supreme Court, Congress, and the President in statutory interpretation. The goal is to construct a model that has some predictive value but that also captures much of the complexity of the legislative process. Specifically, the model must incorporate the dynamic and interactive features of that process, such as the way in which different actors generate information to persuade other actors, while at the same time remaining sensitive to the different preferences of those actors.

For a number of years, positive political theory has been developing equilibrium models of the legislative process' response to agency and executive decisions,[121] but has only recently begun to model the interaction between the Court and Congress.[122] The latter is an area in which law professors may have something to add, because we have done more research in the areas of judicial incentives, preferences, and work product. This Article provides a convenient sample from which to build the outlines of a theory. It shall do so in three sections.

The first section outlines a theory of judicial preferences in statutory interpretation and uses the data from my empirical survey to suggest general relationships between those preferences and committee and legislative preferences in the 1980's and (probably) 1990's. The next section models the interaction between the Supreme Court, Congress, and the President as a sequential game, in which a Court interested in not being overridden can achieve that objective and usually still read its preferences into federal statutes. The last section relaxes that assumption and suggests situations in which the Supreme Court would rationally risk or even prefer statutory overrides of its decisions.

---

to the full Judiciary Committee, which reported the bill favorably to the House on August 12, 1988. H.R. REP. NO. 882, 100th Cong., 2d Sess. (1988).

121. *See* John A. Ferejohn & Charles Shipan, *Congressional Influence on Bureaucracy*, 6 J.L. ECON. & ORGANIZATION 1 (1991) (Special Issue); Steven Mathew, *Veto Threats: Rhetoric in a Bargaining Game*, 104 Q.J. ECON. 347 (1989); Terry Moe, *An Assessment of the Positive Theory of "Congressional Dominance" of Bureaucracy*, 12 LEGIS. STUD. Q. 475 (1987); Weingast & Moran, *supra* note 107.

122. *See* John Ferejohn & Barry R. Weingast, Limitation of Statutes: A Strategic Theory of Interpretation (paper presented at the Conference on Constitutional Law & Economics, Stanford University) (Oct. 25-27, 1990) (on file with author); Brian A. Marks, A Model of Judicial Influence on Congressional Policy-making: *Grove City College v. Bell (1984)* (1989 unpublished Ph.D. dissertation, Washington University) (on file with author).

1. *Supreme Court Preferences in Statutory Interpretation*

What the Supreme Court is trying to do in statutory interpretation has long been a subject of intense controversy, but an emerging academic consensus indicates that statutory interpretation is not dominated by any single approach.[123] The existing literature strongly suggests, for example, that the Court rarely just implements some preexisting "original legislative intent" when it interprets statutes. On the other hand, there is little current academic support for the proposition that the Court simply interprets statutes to implement the Court's own view of what is the best policy. In other words, when interpreting statutes, the Court behaves neither like the traditional vision of a court, nor like the traditional vision of a legislature.

These academic insights are borne out by the Supreme Court's statutory decisions surveyed in this Article, especially those in the survey of decisions from the 1977 through 1983 Terms (Tables 3, 8, and 9). The more than 200 statutory decisions analyzed from that period followed different interpretive methods from case to case. While the Justices emphasized textual plain meaning in some cases, they emphasized legislative history or statutory precedents in others (see Table 5). Indeed, it is often difficult to characterize the approach emphasized in individual decisions, because the Court usually analyzes and relies upon a variety of factors before arriving at a decision.[124]

Notwithstanding the Court's eclectic approach, it is still possible to make some generalizations. This survey, informed by prior scholarship, found that the Supreme Court's interpretation of statutes reflects three different preferences. The first is a preference for implementing the plain meaning of the statutory text (if there is one).[125] Applying the apparent meaning of the text furthers important rule of law values, such as predictability, certainty, and objectivity. The preference for plain meaning is most important for recent and detailed statutes, since they are most likely to have a plain meaning that reflects the preferences of the legislature and sound policy.

The second judicial preference is coherence. The Supreme Court sees itself as preserving, to the extent possible, law's coherence. A reading of the text that

123. Eskridge & Frickey, *supra* note 38; Daniel A. Farber, *Statutory Interpretation and Legislative Supremacy*, 78 GEO. L.J. 281 (1989); William D. Popkin, *The Collaborative Model of Statutory Interpretation*, 61 S. CAL. L. REV. 543 (1988); Richard A. Posner, *The Jurisprudence of Skepticism*, 86 MICH. L. REV. 827 (1988); Cass R. Sunstein, *Interpreting Statutes in the Regulatory State*, 103 HARV. L. REV. 405 (1989); Nicholas S. Zeppos, *Judicial Candor and Statutory Interpretation*, 78 GEO. L.J. 353 (1989).

124. For a detailed elaboration of this point, see Eskridge & Frickey, *supra* note 38, at 345-62.

125. "Our task is to give effect to the will of Congress, and where its will has been expressed in reasonably plain terms, 'that language must ordinarily be regarded as conclusive.'" Griffin v. Oceanic Contractors, Inc., 458 U.S. 564, 570 (1982) (quoting Consumer Prod. Safety Comm'n v. GTE Sylvania, Inc., 447 U.S. 102, 108 (1980)). For other leading, and influential, expressions of this preference, see Pierce v. Underwood, 487 U.S. 552 (1988); TVA v. Hill, 437 U.S. 153, 173, 195 (1978) (holding that plain language of Endangered Species Act requires court to enjoin completion of a federal dam); United States v. American Trucking Ass'ns, 310 U.S. 534, 543 (1940); Caminetti v. United States, 242 U.S. 470, 490 (1917). *See generally* William N. Eskridge, Jr., *The New Textualism*, 37 UCLA L. REV. 621 (1990).

is coherent with other legal authorities is better than an equally plausible textual reading that is incoherent.[126] It is useful to distinguish between horizontal and vertical coherence, both of which are valued by the Court, but which are often in tension.[127] A reading of the text is horizontally coherent if it makes the best sense of the statute as a whole, is consistent with interpretations of similar statutory provisions, and fits with current judicial and legislative policy presumptions. A reading of the text is vertically coherent if it is consistent with the statute's legislative history, its original design and purpose, and prior judicial interpretations of the text. The Court desires horizontal coherence because it makes current statutory law fit together into a seamless web of law and because it believes citizens will understand and accept such law better than checkerboard law.[128] The Court desires vertical coherence because it suggests a rooted tradition from which the Court declares law and because citizens rely on the prior authorities in making decisions.[129]

The third judicial preference is policy based. The Justices bring to the interpretive task ideological frameworks and policy preferences that inevitably influence the choices made.[130] For example, the Court has strong institutional preferences to avoid decisions and rules that it believes itself incompetent to make or believes will overburden the courts operating under scarce resources. Additionally, the Court will implement canons of statutory interpretation that reflect traditional policy preferences. Canons such as the rule of lenity in criminal cases, presumptions against exemption from antitrust and tax laws, and clear statement rules protecting against unannounced waivers of sovereign immunity are particularly important in statutory interpretation.[131] Finally, in difficult cases (ambiguous statutory text, unhelpful legislative history), the political ideology of the particular Justices makes a difference in their statutory interpretations. Ideology seems to have the most influence in cases dealing with politically charged topics, such as discrimination and military and foreign affairs.

It is instructive to compare the Court's apparent preferences with those of Congress and its committees through analysis of the main areas of override activity in the last twelve Congresses. The Supreme Court in this period has

126. For an extended discussion of this point, see RONALD DWORKIN, LAW'S EMPIRE (1986).

127. *See* William N. Eskridge, Jr., *Interpreting Legislative Inaction*, 87 MICH. L. REV. 67, 116 (1988).

128. *See, e.g.*, United States v. Fausto, 484 U.S. 439 (1988) (inferring congressional abrogation of policy in a related statute, over dissent's reliance on continuity with past policy).

129. This is the policy behind the super-strong presumption against overruling statutory precedents. *See, e.g.*, Johnson v. Transportation Agency, 480 U.S. 616, 647-49 (1987) (O'Connor, J., concurring in judgment). It also underlies the Court's various legislative inaction doctrines. *See, e.g.*, Monessen Southwestern Ry. v. Morgan, 486 U.S. 330 (1988).

130. *See* HANS-GEORG GADAMER, TRUTH AND METHOD (Joel Weinsheimer & Donald Marshall trans., 2d rev. ed. 1989), *analyzed in* GEORGIA WARNKE, GADAMER: HERMENEUTICS, TRADITION AND REASON (1987). *See generally* INTERPRETING LAW AND LITERATURE: A HERMENEUTIC READER (Sanford Levinson & Scott Mailloux eds., 1989); *Interpretation Symposium*, 58 S. CAL. L. REV. 1 (1985).

131. These and other canons are discussed in William N. Eskridge, Jr., *Public Values in Statutory Interpretation*, 137 U. PA. L. REV. 1007 (1989), and Sunstein, *supra* note 123.

preferred plain textual meanings, has followed statutory precedents and legislative history unless strongly contradicted, and has been influenced by its concern with a constantly rising caseload, the policies embodied in the canons, and its own conservative ideology. The analysis in this part suggests that Congress and its committees would prefer interpretations that reflected their own political preferences, which are strongly influenced by the Members' own ideological frameworks, their perceptions of constituent preferences, and the pressure and information provided by salient groups, including government groups.

This analysis and the data in Appendix I and Table 4, provides a basis for comparing the preferences of the Court and Congress (during 1967-90) for some of the main policy areas subject to legislative overrides. On the conventional liberal/conservative scale, the Court for most of the period of this study has been more conservative than Congress and its committees on issues involving civil rights, environmental law, federal jurisdiction and procedure, and intergovernmental relations. The Court's relative conservatism in civil rights cases can be attributed to the difficulty of applying old statutes and legislative history to unanticipated problems and to the Court's own strongly conservative preferences about civil rights policy.[132] In contrast, Congress' Democratic majorities have been committed to liberal civil rights enforcement and have been responsive to leading civil rights groups. Similarly, the Democratic Congress is more responsive to environmentalist interest groups than the Court has been. The Court's conservatism in jurisdiction and procedure is mainly due to its institutional policy of interpreting judicial power very conservatively and to its current concerns about excessive caseloads. Congress is not encumbered by these policy limitations and has incentives to provide relevant interest groups greater access to the courts.[133] In cases involving state-federal relations, the Court is strongly influenced by its longstanding commitment to federalism,[134] while Congress is more evenly balanced between its concern for state and local governments and its desire to grant rights and remedies to civil rights, and other, groups.[135]

---

132. Generalizations about the preexisting ideology of the Justices are risky. How can we know what they "really" think, when they only claim to say what Congress thinks? Nonetheless, the conventional wisdom among the legal community holds that the Court's preferences on civil rights have moved steadily to the right after 1971. That wisdom receives empirical support from a study of newspaper editorials at the time of Supreme Court appointments. Jeffrey A. Segal & Albert D. Cover, *Ideological Values and the Votes of U.S. Supreme Court Justices*, 83 AM. POL. SCI. REV. 557 (1989). Confirming evidence can be found in the Court's drift to the right in constitutional civil rights cases.

133. *See, e.g.*, Finley v. United States, 490 U.S. 545 (1989) (expressing institutional reluctance to read federal jurisdiction broadly). Congress promptly overrode *Finley* in the Judicial Improvements Act of 1990, Pub. L. No. 650, § 310, 104 Stat. 5089, 5113-14.

134. *See* Gregory v. Ashcroft, 111 S. Ct. 2395, 2400-01 (1991) (creating "clear statement" rule which creates strong presumption against congressional regulation of core state government functions and officials, such as state judges).

135. This contrast shows up clearly in federal cases finding no congressional abrogation of state Eleventh Amendment immunity, and in their prompt overrides by Congress. *See infra* Appendix I (overrides for Dellmuth v. Muth, 491 U.S. 223 (1989); Atascadero State Hosp. v. Scanlon, 473 U.S. 234 (1985); BV Eng'g v. UCLA, 858 F.2d 1394 (9th Cir. 1988), *cert. denied*, 489 U.S. 1090 (1989)).

Perhaps surprisingly, the Court during this period, on the whole, has been to the left of Congress on issues of substantive criminal law, income tax, and antitrust law. In criminal law, the rule of lenity often impels the Court to demand greater precision from elderly criminal statutes,[136] which Congress, pressured by the Department of Justice, is often willing to provide. Although criminal defendants are not usually represented by well-organized interest groups, tax and antitrust defendants frequently are. This helps explain why the Court is more liberal in those areas: Congress is more immediately responsive than the Court to well-heeled taxpayers and corporate antitrust defendants. And, in each of those areas, the Court, guided by canons against exceptions to tax collection and antitrust policy, has tended to interpret broadly phrased tax and antitrust statutes expansively.[137]

For the period of this study, other statutory areas did not yield predictable divisions between the Court and Congress, for a variety of apparent reasons: There were too few overrides from which to generalize (immigration law, freedom of information law, banking, and traditional labor law). Interest group activity in both the Court and Congress was similarly balanced (bankruptcy law; copyright, trademark, and patent law). The Court's traditions and personal ideologies did not cut strongly in any one direction (bankruptcy law). Moreover, the generalizations made above were and are subject to change over time. For example, in civil rights law, the Court was more liberal than Congress for the early years of this study (1967-71), then shifted right as Congress shifted left (1970's), and has moved even further to the right of Congress in the 1980's.[138]

Notwithstanding these limitations and caveats, what is most striking about this analysis is that one should *expect* Congress and the Supreme Court to have different preferences for statutory interpretation in the large majority of cases. The Court is responsive to the plain meaning and legislative history of statutes even when they are quite old, while Congress is more interested in its own current, rather than historical, preferences. The Court is more concerned about the interconnections in, and overall coherence of, the United States Code than is Congress. The Court's traditions (the canons), institutional concerns, and personal ideological assumptions are significantly different from the interest group pressures on and ideology of Congress. During the period of divided

---

136. *See* United States v. Kozminski, 487 U.S. 931 (1988); McNally v. United States, 483 U.S. 350 (1987); United States v. Campos-Serrano, 404 U.S. 293, 297 (1971) (rule of lenity); *see also* Appendix I (override of *McNally*).

137. *See, e.g.*, National Gerimedical Hosp. & Gerontology Ctr. v. Blue Cross, 452 U.S. 378, 388-89 (1981); Group Life & Health Ins. Co. v. Royal Drug Co., 440 U.S. 205, 231 (1979); United States v. National Ass'n of Sec. Dealers, Inc., 422 U.S. 694, 719-20 (1975); Gordon v. New York Stock Exch., 422 U.S. 659, 682 (1975); United States v. Philadelphia Nat'l Bank, 374 U.S. 321, 348 (1963) (disfavored status of implied antitrust immunities); *see also* United States v. Wells Fargo Bank, 485 U.S. 351 (1988); Oklahoma Tax Comm'n v. United States, 319 U.S. 598, 606 (1943) (disfavored status of implied tax exemptions).

138. *See infra* text accompanying notes 181-209.

government that this country has had since 1969, the ideological differences between the Court and Congress are particularly striking.

If it is true that Congress and the Court often differ markedly in their preferences for the best interpretation of a statute, and if it is further true that interest groups bring about half of the Court's statutory interpretation decisions to the attention of committees generally responsive to Congress' current preferences, then one might have expected many more overrides than have actually occurred in the last twenty-four years. Rather than overriding about five percent of the Court's statutory decisions each year in the 1980's, Congress might have been expected to override several times that number. But that did not happen. For example, in the 101st Congress (1989-90), the Court's habeas corpus decisions, its controversial endorsement of the "bubble concept" in environmental law, and its conservative civil rights decisions were all subject to serious but unsuccessful override attempts.[139]

Why does Congress not override more of the Supreme Court's statutory decisions?[140] The most obvious reason suggested by this study[141] is the existence of conflictual demand patterns. Many Supreme Court statutory decisions involve big stakes and sharply clashing interests. While the losers often have enough clout to bring decisions to the congressional agenda, the winners are also likely to have some influence. In such cases, unless the losers at the Supreme Court level can persuade other groups to be supportive or neutral, their chances of overturning a Supreme Court decision are not promising. This explanation squares with the data generated by the current survey. The Supreme Court's most controversial statutory decisions are usually not overridden because there are strong interest group alignments on both sides of the issues, leaving the Court's decisions firmly intact. The congressional overrides listed in Appendix I tend to involve Supreme Court cases in which the winning interests were not powerful at the time of the override—because the interests are diffuse or outside the political process (decisions benefiting accused criminals) or because the substantive position was weak (*Gilbert*) or had lost force over time (*Boutilier*).

2. *Statutory Interpretation as a Sequential Political Game*

The explanation just posited for the relative dearth of overrides is a troubling one in a representative democracy, for it suggests that the Court is often

139. *See supra* note 4 (describing these failed override attempts).

140. One traditional reason given for Congress' failure to override Supreme Court decisions is that it is "unaware" of them. That is rendered most unlikely by this study's finding that a substantial percentage of the Court's decisions are subjected to committee scrutiny. *See* Table 3. A more plausible reason is that the legislative agenda is not infinitely elastic, and Congress simply does not have the time and resources to override every statutory decision with which it disagrees. This reason, however, fails to account for Congress' tendency to override the less important Supreme Court decisions.

141. Or, more precisely, by Dan Farber in his comments on an earlier draft of this Article.

able to read its preferences into statutes, against the desires of our nationally elected officials. There is, however, another (perhaps complementary) explanation for the Court's ability to avoid congressional overrides, at least in the short term:[142] The Court is attentive to current congressional (and, as will also be shown, presidential) preferences when it interprets statutes.

To explore this hypothesis, think about statutory interpretation as a sequential political game. The game is played across a linear space—here, the possible interpretations of an existing statute—in which a policy position to the right reflects conservative preferences and one to the left reflects liberal preferences. The Supreme Court makes the first move in the game by choosing a point on the policy line (*J*) which represents the Court's preferences as to the best way to interpret the statute. Once the Court has made the first move, the loser(s) in the case will bring the issue to the attention of the relevant congressional committees, which have a "raw" (preexisting) preference about where the policy should be (*C*). If the committees agree with the Court's position ($J = C$), the game ends.[143] If the committees disagree with the Court, they may continue the game by reporting an override bill to their full chambers. The chambers make the next move, reflecting the raw preferences of the median Member (*M*). Thus, Congress may amend the override bill as it likes, in order to bring it into line with its own preferences.[144] The final move is made by the President (*P*), who can veto an override bill if he or she prefers the Court's policy to that of Congress. The presidential veto is, of course, subject to Congress' ability to override the veto by a two-thirds vote in each chamber.

As thus outlined, each player in the game (Court, committees, Congress, President) naively follows its own preexisting preferences about good policy. But the game as actually played is more complicated, as a matter of both strategy and information. The strategic complication arises because a player usually wants the ultimate statutory policy to reflect its own preferences as much as possible in accordance with the rules of the game. Hence, a committee may disagree with the Court's statutory interpretation but still may fail to report an override bill if it would dislike the policy adopted by the full Congress even more. Stated more formally, the committee will have an "indifference point" (*C*(*M*)) where the Court can set policy which the committee likes no more and no less than the opposite policy that would be chosen by the full chamber. The Court itself may strategically compromise its original preferences in order to

142. More than 25% of congressional overrides are for Supreme Court decisions over 10 years old (see Table 1).

143. Here assume that the committee whose jurisdiction covers the Supreme Court's decision has "gatekeeping" power; if it does not report override legislation, Congress has nothing to consider. Also assume that once the gatekeeping committee introduces override legislation, it cannot prevent its chamber from amending it to reflect the chamber's preferences. These are traditional positive political assumptions and are the basis for the works, cited in *supra* notes 121-22, which have most influenced this game theory.

144. This reflects the assumption that the override bill will be considered on at least a partially open-rule basis in Congress, which seems to have been the case during the period of this study. Again, political scientists using such a model, *see* sources in *supra* notes 121-22, make this assumption.

avoid a congressional override, for example, by accommodating the preferences of the President or committees when those players are in a position to protect the Court.

The informational complication arises because each player has some uncertainty about its "raw" (pregame) preferences about statutory policy, and because one object of the game is to gather information that will help resolve its uncertainty about appropriate policy under the statute. Hence, a committee's initial reaction to a Supreme Court statutory interpretation may be skeptical, but after hearings and further information gathering, the committee may decide that the interpretation is defensible or not worth overriding. Under this theory, the Court's ultimate preferences about statutory policy might be influenced by contemporary congressional deliberation and information gathering on the issue.

The above discussion sets forth the broad contours of the "Court/Congress/President Game."[145] Now consider the operation of this sequential game under variations of the players' preferences in concrete policy settings—criminal, tax, and antitrust law, where congressional preferences tend to be more conservative than judicial preferences; jurisdiction and procedure and intergovernmental relations, where congressional preferences have tended to be more liberal than judicial preferences; and civil rights law, where congressional preferences shifted over time from more conservative to more liberal than judicial preferences. Although the discussion is organized around the relative preferences of Congress and the Court, which tend to change fairly slowly and deliberately over time, the preferences of the President, which change more dramatically, are often important in the playing of the game.

a. *The Court/Congress/President Game in Criminal, Tax & Antitrust Law*

Because the Court is influenced by liberal rules of interpretation of criminal, tax, and antitrust statutes, and Congress is more susceptible to conservative interest group pressure (from the Department of Justice, state attorneys general, and private groups), the Court tends to be more liberal than Congress. The judiciary committees during the period of this study tended to be more liberal than their chambers, but not necessarily as liberal as the Court on these issues. Figure 1 maps the relevant preference relationships:

Liberal ________________________________ Conservative
Policy $C(M)$ J C M P Policy

Figure 1. Raw Preferences, $C(M) < J < C < M < P$
Equilibrium Result, $x = J$

145. *See* William N. Eskridge, Jr., *Reneging on History: Playing the Court/Congress/President Civil Rights Game*, 79 CAL. L. REV. 613 (1991) (outlining game in civil rights context).

Because of the Court's willingness to apply the role of lenity against the government when it construes criminal statutes, the Court's preferences, *J*, are usually more liberal than those of the median legislator, *M*. The judiciary committees have raw preferences, *C*, a little to the left of their chamber medians on such issues, but do not tend to be complete outliers.[146] As the nation's chief executive officer, the President, *P*, tends to be more conservative than Congress ($P > M$).

Given the preference configuration in Figure 1, the Court could interpret the statute to reflect its own raw preferences and not be overridden, even though its preferences are somewhat to the left of those of the chamber ($J < M$). This will be the case so long as the Court's preferences are at or to the right of the committee's indifference point, ($C(M)$), that is, the point at which the committee is perfectly indifferent between that point and the chamber median, *M*. In that event, the committee has no incentive to report an override bill, since such a bill could be amended to reflect the median Member's preference, *M*, which the committee may find more distasteful than the Court's policy preference, *J*. So the committee would do nothing, and the Court's preference would be left in place.

This result—no bill for the chamber to consider—endures so long as the Court's preferences are at or to the right of the committee's indifference point, $C(M)$. Thus, so long as $C(M) \leq J$, the Court can simply implement its own preferences and not be overridden. The game changes if the Court's preferences are to the left of the committee's indifference point ($J < C(M)$), as diagrammed in Figure 2:

Liberal Policy	J	$C(M)$	C	M	P	Conservative Policy

Figure 2. Raw Preferences, $J < C(M) < C < M < P$
Equilibrium Result, $J \leq x \leq C(M)$

If the Court implements its preferences, it will trigger an override bill from the committee and probable enactment of the chamber's preferences, *M*. The Court can try to avoid this result by either shifting its own preferences far enough to the right so that the committee will not want to override its interpretation ($x = C(M)$, *J* shifting right), or by trying to persuade the committee to adjust its own preferences to the left by providing it with useful information about the statute ($x = J$, with $C(M)$, *C* shifting left).

146. *See* KREHBIEL, *supra* note 70, at 129 tbl. 4.6.

Note that the figures in the text will simplify Congress into a single chamber, consistent with the political science literature cited in notes 121-22 *supra*.

An example of the phenomenon described in Figure 2 is *United States v. Kozminski*,[147] which interpreted the criminal code's prohibition against "involuntary servitude" to overturn a conviction when much of the evidence of servitude pointed toward psychological pressure rather than physical threats or coercion. The Court's opinion, probably very much to the left of (more protective of criminal defendants than) the probable congressional or committee preferences, reflected traditional judicial preferences in criminal law cases, including attention to the statute's plain meaning, probable original expectations (it was a nineteenth-century statute), and the rule of lenity. But the Court was quick to observe (in dicta) that on retrial the victims' psychological vulnerability would be relevant to the more "overt" coercion allegedly used by the defendants. The Court's apparent willingness to bend its preferences to reflect modern evidence may have been strategic or may have been a genuine effort to accommodate current legislative preferences. In either case, it reflects the fluidity of the Court's preferences, in response to current legislative preferences, on issues of substantive criminal law. Although the Court's opinion was very probably more liberal than were the raw preferences of Congress on this issue, its open accommodation of such views was enough to discourage an override effort.

Note that under the conditions of Figures 1 and 2, the President is not an important player, because he will sign any bill Congress would pass ($P > M > J$). This characterizes the Presidency's position on most issues of criminal and antitrust law for most of this period—but not during the Carter Administration (1977-81), when presidential preferences shifted to the left. Figure 3 reflects the new alignment on at least some criminal law and antitrust issues:

Liberal Policy ——— V J (with P beneath) $C(M)$ C M ——— Conservative Policy

Figure 3. Raw Preferences, $V < J$, $P < C(M) < C < M$
Equilibrium Result, $x = J = P$

When the President is aligned with the Court, as in Figure 3, a new point becomes relevant—the "veto median" (V), namely, that point in each chamber for which one-third of the legislators are on one side, and two-thirds on the other. Under the game mapped by the raw preferences in Figure 3, the Court could implement its own preferences without fear of an override. Even though the Court's preferences are more liberal than those of the committee's indifference point ($J < C(M)$), the committee will not introduce override legislation: The committee knows that the chamber will not act to pass a bill the President

147. 487 U.S. 931 (1988).

will veto unless the chamber can override the veto. And the committee knows that more than a third of the chamber prefers the Court's interpretation to any interpretation the committee and the chamber prefer ($V < J < C < M$). Knowing that it cannot obtain a better policy through override legislation, the committee does nothing.

b. *The Court/Congress/President Game in Federal Jurisdiction, Governmental Relations, and Environmental Law*

Because the Court's traditions in these areas are restrictive, and Congress is more responsive to liberal group pressures (to expand jurisdiction, reform procedure, expand government accountability to citizens, and protect the environment), the Court tended to be more conservative than Congress in these areas during the period of this study. The judiciary committees (and subcommittees) were, on the whole, to the left of their chamber medians, and hence unaligned with the Court on these issues. Figure 4 maps these preference configurations, under the further assumption that the President is neutral or favors Congress (as was usually the case before 1981):

Liberal Policy ———— *C(M)* *C* *M* / *P* *J* ———— Conservative Policy

Figure 4. Raw Preferences, $C < M, P < J$
Equilibrium Result, $M \leq x \leq J$

As in Figures 1-3, Figure 4 shows the relevant committees, *C*, somewhat to the left of the chamber median, *M*. Unlike Figures 1-3, Figure 4 shows the Court's raw preferences, *J*, to the right of those of the chamber median. The location of the Court's preferences vis-à-vis those of the committee and the chamber significantly affects the game. If the Court simply reads its preferences into the statute, it can expect a congressional override, because the committees prefer any policy to the left of the Court's preferred policy, including the policy Congress would adopt ($C < M < J$). Hence, the committees would report override legislation, which Congress would amend to reflect its policy preferences.

Figure 4 roughly describes the relative preferences of the players in the current debate over habeas corpus reform. The Court has been cutting back on *Fay v. Noia*[148] for the last fifteen years, reflecting its institutional concerns about the large volume of habeas cases handled by federal judges. The House

148. 372 U.S. 391 (1963).

Judiciary Committee, generally to the left of both the Court and the House on these issues, sought to override some of the Court's more conservative decisions in 1990,[149] but its override was amended on the House floor to add more conservative provisions.[150] As amended, habeas reform was killed in conference committee by the House conferees, but new override legislation may be successful in the 102d Congress.[151] The 1990 experience suggests that with most habeas issues, the Court has been able to avoid an override by persuading Congress that its increasingly conservative positions are justified, resulting in a shift to the right by Congress.

The Court can also avoid an override if it shifts its preferences in the direction of the chamber median. An unusually dramatic example of this phenomenon was the Court's actions after *Green v. Bock Laundry Machine Co.*[152] *Green* interpreted the Federal Rules of Evidence to permit impeachment of witnesses in civil trials through prior criminal convictions that did not involve perjury of the witnesses. Although the statutory language was not helpful and due process values cut against the Court's interpretation, the Court made a strong case for its interpretation by referring to a traditional common law rule and Congress' probable intent when it redrafted the Rules in 1974.[153] The Court's preferences were certainly more conservative than those held in the current Congress, however. But the Court immediately accommodated Congress' preferences by transmitting an amended version of the Rule within months of *Green*, pursuant to its authority under the Rules Enabling Act.[154] Although a rule change does not put the Court in a position of "interpreting" a statute, it does suggest that the Court was willing to compromise its preferences expressed in *Green*.[155]

For much of the period of this study (especially after 1981), the preferences of the Presidency are to the right of Congress' preferences on issues of jurisdic-

149. *See* H.R. REP. NO. 681(I), 101st Cong., 2d Sess. 123-35 (1990), *reprinted in* 1990 U.S.C.C.A.N. 6472, 6528-41.

150. The Judiciary Committee realized that it did not have the votes to obtain House approval for its habeas corpus provisions and offered its own "diluting" amendments, which were defeated on the floor of the House. 136 CONG. REC. H8870-76 (daily ed. Oct. 4, 1990). The House then passed the more conservative Hyde Amendment, which substituted a habeas corpus title that was on some issues more conservative than the Supreme Court decisions. *Id.* at H8876-82.

151. H.R. 3371, 102d Cong., 1st Sess., tit. xi (1991), as reported by the House Judiciary Committee substantially cuts back on *Fay v. Noia*'s availability of habeas corpus, but is more liberal than the Hyde Amendment adopted by the House in 1990. As an obvious compromise, the new habeas title survived attack from a similar Hyde Amendment in 1991 that would have overridden *Fay v. Noia* altogether. 137 CONG. REC. H7995-8005 (daily ed. Oct. 17, 1991) (Hyde Amendment defeated, 208-218).

152. 490 U.S. 504 (1989).

153. *Id.* at 511-24. *But cf. id.* at 527 (Scalia, J., concurring in judgment) (relying only on most plausible meaning of plain text of statute, but drawing only one vote).

154. The Court transmitted to Congress a proposed revision of Rule 609 in January 1990. *See* 110 S. Ct. cxxviii-cxxxvi (1990). The Rule change went into effect in December 1990, when Congress refrained from deferring the Rule's effective date or rewriting the Rule. *See* 110 S. Ct. c (1990).

155. Note, for example, that the Court arguably lacks the power under the Rules Enabling Act to "repeal" a rule adopted by Congress. If the Court *really* adhered to the *Green* interpretation of congressional intent when redrafting Rule 609, it could not have changed Rule 609 in 1990.

tion and procedure, governmental operation and intergovernmental relations, and environmental policy. Figures 5 and 6 map two versions of this new alignment. Figure 5 describes issues, such as national government operations, where the President is significantly to the right of Congress and somewhat to the right of the Court:

Liberal ______________________________ Conservative
Policy C M J V P Policy

Figure 5. Raw Preferences, $C < M < J < V < P$
Equilibrium Result, $x = J$

Similar to the earlier discussion of Figure 3, when the President's preferences favor those of the Court more than those of Congress, the Court gains greater power to impose its preferences onto statutory policy, because it requires supermajorities in Congress to override both the Court *and* a presidential veto. That is, if the Court's interpretation is at or to the left of the veto median ($J < V$), the relevant committee would tend not to report an override bill, nor would Congress bring the bill to a vote, because the committee and Congress would know that the President's probable veto would be sustained.

An excellent example of this scenario is the ongoing controversy over *Feres v. United States.*[156] There, the Court read the Federal Tort Claims Act to include an immunity from tort suits arising out of military service activities. Congressional hearings through the 1980's were harshly critical of the *Feres* doctrine, especially for medical malpractice in the military, while representatives of the President strongly opposed any effort to override *Feres.*[157] The President apparently had the votes to sustain a veto, for no bill ever passed Congress. The Supreme Court reaffirmed *Feres* in *United States v. Johnson,* reflecting its preference for immunities in military and foreign affairs and for vertical coherence (following precedent). Although the relevant subcommittee

156. 340 U.S. 135 (1950).

157. *See Medical Malpractice Suits for Armed Services Personnel: Hearing on S. 2490 and H.R. 1054 Before the Subcomm. on Courts and Administrative Practice of the Senate Comm. on the Judiciary,* 100th Cong., 2d Sess. (1988) [hereinafter 1988 *Senate* Feres *Hearings*]; *Military Malpractice and Liability for Injuries Resulting from the Atomic Weapons Testing Program: Hearing on H.R. 1054 and H.R. 1341 Before the Subcomm. on Administrative Law and Governmental Relations of the House Comm. on the Judiciary,* 100th Cong., 1st Sess. (1987); *The* Feres *Doctrine and Military Malpractice: Hearing on S. 489 and H.R. 3174 Before the Subcomm. on Administrative Practice and Procedure of the Senate Comm. on the Judiciary,* 99th Cong., 2d Sess. (1986); *Military Medical Malpractice: Hearings on H.R. 1161 Before the Subcomm. on Administrative Law and Governmental Relations of the House Comm. on the Judiciary,* 99th Cong., 1st Sess. (1985); *Medical Malpractice Claims by Armed Forces Personnel: Hearing on H.R. 1942 Before the Subcomm. on Administrative Law and Governmental Relations of the House Comm. on the Judiciary,* 98th Cong., 1st Sess. (1983); *The* Feres *Doctrine as It Relates to Private Claims: Hearing Before the Subcomm. on Agency Administration of the Senate Comm. on the Judiciary,* 97th Cong., 2d Sess. (1982) (heated exchanges between members of Congress and the Departments of State and Justice).

chairs railed against *Johnson*,[158] and a *Feres* override limited to medical malpractice claims passed the House, the President's opposition killed Senate override efforts.

Finally, consider Figure 6, which places the raw preferences of both the Court and the President to the right of the veto median in Congress:

Liberal Policy ——— C M V J / P ——— Conservative Policy

Figure 6. Raw Preferences, $C < M < V < J, P$
Equilibrium Result, $V \leq x \leq J, P$

In this preference configuration, the Court would face an override if it read its raw preferences into the statute. Here, committees have every incentive to report override bills, and Congress could pass a bill setting policy at the veto median, V, that would not be vetoed, because the President would lack the votes to sustain a veto. The Court would then have two options to avoid an override. It could simply compromise its preferences and adopt an interpretation at or near the veto median ($x = V$, with J shifting left), or it could try to persuade a chamber, or at least the veto median, to shift its preferences to the right in light of information the Court would provide about the statute ($x = J$, with V shifting right). If the Court tries the latter, the President may become a useful ally, as a center of media attention and head of one of the political parties.

c. *The Court/Congress/President Game in Civil Rights*

The discussion above has assumed a relatively constant relation between congressional and judicial preferences in the subject areas covered; the big changes in preference configurations for the period of this study have been for the Presidency (compare Figure 1 with Figure 3, and Figure 4 with Figures 5 and 6). Indeed, the Presidency is a relatively more mercurial institution, since a single election can alter its preferences dramatically (as occurred in 1952, 1960, 1968, 1976, and 1980). Preference shifts occur more gradually in Congress and the Court, but they do occur.

For most subject areas, the Court/Congress/President game evolves over time. Not only do the players adjust their raw preferences in the short term to accommodate new information and political pressures, but as their personnel and the political landscape change, the players adjust their absolute preferences *and* their comparative preferences (relative to one another) over time. This

158. *See* 1988 *Senate* Feres *Hearings*, *supra* note 157, at 15-17 (testimony of Rep. Frank to override *Johnson* and adopt the approach of Justice Scalia's dissent in that case).

phenomenon occurs in all subject areas, but has been most dramatic in civil rights policy during this period.[159] During the late Warren Court and early Burger Court (1967-71), the Court's preferences for interpreting civil rights statutes were more liberal than those of Congress and its committees. Figure 1 roughly describes the raw preferences of the players and suggests that the Court then enjoyed relative freedom to read civil rights statutes liberally, without being overridden. During the 1970's, Congress drifted to the left and the Court to the right in their preferences for civil rights policy, and the configuration changed to that shown in Figure 4. As a consequence, the Court was subject to more overrides during that period. After the 1980 election, the President aligned strongly with the Court, and Figures 5 and 6 map the new array of preferences. Protected by the President's veto, the Court more boldly read its raw preferences into civil rights statutes. This culminated in the series of 1989 decisions that have been the subject of override efforts in 1990 and 1991.

Several recent civil rights cases reveal how the Court plays the game as mapped in Figures 5 and 6. In *Patterson v. McLean Credit Union*,[160] the Court interpreted the Civil Rights Act of 1866[161] to provide a cause of action against private employers when they "make or enforce" contracts in ways that discriminate by reason of race, but not when the contract is discriminatory only in actual operation. The Court's opinion was an apparent compromise—on the one hand reaffirming its prior holding that the statute protects African Americans against private refusals to enter contracts, while on the other hand declining to extend its analysis to protect African Americans whose conditions of employment are discriminatory. Based on an amicus brief filed by Members of Congress, which took a very strong position on the first issue but ignored the second, the Court might have believed that such a compromise would satisfy the median Member.[162]

In *Wards Cove Packing Co. v. Atonio*,[163] the Court interpreted Title VII to require that plaintiffs in *Griggs* "disparate impact" cases carry the burden of proving that racial imbalances are the result of specific discriminatory practices. The Court probably realized that its interpretation of Title VII was contrary to the preferences of a substantial majority of legislators in each chamber, but strongly suggested that legislators revise their preferences, lest employers be forced to adopt undesirable quotas.[164] This strategy was probably critical in the defeat of the override effort in the 101st Congress: The President not

159. The analysis in this paragraph is taken from Eskridge, *supra* note 145, and this point is explored further in Part III.A, *infra*.

160. 491 U.S. 164 (1989).

161. Currently codified at 42 U.S.C. § 1981.

162. The amicus brief argued that Runyon v. McCrary, 427 U.S. 160 (1976), should not be overruled, but took no position on the application of *Runyon* to the facts of *Patterson*. Brief for 66 Members of the United States Senate and 118 Members of the United States House of Representatives as *Amici Curiae* in Support of Petitioner, *Patterson* (No. 87-107).

163. 490 U.S. 642 (1989).

164. *Id.* at 652.

only vetoed the override bill, but invoked the quota issue and used it to rally enough Republican Senators to sustain his veto. The political landscape has changed with the 102d Congress and the President abandoned that position, permitting Congress to override *Wards Cove* (as well as *Patterson* and the other 1989 decisions).

3. *A Theory of Congressional Overrides*

The sequential game developed above explains how the Supreme Court often can avoid congressional overrides of its statutory decisions, even when the raw preferences of the Court and Congress might be very different. The Court/Congress/President game then raises the question: Might the Supreme Court avoid overrides altogether by adroitly playing the game? Probably not. The sequential game theory suggests three situations in which the Court's statutory decisions will be overridden.

First, the Court's interpretations will be overridden when congressional preferences change over time.[165] This is why some of the Court's older decisions, such as *Boutilier*, are overridden.[166] These older decisions may have adequately reflected contemporary congressional preferences, but over time society changed, and congressional preferences changed too. Usually, Supreme Court decisions survive such changed circumstances, either because the new circumstances render the decisions irrelevant or because the decisions work well enough within new social frameworks to be regarded as "harmless errors." Changed circumstances, however, may sometimes render a statutory decision not only obsolete, but counterproductive to current congressional policy or productive of confusion in the law.[167] Often in such cases, especially in connection with comprehensive revision or reform bills, Congress overrides the obsolete interpretation.[168] Such overrides are almost always routine affairs,

---

165. Of course, the Court's preferences on an issue might also change over time, in which event the Court might consider "overruling" the statutory precedent. For a suggested connection between the Court's willingness to overrule a statutory precedent and Congress' interest in overriding it, see *infra* Part III.A.1.

166. About 25% of the overriden Supreme Court decisions in Appendix I were decisions rendered more than 10 years before the override.

167. This was the case with *Boutilier*, which was overridden because its view of homosexuality as a "disease" was considered obsolete even by relatively conservative legislators. 135 CONG. REC. S5040-42 (daily ed. May 9, 1989) (Sen. Simpson, R.-Wyo.). More importantly, the obsolescence of *Boutilier* was not harmless error, because the PHS (which no longer would cooperate) opposed the INS (which believed *Boutilier* should be occasionally enforced) on this issue, and the circuits were split as to which agency was acting properly. *Compare* Hill v. INS, 714 F.2d 1470 (9th Cir. 1983) (PHS is correct), *with In re* Longstaff, 716 F.2d 1439 (8th Cir. 1983) (INS is correct).

168. Most of Congress' overrides of recent Supreme Court decisions (within 10 years) have been in legislation either limited to the issue in the overridden decision or close to it. Conversely, most of Congress' overrides of Supreme Court decisions that are more than 10 years old have been in omnibus reconciliation bills and in ambitious statutory recodifications. *See, e.g.*, Bankruptcy Reform Act of 1978, Pub. L. No. 95-598, 92 Stat. 2549 (9 overrides, 7 of them older decisions); Contract Disputes Act of 1978, Pub. L. No. 95-563, 92 Stat. 2383 (2 overrides, 1 of them an older decision); Copyright Act of 1976, Pub. L. No. 94-553, 90 Stat. 2541, 2598 (4 overrides, 1 an older decision): Longshoremen's & Harbor Workers Compensation Act Amendments of 1972, Pub. L. No. 92-576, 86 Stat. 1251 (4 overrides, 3 of them older decisions). These

with no intended criticism of the Court's statutory interpretation. For example, when Congress overrode *Boutilier* as part of its general revision of the immigration law in 1990, the override was treated as a routine policy adjustment, not as an attack on the Court for reading an antihomosexual interpretation into the statute.

Second, the Court may misinterpret congressional preferences or may be unpersuasive in its efforts to inform Congress of constitutional or other concerns. Overrides prompted by such judicial miscalculation usually come swiftly (often within a year or two) and are accompanied by some concern that the Court is not "doing its job." This describes the congressional reaction to *Gilbert*, which interpreted Title VII as not prohibiting pregnancy-based discrimination. The Court rested its decision primarily upon a constitutional precedent which held that depriving women of pregnancy benefits was not gender-based discrimination prohibited by the Equal Protection Clause.[169] The Court's decision also raised the question of whether including pregnancy benefits in a health care package might be unfair to male employees, by providing disproportionately greater health care benefits to female employees. Given Congress' complete failure to deliberate about the sex discrimination provision of Title VII when it enacted the Civil Rights Act in 1964, the Court's opinion raised pertinent constitutional and policy questions that Congress had never considered. Through extensive committee hearings in both chambers, Congress carefully considered the Court's new information to satisfy itself that the Court's concerns were not justified and, therefore, overrode the Court's decision.[170] A similar congressional process responded to the Court's employment discrimination decisions of the 1988 Term (*Wards Cove*, *Patterson*, and others).

Third, and perhaps most importantly, the Court, for institutional reasons, will often invite a congressional override. This point requires elaboration through several examples. In *TVA v. Hill*,[171] the Court interpreted the Endangered Species Act of 1973 to protect the snail darter at the price of halting the nearly complete construction of a $110 million dam. The Court's opinion emphasized the plain meaning of the statute, for which judicial preferences are quite strong, but it is doubtful that this was the Court's real point. The Court's message was an institutional one: You (Congress) have not provided us (the

---

overrides are all collected in Appendix I.

169. General Elec. Co. v. Gilbert, 429 U.S. 125, 134-36 (1976) (relying on Geduldig v. Aiello, 417 U.S. 484 (1974)).

170. *See generally* H.R. CONF. REP. NO. 1786, 95th Cong., 2d Sess. 5 (1978), *reprinted in* 1978 U.S.C.C.A.N. 4765; H.R. REP. NO. 948, 95th Cong. 2d Sess. 5 (1978), *reprinted in* 1978 U.S.C.C.A.N. 4749 (1978); S. REP. NO. 331, 95th Cong., 1st Sess. (1977); *Legislation to Prohibit Sex Discrimination on the Basis of Pregnancy: Hearing on H.R. 5055 and H.R. 6075 Before the Subcomm. on Employment Opportunities of the House Comm. on Education and Labor*, 95th Cong., 1st Sess. (1977); *Discrimination on the Basis of Pregnancy: Hearings on S. 995 Before the Subcomm. on Labor of the Senate Comm. on Human Resources*, 95th Cong., 1st Sess. (1977).

171. 437 U.S. 153 (1978).

Court) with sufficient policy guidance to enable us to administer a system of exceptions to the facially absolute prohibitions in the Endangered Species Act, nor do we have sufficient information or expertise to create these exceptions ourselves (and some of us do not wish to do so). Both the Court and the dissenters called upon Congress to override the Court's decision by statute.[172] Congress did so immediately, establishing an administrative mechanism to consider exemptions from the Act's prohibitions.[173] The statutory override created an administrative mechanism responsive to the political process, something the Court could not have done. The Court in *TVA* expressed rational, and probably exemplary, preferences when it combined a literal statutory interpretation with a call for congressional override.[174] As the foregoing example demonstrates, the Court will sometimes refuse to interpret a statute broadly, especially when such an interpretation would represent a major policy decision that the Court would be more comfortable allowing Congress to make.[175] At other times, however, such signals by the Court do not result in congressional action.

Also exemplifying such institutional signaling are the Court's decisions that apply constitutionally inspired clear statement rules. The most prominent of these rules is the requirement that any congressional abrogation of the states' Eleventh Amendment immunity be explicit on the face of the statute.[176] In the last two years, the Court has invoked this clear statement rule several times to render federal statutory schemes inapplicable to the states, and Congress in return has overridden some of these decisions.[177] A majority of the Court is not unhappy with this sequence of events because the apparent goal of the clear statement rule is to force Congress to decide the issue of state immunity before the Court will find abrogation of Eleventh Amendment interests. If Congress responds by amending the statute to add the requisite language, the Court's goal has been achieved.

172. *Id.* at 195 (majority opinion); *id.* at 210 (Powell, J., dissenting).

173. Endangered Species Act Amendments of 1978, Pub. L. No. 95-632, 92 Stat. 3751 (creating mechanism); *see also* Energy and Water Development Appropriation Act, Pub. L. No. 96-69, 93 Stat. 437, 449 (1979) (reversing result in *TVA* case).

174. *See* William N. Eskridge, Jr., *Spinning Legislative Supremacy*, 78 GEO. L.J. 319, 338-40 (1989). *But see* DWORKIN, *supra* note 126, at 313-54 (arguing that *TVA* dissenters had "best" interpretation, but not considering this institutional dimension).

175. Congress promptly responded to Supreme Court override invitations in Public Employees Retirement System v. Betts, 492 U.S. 158 (1989) (plain meaning interpretation of ADEA); Finley v. United States, 490 U.S. 545 (1989) (refusal to interpret federal jurisdiction statute broadly); McNally v. United States, 483 U.S. 350 (1987) (rule of lenity counsels against expansive judicial interpretation of broad federal criminal statutes, especially when federalism concerns are prominent); Teleprompter Corp. v. CBS, 415 U.S. 394 (1974) (Congress, not Court, should update Copyright Act to reflect new technological developments).

176. *See* Atascadero State Hosp. v. Scanlon, 473 U.S. 234 (1985). The Court's finding of no abrogation of the states' immunity against lawsuits brought under the Rehabilitation Act of 1973 was itself overridden by Congress in the Rehabilitation Act Amendments of 1986, Pub. L. No. 99-506, § 1003 100 Stat. 1807, 1845.

177. *See* Dellmuth v. Muth, 491 U.S. 223 (1989), *overridden by* Education of the Handicapped Act Amendments of 1990, Pub. L. No. 101-476, § 103, 104 Stat. 1103, 1106; BV Eng'g v. UCLA, 858 F.2d 1394 (9th Cir. 1988) (following *Atascadero*), *overridden by* Copyright Remedy Clarification Act, Pub. L. No. 101-553, 104 Stat. 2749 (1990).

III. Implications of the Court/Congress/President Game for Statutory Interpretation Theory and Practice

The Court/Congress/President game developed in Part II provides a realistic theory of the legislative process and the interaction between the Court, Congress, and the President. This model can also serve as the basis for some interesting observations about general theories, as well as specific doctrines, of statutory interpretation. Statutory interpretation traditionally has been viewed as the Court's implementation of the original intent of the enacting Congress. The theoretical debate of the 1980's, however, debunked this traditional view and argued that statutory interpretation usually is, and should be, dynamic.[178]

The description of the Court's preferences in Part II was based upon the insights of dynamic statutory interpretation theory. This theory argues that when the Court interprets statutes it considers arguments based upon plain meaning, horizontal and vertical coherence, and good policy. The Supreme Court cases surveyed in this Article demonstrate the insights of dynamic statutory interpretation. Congress' original intent was critical to very few of the Court's decisions (a rare example is *Boutilier*). In most cases, the Court emphasized such intrinsically evolutive concerns as precedent, the common law, and the ever-changing canons of statutory interpretation (see Tables 6 and 8). The Court/Congress/President game suggests that the Court is a part of the process by which statutory policy is created and that its policy preferences affect public policy, albeit in different ways than Congress' policy preferences.

In at least one respect, however, the game adds a dimension to the interpretive process that dynamic statutory interpretation theory has thus far neglected. It includes an additional feature for the Court's configuration of preferences—a preference that its decisions not be immediately overridden by Congress. Thus, one of the dynamic factors influencing the Court's interpretation of statutes over time is the signals sent to the Court by subsequent Congresses. That idea turns traditional thinking about statutory interpretation on its head.[179] Where they diverge from the Courts' preferences, the expectations of the current Congress and the President are more important to the Court than are the expectations of the enacting Congress.

---

178. *See* DWORKIN, *supra* note 126; T. Alexander Aleinikoff, *Updating Statutory Interpretation*, 87 MICH. L. REV. 238 (1988); William N. Eskridge, Jr., *Dynamic Statutory Interpretation*, 135 U. PA. L. REV. 1479 (1987); Farber, *supra* note 123; Donald C. Langevoort, *Statutory Obsolescence and the Judicial Process: The Revisionist Role of Courts in Federal Banking Regulation*, 85 MICH. L. REV. 672 (1987); Peter C. Schanck, *The Only Game in Town: An Introduction to Interpretive Theory, Statutory Construction, and Legislative Histories*, 38 KAN. L. REV. 815 (1990); Zeppos, *supra* note 123.

179. *See, e.g.*, David Landes & Richard A. Posner, *The Independent Judiciary in an Interest-Group Perspective*, 18 J.L. & ECON. 875 (1975). They argue that the independent federal judiciary was created to facilitate interest group behavior and statutory deals, by enforcing those original deals over time. However, they fail to explain why the courts would want to enforce such deals. It seems more plausible that the Supreme Court would assign greater weight to the preferences of the current and future Congresses (which might override the Court's preferences) than to those of the enacting Congress, particularly if, as often happens, that Congress is long departed.

This is a radical hypothesis.[180] The first section of this part will test this hypothesis by analyzing Supreme Court decisions from the last three decades that interpret civil rights legislation. The analysis will demonstrate that this hypothesis more accurately describes the Court's decisions than does traditional (original intent) theory. The second section will present further evidence supporting this theory by examining the Court's practice of selectively overruling statutory precedents, frequently relying on legislative inaction, and occasionally invoking subsequent legislative history when it interprets statutes. The hypothesis provides a useful framework for thinking about these much-criticized doctrines. The final section will defend the Court's deference to current legislative and presidential preferences against the normative objection that the Court should only consider original legislative preferences. But the Court's practice is vulnerable to objections that it is too deferential to normal politics on the whole and is insufficiently critical of current legislative preferences.

A. *The Court/Congress/President Interaction in Civil Rights Cases, 1967-90*

Civil rights decisions provide a starting point for testing the robustness of the hypothesis that the Court is more responsive to current than to original legislative expectations. The substantial number of such decisions, their political salience, their generation of a number of congressional overrides (see Table 4) and failed override efforts (see Appendix II), and the relatively discernible preferences of the institutional players make these decisions ideal for study. On the other hand, civil rights decisions may be particularly susceptible to this hypothesis, because the rapid changes in civil rights thinking and experience render original legislative expectations less useful in this area than in others, and because constitutional considerations play an important, but not dominant, role in these cases. Notwithstanding these limitations, the sequential game developed in Part II does go far in explaining the interaction between the Court, Congress, and the President in civil rights cases.[181]

1. *Court/Congress/President Interaction, 1966-71*

During the late Warren Court and early Burger Court eras, the Court's raw preferences in civil rights cases were significantly to the left of those in Congress, and somewhat to the left of those in the gatekeeping (labor and judiciary)

180. Note that this hypothesis is *not* that the Court is acting in a dishonest fashion or that it is nothing more than a scheming political institution. Surely, few if any of the Justices see their role as avoiding overrides. Rather, the hypothesis is that *as a group* the Court in the past 24 years has more often—perhaps unconsciously—reflected current, as opposed to historical, congressional preferences when it interprets statutes. Also, note that the Court itself may be rethinking this role. *See infra* Part III.C.

181. *See* Eskridge, *supra* note 145 (analyzing Court's civil rights decisions during this period in more detail).

committees.[182] Thus, the preference configuration sketched in Figure 1 describes the situation between 1967 and 1971. Under the Court/Congress/President game developed in Part II, the preferences of the contemporaneous Congress would not have constrained the Court much, since the Court was protected from legislative override by supportive gatekeeping committees and a very supportive Presidency. In fact, this is what occurred during that period, for the Court not only updated old civil rights statutes to reflect newer legislative preferences, but also interpreted both old and new statutes more liberally than Congress probably would have done on its own.[183] Again, this was possible under the conditions described in Figure 1, because the relevant committees had incentives to protect the Court from overrides. To the extent that the committees' or Congress' raw preferences were subject to persuasion, the Court was backed up by the very persuasive President Lyndon Johnson.

The high point of the Warren Court's liberal interpretation of Reconstruction civil rights laws was *Jones v. Alfred H. Mayer Co.*,[184] which interpreted the Civil Rights Act of 1866, currently codified as 42 U.S.C. § 1982, to provide a remedy for racial discrimination in the sale, leasing, or other conveyance of real or personal property by private parties. *Mayer* essentially overruled the Court's prior understanding that § 1982 only prohibited public laws "providing for discriminatory property arrangements"[185] and was probably contrary to the expectations of the 1866 Congress.[186] It also went well beyond the expectations of the current Congress, which just weeks before *Mayer* had enacted a fair housing statute providing a far less generous remedy to victims of

182. *See* BERNARD SCHWARTZ, SUPER CHIEF: EARL WARREN AND HIS SUPREME COURT—A JUDICIAL BIOGRAPHY 445-50 (1983) (preferences of Warren Court); 2 ENCYCLOPEDIA OF THE AMERICAN CONSTITUTION 848-49 (1986) (describing Court's solidly liberal preferences after Justice Frankfurter's retirement in 1962); *see also* GRAHAM, *supra* note 116; WHALEN & WHALEN, *supra* note 64 (House Judiciary Committee and congressional preferences); Barbara Sinclair, *Agenda, Policy, and Alignment Change from Coolidge to Reagan*, *in* CONGRESS RECONSIDERED 291, 301-04 (Laurence C. Dodd & Bruce I. Oppenheimer eds., 3d ed. 1985) (Congress' preferences).

The House Judiciary Committee was strongly to the left of the House as a whole (and maybe as far left as the Warren Court) on some issues under the chairmanship of Representative Celler from 1955 to 1973. *See* WHALEN & WHALEN, *supra* note 64, at 29-67. The Senate Judiciary Committee through the 1960's was chaired by a Southern conservative and was evenly split between pro- and anti-civil rights Senators. But the Senate Democratic leadership (led by liberal Majority Leader Mansfield) and the Senate Labor Committee were pro-civil rights. *See, e.g.*, 29 CONG. Q. ALMANAC 44 (1963).

183. *See* Griggs v. Duke Power Co., 401 U.S. 424 (1971) (interpreting Civil Rights Act of 1964 to prohibit employment practices having "disparate impact" on minorities); Allen v. State Bd. of Elections, 393 U.S. 544 (1969) (interpreting Voting Rights Act of 1965 to invalidate de minimis dilution of minority voting); United States v. Guest, 383 U.S. 745 (1966) (interpreting Enforcement Act of 1870 to criminalize some private conspiracies to deprive people of civil rights); Louisiana v. United States, 380 U.S. 145 (1965) (interpreting Enforcement Act of 1870 in accordance with Court's new Fifteenth Amendment jurisprudence).

184. 392 U.S. 409 (1968).

185. *See id.* at 451-52 (Harlan, J., dissenting).

186. *Id.* at 454-76; *see also* CHARLES FAIRMAN, RECONSTRUCTION AND REUNION, 1864-88, PART I, at 1258-59 (1971); Gerhard Casper, Jones v. Mayer*: Clio, Bemused and Confused Muse*, 1968 SUP. CT. REV. 89 (examining *Mayer* in light of legislative history of 1866 Civil Rights Act).

housing discrimination.[187] But the Court's interpretation was acceptable to the gatekeeping committees in Congress, which protected it from legislative override.[188]

2. *Court/Congress/President Interaction, 1972-81*

The Court's raw preferences in civil rights cases moved sharply to the right after 1971,[189] just as Congress' raw preferences were moving to the left.[190] Thus the preference configuration sketched in Figure 4 is applicable, and the model predicts more tension between the Court and the current Congress. This is precisely what happened. This period saw several important congressional overrides of the Supreme Court's statutory civil rights decisions,[191] mainly because a Court to the right of Congress and even more to the right of the gatekeeping committees had no margin of error in predicting or transforming congressional preferences. In all but one of the overridden decisions, the Court had no signals from Congress as to its current preferences, and therefore simply read its own preferences into the statutes.[192]

More importantly, in several civil rights decisions the Court directly or indirectly suggested that it was adjusting its raw preferences to reflect those of the current, rather than the enacting, Congress. The best example is *Runyon v. McCrary*,[193] which reaffirmed *Mayer* and applied its interpretation of the property rights provision of the 1866 Act (now § 1982) to the contract rights

---

187. Pub. L. No. 90-284, 82 Stat. 73, 81 (1968); *see* Eskridge, *supra* note 174, at 340-43.

188. In 1971-72, floor amendments in both the Senate and the House sought to override *Mayer*'s interpretation as it pertained to the contracting provision of the 1866 Act (now codified at 42 U.S.C. § 1981). The Senate defeated the floor amendment upon a tie vote in which the tiebreaking Senator agreed to a highly unusual "live pair," 118 CONG. REC. 3373, 3965 (1972), but the House adopted a similar one, 117 CONG. REC. 31973, 32111 (1971). The conference committee, dominated by House and Senate committee members who had opposed the override from the beginning, then quietly dropped the override provision. H.R. CONF. REP. No. 899, 92d Cong., 2d Sess. 17 (1972).

189. When Justices Powell and Rehnquist started casting votes in 1972, the Court's center of gravity moved sharply to the right. *See* Segal & Cover, *supra* note 132, at 560.

190. *See* Sinclair, *supra* note 182, at 306-11 (finding big jump in civil liberties support scores for congressional Democrats from 1969-72 to 1981-82).

191. *See* City of Mobile v. Bolden, 446 U.S. 55 (1980), *overridden by* Voting Rights Act Amendments of 1982, Pub. L. No. 97-205, § 3, 96 Stat. 131, 134; United Airlines v. McMann, 434 U.S. 192 (1977), *overridden by* Age Discrimination in Employment Act Amendments of 1978, Pub. L. No. 95-256, 92 Stat. 189; General Elec. Co. v. Gilbert, 429 U.S. 125 (1976), *overridden by* Pregnancy Discrimination Act of 1978, Pub. L. No. 95-555, 92 Stat. 2076; Alyeska Pipeline Serv. Co. v. Wilderness Soc'y, 421 U.S. 240 (1975), *overridden by* Civil Rights Attorney's Fees Awards Act of 1976, Pub. L. No. 94-559, 90 Stat. 2641.

192. Thus, *Gilbert* interpreted the gender discrimination provisions of Title VII, for which there was no useful legislative history or subsequent congressional action, using reasoning from its constitutional precedent, Geduldig v. Aiello, 417 U.S. 484 (1974). Similarly, the Court in *Bolden* had no reliable legislative signals for Congress' expectations in the Voting Rights Act and simply applied its Fifteenth Amendment jurisprudence to the issues. *Alyeska* interpreted the old federal costs statute and *relied* on subsequent congressional signals, namely the enactment of *specific* fee-shifting statutes, to conclude that the general costs statute did not authorize fee shifting generally. Only in *McMann* was there evidence of current congressional preferences, but it consisted of a committee report issued shortly before the Court's opinion was handed down, and after the case was argued.

193. 427 U.S. 160 (1976).

provision of the Act (now § 1981). The Court's willingness to do so, by a seven-to-two vote, was expressly premised upon the Court's belief that Congress in 1971-72 had signaled its approval of the application of *Mayer* to § 1981.[194] Moreover, two of the majority Justices wrote special concurring opinions suggesting that they thought *Mayer* was in fact wrongly decided but that stare decisis, reinforced by current expressions of legislative preferences, impelled them to go along with a liberal interpretation of the 1866 Act.[195]

A number of other decisions in the late 1970's relied on the Court's perception of current legislative preferences to reach results that were probably more liberal than the Court's preferences otherwise would have been.[196] Indeed, this hypothesis provides a cogent explanation for *United Steelworkers v. Weber*,[197] which interpreted Title VII to allow voluntary affirmative action. One of the Justices in the *Weber* majority had voted the year before against the constitutionality of state-sponsored affirmative action,[198] and a second Justice explained his vote as a response to societal developments that had overtaken the original congressional expectations.[199] Both of these Justices, and probably others in the majority, conceded the dissent's view that the Court's holding had little support in the original congressional understanding,[200] but were sensitive to the pressures for affirmative action created by *Griggs* and to the approval of *Griggs* voiced by the gatekeeping committees in 1971. For this reason, a Court critical of affirmative action in constitutional cases interpreted the Civil Rights Act of 1964 to allow a much broader range of preferential programs than one would expect.

To generalize this point, the Burger Court produced results in constitutional cases—where there was little chance of an override—that were discernibly more

194. *Id.* at 174-75 & n.11. I consider the evidence of legislative approval cited by the Court to be unreliable. *See* Eskridge, *supra* note 127.

195. 427 U.S. at 186-89 (Powell, J., concurring); *id.* at 189-92 (Stevens, J., concurring). A third Justice in the majority, conservative Chief Justice Burger, probably would have voted with the dissenters if the Court had split 4-4. It is common knowledge, especially after *The Brethren*, that Chief Justice Burger often voted with liberal majorities simply to control the assignment of the opinion. BOB WOODWARD & SCOTT ARMSTRONG, THE BRETHREN 64-65 (1979).

196. *See, e.g.*, Cannon v. University of Chicago, 441 U.S. 677, 685-87, 694-708 (1979) (Court split 5-1-3; key argument for majority was apparent congressional assumption that Title IX included private cause of action); Monell v. New York City Dept. of Social Servs., 436 U.S. 658 (1978) (7-2 Court relied upon recent legislative assumptions to overrule line of § 1983 cases); United States v. Board of Comm'rs, 435 U.S. 110, 131-35 (1978) (5-1-3 Court endorsed liberal interpretation of Voting Rights Act, based in part on congressional understanding when Act was renewed in 1975); Franks v. Bowman Transp. Co., 424 U.S. 747 (1976) (5-1-2 Court allowed affirmative remedies in Title VII cases and relied on discussions underlying 1972 amendments). *But see* International Bhd. of Teamsters v. United States, 431 U.S. 324 (1977) (Marshall, J., dissenting).

197. 443 U.S. 193 (1979).

198. Justice Stewart, the fifth vote in the 5-2 split for *Weber*, was part of the five-Justice majority invalidating the affirmative action plan in University of Cal. Regents v. Bakke, 438 U.S. 265 (1978). Justices Stevens and Powell, who did not participate in *Weber*, were also part of the *Bakke* majority.

199. *Weber*, 443 U.S. at 209-16 (Blackmun, J., concurring).

200. *Id.* at 228-55 (Rehnquist, J., dissenting). Academics tend to agree with the dissent on this issue. *See* GRAHAM, *supra* note 116; Farber, *supra* note 123, at 303; Bernard D. Meltzer, *The* Weber *Case: The Judicial Abrogation of the Antidiscrimination Standard in Employment*, 47 U. CHI. L. REV. 423 (1980).

conservative than the results it reached in analogous cases of statutory interpretation.[201] This fact provides further support for the hypothesis. The Burger Court's greater liberalism in statutory cases cannot credibly be attributed to textual plain meaning or to original legislative expectations, which cut very much against its interpretations, or to any great sympathy for civil rights legislation. Instead, the Court seems, perhaps unconsciously, to have molded its preferences in statutory cases (but not so much in constitutional cases) to accommodate the more liberal preferences of Congress and the President in the late 1970's.

3. *Court/Congress/President Interaction, 1981-90*

The Court's behavior after 1981 provides strong support for this hypothesis. There was just one change in the Court's personnel between 1975 and 1986, the replacement of moderately conservative Justice Stewart with the slightly more conservative Justice O'Connor. Hence, the Court's raw preferences remained just about the same throughout that period, and Congress' raw preferences did not markedly change.[202] The significant change was the election of a conservative President. Hence, after 1981, Figures 5 and 6 represent the configuration of raw preferences on civil rights issues.

This hypothesis would predict that the Court would shift to the right in its interpretation of civil rights statutes. The Court would be protected from congressional overrides by a presidential veto, unless the Court took a position that not even a third of either chamber could accept. This is apparently what happened: Within a few years the Court handed down a series of narrowing constructions for Title VII and other recent civil rights statutes,[203] as well as for § 1983 and other nineteenth century civil rights statutes.[204] An examina-

201. Contrast *Weber* with *Bakke*. The disparity became even stronger in the 1980's. *Compare* Johnson v. Transportation Agency, 480 U.S. 616 (1987) (articulating very expansive view of *Weber*) *with* Wygant v. Jackson Bd. of Educ., 476 U.S. 267 (1986) (articulating stingier view of affirmative action in constitutional cases). Also contrast the Burger Court's willingness to look at effects upon racial groups to find actionable discrimination in statutory cases, such as *Griggs*, with its focus only upon intentional conduct to find discrimination in constitutional cases. *See* Arlington Heights v. Metropolitan Hous. Corp., 429 U.S. 252 (1977); Washington v. Davis, 426 U.S. 229 (1976).

202. The Republicans gained control of the Senate from 1981-87, thereby moving Congress to the right. The move, however, was only a small one. For example, although chaired by conservative Republicans Thurmond and Hatch, the Senate Judiciary and Human Resources Committees retained pro-civil rights majorities.

203. *See, e.g.*, Smith v. Robinson, 468 U.S. 992 (1984) (6-3 decision) (construing Education of the Handicapped Act and Rehabilitation Act narrowly); Firefighters Local Union No. 1784 v. Stotts, 467 U.S. 561 (1984) (6-3 decision) (construing Title VII narrowly); Grove City College v. Bell, 465 U.S. 555 (1984) (6-3 decision) (construing Title VII narrowly); Arizona Governing Comm. for Tax Deferred Annuity v. Norris, 463 U.S. 1073 (1983) (4-1-4 decision) (extending liberal Pregnancy Discrimination Act of 1978 interpretation to insurance companies, but only prospectively); City of Lockhart v. United States, 460 U.S. 125 (1983) (6-2-1 decision) (construing Voting Rights Act narrowly); American Tobacco Co. v. Patterson, 456 U.S. 63 (1982) (5-4 decision) (construing exception to Title VII broadly).

204. *See* General Bldg. Contractors Ass'n v. Pennsylvania, 458 U.S. 375 (1982) (6-1-2 decision) (interpreting § 1981 narrowly); City of Memphis v. Greene, 451 U.S. 100 (1981) (6-3 decision) (interpreting

tion of all the civil rights statutory decisions during this period reveals a clear overall trend toward more conservative voting divisions on the Court after 1980.[205] Although the Court still handed down some liberal decisions, they tended to be on issues where the Court felt constrained by precedent or where Congress had sent strong signals that conservative results could be overridden by veto-proof margins.[206]

The balance between conservative and liberal interpretations of civil rights statutes shifted to the right after 1981 due to the Court's perception that a conservative President gave it more leeway to reach conservative results.[207] The Court's preferences shifted further to the right after 1986 because of personnel changes,[208] which resulted in six decisions in May and June 1989 (including *Patterson* and *Wards Cove*) that triggered the override efforts in the 101st and 102d Congresses. The conservative Court might have been testing

---

§ 1982 narrowly).

In May 1981, Senator Hatch's Subcommittee on the Constitution of the Senate Judiciary Committee held hearings on bills to override the Burger Court's liberal interpretations of § 1983 in Maine v. Thiboutot, 448 U.S. 1 (1980), and Owen v. City of Independence, 445 U.S. 622 (1980). *See Municipal Liability Under 42 U.S.C. § 1983: Hearings Before the Subcomm. on the Constitution of the Senate Comm. on the Judiciary*, 97th Cong., 1st Sess. 1-2 (1981) [hereinafter *Municipal Liability*]. By July of that year, the Supreme Court had narrowed both decisions with fresh, and markedly more conservative, interpretations of § 1983 in Middlesex County Sewerage Auth. v. National Sea Clammers Ass'n, 453 U.S. 1 (1981), and City of Newport v. Fact Concerns, Inc., 453 U.S. 247 (1981). This was noted with enthusiasm in the *Municipal Liability*, *supra*, at 380, 404-06, 444, 450-52, 458.

205. Consider the following data, drawn from the Supreme Court's decisions from the 1977 through 1983 Terms, which were the basis for Table 4:

Interpretations of Modern Civil Rights Statutes	Supreme Court Decisions 1977 to 1979 Terms	Supreme Court Decisions 1980 to 1983 Terms
Liberal	10 Decisions	11 Decisions
Conservative	6 Decisions	12 Decisions
No Clear Division	1 Decision	11 Decisions
Interpretations of Reconstruction Era Statutes		
Liberal	7 Decisions	5 Decisions
Conservative	6 Decisions	14 Decisions
No Clear Division	7 Decisions	9 Decisions

This data suggests that after 1980 the balance of power on the Court shifted toward more conservative interpretations of both modern and nineteenth-century civil rights statutes. The shift is particularly strong for the older statutes, perhaps because they are so open ended that there is more room for the Justices' personal political philosophies to play a critical role.

206. The most notably liberal decisions were Johnson v. Transportation Agency, 480 U.S. 616 (1987) (reaffirming *Weber*); School Bd. v. Arline, 480 U.S. 273 (1987); Bob Jones Univ. v. United States, 461 U.S. 574 (1983), all of which relied explicitly upon subsequent congressional signals.

207. The Court did not, of course, always prevail in this period, for it dramatically failed to hit the veto median in Grove City College v. Bell, 465 U.S. 555 (1984), which was overridden by the Civil Rights Restoration Act of 1987, Pub. L. No. 100-259, 102 Stat. 28 (1988).

208. These changes consisted of the replacement of conservative Chief Justice Burger by the more conservative Chief Justice Rehnquist in 1986, of Justice Rehnquist by the more conservative Justice Scalia in 1986, of moderately conservative Justice Powell by the more conservative Justice Kennedy in 1987, and of liberal Justice Brennan by the less liberal Justice Souter in 1990.

Congress to discover the veto median on these issues,[209] which Congress has now provided. Section C of this part will consider another explanation for what the Court was doing in these cases.

B. *Rethinking Doctrines of Statutory Interpretation: Strong Stare Decisis, Legislative Inaction, and Subsequent Legislative History*

The Court/Congress/President game provides a fresh way of thinking about several doctrines of statutory interpretation that scholars have scorned, but that the Court has followed. These are: (1) the super-strong presumption of correctness of statutory precedents; (2) the ratification of an authoritative statutory interpretation by legislative inaction; and (3) the use of subsequent legislative history. The Court's selective invocation of these doctrines follows the pattern suggested by my model. That is, the Court usually will invoke strong stare decisis when the Court has reason to believe that current legislative majorities support the precedent and will tend not to invoke it when there are strong doubts that this is what Congress prefers. The Court will invoke legislative inaction and subsequent legislative history as evidence of statutory meaning when it believes that they provide reliable evidence of current congressional preferences regarding an issue of interpretation.

The hypothesis that the Court is attentive to current congressional and presidential preferences provides an interesting and useful way of thinking about these often-criticized doctrines. In turn, these patterns support the hypothesis that the Court is more responsive to current congressional preferences than to the preferences of the enacting Congress in statutory interpretation cases.

1. *Super-Strong Presumption of Correctness for Statutory Precedents*

The Supreme Court has long held that statutory precedents are entitled to a greater stare decisis effect than either constitutional or common law precedents, in part because Congress and not the Court should have the primary responsibility for overriding statutory precedents.[210] Scholars have been critical of this "super-strong presumption of correctness" for statutory precedents, in part because it is not realistic to expect Congress to know about and

209. For example, in *Patterson*, the Court unanimously declined to overrule *Runyon*, in response to unequivocal congressional hostility to such a move (signaled in an amicus brief), but gave the decision a narrow reading that the Court might have believed would survive congressional scrutiny. Patterson v. McLean Credit Union, 491 U.S. 164 (1989).

210. Burnet v. Coronado Oil & Gas Co., 285 U.S. 393, 405-07 (1932) (Brandeis, J., dissenting); *see also* Cleveland v. United States, 329 U.S. 14, 18 (1946); Apex Hosiery Co. v. Leader, 310 U.S. 469, 488-89 (1940); Erie R.R. Co. v. Tompkins, 304 U.S. 64, 77-78 (1938); Edward H. Levi, *An Introduction to Legal Reasoning*, 15 U. CHI. L. REV. 501, 540 (1948).

respond to the Court's statutory precedents,[211] and in part because the Court invokes it so selectively.[212] The empirical study described in this Article suggests that the first criticism has been too harsh. Congress is aware of the Court's statutory decisions and actively considers almost half of them in legislative hearings, but does not respond to most of them.

The second criticism may also be too harsh, because the analysis in this Article suggests an underlying coherence to the Court's invocation of the super-strong presumption. The Court will not overrule a statutory precedent that seems to enjoy support in the current Congress, but will consider overruling a statutory precedent that the Court has reason to believe the current Congress would not protect with an override. In other words, the Supreme Court does abandon the super-strong presumption, but only when it thinks the precedent is no longer politically viable.[213]

Two recent statutory stare decisis decisions illustrate this point. In *Patterson*, a unanimous Court reaffirmed *Runyon*'s and *Alfred H. Mayer*'s interpretations of the Civil Rights Act of 1866, even though several Justices believed those cases were wrongly decided.[214] The Court invoked the super-strong presumption of correctness for statutory precedents, but made it clear that the key reason for its refusal to disturb the precedent was its consistency with Congress' current commitment to ending racial discrimination.[215]

The year before *Patterson*, another unanimous Court overruled a line of statutory precedents involving appellate jurisdiction in *Gulfstream Aerospace Corp. v. Mayacamas Corp.*[216] The Court did not mention either the super-strong presumption of correctness for statutory precedents or the possibility of congressional action, even though several override bills introduced in 1987 were then being given serious congressional consideration.[217] While it is hard to

211. *See* REED DICKERSON, THE INTERPRETATION AND APPLICATION OF STATUTES 252-55 (1975); Frank H. Easterbrook, *Stability and Reliability in Judicial Decisions*. 73 CORNELL L. REV. 422, 425-29 (1988); Earl Maltz, *The Nature of Precedent*, 66 N.C. L. REV. 367, 388-89 (1988).

212. William N. Eskridge, Jr., *Overruling Statutory Precedents*, 76 GEO. L.J. 1361, 1427-39 (1988), lists 26 Supreme Court decisions explicitly overruling statutory precedents between 1961 and 1987, another 24 implicitly overruling statutory precedents, and another 35 significantly curtailing statutory precedents or overruling their reasoning. *See also* Lawrence C. Marshall, *"Let Congress Do It": The Case for an Absolute Rule of Statutory Stare Decisis*, 88 MICH. L. REV. 177 (1989) (arguing that the Court should never overrule statutory precedents).

213. If this reformulation is correct, the Court's traditional rationale for the super-strong presumption is backwards. If the Court can undo the damage of a statutory precedent that is no longer politically popular, it will overrule the precedent. Only if the Court has reason to believe Congress would still support the precedent will it refuse to reconsider the precedent.

214. Patterson v. McLean Credit Union, 491 U.S. 164 (1989).

215. *Id.* at 174. The Court disclaimed reliance on legislative acquiescence, *id.* at 175 n.1, but its invocation of contemporary values is an obvious reference to the values held by Congress as well as the electorate. Although the Court did not rely on the amicus brief filed by dozens of Members of Congress, *supra* note 162, it might have been influenced by the very substantial congressional support for *Runyon*.

216. 485 U.S. 271 (1988) (overruling Ettelson v. Metropolitan Life Ins. Co., 317 U.S. 188 (1942), and Enelow v. New York Life Ins. Co., 293 U.S. 379 (1935)).

217. Override provisions for the *Enelow-Ettelson* doctrine were included in H.R. 3152, 100th Cong., 1st Sess. (1987), and S. 1482, 100th Cong., 1st Sess. (1987), at the behest of the Judicial Conference. *See generally Court Reform and Access to Justice Act: Hearings Before the Subcomm. on Courts, Civil Liberties,*

tell whether the Court was fully aware of how close Congress was to overriding the old decisions, the Court's eagerness to overrule them—and to deny them any special stare decisis—probably represented its (correct) impression that they enjoyed little or no current legislative support.

The point of this comparison can be generalized. On the one hand, when the Court has explicitly overruled its statutory precedents in the last thirty years, it has usually had good reason to believe that the precedents no longer reflected congressional preferences. Indeed, the Court has often cited inconsistent statutory developments as a reason to overrule such precedents.[218] Even where the Court has not cited subsequent statutory developments, it can sometimes be inferred that negative congressional signals contributed to the Court's willingness to overrule precedents.[219]

It is noteworthy that Congress has never during this period overridden any of the 30 Supreme Court decisions overruling statutory precedents.[220] The most likely override is *Fay v. Noia*,[221] which was an important target of the 1990 habeas revisions deleted in conference committee. Consistent with congressional restiveness over *Fay*, the Court itself has been trimming it back for fifteen years,[222] and the Court's recent habeas decisions track Congress' concern with the federalism values undermined in *Fay*.

On the other hand, when the Court has invoked the super-strong presumption to rebuff a serious challenge to a statutory precedent, there has often been tangible evidence that the precedent enjoyed substantial support in recent Congresses.[223] For example, the Court in *United States v. Johnson*[224] recent-

and the Administration of Justice of the House Comm. on the Judiciary, 100th Cong., 1st & 2d Sess. 33 (1987-88). After the Supreme Court overruled these decisions in *Mayacamas*, the general override was dropped by the House Judiciary Committee, though it retained a specific override for Baltimore Contractors, Inc. v. Bodinger, 348 U.S. 176 (1955), which applied only to arbitration cases. *See* H.R. REP. NO. 889, 100th Cong., 2nd Sess. (1988), *reporting* H.R. 4807, 100th Cong., 2d Sess. (1988); 133 CONG. REC. E1508 (daily ed. Apr. 23, 1987).

218. *See* Eskridge, *supra* note 212, at 1427-29 app. A (10 of 26 Supreme Court decisions overruling statutory precedents note subsequent statutory developments as one reason for overruling).

219. For example, the Court's per se invalidation of vertical restraints under the Sherman Act in United States v. Arnold, Schwinn & Co., 388 U.S. 365 (1967), came under increasing fire in Congress during the 1970's and generated a host of proposals to exempt various industries (such as soft drinks and beer) from the per se rule. For proposals protecting the soft drink industry, see H.R. 3567, 97th Cong., 1st Sess. (1979); S. 1483, 95th Cong., 1st Sess. (1975); S. 3421, 94th Cong., 1st Sess. (1973); H.R. 6684, 94th Cong., 1st Sess. (1973); S. 978, 93d Cong., 1st Sess. (1971); H.R. 16,916, 93d Cong., 2d Sess. (1972). This may have contributed to the Court's willingness to overrule *Schwinn* in Continental T.V., Inc. v. GTE Sylvania, Inc., 433 U.S. 36 (1977). Notwithstanding *GTE Sylvania*, Congress still overrode *Schwinn* in the Soft Drink Interbrand Competition Act, Pub. L. No. 96-308, 94 Stat. 939 (1980).

220. *See* Eskridge, *supra* note 212, at 1427-29 app. A (collecting cases); Rodriguez de Quijas v. Shearson/American Express, Inc., 490 U.S. 477 (1989); Gulfstream Aerospace Corp. v. Mayacamas, 485 U.S. 271 (1988); Lee v. Florida, 392 U.S. 378 (1968).

221. 372 U.S. 391, 435-36 (1963), *overruling* Darr v. Burford, 339 U.S. 200, 208 (1950).

222. Starting with Wainright v. Sykes, 433 U.S. 72, 87-88 (1977); *see id.* at 94-96 (Stevens, J., concurring); *id.* at 98-99 (White, J., concurring in judgment); *id.* at 102-09 (Brennan, J., author of *Fay*, dissenting).

223. *See, e.g.*, Johnson v. Transportation Agency, 480 U.S. 616, 629 n.7 (1987) (refusing to consider overruling *Weber*, because there is no sentiment in Congress to override precedent); Patsy v. Board of Regents, 457 U.S. 496, 501 & n.3 (1982) (refusing to reconsider § 1983 precedent, in part because of

ly refused to overrule *Feres* over the objections of a strong dissent. An important reason cited by the Court was Congress' failure, over a forty-year period, to derogate from *Feres* immunity in any way, notwithstanding numerous proposals to do so. As if to confirm the Court's judgment, legislative efforts to override *Feres* through the 1980's have been unsuccessful.

2. *Interpreting Legislative Inaction*

The Court has long maintained that "legislative inaction" might ratify or bolster statutory interpretations reached not only by the Supreme Court, but also by lower courts or agencies. Specifically, the Court often gives special deference to an interpretation that Congress has left in place notwithstanding legislative hearings on the issue, reenactment of the underlying statute, and proposals in committee or on the floor to reject that interpretation.[225] Like the Court's special stare decisis rule, its legislative inaction rules have been criticized by academics on the grounds that the rules are unrealistic and that the Court only selectively invokes them.[226] Again, these criticisms may be overstated, because the Court's practice has been to invoke the legislative inaction doctrines mainly when it has found some indication that there is insufficient support in Congress for overriding the contested interpretation.

Perhaps the most criticized case invoking special stare decisis for statutory precedents and the legislative inaction doctrines is *Flood v. Kuhn*.[227] A badly divided Supreme Court was "loath" to overrule its own Sherman Act precedents giving baseball an exemption from the antitrust laws, "when Congress, by its positive inaction, has allowed those decisions to stand for so long and, far beyond mere inference and implication, has clearly evinced a desire not to disapprove them legislatively."[228] Although the Court's opinion left antitrust law in a state of incoherence (since other professional sports were covered by the antitrust laws), the Court would not act. The precedents were surely ques-

congressional reliance); Flood v. Kuhn, 407 U.S. 258, 281 (1972) (refusing to reconsider Sherman Act precedent, in part because Congress had extensively considered issue and focused attention on expanding precedent rather than overriding it).

For most, and perhaps all, of the other leading decisions explicitly invoking the super-strong presumption, a case can be made that the statutory issue was sufficiently controversial that Congress would not itself have overridden the precedent in dispute. For example, although the Court in Illinois Brick Co. v. Illinois, 431 U.S. 720, 736 (1977), did not mention congressional approval of the challenged precedent, Hanover Shoe, Inc. v. United Shoe Mach. Corp., 392 U.S. 481 (1968), subsequent hearings suggest that Congress would not have overridden it. *See* 1979 *House* Illinois Brick *Hearings*, *supra* note 100.

224. 481 U.S. 681 (1987).

225. *See* Eskridge, *supra* note 127, at 125-37 (appendices collecting cases).

226. DICKERSON, *supra* note 211, at 181; HART & SACKS, *supra* note 52, at 1394-1401; Reed Dickerson, *Statutory Interpretation: Dipping into Legislative History*, 11 HOFSTRA L. REV. 1125, 1133 (1983); John C. Grabow, *Congressional Silence and the Search for Legislative Intent: A Venture into "Speculative Unrealities,"* 64 B.U. L. REV. 737 (1984); Laurence Tribe, *Toward a Syntax of the Unsaid: Construing the Sounds of Congressional and Constitutional Silence*, 57 IND. L.J. 515 (1982).

227. 407 U.S. 258 (1972).

228. *Id.* at 283-84.

tionable, but the Court perceived that Congress supported them. That was the point of the Court's emphasis on "positive inaction." Congress not only deliberated about baseball's antitrust exemption and failed to override it, but the proposals that enjoyed the most support were ones that would have *expanded* baseball's exemption to other sports and would not have *constricted* the exemption the Court had given baseball.[229] Hence, the Court left the prior interpretation in place. As in other cases, the Court's political instincts were correct, for subsequent legislative hearings in *Flood* revealed little interest in overturning the decision.[230]

A similar point can be made about Supreme Court decisions bolstering agency interpretations by reference to current congressional preferences. Responding to court challenges, the Internal Revenue Service (IRS) in 1970-71 amended its regulations to disallow income tax exemptions to educational institutions that discriminate on the basis of race. The new IRS position was probably not the one that the original enacting Congress would have adopted, but Congress in the 1970's rejected all efforts to reverse the new rules, though it did hamper the agency's efforts to devote significant resources to enforcing the regulation.[231]

In *Bob Jones University v. United States*,[232] a virtually unanimous Supreme Court upheld the agency's antidiscrimination regulation, with heavy reliance on Congress' supportive stance during the 1970's.[233] Like *Flood*, *Bob Jones* drew from the record of Congress' deliberations the inference that Congress was happy with the agency's regulation on its face. A year later, in *Allen v. Wright*,[234] the Court turned back efforts to challenge the agency's

229. Bills were introduced and hearings held on sports exemptions to the antitrust laws in 1957, 1958, 1959, 1960, 1964, and 1965. Brief for Respondents at 32-36, *Flood* (No. 71-32). Most of the serious proposals sought to expand baseball's exemption to other sports. In 1958, the House passed one such bill, H.R. 10378, 85th Cong., 2d Sess. (1958) (Senate took no action). In 1960 and 1964, a Senate committee recommended similar legislation, and in 1965, the Senate passed a bill expanding baseball's exemption to other sports, S. 950, 89th Cong., 2d Sess. (1965) (House took no action).

230. *See Antitrust Policy and Professional Sports: Oversight Hearings Before the Subcomm. on Monopolies and Commercial Law of the House Comm. on the Judiciary*, 97th Cong., 1st & 2d Sess. (1981-82). Although the Department of Justice enthusiastically supported overriding *Flood*, *id.* at 29, no other group backed up the Department's position, and the subcommittee spent most of the hearings exploring issues in other sports.

231. Specifically, after the IRS issued regulations in 1978-79 placing burdens on schools with low percentages of black students to "prove" their nondiscrimination, Congress attached the Ashbrook Amendment to a 1980 appropriations statute, barring the IRS from implementing the regulations. Other "back door" restrictions followed. *See IRS Tax Exemptions and Segregated Private Schools: Hearing Before the Subcomm. on Civil and Constitutional Rights of the House Comm. on the Judiciary*, 97th Cong., 2d Sess. 49-50 (1982) (hearings preceding but cognizant of Court's forthcoming decision in *Bob Jones*).

232. 461 U.S. 574 (1983).

233. *Id.* at 599-602 (majority opinion by Burger, C.J., for eight Justices); *see also id.* at 607 (Powell, J., concurring).

234. 468 U.S. 737 (1984).

refusal to enforce its regulation very vigorously, again in accord with recent congressional signals.[235]

3. *Subsequent Legislative History*

In its analysis of a statute's legislative history, the Court sometimes consults legislators' post-enactment statements about the statute.[236] Even defenders of the use of such "subsequent" legislative history have criticized the Court's practice.[237] They argue that the Court invokes it arbitrarily[238] and that such materials are unreliable. However, the Court/Congress/President game developed in this Article suggests an underlying reason for the Court's invocation of subsequent legislative history: The Court is particularly interested in such material if it is persuasive evidence of recent congressional preferences and of the probability of a legislative override.

Thus, while the Court does not rely on subsequent legislative history to illuminate the enacting Congress' expectations, it does consider subsequent history when the history illuminates the probable desires of the current Congress.[239] This is particularly important when the Court's preferences are otherwise substantially to the right of those in Congress (the configuration of preferences in Figures 4 and 6). For example, in 1987, the Supreme Court in *School Board v. Arline*[240] interpreted the Rehabilitation Act of 1973 to prohibit discrimination against a person afflicted with contagious tuberculosis. This was a very liberal interpretation of the statute by a very conservative Court. As the dissenting opinion suggested,[241] the liberal result was hardly compelled by the vague statutory language, the generalized legislative history, or the Court's own precedents. Instead, the Court's opinion rested upon subsequent agency regulations that "were drafted with the oversight and approval of

---

235. *Allen*, however, was a case of constitutional standing, not statutory interpretation, in which the Court made it difficult for citizens to sue the IRS to force it to enforce its regulation.

236. "[W]hile the views of subsequent Congresses cannot override the unmistakable intent of the enacting one, such views are entitled to significant weight and particularly so when the precise intent of the enacting Congress is obscure." Seatrain Shipbuilding Corp. v. Shell Oil Co., 444 U.S. 572, 596 (1980) (citations omitted); *see also* Andrus v. Shell Oil Co., 446 U.S. 657, 666 n.8 (1980).

237. *See* Dickerson, *supra* note 226, at 1146; Patricia M. Wald, *Some Observations on the Use of Legislative History in the 1981 Supreme Court Term*, 68 IOWA L. REV. 195, 205 (1983).

238. *Compare* cases cited *supra* note 236 *with* Mackey v. Lanier Collections Agency & Serv., 486 U.S. 825, 840 (1988); Consumer Prod. Safety Comm'n v. GTE Sylvania, Inc., 447 U.S. 102, 117-18 (1980); United States v. Price, 361 U.S. 304, 313 (1960) (leading case, using frequently quoted language that "the views of a subsequent Congress form a hazardous basis for inferring the intent of an earlier one").

239. *See, e.g.*, Bowen v. Yuckert, 482 U.S. 137, 148-52 (1987) (interpreting Social Security Act in light of Social Security Disability Benefits Reform Act of 1984); North Haven Bd. of Educ. v. Bell, 456 U.S. 512, 530-35 (1984) (following HEW regulations considered by Congress and not overruled, notwithstanding congressional deliberation and proposals to override regulations); Cannon v. University of Chicago, 441 U.S. 677, 686 & n.7 (1979) (relying on subsequent legislative signals to find private cause of action in Title IX).

240. 480 U.S. 273 (1987).

241. *Id.* at 289-93 (Rehnquist, J., dissenting).

Congress," and hence, considered probative.[242] The subsequent legislative history was, in the sequential game modeled here, important to the Court as evidence that Congress (perhaps by veto-proof margins) favored a liberal approach to the Rehabilitation Act.[243] It is also noteworthy that *Arline* came to the Court one year after the Court suffered three reversals of its statutory decisions failing to protect the rights of the disabled.[244]

The Court's refusal to credit subsequent legislative history traditionally has meant that the Court does not consider the legislative history to be a reliable source of current congressional preferences or (for the reasons developed above) that it wants to invite an override. Both reasons were implicated in the Court's refusal to credit subsequent legislative history in *TVA v. Hill*. In *TVA*, the petitioner argued that the Endangered Species Act permitted exceptions for an almost-completed dam, and that Congress' continuing appropriations for the dam after the snail darter problem arose were evidence that Congress did not consider the dam threatened by the Act.[245] The Court ruled that this evidence was not a reliable indicator of congressional preferences, since legislators do not scrutinize appropriations measures for substantive statutory developments. Another probable reason was that the Court believed the best solution of the snail darter and other similar dilemmas was a statutory override, which the Court invited in its opinion.

In sum, this Article's game theory analysis suggests that the Court has used the foregoing doctrines of statutory interpretation in a relatively systematic, rather than haphazard, way. Specifically, the Court's invocation of special stare decisis for statutory precedents, legislative inaction, and subsequent legislative history is a signal that it is readjusting its own preferences to avoid an override—in light of signals from post-enactment Congresses. Moreover, the Court has been quite astute in its perceptions about such evidence, for the Court's decisions relying upon these doctrines are rarely overridden by Congress. The Court's use of these doctrines supports the hypothesis that the Court tends to be more attentive to the preferences of the current Congress than to those of the enacting Congress.

---

242. *Id.* at 279 (majority opinion) (relying on Consolidated Rail Corp. v. Darrone, 465 U.S. 624, 634-35 (1984)); *see also id.* at 285 n.14 (relying on 1978 amendments to Act).

243. In the Civil Rights Restoration Act of 1988, Pub. L. No. 100-259, § 9, 102 Stat. 28, 31-32, Congress amended the Rehabilitation Act essentially to codify *Arline*. *See also* Fair Housing Amendments Act of 1988, Pub. L. No. 100-430, § 6(a), 102 Stat. 1619, 1620.

244. *See* Rehabilitation Act Amendments of 1986, Pub. L. No. 99-506, 100 Stat. 1807 (overriding Atascadero State Hosp. v. Scanlon, 473 U.S. 234 (1985)); Air Carrier Access Act of 1986, Pub. L. No. 99-435, 100 Stat. 1080 (overriding United States Dep't of Transp. v. Paralyzed Veterans of Am., 477 U.S. 597 (1986)); Handicapped Children's Protection Act of 1986, Pub. L. No. 99-372, 100 Stat. 796 (overriding Smith v. Robinson, 468 U.S. 992 (1984)).

245. *See* Brief for TVA at 7-18, TVA v. Hill, 437 U.S. 153 (1978) (No. 76-170) (survey of House and Senate Appropriations Committees' monitoring of dam situation, with full knowledge of snail darter problem).

C. *Should the Court Be Playing the Court/Congress/President Game?*

If the Court is more responsive to the preferences of the current Congress than to those of the enacting Congress, the question remains: Should the Court be playing such a game? To lawyers, this game may seem like an "unjudicial," if not highly irregular, way for the Court to carry out its statutory interpretation duties, which have in the legal literature traditionally been characterized as a search for Congress' "intent" or application of a statute's "plain meaning." Even modern scholars of dynamic statutory interpretation are sometimes reluctant to acknowledge the pull of subsequent legislative signals.[246]

But to political theorists and economists this game is not so remarkable. According to traditional political theory, the Court's willingness to consider current legislative preferences and its desire to avoid legislative overrides rests upon a specific and widely held ideology[247] regarding the Court's role in our political system.[248] Under this ideology, the Court is part of our nation's pluralist political system, just as Congress and the President are. Like the other branches, the Court plays a specialized role in the overall lawmaking process, but a role that facilitates rather than obstructs the operation of the pluralist system. The Court is, therefore, not normally "countermajoritarian," though sometimes it may push our pluralism to make adjustments ensuring the participation of relevant groups (and hence the perpetuation of pluralism and the stability it brings).[249] This vision sees a limited but important role for the Court as constitutional interpreter and a most important role for the Court as statutory interpreter. As statutory interpreter, the Court is a faithful agent of majoritarian policymaking and carries out statutory policies as Congress desires.

An ambiguity rests in the lessons of this traditional ideology. If the Court is to be a facilitator of majoritarian policies, it is unclear which majority it should obey. Should it obey the congressional majority that enacted the statute or the majority in the current Congress, which may not be willing to enact

---

246. *See, e.g.*, Farber, *supra* note 123 (favoring dynamic statutory interpretation, except where it runs against the clear import of both the plain textual meaning and the original intent of Congress).

247. By "ideology," I do not mean a crude liberal/conservative political strategy, but a holistic cultural understanding of the power dynamics and institutional roles in our polity.

248. The leading explicit statement is Robert A. Dahl, *Decision Making In a Democracy: The Role of the Supreme Court As a National Policy-Maker*, 6 J. PUB. L. 279, 293-94 (1957), which argues that the Supreme Court is inevitably part of the national political coalition and cannot be expected to perform the "countermajoritarian" functions often expected of it. Dahl's thesis is implicit in some of *The Federalist Papers*, *see, e.g.*, THE FEDERALIST NO. 78 (Alexander Hamilton), and in much leading scholarship about the role of federal courts, most notably JOHN H. ELY, DEMOCRACY AND DISTRUST (1980); HART & SACKS, *supra* note 52; RICHARD A. POSNER, THE FEDERAL COURTS: CRISIS AND REFORM (1985).

249. Thus, the Court might aggressively intervene to ensure that "discrete and insular minorities" are not excluded from the political system, lest they abandon the system and work against its stability. *See generally* ELY, *supra* note 248 (purpose of judicial review is "representation reinforcing" rather than imposing constitutional values). Under this theory, the Court's commitment to desegregation in the 1950's makes sense as a pluralist strategy to ensure participation in politics by all groups in society. *Cf.* Derrick A. Bell, Jr., Brown v. Board of Education *and the Interest-Convergence Dilemma*, 93 HARV. L. REV. 518, 524-26 (1980) (arguing that *Brown* was part of elites' strategy of co-opting minorities).

anything like the original statute? The Court cannot ignore either Congress. It needs to pay attention to the preferences of the enacting Congress, not just to assert "rule of law" values, but also to reassure interest groups that, when they receive legislation from Congress, their legislative deal will not entirely collapse over time.[250] But the Court also needs to pay attention to the preferences of the current Congress, to facilitate the efficient operation of pluralism. If the Court completely ignored current legislative preferences and interest group configurations, Congress would have to revisit statutes constantly to update them—a job the Court can perform more efficiently for a wide range of issues. Because most of the statutory issues decided by the Court are those for which there is no completely verifiable "deal" in the enacting Congress, the preferences of the current Congress are usually more important for the Court than are the preferences of the enacting Congress.

The evidence suggests that during the time frame of this Article (1967-90), the Court has tacitly followed the ideology just described. This may be changing, however.[251] Voices within the Court itself are openly questioning this traditional ideology, and academics and judges writing about issues of statutory interpretation are criticizing the Court for its practices in the pluralist system. A discussion of the normative desirability of the Court's pluralist ideology first should focus upon the now-ascendant "formalist" ideology. Formalism offers both a critique of the Court's traditional approach and an affirmative new approach. The difficulties with formalism suggest a different, "normative" critique, which argues that the Court ought to challenge the pluralist system more often to protect values not protected by normal politics.

Formalism argues that constitutional "rule of law" values require the Court to follow only the statutory language as understood by both Congress and the President at the time of enactment. Under formalist ideology, the Court's role in statutory interpretation is not to facilitate the dominant political coalition's evolving preferences, but to protect the formal structures of our democracy. This argument places great weight on the Constitution's requirement of bicameralism and presentment before "law" can be changed.[252] Traditionally this critique argued that statutory interpretation is limited to discerning Congress' original intent, but recent voices on the Court, most notably that of Justice

250. Professors Landes and Posner argue that an independent judiciary might be viewed as protecting the integrity of interest group deals over time. *See* Landes & Posner, *supra* note 179. This is an important insight but does not tell the whole story.

251. For early soundings, see Richard Pildes, Note, *Intent, Clear Statements and the Common Law: Statutory Interpretion in the Supreme Court*, 95 HARV. L. REV. 892 (1982).

252. U.S. CONST. art. I, § 7 (bicameralism and presentment requirements for Congress to enact "laws"). For stringent formalist application of the bicameralism and presentment requirements to the issues in this Article, see Green v. Bock Laundry Machine Co., 490 U.S. 504, 527 (1989) (Scalia, J., concurring in judgment); Public Citizen v. United States Dep't of Justice, 491 U.S. 440, 467 (1989) (Kennedy, J., concurring in judgment); Thompson v. Thompson, 484 U.S. 174, 191-92 (1988) (Scalia, J., concurring in judgment); INS v. Cardoza-Fonseca, 480 U.S. 421, 452-53 (1987) (Scalia, J., concurring in judgment).

Scalia, have recast this critique by focusing on the statutory text.[253] Changes in the Court's personnel in the last five years have yielded a Court more sympathetic to such formalist arguments than any other Court since the 1930's.[254]

The formalist group on the Court is not interested in the preferences of the current Congress. Thus, they have vigorously attacked the traditional doctrines by which the Court has explicitly considered post-enactment congressional preferences. Specifically, they have been more prone to revise statutory precedents for which current Congresses are sympathetic,[255] to reject arguments relying on current congressional acquiescence,[256] and to scorn subsequent legislative history.[257] Moreover, this formalist group is much more aggressive in using the canons as critical tools for interpreting statutes, especially those drawn from structural constitutional principles.[258]

Not surprisingly, Congress is more likely to override Supreme Court statutory decisions following such a formalist approach. Appendix III and the summary in Table 6 present systematic evidence of this phenomenon, which has also been noted by Justice Stevens, the Court's staunchest exponent of traditional pluralist ideology.[259] Justice Stevens strongly objects that the Court "do[es] the country a disservice when [it] needlessly ignore[s] persuasive evidence of Congress' actual purpose and require[s] it 'to take the time to revisit the matter' and to restate its purpose in more precise English."[260]

While aware that the Court has often followed the preferences of current Congresses, formalists believe the Court is doing the country a greater service

253. For analytical descriptions of Justice Scalia's jurisprudence of statutory interpretation, see Eskridge, *supra* note 127; Daniel A. Farber & Philip P. Frickey, *Legislative Intent and Public Choice*; 74 VA. L. REV. 423 (1988); Stephen F. Ross, *Reaganist Realism Comes to Detroit*, 1989 U. ILL. L. REV. 399; Patricia M. Wald, *The Sizzling Sleeper: The Use of Legislative History in Construing Statutes in the 1988-89 Term of the United States Supreme Court*, 39 AM. U. L. REV. 277 (1990); Nicholas S. Zeppos, *Justice Scalia's Textualism: The "New" New Legal Process*, 12 CARDOZO L. REV. 1597 (1991).

254. Justice Rehnquist (who generally favors original intent) was elevated to Chief Justice in 1986; Justice Rehnquist was replaced by Justice Scalia (an ardent textualist); Justice Kennedy (a sometime textualist) replaced Justice Powell (an accommodationist) in 1987. It is not clear how sympathetic newly appointed Justices Souter and Thomas will be to the formalist vision, but it is highly likely that they will be more sympathetic than Justices Brennan and Marshall, whom they replaced. Justices White and O'Connor are sometimes sympathetic to formalist arguments.

255. *See, e.g.*, Johnson v. Transportation Agency, 480 U.S. 616, 657, 677 (1987) (Scalia, J., dissenting).

256. *See id.* at 672 (Scalia, J., dissenting). *Compare* Patterson v. McLean Credit Union, 491 U.S. 164, 200 (Brennan, J., concurring in part and dissenting in part) (arguing that *Runyon v. McCrary* ought to receive heightened stare decisis treatment because subsequent Congresses had signaled approval after deliberation and study) *with id.* at 175 n.1 (Kennedy, J.) (refusing to consider evidence of legislative acquiescence).

257. *See, e.g.*, Public Employees Retirement Sys. v. Betts, 492 U.S. 158, 168 (1989) (Kennedy, J.) ("We have observed on more than one occasion that the interpretation given by one Congress (or a committee or Member thereof) to an earlier statute is of little assistance in discerning the meaning of that statute." (citations omitted)); Mackey v. Lanier Collection Agency & Serv., 486 U.S. 825, 838-41 (1988) (White, J.).

258. *See* Eskridge, *supra* note 125, at 663-66.

259. *See* West Virginia Univ. Hosps., Inc. v. Casey, 111 S. Ct. 1138, 1153-56 (1991) (Stevens, J., dissenting).

260. *Id.* at 1155 (citation omitted).

when it ignores evidence of subsequent congressional purposes and attitudes. They argue that the Court should refuse to do Congress' job. If a statute falls out of date in relation to newer congressional preferences or newer problems, formalists argue that the Constitution requires any revision of the statute to go through the processes of bicameralism and presentment. The empirical study described in Part I of this Article lends some support for this argument because it shows that Congress is well aware of the Court's statutory decisions and often will override those it disagrees with.[261] Congress already overrides many of the plain meaning decisions[262] and could probably override more decisions if it enlarged the staffs of the judiciary committees and the labor committees in each chamber.[263]

Moreover, several of the case studies described in this Article suggest that formalist ideology has some advantages. Consider the example of employment policies that raise questions of disparate impact and affirmative action. While these issues were not squarely debated or addressed in the Civil Rights Act of 1964,[264] the Court still made the tough policy choices in *Griggs* and *Weber*. Because the gatekeeping committees supported the Court's resolutions, Congress never meaningfully debated these issues. When *Wards Cove* brought *Griggs* and *Weber* into question, these issues moved to the legislative agenda, where they have been discussed hotly. Whatever the legislative resolution of these issues, it may be more satisfying, in a democracy, for the elected legislature rather than the unelected Justices to make and debate the policy choices.

Formalism raises important questions about the Court's traditional accommodationist approach to statutory interpretation and makes an attractive case for a more confrontational approach. However, there are several problems with such a strategy of confrontation. One problem arises out of the nature of formalist reasoning and raises the question of whether the Court's formalists have really made out a case for rejecting the Court's traditional accommodationist attitude. To make its case, formalism must root its argument in an authoritative source. The obvious source for the Court's formalism is the Constitution, but the Constitution offers little if any support for such a vision of statutory interpretation.[265] Nothing in the text of the Constitution provides reliable support for formalism. Article III simply defines the duties of the Supreme Court as entailing the "judicial Power," which tells us little about proper considerations in statutory interpretation. Article I's bicameralism and presentment requirements, much relied upon by the new formalists, tell us nothing

261. *See* Tables 1, 2 and 3.
262. *See* Tables 6 and 8.
263. *See* Table 4.
264. See GRAHAM, *supra* note 116, for an excellent discussion of the evolution of debate (almost entirely outside Congress) from 1961 to 1971.
265. *See* Eskridge, *supra* note 125, at 670-78.

about the Court's proper approach to statutory interpretation, as the Court itself suggested in *INS v. Chadha*.[266]

The discussions surrounding the adoption of the Constitution also fail to provide persuasive support for formalism. Indeed, there is some indication that the Framers would have expected the Court to interpret statutes to reflect contemporary policy and reasonableness.[267] Without authoritative support for its ideology of confrontation, the formalist critique is not only incoherent, but presents others with no substantial reason to supplant the Court's traditional ideology of accommodation.

A second problem with the formalist critique is that it requires the Court to act in a more countermajoritarian manner than its traditional approach. Both traditional and formalist ideologies view the Court as Congress' "agent" in statutory interpretation. Like commercial agents in the real world, the Court's role is a subordinate one, implementing directives issued by the principal (Congress) over time. Like principals in the real world, Congress makes the big choices and expects its agent to implement them. The question then becomes one of who is a better agent, the accommodationist who keeps one eye on the principal's current as well as historical preferences, or the formalist, who only has eyes for the principal's original intent or for the plain terms of the written directives? Obviously the principal would rather have the agent who follows the dynamic purpose of his directives, rather than their strict, literal meaning.

This principal-agent analysis has some application to institutions like Congress. When the Court denies civil rights to groups Congress intended to help, or when the Court obstructs a statutory scheme, the damage, even if short term (i.e., there is a quick override), is often irreparable. When the principal is a complex institution like Congress or the President, many mistakes will

---

266. 462 U.S. 919 (1983). *Chadha* invalidated the legislative veto as an effort by *Congress* to make new "laws" without going through bicameral approval and presentment to the President and, therefore, said nothing about the role of the Court to interpret the "laws." Indeed, the Court explicitly approved of highly dynamic executive branch "lawmaking" pursuant to a congressional delegation, because executive activity is regulated under Article II, not Article I. *Id.* at 953 n.16. Obviously, the same point could be made about the Supreme Court's "lawmaking" through statutory interpretation.

267. The English Humanist tradition of the eighteenth century, which was influential for many of the Framers, emphasized the rule of Heydon's Case, 76 Eng. Rep. 637, 638 (K.B. 1584):

> the office of all the Judges is always to make such [] construction as shall suppress the mischief [addressed by the statute], and advance the remedy, and to suppress subtle inventions and evasions for continuance of the mischief . . . and to add force and life to the cure and remedy, according to the true intent of the makers of the Act, *pro bono publico*.

Even much more conservative thinkers such as Blackstone stated that "where some collateral matter arises out of the general words [of a statute], and happens to be unreasonable, there the judges are in decency to conclude that this consequence was not foreseen by the parliament, and therefore they are at liberty to expound the statute by equity," as in *Heydon's Case*. 1 WILLIAM BLACKSTONE, COMMENTARIES *91. *The Federalist Papers* echo Blackstone in arguing that courts ought to interpret "unjust and partial" laws by "mitigating the severity and confining the operation of such laws." THE FEDERALIST NO. 78, at 470 (Alexander Hamilton) (Clinton Rossiter ed., 1961).

never be corrected.[268] Because Congress does not have an infinitely elastic agenda, the Court's effort to push more items onto the legislative agenda necessarily pushes other items off of it. It is arguably countermajoritarian for the Court to make Congress legislate repeatedly on matters that Congress thought were closed.

This difficulty is compounded by the democratic process' reliance on the Court's past practice. Since 1937, it appears that the Court has generally been in sync with the pluralist political process in statutory interpretation.[269] During this period, Congress has enacted thousands of statutes, which were surely written and implemented with the baseline assumption that the Court (or, increasingly, an agency) would interpret the statutes over time to carry out Congress' overall goals in a practical fashion. If, as formalists such as Justice Scalia suggest, the Court in the 1990's were to replace its accommodationist philosophy with a more confrontational one, the Court's move would be tantamount to a game of "bait and switch"—one that lures the mark into enacting a statute by holding out the promise of helpful dynamic interpretation (bait), but then eviscerates the statute over time by stingy interpretation (switch).

Consider the following example of bait and switch. The Court has long recognized that Congress can abrogate the states' Eleventh Amendment immunity from lawsuits pursuant to a federal statutory scheme. In 1985, the Court changed the rule to require Congress to make "its intention unmistakably clear in the language of the statute," in order to abrogate Eleventh Amendment immunity.[270] In the last several Terms, the Court relied on this rule to carve the states out of several important statutory schemes.[271]

In *Dellmuth v. Muth*,[272] the Court held that the Education of the Handicapped Act (EHA) of 1975 did not abrogate state immunity. The Court reached this result even though the law imposed substantive obligations directly on the states, included the states in its jurisdictional grant, and included legislative discussion assuming that the states could be sued. After the Supreme Court changed the clear statement rule in 1985, Congress responded in 1986 with a broad textual abrogation of state immunity for statutes protecting the disabled.[273] Yet in *Dellmuth*, the Court held not only that the EHA did not meet the more stringent test for abrogation, but that the 1986 statute made clear

268. For example, recall the preference configuration described in Figure 1. When the gatekeeping committee of either chamber favors the Court's countermajoritarian interpretation about as much as it favors the chamber's preferred interpretation, it will have few or no incentives to introduce override legislation. In those not insubstantial number of cases, strong countermajoritarian statutory interpretations can survive.

269. This ambitious generalization is based upon the present study, which covers the period 1967-90, and the political science scholarship cited *supra* note 55, as well as Dahl, *supra* note 248, which covers the period before the 1960's. The key date is 1937, the beginning of the end of the *Lochner* era.

270. Atascadero State Hosp. v. Scanlon, 473 U.S. 234, 242 (1985), *overridden by* Rehabilitation Act Amendments of 1986, Pub. L. No. 99-506, § 1003, 100 Stat. 1807, 1845.

271. *See* Hoffman v. Connecticut Dep't of Income Maintenance, 492 U.S. 96 (1989) (Bankruptcy Act); Will v. Michigan Dep't of State Police, 491 U.S. 58 (1989) (§ 1983).

272. 491 U.S. 223 (1989).

273. 42 U.S.C. § 2000d-7(a)(1) (1988).

Congress' "intent" not to abrogate state immunity in lawsuits filed before 1986.[274] Congress overrode *Dellmuth* in 1990.[275] That Congress had to pass the same statute three times to achieve its original goal is quite striking. Although the new formalists proclaim the "obligation" of the Court "to conduct [its] exegesis [of statutes] in a fashion which fosters the democratic process,"[276] the formalist ideology may undercut the democratic process in many cases.

A final, and related, problem with formalism is that it does not appear to be a "neutral" alternative to the Court's traditional accommodationist ideology. Rather, formalism appears to be structurally biased in ways that are difficult to defend. By requiring Congress to revisit statutes that are imperfectly drafted or that do not precisely address new versions of the problem they were enacted to solve, formalism substantially raises the costs of passing statutes. If statutes are more costly to write and rewrite, fewer of them will exist. Formalism in this way embodies a relatively antigovernmental philosophy. This may reflect the libertarian bias of some formalists[277] or their belief in the distributive theory of politics,[278] both of which are deeply controversial views. In any event, their ideology systematically works against majoritarian regulation.[279]

The present study points to another structural bias in formalism, derived from its pride in kicking statutory issues back to Congress. Tables 7 and 9 suggest asymmetries in Congress' willingness to override Supreme Court statutory decisions. The United States, big business, state and local governments, organized employee groups, women's organizations, and environmentalists are best able to obtain override legislation when they lose Supreme Court statutory cases. More diffuse interests are less able to do this. In other words, a Court that has adopted formalism would systematically benefit established interest groups at the expense of diffuse groups and minorities. Thus, an odd consequence of formalism is that it would considerably strengthen the Court's already strong pro-government bias.

274. *Compare Dellmuth*, 491 U.S. at 231-32 (majority opinion) (relying solely on plain meaning of statutory text) *with id.* at 238 (Brennan, J., dissenting) (looking to structure and implications of entire statute).

275. Education of the Handicapped Act Amendments of 1990, Pub. L. No. 101-476, § 1103, 104 Stat. 103, 1106.

276. United States v. Taylor, 487 U.S. 326, 337 (1988) (Scalia, J., concurring).

277. *See, e.g.*, Frank H. Easterbrook, *Statute's Domains*, 50 U. CHI. L. REV. 533 (1983) (supporting statutory construction only when statute either plainly addresses problem or requires judges to supply construction).

278. *See, e.g.*, Frank H. Easterbrook, *The Supreme Court, 1983 Term—Foreword: The Court and the Economic System*, 98 HARV. L. REV. 4 (1984) (arguing that judges should attend more to economics of legislative process).

279. The formalists on the current Court add a further bias in their enthusiastic espousal of the *Chevron* doctrine that courts should defer to agency interpretations of statutes they are charged with implementing. This bias suggests their preference for presidential over congressional lawmaking, a preference which is contrary to the structure of lawmaking contemplated in Article I, Section 7 of the Constitution itself. *See* William N. Eskridge, Jr. & John Ferejohn, *The Article I, Section 7 Game*, 80 GEO. L.J. (forthcoming 1992).

This last line of analysis suggests a very different critique of the Court/Congress/President game—that the Court's traditional ideology is too accommodationist and too uncritical of the pluralist system.[280] There are two ways of expressing this critique, one that is "representation reinforcing"[281] and one that is 'normativist."[282] The representation-reinforcing version would argue that many interests are left out of our pluralist political system. To enhance our system's representation of such interests, the Court should act in a countermajoritarian fashion that provides a voice for those who are not heard. The normativist version would argue that certain fundamental values are neglected in the political process, and the Court can protect those values, or at least force attention to them, through statutory interpretation. Since these two expressions are interrelated, this section will simply refer to them both as "normativist."

A normativist analysis would engage in a statutory interpretation much different from the Court's traditional approach. Recall *Boutilier v. INS*,[283] in which the Court interpreted the immigration law's exclusion of people afflicted with "psychopathic personality" as excluding all lesbians, gay men, and bisexuals. The Court's result strained the "plain meaning" of the statute's text, but accurately read the political situation in 1967 to suggest that the original anti-homosexual "deal" between the PHS and key players in Congress was still in force.[284] If the Court's goal was to avoid overrides and mirror the dominant political feelings of the day, then *Boutilier* succeeded.

Yet *Boutilier* was normatively questionable. By going out of its way to interpret an ambiguous statute to exclude lesbians, gay men, and bisexuals,[285] the Court made it easier for the political process to persecute a vulnerable minority, which was virtually invisible in the political process. If ever the interests of lesbians, gay men, and bisexuals were going to be heard in 1967, the Court would have had to supply the forum and a considerable amplifier. Not least of all, *Boutilier* added the sanction of Court-determined "rule of law" to the historical discrimination against gay men, lesbians, and bisexuals in this

---

280. *The Federalist Papers* suggest that the role of the Court is to "mitigat[e] the severity and confin[e] the operation" of "partial and unjust" laws. THE FEDERALIST NO. 78, at 470 (Alexander Hamilton) (Clinton Rossiter ed., 1961).

281. *See* ELY, *supra* note 248.

282. *See* Eskridge & Peller, *supra* note 68, at 743-47; William N. Eskridge, Jr., *Metaprocedure*, 98 YALE L.J. 945, 964 (1989) (reviewing ROBERT COVER, ET AL., PROCEDURE (1988)).

283. 387 U.S. 118 (1967).

284. The Court had very good evidence for that supposition. The Ninth Circuit in Rosenberg v. Fleuti, 302 F.2d 652 (9th Cir. 1962), *vacated and remanded on other grounds*, 374 U.S. 449 (1963), had interpreted the "plain meaning" of the statute not to cover gay men and lesbians. Congress reacted promptly to the decision, with a statute adding "sexual deviation" to the list of exclusions in the Act of Oct. 3, 1965, Pub. L. No. 89-236, § 15(b), 79 Stat. 911, 919. Although the 1965 Act did not apply to Boutilier, the recent political signals surely informed the Court's interpretation.

285. Clive Michael Boutilier was not even a "homosexual," as we now understand the term, but rather was "bisexual." Unrebutted medical evidence stated that Boutilier had sexual relations with both men and women equally. *See* Boutilier v. INS, 363 F.2d 488, 499 (2d Cir. 1966) (Moore, J., dissenting).

country. In short, *Boutilier* was normatively unjustifiable, even if politically expedient. Even at the risk of an override and adverse criticism, the Court should have interpreted the ambiguous statute to protect the interests of the dispossessed and to avoid irrational discrimination.

Normativism is an attractive vision for a Court constantly engaged in statutory interpretation. Like formalism, it confronts the existing political process with discordant statutory interpretations and challenges the process to override. Unlike formalism, normativism carries with it powerful justifications for supplementing or replacing the Court's traditional approach. It succeeds as an alternative for some of the reasons that formalism fails.

Perhaps surprisingly, normativist—rather than either pluralist or formalist—assumptions make the best sense out of the Constitution. The structure of the Constitution itself is strikingly inconsistent with the agency metaphor favored by both pluralist and formalist ideologies. The Court is featured as an independent branch of government, not as a satrapy of Congress. The metaphor that is more consistent with the separation of powers resonant in the Constitution is that of "partnership" rather than "agency."[286] That is, Congress, the President, and the Court are partners in the creation of public policy, the first making the laws (Article I), the second enforcing the laws (Article II), and the third interpreting the laws (Article III). Article III assures the Court of life tenure and no diminishment of salary, so that the Court has the freedom to reflect upon and criticize the political process as a coequal partner. Alexander Hamilton anticipated normativism in *The Federalist No. 78*, when he argued that a critical role for the Court in statutory interpretation is to interpret "partial and unjust" laws by "mitigating the severity and confining the operation of such laws."[287]

While normativism may be more consistent with the text, structure, and traditions of the Constitution, it is subject to the other two objections to formalist ideology, namely, countermajoritarian tendencies and nonneutrality. But these objections are not as problematic for normativism as they are for formalism, which claims to be more "democracy-enhancing" and "neutral" than the Court's traditional pluralist ideology. Normativism posits that neutrality is not possible and that countermajoritarianism is necessary to our political process.

An impressive body of legal literature is in the process of justifying normativism as an alternative to the traditional pluralist vision.[288] The empiri-

286. *See generally* DAVID EPSTEIN, THE POLITICAL THEORY OF THE FEDERALIST 189-91 (1984).

287. THE FEDERALIST NO. 78, at 469 (Alexander Hamilton) (Clinton Rossiter ed., 1961).

288. *See, e.g.*, DWORKIN, *supra* note 126; CASS R. SUNSTEIN, AFTER THE RIGHTS REVOLUTION (1990); Anthony E. Cook, *Beyond Critical Legal Studies: The Reconstructive Theology of Dr. Martin Luther King, Jr.*, 103 HARV. L. REV. 985 (1990); Robert Cover, *The Supreme Court, 1982 Term—Foreword: Nomos and Narrative*, 97 HARV. L. REV. 4 (1983); Harold McDougall, *Social Movements, Law, and Implementation: A Clinical Dimension for the New Legal Process*, 75 CORNELL L. REV. 83 (1989); Frank Michelman, *Law's Republic*, 97 YALE L.J. 1493 (1988); Martha Minow, *The Supreme Court, 1986 Term—Foreword: Justice Engendered*, 101 HARV. L. REV. 10 (1987); Suzanna Sherry, *Civic Virtue and the Feminine Voice in Constitutional Adjudication*, 72 VA. L. REV. 543 (1986).

cal research reported in this Article is relevant to this literature in several ways. To begin with, the override data compiled here, especially that in Tables 7 and 9 (the ability of "losers" in Supreme Court cases to obtain congressional overrides), supports the proposition that our political system is not meaningfully "pluralist." It lends some support to the views of political scientists who argue that "[t]he flaw in the pluralist heaven is that the heavenly chorus sings with a strong upper-class accent,"[289] for the poor, the ordinary, and the diffused are seldom heard by our Congress when their interests lose in Supreme Court statutory cases.

But the data suggest a much more complicated political system than one in which the "haves come out ahead."[290] It is a system in which government "insiders" (federal employees, state and local governments, federal agencies, the executive departments) often do a lot better than "outsiders," even wealthy outsiders. It is a system in which middle class "minority" groups (noncitizens, women, the disabled) can do better than "established" business interests and diffuse groups such as consumers.

If Hamilton's words[291] mean anything today, they should at least mean that the Court can serve as the "conscience" of the nation's pluralism by bringing attention to interests that go unrepresented in Washington and values that are overlooked.[292] A further lesson of the present study is that the Court's stance significantly affects the way public policy develops in this country.[293] What this Article suggests is that because of the informational features of the Court's statutory interpretation, the Court can influence political preferences by framing statutory issues in a different way, by presenting those issues in a concrete (and probably unanticipated) factual setting, and by raising arguments of public policy not considered by the political process.

Interestingly, the Court's traditional practice in statutory interpretation offers traces of a normativist approach in some of its "clear statement rules," long a mainstay of Anglo-American statutory interpretation.[294] To take the best example, the rule of lenity requires that the Court interpret ambiguous criminal prohibitions in favor of the accused and against the government. This rule serves the representation-reinforcing goal of protecting a relatively powerless group (people accused of committing crimes) and the normativist goal of

---

289. SCHATTSCHNEIDER, *supra* note 58, at 35.

290. For example, organized workers (not a big "have" group) do about as well in obtaining overrides as organized businesses (the big "have" group). *See* Tables 7 and 9. Unions and public employees often obtain overrides, and (perhaps just as important) when such groups intensely oppose an override they have a better track record than do business groups.

291. The Court should interpret "partial and unjust" laws by "mitigating the severity and confining the operation of such laws." THE FEDERALIST NO. 78, at 469 (Alexander Hamilton) (Clinton Rossiter ed., 1961).

292. A theme best developed in Minow, *supra* note 288.

293. Aside from the usually mentioned reasons that the Court's interpretation is accepted as the presumptive starting point for any discussion of a statute and that the political process usually defers to the Court's judgment.

294. *See* Eskridge, *supra* note 131; Sunstein, *supra* note 123.

injecting due process values of notice, fairness, and proportionality into the political process.[295] The rule of lenity also seems to make a difference in the Court's decisions. For example, the rule appears to trump the Court's traditionally accommodationist attitude toward current congressional preferences.[296] This is normatively attractive, because the rule embodies worthy values and because its beneficiaries are too easily brushed aside in the legislative process.

From a normativist perspective, the problem with the Court's practice is that few of the clear statement rules are as sensible as the rule of lenity. Many of the rules—against waivers of federal sovereign immunity, against federal abrogation of state Eleventh Amendment immunity, against federal regulation of the states—protect values and interests that are already well protected by the national political process. Other rules—against extraterritorial application of federal law and in favor of common law baselines—rest upon outdated, often pre-industrial, assumptions. Still other rules—in favor of groups outside the political process and in favor of proportionality—are good rules that are not authoritatively accepted or regularly invoked by the Court.

Return to *Boutilier*. Boutilier was expelled from the United States because the Court found his sexuality evidence of "psychopathic personality" exclusion in the immigration statute. Justice Brennan dissented from that interpretation and adopted the reasoning of Judge Moore in the lower court.[297] Judge Moore's dissent was a classic normativist move in statutory interpretation, for it focused attention on the facts of the case, subjected the pluralist values to substantive critique, and spoke for the victims whose voices had not effectively been heard in the political process. Had the Supreme Court adopted Judge Moore's position, a congressional override would have been *probable*. But it is *possible* that the political process would have been enlightened—or shamed—by a Court opinion precisely analyzing the medical term "psychopathic personality," in light of the developing medical literature. Instead, the Court added the sanction of law to poor policy.

One lesson of the theory and practice described in this Article is that the Court can provide leadership to Congress when it can express a perspective that has not been heard. Sometimes by resisting the political process, the Court can transform the preferences of the players, or at least initiate a debate that will, in turn, transform their preferences.

295. *see generally* ESKRIDGE & FRICKEY, *supra* note 51, at 658-76; J. WILLARD HURST, DEALING WITH STATUTES 64-65 (1982); POSNER, *supra* note 248, at 283-84.

296. Congress frequently overrides the Court's lenient interpretations of federal criminal statutes. *See supra* notes 89-90.

297. *Boutilier*, 387 U.S. 118, 125 (1967) (Brennan, J., dissenting) (relying on Boutilier v. INS, 363 F.2d 488, 497 (2d Cir. 1966) (Moore, J., dissenting)). Justices Douglas and Fortas filed a separate dissenting opinion, *id.* at 125.

IV. Conclusion

The empirical and theoretical discussion in this Article may contribute to a more systematic analysis of the interaction between the Court, Congress, and the President in the creation of public policy in the United States. Although the data here only pertain to federal statutory interpretation cases, the same analysis could apply to agency lawmaking, federal common law, and federal constitutional law.[298] One point of the analysis is that the Court's role in American lawmaking is intrinsically political and not neutral and that other institutions should be aware of that reality. This analysis has a range of implications for the theory and operation of public policy in this country.

The Court's dynamic statutory interpretation takes on new meaning in light of this study. The evolution of statutes is influenced not just by changing circumstances, but also by changing preferences in the political system. Dynamic statutory interpretation theory has established that the Court does not and cannot tie its interpretive practice meaningfully to original legislative intent. This study suggests, further and perhaps surprisingly, that current legislative expectations are usually more important to the Court than original legislative expectations. Furthermore, these conclusions are defensible against formalist attack, but subject to the normativist reservation that the Court should be more critical of the political preferences to which it defers. Consistent with recent literature, this Article views the canons of statutory interpretation as one mode for the Court's critical reflection.

The analysis in this Article is more important for Congress, which should be thinking more systematically about its dynamic interaction with the Court and the President. To begin with, Congress should be aware that judicial interpretations of the statutes it enacts are not going to be faithful to its original expectations[299]—the Court will be more responsive to the expectations of future Congresses and to values (such as plain meaning and due process) that it particularly treasures. Given this, Congress has much stronger incentives to monitor judicial decisionmaking than it has traditionally realized. Congress' need to monitor judicial decisions is particularly strong in a period of divided government when the Court is aligned with the President on many policy matters.

Moreover, Congress can be assured that most controversial Supreme Court decisions will come to its attention and that the relevant committees do a good job of monitoring Supreme Court decisions. Congress, however, should be

298. I am currently conducting an empirical study, similar to this one, surveying congressional "responses" (not just overrides) to Supreme Court constitutional decisions.

299. This came as a surprise to some of the Members during former Congressman Kastenmeier's hearings on statutory interpretation in 1990. *See Statutory Interpretation and the Uses of Legislative History: Hearings Before the Subcomm. on Courts, Intellectual Property, and the Administration of Justice of the House Comm. on the Judiciary*, 101st Cong., 2d Sess. (1990).

concerned that it is aware of relatively few lower court decisions. Just as the present study shows impressive congressional activity in connection with Supreme Court decisions, it shows an unimpressive knowledge of and response to the far more numerous lower federal court statutory interpretation decisions. Even a Supreme Court per curiam opinion, or a memorandum reflecting an evenly split Court, is more likely to trigger congressional attention than important en banc decisions in the federal circuits. Congress needs to monitor these lower court decisions more effectively, and a promising beginning is the trial project by Dr. Robert Katzmann, who is setting up a computer link between the clerk's office of the District of Columbia Circuit and the staffs of the relevant congressional committees.[300]

Congress should also be concerned that its monitoring of Supreme Court statutory decisions yields few overrides. All but one of the six preference configurations explored in this Article (all but Figure 4) reveal the significant power of the Court to read its own raw preferences into statutes without congressional override. This is particularly troubling today, when the raw preferences of Congress and the Court are very far apart, when the Court is becoming a preference outlier without significant dissenting voices, and when the Court's preferences can be backed up by a presidential veto (the divided government problem). Even if a President with preferences similar to those in Congress were elected, Congress could still expect provocatively conservative Supreme Court decisions yielding Court/Congress conflict in the areas of civil rights, environmental law, immigration, government liability for constitutional and ordinary torts, and federal jurisdiction and procedure.

Congress ought to be particularly alert to any movement within the Court toward Justice Scalia's formalist critique of the Court's traditional practice. Given the Court's institutional history, I am not sure that Justice Scalia's formalist vision will make much headway in the Court. But to the extent that it does, there will be much more conflict between the Court and Congress in the 1990's—with more overrides and more acrimony. Congress will search for ways to deal with a Court no longer willing to "play the game." In that event, Congress should consider setting up "councils of revision" specializing in override legislation within the legislature, and should consider transferring primary decisionmaking power to agencies over which Congress has more leverage.

A final conclusion to be drawn from the present analysis is the critical role of the Presidency in statutory interpretation. The President is now truly imperial in issues of statutory interpretation, through two powers given the office by the Constitution—the power to appoint Supreme Court Justices[301] and to veto

300. This is described in Robert A. Katzmann, *Congress, the Courts and Statutory Cases: A Challenge For Positive Political Theory*, 80 GEO. L.J. (forthcoming Feb. 1992).

301. U.S. CONST. art. II, § 2, cl. 2.

legislation[302]—and one power given the office by the Court—the power of executive agencies to issue presumptively valid interpretations of statutes.[303] Thus, a Presidency that has grown increasingly conservative since 1968 has appointed a Court that is increasingly conservative, has used the veto power to protect at least some of the Court's conservative statutory interpretations (and thereby raise the cost of successful overrides), and has used agency rulemaking as a means for trimming back statutory policy. At this point in our history of divided government, the big winner is the Court/Congress/President game is the President.

302. *Id.* art. I, § 7, cls. 2-3.
303. Chevron, U.S.A., Inc. v. Natural Resources Defense Council, 467 U.S. 837 (1984).

A Methodological Introduction to the Three Appendices

The following three appendices report the raw data upon which Tables 1 through 9 and much of the discussion in this Article are based. This introduction describes the methodology used in compiling these appendices, the limits of the methodology, and some of the choices made.

A. *Appendix I: Overrides, 1967-90*

Appendix I collects statutes in the 89th through 101st Congresses in which Congress knowingly overrode federal court interpretations of federal statutes. This Appendix does not report statutory overrides of, or responses to, the Supreme Court's decisions interpreting the Constitution[304] or its common law decisions.[305] The Appendix does report overrides of Supreme Court decisions resting upon both statutory and constitutional grounds.

The *United States Code Congressional and Administrative News (U.S.C.C.A.N.)* collects the main committee reports (and sometimes floor explanations) for most of the public laws enacted by Congress in any given year. Committee reports, including conference committee reports, routinely discuss judicial decisions affected by proposed statutory provisions, usually in their section-by-section analyses. My research assistants and I searched the reports printed in *U.S.C.C.A.N.* for the period 1967-90, noting every reference to a Supreme Court or other judicial interpretation of federal statutes that the reports described as being "overruled," "modified," or "clarified" by a provision in the proposed statute. I then correlated these references to provisions in the enacted public law, weeding out references to provisions that did not override a decision in any substantial way or that were not ultimately enacted.

This method has a number of gaps. Not all public laws generate committee reports. Not all of the overrides are reflected in committee reports. Not all committee reports are reprinted in *U.S.C.C.A.N.* To fill in at least some of these gaps, I did an extensive (but not comprehensive) search of committee reports reproduced on microfiche by the Congressional Information Service, examined the hearings conducted by the House and Senate Judiciary Committees in the period 1979-88, and consulted secondary sources.[306]

---

304. *See, e.g.*, Veterans Judicial Review Act, Pub. L. No. 100-687, § 104, 102 Stat. 4105, 4108-09 (1988) (overriding Walters v. National Ass'n of Radiation Survivors, 473 U.S. 305 (1985)); Privacy Protection Act of 1980, Pub. L. No. 96-440, 94 Stat. 1879 (overriding Zurcher v. Stanford Daily, 436 U.S. 547 (1978)).

305. Federal Employees Liability Reform & Tort Compensation Act of 1988, Pub. L. No. 100-691, 102 Stat. 1568 (overriding Westfall v. Erwin, 484 U.S. 292 (1988)); Amendments to Federal Rules of Evidence, Pub. L. No. 93-595, § 1, 88 Stat. 2215, 2236 (1974) (new Rule 803(3)) (overriding Mutual Life Ins. Co. v. Hillmon, 145 U.S. 285 (1892)).

306. Particularly helpful was Solimine & Walker, *supra* note 5.

I have made a number of choices that should be explicitly noted. First, I have included as "overrides" statutes that "modified" the holding or reasoning of a federal statutory decision. The statute does not have to have entirely nullified the court's statutory decision for me to have counted it as an override.[307] So long as key players in Congress were clearly reacting to a statutory decision, I have counted the statute as an override. Generally, I have counted as overrides only those statutes whose legislative history mentions overridden cases by name. I deviated from this policy for a few overrides of Supreme Court cases because the overrides are clearly linked to the Supreme Court cases in the relevant communities of interpretation.[308]

Second, I have not included as overrides statutes that contain legislative history rejecting a federal statutory decision but that did not proceed to change the text of the *United States Code* to override the decision.[309] Nor do I include as overrides statutes only requiring agency reports or agency follow up on the implications of statutory precedents, rather than changing the text of the statutes.[310]

Third, I have not included as overrides statutes that "codified" or "endorsed" federal statutory decisions. There must have been disapproval of the decision or its consequences for the statute to count as an override.[311] A

---

307. *See, e.g.*, Soft Drink Interbrand Competition Act, Pub. L. No. 96-308, 94 Stat. 939 (1980) (overriding United States v. Arnold Schwinn & Co., 388 U.S. 365 (1967), but only for soft drink industry); Deepwater Port Act of 1974, Pub. L. No. 93-617, 88 Stat. 2126 (overriding procedural rules of Zahn v. Int'l Paper Co., 414 U.S. 291 (1973) (overriding Eisen v. Carlisle & Jacquelin, 417 U.S. 156 (1974), but only for Port Act cases).

308. *See* Immigration Act of 1990, Pub. L. No. 101-649, § 601, 104 Stat. 4978, 5067 (overriding Boutilier v. INS, 387 U.S. 118 (1967), with legislative history only focusing on lower court decision following *Boutilier*); Child Sexual Abuse & Pornography Act of 1986, Pub. L. No. 99-628, § 5(b)(1), 100 Stat. 3511 (overriding Caminetti v. United States, 242 U.S. 470 (1971), but not mentioning decision); Firearm Owners' Protection Act, Pub. L. No. 99-308, § 105, 100 Stat. 449, 459 (1986) (overriding Dickerson v. New Banner Inst., Inc., 460 U.S. 109 (1984), but not mentioning decision).

309. For example, the House report for the Omnibus Budget Reconciliation Act of 1989, Pub. L. No. 101-239, 103 Stat. 2106, rejects the Supreme Court's interpretation of ERISA in Pilot Life Ins. Co. v. Dedeaux, 481 U.S. 41 (1987). *See* H.R. REP. NO. 247, 101st Cong., 1st Sess. 55-56 (1989), *reprinted* in 1989 U.S.C.C.A.N. 1947-49. But there is no change in the statute to reflect this rejection. Hence, I have not included this as a statutory override.

310. *See* Housing & Community Development Act of 1987, Pub. L. No. 100-242, § 102(b), 101 Stat. 1815, 1820 (calling for Comptroller General report, in response to congressional doubts about Wright v. Roanoke Dev. & Hous. Auth., 479 U.S. 418 (1987) *see also* 1987 U.S.C.C.A.N. 3461 (Conf. Rep.)); Insider Trading Sanctions Act of 1984, Pub. L. No. 98-376, 98 Stat. 1264 (1984) (House Report directs SEC to monitor impact of Dirks v. SEC, 463 U.S. 636 (1983), and report back to committee H.R. REP. NO. 98-355, 98th Cong., 2d Sess. 15 (1984), *reprinted in* 1984 U.S.C.C.A.N. 2288).

311. For example, Congress essentially built upon and expanded upon the Court's decision to protect victims of contagious diseases in School Board v. Arline, 480 U.S. 273 (1987), when it enacted the Civil Rights Restoration Act of 1988, Pub. L. No. 100-259, § 9, 102 Stat. 28, 31-32. Although Walker & Solimine, *supra* note 5, count this as a congressional response to *Arline* because the statute expanded *Arline*'s holding, I do not count it as an override because there was no congressional disapproval of the decision; Congress was only using it as a "building block" for public policy.

harder choice was whether a statute indirectly "responding" to a decision Congress does not like counts as an override. Generally not.[312]

B. *Appendix II: Judiciary Committee Hearings, 1979-88*

Appendix II collects the Supreme Court cases that were subject to scrutiny in hearings before the House or Senate Judiciary Committees for the 96th through 100th Congresses (1979-88). The appendix lists Supreme Court decisions (often clustered, if they all relate to the same statutory issue), any override bills aimed at those decisions, and the ultimate disposition of the override bills.

The methodology here was quite simple. I read through the Library of Congress' collection of House and Senate Judiciary Committee hearings for the 96th through 100th Congresses. The Library of Congress keeps the hearings all together and arranges them in sequential numerical order, so that any gaps in coverage can be readily noted. Obviously, I did not read hearings that were clearly unrelated to statutory interpretation issues (which was about half of them), nor did I read the hearings carefully for substance. I just looked for scrutiny of Supreme Court decisions and studied the more important hearings.

The hearings note and usually reprint the bills on which they are focused, and this was my main source for the override bills. Hence, my study does not report override bills that were not the focus of hearings. On the other hand, I have listed a few cases that were scrutinized in hearings, but for which there were no override bills reported in the hearings. What was important was the House or Senate Judiciary Committees' scrutiny of Supreme Court statutory decisions.

I determined the ultimate fate of the override bills primarily through the LEGISLATE computer service at the Library of Congress. Unhappily, this service leaves much to be desired. Sometimes, for example, an override bill is left to die in committee, while an equivalent provision is inserted into another bill, through amendment or so forth; LEGISLATE does not catch these developments. I have caught as many of these anomalies as possible (often through reference in subsequent hearings), but gaps no doubt remain.

C. *Appendix III: Characteristics of Overridden Supreme Court Decisions*

---

312. For example, the Supreme Court in Sears, Roebuck & Co. v. Stiffel Co., 376 U.S. 225 (1964), and Compco Corp. v. Day-Brite Lighting, Inc., 376 U.S. 234 (1964), ruled that federal patent law preempted most state regulation of sound recordings, even though federal law did not itself provide protection. Congress responded by amending federal patent law to protect sound recordings. Although Congress amended the statute specifically in response to the Supreme Court decisions and did not like the policy resulting from those decisions, *see* H.R. REP. NO. 487, 92d Cong., 1st Sess. (1971), *reprinted in* 1971 U.S.C.C.A.N. 1566, 1577-78, I have not included this action as an override of the Supreme Court decisions because the statutory amendment left their rulings completely in place (state law remained preempted). I consider this a very close call.

Appendix III lists the 121 overridden Supreme Court decisions collected in Appendix I, indicates in parentheses the dates of the decisions, and indicates in brackets the dates of the congressional overrides. In the three remaining columns, Appendix III makes some crude characterizations of those decisions. Most of the characterizations are self-explanatory, but a few words are in order.

1. *Voting Split*

The "voting split" column reports how the Court divided, with the Court majority being first, followed by the number of dissenters, followed by the number of Justices concurring only in the judgment (if applicable). Hence, "7-2" means there were seven Justices in the majority and two in dissent; "6-2-1" means there were six Justices in the majority, two in dissent, and one concurring in the judgment. I have characterized the ideology of the voting split in brackets. Ideology is measured in conventional terms, with Justices Brennan and Marshall as "liberals" and Justice Rehnquist as a "conservative." If the Court divided ideologically and the conservatives won (Rehnquist in the majority, Brennan and Marshall in dissent), I have reported "Con./Lib." If the Court issues no opinion, was unanimous, or did not split along ideological lines (e.g., Brennan and Rehnquist vote together), I have signified that as "No Split."

2. *Primary Reasoning*

The "primary reasoning" column reports the most important justification invoked by the Court to support its interpretation of the statute. The choices are:

- *Plain Meaning*, when the Court relies on the most natural meaning of the statutory text, in light of standard rules of syntax and grammar, accepted dictionaries, and the structure and other provisions of the statute (the whole act).

- *Legislative History*, when the Court relies on the discussion (usually within Congress) surrounding the enactment of the statute.

- *Precedents*, when the Court relies on its own precedents interpreting the statute or related statutes.

- *Canons*, when the Court relies on the canons of statutory construction, traditional presumptions, and clear statement rules of statutory interpretation.

- *Purpose*, when the Court relies on the policy or purpose of the statute.

- *Common Law*, when the Court relies on common law baselines.

Sometimes, it was hard to determine the Court's "primary" basis for decision. In such instances, I usually list the two most important justifications

3. *Winners/Losers*

The "winners/losers" column reports my characterization of the groups that essentially won and lost each case, measured in terms of the decision's effect upon their interests. Often this corresponds to the parties in the case (for example, the United States), but sometimes I have extrapolated from the parties to the groups that are more generally helped or hurt by the decision. I have tried to be conservative in these extrapolations.

I have identified the raw "groups" whose "interests" are harmed by each Supreme Court decision. The raw groups identified are:

• *United States*, when the government or one of its agencies or officers lost the case against a criminal defendant, government contractor, tort victim, regulated industry, taxpayer, etc. (I have not counted the U.S. as the losing interest when it intervened to support a private interest's interpretation.) Interests represented by the Solicitor General (at the Court) and executive agencies or departments (in Congress) fall within this category.

• *Diffuse Citizenry*, when the case harmed the interests of most or all Americans in a similar or random way, including decisions against the interests of government tort victims, antitrust plaintiffs, FOIA applicants, consumers, and general litigants. Interests represented by the Consumer's Union, Common Cause, or the ACLU fall within this category.

• *Organized Business*, when the case harms the interests of a well organized industry or trade group. Interests represented by the Chamber of Commerce, the Business Roundtable, or a more specialized industry group fall within this category.

• *State & Local Government*, when state and local governments directly lost cases against criminal defendants, constitutional tort victims, antitrust plaintiffs or defendants, etc. Interests represented by the Association of State and Local Governments, or Association of State Attorney Generals fall within this category.

• *Organized Workers*, when a decision injured the interests of unions, retired workers, or government employees. Interests represented by AFL-CIO and specific unions, American Association of Retired Persons, or government employee unions fall within this category.

• *Women*, when a decision injured the interests of women as a group. Interests represented by the National Organization for Women, various ad hoc groups, or Planned Parenthood fall within this category.

• *Disabled*, when a decision injured the interests of Americans who have physical or mental disabilities. Interests represented by the ACLU or various special groups fall within this category.

• *Environmentalists*, when a decision failed to protect the environment. Interests represented by the Sierra Club, Environmental Defense Fund, Natural Resources Defense Council, etc. fall within this category.

• *Veterans*, when a decision failed to protect Americans who served in the armed forces. Interests represented by Veterans of Foreign Wars or various special issue groups fall within this category.

• *Noncitizens*, when a decision made it harder for noncitizens to enter into or remain in this country. Interests represented by the Immigration Bar fall within this category.

• *Minorities*, when a decision failed to recognize or enforce a statutory right or remedy sought by a group traditionally discriminated against because of its race, ethnicity, or sexual orientation. Interests represented by the Lawyers' Committee on Civil Rights and the ACLU (generally), the NAACP and Urban League (African Americans), MALDEF (Mexican Americans), Human Rights Campaign Fund (lesbians and gay men) fall within this category.

• *The Poor*, when a decision upheld or created a role disproportionately affecting people below the poverty line. Interests represented by the ACLU and specialized issue groups fall within this category.

APPENDIX I

CONGRESSIONAL OVERRIDES OF JUDICIAL INTERPRETATIONS OF FEDERAL STATUTES (1967-1990)

CONGRESSIONAL OVERRIDES	SUPREME COURT DECISION	PRIMARY REASONING
	101ST CONGRESS	
Judicial Improvements Act of 1990, Pub.L.No. 101-650, § 310, 104 Stat. 5089, 5113-14 (1990)	Finley v. United States, 490 U.S. 545 (1989)	Gap in federal jurisdiction rules. 1990 U.S.C.C.A.N. 6873-76 (H.R. Rep.)
Immigration Act of 1990, Pub.L.No. 101-649, § 601, 104 Stat. 4978, 5067 (1990)	Matter of Longstaff, 716 F.2d 1439 (5th Cir. 1983); also Boutilier v. INS, 387 U.S. 118 (1967)	Outdated health-based rules. 1990 U.S.C.C.A.N. 6736 (H.R. Rep.)
Crime Control Act of 1990, Pub.L.No. 101-647, 104 Stat. 4789 (1990)		
§ 3102, 104 Stat. at 4916	In re Cain, 96 B.R. 115 (Bankr. N.D. Ohio 1988), et al.	Bad policy. 1990 U.S.C.C.A.N. 4069-70 (S. Rep.)
§ 3103, 104 Stat. at 4916	Pennsylvania Dep't of Pub. Welfare v. Davenport, 495 U.S. 552 (1990)	Bad policy. 1990 U.S.C.C.A.N. 6570-71 (H.R. Rep.); *id.* at 4071 (S. Rep.)
Independent Safety Board Act Amendments of 1990, Pub.L.No. 101-641, § 3, 104 Stat. 4654 (1990)	Woulfe v. United States, No. 89-7822 (N.D. Ill. Nov. 20, 1989)	Bad interpretation. 1990 U.S.C.C.A.N. 6380 (S. Rep.)
Antitrust Amendments Act of 1990, Pub.L.No.101-588, § 2, 104 Stat. 2879 (1990)	TRW, Inc. v. FTC, 647 F.2d 942, 948 (9th Cir. 1981), et al.	Bad policy. 1990 U.S.C.C.A.N. 4104 (S. Rep.)
Inventions in Outer Space, Pub.L.No. 101-580, 104 Stat. 2863 (1990)	Decca Ltd. v. United States, 191 U.S.P.Q. 439 (Ct.Cl. 1976); see Deepsouth Packing Co. v. Laitram, 406 U.S. 518, 531 (1972)	Bad policy. 1990 U.S.C.C.A.N. 4060-61 (S. Rep.)
Copyright Remedy Clarification Act, P.L.No. 101-553, 104 Stat. 2749 (1990)	BV Engineering v. UCLA, 858 F.2d 1394 (9th Cir. 1988), et al.; see Atascadero St. Hosp. v. Scanlon, 473 U.S. 234 (1985)	Bad interpretation based upon bad Supreme Court cases. 1990 U.S.C.C.A.N. 3950-55 (H.R. Rep.)
Clean Air Act, Amendments, Pub.L.No. 101-549, 104 Stat. 2399 (1990)		
§ 101(c)(3), 104 Stat. at 2406-07	Abramowitz v. EPA, 832 F.2d 1071 (9th Cir. 1987)	Bad policy. 1990 U.S.C.C.A.N. 3408 (S. Rep.)
§ 228(b), 104 Stat. at 2507-08	Ced's Inc. v. EPA, 745 F.2d 1092 (7th Cir. 1984)	Bad policy. 1990 U.S.C.C.A.N. 3509 (S. Rep.)
§ 228(d), 104 Stat. at 2510-11	United States v. Hill Petroleum, No. 85-0184C (W.D. La. July 29, 1986)	Bad policy. 1990 U.S.C.C.A.N. 3512 (S. Rep.)
§ 701, 104 Stat. at 2679 (new § 113(e))	United States v. SCM Corp., 667 F. Supp. 1110 (D.Md. 1987); United States v. Kaiser Steel, No.82-2623-IH (C.D.Cal. Jan. 17, 1984)	Bad policy. 1990 U.S.C.C.A.N. 3749 (S. Rep.)
§ 706, 104 Stat. at 2682	West Penn Power Co. v. EPA, 860 F.2d 581 (3d Cir. 1988)	Bad interpretation. 1990 U.S.C.C.A.N. 3755 (S. Rep.)
§ 707(g), 104 Stat. at 2683	Gwaltney v. Chesapeake Bay Foundation, 484 U.S. 49 (1984)	Bad policy. 136 CONG. REC. S18040 (daily ed. Oct. 24, 1990) (explanation of conference agreement)
§ 707(h), 104 Stat. at 2683-84	New York v. Thomas, 613 F. Supp. 1472 (D.D.C. 1985), rev'd on other grounds, 802 F.2d 1443 (D.C. Cir. 1986)	Bad policy. 1990 U.S.C.C.A.N. 3758 (S.Rep.)
National Defense Authorization Act for FY 1991, Pub.L.No. 101-510, § 555, 104 Stat. 1485, 1569-70 (1990)	Unnamed judicial decisions interpreting Uniformed Servs. Former Spouses Protection Act	Bad interpretation. 1990 U.S.C.C.A.N. 3166 (Conf. Rep.)

Omnibus Budget Reconciliation Act of 1990, Pub.L.No. 101-508, 104 Stat. 1388 (1990)		
§ 6208, 104 Stat. at 1388-307 to -308	Secretary of the Interior v. California, 464 U.S. 312 (1984)	Bad policy. 1990 U.S.C.C.A.N. 2675-77 (Conf. Rep.)
§ 11323(a), 104 Stat. at 1388-464	Commissioner v. Danileson, 378 F.2d 771 (3d Cir. 1967), et al.	Confusing caselaw. 1990 U.S.C.C.A.N. 2351-53 (H.R. Rep.)
Education of the Handicapped Act Amendments of 1990, Pub.L. No. 101-476, § 103, 104 Stat. 1103, 1106 (1990)	Dellmuth v. Muth, 491 U.S. 223 (1989)	Bad interpretation and bad policy. 1990 U.S.C.C.A.N. 1734 (H.R. Rep.)
Older Workers Benefit Protection Act, Pub.L. No. 101-433, 104 Stat. 978 (1990)	Public Employees Ret. Sys. of Ohio v. Betts, 492 U.S. 158 (1989)	Bad interpretation. 1990 U.S.C.C.A.N. 1510, 1522-23, 1534-35 (S. Rep.)
Radiation Exposure Compensation Act, Pub.L.No. 101-426, 104 Stat. 920 (1990)	United States v. Allen, 816 F.2d 1417 (10th Cir. 1987); Begay v. United States, 591 F. Supp. 991 (D.Ariz. 1984), aff'd, 768 F.2d 1059 (9th Cir. 1985)	Unfair interpretation. 1990 U.S.C.C.A.N. 1370-71 (H.R.Rep.)
Civil Service Due Process Amendments, Pub.L.No. 101-376, 104 Stat. 461 (1990)	United States v. Fausto, 484 U.S. 439 (1988)	Bad policy. 1990 U.S.C.C.A.N. 698 (H.R.Rep.)
Financial Institutions Reform, Recovery, and Enforcement Act of 1989, Pub.L.No. 101-73, 103 Stat. 183 (1989)		
§ 212(a), 103 Stat. at 225-30 (new § 11(d)(3)-(7))	Coit Indep. Joint Venture v. FSLIC, 489 U.S. 561 (1989)	Address concerns raised by Supreme Court. 1989 U.S.C.C.A.N. 214-15 (H.R. Rep.)
§ 212(a), 103 Stat. at 240	Continental Cas. v. Allen, 710 F.Supp. 1088 (N.D. Tex. 1989)	Bad policy. 1989 U.S.C.C.A.N. 212-13 (H.R. Rep.)
§ 902, 103 Stat. at 450-53	Larimore v. Comptroller of the Currency, 789 F.2d 1244 (7th Cir. 1986)	Confusion in law. 1989 U.S.C.C.A.N. 264 (H.R. Rep.)
§ 903, 103 Stat. at 453-57	Stoddard v. Board of Gov'rs, 868 F.2d 1308 (D.C. Cir. 1989)	Confusion in law. 1989 U.S.C.C.A.N. 264-65 (H.R. Rep.)
	100TH CONGRESS	
Marine Mammal Protection Act Amendments of 1988, Pub.L.No. 100-711, § 2, 102 Stat. 4755 (1988)	Kokechik Fishermen's Ass'n v. Secretary of Commerce, 839 F.2d 795 (D.C.Cir. 1988)	Bad policy. 1988 U.S.C.C.A.N. 6162, 6178-79 (H.R. Rep.)
Insider Trading & Securities Fraud Enforcement Act of 1988, Pub.L.No. 100-704, 102 Stat. 4677 (1988)		
§ 3(b)(2), 102 Stat. at 4680	Carpenter v. United States, 484 U.S. 19 (1987)	Issue unresolved by equally divided Court. 1988 U.S.C.C.A.N. 6047 (H.R. Rep.)
§ 5, 102 Stat. at 4680-81	Moss v. Morgan Stanley, 719 F.2d 5 (2d Cir. 1983)	Bad policy. 1988 U.S.C.C.A.N. 6075-76 (H.R. Rep.)
Patent & Trademark Office Authorization, Pub.L.No. 100-703, § 201, 102 Stat. 4674, 4676 (1988)	United States v. Morton Salt, 338 U.S. 632 (1950)	Bad policy. *Patent Licensing Reform Act of 1988: Hearing Before the Subcomm. on Courts, Civil Liberties & the Admin. of Justice of the House Comm. on the Judiciary*, 100th Cong., 2d Sess. 67 (1988)
Judicial Improvements & Access to Justice Act, Pub.L.No. 100-702, 102 Stat. 4642 (1988)		
§ 501, 102 Stat. at 4652	Bowen v. Massachusetts, 487 U.S. 879 (1988); Hohri v. United States, 482 U.S. 64 (1987)	Confused/unclear law. 1988 U.S.C.C.A.N. 6012-14 (H.R. Rep.)

§ 801, 102 Stat. at 4657	United States v. Evans, 526 F.2d 701 (5th Cir. 1976); United States v. Hill, 480 F. Supp. 1223 (S.D. Fla. 1979)	Bad policy. 1988 U.S.C.C.A.N. 6024 (H.R. Rep.)
§ 1007, 102 Stat. at 4667	In re Cement & Concrete Antitrust Litigation, 515 F. Supp. 1076 (D.Ariz. 1981)	Excessively technical policy. 1988 U.S.C.C.A.N. 6029 (H.R. Rep.)
§ 1019, 102 Stat. at 46	Baltimore Contractors, Inc. v. Bodinger, 348 U.S. 176 (1955)	Clarification of outdated rule. 133 CONG. REC. E1509 (daily ed. Apr. 23, 1987)
Anti-Drug Abuse Act of 1988, Pub.L.No. 100-690, § 7603, 102 Stat. 4181, 4508 (1988)	McNally v. United States, 483 U.S. 350 (1987)	Bad policy. 134 CONG. REC. S17376 (daily ed. Nov. 10, 1988)
Ocean Dumping Ban Act of 1988, Pub.L.No. 100-688, 102 Stat. 4139 (1988)	City of New York v. EPA, 543 F. Supp. 1084 (S.D.N.Y. 1981)	Bad policy. 1988 U.S.C.C.A.N. 5869-70 (S. Rep.)
Veterans' Judicial Review Act–Veterans' Benefits Improvement Act of 1988, Pub.L.No. 100-687, Tit. II & III, 102 Stat. 4105, 4109-22 (1988)	Traynor v. Turnage, 485 U.S. 535 (1988)	Bad policy. 1988 U.S.C.C.A.N. 5801-04 (H.R. Rep.)
Trademark Law Revision Act of 1988, Pub.L.No. 100-667, 102 Stat. 3935 (1988)		
§§ 128-130, 102 Stat. at 3944-45	Blau Plumbing, Inc. v. S.O.S. Fix-it, Inc., 781 F.2d 604 (7th Cir. 1986); Standard Terry Mills Inc. v. Shen Mfg. Co. 803 F.2d 778 (3d Cir. 1986)	Resolve split in circuits and update statute. 1982 U.S.C.C.A.N. 5601-02 (S. Rep.)
§ 132, 102 Stat. at 3946	Bernard Food Indus. v. Dietene Co., 415 F.2d 1279 (7th Cir. 1969)	Bad policy. 1988 U.S.C.C.A.N. 5603 (S. Rep.)
Satellite Home Viewer Act of 1988, Pub.L.No. 100-667, 102 Stat. 3935 (1988)	Eastern Microwave, Inc. v. Doubleday Sports, Inc., 691 F.2d 125 (2d Cir. 1982); Pacific & Southern Co. v. SBN, 694 F. Supp. 1565 (N.D. Ga. 1988)	Unanticipated policy problem. 1988 U.S.C.C.A.N. 5616 & 5642 (two H.R. Reps.)
Technical & Miscellaneous Revenue Act of 1988, Pub.L.No. 100-647, § 3041, 102 Stat. 3342, 3640-41 (1988)	Peterson Est. v. Comm'r, 90 T.C. #18 (1988), et al.	Bad policy. 1988 U.S.C.C.A.N. 4977 (S. Rep.)
McKinney Homeless Assistance Amendments Act of 1988, Pub.L.No. 100-628, § 1006, 102 Stat. 3224, 3265 (1988)	Drake v. Pierce, 698 F. Supp. 1523 (W.D. Wash. 1988)	Bad policy. 1988 U.S.C.C.A.N. 4477-78 (Conf. Rep.)
Review of Tribal Constitutions & Bylaws, Pub.L.No. 100-581, 102 Stat. 2938 (1988)	Coyote Valley Band of Pomo Indians v. United States, 639 F. Supp. 165 (E.D. Cal. 1986)	More flexible policy. 1988 U.S.C.C.A.N. 3909 (S. Rep.)
Intellectual Property Licenses in Bankruptcy, Pub.L.No. 100-506, 102 Stat. 2538 (1988)	Lubrizol Enterprises, Inc. v. Richmond Metal Finishers, Inc., 765 F.2d 1043 (4th Cir. 1985)	Bad policy. 1988 U.S.C.C.A.N. 3201-02 (S. Rep.)
Indian Gaming Regulatory Act, Pub.L.No. 100-497, 102 Stat. 2467 (1988)	California v. Cabazon Band of Mission Indians, 480 U.S. 202 (1987)	Rationalizing federal law. 1988 U.S.C.C.A.N. 3072-76 (S. Rep.)
Indian Self-Determination & Education Assistance Act Amendments of 1988, Pub.L.No. 100-472, § 206, 102 Stat. 2285, 2294-95 (1988)	Busby Sch. of the N. Cheyenne Tribe v. United States, 8 Ct.Cl. 596 (1985); Appeals of Papago Indian Tribe of Ariz., IBCA-1962 & 1966 (1986)	Unequal application of federal law. 1988 U.S.C.C.A.N. 2653-55 (S. Rep.)
Abandoned Shipwreck Act of 1987, Pub.L.No. 100-298, 102 Stat. 432 (1988)	Treasure Salvors, Inc. v. Unidentified Wrecked & Abandoned Sailing Vessel, 569 F.2d 330 (5th Cir. 1978), et al.	Split in courts, bad policy. 1988 U.S.C.C.A.N. 371 (H.R. Rep.)
Prescription Drug Marketing Act of 1987, Pub.L.No. 100-293, § 4, 102 Stat. 95, 96 (1988)	United States v. Park, 421 U.S. 658 (1975)	Unfair policy. 1988 U.S.C.C.A.N. 59-60 (S. Rep.)

Civil Rights Restoration Act of 1987, Pub.L.No. 100-259, 102 Stat. 28 (1988)	Grove City College v. Bell, 465 U.S. 555 (1984); Consolidated Rail Corp. v. Darrone, 465 U.S. 624, 635-36 (1984) (leaving issue open)	Bad interpretation. 1988 U.S.C.C.A.N. 3-6 (S. Rep.)
Computer Security Act, Pub.L.No. 100-235, § 8, 101 Stat. 1724, 1730 (1987).	SDC v. Mathews, 542 F.2d 1116 (9th Cir. 1976).	Bad interpretation, bad policy. 1987 U.S.C.C.A.N. 3157, 3183 & nn.44-45.
Foreign Relations Authorization Act, FY 1988-89, Pub.L.No. 100-204, 101 Stat. 1331, 1399 (1987).	Reagan v. Abourezk, 85 F.2d 1043 (D.C. Cir. 1986).	Constitutional concerns. 1987 U.S.C.C.A.N. 2357 (S. Rep.) & 2423 (Conf. Rep.).
Omnibus Budget Reconciliation Act of 1987, Pub.L.No. 100-203, 101 Stat. 1330 (1987)		
§ 9307(d), 101 Stat. 1330-357	AMP, Inc. v. United States, 820 F.2d 612 (3d Cir. 1987)	Policy coherence. 1987 U.S.C.C.A.N. 2313-614 (H.R. Rep.)
§ 9343(c), 101 Stat. at 1330-372	Calfee, Halter & Griswold v. Comm'r, 88 T.Ct. No. 35 (1987).	Bad interpretation. 1987 U.S.C.C.A.N. 2313-1636 (H.R. Conf. Rep.).
§ 10103, 101 Stat. 1330-86	Porter v. Comm'r, 88 T.Ct. No. 28 (1987)	Unfair policy. 1987 U.S.C.C.A.N. 2313-654 (H.R. Rep.)
§ 10222, 101 Stat. 1330-410 to -411	Woods Inv. Co. v. Comm'r, 85 T.Ct. 274 (1985).	Unfair policy. 1987 U.S.C.C.A.N. 2313-703-705 (H.R. Rep.), 2313-1706-1709 (Conf. Rep.)
§ 10225, 101 Stat. 1330-413	Textron, Inc. v. United States, 561 F.2d 1023 (1st Cir. 1977)	Unfair tax policy. 1987 U.S.C.C.A.N. 2313-711 (H.R. Rep.) & 2313-1717 (Conf.Rep.)
§ 10402, 101 Stat. 1330-431 to -432	Estate of John G. Boykin, 53 T.C.M. 345 (1987)	Unfair policy. 1987 U.S.C.C.A.N. 2313-658 to -660 (H.R. Rep.) & 2313-1740 to -1743 (Conf.Rep.)
Criminal Fine Improvements Act, Pub.L.No. 100-185, § 3, 101 Stat. 1279 (1987)	United States v. King, 824 F.2d 313 (4th Cir. 1987); United States v. Mayberry, 774 F.2d 1018 (10th Cir. 1985)	Policy coherence. 1987 U.S.C.C.A.N. 2140 (H.R. Rep.)
Competitive Equality Banking Act, Pub. L. No. 100-86, 101 Stat. 552 (1987)		
§ 101(a), 101 Stat. at 554	Unnamed 11th Circuit case	Bad policy. 1987 U.S.C.C.A.N. 497 (S. Rep.)
§ 108, 101 Stat. at 579	M&M Leasing Corp. v. Seattle First Nat'l Bank, 563 F.2d 1377 (9th Cir. 1977)	Bad policy. 1987 U.S.C.C.A.N. 533 (S.Rep.), 612 (Conf. Rep.)
Water Quality Act, Pub.L.No. 100-4, 101 Stat. 7 (1987)		
§ 306, 101 Stat. at 35-36	Chemical Mfrs. Ass'n v. NRDC, 470 U.S. 116 (1985)	Bad policy. 1987 U.S.C.C.A.N. 22-25 (floor remarks)
§ 406(e), 101 Stat. at 73	NRDC v. EPA, 790 F.2d 289 (3d Cir. 1986)	Policy fairness. 1987 U.S.C.C.A.N. 40 (floor remarks)
	99TH CONGRESS	
Nat'l Defense Auth. Act for FY 1987, Pub.L.No. 99-661, § 952, 100 Stat. 3816, 3945-49 (1986)	Cutler-Hammer, Inc. v. United States, 416 F.2d 1306 (1969); United States v. Rogerson, 785 F.2d 296 (Fed. Cir. 1986)	Policy unfairness, bad interpretation. 1986 U.S.C.C.A.N. 6462-63 (S. Rep.) & 6568-69 (Conf. Rep.)
Health Programs, Pub.L.No. 99-660, § 2122, 100 Stat. 3743 (1986)	Givens v. Lederle, 556 F.2d 1341 (5th Cir. 1977), et al.	Bad policy. 1986 U.S.C.C.A.N. 6368 (H.R. Rep.)
Sexual Abuse Act of 1986, Pub.L.No. 99-654, § 2, 100 Stat. 3660, 3660-63 (1986)	Williams v. United States, 327 U.S. 711 (1946)	Bad policy. 1986 U.S.C.C.A.N. 6188 & nn.15-16, 6194-6200 (H.R. Rep.)
Criminal Law & Procedure Technical Amendments Act of 1986, Pub.L.No. 99-646, 100 Stat. 3592 (1986)		

§ 61, 100 Stat. at 3614	United States v. Dawlett, 787 F.2d 771 (1st Cir. 1986)	Bad policy. 1986 U.S.C.C.A.N. 6153 (H.R. Rep.)
§ 63, 100 Stat. at 3614-15	United States v. Lopez-Flores, 592 F.Supp. 1302 (W.D.Tex.1984)	Bad policy. 1986 U.S.C.C.A.N. 6153 (H.R. Rep.)
§ 68, 100 Stat. at 3616	United States v. Carpenter, 611 F.2d 113 (5th Cir. 1980); United States v. Culbert, 548 F.2d 1355 (9th Cir.1977)	Split in circuits. 1986 U.S.C.C.A.N. 6155-56 (H.R. Rep.)
Emergency Wetlands Resources Act of 1986, Pub.L. No. 99-645, § 501, 100 Stat. 3582, 3590 (1986)	United States v. Wulff, 758 F.2d 1121 (6th Cir. 1985)	Bad policy. 1986 U.S.C.C.A.N. 6128 (S.Rep.)
Futures Trading Act of 1986, Pub.L.No. 99-641, § 103, 100 Stat. 3556, 3557 (1986)	CFTC v. Nahas, 738 F.2d 487 (D.C. Cir. 1984)	Bad policy. 1986 U.S.C.C.A.N. 6010 (H.R. Rep.)
Child Sexual Abuse & Pornography Act of 1986, Pub.L. No. 99-628, § 5(b)(1), 100 Stat. 3510-11 (1986)	Caminetti v. United States, 242 U.S. 470 (1917), aff'd, Cleveland v. United States, 329 U.S. 14 (1946)	Outdated policy. 1986 U.S.C.C.A.N. 5958 (H.R. Rep.)
Immigration Reform & Control Act of 1986, Pub.L.No. 99-603, 100 Stat. 3359 (1986)		
§ 112, 100 Stat. at 3381-83	United States v. Anaya, 509 F.Supp. 2289 (S.D. Fla.), aff'd, 685 F.2d 1272 (11th Cir. 1982)	Bad and ambiguous policy. 1986 U.S.C.C.A.N. 5669-70 (H.R. Rep.)
§ 315(b), 100 Stat. at 3439-40	INS v. Phinpathya, 464 U.S. 183 (1984)	Bad policy. 1986 U.S.C.C.A.N. 5728 (H.R. Rep.)
Quiet Title Actions, Pub.L.No. 99-598, 100 Stat. 3351 (1986)	Block v. North Dakota, 461 U.S. 273 (1983)	Bad policy. 1986 U.S.C.C.A.N. 5643-44 (H.R. Rep.)
Age Discrimination in Employment Amendments of 1986, Pub.L.No. 99-592, 100 Stat. 3342 (1986)	Johnson v. Mayor & City Council of Baltimore, 472 U.S. 353 (1985)	Clarify policy. 1986 U.S.C.C.A.N. 5632, 5639 (H.R. Rep.); also 131 CONG. REC. S14044 (daily ed. Oct. 24, 1983)
Freedom of Information Reform Act of 1986, §§ 1801-1804 of the Anti-Drug Abuse Act of 1986, Pub.L.No. 99-570, 100 Stat. 3207, 3207-48 (1986)	Sladek v. Bensinger, 605 F.2d 899 (5th Cir. 1979), et al.	Bad policy. *Freedom of Information Act: Hearing Before the Subcomm. on Technology & the Law of the Senate Comm. on the Judiciary*, 100th Cong., 2d Sess. 60 & n.38
	Jordan v. United States Dep't of Justice, 591 F.2d 753 (D.C. Cir. 1978) (en banc), et al.	Bad policy. *Freedom of Information Act: Hearing Before the Subcomm. on Technology & the Law of the Senate Comm. on the Judiciary*, 100th Cong., 2d Sess. 62
False Claims Amendments Act of 1986, Pub.L.No. 99-562, 100 Stat. 3153 (1986)		
§ 2(7), 100 Stat. at 3153-54	Olson v. Mellon, 4 F.Supp. 947 (W.D.Pa.1933), aff'd, 71 F.2d (3d Cir. 1934)	Split in circuits. 1986 U.S.C.C.A.N. 5283-84 (S. Rep.)
	United States v. Aerodex, Inc, 469 F.2d 1003 (5th Cir. 1972)	Bad policy. 1986 U.S.C.C.A.N. 5284 (S. Rep.)
	United States v. Azzarelli Constr. Co., 647 F.2d 757 (7th Cir. 1981), et al.	Bad policy. 1986 U.S.C.C.A.N. 5286-87 (S. Rep.)
§ 5, 100 Stat. at 3158	United States v. Ueber, 299 F.2d 310 (6th Cir. 1962), et al.	Bad policy. 1986 U.S.C.C.A.N. 5295-96 (S. Rep.)
§ 6, 100 Stat. at 3159-68	United States v. Sells Eng'g Co., 463 U.S. 418 (1983); United States v. Baggot, 463 U.S. 476 (1983)	Bad policy. 1986 U.S.C.C.A.N. 5298-99 (S. Rep.)
Tax Reform Act of 1986, Pub.L.No. 99-514, 100 Stat. 2085 (1986)		

§ 631, 100 Stat. at 2269-75	General Utilities & Operating Co. v. Helvering, 296 U.S. 200 (1935)	Bad policy. See 1986 U.S.C.C.A.N. 4286-87, 4292-93 (Conf. Rep.)
§ 821, 100 Stat. at 2372	Orange & Rockland Utils. v. Comm'r, 86 T.Ct. No. 14 (1986), et al.	Bad policy. 1986 U.S.C.C.A.N. 4410-12 (Conf. Rep.)
§ 1004, 100 Stat. at 2388	Miller v. Comm'r, 733 F.2d 399 (6th Cir. 1984), et al.	Bad policy. 1986 U.S.C.C.A.N. 4430-31 (Conf. Rep.)
§ 1501, 100 Stat. at 2732-43	Asphalt Prods. Co. v. Comm'r, 796 F.2d 843 (6th Cir. 1986)	Bad interpretation. 1986 U.S.C.C.A.N. 4870 n.3 (Conf. Rep.)
§ 1535, 100 Stat. at 2750	DeMartino v. Comm'r, T.C. Memo. 1986-263, et al.	Bad interpretation and bad policy. 1986 U.S.C.C.A.N. 4884 (Conf. Rep.)
Electronic Communications Privacy Act, Pub.L.No. 99-508, 100 Stat. 1848 (1986)		
§ 101(b)(2), 100 Stat. at 1850	Boddie v. ABC, 731 F.2d 333 (6th Cir. 1984), et al.	Constitutional problems. 1986 U.S.C.C.A.N. 3571 (S. Rep.)
§ 301(a), 100 Stat. at 1868-72	United States v. New York Tel. Co., 434 U.S. 159 (1977), et al.	Constitutional problems and bad policy. 1986 U.S.C.C.A.N. 3556, 3567-68 (S. Rep.)
Rehabiliation Act Amendments, Pub.L.No. 99-506, 100 Stat. 1807 (1986)	Atascadero State Hosp. v. Scanlon, 473 U.S. 234 (1985)	Bad interpretation. S. REP. No. 388, 99th Cong., 2d Sess. 27 (1986)
Superfund Amendments & Reauthorization Act of 1986, Pub.L.No. 99-499, 100 Stat. 1613 (1986)		
§ 114, 100 Stat. at 1652-53	Exxon Corp. v. Hunt, 475 U.S. 355 (1986)	Bad policy. 1986 U.S.C.C.A.N. 3318 (Conf. Rep.)
§ 127(d), 100 Stat. at 1693	Middlesex County Sewerage Auth. v. National Sea Clammers Ass'n, 453 U.S. 1 (1981)	Bad policy. 1986 U.S.C.C.A.N. 3352-53 (Conf. Rep.)
Air Carrier Access Act of 1986, Pub.L.No. 99-435, 100 Stat. 1080 (1986)	United States Dep't Transp. v. Paralyzed Veterans of America, 477 U.S. 597 (1986)	Policy fairness. 1986 U.S.C.C.A.N. 2329-30 (S. Rep.)
Handicapped Children's Protection Act of 1986, Pub.L. No. 99-372, 100 Stat. 796 (1986)	Smith v. Robinson, 468 U.S. 992 (1984); also Marek v. Chesney, 473 U.S. 1 (1985) (overidden in part)	Bad interpretation. 1986 U.S.C.C.A.N. 1799 (Conf. Rep.)
Judicial Improvements Act of 1985, Pub.L.No. 99-336, § 3, 100 Stat.633, 637 (1986)	Lambert Run Coal Co. v. B&O R. Co., 258 U.S. 377 (1922), aff'd in Franchise Tax Bd v. Construction Trust, 463 U.S. 1, 24 (1983)	Obsolescent rule. 1986 U.S.C.C.A.N. 1553 (H.R. Rep.)
Firearm Owners' Protection Act, Pub.L.No. 99-308, § 105, 100 Stat. 449, 459 (1986)	Dickerson V. New Banner Inst., Inc., 260 U.S. 103 (1983)	Bad policy. 1986 U.S.C.C.A.N. 1354-55 (H.R. Rep.)
Comprehensive Omnibus Budget Reconciliation Act of 1986, Pub.L.No. 99-272, § 11007(a), 100 Stat. 82, 244 (1986)	In re Bastian Co., 45 Bankr.L.Rep. 717 (W.D.N.Y. 1985)	Bad interpretation. 1986 U.S.C.C.A.N. 699 (H.R. Rep.)
California-Nevada Boundary, Pub.L.No. 99-200, 99 Stat. 1663 (1985)	California v. Nevada, 447 U.S. 125 (1980)	Litigation inappropriate. § 1, 99 Stat. 1663
Dep't of Defense Auth. Act, 1986, Pub.L.No. 99-145, § 512, 99 Stat. 583, 623-27 (1985)	Doughtery v. Lehman, 688 F.2d 158 (3d Cir. 1982)	Bad policy. 1985 U.S.C.C.A.N. 484-85 (H.R. Rep.)
Equal Access to Justice Act, Extension & Amendment, Pub.L.No. 99-80, 99 Stat. 183 (1985)		
§ 1(a), (c), 99 Stat. at 183-84	Spencer v. NLRB, 712 F.2d 539 (D.C. Cir. 1983), et al.	Bad interpretation. 1985 U.S.C.C.A.N. 139-41 (H.R. Rep.)

§ 1(c)(2), 99 Stat. at 184	Fidelity Constr. Co. v. United States, 700 F.2d 1379 (Fed. Cir. 1983)	Bad policy. 1985 U.S.C.C.A.N. 144 (H.R. Rep.)
§ 2, 99 Stat. at 184-85	Tulalip Tribes of Washington v. FERC, 749 F.2d 1367 (9th Cir. 1984)	Bad policy. 1985 U.S.C.C.A.N. 145 (H.R. Rep.)
§ 2(c)(2)(G), 99 Stat. at 185	Auke Bay Concerned Citizens' Advisory Council v. Marsh, 755 F.2d 717 (9th Cir. 1985)	Overly technical approach. 1985 U.S.C.C.A.N. 146 (H.R. Rep.)
§ 2(c)(2)(H), 99 Stat. at 185	Cases holding EAJA inapplicable to condemnation proceedings (no list)	Bad policy. 1985 U.S.C.C.A.N. 147 (H.R. Rep.)
Export Administration Amendments Act of 1985, Pub.L.No. 99-64, § 113(5), 99 Stat. 120, 148-50 (1985)	United States v. Swarovski, 557 F.2d 40 (2d Cir. 1977)	Bad policy. 1986 U.S.C.C.A.N. 126 (Conf. Rep.)

98TH CONGRESS

Patent Law Amendments of 1984, Pub.L.No. 98-622, 98 Stat. 3383 (1984)		
§ 101, 98 Stat. at 3383	Deepsouth Packing Co. v. Laitram Corp., 406 U.S. 518 (1972)	Bad policy. 1984 U.S.C.C.A.N. 5828 (section-by-section floor analysis)
§ 103, 98 Stat. at 3384	In re Clemens, 622 F.2d 1029 (C.C.P.A. 1980); In re Bass, 474 F.2d 1276 (C.C.P.A. 1973)	Bad policy. 1984 U.S.C.C.A.N. 5833-34 (section-by-section floor analysis)
Trademark Clarification Act, Pub.L.No. 98-620, § 102, 98 Stat. 3335 (1984)	Anti-Monopoly, Inc. v. General Mills Fun Group, Inc., 684 F.2d 1316 (9th Cir. 1982)	Bad interpretation, and bad policy. 1984 U.S.C.C.A.N. 5720-27 (S. Rep.)
Trade & Tariff Act of 1984, Pub.L.No. 98-573, § 210(a), 98 Stat. 2948, 2977 (1984)	United States v. Heraeus-Amersil, Inc., 671 F.2d 1356 (C.C.P.A. 1982)	Bad policy. 1984 U.S.C.C.A.N. 5027 (H.R. Rep.)
Cable Communications Policy Act of 1984, Pub.L.No. 98-549, § 5, 98 Stat. 2779, 2802-03 (1984)	Chartwell Communications Group v. Westbrook, 637 F.2d 459 (6th Cir. 1980)	Bad policy. 1984 U.S.C.C.A.N. 4745-52 (floor colloquy)
Local Government Antitrust Act of 1984, Pub.L.No.98-544, 98 Stat. 2750 (1984)	Community Communications Co. v. City of Boulder, 455 U.S. 40 (1982); City of Lafayette v. Louisiana Power & Light, 435 U.S. 389 (1978)	Bad interpretation and bad policy. 1984 U.S.C.C.A.N. 4603-08 (H.R. Rep.)
Central Intelligence Information Act, Pub.L. No. 98-477, § 2(c), 98 Stat. 2209, 2211-12 (1984)	Terkel v. Kelly, 599 F.2d 214 (7th Cir. 1979); Painter v. FBI, 615 F.2d 689 (6th Cir. 1980)	Bad interpretation and bad policy. 1984 U.S.C.C.A.N. 3786-88 & 3791 (H.R. Rep.)
Comprehensive Crime Control Act of 1984, Pub.L.No. 98-473, 98 Stat. 1837 (1984)		
§ 212(a), 98 Stat. at 2000	United States v. Segal, 549 F.2d 1293, 1301 (9th Cir. 1977)	Bad reasoning. 1984 U.S.C.C.A.N. 3309-10, 3312 (S. Rep.)
	Smith v. United States, 143 F.2d 228 (9th Cir. 1944)	Bad policy. 1984 U.S.C.C.A.N. 3320 (S. Rep.)
§ 1005, 98 Stat. at 2138-39	Busic v. United States, 446 U.S. 398 (1980); Simpson v. United States, 435 U.S. 6, 10 (1978)	Bad policy. 1984 U.S.C.C.A.N. 3490, 3493 n.3 (S. Rep.)
§ 1103, 98 Stat. at 2143	United States v. Brown, 688 F.2d 596 (9th Cir. 1982)	Bad policy. 1984 U.S.C.C.A.N. 3509 (S. Rep.)
§ 1104, 98 Stat. at 2143-44	United States v. Loschiavo, 531 F.2d 659 (2d Cir. 1976), et al.	Bad policy. 1984 U.S.C.C.A.N. 3510-11 (S. Rep.)
§ 1106, 98 Stat. at 2145	United States v. Kaplan, 586 F.2d 980 (2d Cir. 1978), et al.	Bad policy. 1984 U.S.C.C.A.N. 3514 (S. Rep.)
§ 1107, 98 Stat. at 2145-46	Williams v. United States, 458 U.S. 279 (1982); United States v. Maze, 414 U.S. 395 (1974)	Bad policy. 1984 U.S.C.C.A.N. 3517-19 (S. Rep.)
§ 1109(a), 98 Stat. at 2147-48	United States v. Bedwell, 456 F.2d 448 (8th Cir. 1972)	Bad policy. 1984 U.S.C.C.A.N. 3521 (S. Rep.)

§ 1204(a), 98 Stat. at 2152	United States v. Lember, 319 F.Supp. 249 (E.D. Va. 1970)	Bad policy. 1984 U.S.C.C.A.N. 3538 (S. Rep.)
§ 1206, 98 Stat. at 2153	United States v. Sam Goody, Inc., 675 F.2d 17 (2d Cir.1982), et al.	Bad policy. 1984 U.S.C.C.A.N. 3541-44 (S. Rep.)
§ 1503(2), 98 Stat. at 2182	Playboy Enterprises v. Baccarat Clothing Co., 692 F.2d 1272 (9th Cir. 1982)	Bad policy. 1984 U.S.C.C.A.N. 3631-32 (S. Rep.)
Longshore & Harbor Workers' Compensation Act Amendments of 1984, Pub.L.No. 98-426, § 4, 98 Stat. 1639, 1641 (1984)	Washington Metropolitan Area Transit Authority v. Johnson, 467 U.S. 925 (1984)	Bad interpretation. 1984 U.S.C.C.A.N. 2774 (Conf. Rep.)
Drug Price Competition & Patent Term Restoration Act, Pub.L.No. 98-417, § 202, 98 Stat. 1585, 1603 (1984)	Roche Prods. v. Bolar Pharmaceutical Co., 733 F.2d 858 (Fed. Cir. 1984)	Bad policy. 1984 U.S.C.C.A.N. 2678-79 (H.R. Rep.)
Insider Trading Sanctions Act of 1984, Pub.L.No. 98-376, § 2, 98 Stat. 1264 (1984)	SEC v. MacDonald, 699 F.2d 47 (1st Cir. 1983)	Bad policy. 1984 U.S.C.C.A.N. 2284-85 (H.R. Rep.)
Deficit Reduction Act of 1984, Pub.L.No. 98-369, 98 Stat. 494 (1984)		
§ 65, 98 Stat. at 584	Comm'r v. Kelly, 293 F.2d 904 (5th Cir. 1961)	Bad policy. 1984 U.S.C.C.A.N. 1536 (Conf. Rep.)
§ 77, 98 Stat. at 595-97	Starker v. United States, 602 F.2d 1341 (9th Cir. 1979)	Bad policy.1984 U.S.C.C.A.N. 895-98 (H.R. Rep.)
§ 79, 98 Stat. at 597	Raphan v. United States, 3 Ct.Cl. 457 (1983)	Bad policy. 1984 U.S.C.C.A.N. 899-900 (H.R. Rep.)
§ 82, 98 Stat. at 598	Edward L. Stephenson Trust v. Comm'r, 81 T.C. 22 (1983)	Bad policy. 1984 U.S.C.C.A.N. 902-03 (H.R. Rep.)
§ 91, 98 Stat. at 598-601	Harold v. Comm'r, 192 F.2d 1002 (4th Cir. 1951); Crescent Wharf v. Comm'r, 518 F.2d 772 (9th Cir. 1975)	Bad policy. 1984 U.S.C.C.A.N. 915 (H.R. Rep.)
§ 95, 98 Stat. at 616	Insilco Corp. v. Comm'r, 73 T.C. 589 (1980)	Bad policy. 1984 U.S.C.C.A.N. 1585-86 (Conf. Rep.)
§ 131, 98 Stat. at 662-64	Dittler Bros. v. Comm'r, 72 T.C. 896, 915 (1979)	Bad policy. 1984 U.S.C.C.A.N. 969, 971 (H.R. Rep.)
§ 159, 98 Stat. at 696	United States v. Williams, 644 F.2d 696 (8th Cir. 1981)	Bad policy. 1984 U.S.C.C.A.N. 1689 (Conf. Rep.)
§ 172(a), 98 Stat. at 699-703	Beaton v. Comm'r, 664 F.2d 315 (1st Cir. 1981); J. Simpson Dean v. Comm'r, 35 T.C. 1083 (1961), et al.	Bad policy. 1984 U.S.C.C.A.N. 1019-21 (H.R. Rep.)
	Greenspun v. Comm'r, 72 T.C. 931, aff'd, 670 F.2d 123 (9th Cir. 1982)	Bad policy. 1984 U.S.C.C.A.N. 1699-1712 (Conf. Rep.)
§ 211(a), 98 Stat. at 740-41	Comm'r v. Standard Life & Accid. Ins. Co., 433 U.S. 148 (1977)	Bad policy. 1984 U.S.C.C.A.N. 1072-73 (H.R. Rep.) & 1748-53 (Conf.Rep.)
§ 421, 98 Stat. at 793-95	United States v. Davis, 370 U.S. 65 (1962)	Bad policy. 1984 U.S.C.C.A.N. 1134-35 (H.R. Rep.) & 1804 (Conf. Rep.)
§ 1026, 98 Stat. at 1031	Diedrich v. Comm'r, 457 U.S. 191 (1982)	Fairness adjustment. 1984 U.S.C.C.A.N. 1328-29 (H.R. Rep.) & 1929-30 (Conf. Rep.)
§ 1051, 98 Stat. at 1044-45	Kamanski v. Comm'r, 477 F.2d 452 (9th Cir. 1973)	Bad policy. 1984 U.S.C.C.A.N. 1329-32 (H.R. Rep.) & 1952 (Conf. Rep.)
Bankruptcy Amendments & Federal Judgeship Act of 1984, Pub.L.No. 98-353, 98 Stat. 333, 390-91 (1984)	NLRB v. Bildisco & Bildisco, 465 U.S. 513 (1984)	Bad policy. 130 CONG. REC. 14851-52 & 17151-59 (1984)
Shipping Act of 1984, Pub.L.No. 98-237, § 7, 98 Stat. 67, 73-74 (1984)	FMC v. Aktiebolaget Svenska Amerika Linien, 309 U.S. 238 (1968); Carnation Co. v. Pacific Westbound Conf., 383 U.S 213 (1966)	Bad policy. 1984 U.S.C.C.A.N. 174, 222-23 (Conf. Rep.)

FCC Authorization Act of 1983, Pub.L.No. 98-214, § 4, 97 Stat. 1467-68 (1983)	Western Broadcasting Co. v. FCC, 674 F.2d 4 (D.C. Cir. 1982)	Bad policy. 1983 U.S.C.C.A.N. 2232 (H.R. Rep.)
Supplemental Approps. Act of 1983, Pub.L.No. 98-63, ch. VII, 97 Stat. 301, 323-24 (1983)	Meade Township v. Andrus, 695 F.2d 1006 (6th Cir. 1982)	Bad policy. 1983 U.S.C.C.A.N. 1309 (S. Rep.)
Social Security Amendments of 1983, Pub.L.No. 98-21, § 327, 97 Stat. 65, 126-27 (1983)	Rowan Companies, Inc. v. United States, 452 U.S. 247 (1981)	Bad reasoning. 1983 U.S.C.C.A.N. 183 (S. Rep.), 299-300 (H.R. Rep.), 438 (Conf. Rep.)
	97TH CONGRESS	
Misc. Tax & ERISA Provisions, Pub.L.No. 97-473, § 301, 96 Stat. 2605, 2611-12 (1982)	Agsalud v. Standard Oil of Calif., 454 U.S. 801 (1981), aff'g mem., 633 F.2d 760 (9th Cir. 1980)	Bad policy. 1982 U.S.C.C.A.N. 4595 (S. Rep.) & 4603 (Conf. Rep.)
Futures Trading Act of 1982, Pub.L.No. 97-444, 96 Stat. 2294 (1982)		
§ 101, 96 Stat. at 2294-96	Board of Trade of the City of Chicago v. SEC, 677 F.2d 1137 (7th Cir. 1982)	Interpretation violates agency agreement. 1982 U.S.C.C.A.N. 3889, 3929 (H.R. Rep.)
§ 225, 96 Stat. at 2315-16	Board of Trade of the City of Chicago v. CFTC, 605 F.2d 1016 (7th Cir. 1979)	Bad policy. 1982 U.S.C.C.A.N. 3906-09 (H.R. Rep.)
NRC Authorization Act, Pub.L.No. 97-415, § 12, 96 Stat. 2067, 2073-74 (1982)	Sholly v. United States Nuclear Regulatory Comm'n, 651 F.2d 780 (D.C. Cir. 1980) (per curium)	Bad policy. 1982 U.S.C.C.A.N. 3598 (S. Rep.)
Antitrust Reciprocity Act, Pub.L.No. 97-393, 96 Stat. 1964 (1982)	Pfizer, Inc. v. Gov't of India, 434 U.S. 308 (1978)	Bad policy. 1982 U.S.C.C.A.N. 3495, 3500-01 (H.R. Rep.)
Endangered Species Act Amendments of 1982, Pub.L.No. 97-304, § 5, 96 Stat. 1411, 1421-22 (1982)	Defenders of Wildlife, Inc. v. Endangered Species Scientific Auth., 659 F.2d 168 (D.C. Cir. 1981)	Bad policy. 1982 U.S.C.C.A.N. 2829 (H.R. Rep.) & 2869 (Conf. Rep.)
Communications Amendments of 1982--National Telecommunications and Information Administration, Pub.L. No. 97-259, 96 Stat. 1087, 1099 (1982)	Reston v. FCC, 492 F.Supp. 697 (D.D.C. 1980)	Bad policy. 1982 U.S.C.C.A.N. 2304 (Conf. Rep.)
Dep't of Defense Authorization Act of 1983, Pub.L.No. 97-252, § 1002, 96 Stat. 718, 730-35 (1982)	McCarty v. McCarty, 453 U.S. 210 (1981)	Unfair policy. 1982 U.S.C.C.A.N. 1570 (Conf.Rep.)
Tax Equity & Fiscal Responsibility Act of 1982, Pub.L.No. 97-248, 96 Stat. 324 (1982)		
§ 224, 96 Stat. at 485-90	Kimbell-Diamond Milling Co. v. Comm'r, 14 T.C. 74, aff'd, 187 F.2d 718 (5th Cir. 1951)	Bad policy. 1982 U.S.C.C.A.N. 1309-14 (Conf. Rep.)
§ 228, 96 Stat. at 493	Rickey v. United States, 592 F.2d 1251 (5th Cir. 1979)	Bad policy. 1982 U.S.C.C.A.N. 1319 (Conf. Rep.)
Voting Rights Act Amendments of 1982, Pub.L.No. 97-205, § 3, 96 Stat. 131, 134 (1982)	City of Mobile v. Bolden, 446 U.S. 55 (1980)	Bad interpretation. 1982 U.S.C.C.A.N. 179, 193-204 (S. Rep.)
Federal Tort Claims--National Guard, Pub.L.No. 97-124, 95 Stat. 1666 (1981)	Maryland v. United States, 381 U.S. 41 (1965)	Bad policy. *Federal Tort Claims Act: Hearings Before the Subcomm. on Agency Admin. of the Senate Comm. on the Judiciary*, 97th Cong., 1st & 2d Sess. 34, 86-88 (1981-82).
Immigration & Nationality Act Amendments of 1981, Pub.L.No. 97-116, § 8, 95 Stat. 1611, 1616 (1981)	Reid v. INS, 420 U.S. 619 (1975); INS v. Errico, 385 U.S. 214 (1966)	Confusing Court precedents. 1981 U.S.C.C.A.N. 2593-94 (H.R. Rep.)
Dep't of Defense Authorization Act of 1982, Pub.L.No. 97-86, § 905, 95 Stat. 1099, 1114-16 (1981)	United States v. Banks, 383 F.Supp. 368 (D.S.D. 1974); United States v. Jaramillo, 380 F.Supp. 1375 (D. Neb.), appeal dismissed, 510 F.2d 808 (8th Cir. 1975)	Bad policy and update old statute. 1981 U.S.C.C.A.N. 1788, 1790 (H.R. Rep.)

Military Justice Amendments of 1981, Pub.L.No. 97-81, 95 Stat. 1085 (1981)		
§ 4, 95 Stat. at 1038	United States v. Furgason, 6 M.J. 844 (CMR 1979), et. al.	Unfair policy. 1981 U.S.C.C.A.N. 1521 (S. Rep.)
§ 5, 95 Stat. at 1088-89	United States v. Larneard, 3 M.J. 76 (CMA 1977)	Bad policy. 1981 U.S.C.C.A.N. 1517-18 (S. Rep.)
Lacey Act Amendments of 1981, Pub.L.No. 97-79, 95 Stat. 1073 (1981)		
§ 2(a), 95 Stat. at 1073	United States v. Wingate, No. 76-20M (M.D. Fla. June 18, 1976)	Bad interpretation. 1981 U.S.C.C.A.N. 1752 (S. Rep.)
§ 2(d), 95 Stat. at 1073	United States v. Molt, 599 F.2d 1217 (3d Cir. 1979)	Bad policy. 1981 U.S.C.C.A.N. 1753 (S. Rep.)
Marine Mammal Protection Act, Pub.L.No. 97-58, § 2(2), 95 Stat. 979, 981 (1981)	People of Togiak v. United States, 470 F.Supp. 423 (D.D.C 1979)	Bad policy. 1981 U.S.C.C.A.N. 1470 (H.R. Rep.)
Omnibus Budget Reconciliation Act of 1981, Pub.L.No. 97-35, 95 Stat. 357 (1981)		
§§ 1118(e)(3) & 1119(d), 95 Stat. at 631-32, 633	Gebbie v. United States R.R. Retirement Bd., 631 F.2d 512 (7th Cir. 1980)	Bad policy. 1981 U.S.C.C.A.N. 1224-26 (Conf. Rep.)
§ 2312, 95 Stat. at 853	Burns v. Alcala, 420 U.S. 575 (1975)	Bad policy. 1981 U.S.C.C.A.N. 780-81 (S. Rep.)
Economic Recovery Tax Act of 1981, Pub.L.No.97-34, 95 Stat. 172 (1981)		
§ 266, 95 Stat. at 265-66	Consolidated Freight Lines, Inc. v. Comm'r, 37 BTA 576 (1938), aff'd, 101 F.2d 813 (9th Cir. 1938)	Special relief. 1981 U.S.C.C.A.N. 206 (S. Rep.)
§ 507, 95 Stat. at 333	Teh v. Comm'r, 260 F.2d 489 (9th Cir. 1952); Comm'r v. Pittston Co., 252 F.2d 344 (2d Cir. 1958)	Bad policy. 1981 U.S.C.C.A.N. 266-67 (S. Rep.)
	96TH CONGRESS	
Miscellaneous Revenue Act of 1980, Pub.L.No. 96-605, § 107, 94 Stat. 3521, 3524 (1980)	Comm'r v. Kowalski, 434 U.S. 77 (1977)	Unfair policy. 1980 U.S.C.C.A.N. 7311 (S. Rep.)
Pub.L.No. 96-598, § 1, 94 Stat. 3485, 3485-86 (1980)	Great Olympic Tire Co. v. U.S., 597 F.2d 449 (5th Cir. 1979)	Bad policy. 1980 U.S.C.C.A.N. 7201-02 & n.2 (S. Rep.)
Pub.L.No. 96-596, § 2, 94 Stat. 3469, 3469-74 (1980)	Adams v. Comm'r, 72 T.C. 81 (1979)	Bad policy. 1980 U.S.C.C.A.N. 7191-92 & n.4 (S. Rep.)
Bankruptcy Tax Act of 1980, Pub.L.No. 96-589, § 5(f), 94 Stat. 3389, 3406 (1980)	Meyer v. Comm'r, 383 F.2d 883 (8th Cir. 1967)	Bad policy. 1980 U.S.C.C.A.N. 7058 & n.9 (S. Rep.)
Alaska National Interest Lands Conservation Act, Pub.L.No. 96-487, § 1323, 94 Stat. 2371, 2488 (1980)	Utah v. Andrus, Civ. 79-0037 (D. Ut. Oct. 1, 1979)	Legal uncertainty. 1980 U.S.C.C.A.N. 5254 (S. Rep.)
Federal Question Jurisdictional Amendments Act of 1980, Pub.L.No. 96-486, 94 Stat. 2369 (1980)	Snyder v. Harris, 294 U.S. 332 (1969)	Unfair policy. 1980 U.S.C.C.A.N. 5064 & n.2 (H.R. Rep.)
Equal Access to Justice Act, Title II of the Small Business Export Expansion Act of 1980, Pub.L.No. 96-481, 94 Stat. 2321, 2325-30 (1980)	Peolo v. Farmers Homes Admin., 562 F.2d 744 (D.C. Cir. 1977), et al.; also Alyeska Pipeline v. Wilderness Soc'y, 421 U.S. 240 (1975)	Bad policy. 1980 U.S.C.C.A.N. 4996, also 4985 (H.R. Rep.)
Installment Sales Revision Act of 1980, Pub.L.No. 96-471, 94 Stat. 2247 (1980)		
§ 2(a), 94 Stat. at 2247-51	Kirschenmann v. United States, 488 F.2d 270 (9th Cir. 1973), et al.	Confusion in law. 1980 U.S.C.C.A.N. 4702-04 & n.4 (S. Rep.)

	Baltimore Baseball Co. v. United States, 481 F.2d 1283 (Ct.Cl. 1973)	Bad policy. 1980 U.S.C.C.A.N. 4704-05 & n.8 (S. Rep.)
§ 2(a), 94 Stat. at 2247-48	Pacific Nat'l Co. v. Welch, 304 U.S. 191 (1938)	Bad policy. 1980 U.S.C.C.A.N. 4705-06 & n.10 (S. Rep.)
§ 2(a), 94 Stat at 2248-50	Rushing v. Comm'r, 441 F.2d 593 (5th Cir. 1971), et al.	Confusion in law. 1980 U.S.C.C.A.N. 4707-09 (S. Rep.)
§ 2(a), 94 Stat. at 2250	J.K. Griffith, 73 T.C. No. 76 (Feb. 28, 1980)	Bad policy. 1980 U.S.C.C.A.N. 4712-13 & n.22 (S. Rep.)
§ 2(a), 94 Stat. at 2253	Miller v. Usry, 160 F.Supp. 368 (W.D. La. 1958)	Bad policy. 1980 U.S.C.C.A.N. 4721 (S. Rep.)
Staggers Rail Act of 1980, Pub.L.No. 96-448, 94 Stat. 1895 (1980)		
§ 226, 94 Stat. at 1930-31	Atchison, Topeka & Santa Fe R.R. v. ICC, 617 F.2d 485 (7th Cir. 1980)	Bad policy. 1980 U.S.C.C.A.N. 4151 (Conf. Rep.)
§ 506, 94 Stat. at 1956	Maloof v. United Transp. Union, No. 78-3797 (E.D.Pa. Mar. 27, 1980)	Bad interpretation. 1980 U.S.C.C.A.N. 4166 (Conf. Rep.)
Customs Courts Act of 1980, Pub.L.No. 96-417, § 201, 94 Stat. 1727, 1728-30 (1980)	Sneaker Circus v. Carter, 566 F.2d 396 (2d Cir. 1977); Consumers Union v. Comm. for Implementation of Textile Agreements, 561 F.2d 872 (D.C. Cir. 1977), et al.	Bad policy. 1980 U.S.C.C.A.N. 3741 (H.R. Rep.)
Antitrust Procedural Improvements Act of 1980, Pub.L.No. 96-349, 94 Stat. 1154 (1980)		
§ 2, 94 Stat. at 1154-56	United States v. GAF Corp., 596 F.2d 10 (2d Cir. 1979)	Need for legislative elaboration. 1980 U.S.C.C.A.N. 2716 (H.R. Rep.)
§ 3, 94 Stat. at 1156	Kiefer v. Las Vegas Hacienda, Inc., 404 F.2d 1163 (7th Cir. 1968), et al.	Bad policy. *Antitrust Procedural Improvements & Jurisdictional Amendments: Hearings Before the Subcomm. on Monopolies & Commercial Law of the House Comm. on the Judiciary*, 96th Cong., 1st Sess. 23 & n.60 (1979)
§ 4, 94 Stat. at 1156-57	TWA v. Hughes, 449 F.2d 51 (2d Cir. 1971), rev'd on other grounds, 409 U.S. 363 (1973)	Bad policy. 1980 U.S.C.C.A.N. 2769 (H.R. Rep.)
§ 5, 94 Stat. at 1157	Illinois v. General Paving Co., 590 F.2d 680 (7th Cir. 1979)	Bad policy. 1980 U.S.C.C.A.N. 2754 (H.R. Rep.)
§ 6, 94 Stat. at 1157-58	United States v. American Building Maintenance Indus., 422 U.S. 271 (1975)	Remove anomaly in law. 1980 U.S.C.C.A.N. 2732 (H.R. Rep.)
Soft Drink Interbrand Competition Act, Pub.L.No. 96-308, 94 Stat. 939 (1980)	United States v. Arnold, Schwinn & Co., 388 U.S. 365 (1967); see Continental T.V. Inc. v. GTE Sylvania Inc., 433 U.S. 36 (1977)	Need clarification for one industry. 1980 U.S.C.C.A.N. 2373-74 (H.R. Rep.)
Civil Rights of Institutionalized Persons Act, Pub.L.No. 96-247, 94 Stat. 349 (1980)	United States v. Mattson, 600 F.2d 1295 (9th Cir. 1979); United States v. Solomon, 563 F.2d 1121 (4th Cir. 1977)	Bad policy. 1980 U.S.C.C.A.N. 789 (S. Rep.)
Pub.L.No. 96-170, 93 Stat. 1284 (1979)	District of Columbia v. Carter, 409 U.S. 418 (1972)	Update statutory policy. 1979 U.S.C.C.A.N. 2609-10 (H.R. Rep.)
Pub.L.No. 96-135, 93 Stat. 1056 (1979)	Mescalero Apache Tribe v. Hickel, 432F.2d 956 (10th Cir. 1970)	Bad policy. 1979 U.S.C.C.A.N. 2077 (H.R. Rep.)
Dep't of Justice Appropriation Act, FY 1980, Pub.L.No. 96-132, § 14, 93 Stat. 1040, 1048 (1979)	Clay Simmons v. United States, No. 77-75-5 (D.N.Mex.)	Bad interpretation. 1979 U.S.C.C.A.N. 2039-40 (S. Rep.)
Dep't of Defense Authorization Act, 1980, Pub.L.No. 96-107, § 801(a), 93 Stat. 803, 810-11 (1979)	United States v. Russo, 1 M.J. 134 (CMA 1975); also United States v. Harrison, 5 M.J. 476, 481 (CMA 1978), et al.	Bad policy. 1979 U.S.C.C.A.N. 1827-28 (S. Rep.)

Panama Canal Act of 1980, Pub.L.No. 96-70, § 1411, 93 Stat. 452, 485 (1979)	United Fruit Co. v. Panama Canal Co., 243 F.Supp. 410 (D.Canal Zone 1965)	Bad policy. 1979 U.S.C.C.A.N. 1067 (H.R. Rep.)
Energy and Water Development Appropriation Act, 1980, Pub.L.No. 96-69, Tit. IV, 93 Stat. 437, 449 (1979)	TVA v. Hill, 437 U.S. 153 (1978)	Bad policy. H.R. Conf. Rep. No. 388, 96th Cong., 1st Sess. (1979)
Trade Agreements Act of 1979, Pub.L.No. 96-39, § 101, 93 Stat. 144, 181-82 (1979)	Voss Int'l v. United States, C.D. 4801 (May 7, 1979)	Bad policy. 1979 U.S.C.C.A.N. 480 (S. Rep.)
	95TH CONGRESS	
Endangered Species Act Amendments of 1978, Pub.L.No. 95-632, § 7, 92 Stat. 3751, 3752-60 (1978)	TVA v. Hill, 437 U.S. 153 (1978)	Need for more flexible policy. 1978 U.S.C.C.A.N. 9453, 9460-63 (H.R. Rep.)
Revenue Act of 1978, Pub.L.No. 95-600, § 365, 92 Stat. 2763, 2854-55 (1978)	Bongiovanni v. Comm'r, 470 F.2d 921 (2d Cir 1972); Thatcher v. Comm'r, 533 F.2d 114 (9th Cir. 1976)	Split in the circuits. 1978 U.S.C.C.A.N. 6946-48 (S.Rep.)
Bankruptcy Reform Act of 1978, Pub.L.No. 95-598, 92 Stat. 2549 (1978)		
§ 101, 92 Stat. at 2449-50	In re Freight Drivers Local 600, 3 Bankr.Ct. Dec. 528 (E.D.Mo.1977)	Bad policy. 1978 U.S.C.C.A.N. 6266 (H.R. Rep.)
§ 101, 92 Stat. at 2555	Toucey v. N.Y. Life Ins. Co., 314 U.S. 1 (1941)	Bad policy. 1978 U.S.C.C.A.N. 5815 (S. Rep.) & 6274 (H.R. Rep.)
§ 101, 92 Stat. at 2557	In re Bank of Crowell, 53 F.Supp. 682 (N.D. Tex. 1931)	Bad policy. 1978 U.S.C.C.A.N. 6157-58 (H.R. Rep.)
§ 101, 92 Stat. at 2564	Massachusetts Mut. Life Ins. Co. v. Brock, 405 F.2d 429 (5th Cir. 1968)	Bad policy. 1978 U.S.C.C.A.N. 6442, 6511 (floor debate)
§ 101, 92 Stat. at 2564	In re Beverly Crest Convalescent Hosp, Inc., 548 F.2d 817 (9th Cir. 1976)	Bad policy. 1978 U.S.C.C.A.N. 6286 (H.R. Rep.)
§ 101, 92 Stat. at 2579-80	In re Illinois Art Indus., Inc., 27 F. Supp. 334 (W.D.Mich. 1939)	Bad policy. 1978 U.S.C.C.A.N. 6153 (H.R. Rep.)
§ 101, 92 Stat. at 2584	United States v. Embassy Restaurant, 359 U.S. 29 (1958)	Bad policy. 1978 U.S.C.C.A.N. 5855 (S. Rep.) & 6313 (H.R. Rep.)
§ 101, 92 Stat. at 2590-91	Birkett v. Columbia Bank, 195 U.S. 345 (1904)	Bad policy. 1978 U.S.C.C.A.N. 6453 (S. Rep.) & 6522 (H.R. Rep.)
§ 101, 92 Stat. at 2591	In re Waller, 494 F.2d 447 (6th Cir. 1974), et al.	Bad policy. 1978 U.S.C.C.A.N. 5865 (S. Rep.) & 6320 (H.R. Rep.)
§ 101, 92 Stat. at 2591	Tinker v. Colwell, 139 U.S. 473 (1902)	Bad policy. 1978 U.S.C.C.A.N. 5865 (S. Rep.) & 6320-21 (H.R. Rep.)
§ 101, 92 Stat. at 2594	Lines v. Frederick, 400 U.S. 18 (1970); Lockwood v. Exchange Bank, 190 U.S. 294 (1908)	Bad policy. 1978 U.S.C.C.A.N. 5868 (S. Rep.) & 6324 (H.R. Rep.)
§ 101, 92 Stat. at 2595-96 & 1601-02	Fort Pitt Coal & Coke Co. v. Diser, 239 F. 443 (6th Cir. 1917)	Bad policy. 1978 U.S.C.C.A.N. 6160 (H.R. Rep.)
§ 101, 92 Stat. at 2596	In re Federals, Inc., 553 F.2d 509 (6th Cir. 1977)	Bad policy. 1978 U.S.C.C.A.N. 6456 (H.R. Rep.) & 6525 (S. Rep.)
§ 101, 92 Stat. at 2598-99	In re King Porter Co., 446 F.2d 722 (5th Cir. 1971)	Bad policy. 1978 U.S.C.C.A.N. 5875 (S. Rep.) & 6330 (H.R. Rep.)
§ 101, 92 Stat. at 2599-2600	DuBay v. Williams, 417 F.2d 1277 (9th Cir. 1966); Grain Merchants v. Union Bank & Savs., 408 F.2d 209 (7th Cir. 1969)	Bad policy. 1978 U.S.C.C.A.N. 5874-75 (S. Rep.) & 6330 (H.R. Rep.)
§ 101, 92 Stat. at 2619	In re Rosenbaum Grain Corp., 112 F.2d 315 (7th Cir. 1940)	Bad policy. 1978 U.S.C.C.A.N. 5892 (S. Rep.)

§ 101, 92 Stat. at 2624	American United Mut. Life Ins. Co. v. City of Aron Park, 311 U.S. 138 (1940)	Bad policy. 1978 U.S.C.C.A.N. 6465 (H.R. Rep.) & 6534 (S. Rep.)
§ 101, 92 Stat. at 2632	St. Joe Paper Co. v. Atlantic Coast Line, 347 U.S. 298 (1954)	Bad policy. 1978 U.S.C.C.A.N. 5905 (H.R. Rep.)
§ 101, 92 Stat. at 2635	Aladdin Hotel Corp. v. Bloom, 200 F.2d 627 (8th Cir. 1953)	Bad policy. 1978 U.S.C.C.A.N. 6367 (H.R. Rep.)
§ 213, 92 Stat. at 2661	United States v. Kras, 409 U.S. 434 (1973)	Bad policy. 1978 U.S.C.C.A.N. 6404 (H.R. Rep.)
Contract Disputes Act of 1978, Pub.L.No. 95-563, 92 Stat. 2383 (1978)		
§ 10(a), 92 Stat. at 2388	United States v. Bianchi & Co., 373 U.S. 709 (1963)	Bad policy. 1978 U.S.C.C.A.N. 5239-40 (S. Rep.)
§§ 8(g) & 14(h), 92 Stat. at 2387 & 2390	S & E Contractors, Inc. v. United States, 406 U.S. 1 (1972)	Bad policy. 1978 U.S.C.C.A.N. 5237-38 (S. Rep.)
Pregnancy Discrimination Act of 1978, Pub.L.No. 95-555, 92 Stat. 2076 (1978)	General Elec. Co. v. Gilbert, 429 U.S. 125 (1976)	Bad interpretation and bad policy. 1978 U.S.C.C.A.N. 4750-52 (H.R. Rep.)
Foreign Intelligence Surveillance Act of 1978, Pub.L.No. 95-511, 92 Stat. 1783 (1978)	United States v. United States Dist. Court, 407 U.S. 297 (1972)	Fill in statutory gap. 1978 U.S.C.C.A.N. 3910-16 (S.Rep.)
Airline Deregulation Act of 1978, Pub.L.No. 95-504, § 30, 92 Stat. 1705, 1731 (1978)	Hughes Tool Co. v. TWA, 409 U.S. 363 (1973)	Bad policy. 1978 U.S.C.C.A.N. 3754 (H.R. Rep.) & 3792 (Cong. Rep.)
Pub.L.No. 95-502, Title III, 92 Stat. 1693, 1702-03 (1978)	Clarence LaBelle Post No. 217 v. United States, 580 F.2d 270 (8th Cir. 1978), et al.	Bad policy. 1978 U.S.C.C.A.N. 3716-17 (H.R. Rep.)
Income Taxes, Fringe Benefits, Regulations, Pub.L.No. 95-427, § 3, 92 Stat. 996, 996-97 (1978)	Comm'r v. Kowalski, 434 U.S. 77 (1977)	Fairness. 1978 U.S.C.C.A.N. 2512-13 (H.R. Rep.)
Regional Rail Reorganization Act of 1973 Amendments, Pub.L.No. 95-597, 92 Stat. 2547 (1978)	In Re Erie Lackawanna Ry. Co., 548 F.2d 621 (6th Cir. 1977)	Bad policy. 1978 U.S.C.C.A.N. 5781-82 (S. Rep.)
Age Discrimination in Employment Act Amendments of 1978, Pub.L.No. 95-256, 92 Stat. 189 (1978)		
§ 2, 92 Stat. at 189	McMann v. United Airlines, 434 U.S. 192 (1977)	Bad interpretation. 1978 U.S.C.C.A.N. 529 (Conf. Rep.)
§ 4(b), 92 Stat. at 190-91	Ott v. Midland-Ross Corp., 523 F.2d 1367 (6th Cir. 1975), et al.	Bad policy. 1978 U.S.C.C.A.N. 515 (S. Rep.) & 533-34 (Conf. Rep.)
§ 4(c), 92 Stat. at 191	Usery v. Sun Oil Co., 423 F.Supp. 125 (N.D. Tex. 1976)	Bad policy. 1978 U.S.C.C.A.N. 516 (S. Rep.) & 534-35 (Conf. Rep.)
Clean Water Act of 1977, Pub.L.No. 95-217, §§ 61 & 67(b), 91 Stat. 1566, 1598, 1606 (1977)	Minnesota v. Hoffman, 543 F.2d 1198 (9th Cir. 1976)	Bad interpretation. 1977 U.S.C.C.A.N. 4393 (S. Rep.)
Food & Agriculture Act of 1977, Pub.L.No. 95-113, 91 Stat. 913 (1977)		
§ 1301, 91 Stat. at 962-63 (new § 5(d))	Hein v. Burns, 402 F.Supp. 398 (S.D.Iowa 1975), rev'd, 429 U.S. 288 (1977), et al.	Bad interpretation and bad policy. 1977 U.S.C.C.A.N. 2003-05 (H.R. Rep.)
Ibid.	Compton v. Tennessee Dep't of Pub. Welf., 532 F.2d 561 (6th Cir. 1976)	Bad policy. 1977 U.S.C.C.A.N. 2008 (H.R. Rep.)
Ibid.	Thomas v. Butz, No. 73-336 (D.Ariz. Jan. 20, 1976)	Bad policy. 1977 U.S.C.C.A.N. 2012 (H.R. Rep.)
Clean Air Act Amendments of 1977, Pub.L.No. 95-95, 91 Stat. 685 (1977)		
§ 116, 91 Stat. at 711	Hancock v. Train, 426 U.S. 167 (1976)	Bad interpretation. 1977 U.S.C.C.A.N. 1277-78 (H.R. Rep.)

§ 120, 91 Stat. at 720	Northern States Power Co. v. State of Minn., 447 F.2d 1143 (8th Cir. 1971), aff'd, 405 U.S. 1035 (1972)	Bad policy. 1977 U.S.C.C.A.N. 1524 (Conf. Rep.)
§ 127, 91 Stat. at 731 ff.	Fri v. Sierra Club, 412 U.S. 541 (1973), aff'g by equally divided Court, 344 F. Supp. 253 (D.D.C. 1972)	Preserve decision against possible Supreme Court reconsideration. 1977 U.S.C.C.A.N. 1183 (H.R. Rep.), also 1479 (views Reps. Devine et al.)
§ 305, 91 Stat. at 772-77	Kennecott Copper Corp. v. EPA, 462 F.2d 846 (D.C. Cir. 1972)	Address concerns implicit in these decisions. 1977 U.S.C.C.A.N. 1397-98 (H.R. Rep.)
§ 305(c)(3), 91 Stat. at 776	Investment Co. Inst. v. Board of Gov'rs, 551 F.2d 1270 (D.C. Cir. 1977) (dicta)	Bad policy. 1977 U.S.C.C.A.N. 1401 (H.R. Rep.)
	94TH CONGRESS	
Federal Land Policy and Management Act of 1976, Pub.L.No. 94-579, § 704(a), 90 Stat. 2743, 2792 (1976)	United States v. Midwest Oil Co., 236 U.S. 459 (1915)	Bad policy. 1976 U.S.C.C.A.N. 6203 (H.R. Rep.)
Pub.L.No. 94-577, 90 Stat. 2729 (1976)	Wingo v. Wedding, 418 U.S. 461 (1974)	Bad interpretation. 1976 U.S.C.C.A.N. 6164-66 (H.R. Rep.)
Pub.L.No. 94-574, 90 Stat. 2721 (1976)		
§ 1, 90 Stat. at 2721	Litell v. Morton, 445 F.2d 1207 (4th Cir. 1971), et al.	Bad policy. 1976 U.S.C.C.A.N. 6131 n.33 (H.R. Rep.)
§ 3, 90 Stat. at 2721-22	Town of East Haven v. Eastern Airlines, 28 F. Supp. 507 (D. Conn. 1968)	Bad policy. 1976 U.S.C.C.A.N. 6139 (H.R. Rep.)
Pub.L.No. 94-568, 90 Stat. 2697 (1976)	McGlotten v. Connally, 338 F. Supp. 448 (D.D.C. 1972)	Bad policy. 1976 U.S.C.C.A.N. 6057-58 (S. Rep.)
The Civil Rights Attorney's Fees Awards Act of 1976, Pub.L.No. 94-559, 90 Stat. 2641 (1976)	Alyeska Pipeline Serv.Co. v. Wilderness Soc'y, 421 U.S. 240 (1975)	Bad policy, fill "anomalous gaps" in civil rights. 1976 U.S.C.C.A.N. 5909-12 (S. Rep.)
Copyrights Act, Pub.L.No. 94-553, 90 Stat. 2541 (1976)		
§ 101, 90 Stat. at 2541-44	White-Smith Publ. Co. v. Apollo Co., 209 U.S. 1 (1908)	Bad policy. 1976 U.S.C.C.A.N. 5665 (H.R. Rep.)
§ 110, 90 Stat. at 2549-50	Twentieth Century Music Corp. v. Aiken, 422 U.S. 151 (1975) (reasoning)	Bad policy. 1976 U.S.C.C.A.N. 5700-01 (H.R. Rep.)
§ 108, 90 Stat. at 2546-48	Williams & Wilkins Co. v. United States, 420 U.S. 376 (1975), aff'g by an equally divided Court, 487 F.2d 1345 (Ct. Cl. 1973)	Bad policy. 1976 U.S.C.C.A.N. 5688-92 (H.R. Rep.)
§ 111, 90 Stat. at 2550-58	Teleprompter Corp. v. CBS, Inc., 415 U.S. 394 (1974); Fortnightly Corp. v. United Artists Television, Inc., 39 U.S. 390 (1968)	Bad policy. 1976 U.S.C.C.A.N. 5703 (H.R. Rep.)
§ 411, 90 Stat. at 2583	Vacheron & Constantin-Le Coultre Watches, Inc. v. Benrus Watch Co., 260 F.2d 637 (2d Cir. 1958)	Bad policy. 1976 U.S.C.C.A.N. 5773 (H.R. Rep.)
Pub.L.No. 94-489, 90 Stat. 2358 (1976)	Descomp v. Sampson, 377 F.Supp. 254 (D. Del. 1974), et al.	Bad interpretation. 1976 U.S.C.C.A.N. 5212 (H.R. Rep.)
Pub.L.No. 94-464, 90 Stat. 1985 (1976)	Henderson v. Bluemink, 511 F.2d 399 (D.C. Cir. 1974)	Bad policy. 1976 U.S.C.C.A.N. 4445-46 (S. Rep.)
Tax Reform Act of 1976, Pub.L.No. 94-455, 90 Stat. 1520 (1976)		
§ 208, 90 Stat. at 1541-42	Various unnamed Tax Court decisions	Bad policy. 1976 U.S.C.C.A.N. 2992-96 (H.R. Rep.)
§ 601(a), 90 Stat. at 1569-72	George H. Newi, T.C. Memo. 1969-131, aff'd, 432 F.2d 998 (2d Cir. 1970)	Split authority. 1976 U.S.C.C.A.N. 3050-56 (H.R. Rep.) & 3576-82 (S. Rep.)

§ 1051, 90 Stat. at 1643-47	Burke Concrete Accessories, Inc., 56 T.C. 588 (1971)	Bad policy. 1976 U.S.C.C.A.N. 3151-52 & n.42 (H.R. Rep.) & 3710 n.36 (S. Rep.)
§ 1201(a), 90 Stat. at 1660-67	Tax Analysts & Advocates v. IRS, 505 F.2d 350 (D.C. Cir. 1974)	Bad policy. 1976 U.S.C.C.A.N. 3209-12 (H.R. Rep.)
§ 1204(b), 90 Stat. at 1696-97	Laing v. United States, 496 F.2d 853 (2d Cir. 1974)	Bad policy. 1976 U.S.C.C.A.N. 3197-99 (H.R. Rep.) & 3793 (S. Rep.)
§ 1306(a), 90 Stat. at 1717-20	Bob Jones Univ. v. Simon, 416 U.S. 725 (1974); Alexander v. "Americans United" Inc., 416 U.S. 752 (1974)	Harsh policy. 1976 U.S.C.C.A.N. 3179-80 & n.4 (H.R. Rep.) & 4009-12 (S. Rep.)
§ 2009(a), 90 Stat. at 1893	United States v. Byrum, 408 U.S. 125 (1972)	Bad interpretation and incoherence with tax policy. 1976 U.S.C.C.A.N. 3418-19 (H.R. Rep.)
§ 2009(d), 90 Stat. at 1896	Estate of Bray v. Comm'r, 396 F.2d 452 (6th Cir. 1968), et al.	Unfair policy. 1976 U.S.C.C.A.N. 3425-26 (H.R. Rep.)
§ 2101(b), 90 Stat. at 1899	Park Place, Inc., 57 T.Ct. 767 (1972)	Bad interpretation. 1976 U.S.C.C.A.N. 3826 (S. Rep.)
Hart-Scott-Rodino Antitrust Improvements Act of 1976, Pub.L.No. 94-435, 90 Stat. 1383 (1976)		
§ 102, 90 Stat. at 1384-87	United States v. Union Oil Co. of Calif., 343 F.2d 29 (9th Cir. 1965)	Bad policy. 1976 U.S.C.C.A.N. 2615 (H.R. Rep.)
§ 301, 90 Stat. at 1394-96	California v. Frito-Lay, 474 F.2d 774 (9th Cir. 1973)	Bad policy. 1976 U.S.C.C.A.N. 2574-78 (H.R. Rep.)
§ 302(3), 90 Stat. at 1396	Decorative Stone Co. v. Building Trades Council, 23 F.2d 426 (2d Cir. 1928)	Bad policy. 1976 U.S.C.C.A.N. 2588-90 (H.R. Rep.)
Pub.L.No. 94-416, 90 Stat. 1275 (1976)	New Mexico v. United States, 148 F.Supp. 508 (D.N.M. 1957)	Bad policy. 1976 U.S.C.C.A.N. 2369-71 (H.R. Rep.)
Government in the Sunshine Act, Pub.L.No. 94-409, 90 Stat. 1241 (1976)		
§ 5(b), 90 Stat. at 1247-48	Administrator v. Robertson, 422 U.S. 255 (1972)	Bad interpretation. 1976 U.S.C.C.A.N. 2204-05 (H.R. Rep.) & 2250 (Conf. Rep.)
§ 5(c), 90 Stat. at 1247-48	Aviation Consumer Action Project v. Washburn, 535 F.2d 101 (D.C. Cir. 1976)	Bad policy. 1976 U.S.C.C.A.N. 2262 (Conf. Rep.)
Wild and Scenic Rivers Act, Pub.L.No. 94-407, 90 Stat. 1238 (1976)	North Carolina v. FPC, No. 74-1941 (D.C.Cir. 1976)	Bad policy. 1976 U.S.C.C.A.N. 2174 (H.R. Rep.)
Overseas Citizens Voting Rights Act of 1975, Pub.L.No. 94-203, 89 Stat. 1142 (1975)	Hardy v. Lomenzo, 349 F.Supp. 617 (S.D.N.Y. 1972)	Bad policy. 1975 U.S.C.C.A.N. 2361 (H.R. Rep.)
Pub.L.No. 94-83, 89 Stat. 424 (1975)	Conservation Soc'y v. Secretary, 508 F.2d 927 (2d Cir. 1974)	Practical problems. 1975 U.S.C.C.A.N. 869-70 (S. Rep.)
Voting Rights Act of 1965 – Extension, Pub.L.No. 94-73, § 402, 89 Stat. 400, 404 (1975)	Alyeska Pipeline Serv. Co. v. Wilderness Soc'y, 471 U.S. 240 (1975)	Bad policy. 1975 U.S.C.C.A.N. 807-10 (S. Rep.)
Securities Acts Amendment of 1975, Pub.L.No. 94-29, 89 Stat. 97 (1975)		
§ 17(3), 89 Stat. at 155	In re Nat'l Student Marketing Corp., 368 F.Supp. 1311 (J.P.M.L. 1973)	Bad policy. 1975 U.S.C.C.A.N. 251-55 (S. Rep.)
§ 28(1), 89 Stat. at 164-65	Rosenfeld v. Black, 445 F.2d 1337 (2d Cir. 1971)	Bad policy. 1975 U.S.C.C.A.N. 249 (S. Rep.)
	93D CONGRESS	
Magnuson-Moss Warranty - FTC Improvement Act, Pub.L.No. 93-637, 88 Stat. 2183 (1974)		

§ 201, 88 Stat. at 2545	Bunte Bros. v. FTC, 312 U.S. 349 (1941)	Bad policy. 1974 U.S.C.C.A.N. 7712-13 (H.R. Rep.)
§ 202, 88 Stat. at 2193-98	National Petroleum Refiners Ass'n v. FTC, 340 F.Supp. 134 (D.D.C. 1972), rev'd 482 F.2d 672 (D.C.Cir. 1973)	Bad policy. 1974 U.S.C.C.A.N. 7715 (H.R. Rep.)
1974, Pub.L.No. 93-627, 88 Stat. 2126 (1974)	Zahn v. Int'l Paper Co., 414 U.S. 291 (1973) (overridden for Port Act claims only); Eisen v. Carlisle & Jacquelin, 417 U.S. 156 (1974) (similar)	Bad policy. 1974 U.S.C.C.A.N. 7556-57 (S. Rep.)
Pub.L.No. 93-600, 88 Stat. 1955 (1974)	Fleishmann Distiller Corp. v. Maier Brewing Co., 386 U.S. 714 (1967)	Bad policy. 1974 U.S.C.C.A.N. 7133-36 (S. Rep.)
Pub.L.No. 93-512, 88 Stat. 1609 (1974)	Edwards v. United States, 334 F.2d 360 (5th Cir. 1964)	Bad policy. 1974 U.S.C.C.A.N. 6[illegible] (H.R. Rep.)
Freedom of Information Act Amendments of 1974, Pub.L.No. 93-502, §§ 1(b)(2) & 2(a), 88 Stat. 1561, 1561-62, 1563 (1974)	EPA v. Mink, 410 U.S. 73 (1973)	Bad interpretation. 1974 U.S.C.C.A.N. 6272 (H.R. Rep.) & 6290 (Conf. Rep.)
Antihijacking Act of 1974, Pub.L.No. 93-366, § 104(b), 88 Stat. 409, 411 (1974)	United States v. Pliskow, 354 F.Supp. 369 (E.D. Mich.), aff'd, 480 F.2d 957 (6th Cir. 1973)	Bad policy. 1974 U.S.C.C.A.N. 3979-80 (H.R. Rep.)
	United States v. Clark, 19 C.M.A. 62 (1969)	Bad policy. 1974 U.S.C.C.A.N. 3980 (H.R. Rep.)
Energy Supply & Environmental Coordination Act of 1974, Pub.L.No. 93-319, 88 Stat. 246 (1984)	Buckeye Power, Inc. v. EPA, No. 72-1628 (6th Cir. 1973)	Bad policy. 1974 U.S.C.C.A.N. 3286 (H.R. Rep.)
Fair Labor Standards Amendment of 1974, Pub.L.No. 93-259, § 6(a)(1)-(2), 88 Stat. 55, 58-59 (1974)	Employees of the Dep't of Pub. Health v. Missouri, 411 U.S 279 (1973)	Bad policy. 1974 U.S.C.C.A.N. 2853 (H.R. Rep.)
Pub.L.No. 93-201, 87 Stat. 838 (1973)	Gulf Canal Lines v. United States, 386 U.S. 348 (1967) (per curiam), aff'g, 258 F.Supp. 864 (S.D. Tex. 1966)	Bad policy. 1974 U.S.C.C.A.N. 2925 (S. Rep.)
Trans-Alaska Pipeline Authorization Act, Pub.L.No. 93-153, 87 Stat. 576 (1973)	Wilderness Soc'y v. Morton, 479 F.2d 842 (D.C. Cir. 1973)	Bad policy. 1973 U.S.C.C.A.N. 2417-19 (H.R. Rep.)
	92D CONGRESS	
Longshoremen's & Harbor Workers Compensation Act Amendments of 1972, Pub.L.No. 92-576, § 18, 86 Stat. 1251, 1263 (1972)	Seas Shipping Co. v. Sieracki, 328 U.S. 25 (1946)	Unfair policy. 1972 U.S.C.C.A.N. 4702-05 (H.R. Rep.)
	Ryan Stevedoring Co. v. Pan Atlantic S.S. Corp., 350 U.S. 124 (1956)	Bad policy. 1972 U.S.C.C.A.N. 4702-04 (H.R. Rep.)
	Jackson v. Lykes Bros. S.S. Co., 386 U.S. 371 (1967); Reed v. S.S. Yaka, 373 U.S. 410 (1963)	Unfair policy. 1972 U.S.C.C.A.N. 4705 (H.R. Rep.)
Pub.L.No. 92-415, 86 Stat. 652 (1972)	Anthony Grace & Sons, Inc. v. United States, 345 F.2d 808 (Ct.Cl. 1965), rev'd, 384 U.S. 424 (1966)	Bad policy. 1972 U.S.C.C.A.N. 3118 (S. Rep.)
Pub.L.No. 92-140, 85 Stat. 391 (1971)	Capitol Records, Inc v. Mercury Records Corp., 221 F.2d 657 (2d Cir. 1955)	Regulatory gap. 1971 U.S.C.C.A.N. 1577 (H.R.Rep., DOJ Letter)
Equal Employment Opportunity Amendment of 1972, Pub.L.No. 92-261, § 217, 86 Stat. 103, 104 (1972)	Dewey v. Reynolds Metals Co., 402 U.S. 689 (1971), aff'g by an equally divided Court, 429 F.2d 325 (6th Cir. 1970)	Bad policy. 118 CONG. REC. 1861-62 (1972) (House); *id.* at 228 (Senate)
Revenue Act of 1971, Pub.L.No. 92-178, 85 Stat. 497 (1971)		

§ 307, 85 Stat. at 524	"A recent court case" (unnamed)	Bad policy. 1971 U.S.C.C.A.N. 1863 (H.R. Rep.), 1976 (S. Rep.), 1065 (Conf. Rep.)
§ 312, 85 Stat. at 526	"Recent court decisions" (unnamed)	Bad policy. 1971 U.S.C.C.A.N. 1981 (S. Rep.), 1066 (Conf. Rep.)
Amendments to the Military Selective Service Act of 1967, Pub.L.No. 92-129, 85 Stat. 348 (1971)	Toussie v. United States, 397 U.S. 112 (1970)	Bad policy. 1971 U.S.C.C.A.N. 1455-56 (S. Rep.)
Pub.L.No. 92-79, 85 Stat. 285 (1971)	United States v. Carver, 260 U.S. 482 (1923); Dampskibsselskabet Dannebrog v. Signal Oil & Gas Co., 310 U.S. 268 (1940)	Bad policy. 1971 U.S.C.C.A.N. 1367-68 (H.R. Rep.)
	91st Congress	
Pub.L.No. 91-679, 84 Stat. 2063 (1970)	Louise M. Scudder, 48 T.C. 36, 41 (1967)	Unfair policy. 1970 U.S.C.C.A.N. 60 90-91 (S. Rep.)
Investment Company Amendments Act of 1970, Pub.L.No. 91-547, 84 Stat. 1413-36 (1970)	Investment Co. Inst. v. Camp, No. 1083-66 (D.D.C. Sept 27, 1967)	Legal uncertainty. 1970 U.S.C.C.A.N. 4907 (S. Rep.)
Pub.L.No. 91-467, § 7, 84 Stat. 990, 992-93 (1970)	Unnamed lower court decisions	Split in circuits. 1970 U.S.C.C.A.N. 4161-62 (H.R. Rep.)
Organized Crime Control Act of 1970, Pub.L.No. 91-452, 84 Stat. 922 (1970)		
§ 201(a), 84 Stat. at 926-28	In re McElrath, 248 F.2d 612 (D.C. Cir. 1957)	Bad policy. 1970 U.S.C.C.A.N. 4018 (H.R. Rep.)
§ 702(a), 84 Stat. at 935-36	Alderman v. United States, 394 U.S. 165 (1968)	Bad policy. 1970 U.S.C.C.A.N. 4027 (H.R. Rep.)
Pub.L.No. 91-376, § 8(a), 84 Stat. 787, 790 (1970)	Wellman v. Whittier, 259 F.2d 163 (D.C. Cir. 1958), et al.	Bad interpretation. 1970 U.S.C.C.A.N. 3729-31 (H.R. Rep.)
Newspaper Preservation Act of 1970, Pub.L.No. 91-353, 84 Stat. 466 (1970)	Citizen Publishing Co. v. United States, 394 U.S. 131 (1969)	Unfair, bad policy 1970 U.S.C.C.A.N. 3547 (H.R. Rep.)
Pub.L.No. 91-350, 84 Stat. 449 (1970)	Kyer v. United States, 369 F.2d 714 (Ct. Cl. 1966), et al.	Regulatory gap. 1970 U.S.C.C.A.N. 3477-79 (H.R. Rep.)
Pub.L.No. 91-376, § 8(a), 84 Stat. 787, 790 (1970)	Tracy v. Gleason, 379 F.2d 469 (D.C.Cir. 1967), et al.	Bad interpretation. 1970 U.S.C.C.A.N. 3729-31 (H.R. Rep.)
Tax Reform Act of 1969, Pub.L.No. 91-172, 83 Stat. 487 (1969)		
§ 121, 83 Stat. at 536-49	University Hill Found., 51 T. Ct. 548 (1969)	Bad policy. 1969 U.S.C.C.A.N. 1690-91 (H.R. Rep.) & 2092-93 (S. Rep.)
§ 121(b), 83 Stat. at 537-44	Various unnamed court decisions	Split in courts. 1970 U.S.C.C.A.N. 2103 (S. Rep.), 2405 (Conf. Rep.)
§ 414, 83 Stat. at 612	Various unnamed court decisions	Split in courts. 1970 U.S.C.C.A.N. 2181 (S. Rep.), 2423 (Conf. Rep.)
§ 504, 83 Stat. at 632-33	Santa Fe R. v. United States, 378 F.2d 72 (7th Cir. 1967)	Unfair policy. 1970 U.S.C.C.A.N. 2221 (S. Rep.), 2430 (Conf. Rep.)
§ 516(b), 83 Stat. at 646	Maurer v. United States, 284 F.2d 122 (10th Cir. 1960)	Confusion in law. 1969 U.S.C.C.A.N. 1810-12 (H.R. Rep.) & 2240-41 (S. Rep.)
§ 516(c), 83 Stat. at 647	Moberg v. Comm'r, 305 F.2d 800 (5th Cir. 1962), et al.	Split in circuits. 1969 U.S.C.C.A.N. 1813-17 (H.R. Rep.) & 2241-46 (S. Rep.)
	90th Congress	
Military Justice Act of 1968, Pub.L.No. 90-632, 82 Stat. 1335 (1968)		

§ 2(17), 82 Stat. at 1339	United States v. Cleveland, 15 C.M.A. 213 (1965), et al.	Unfair practice. 1968 U.S.C.C.A.N. 4511 (S. Rep.)
§ 2(24), 82 Stat. at 1341	United States v. May, 10 C.M.A. 358 (1959)	Unjust policy. 1968 U.S.C.C.A.N. 4513-14 (H.R. Rep.)
False Representations by Mail Act, Pub.L.No. 90-590, 82 Stat. 1153 (1968)	Reilly v. Pinkus, 338 U.S. 269 (1959)	Bad policy. 1968 U.S.C.C.A.N. 4295 (H.R. Rep.), 4298 (Postm. Gen'l), 4299 (Att'y Gen'l)
Pub.L.No. 90-537, 82 Stat. 885 (1968)	Arizona v. Calif., 373 U.S. 546 (1963)	Elaborate on Supreme Court decree. 1968 U.S.C.C.A.N. 3668-69 (H.R. Rep.); see *id.* at 3735 (dissenting view, that law all but negates Supreme Court decree)
Pub. L.No. 90-535, 82 Stat. 885 (1968)	Streett v. United States, 331 F.2d 151 (8th Cir. 1964)	Bad policy. 1968 U.S.C.C.A.N. 3654-55 (H.R. Rep.)
Pub.L.No. 90-514, 82 Stat. 867 (1968)	World Airways, Inc. v. Pan American World Airways, Inc., 391 U.S. 461 (1968), aff'g by an equally divided Court, 380 F.2d 1770 (2d Cir. 1967)	Split circuits, confused law. 1968 U.S.C.C.A.N. 3595 (H.R. Rep.)
Pub.L.No. 90-446, 82 Stat. 474-75 (1968)	Denver Union Stock Yard Co. v. Prod'rs Livestock Marketing Ass'n, 356 U.S. 282, 289 (1958)(reasoning not result)	Bad policy. 1968 U.S.C.C.A.N. 2866-67 (S. Rep.) & 2868 (Dep't Agric.)
Pub.L.No. 90-433, 82 Stat. 448-49 (1968)	Northwest Agric. Coop Ass'n, Inc. v. ICC, 350 F.2d 252 (9th Cir. 1966)	Bad policy. 1968 U.S.C.C.A.N. 2768-69 (H.R. Rep.), 2777 (Sec'y Army) & 2774-75 (Dep't Ag.)
Pub.L.No. 90-369, 82 Stat. 279 (1968)	In re Noland, 185 F.Supp. 948 (D.Neb. 1960)	Unfair policy. 1968 U.S.C.C.A.N. 2446 (S. Rep.)
Civil Rights Act of 1968, Pub.L.No. 90-284, § 101, 82 Stat. 73-77 (1968)	United States v. Guest, 383 U.S. 745, 754-55 (1966) (dicta)	Clarify law. 1968 U.S.C.C.A.N. 1840-41 (S. Rep.)
Pub.L.No. 90-237, 81 Stat. 765 (1967)		
§ 2(a), 81 Stat. at 765	National Coun. of Am.-Sov. Friendship, Inc. v. SACB, 322 F.2d 375 (D.C. Cir. 1963)	Clarify legislative intent. 1967 U.S.C.C.A.N. 2669-70 (H.R. Rep.)
§ 10(b), 81 Stat. at 768-71	Labor Youth League v. SACB, 322 F.2d 364 (D.C.Cir. 1963)	Solve mootness problem. 1967 U.S.C.C.A.N. 2673-75 (H.R. Rep.)
Pub.L.No. 90-158, 81 Stat. 516 (1967)	Lane v. Haytian Corp. of Am., 117 F.2d 216 (2d Cir. 1941)	Bad policy. 1967 U.S.C.C.A.N. 2009-10 (S. Rep., quoting H.R. Rep.)
Pub.L.No. 90-123, 81 Stat. 362 (1967)	United States v. Scoratow, 137 F.Supp. 620 (W.D. Pa. 1956)	Bad policy. 1967 U.S.C.C.A.N. 1761 (H.R. Rep.)
Pub.L.No. 90-108, 81 Stat. 275-78 (1967)	Feeley v. District of Columbia, 387 F.2d 216 (D.C. Cir. 1967); Smith v. District of Columbia, 387 F.2d 233 (D.C. Cir. 1967)	Gap in law. 1967 U.S.C.C.A.N. 1742 (H.R. Rep.)
Military Selective Service Act of 1967, Pub.L.No. 90-40, § 1(7), 81 Stat. 100, 104 (1967)	United States v. Seeger, 380 U.S. 163 (1964)	Bad policy. 1967 U.S.C.C.A.N. 1333-34 (H.R. Rep.) & 1359-60 (Conf. Rep.)

APPENDIX II

SUPREME COURT DECISIONS SCRUTINIZED IN HOUSE & SENATE JUDICIARY COMMITTEE HEARINGS (1979 - 1988)

This Appendix lists Supreme Court statutory interpretation decisions subject to hearings in the House or Senate Judiciary Committees and Subcommittees, which considered overruling or modifying the decisions. No effort was made to find every bill that responded to a Supreme Court decision; only those bills that were the subject of hearings are listed. The Appendix covers the ten-year period of the 96th through 100th Congresses.

SUPREME COURT DECISIONS	OVERRIDE BILLS (CONGRESS)	ULTIMATE DISPOSITION OF OVERRIDE BILLS
Bowen v. Massachusetts, 487 U.S. 879 (1988); United States v. Hohri, 482 U.S. 64 (1987)	H.R. 3152 (100C)	Pub. L. No. 100-702 (1988)
Forrester v. White, 484 U.S. 219 (1988); Stump v. Sparkman, 435 U.S. 349 (1978)	Senate Hearings (100C)	No bill
McNally v. United States, 483 U.S. 350 (1987)	H.R. 3089 (100C) H.R. 3050 (100C)	Bills die Subcomm., override included in Pub. L. No. 100-690 (1988)
	S. 2793 (100C) S. 1898 (100C) S. 1837 (100C)	Similar to House
United States v Stanley, 483 U.S. 669 (1987); United States v. Johnson, 481 U.S. 681 (1987)	S. 2490 (100C)	Dies Subcomm.
Agency Holding Corp. v. Malley-Duff & Assocs., 483 U.S. 143 (1987)	S. 1523 (100C)	Comm. reports, dies Senate Calendar
Shearson/American Express, Inc. v. McMahon, 482 U.S. 220 (1987)	S. 1523 (100C)	Comm. reports, dies Senate Calendar
	H.R. 4920 (100C)	Dies Subcomm.
Cargill, Inc. v. Montfort of Colo., Inc., 479 U.S. 104 (1986)	S. 1407 (100C)	Dies Subcomm.
Kelly v. Robinson, 479 U.S. 104 (1986)	House Hearings (100C)	No Bill
United States v. Mechanik, 475 U.S. 66 (1986)	H.R. 2515 (100C) H.R. 5367 (99C)	Dies Subcomm. Dies Comm.
Square D Co. v. Niagara Frontier Tariff Bureau, Inc., 476 U.S. 409 (1986); Keogh v. Chicago & Northwestern Ry., 260 U.S. 156 (1922)	H.R. 941 (100C) S. 443 (100C)	Dies Subcomm. Dies Subcomm.
Sedima, S.P.R.L. v. Imrex Co., 473 U.S. 479 (1985)	S. 1523 (100C)	Comm. reports, dies Senate Calendar
	H.R. 3240 (100C) H.R. 2983 (100C) H.R. 4920 (100C) H.R. 4923 (100C)	All 100C House bills die Subcomm.

	H.R. 2943 (99C) H.R. 5445 (99C)	Passes House but dies on Senate floor
United States v. Shearer, 473 U.S. 52 (1985); Chappell v. Wallace, 462 U.S. 296 (1983); Feres v. United States, 340 U.S. 135 (1950)	H.R. 1054 (100C) S. 2490 (100C)	Passes House dies Senate Subcomm. Dies Subcomm.
	H.R. 1161 (99C) H.R. 3174 (99C) S. 489 (99C)	H.R. 3174 passes House dies Senate Comm.
United States v. Varig Airlines, 467 U.S. 797 (1984)	H.R. 3872 (100C)	Dies Subcomm.
Pulliam v. Allen, 466 U.S. 522 (1984); Supreme Court of Virginia v. Consumers Union, 446 U.S. 719 (1980)	S. 1512 (100C) S. 1515 (100C) S. 1482 (100C)	Dies Subcomm. Dies Subcomm. *Pulliam* override deleted from Pub. L. No. 100-702
	S. 1794 (99C) S. 1795 (99C)	Dies Subcomm. Dies Comm.
Blum v. Stenson, 465 U.S. 886 (1984); Hensley v. Eckerhart, 461 U.S. 424 (1983); Maher v. Gagne, 448 U.S. 122 (1980)	S. 1580 (99C) H.R. 3181 (99C)	Dies Subcomm. Dies Subcomm.
	H.R. 5757 (98C) S. 2802 (98C)	Dies Subcomm. Dies Subcomm.
Monsanto Co. v. Spray-Rite Serv. Corp., 465 U.S. 752 (1984)	H.R. 585 (100C)	Passes House, dies Senate Comm.
	S. 430 (100C)	Comm. reports but dies Senate floor
	H.R. 5293 (99C)	Dies Comm.
Grove City College v. Bell, 465 U.S. 555 (1984); Consolidated Rail Corp. v. Darrone, 465 U.S. 624 (1984); North Haven Bd. of Educ. v. Bell, 456 U.S. 512 (1982)	S. 557 (100C)	Pub. L. No. 100-259 (1988)
	H.R. 700 (99C)	Comm. reports but dies House Calendar
	S. 431 (99C) H.R. 5490 (98C)	Dies Comm. Passes House, dies Senate floor
	S. 2568 (98C)	Dies Comm.
NLRB v. Bildisco & Bildisco, 465 U.S. 513 (1984)	H.R. 4908 (98C) H.R. 5174 (98C)	Pub. L. No. 98-353 (1984)
Sony Corp. of Am. v. Universal City Studios, Inc., 464 U.S. 417 (1984)	H.R. 2911 (99C) S. 1739 (99C)	Dies Subcomm. Dies Subcomm.
	H.R. 175 (98C) H.R. 1029 (98C) H.R. 1030 (98C) S. 31 (98C) S. 33 (98C) S. 175 (98C)	All 98C bills die Subcomm. or Comm.
	H.R. 5705 (97C) S. 1758 (97C)	Dies Subcomm. Dies Comm.
INS v. Phinpathya, 464 U.S. 183 (1984)	H.R. 4823 (99C)	Pub. L. No. 99-603 (1986)
Jefferson Parish Hosp. Dist. No. 2 v. Hyde, 466 U.S. 2 (1984); United States v. Loew's, Inc., 371 U.S. 38 (1962); International Salt Co. v. United States, 332 U.S. 392 (1947)	H.R. 557 (100C) S. 438 (100C)	Dies Subcomm. Passes Senate, dies House Comm.
Ruckelshaus v. Sierra Club, 463 U.S. 680 (1983)	House Hearings (99C)	No Bill
United States v. Sells Engineering, Inc., 463 U.S. 418 (1983); United States v. Baggott, 463 U.S. 476 (1983)	H.R. 3340 (99C) S. 1676 (99C)	Pub. L. No. 99-562 (1986)

First Nat'l City Bank v. Banco Para el Comercio Exterior de Cuba, 462 U.S. 611 (1983)	Senate Hearings (100C)	No bill
Block v. North Dakota, 461 U.S. 273 (1983)	H.R. 2484 (99C)	Pub. L. No. 99-598 (1986)
	H.R. 3917 (98C)	Dies Subcomm.
	S. 2750 (98C)	Dies Comm.
Lockheed Aircraft Corp. v. United States, 460 U.S. 190 (1983)	H.R. 2378 (100C)	Dies Subcomm.
	H.R. 1623 (99C)	Dies Subcomm.
	H.R. 4083 (98C)	Clean bill
	H.R. 4199 (98C)	Clean bill
	H.R. 5883 (98C)	Dies Comm.
	S. 1839 (97C)	Dies Subcomm.
Williams v. United States, 458 U.S. 279 (1982); United States v. Maze, 414 U.S. 395 (1974)	H.R. 5405 (98C)	Pub. L. No. 98-473 (1984)
	H.R. 5872 (98C)	
	S. 1762 (98C)	
Union Labor Life Ins. Co. v. Pireno, 458 U.S. 119 (1982); Group Life & Health Ins. Co. v. Royal Drug Co., 440 U.S. 205 (1979)	H.R. 1766 (100C)	Dies Subcomm.
	S. 808 (100C)	Dies Subcomm.
United States Dep't of State v. Washington Post Co., 456 U.S. 595 (1982)	S. 774 (98C)	Passes Senate, dies House Gov't Ops. Comm.
Engle v. Isaac, 456 U.S. 107 (1982); Rose v. Lundy, 455 U.S. 509 (1982); United States v. Frady, 456 U.S. 152 (1982); Wainright v. Sykes, 433 U.S. 72 (1977)	S. 238 (99C)	Dies Comm.
	S. 829 (98C)	Dies Subcomm.
	H.R. 4419 (97C)	Dies Subcomm.
	H.R. 6050 (97C)	Dies Subcomm.
	S. 653 (97C)	Dies Subcomm.
	S. 2216 (97C)	Dies Subcomm.
White v. New Hampshire Dep't of Employment Sec., 455 U.S. 445 (1982)	H.R. 5757 (98C)	Dies Subcomm.
	S. 2802 (98C)	Dies Subcomm.
Community Communications Co. v. City of Boulder, 455 U.S. 40 (1982); City of LaFayette v. Louisiana Power & Light Co., 435 U.S. 389 (1978)	H.R. 6027 (98C)	Pub. L. No. 98-544 (1984)
	S. 1578 (98C)	
Polk County v. Dodson, 454 U.S. 312 (1981)	S. 829 (98C)	Dies Subcomm.
Fair Assessment in Real Estate Ass'n v. McNary, 454 U.S. 100 (1981)	H.R.2953 (100C)	Comm. reports, dies House floor
City of Newport v. Fact Concerts, Inc., 453 U.S. 247 (1981); Middlesex County Sewerage Auth. v. National Sea Clammers Ass'n, 453 U.S. 1 (1981)	House Hearings (98C)	No Bill
United States v. Turkette, 452 U.S. 576 (1981)	H.R. 2517 (99C)	Passes House, dies Senate floor
	H.R. 5445 (99C)	
	H.R. 1647 (97C)	Dies Subcomm.
	H.R. 4711 (97C)	Dies Subcomm.
Texas Indus., Inc. v. Radcliff Materials, Inc., 451 U.S. 630 (1981)	S. 635 (100C)	Dies Subcomm.
	S. 1300 (99C)	Comm. reports, dies Senate Calendar
	S. 380 (98C)	Dies Subcomm.
	H.R. 1242 (97C)	Dies Subcomm.
	H.R. 4072 (97C)	Dies Subcomm.
	H.R. 5794 (97C)	Dies Subcomm.
	S. 995 (97C)	Comm. reports, dies Senate floor
City of Milwaukee v. Illinois, 451 U.S. 304 (1981)	House Hearings (99C)	No Bill
	H.R. 2867 (98C)	Comm. reports, but override dropped from Pub. L. No. 98-616 (1984)
	H.R. 6307 (97C)	Passes House, dies Senate floor

Delta Air Lines v. August, 450 U.S. 346 (1981)	H.R. 5757 (98C) S. 2802 (98C)	Dies Subcomm. Dies Subcomm.
Firestone Tire & Rubber Co. v. Risjord, 449 U.S. 368 (1981); Cohen v. Beneficial Indus. Loan Corp., 337 U.S. 541 (1949)	H.R. 3152 (100C)	Cohen override deleted in Comm.
Sumner v. Mata, 449 U.S. 539 (1981)	H.R. 6050 (97C) S. 2216 (97C)	Dies Subcomm. Dies Subcomm.
EPA v. National Crushed Stone Ass'n, 449 U.S. 64 (1981); Udall v. Tallman, 380 U.S. 1 (1965)	S. 1080 (98C) H.R. 746 (97C)	Dies Senate Calendar Comm. reports, dies House Calendar
	S. 1080 (97C)	Passes Senate, dies House Calender
Dawson Chem. Co. v. Rohm & Haas Co., 448 U.S. 176 (1980); Zenith Radio Corp. v. Hazeltine Research, Inc., 395 U.S. 100 (1969); Brulotte v. Thys Co., 379 U.S. 29 (1964)	H.R. 1155 (100C) S. 1200 (100C)	*Zenith* override dropped from bills
Maine v. Thiboutot, 448 U.S. 1 (1980); Miller v. Youakim, 440 U.S. 125 (1979); Van Lare v. Hurley, 421 U.S. 338 (1975); Townsend v. Swank, 404 U.S. 282 (1971); King v. Smith, 392 U.S. 309 (1968)	H.R. 4086 (100C) S. 436 (99C) S. 584 (97C)	Dies in Subcomm. Dies Subcomm. Dies Subcomm.
United States v. Raddatz, 447 U.S. 667 (1980)	S. 653 (97C)	Dies Subcomm.
Diamond v. Chakrabarty, 447 U.S. 303 (1980)	House Hearings (100C)	No Bill
Standefer v. United States, 447 U.S. 10 (1980)	H.R. 1647 (97C) H.R. 4711 (97C) H.R. 6915 (96C)	Dies Subcomm. Dies Subcomm. Comm. reports
Board of Regents v. Tomanio, 446 U.S. 478 (1980)	S. 990 (97C)	Dies Subcomm.
Busic v. United States, 446 U.S. 398 (1980); Simpson v. United States, 435 U.S. 6 (1978)	H.J. Res. 648 (98C) S.J. Res. 356 (98C)	Pub. L. No. 98-473 (1984)
	H.R. 6915 (96C)	Comm. reports
City of Mobile v. Bolden, 446 U.S. 55 (1980)	H.R. 3112 (97C) H.R. 3198 (97C) S. 1992 (97C)	Pub. L. No. 97-205 (1982)
Carlson v. Green, 446 U.S. 14 (1980); Davis v. Passman, 442 U.S. 228 (1979)	H.R. 595 (98C) H.R. 3142 (98C)	Dies Comm.
	H.R. 24 (97C) H.R. 7034 (97C) S. 1775 (97C)	Clean bill Dies Comm. Dies Comm.
Owen v. City of Independence, 445 U.S. 622 (1980)	S. 436 (99C) S. 585 (97C)	Dies Comm. Dies Subcomm.
Kissinger v. Reporters Comm. for Freedom of the Press, 445 U.S. 136 (1980); Forsham v. Harris, 445 U.S. 169 (1980)	S. 1730 (97C) S. 1751 (97C)	Comm. reports, dies Senate Calendar
California Retail Liquor Dealers Ass'n v. Midcal Aluminum, Inc., 445 U.S. 97 (1980)	House Hearings (100C)	No Bill
Ferri v. Ackerman, 444 U.S. 193 (1979)	H.R. 3004 (99C)	Pub. L. No. 99-651 (1986)
	H.R. 3233 (98C) H.R. 4307 (98C) S. 2420 (98C)	Override dropped from Pub. L. No. 98-479 (1984)
	S. 829 (98C) H.R. 3060 (97C) S. 2617 (96C)	Dies Subcomm. Dies Subcomm. Dies Comm.
United Steelworkers v. Weber, 443 U.S. 193 (1979); Griggs v. Duke Power Co., 401 U.S. 424 (1971); Regents of the Univ. of Calif. v. Bakke, 438 U.S. 265 (1978)	S.J. Res 41 (97C)	Dies Subcomm.

Moore v. Sims, 442 U.S. 415 (1979); Younger v. Harris, 401 U.S. 37 (1971)	S. 990 (97C)	Dies Subcomm.
Ulster County Ct. v. Allen, 442 U.S. 190 (1979)	S. 1437 (97C)	Comm. reports, dies Senate floor
Chrysler Corp. v. Brown, 441 U.S. 281 (1979)	S. 774 (98C)	Passes Senate, dies House Gov't Ops. Comm.
	S. 1247 (97C) S. 1730 (97C) S. 1751 (97C)	Comm. reports, dies Senate Calendar
Dalia v. United States, 441 U.S. 238 (1979)	H.R. 1647 (97C) H.R. 4711 (97C)	Dies Subcomm. Dies Subcomm.
	S. 1717 (96C) S. 1815 (96C)	Passes Senate, dies House Subcomm.
Gladstone, Realtors v. Village of Bellwood, 441 U.S. 91 (1979)	House Hearings (96C)	No Bill
Broadcast Music, Inc., v. Columbia Broadcasting System, Inc., 441 U.S. 1 (1979)	S. 698 (100C) H.R. 3521 (99C) S. 1980 (99C)	Dies Subcomm. Dies Subcomm. Dies Subcomm.
Quern v. Jordan, 440 U.S. 332 (1979); Edelman v. Jordan, 415 U.S. 651 (1974)	S. 990 (97C)	Dies Subcomm.
Owen Equip. & Erection Co. v. Kroger, 437 U.S. 365 (1978)	H.R. 1046 (96C)	Override dropped from Pub.L.No. 96-82 (1979)
NLRB v. Robbins Tire & Rubber Co., 437 U.S. 214 (1978)	S. 1751 (97C)	Comm. reports, dies Senate Calendar
Monell v. New York City Dep't of Social Servs., 436 U.S. 658 (1978)	S. 585 (97C)	Dies Subcomm.
City of Los Angeles, Dep't of Water & Power v. Manhart, 435 U.S. 702 (1978)	S. 2477 (96C)	Dies Subcomm.
United States v. Culbert, 435 U.S. 371 (1978)	H.R. 6915 (96C)	Comm. reports
J.W. Bateson Co. v. United States, 434 U.S. 586 (1978)	H.R. 3356 (100C)	Dies Subcomm.
Christiansburg Garment Co. v. EEOC, 434 U.S. 412 (1978)	Senate Hearings (97C)	No Bill
Pfizer, Inc. v. Government of India, 434 U.S. 308 (1978)	S. 816 (97C)	Pub. L. No. 97-393 (1982)
United States v. New York Tel. Co., 434 U.S. 159 (1977)	H.R. 3378 (99C) H.R. 4952 (99C) S. 1667 (99C)	Pub. L. No. 99-508 (1986)
	H.R. 6343 (98C) H.R. 6915 (96C)	Dies Subcomm. Comm. reports
Continental T.V., Inc. v. GTE Sylvania, Inc., 433 U.S. 36 (1977)	H.R. 1108 (99C) S. 412 (99C)	Dies Subcomm. Comm. reports, dies Senate Calendar
	S. 1680 (98C)	Dies Comm.
Illinois Brick Co. v. Illinois, 431 U.S. 720 (1977); Hanover Shoe, Inc. v. United Shoe Mach. Corp., 392 U.S. 481 (1968)	S. 2481 (99C) H.R. 2244 (98C) S. 915 (98C)	Dies Comm. Dies Subcomm. Dies Comm.
	H.R. 2060 (96C) H.R. 2204 (96C) S. 300 (96C)	Dies Comm. Dies Comm. Comm. reports, dies on Senate Calendar
Stencel Aero Eng'g Corp. v. United States, 431 U.S. 666 (1977)	H.R. 2378 (100C) H.R. 1623 (99C) S. 1254 (99C) H.R. 4083 (98C) H.R. 4199 (98C) H.R. 5883 (98C)	Dies Subcomm. Dies Subcomm. Dies Comm. Clean bill Clean bill Dies Comm.

Stencel Aero Eng'g Corp. v. United States, 431 U.S. 666 (1977) (cont'd)	S. 1839 (98C) H.R. 1504 (97C) S. 1839 (97C) H.R. 5351 (96C) H.R. 5358 (96C)	Dies Comm. Dies Subcomm. Dies Subcomm. Dies Subcomm. Dies Subcomm.
Arlington Heights v. Metropolitan Hous. Corp., 429 U.S. 252 (1976)	S. 506 (96C)	Comm. reports, dies Senate floor
Department of the Air Force v. Rose, 425 U.S. 352 (1976)	S. 1751 (97C)	Comm. reports, dies Senate Calendar
Simon v. Eastern Ky. Welfare Rights Org., 426 U.S. 26 (1976); Warth v. Seldin, 422 U.S. 490 (1975); Schlesinger v. Reservists Comm. to Stop the War, 418 U.S. 208 (1974); Linda R.S. v. Richard D., 410 U.S. 614 (1973)	S. 680 (96C)	Dies Comm.
Day & Zimmerman, Inc. v. Challoner, 423 U.S. 3 (1975); Klaxon Co. v. Stentor Elec. Mfg. Co., 313 U.S. 487 (1941)	H.R. 4087 (100C)	Comm. reports but override dropped from Pub. L. No. 100-702 (1988)
United States v. American Building Maintenance Indus., 422 U.S. 271 (1975)	H.R. 4049 (96C) S. 390 (96C)	Pub. L. No. 96-349 (1980)
Alyeska Pipeline Serv. Co. v. Wilderness Soc'y, 421 U.S. 240 (1975)	H.R. 5612 (96C) S. 3186 (96C) S. 265 (96C)	Pub. L. No. 96-481 (1980)
United States v. Feola, 420 U.S. 671 (1975)	H.R. 6915 (96C)	Comm. reports, dies House Calendar
	S. 1723 (96C)	Dies Comm.
Reid v. INS, 420 U.S. 619 (1975); INS v. Errico, 385 U.S. 214 (1966)	H.R. 4327 (97C)	Pub. L. No. 97-116 (1981)
	H.R. 5087 (96C) S. 1763 (96C)	Dies Subcomm.
F.D. Rich Co. v. United States, 417 U.S. 116 (1974)	H.R. 3356 (100C)	Dies Subcomm.
Zahn v. Int'l Paper Co., 414 U.S. 291 (1973)	H.R. 4807 (100C)	Comm. reports, but override dropped from Pub. L. No. 100-702 (1988)
United States v. Enmons, 410 U.S. 396 (1973)	H.R. 1514 (98C) S. 462 (98C) H.R. 3047 (97C) S. 613 (97C) S. 1722 (96C)	Dies Subcomm. Dies Comm. Dies Subcomm. Dies Subcomm. Comm. reports, dies Senate Calendar
Kleindienst v. Mandel, 408 U.S. 753 (1972)	H.R. 1119 (100C) H.R. 4427 (100C)	Comm. reports but dies House Calendar
Flood v. Kuhn, 407 U.S. 258 (1972); Toolson v. New York Yankees, 346 U.S. 356 (1953); Federal Baseball Club v. National League, 259 U.S. 200 (1922)	H.R.3287 (97C)	Dies Subcomm.
Deepsouth Packing Co. v. Laitram Corp., 406 U.S. 518 (1972)	H.R. 5041 (98C) H.R. 4526 (98C) H.R. 4814 (98C) S. 1535 (98C) S. 1841 (98C)	Pub. L. No. 98-462 (1984)
United States v. Bass, 404 U.S. 336 (1971)	S. 1722 (96C)	Comm. reports, dies Senate Calendar
United States v. Campos-Serrano, 404 U.S. 293 (1971)	S. 1722 (96C)	Comm. reports, dies Senate Calendar

Lear, Inc. v. Adkins, 395 U.S. 653 (1969)	H.R. 4529 (98C) S. 1535 (98C) S. 1841 (98C)	Override dropped from Pub. L. No. 98-462 (1984)
Federal Maritime Comm'n v. Aktiebolaget Svenska Amerika Linien, 390 U.S. 238 (1968); Carnation Co. v. Pacific Westbound Conf., 383 U.S. 213 (1966)	H.J. Res. 478 (98C) H.R. 1878 (98C) S. 47 (98C)	Pub. L. No. 98-237 (1984)
	H.R. 4374 (97C)	Passes House, dies Senate Calendar
	S. 1593 (97C)	Comm. reports, dies Senate Calendar
	H.R. 6899 (96C)	Comm. reports, dies House Calendar
United States v. Arnold, Schwinn & Co., 388 U.S. 365 (1967)	H.R. 3567 (96C) H.R. 3573 (96C) S. 598 (96C)	Pub. L. No. 96-308 (1980)
Walker v. City of Birmingham, 388 U.S. 307 (1967); United States v. United Mine Workers, 330 U.S. 258 (1947)	H.R. 1647 (97C) H.R. 4711 (97C)	Dies Subcomm. Dies Subcomm.
	H.R. 6915 (96C)	Comm. reports, dies House Caldendar
	S. 1722 (96C)	Comm. reports, dies Senate Calendar
Boutilier v. INS, 387 U.S. 118 (1967)	H.R. 1119 (100C) H.R. 4427 (100C)	Comm. reports but dies House Calendar [Override adopted Pub. L. No. 101-649 (1990)]
	H.R. 4509 (98C) H.R. 5227 (98C)	Dies Subcomm. Dies Subcomm.
FTC v. Procter & Gamble Co., 386 U.S. 568 (1967); United States v. Von's Grocery Co., 384 U.S. 270 (1966); United States v. Pabst Brewing Co., 384 U.S. 546 (1966); FTC v. Consolidated Foods, 380 U.S. 592 (1965)	H.R. 4247 (99C) S. 2160 (99C)	Dies Subcomm. Dies Comm.
Maryland v. United States, 381 U.S. 41 (1965)	H.R. 3799 (97C) S. 267 (97C)	Pub. L. No. 97-124 (1981)
	S. 1858 (96C)	Passes Senate, dies House Comm.
Fay v. Noia, 372 U.S. 391 (1963); Townsend v. Sain, 372 U.S. 293 (1963)	H.R. 6050 (97C) S. 2216 (97C)	Dies Subcomm. Dies Subcomm.
Rosenberg v. Fleuti, 374 U.S. 449 (1963)	H.R. 2921 (100C)	Dies Subcomm.
Scales v. United States, 367 U.S. 203 (1961); Dennis v. United States, 341 U.S. 494 (1951)	S. 1722 (96C)	Comm. reports, dies Senate Calendar
Toth v. Quarles, 350 U.S. 11 (1955)	S. 1722 (96C)	Comm. reports, dies Senate Calendar
Baltimore Contractors v. Bodinger, 348 U.S. 176 (1955); Ettelson v. Metropolitan Life Ins., 317 U.S. 188 (1942); Enelow v. New York Life Ins., 293 U.S. 379 (1935)	H.R. 3152 (100C) H.R. 4807 (100C)	*Bodinger* override adopted in Pub. L. No. 100-702 (1988); other overrides dropped in conference
United States v. Harriss, 347 U.S. 612 (1954)	H.R. 81 (96C) H.R. 128 (96C) H.R. 1979 (96C) H.R. 2302 (96C) H.R. 2497 (96C) H.R. 2613 (96C)	All bills die in Comm.
Brown v. Allen, 344 U.S. 443 (1953)	S. 1762 (98C) S. 238 (99C) S. 829 (98C) H.R. 6050 (97C) S. 2216 (97C)	Clean bill Dies Comm. Dies Subcomm. Dies Subcomm. Dies Subcomm.

Kawakita v. United States, 343 U.S. 717 (1952)	S. 1722 (96C)	Comm. reports, dies Senate Calendar
Feres v. United States, 340 U.S. 135 (1950)	H.R. 1054 (100C)	Passes House, dies Senate subcomm.
	H.R. 1161 (99C)	Clean bill
	H.R. 3174 (99C)	Passes House, dies Senate Comm.
	S. 489 (99C)	Dies Comm.
	H.R. 1942 (98C)	Dies Subcomm.
United States v. Morton Salt, 338 U.S. 632 (1950)	H.R. 1647 (97C)	Dies Subcomm.
	H.R. 4711 (97C)	Dies Subcomm.
Pinkerton v. United States, 328 U.S. 640 (1946)	H.R. 1647 (97C)	Dies Subcomm.
	H.R. 4711 (97C)	Dies Subcomm.
	H.R. 6915 (96C)	Comm. reports, dies House Calendar
Williams v. United States, 327 U.S. 711, 715 (1946); Mills v. United States, 164 U.S. 644, 648-49 (1896)	H.R. 596 (99C)	Pub. L. No. 99-654 (1986)
	H.R. 4745 (99C)	
	H.R. 4876 (98C)	Clean bill
	H.R. 6284 (98C)	Comm. reports, override dropped from final legislation
	H.R. 5703 (97C)	Comm. reports but dies House Calendar
	H.R. 6915 (96C)	Comm. reports but dies House Calendar
Screws v. United States, 325 U.S. 91 (1945)	H.R. 1647 (97C)	Dies Subcomm.
	H.R. 4711 (97C)	Dies Subcomm.
	H.R. 6915 (96C)	Comm. reports, dies House Calendar
	S. 1722 (96C)	Comm. reports, dies Senate Calendar
Morton Salt Co. v. G.S. Suppiger Co., 314 U.S. 488 (1942)	H.R. 4972 (100C)	Pub. L. No. 100-703 (1988)
Klaxon v. Stentor Elec. Mfg. Co., 313 U.S. 487 (1941)	S. 1996 (100C)	Dies Subcomm.
United States v. Norris, 300 U.S. 564 (1937)	S. 1722 (96C)	Comm. reports, dies Senate Calendar
Valentine v. United States ex rel. Neidecker, 299 U.S. 5 (1936)	S. 1639 (97C)	Dies Comm.
	S. 1722 (96C)	Comm. reports, dies Senate Calendar
Hudson v. United States, 272 U.S. 451 (1926)	S. 1981 (96C)	Comm. reports, dies Senate Calendar
John Bad Elk v. United States, 177 U.S. 529 (1900)	S. 1722 (96C)	Comm. reports, dies Senate Calendar
Keck v. United States, 172 U.S. 434 (1899)	H.R. 6915 (96C)	Comm. reports, dies House Calender
Davis v. United States, 160 U.S. 469 (1895)	H.R. 1329 (98C)	Clean bill
	H.R. 1280 (98C)	Clean bill
	H.R. 3336 (98C)	Comm. reports, dies House floor
	S. 1762 (98C)	Clean bill
	S. 829 (98C)	Dies Subcomm.

Appendix III

Supreme Court Statutory Decisions Overridden by Congress (1967 -1990)

This Appendix lists Supreme Court statutory interpretation decisions that were overridden by the 96th through 100th Congresses. The full citations to these decisions, and to their override statutes, can be found in Appendix I. This Appendix III then provides further information about these Supreme Court decisions.

Decision [Override Year]	Voting Split [Pol. Split]	Primary Reasoning	Winners/Losers
Davenport, 1990 [1990]	7-2 [No Split]	Plain Meaning	Persons Accused of Welfare Fraud/ State Collections Agencies and Creditors
Betts, 1989 [1990]	7-2 [Con./Lib.]	Plain Meaning	Employer Pension Plans/Retired Employees
Dellmuth, 1989 [1990]	5-4 [Con./Lib.]	Plain Meaning & Canons	States/Disabled Children
Coit, 1989 [1990]	7-2-0 [No Split]	Plain Meaning	Creditors of Failed Savings & Loans/FSLIC
Finley, 1989 [1990]	5-4 [Con./Lib.]	Plain Meaning	U.S./Tort Victims with Claims against U.S. & Local Gov't
Traynor, 1988 [1988]	4-3 [Con./Lib.]	Legislative History & Canons	Veterans Admin./Alcoholic Veterans
Fausto, 1988 [1990]	5-3 [Con./Lib.]	Plain Meaning & Canons	U.S./Federal Employees
Bowen, 1988 [1988]	5-1-3 [Con./Lib.]	Legislative History	States/HHS
McNally, 1987 [1988]	7-2 [No Split]	Legislative History & Canons	Allegedly Fraudulent State Officials/Dep't of Justice
Gwaltney, 1987 [1990]	6-3 [Lib./Con.]	Plain Meaning	Industrial Polluters/ Environmentalists & EPA
Cabazon Band, 1987 [1988]	6-3-0 [No Split]	Canons	Indian Tribes/States
Hohri, 1987 [1988]	8-0 [No Split]	Legislative History	Federal Circuit/Federal Courts of Appeals & Confused Litigants
Carpenter, 1987 [1988]	4-4 [Not Recorded]	No Opinion	People Accused of Securities Fraud/U.S. & SEC
Paralyzed Veterans, 1986 [1986]	6-3 [Con./Lib.]	Plain Meaning	Airlines/Disabled Passengers
Exxon Corp., 1986 [1986]	7-1 [No Split]	Legislative History	U.S. & Industrial Polluters/States & Enviromentalists
Marek, 1985 [1986]	6-3 [Con./Lib.]	Canons	§ 1983 Defendants/ § 1983 Plaintiffs
NRDC, 1985 [1987]	5-4 [Con./Lib.]	Legislative History & Canons	EPA & Manufact'rs/ Environmentalists
Johnson, 1985 [1986]	9-0 [No Split]	Legislative History	Local Firefighters/State & Local Gov'ts

Atascadero, 1985 [1986]	5-4 [Con./Lib.]	Plain Meaning & Canons	States/Disabled Workers
Block, 1985 [1986]	8-1 [No Split]	Legislative History & Canons	U.S./States
Grove City, 1984 [1988]	7-2 [Con./Lib.]	Purpose & Plain Meaning	Colleges with Gender Discrimination/Female Students & Women's Groups
Darrone, 1984 [1988]	9-0 [No Split]	Precedent	Issue Unresolved - Winners/Losers Unclear
Phinpathya, 1984 [1986]	6-3 [Con./Lib.]	Plain Meaning	INS/Immigrants Leaving U.S. Temporarily
Robinson, 1984 [1986]	6-3 [Con./Lib.]	Legislative History	Local School Districts/ Disabled Children
Sec'y Interior, 1984 [1990]	5-4 [Con./Lib.]	Legislative History	Dep't Interior & Oil & Gas Interests/State & Environmentalists
Washington Metro., 1984 [1984]	6-3 [No Split]	Purpose	Gov't Contractors/Employees of Subcontractor Injured on Job
Bildisco, 1984 [1984]	5-4 [Con./Lib.]	Plain Meaning	Failing Companies/Unions & Employees
Dickerson, 1983 [1986]	5-4 [No Split]	Plain Meaning & Purpose	Dep't of Justice & Gun Control Advocates/ Convicts with Expungements
Sells, 1983 [1986]	5-4 [Lib./Con.]	Legislative History	Grand Jury Witnesses Investigated/Dep't of Justice
Baggott, 1983 [1986]	8-1 [Lib./Con.]	Legislative History	Grand Jury Witns. Investigated/IRS
Diedrich, 1982 [1984]	8-1 [No Split]	Precedents	IRS/Donors Property Relying on Text & Lower Courts
City of Boulder, 1982 [1984]	5-3 [Lib./Con.]	Precedents	Antitrust Plaintiffs/Local Gov'ts
Williams, 1982 [1984]	5-4 [Lib./Con.]	Canons	Check Kiting Defendants/Dep't of Justice & Banks
Rowan, 1981 [1983]	6-3 [Con./Lib.]	Plain Meaning & Legislative History	Employers/IRS & Employees
Agsalud, 1981 [1982]	Memorandum [No Split]	No Opinion	Employers in Hawaii/Hawaii & Employees
McCarty, 1981 [1982]	8-1 [No Split]	Plain Meaning & Legislative History	Retired Military Personnel/Spouses Owed Support & States
Sea Clammers, 1981 [1986]	7-2 [No Split]	Precedents	Industrial Polluters/ Environmentalists
California v. Nevada, 1980 [1986]	9-0 [No Split]	Practical Construction	California/Nevada
Busic, 1980 [1984]	6-3 [Lib./Con.]	Legislative History	Felons with Firearms/ Dep't of Justice
Bolden, 1980 [1982]	4-2-3 [Con./Lib.]	Constitutional Precedents	White Voters in South/Black Voters
City of Lafayette, 1978 [1984]	5-4 [Lib./Con.]	Plain Meaning & Canons	Antitrust Plaintiffs/Local Gov'ts
Pfizer, 1978 [1982]	5-3 [Lib./Con.]	Purpose & Canons	Foreign States/Antitrust Defendants

TVA v. Hill, 1978 [1978, 1979]	6-3 [Lib./Con.]	Plain Meaning	Environmentalists/TVA & Tennessee
Simpson, 1978 [1984]	8-1 [Lib./Con.]	Legislative History & Canons	Felons with Firearms/ Dep't of Justice & Banks
New York Tel., 1977 [1986]	6-3 [Con./Lib.]	Plain Meaning & Legislative History	Dep't of Justice/Criminal Suspects Subject to Wiretaps
Standard Life, 1977 [1984]	6-2-0 [No Split]	Plain Meaning	Insurance Comps. & NAIC/IRS
Kowalski, 1977 [1980]	7-2 [No Split]	Canons	IRS/State Troopers & Employees with Meal Allowances
McMann, 1977 [1978]	7-2 [Con./Lib.]	Plain Meaning & Legislative History	Employers/Older Employees
Hancock, 1976 [1978]	7-2 [Lib./Con.]	Legislative History & Canons	Federally Owned Facilities/ Environmentalists
Gilbert, 1976 [1978]	6-3 [Con./Lib.]	Constitutional Precedents	Employers/Female Employees
Park, 1975 [1988]	6-3 [No Split]	Precedents	Corporate Officials/ Dep't of Justice
Reid, 1975 [1981]	6-2 [Con./Lib.]	Plain Meaning	INS/Illegal Aliens with Children in U.S.
Alcala, 1975 [1981]	7-1 [Con./Lib.]	Plain Meaning & Purpose	States/Pregnant Women on Welfare
Alyeska, 1975 [1976 & 1980]	5-2 [Con./Lib.]	Plain Meaning & Canons	Corporate & Gov't Defendants/Small Claim & Civil Rights Plaintiffs
Wilkins, 1945 [1976]	4-4 [No Split]	No Opinion	Researchers & Academics/ Publishers & Authors of Copyrighted Works
American Building, 1975 [1980]	6-3 [Con./Lib.]	Plain Meaning	Local Companies/Dep't of Justice & Antitrust Plaintiffs
Aiken, 1975 [1976]	6-1-2 [Con./Lib.]	Precedents	Radio & T.V. & Receivers/Copyright Holders
Bob Jones, 1974 [1976]	8-0 [No Split]	Plain Meaning	IRS/§ 501 Exempt Institutions
"Americans United," 1974 [1976]	7-1 [No Split]	Plain Meaning	IRS/§ 501 Exempt Institutions
Maze, 1974 [1984]	5-4 [No Split]	Precedents	Bank Card Fraud Defendants/Dep't of Justice & Banks
Teleprompter, 1974 [1976]	6-3 [No Split]	Precedent	Radio & T.V. & Receivers/Copyright Holders
Wingo, 1974 [1976]	7-2 [Lib./Con.]	Precedent & Canons	Habeas Claimants/Fed'l Magistrates
Eisen, 1974 [1974]	6-3 [Con./Lib.]	Plain Meaning & Precedents	Corporate Defendants/Small Claim Plaintiffs
Mink, 1973 [1974]	5-3 [Con./Lib.]	Plain Meaning	Executive Branch/ Citizens Seeking Information & Members Congress
Missouri, 1973 [1974]	8-1 [No Split]	Legislative History & Canons	States/State Employees
Zahn, 1973 [1974]	6-3 [Con./Lib.]	Precedents	Corporate Defendants/Small Claim Plaintiffs

Sierra Club, 1973 [1976]	4-4 [No Record]	No Opinion	Environmentalists/ Industrial Polluters
Hughes Tool, 1973 [1976]	6-2 [Lib./Con.]	Precedent	Antitrust Defendants/ Antitrust Plaintiffs
Kras, 1973 [1978]	5-4 [Con./Lib.]	Legislative History & Precedent	Creditors & U.S./Indigents
Carter, 1972 [1979]	9-0 [No Split]	Legislative History	District of Columbia/Victims Const'l Torts
Deepsouth, 1972 [1984]	5-4 [Lib./Con.]	Common Law & Canons	Holders of Combination Patents/Extraterritorial Competitors
Byrum, 1972 [1976]	6-3 [No Split]	Precedents	Taxpayers with Trusts/ IRS
Robertson, 1972 [1976]	5-2-2 [Con./Lib.]	Canons	FAA/Citizens Seeking Info.
S & E Contractors, 1972 [1978]	5-3 [Con./Lib.]	Purpose	Gov't Contractors/U.S.
United States District Court, 1972 [1978]	5-3-0 [No Split]	Plain Meaning & Legislative History	Persons Subject to Suveillance/Dep't of Justice & FBI
Dewey, 1971 [1972]	Mem. [No Split]	No Opinion	Companies/ Religious Employees
Toussie, 1970 [1971]	6-3 [Lib./Con.]	Canons	Draft Dodgers/Selective Service
Lines, 1970 [1978]	4-2 [No Split]	Purpose	Working Bankrupts/ Creditors
Citizen Publishing, 1969 [1970]	6-1-1 [Lib./Con.]	Precedents	Dep't of Justice & Antitrust Plaintiffs/Failing Newspapers
Snyder v. Harris, 1969 [1980]	7-2 [Con./Lib.]	Precedents	Defendants/ Plaintiffs with Small Claims
Fortnightly, 1968 [1976]	5-1 [No Split]	Purpose	Radio & T.V. & Receivers/Copyright Holders
Pan Am, 1968 [1968]	4-4 [No Record]	No Opinion	Not Clear
Svenska, 1968 [1984]	8-0 [No Split]	Canons	Antitrust Plaintiffs/Shipping Cartels
Alderman, 1968 [1971]	5-1-3 [Con./Lib.]	Constitutional Precedents	Dep't of Justice/ Co-Defendants of Wiretapped Defendants
Fleishmann, 1967 [1974]	8-1 [No Split]	Canons	Random Litigants/Same
Lykes Bros., 1967 [1972]	7-2 [Lib./Con.]	Precedent	Longshoremen/ Shipowners
Boutilier, 1967 [1990]	6-3 [Con./Lib.]	Legislative History	INS/Bisexuals, Gay Men, Lesbians
Schwinn, 1967 [1980]	5-2 [Lib./Con.]	Legislative History	Dep't of Justice & Retailers/ Manufacturers with Vert. Arrangem'ts
Gulf Coastal, 1967 [1974]	9-0 [No Split]	No Opinion	ICC/ Water Carriers
Errico, 1966 [1981]	6-3 [Lib./Con.]	Purpose & Legislative History	Illegal Aliens w/Relatives in U.S./INS
Guest, 1966 [1968]	6-3 [Con./Lib.]	Canons & Precedent	Private Persons Attacking Civil Rights Workers/ Civil Rights Victims

Carnation, 1966 [1984]	9-0 [No Split]	Canons & Legislative History	Antitrust Plaintiffs/Shipping Industry
Seeger, 1965 [1967]	9-0 [No Split]	Legislative History	Conscientious Objectors/Selective Service
Maryland v. United States, 1965 [1984]	8-1 [No Split]	Legislative History	U.S./National Guard Personnel Injured in Tort
Arizona v. Calif., 1963 [1968]	4-2-1 [No Split]	Legislative History	Dep't Interior & U.S./Various State Water Claimants
S.S. Yaka, 1963 [1972]	7-2 [Lib./Con.]	Precedent	Longshoremen/ Shipowners
Bianchi, 1963 [1978]	7-2 [No Split]	Legislative History	Federal Dep'ts/ Federal Contractors
Davis, 1962 [1984]	7-0 [No Split]	Purpose & Canons	IRS/Divorcing Couples
Denver Union, 1958 [1968]	6-3 [Lib./Con.]	Canons	Market Agencies at Stockyards/Stockyard Companies
Embassy, 1958 [1978]	6-3 [Con./Lib.]	Precedents	Employers/Union Welfare Funds & Employees
Ryan Stevedoring, 1956 [1972]	5-4 [Con./Lib.]	Purpose	Shipowners/Contractors
Bodinger, 1955 [1988]	6-1-2 [Con./Lib.]	Precedent	Random Litigants/same
St. Joe Paper, 1954 [1978]	4-3 [No Split]	Legislative History & Purpose	Creditors & Rivals for Rail Merger/ICC & Railroads Wanting Merger
Pinkus, 1949 [1968]	8-0 [No Split]	Plain Meaning & Precedent	Mail Order Shippers/Post Office & Dep't of Justice
Sieracki, 1946 [1972]	5-3 [Lib./Con.]	Purpose & Precedent	Stevedores Employed by Indep. Contractor/ Shipowner
Williams, 1946 [1986]	9-0 [No Split]	Precedent	Alleged Rapists/ Victims of Rape
Morton Salt, 1941 [1988]	8-0 [No Split]	Precedent & Purpose	Patent Holders/ Patnet Licenses
Toucey, 1941 [1978]	5-3 [No Split]	Canons	Random Litigants/Same
Bunte Bros., 1941 [1974]	6-3 [Con./Lib.]	Practical Construction	Local Businesses/FTC
Aron Park, 1940 [1978]	9-0 [No Split]	Practical Construction	Creditors in Bankruptcy/ Debtors
Signal Oil, 1940 [1971]	9-0 [No Split]	Purpose	Supplies to Ships/ Ship Owners
Welch, 1938 [1980]	7-0 [No Split]	Plain Meaning	IRS/Companies Selling Lots Under Installment Sales
General Utilities, 1935 [1986]	9-0 [No Split]	Canons	Taxpayers/IRS
Carver, 1923 [1971]	9-0 [No Split]	Plain Meaning	Shipowners/ Suppliers to Ships
Lambert, 1922 [1986]	8-0 [No Split]	Practical Construction	Random Litigants/Same
Caminetti, 1917 [1986]	6-3 [No Split]	Plain Meaning	United States/ Defendants Accused of Fornication
Midwest Oil, 1915 [1976]	5-3 [No Split]	Practical Construction	President & Environmentalists/ Western Oil Developers
Apollo Co., 1908 [1976]	9-0 [No Split]	Precedents & Legislative History	Makers of Player Pianos & Music Rolls/Composers

Lockwood, 1908 [1978]	9-0 [No Split]	Plain Meaning	Bankrupt Persons/Creditors & Banks
Birkett, 1904 [1978]	9-0 [No Split]	Practical Construction	Bankruptcy Creditors/Debtors
Tinker, 1902 [1978]	6-3 [Con./Lib.]	Precedents	Bankrupt's Spouse Judgment Creditor/ Business Creditors

[17]

The Logic of Strategic Defection: Court–Executive Relations in Argentina Under Dictatorship and Democracy

GRETCHEN HELMKE *University of Notre Dame*

Building on the separation-of-powers approach in American politics, this article develops a new micro-level account of judicial decision-making in contexts where judges face institutional insecurity. Against conventional wisdom, I argue that under certain conditions the lack of judicial independence motivates judges to "strategically defect" against the government once it begins losing power. The result is a reverse legal–political cycle in which antigovernment decisions cluster at the end of weak governments. Original data on more than 7,500 individual decisions by Argentine Supreme Court justices (1976–1995) are used to test hypotheses about why, when, and in which types of cases judges are likely to engage in strategic defection. Consistent with the theory's predictions, the results of the analysis show a significant increase in antigovernment decisions occurring at the end of weak dictatorships and weak democratic governments. Examining subsets of decisions and controlling for several additional variables further corroborate the strategic account.

All judges are politicians, whether they know it or not.

Enrique Petracchi, Argentine Supreme Court Justice, 1983–present (Abramovich 1992)

Why do judges rule against the government? Standard answers suggest that judges do so only if they are independent (Larkins 1998; Stotzsky 1993). Although contemporary scholars disagree over how to define and measure judicial independence,[1] the assumption that it is a necessary, if insufficient, condition for a functioning system of interbranch checks and balances has remained unquestioned since Hamilton's ([1787] 1961, 471) eloquent observation that judges who lack independence will rarely "hazard the displeasure" of those in power. Yet even casual observation of judicial behavior in institutionally insecure environments suggests that the facts do not fully support this assertion. From Franco's authoritarian Spain, where judges routinely expressed views at odds with the government, to countries such as Guatemala and Peru, where judges refused to legitimize *autogolpes* (self-coups) staged by sitting executives, to Argentina, where judges have sent to prison the very politicians by whom they were appointed, evidence suggests that judicial decision-making varies a great deal even where the basic institutional requisites for independence are conspicuously absent.

If the existing literature offers little insight into why dependent judges sometimes serve to check their governments, how can we make sense of this behavior? I develop one set of answers to this question by building on the emerging separation-of-powers approach in American politics. In contrast to legalistic approaches that assume apolitical judges and approaches that focus on judges' attitudes or ideologies, the separation-of-powers approach treats judges as rational decision-makers who are constrained by other institutional actors (see, e.g., Epstein and Knight 1996, 1998; Ferejohn and Weingast 1992; and Spiller and Gely 1990). Whereas strategic approaches in the American politics literature have been criticized on the grounds that judges are relatively insulated from the alleged pressures imposed by other actors (Segal 1997), I argue that precisely because such institutional protections are in short supply in many parts of the developing world, the separation-of-powers approach should prove particularly compelling for analyzing judicial behavior beyond the American context.

Extending the separation-of-powers approach to new institutional settings yields several intuitive but novel predictions about judges' reactions to their political environment. Most fundamentally, in stark contrast to the conventional wisdom sketched above, I argue that under certain conditions the very *lack* of independence motivates judges to challenge the other branches of government. Specifically, once the government in office begins to lose power, judges who lack institutional security begin facing incentives to increase their antigovernment rulings to distance themselves from a weakening government. I refer to this phenomenon as strategic defection. Taking into account factors such as the degree of institutional security that judges face, the number of relevant political actors, and the timing of sanctions, the theory of strategic defection predicts a reverse legal–political cycle in which antigovernment decisions increase at the end of weak governments and are handed down by the very judges whom the government

---

Gretchen Helmke is Assistant Professor, Department of Political Science, University of Notre Dame, 217 O'Shaughnessy Hall, Notre Dame, IN 46556 (ghelmke@nd.edu).

The author gratefully acknowledges support from the National Science Foundation (SBR-9617896) and the SSRC. My deepest thanks go to Carlos Acuña, Jim Alt, Martin Böhmer, Delia Boylan, Daniel Brinks, Gregory Caldeira, Pedro Cavallero, Mark Chaves, Lee Epstein, Russ Faeges, Barry Friedman, Andy Gould, Scott Mainwaring, Jonathan Katz, Jack Knight, David Laitin, Steve Levitsky, Douglass North, Gerry Rosenberg, Mitch Sanders, Catalina Smulovitz, Rich Snyder, Lyn Spillman, Susan Stokes, Neal Tate, Georg Vanberg, Ashutosh Varshney, Jennifer Widner, Jakub Zielinski, and anonymous reviewers for comments and encouragement on early drafts of this article and to Pablo Lafuente for excellent research assistance.

[1] For surveys of competing definitions of judicial independence and problems of measurement, see Larkins 1996, Rosenberg 1992, and Tate and Haynie 1994.

had earlier appointed. The logic of strategic defection offers an important but heretofore undertheorized mechanism for analyzing a variety of interinstitutional behaviors under dictatorships and democracies alike.

The Argentine Supreme Court presents a textbook case for examining the theory of strategic defection. Despite the constitutional guarantee of lifetime tenure for Argentine Supreme Court justices, the decades of political instability that plagued Argentina from the 1930s through the 1980s resulted in the *de facto* norm of removing and replacing the members of the Supreme Court with each regime transition. In the period examined here, the Court was replaced *en masse* by the military following the coup in 1976 and again by the incoming democratic government of Raul Alfonsín in 1983. This institutional insecurity continued even as democracy consolidated. As recently as 1990 newly elected president Carlos Menem gained control over the Court through a court-packing scheme that ultimately enabled him to appoint six of the nine justices to the bench.

THE SEPARATION-OF-POWERS APPROACH IN A COMPARATIVE PERSPECTIVE: THE THEORY OF STRATEGIC DEFECTION

In extending the separation-of-powers framework beyond the United States, I begin with three observations. First, in many parts of the developing world, judges face threats far greater than simply having their decisions overturned. In such contexts, sanctions range from impeachment, removal, and court-packing to criminal indictment, physical violence, and even death. Compared to American justices, who serve an average of 16.3 years on the bench, in Argentina in the post-Perón period, the average length of tenure has been a mere 5.6 years (see Table 1). Although judges stepped down for a variety of reasons throughout each of the three governments, multiple resignations clustered at the end of both the military and the first democratic government of Alfonsín suggest that incoming governments in Argentina routinely get rid of their predecessors' judges despite constitutional guarantees.

Second, in many developing countries the *de facto* concentration of power in the executive branch eclipses the formal institutional judicial sanctioning powers granted to the legislature. This is particularly true in Latin America, where despite constitutional guarantees, the functional separation of powers is notoriously weak or absent and power is concentrated heavily in the executive branch (O'Donnell 1994). The weakness of these other institutions thus also tends to increase dramatically the threat judges face, for sanctions against the judges are unlikely to be successfully blocked by third-party actors such as the legislature.

TABLE 1. Characteristics of Argentine Supreme Court Justices' Tenure, 1976–1995

Name of Justice	Dates	Government	Departure	Tenure (Months)
Horacio Herredia	1976–78	Videla*	Deceased	24
Frederico Escalada	1976	Videla*	Resigned	9
Adolfo Gabrielli	1976–83	Videla*	Resigned**	94
Alejandro Caride	1976–77	Videla*	Resigned	21
Abelardo Rossi	1976–83	Videla*	Resigned**	94
Pedro Frías	1976–81	Videla*	Resigned	69
Elías Guastavino	1978–83	Videla*	Resigned**	72
Emilio Daireaux	1977–80	Videla*	Deceased	36
César Black	1980–82	Videla*	Resigned	24
Carlos Renom	1982–83	Galtieri*	Resigned	24
Julio Martínez Vivot	1983	Bignone*	Resigned*	12
Emilio Gnecco	1983	Bignone*	Resigned*	12
Genaro Carrió	1983–85	Alfonsín	Resigned	24
José Caballero	1983–90	Alfonsín	Resigned*	84
Augusto Belluscio	1983–	Alfonsín		192
Carlos Fayt	1983–	Alfonsín		192
Enrique Petracchi	1983–	Alfonsín		192
Jorge Bacqué	1985–90	Alfonsín	Resigned**	60
Julio Oyanarte	1990–91	Menem	Resigned	12
Ricardo Levene	1990–95	Menem	Retired	67
Mariano Cavagna Martínez	1990–93	Menem	Resigned	36
Rodolfo Barra	1990–93	Menem	Resigned	36
Julio Nazareno	1990–	Menem		108
Eduardo Moliné O'Connor	1990–	Menem		108
Antonio Boggiano	1991–	Menem		96
Gustavo Bossert	1993–	Menem		72
Guillermo López	1993–	Menem		72
Adolfo Vázquez	1995–	Menem		48
				(Average = 67.5)

Source: Compiled from data in Carrió 1996; Miller, Gelli, and Cayuso 1995; and Poder Cuidadano 1997.
Note: *Judges appointed during the dictatorship; **judges who resigned during a political transition.

American Political Science Review Vol. 96, No. 2

FIGURE 1. The Executive Selecting and Sanctioning Game

```
-----------I----------------I-----------------I-------------------------I--------------> Time
           G1               C                 N                         G2
           Select           Decide            Determine Next            Sanction
           Justices         For/Against       Government                Justices
```

FIGURE 2. (A) Policy Preferences without Intertemporal Conflict; (B) Policy Preferences with Intertemporal Conflict

```
A  SQ---------------------------G1-----------------------G2-------------------------------->Policy

B  G1---------------------------SQ-----------------------G2-------------------------------->Policy
```

Third, in many developing countries the primary threat to judges comes not from incumbent governments but from incoming ones. This follows from the fact that those with the greatest incentives to sanction justices are not those who appoint them but, rather, those who succeed the appointing government. Theoretically, this means that the appropriate locale of what Ferejohn and Weingast (1992) refer to as the "intertemporal conflict of interest" shifts from one between *past* and *current* governments to one based on the *current*, incumbent executive and the *future*, incoming executive. Under this alternative scenario judges face incentives to curry favor not with the current government but, rather, with the future government.

Taken together, the first two points suggest that judges' incentives to engage in strategic behavior in developing democracies are potentially far greater than in developed democracies. The third point implies a difference based not on mere degree but, rather, on the particular repertoire of strategic behavior that emerges. When judges believe that they are constrained by incoming governments who oppose the incumbent government, their best response may not be to support the current government (e.g. Epstein and Knight 1996) but, rather, to defect from it.

Figure 1 provides a basic strategic setting that illustrates the logic of strategic defection. The figure depicts a sequence of decisions with the current government (G1) moving first, the court (C) second, Nature (N) third, and the future government (G2) fourth. In the first stage, the current government acts by selecting justices for the court. In the second stage, these justices rule on policies of this government, either upholding or overruling the policies of the government.[2] In the third stage, Nature selects the next government, with a probability p that the incumbents will remain and $1 - p$ that opponents will take office. In the fourth and final stage, the future government decides whether to sanction the court based on the court's decisions made under the previous government.

For the sake of simplicity, assume that the basic rule that guides the actors' choices is that if the court has decided cases close to the views of the incoming government, the future government will be less likely to sanction the justices. If the court has decided cases against the views of the new incumbents, however, the future government will be more likely to sanction the justices.[3]

The first implication is that in only two circumstances will the incoming government be unlikely to sanction justices who continued to rule in favor of the previous government. The first condition is when the current government itself is strong and able to maintain itself in power; that is, G1 = G2. The second is when the incumbents lose to the opposition, but the location of the new government's ideal points is such that it prefers G1 to SQ, where SQ is the status quo (see Figure 2A). Such a circumstance might obtain, for example, if there are relatively few policy differences between the outgoing and the incoming governments. In these circumstances, incoming governments will have little incentive to punish their opponents' court, even if the court that served under the previous government continues to rule in its favor.

In all other circumstances, future governments will have incentives to sanction justices who continued to rule in favor of the previous government. If the incoming government opposes the policies of its predecessors such that it prefers that its opponents' policies do not become law, then, in effect, the future government can be said to favor the status quo (that is, the condition that obtains whenever the policies of the current government are not enacted). In short, future rulers will have an incentive to sanction justices loyal to the previous government (judges whose decisions fall between G1 and SQ) whenever SQ is between G1 and G2 (see Figure 2B).

I am now in a position to propose a new set of answers to the question of why, when, and in which cases judges who lack independence are likely to rule against the government. Assuming that judges wish to avoid sanctions, loyalty to the current government clearly may not be the best strategy. Instead, once the government in office begins to lose power, judges will face incentives to engage in strategic defection.[4] Stated as a testable hypothesis, the first prediction is as follows.

HYPOTHESIS 1. *Judges will increase their rulings against the current government once the prospect emerges that the current government will lose power.*

Moreover, to the extent that judges use strategic defection to mitigate the sanctions they face, it follows

[2] The assumption that the court has a dichotomous choice is simplifying, as judges may decide neither strictly for nor strictly against the government. I assume that governments have well-defined, stable, single-peaked preferences in a unidimensional policy space.

[3] A more general assumption is that judges are uncertain about the incoming government's type. If an incoming government cares about legitimacy, it might not sanction judges regardless of what the judges do. But if judges are uncertain about the next government, strategic defection will never hurt them and could help them.

[4] Further research on justices' motives, such as seeking to enhance their legal reputations, should examine judges' behavior where the preferences of the legal community and the incoming government diverge. Judges seeking to enhance their legal reputation should appeal to the legal community regardless of the political environment.

that defection should occur in cases about which the opposition is likely to care most. Thus, the second prediction can be stated as follows.

HYPOTHESIS 2. *All else equal, judges will concentrate their defection in cases that are considered most important to the incoming government.*

Evidence would be inconsistent with these hypotheses if judges facing sanctions remained loyal to the outgoing government or if antigovernment decisions were limited to relatively minor cases.

DATA AND RESEARCH DESIGN

Elsewhere, I have tested the theory of strategic defection by considering high-profile cases such as the reelection case involving Menem's bid for a third term in office in 1999 (Helmke n.d.). Here I use new individual-level data on the Argentine Supreme Court justices' decisions between 1976 and 1995, contained in the *Argentine Supreme Court Decisions Database* (ASCD), which I constructed.[5] I compare the behavior of justices in periods of relative institutional security to their behavior in periods of relative insecurity. Inferences about strategic defection are thus based not simply on the total percentage of antigovernment decisions, which may be affected by any number of factors, but on whether the willingness of judges to rule against the government *changes* relative to changes in their political environment. In this section I briefly describe the organization and decision-making process of the Argentine Supreme Court, explain how the data needed to test the hypotheses were gathered, and discuss the operationalization of several key variables.

The Argentine Judiciary and the ASCD Database

The Argentine Supreme Court (*Corte Suprema de Justicia de la Nación*) stands at the head of a federal judiciary established by the Constitution of 1853, modeled on the United States Constitution, and recently reformed in 1994. The Argentine Supreme Court is the highest court in the country, with original and appellate jurisdiction over all federal questions. In 1887, the Court established through its own jurisprudence the power of judicial review. It cannot exercise abstract review. Once a case arrives at the Argentine Supreme Court it is circulated among the nine justices,[6] who may either sign the draft opinion or write a separate opinion. The order in which a justice receives the case depends on the type of appeal filed.[7] Justices meet either weekly or biweekly in sessions called *acuerdos*, mainly to sign opinions and occasionally to discuss cases. There are no oral proceedings and the records of weekly meetings are not publicly available. Moreover, the norm is that while all of the justices who agree with the opinion of the majority sign it, the actual "author" of the opinion remains anonymous (Carrió 1996). Nevertheless, for all full opinions[8] the judges in the majority are listed at the end of the opinion and the identities of those justices who sign separate dissents and concurrences are also clear, allowing me to code the individual justices' positions.

One of the main challenges involved in constructing the database was developing a reliable and systematic method for selecting cases in which the government had an identifiable interest. Unlike the U.S. Supreme Court, the Argentine Supreme Court decides thousands of cases annually.[9] Many of these are relatively unimportant legally and politically, raising the issue of which cases were most appropriate for evaluating the strategic behavior of Argentine justices. After considering several alternatives,[10] I used the indexes contained in the back of each volume of Argentine Supreme Court decisions (*Fallos de la Corte Suprema de Justicia de la Nación*) to generate a complete list of cases that met one or both of the following criteria: (1) the case named the state as a party and (2) the case named a decree passed by the current executive. Using these two criteria ensured that all cases in which the government had an interest would be selected. By coding additional information on case type, appeals brought by the government, and types of issues (described below), I can address the concern that the government may not care equally about winning all of the cases in which it is a party or in which the legality of a particular decree is at stake. The total number of individual votes based on these cases is 7,562.[11] These votes are coded

[5] The ASCD database provides the first systematic collection of information on judicial decision-making in contemporary Latin America. See Molinelli, Palanza, and Sin 1999 for additional data, analyzed in Iaryczower, Spiller, and Tomassi 2000.

[6] Congress determines the number of justices. There were five justices under the military and Alfonsín, and nine under Menem. Two Alfonsín appointees resigned in 1990, allowing Menem to appoint six new justices, or a majority, upon taking office.

[7] In cases that reach the Court on grounds of arbitrariness granted by the appeals courts (*recurso extraordinario*), the order of circulation is determined randomly. In cases where lower courts denied the appeal (*recurso de queja*) or cases involving more than 800,000 pesos (*recurso ordinario*), the Chief Justice determines the order, although in practice another justice may set the agenda (anonymous interview, Buenos Aires, July 2001).

[8] All judicial decisions are either full or summary opinions. However, because justices do not sign summary opinions, individual votes can be coded only for full opinion cases.

[9] From 1974 to 1994 the annual number of cases entering the Court averaged between 4,000 and 6,000, but it has risen to more than 36,000 cases since 1997 (FORES 1988, 1/3; Corte Suprema de Justicia de la Nación Secretaria Letrada de Estadisticas 1998; Molinelli, Palanza, and Sin 1999, 710). Each justice currently receives an average of 50 cases per day (anonymous interview, Buenos Aires, July 2001).

[10] Coding all decisions and randomly selecting cases yielded too many cases with no identifiable interest for the government. Efforts to replicate Dahl's (1957) method also failed, as there is no necessary overlap between constitutional cases and cases where one could identify the interest of the government (but see Molinelli, Palanza, and Sin 1999).

[11] Individual justices votes are recorded on a total of 932 cases, with 325 cases under the military government, 278 cases under Alfonsín, and 329 cases under Menem.

dichotomously according to whether the justice voted in favor of or against the government.[12]

Regime, Government, and Political Timing

Testing the strategic defection explanation requires, first and foremost, a measure of the judges' expectations about the threats they face and the ability of the incumbent government to remain in power. Because it is impossible to measure directly the justices' beliefs about their own and the government's future, I generate proxy measures for the justices' expectations by drawing on primary and secondary accounts of political events during the three governmental periods examined. Each entry contained in the ASCD database records the exact date on which the decision was officially handed down. Based on this information, I created a series of dichotomous timing variables that allow me to model the changes in the justices' perceptions about their political environment. Under the military, the earliest plausible beginning for the transitional period in which judges would have expected the military to lose power was two years prior to the regime change.[13] Under the two democratic governments examined, the midterm parliamentary elections two years before the presidential elections serve as the earliest cutoff points for establishing the transitional period.[14] Beginning with the two-year cutoff point, I then capture each transition by creating a series of dummy variables with adjusted cutoff points at eighteen, twelve, 6, and 3 months. These cutoff points generate a series of *transition* variables—*final 24 months*, *final 18 months*, *final 12 months*, *final 6 months*, *final 3 months*—which allow me to assess how judges' behavior changes as an election approaches and a change to a new government becomes increasingly likely. I assign a value of one to all decisions falling within the periods of the transitions. All other decisions take a value of Zero.[15]

Additional Control Variables: Case Importance, Composition, Issue Categories

All of the individual votes analyzed in this article are based on full opinion cases. Thus, the data on individual decisions already deal with a subset of cases considered sufficiently relevant by the justices to warrant a full opinion. To provide additional measures of case importance, I constructed four dummy variables.[16] The first variable, *Decree*, provides a rough measure of importance based on political rather than legal criteria. Because these cases involve only decrees passed by the sitting government, this measure distinguishes decisions that deal with timely political issues from decisions involving the government as a litigant, which, as result of case backlog, may be less important by the time the cases reach the Supreme Court. The second variable, *Salient Decree*, takes account of the fact that not all decrees passed are necessarily of equal importance (e.g., Ferreira Rubio and Gorretti 1998). To deal with this concern, I selected a subset of the decree cases that dealt with issues considered to be especially relevant under each of the three governments, including cases involving issues of constitutional interpretation, amparo cases,[17] and habeas corpus cases. To address the further concern that the government may not care equally about winning all cases, I constructed *Appeal* as a dichotomous variable that distinguishes cases in which the government lost in the lower court and filed an appeal to bring the case to the Supreme Court. Finally, to measure the Court's level of effort as an indicator of importance, the fourth variable, *Overturn*, distinguishes cases where the Court had to overturn a favorable decision handed down by a lower court to rule against the government from cases where it upheld a negative decision. To account for individual-specific effects, I include dummy variables for each judge on the Court at the time the decision was handed down. Additional dummy variables are included to deal with the possible effects of the Court's composition and the mix of cases coming before the Court. The Appendix includes a complete list of the issue variables used in the analysis.

EVALUATING STRATEGIC MODELS OF JUDICIAL DECISION-MAKING ON THE ARGENTINE SUPREME COURT

Confidence in inferences about strategic defection increases as alternative explanations for such change can be ruled out.[18] For example, if the mix of cases being

---

[12] Decisions decided against the state on the merits that make important concessions to the government are coded "partially against." Decisions decided for the state on the merits but that make important concessions to the other litigant are coded "partially for." Because less than 1% of the cases contain partial votes, here I recoded the "partially against" decisions as "against" and the "partially for" decisions as "for."

[13] Although there was great uncertainty about the democratic transition (Munck 1998; O'Donnell and Schmitter 1986), by 1981 the opening of dialogue with the opposition, mass human rights protests, the palace coup against Viola, and the failing economy suggested that the military regime could lose power (Nino 1996). In Argentina's leading law journals the future fate of the military's justices was debated, suggesting that the justices were aware of the threat they faced if the military left power (Carrió 1996).

[14] During the last two years (1987–1989), Alfonsín's government was crippled by labor strikes (McGuire 1997), mass protests, military rebellions, and successive rounds of hyperinflation. The Radicals lost seats in the 1987 midterm elections, and Alfonsín's approval ratings fell steadily, from 42% in April 1987 to 9% prior to the 1989 election (Catterberg 1991). Menem's popularity grew during the first administration (Levitsky n.d.; Stokes 2001). In 1993 the Peronist Party swept the midterm elections. The 1994 constitutional reforms changed the presidential term from a single six-year term to two four-year terms, allowing Menem to win a second term in 1995 (Acuña 1995).

[15] The theoretical justification for treating the timing variables as dichotomous is that it is not the elapsing of time *per se* that increases the probability of antigovernment decisions but, rather, the judges' perception that the government will lose power. Dummy variables model the change in the judges' perception as discontinuous.

[16] The descriptive statistics for each of these dummy variables are listed in Table 3.

[17] The *recurso de amparo* accelerates judicial review to remedy a government's abuse of constitutional guarantees (Rogers and Wright-Carozza 1995, 168)

[18] Ideally, to evaluate the strategic account one would use an independent measure of the justices' attitudes, for example, a

decided by judges is relatively stable over time, a significant increase in antigovernment decisions clustered at the end of a government's term cannot be fully explained by a nonstrategic account. Put differently, the null hypothesis is that if the mix of cases is stable and judges are not reacting strategically to changes in their political environment, then antigovernment decisions should occur at approximately the same rate throughout the government's term.

Timing

The timing hypothesis states that when judges lack secure tenure, antigovernment decisions will increase once judges perceive that the government in office is beginning to lose power. Given the evidence regarding the growing weakness of the military and Alfonsín governments, the specific prediction is that judges during both periods began to turn against the government once it began to lose power. As discussed above, I examine this shift in justices' perceptions between two years and three months prior to the change in government. For the third period examined, the relative strength of the first Menem administration suggests that the justices lacked similar incentives to defect at the end of Menem's first term. Thus, evidence would be consistent with the timing hypothesis if antigovernment decisions increased at the end of the first two governments but not at the end of the third government.[19]

Figure 3, showing trends in antigovernment decisions by year across each of the three governments, strongly supports the patterns predicted by the first strategic defection hypothesis. Under both the military and the Alfonsín governments, judges increased their antigovernment rulings during the last two years of each government as it became increasingly likely that the incumbents would lose power. Under the military regime in the years through 1980, judges ruled against the government in 36% of cases on average. But in 1982 and 1983, once it became likely that a transition would occur, judges increased their percentage of antigovernment rulings considerably, to 48 and 46%. Under the Alfonsín government, antigovernment rulings also began at a relatively low level and then rose as the government became increasingly weak. From 1983 to 1987, antigovernment rulings occurred in only about 37% of all decisions. In 1988 and 1989, antigovernment rulings rose to an average of 47% of all judicial decisions.

FIGURE 3. Percentage of Antigovernment Individual Judicial Decisions by Year

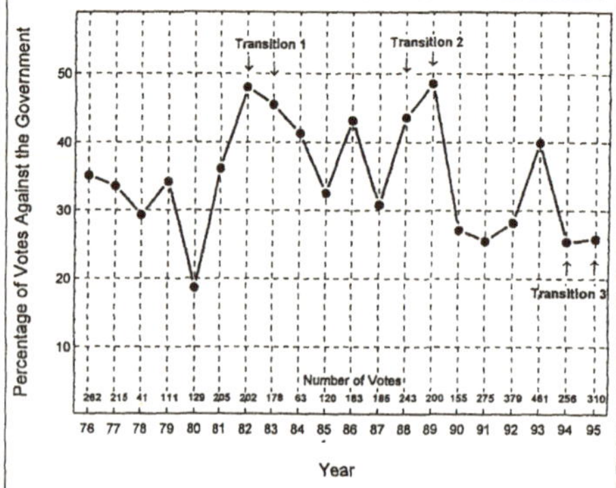

Note: Based on justices' votes in full opinion cases.

In contrast, during the first Menem government (1989–1995), when the justices did not face a credible threat, there was no increase in antigovernment decisions. Indeed, consistent with the logic of strategic defection, the patterns in the individual-level data show that as Menem became increasingly popular and as it became more likely that he would stand for a second term, the percentage of antigovernment decisions declined. Under Menem, the percentage of antigovernment rulings began at roughly the same level as in the early years of the two previous governments, increased to 40% in 1993, but then fell to roughly 25% during the last two years of Menem's first administration. This was a period of success for Menem's economic policies and an increasing likelihood of Menem's bid for reelection.

To delve further into the relationship between changes in the political environment and changes in patterns of judicial decision-making, I employed a series of logit models.[20] The results for each period are presented in Table 2. Beginning with the military period, the results for Models 1–6 overwhelmingly support the timing hypothesis. Consistent with the prediction that judges would increasingly decide cases against weak governments, every transition coefficient for the military period contained in Models 1, 2, and 3 is negative and statistically significant at the $p \leq 0.05$ level or better. Calculating the marginal effects for these coefficients reveals that in the 24, 18, and 12 months prior to the regime transition, the likelihood of the justices voting against the government increased by 20, 21, and seven percentage points, respectively. Somewhat less convincing are the results of Models 4 and 5, which examine the decisions of judges during only the last six- and three-month periods prior to the regime transition. Here the coefficients are also negative but fall short of statistical significance. One interpretation,

liberal–conservative scale is used in the American literature (Segal 1997). No comparable data on judicial preferences exist for developing countries. Assuming that governments appoint like-minded judges, the fact that each Argentine government selected its own majority partially alleviates this problem.

[19] Using timing variables raises ambiguities for the strategic account: Justices may rule against unpopular governments to build popular support (Epp 1998; Gibson, Caldeira, and Baird 1998). However, to the extent that democratically elected incoming governments reflect the public's views, this is hardly at odds with a strategic account (Epstein and Knight 1998; Stimson, Mackuen, and Erikson 1995; Vanberg 2000, 2001). Future research can further determine whether changes in public opinion are *sufficient* to cause a change in the behavior of the Court by examining judges' decisions in cases where the government's and the public's preferences diverge.

[20] I calculated descriptive statistics with SPSS 10.0; all logit models used STATA 6.0.

TABLE 2. Individual Supreme Court Justices' Antigovernment Votes by Time to Transition

	Final 24 Months	Final 18 Months	Final 12 Months	Final 6 Months	Final 3 Months	Final 3 vs. Pre-24 Months
			Military Government, 1976–83			
	Model 1	Model 2	Model 3	Model 4	Model 5	Model 6
Constant	0.51*	0.49*	0.49*	0.49*	0.49*	0.49*
	(0.24)	(0.24)	(0.24)	(0.24)	(0.24)	(0.24)
Transition	−0.81***	−0.85***	−0.38*	−0.11	−0.29	−0.61*
	(0.15)	(0.15)	(0.17)	(0.22)	(0.26)	(0.27)
N	1,339	1,318	1,318	1,318	1,318	1,037
Significance of χ^2	0.001	0.001	0.399	0.769	0.685	0.432
			Alfonsín Government, 1983–89			
	Model 7	Model 8	Model 9	Model 10	Model 11	Model 12
Constant	0.90***	0.75**	0.71**	0.63**	0.63**	0.59*
	(0.22)	(0.22)	(0.22)	(0.22)	(0.22)	(0.28)
Transition	−0.39**	−0.30*	−0.40*	−0.39	−0.59*	−0.62*
	(0.13)	(0.15)	(0.16)	(0.23)	(0.26)	(0.27)
N	989	837	837	837	837	552
Significance of χ^2	0.014	0.170	0.141	0.379	0.207	0.311
			Menem Government, 1989–95			
	Model 13	Model 14	Model 15	Model 16	Model 17	Model 18
Constant	0.45***	0.44***	0.40***	0.44***	0.46***	0.42***
	(0.09)	(0.09)	(0.08)	(0.08)	(0.08)	(0.09)
Transition	0.09	0.10	0.48**	0.49*	0.13	0.28
	(0.13)	(0.13)	(0.17)	(0.23)	(0.24)	(0.26)
N	1,640	1,613	1,640	1,640	1,640	1,272
Significance of χ^2	0.001	0.001	0.001	0.001	0.001	0.001

Note: The unit of analysis is a justice's vote in a (full opinion) decision, coded 0 = against the government or 1 = for the government. Transition is measured as described in the column headings. Cell entries are logistic regression coefficients. Dummy variables for each justice are included in each model, but the results are not presented here. Standard errors are in parentheses. $^*p \leq 0.05$; $^{**}p \leq 0.01$; $^{***}p \leq 0.001$ (two-tailed test).

somewhat troubling from the perspective of strategic defection, is that the willingness of justices to decide cases against the government peaks at the beginning of the transitional period but declines in the final months before the regime change. A different interpretation is that when the timing cutoff points are altered, the model ends up lumping the previous transitional period effects into the pretransitional period, thus decreasing the effects of moving from one period to another. This could also explain why the likelihood declines from 21 to 7 percentage points when moving from the 18- to the 12-month period prior to the transition.

To examine which of these two interpretations provides the better explanation, I excluded all decisions between 24 and 4 months prior to the end of the regime, thus enabling me to compare directly the period in which judges had the least information about the prospects of the sitting government (before the last two years) to the period in which judges had the most information (the last three months). The results clearly favor the second interpretation. Consistent with the strategic account, the coefficient, *final 3 vs. pre-24 months*, for Model 6 (−0.61) is negative and statistically significant, suggesting that as the transition drew near, justices were continuing to defect against the government. According to the marginal effects, compared to the first five years of the dictatorship, in the final three months of the transitional period justices were more likely to vote against the government by 15 percentage points.

Repeating the analysis for the second period under the new democratic government of Raul Alfonsín yields equally impressive results. In Table 2, all of the coefficients from Models 7–12 are negative, and with the exception of the six-month transition variable (−0.39), all are statistically significant. Indeed, the statistical significance of the coefficient (−0.59) in Model 11 shows that even without excluding the interim period, justices in the final three months of the Alfonsín regime were significantly more likely to rule against the government. The willingness of judges to rule against the government increased by approximately 9 percentage points for each cutoff point, reaching to 15 percentage points in the final three months prior to the 1989 presidential election compared to the period prior to the 1987 midterm elections.

Shifting the focus to the decision-making pattern among judges under the government of Carlos Menem,

TABLE 3. Number and Percentage of Individual Antigovernment Judicial Decisions by Year in Decree Cases, Salient Decree Cases, Government Appeals Cases, Cases Overturning Second Instance Court, and Habeas Cases

	% Against (*N*)				
Year	Decree	Salient Decree	Govt. Appeals	Overturning 2nd Instance	Habeas
1976	— (0)	— (0)	53% (87)	26% (175)	— (0)
1977	0% (13)	0% (13)	46% (79)	18% (103)	— (0)
1978	0% (3)	0% (3)	100% (4)	22% (37)	— (0)
1979	19% (21)	19% (21)	68% (37)	21% (62)	100% (4)
1980	17% (24)	17% (24)	37% (41)	11% (85)	— (0)
1981	24% (38)	24% (38)	50% (103)	25% (92)	0% (11)
1982[a]	48% (100)	45% (95)	64% (86)	33% (101)	69% (39)
1983[a]	51% (75)	48% (71)	66% (82)	29% (93)	100% (3)
1984	13% (32)	13% (32)	74% (19)	27% (44)	— (0)
1985	17% (29)	21% (24)	55% (40)	12% (50)	— (0)
1986	58% (47)	64% (42)	57% (75)	32% (77)	— (0)
1987	25% (103)	27% (98)	53% (49)	29% (93)	— (0)
1988[a]	35% (102)	40% (92)	43% (63)	48% (105)	0% (5)
1989[a]	67% (51)	67% (46)	58% (77)	43% (106)	— (0)
1990	19% (63)	21% (57)	36% (44)	7% (56)	0% (5)
1991	14% (37)	14% (28)	27% (113)	25% (111)	— (0)
1992	40% (101)	41% (92)	27% (151)	22% (126)	— (0)
1993	37% (248)	36% (237)	53% (186)	30% (152)	— (0)
1994[a]	30% (178)	30% (178)	26% (70)	22% (101)	— (0)
1995[a]	25% (185)	25% (166)	42% (98)	18% (119)	— (0)
Total	34% (145)	34% (133)	45% (1,504)	26% (1,888)	51% (67)

[a] Transitional period.

the evidence presented in Table 2 overwhelmingly supports the prediction for null cases consistent with the theory of strategic defection. As expected, none of the coefficients in Models 13–18 is negative, confirming the expectation that antigovernment decisions would not increase at the end of Menem's highly successful first government. Indeed, in the midst of Menem's run for reelection, the coefficients (0.48 and 0.49) for the final year and the final six months before the end of this first term show that justices were significantly *more* likely to support the government in its last year prior to Menem's reelection. The marginal effect of the last year on the justices' behavior was to increase by 11 percentage points the justices' willingness to hand down a favorable governmental decision. Although it is difficult to distinguish here between strategic and sincere behavior, the fact that the justices under Menem increased their progovernmental decisions in the final year before his reelection fits well within the longstanding suspicion that insecure tenure amplifies the willingness of judges to curry favor with the government, but only when governments themselves are seen as likely to remain in power. In sum, the patterns in the data on judicial decisions under each of the three governments support the prediction that when judges face uncertain futures, they increasingly decide cases against the outgoing government.[21]

Importance

I now turn to the second main hypothesis, which predicts that when judges defect, they will do so in the most important cases. Table 3 provides information on the behavior of Argentine judges in the most important decisions they make. Among decisions involving decrees and in the subset of salient decree decisions, these data show large increases in antigovernment decisions clustered at the end of the first and second transition periods. In each of the first two groups, the overall number of decisions increased as the cases involving decrees passed by the executive reached the Court, and, quite dramatically, so did the percentage of antigovernment decisions, as shown by the jump from 21% in 1981 to 48 and 51% in 1982 and 1983, respectively. A similar trend occurred at the end of the Alfonsín government, with the sole exception of 1986, when antigovernment decisions peaked. Also in line with the theory of strategic defection is that antigovernment decisions among both groups of decree cases did not exhibit a similar pattern under Menem.

The findings for the three additional categories are somewhat more mixed. In cases where the government clearly had an interest in appealing a negative lower court decision, the percentage of antigovernment decisions increased only modestly in the first transition and actually declined to its lowest level in 1988. The subset

[21] Logit regression models were estimated comparing the last two years of the previous government to the first two years of the next government in the second and third transition periods. Both coefficients (0.42 and 0.40) were significant at the 0.05 level, showing that justices defect more at the end of the governments' terms.

TABLE 4. Antigovernment Votes by Time to Transition in Decree Cases, Salient Decree Cases, Government Appeals Cases, and Cases Overturning Second Instance Court

	Decree	Salient Decree	Govt. Appeals	Overturn 2nd Instance
	Military Government, 1976–83			
	Model 19	Model 20	Model 21	Model 22
Constant	1.10 (1.15)	1.39 (1.19)	0.24 (0.40)	0.85* (0.35)
Final 24 months	−2.52*** (0.64)	−2.46*** (0.64)	−0.93*** (0.24)	−0.67** (0.23)
N	176	172	515	748
Significance of χ^2	0.001	0.001	0.085	0.059
	Alfonsín Government, 1983–89			
	Model 23	Model 24	Model 25	Model 26
Constant	1.44 (0.44)***	1.30*** (0.45)	−0.20 (0.40)	1.51*** (0.35)
Final 24 months	−0.63* (0.26)	−0.63** (0.27)	0.25 (0.23)	−0.86*** (0.20)
N	263	248	323	470
Significance of χ^2	0.067	0.130	0.777	0.001
	Subset of Four Military-Era Justices, 1976–83			
	Model 27	Model 28	Model 29	Model 30
Constant	2.34*** (0.60)	2.34*** (0.60)	0.05 (0.13)	1.36*** (0.14)
Final 24 months	−2.34*** (0.63)	−2.26*** (0.63)	−0.89*** (0.23)	−0.59** (0.22)
N	148	144	354	480
Significance of χ^2	0.001	0.001	0.001	0.008

Note: The unit of analysis is a justice's vote in a (full opinion) decision, coded 0 = against the government or 1 = for the government. Cell entries are logistic regression coefficients. Dummy variables for each justice are included in each model, but the results are not presented here. Standard errors are in parentheses. $^*p \leq 0.05$; $^{**}p \leq 0.01$; $^{***}p \leq 0.001$ (two-tailed test).

of decisions in which the justices had to overturn a pro-government decision supports the theory of strategic defection, particularly for the second transition, when the percentage of antigovernment decisions increased dramatically, from an average of 25% in the first four years to 45% in the government's final two years. Undoubtedly as a result of the Dirty War waged by the military against "subversives" in the late 1970s, most habeas corpus cases were concentrated under the military government. Despite the relatively small number of decisions in this category, the jump from 0% in 1981 to 69% in 1982 strongly supports the idea that when defection occurs, it is in the most politically charged cases.

Logistic regression models estimated for each subset of cases under the military and Alfonsín governments (Table 4) confirm these overall patterns. All of the coefficients for the final 24 months for the first transition are negative, with three of the four coefficients achieving statistical significance at the 0.001 level. The likelihood of antigovernment decisions increased by 56 percentage points among decree cases, by 55 percentage points among the salient decree cases, by 23 percentage points among government appeals cases, and by 16 percentage points among cases overturning a favorable lower court decision.

Consistent with the overall patterns identified in Table 3 for the Alfonsín period, three of the four timing coefficients in Table 4 are also negative. For this period, the likelihood of handing down an antigovernment decision in decree cases, salient decree cases, and cases where the decision of the lower court had favored the government increased by 12, 12, and 16 percentage points, respectively, during the final two years of the Alfonsín government. Overall, the data reveal systematic support for the hypothesis that when judges defect, they do so in the most important cases.

Assessing Alternative Explanations

Composition. I now consider two sets of competing explanations for the increase in antigovernment decisions. The first alternative explanation is that changes in the composition of the Court during each of the governments' terms may account for the increase in antigovernment decisions. If the composition of the Court changed during a single government's tenure, how can one know whether the increase in the justices' votes against the government was driven by strategic defection or by the replacement of justices?

Because the composition of the Court remained stable during Alfonsín's government between 1983 and 1989, a compositional explanation for the observed change in voting pattern of the judges is relevant only for the military period. Between 1976 and 1983 there were no fewer than 10 compositions of the Supreme Court (Molinelli, Palanza, and Sin 1999, 703). Of the 12 justices who sat on the bench during this period, only two remained during the entire military regime (Justices Gabrielli and Rossi) and only four sat on the bench during portions of both the pretransitional and the transitional periods (Justices Gabrielli, Rossi, Guastavino, and Black).

To deal with the possibility that only later appointees ruled against the government, I reestimated several of the previous models to examine the impact of timing and case importance only for the subset of the four justices who served during both periods. Similar to the findings for the full set of judges' decisions, the coefficients for each of the final 24 months timing variables are statistically significant, with the subset of justices increasing their antigovernment decisions in the last two years of the military government by 41 percentage points in decree cases, by 39 percentage points in the salient decree cases, by 21 percentage points in government appeals cases, and by 11 percentage points in overturning cases (see Table 4). These results suggest that the increase in antigovernment decisions cannot be explained away by the changing composition of the Court at the end of the dictatorship.[22]

Mix of Cases. The second set of alternative explanations is that the increase in antigovernment decisions at the end of weak governments was driven by changes in the types of cases coming before the court. One plausible alternative hypothesis is that if governments acted less legally at the end of their terms, then the increased rulings against the government might be due to changes in the cases themselves, not strategic defection. While plausible, this interpretation does not square fully with what is known about the actions of recent Argentine governments. For example, it is highly dubious whether increasing illegality explains the actions of the Court at the end of the military period. Cases involving the most egregious violations of human and civil rights began coming to the Court immediately after the military seized power.[23] Thus, what changed was not the legality of these cases but, rather, the decisions of the justices.

To test this claim, I isolated the cases that involved writs of habeas corpus filed on behalf of prisoners detained or "disappeared" by the military and estimated a separate logit model (not shown here) with a constant, final 24 months, *habeas*, and an interaction term, *final 24 months* $*$ *habeas*. Consistent with a strategic interpretation, the coefficient for the interaction term is negative and significant at the $p \leq 0.05$ level, but the coefficient for the *habeas* term is indistinguishable from zero. In other words, in nontransitional periods habeas cases were no more or less likely than all other types of cases to be decided against the government, but in transition periods they were more likely to be decided against the government. Thus, the judges' willingness to decide against the government in habeas corpus cases coincided not with a change in the legality of the cases per se, but with the unraveling of the military dictatorship.

A somewhat different alternative explanation posits that regardless of the legality of the government's actions, the mix of cases coming before the Court may have included more that were likely to be decided against the government. To examine this possibility, I ran logistic regressions for each of the first two final 24-month transitional periods with all of the 19 issue variables contained in the database.[24] The results in Table 5 suggest that a change in the mix of cases does not erase the timing effect predicted by the theory of strategic defection. Consistent with the strategic argument, Model 31 shows that during the first transitional period under the military, controlling for the issue categories has virtually no effect. The coefficient for the final 24 months under the military (−0.83) remains negative and significant at the $p \leq 0.001$ level.

For the second final 24-month transitional period Model 32 shows that cases involving several types of issues (*armed forces retire, customs, emergency, federal, procedures*, and *public administration hiring/firing*) were significantly more likely to be decided against the government.[25] Thus, I constructed a new dummy variable (*Issue Group*), which subsumes all of the issues with negative and significant coefficients. Inconsistent with the alternative explanation, however, the coefficient from the second timing variable (−0.31) remains negative and significant at the $p \leq 0.05$ level. Although less impressive than the findings for the first transition, the data show that when controls for cases of a type more likely to be decided against the government were introduced, the justices still increased their decisions against the government during the second transition period by a margin of six percentage points.

CONCLUSION

Scholars have long assumed that only judges free of political pressure and manipulation are capable of ruling against the government. In many parts of the world, this explains why judges who lack institutional security support incumbent governments but not why they also make decisions that go against the government. I have argued instead that under certain conditions institutional insecurity may be the very reason why judges rule against the rulers. Once the incumbent government begins to lose power, judges who lack institutional security face incentives to distance themselves from the outgoing government by ruling against it, engaging in strategic defection. The results reported here strongly support the strategic defection account: Under both dictatorship and democracy Argentine judges tended

[22] Only the dummy variables for Justices Black and Renom were statistically significant. That these justices were among the last to be appointed undermines the view that later appointees were more likely to vote against the military than earlier appointees.

[23] During the military period 4% of cases dealt with writs of habeas corpus. Among the leading human rights cases under the military were *Ercoli* (1976), *Lokman* (1977), *Pérez de Smith* (1977), *Timerman* (1978, 1979), and *Zamorano* (1977) (Carrió 1996).

[24] The vast majority of cases (85%) includes only one or two issues.

[25] To deal with the separate question of whether the effects of the changing political environment obtained across different issues, I ran separate logistic regressions for each issue category with the votes of justices as the dependent variable and the 24-month timing variable as the independent variable. Although the timing variable achieved statistical significance in some issue categories and not in others, in none of the issue categories did the justices increase their support for the outgoing government.

TABLE 5. Individual Supreme Court Justices' Antigovernment Votes, Controlling for Changing Mix of Cases

Independent Variable	Model 31	Model 32	Model 33
Constant	0.68* (0.29)	0.77** (0.29)	1.23*** (0.23)
Final 24 months (military)	−0.83*** (0.17)		
Final 24 months (Alfonsín)		−0.13 (0.16)	−0.31* (0.14)
Military (hiring/firing)	−0.44 (0.43)	0.24 (0.26)	
Military (other)	0.28 (0.23)	−1.00*** (0.29)	
Amparo	1.23*** (0.32)	−1.02*** (0.28)	
Monetary claims	−0.19 (0.15)	−0.04 (0.18)	
Constitutional issues	0.81*** (0.22)	0.61** (0.22)	
Customs	−1.05** (0.31)	−1.92** (0.56)	
Emergency powers	0.25 (0.98)	−1.09* (0.56)	
Federal–provincial	−1.55* (0.73)	−0.49 (0.28)	
Federal (other)	1.05 (0.64)	0.95 (0.56)	
Habeas corpus	−0.99** (0.33)		
Interpretation	0.09 (0.15)	0.04 (0.17)	
Judiciary	0.59 (0.47)	−0.12 (0.42)	
Jurisdiction	−0.35 (0.47)	1.30** (0.43)	
Procedures	−0.14 (0.27)	−1.23*** (0.29)	
Property	−0.54 (0.35)		
Public employees (hiring/firing)	−0.49* (0.22)	−0.72* (0.32)	
Public employees (other)	−0.50* (0.24)	0.30 (0.29)	
Taxes	−0.83** (0.25)	0.07 (0.31)	
Issue group			−1.23*** (0.16)
N	1,335	971	989
Significance of χ^2	0.001	0.001	0.001

Note: The unit of analysis is a justice's vote in a (full opinion) decision, coded 0 = against the government or 1 = for the government. Cell entries are logistic regression coefficients. Dummy variables for each justice are included in each model, but the results are not presented here. Standard errors are in parentheses. $^{*}p \leq 0.05$; $^{**}p \leq 0.01$; $^{***}p \leq 0.001$ (two-tailed test).

to support governments when governments were strong and to desert them when they grew weak.

Several broader implications emerge from examining judicial behavior under institutional insecurity. The analysis not only reveals that there is more than one way in which checks and balances can emerge, but also suggests that the nature of checks and balances may differe depending on whether they are induced by secure or insecure tenure. Students of the U.S. Supreme Court have long observed that secure tenure tends to produce judges who are backward-looking or conservative (Dahl 1957). A major area of debate among scholars of the U.S. judiciary is whether courts can be at the forefront of social change (McCann 1994; Rosenberg 1991; Schultz 1998). Although much work remains to be done on the relationship between civil society and courts beyond the United States, this analysis suggests a new mechanism by which even a Court that lacks basic institutional security may become forward-looking and even progressive, depending, of course, on the nature of the incoming government. Under such conditions, it may be that social movements *should* choose a legal course of action, if only to speed up or reinforce an expected policy shift in that direction. This may explain why, despite the overall lack of confidence in the independence of the judiciary, many social movements in Argentina have sought redress through the courts (Brysk 1994).

The flip side of insecure tenure, however, is that when the incumbent government is secure the court is completely captured. This may be good news to some democratic critics of the court who argue that judges should not be allowed to overrule the will of the people, but it is more problematic in a context where elected representatives do not necessarily respect that will. Under conditions of insecure tenure, judges are continually and directly affected by politics. If one thinks of judges as part legalist, part politician, then under conditions of insecure tenure the latter role tends to dominate the former. Thus, in addition to suffering from the same institutional deficits as their tenured counterparts (i.e., having neither the purse nor the sword), the legitimacy of judges is compromised by their subservience to the government of the day. Moreover, when political influence is limited to selection, the question remains whether judges will actually prove loyal. Politicians may fail to anticipate all issues that will come before the court, or judges may turn out differently than expected. The possibility that judges will eventually be able to operate independently of political considerations is absent under conditions of insecure tenure, where the mechanisms of control and influence are contemporaneous and thus comparatively more effective.

The foregoing analysis does not imply that insecure judicial tenure automatically increases the power of all political actors. It does not. Notably, the power of executives does not uniformly increase where institutional insecurity obtains. On the contrary, insecure tenure may be one of the very mechanisms by which presidential power is reduced: Just when executives are most in need of a loyal court, they are least likely to get one. That Latin American presidents are not all-powerful is familiar to scholars of presidentialism (Shugart and Carey 1992). Strategic defection provides a new twist on this phenomenon by explaining why even the most loyal supporters of presidents turn against them once they begin to lose power. Moreover, to the extent that institutional insecurity obtains more broadly, the analysis reported here establishes a new agenda for explaining the behavior of various other institutional actors who may face similar incentives to defect strategically from weak presidents, such as legislators, bureaucrats, and nonindependent central bankers.

Finally, with respect to broader questions about democratic consolidation and the rule of law, strategic defection offers no panacea. Strategic defection may lead to progressive decisions in some contexts, but so too might things work in the other direction. The character of decisions depends not on the judges' sincere reading of the law, but on their ability to adjust their interpretation of the law in light of the values and preferences of the incoming government. Thus, even though judges challenge governments, as long as insecure tenure obtains and judges are forced to take into account political actors' views, the rule of law will continue to prove elusive.

APPENDIX

The issue variables are coded as follows. *Military (hiring/firing)* = 1 when the case involved the hiring or firing of military personnel. *Military (other)* = 1 when the case involved any military issue that is not hiring or firing. *Amparo* = 1 when a case involved an injunction against the government (referred to in Latin American law as a writ of amparo). *Monetary claims* = 1 when the case involved monetary claims made by or against the state. *Constitutional issues* = 1 when the case involved a federal or provincial constitutional question. *Customs* = 1 when the case involved customs claims. *Emergency powers* = 1 when the case involved the emergency powers of the executive contained in Article 23 of the 1853 Constitution. *Federal–provincial* = 1 when the case involved a dispute between the federal and the provincial governments. *Federal (other)* = 1 when the case involved a federal question not subsumed by the other variables. *Habeas corpus* = 1 when a case involved a writ of habeas corpus. *Interpretation* = 1 when the case involved a federal statutory interpretation. *Judiciary* = 1 when the case involved judicial salaries, hiring and firing, or promotion. *Jurisdiction* = 1 when a case involved a question of jurisdiction. *Procedures* = 1 when the case involved criminal procedures and due process. *Property* = 1 when the case involved private property. *Public employees (hiring/firing)* = 1 when the case involved the hiring or firing of any nonmilitary public employee. *Public employees (other)* = 1 when the case involved any nonmilitary public employee and was not about hiring or firing. *Taxes* = 1 when the case involved federal taxes.

REFERENCES

Abramovich, Victor. 1992. "Todos los Jueces Son Crustáceos" ["All Judges Are Like Crabs"]. *No Hay Derecho* [*There Is No Law*] 3. No. 8 (December)

Acuña, Carlos, ed. 1995. *La Nueva Matriz Politica Argentina* [*The New Argentine Political Matrix*]. Buenos Aires: Nueva Visión.

Baglini, Raúl, and Andrés D'Ambrosio. 1993. *Juicio a la Corte* [Impeach the Court]. Buenos Aires: n.p.

Brysk, Alison. 1994. *The Politics of Human Rights in Argentina: Protest, Change, and Democratization*. Stanford, CA: Stanford University Press.

Carrió, Alejandro. 1996. *La Corte Suprema y Su Independencia* [*The Supreme Court and Its Independence*]. Buenos Aires: Abeledo-Perrot.

Catterberg, Edgardo R. 1991. *Argentina Confronts Politics*. Boulder, CO: L. Rienner.

Corte Suprema de Justicia de la Nación Secretaria Letrada de Estadisticas. 1998. *Expedientes Ingresados en la Corte Suprema de Justicia de la Nacion por Año* [Cases Entering the Supreme Court per Year]. Buenos Aires.

Dahl, Robert. 1957. "Decision-Making in a Democracy: The Supreme Court as a National Policymaker." *Journal of Public Law* 6: 279–95.

Epp, Charles R. 1998. *The Rights Revolution: Lawyers, Activists, and Supreme Courts in Comparative Perspective*. Chicago: University of Chicago Press.

Epstein, Lee, and Jack Knight. 1996. "On the Struggle for Judicial Supremacy." *Law and Society Review* 30 (1): 87–120.

Epstein, Lee, and Jack Knight. 1998. *The Choices Justices Make*. Washington, DC: Congressional Quarterly Press.

Fallos de la Corte Suprema de Justicia de la Nacion [*Cases in the Supreme Court of the Nation*]. Various years. Buenos Aires.

Ferejohn, John A., and Barry Weingast. 1992. "A Positive Theory of Statutory Interpretation." *International Review of Law and Economics* 12.

Ferreira Rubio, Delia, and Matteo Goretti. 1998. "When the President Governs Alone: The *Decretazo* in Argentina, 1989–93." *In Executive Decree Authority*, ed. John M. Carey and Matthew Soberg Shugart. Cambridge: Cambridge University Press.

FORES (Foro de Estudios sobre la Administración de Justicia). 1988. *Diagnostico de la Justicia Argentina* [Report of the Argentine Judiciary].

Gibson, James L., Gregory A. Caldeira, and Vanessa A. Baird. 1998. "On the Legitimacy of National High Courts." *American Political Science Review* 92 (June): 343–58.

Hamilton, Alexander. 1961 [1787]. *The Federalist Papers*, ed. C. Rossiter. New York.

Helmke, Gretchen. N.d. "Checks and Balances by Other Means: The Argentine Judiciary in the 1990s." *Comparative Politics*. Forthcoming.

Iaryczower, Matías, Pablo Spiller, and Mariano Tomassi. 2000. "Judicial Decision-Making in Unstable Environments: Argentina 1935–1998." Paper presented at the Annual Conference on the Scientific Study of Judicial Politics, Ohio State University.

Larkins, Christopher M. 1996. "Judicial Independence and Democratization: A Theoretical and Conceptual Analysis." *American Journal of Comparative Law* 44 (4): 605–26.

Larkins, Christopher M. 1998. "The Judiciary and Delegative Democracy in Argentina." *Comparative Politics* 30: 423–43.

Levitsky, Steven Robert. N.d. *Transforming Labor-Based Parties in Latin America: Argentine Peronism in Comparative Perspective*. New York: Cambridge University Press. Forthcoming.

McCann, Michael W. 1994. *Rights at Work: Pay Equity Reform and the Politics of Legal Mobilization*. Chicago: University of Chicago Press.

McGuire, James A. 1997. *Peronism without Peron: Unions, Parties, and Democracy in Argentina*. Stanford, CA: Stanford University Press.

Miller, Jonathon, María Angélica Gelli, and Susana Cayuso. 1995. *Constitución y Poder Político Jurisprudencia de la Corte Suprema y Técnicas para su Interpretación* [*The Constitution and Political Power: The Supreme Court's Jurisprudence and Methods of Interpretation*]. Buenos Aires: Astrea.

Molinelli, N. Guillermo, M. Valeria Palanza, and Gisela Sin. 1999 *Congreso, Presidencia, y Justicia en Argentina* [*Congress, the Presidency, and the Judiciary in Argentina*]. Buenos Aires: CEDI.

Munck, Gerardo L. 1998. *Authoritarianism and Democratization: Soldiers and Workers in Argentina, 1976–1983* University Park: Pennsylvania State University Press

Nino, Carlos Santiagó. 1996. *Radical Evil on Trial*. New Haven, CT: Yale University Press.

O'Donnell, Guillermo. 1994 "Delegative Democracy" *Journal of Democracy* 5: 1.

O'Donnell, Guillermo, and Philippe C Schmitter 1986 *Transitions from Authoritarian Rule: Tentative Conclusions about Uncertain Democracies*. Baltimore, MD: Johns Hopkins University Press.

Poder Cuidadano. 1997. *Quien es Quien en el Poder Judicial* [*Who Is Who in the Judiciary*] Buenos Aires: Perfil Libros.

Rogers, William D., and Paolo Wright-Carozza. 1995. *La Corte Suprema de Justicia y la Seguridad Jurídica* [*The Supreme Court of Justice and Juridical Security*]. Buenos Aires: Editorial Ábaco de Rodolfo Depalma.

Rosenberg, Gerald N. 1991. *The Hollow Hope. Can Courts Bring about Social Change*? Chicago IL: University of Chicago Press.

Rosenberg, Gerald N. 1992. "Judicial Independence and the Reality of Political Power." *Review of Politics* 54 (3): 369–88.

Schultz, David A., ed. 1998. *Leveraging the Law: Using the Courts to Achieve Social Change*. New York: Peter Lang.

Segal, Jeffrey A. 1997. "Separation-of-Powers Games in the Positive Theory of Congress and Courts." *American Political Science Review* 91: 28–44.

Shugart, Matthew Soberg, and John H. Carey. 1992 *Presidents and Assemblies. Constitutional Design and Electoral Dynamics* New York: Cambridge University Press

Spiller, Pablo T., and Rafael Gely 1990. "A Rational Choice Theory of Supreme Court Statutory Decisions with Applications to the *State Farm* and *Grove City* Cases." *Journal of Law, Economics, and Organization* 6 (2): 263–300.

Stimson, James A., Michael B Mackuen, and Robert S Erikson. 1995 "Dynamic Representation." *American Political Science Review* 89: 543–65.

Stokes, Susan C. 2001. *Mandates and Democracy: Neoliberalism by Surprise in Latin America* Cambridge: Cambridge University Press

Stotzky, Irwin P., ed. 1993. *Transition to Democracy in Latin America The Role of the Judiciary* Boulder, CO: Westview Press.

Tate, C. Neal, and Stacia Haynie. 1994. "Building a Scientific Comparative Judicial Politics and Arousing the Dragons of Antiscientism." *Law and Society Review* 28: 377–94.

Vanberg, Georg. 2000. "Establishing Judicial Independence in West Germany: The Impact of Opinion Leadership and the Separation of Powers." *Comparative Politics* 32: 333–53.

Vanberg, Georg. 2001. "Legislative-Judicial Relations: A Game Theoretic Approach to Constitutional Review." *American Journal of Political Science* 45: 346–61.

Part IV
The Role of Courts in Democracies

[18]

DECISION-MAKING IN A DEMOCRACY: THE SUPREME COURT AS A NATIONAL POLICY-MAKER

Robert A. Dahl*

To CONSIDER THE SUPREME COURT OF THE UNITED STATES strictly as a legal institution is to underestimate its significance in the American political system. For it is also a political institution, an institution, that is to say, for arriving at decisions on controversial questions of national policy. As a political institution, the Court is highly unusual, not least because Americans are not quite willing to accept the fact that it *is* a political institution and not quite capable of denying it; so that frequently we take both positions at once. This is confusing to foreigners, amusing to logicians, and rewarding to ordinary Americans who thus manage to retain the best of both worlds.

I

A policy decision might be defined as an effective choice among alternatives about which there is, at least initially, some uncertainty. This uncertainty may arise because of inadequate information as to (a) the alternatives that are thought to be "open"; (b) the consequences that will probably ensue from choosing a given alternative; (c) the level of probability that these consequences will actually ensue; and (d) the relative value of the different alternatives, that is, an ordering of the alternatives from most preferable to least preferable, given the expected consequences and the expected probability of the consequences actually occurring. An *effective* choice is a selection of the most preferable alternative accompanied by measures to insure that the alternative selected will be acted upon.

No one, I imagine, will quarrel with the proposition that the Supreme Court, or indeed any court, must make and does make policy decisions in this sense. But such a proposition is not really useful to the question before us. What is critical is the extent to which a court can and does make policy decisions by going outside established "legal" criteria found in precedent,

* Eugene Meyer Professor of Political Science, Yale University; author, A Preface to Democratic Theory (1956) and other works.

statute, and constitution. Now in this respect the Supreme Court occupies a most peculiar position, for it is an essential characteristic of the institution that from time to time its members decide cases where legal criteria are not in any realistic sense adequate to the task. A distinguished associate justice of the present Court has recently described the business of the Supreme Court in these words:

> It is essentially accurate to say that the Court's preoccupation today is with the application of rather fundamental aspirations and what Judge Learned Hand calls "moods," embodied in provisions like the due process clauses, which were designed not to be precise and positive directions for rules of action. The judicial process in applying them involves a judgment . . . . that is, on the views of the direct representatives of the people in meeting the needs of society, on the views of Presidents and Governors, and by their construction of the will of legislatures the Court breathes life, feeble or strong, into the inert pages of the Constitution and the statute books.[1]

Very often, then, the cases before the Court involve alternatives about which there is severe disagreement in the society, as in the case of segregation or economic regulation; that is, the setting of the case is "political." Moreover, they are usually cases where competent students of constitutional law, including the learned justices of the Supreme Court themselves, disagree; where the words of the Constitution are general, vague, ambiguous, or not clearly applicable; where precedent may be found on both sides; and where experts differ in predicting the consequences of the various alternatives or the degree of probability that the possible consequences will actually ensue. Typically, in other words, although there may be considerable agreement as to the alternatives thought to be open [(a)], there is very serious disagreement as to questions of fact bearing on consequences and probabilities [(b) and (c)], and as to questions of value, or the way in which different alternatives are to be ordered according to criteria establishing relative preferability [(d)].

If the Court were assumed to be a "political" institution, no particular problems would arise, for it would be taken for granted that the members of the Court would resolve questions of fact and value by introducing assumptions derived from their own predispositions or those of influential clienteles and constituents. But, since much of the legitimacy of the Court's decisions rests upon the fiction that it is not a political institution but exclusively a legal one, to accept the Court as a political institution would solve one set of problems at the price of creating another. Nonetheless, if it is true that

[1] Frankfurter, The Supreme Court in the Mirror of Justices, 105 U. of Pa. L. Rev. 781, 793 (1957).

the nature of the cases arriving before the Court is sometimes of the kind I have described, then the Court cannot act strictly as a legal institution. It must, that is to say, choose among controversial alternatives of public policy by appealing to at least some criteria of acceptability on questions of fact and value that cannot be found in or deduced from precedent, statute, and Constitution. It is in this sense that the Court is a national policy-maker, and it is this role that gives rise to the problem of the Court's existence in a political system ordinarily held to be democratic.

Now I take it that except for differences in emphasis and presentation, what I have said so far is today widely accepted by almost all American political scientists and by most lawyers. To anyone who believes that the Court is not, in at least some of its activities, a policy-making institution, the discussion that follows may seem irrelevant. But to anyone who holds that at least one role of the Court is as a policy-making institution in cases where strictly legal criteria are inadequate, then a serious and much debated question arises, to wit: Who gets what and why? Or in less elegant language: What groups are benefited or handicapped by the Court and how does the allocation by the Court of these rewards and penalties fit into our presumably democratic political system?

II

In determining and appraising the role of the Court, two different and conflicting criteria are sometimes employed. These are the majority criterion and the criterion of Right or Justice.

Every policy dispute can be tested, at least in principle, by the majority criterion, because (again: in principle) the dispute can be analyzed according to the numbers of people for and against the various alternatives at issue, and therefore according to the proportions of the citizens or eligible members who are for and against the alternatives. Logically speaking, except for a trivial case, every conflict within a given society must be a dispute between a majority of those eligible to participate and a minority or minorities; or else it must be a dispute between or among minorities only.[2] Within certain limits, both possibilities are independent of the number of policy alternatives at issue, and since the argument is not significantly affected by the number of alternatives, it is convenient to assume that each policy dispute represents only two alternatives.[3]

2 Provided that the total membership of the society is an even number, it is technically possible for a dispute to occur that divides the membership into two equal parts, neither of which can be said to be either a majority or minority of the total membership. But even in the instances where the number of members is even (which should occur on the average only half the time), the probability of an exactly even split, in any group of more than a few thousand people, is so small that it may be ignored.

3 Suppose the number of citizens, or members eligible to participate in collective decisions, is n. Let each member indicate his "most preferred alternative." Then it is obvious that

If everyone prefers one of two alternatives, then no significant problem arises. But a case will hardly come before the Supreme Court unless at least one person prefers an alternative that is opposed by another person. Strictly speaking, then, no matter how the Court acts in determining the legality or constitutionality of one alternative or the other, the outcome of the Court's decision must either (1) accord with the preferences of a minority of citizens and run counter to the preferences of a majority; (2) accord with the preferences of a majority and run counter to the preferences of a minority; or (3) accord with the preferences of one minority and run counter to the preferences of another minority, the rest being indifferent.

In a democratic system with a more or less representative legislature, it is unnecessary to maintain a special court to secure the second class of outcomes. A case might be made out that the Court protects the rights of national majorities against local interests in federal questions, but so far as I am aware, the role of the Court as a policy-maker is not usually defended in this fashion; in what follows, therefore, I propose to pass over the ticklish question of federalism and deal only with "national" majorities and minorities. The third kind of outcome, although relevant according to other criteria, is hardly relevant to the majority criterion, and may also be passed over for the moment.

One influential view of the Court, however, is that it stands in some special way as a protection of minorities against tyranny by majorities. In the course of its 167 years, in seventy-eight cases, the Court has struck down eighty-six different provisions of federal law as unconstitutional,[4] and by interpretation it has modified a good many more. It might be argued, then, that in all or in a very large number of these cases the Court was, in fact,

the maximum number of most preferred alternatives is *n*. It is equally obvious that if the number of most preferred alternatives is more than or equal to *n*/2, then no majority is possible. But for all practical purposes those formal limitations can be ignored, for we are dealing with a large society where the number of alternatives at issue before the Supreme Court is invariably quite small. If the number of alternatives is greater than two, it is theoretically possible for preferences to be distributed so that no outcome is consistent with the majority criterion, even where all members can rank all the alternatives and where there is perfect information as to their preferences; but this difficulty does not bear on the subsequent discussion, and it is disregarded. For an examination of this problem, consult Arrow, Social Choice and Individual Values (1951).

4 Actually, the matter is somewhat ambiguous. There appear to have been seventy-eight cases in which the Court has held provisions of federal law unconstitutional. Sixty-four different acts in the technical sense have been construed, and eighty-six different provisions in law have been in some respects invalidated. I rely here on the figures and the table given in Library of Congress, Legislative Reference Service, Provisions of Federal Law Held Unconstitutional By the Supreme Court of the United States 95, 141-47 (1936), to which I have added United States v. Lovett, 328 U.S. 303 (1946), and United States ex rel. Toth v. Quarles, 350 U.S. 11 (1955). There are some minor discrepancies in totals (not attributable to the differences in publication dates) between this volume and Acts of Congress Held Unconstitutional in Whole or in Part by the Supreme Court of the United States, in Library of Congress, Legislative Reference Service, The Constitution of the United States of America, Analysis and Interpretation (Corwin ed., 1953). The difference is a result of classification. The latter document lists seventy-three acts held unconstitutional (to which Toth v. Quarles, supra, should be added) but different sections of the same act are sometimes counted separately.

defending the rights of some minority against a "tyrannical" majority. There are, however, some exceedingly serious difficulties with this interpretation of the Court's activities.

III

One problem, which is essentially ideological in character, is the difficulty of reconciling such an interpretation with the existence of a democratic polity, for it is not at all difficult to show by appeals to authorities as various and imposing as Aristotle, Locke, Rousseau, Jefferson, and Lincoln that the term democracy means, among other things, that the power to rule resides in popular majorities and their representatives. Moreover, from entirely reasonable and traditional definitions of popular sovereignty and political equality, the principle of majority rule can be shown to follow by logical necessity.[5] Thus to affirm that the Court supports minority preferences against majorities is to deny that popular sovereignty and political equality, at least in the traditional sense, exist in the United States; and to affirm that the Court *ought* to act in this way is to deny that popular sovereignty and political equality *ought* to prevail in this country. In a country that glories in its democratic tradition, this is not a happy state of affairs for the Court's defenders; and it is no wonder that a great deal of effort has gone into the enterprise of proving that, even if the Court consistently defends minorities against majorities, nonetheless it is a thoroughly "democratic" institution. But no amount of tampering with democratic theory can conceal the fact that a system in which the policy preferences of minorities prevail over majorities is at odds with the traditional criteria for distinguishing a democracy from other political systems.[6]

Fortunately, however, we do not need to traverse this well-worn ground; for the view of the Court as a protector of the liberties of minorities against the tyranny of majorities is beset with other difficulties that are not so much ideological as matters of fact and logic. If one wishes to be at all rigorous about the question, it is probably impossible to demonstrate that any particular Court decisions have or have not been at odds with the preferences of a "national majority." It is clear that unless one makes *some* assumptions as to the kind of evidence one will require for the existence of a set of minority and majority preferences in the general population, the view under consideration is incapable of being proved at all. In any strict sense, no adequate evidence exists, for scientific opinion polls are of relatively recent origin, and national elections are little more than an indication of the first preferences of a number of citizens—in the United States the number ranges between about

5 Dahl, A Preface to Democratic Theory, c. 2 (1956).
6 Compare Commager, Majority Rule and Minority Rights (1943).

forty and sixty per cent of the adult population—for certain candidates for public office. I do not mean to say that there is no relation between preferences among candidates and preferences among alternative public policies, but the connection is a highly tenuous one, and on the basis of an election it is almost never possible to adduce whether a majority does or does not support one of two or more policy alternatives about which members of the political elite are divided. For the greater part of the Court's history, then, there is simply no way of establishing with any high degree of confidence whether a given alternative was or was not supported by a majority or a minority of adults or even of voters.

In the absence of relatively direct information, we are thrown back on indirect tests. The eighty-six provisions of federal law that have been declared unconstitutional were, of course, initially passed by majorities of those voting in the Senate and in the House. They also had the president's formal approval. We could, therefore, speak of a majority of those voting in the House and Senate, together with the president, as a "lawmaking majority." It is not easy to determine whether any such constellation of forces within the political elites actually coincides with the preferences of a majority of American adults or even with the preferences of a majority of that half of the adult population which, on the average, votes in congressional elections. Such evidence as we have from opinion polls suggests that Congress is not markedly out of line with public opinion, or at any rate with such public opinion as there is after one discards the answers of people who fall into the category, often large, labelled "no response" or "don't know." If we may, on these somewhat uncertain grounds, take a "lawmaking majority" as equivalent to a "national majority," then it is possible to test the hypothesis that the Supreme Court is shield and buckler for minorities against national majorities.

Under any reasonable assumptions about the nature of the political process, it would appear to be somewhat naive to assume that the Supreme Court either would or could play the role of Galahad. Over the whole history of the Court, on the average one new justice has been appointed every twenty-two months. Thus a president can expect to appoint about two new justices during one term of office; and if this were not enough to tip the balance on a normally divided Court, he is almost certain to succeed in two terms. Thus, Hoover had three appointments; Roosevelt, nine; Truman, four; and Eisenhower, so far, has had four. Presidents are not famous for appointing justices hostile to their own views on public policy nor could they expect to secure confirmation of a man whose stance on key questions was flagrantly at odds with that of the dominant majority in the Senate. Justices are typically men who, prior to appointment, have engaged in public life and have committed themselves publicly on the great questions of the day. As Mr. Justice Frankfurter has recently reminded us, a surprisingly large proportion of the justices, particularly of the great justices who have left their stamp upon the decisions of the Court, have had little or no prior judicial experience.[7] Nor have the justices—certainly not the great justices—been timid men with a passion for anonymity. Indeed, it is not too much to say that if justices were appointed primarily for their "judicial" qualities without regard to their basic attitudes on fundamental questions of public policy, the Court could not play the influential role in the American political system that it does in reality play.

The fact is, then, that the policy views dominant on the Court are never for long out of line with the policy views dominant among the lawmaking majorities of the United States. Consequently it would be most unrealistic to suppose that the Court would, for more than a few years at most, stand against any major alternatives sought by a lawmaking majority. The judicial agonies of the New Deal will, of course, quickly come to mind; but Mr. Roosevelt's difficulties with the Court were truly exceptional. Generalizing over the whole history of the Court, the chances are about one out of five that a president will make one appointment to the Court in less than a year, better than one out of two that he will make one within two years, and three out of four that he will make one within three years. Mr. Roosevelt had unusually bad luck: he had to wait four years for his first appointment; the odds against this long an interval are four to one. With average luck, the battle with the Court would never have occurred; even as it was, although

TABLE 1

The Interval Between Appointments to the Supreme Court.

Interval in Years	Per Cent of Total Appointments	Cumulative Per Cent
Less than 1	21	21
1	34	55
2	18	73
3	9	82
4	8	90
5	7	97
6	2	99
—	—	—
12	1	100
Total	100	100

Note: The table excludes the six appointments made in 1789. Except for the four most recent appointments, it is based on data in the Encyclopedia of American History 461-62 (Morris ed., 1953). It may be slightly inaccurate because the source shows only the year of appointment, not the month. The twelve-year interval was from 1811 to 1823.

7 Frankfurter, op. cit. supra note 1, at 782-84.

the "court-packing" proposal did formally fail, by the end of his second term Mr. Roosevelt had appointed five new justices and by 1941 Mr. Justice Roberts was the only remaining holdover from the Hoover era.

It is to be expected, then, that the Court is least likely to be successful in blocking a determined and persistent lawmaking majority on a major policy and most likely to succeed against a "weak" majority; e.g., a dead one, a transient one, a fragile one, or one weakly united upon a policy of subordinate importance.

IV

An examination of the cases in which the Court has held federal legislation unconstitutional confirms, on the whole, our expectations. Over the whole history of the Court, about half the decisions have been rendered more than four years after the legislation was passed.

TABLE 2

Percentage of Cases Held Unconstitutional Arranged by Time Intervals Between Legislation and Decision.

Number of Years	New Deal Legislation %	Other %	All Legislation %
2 or Less	92	19	30
3 - 4	8	19	18
5 - 8	0	28	24
9 - 12	0	13	11
13 - 16	0	8	6
17 - 20	0	1	1
21 or More	0	12	10
Total	100	100	100

Of the twenty-four laws held unconstitutional within two years, eleven were measures enacted in the early years of the New Deal. Indeed, New Deal measures comprise nearly a third of all the legislation that has ever been declared unconstitutional within four years after enactment.

TABLE 3

Cases Holding Legislation Unconstitutional Within Four Years After Enactment.

Interval in Years	New Deal No.	New Deal %	Other No.	Other %	Total No.	Total %
2 or Less	11	29	13	34	24	63
3 to 4	1	3	13	34	14	37
Total	12	32	26	68	38	100

It is illuminating to examine the cases where the Court has acted on legislation within four years after enactment—where the presumption is, that is to say, that the lawmaking majority is not necessarily a dead one. Of the twelve New Deal cases, two were, from a policy point of view, trivial; and two, although perhaps not trivial, were of minor importance to the New Deal program.[8] A fifth[9] involved the NRA, which was to expire within three weeks of the decision. Insofar as the unconstitutional provisions allowed "codes of fair competition" to be established by industrial groups, it is fair to say that President Roosevelt and his advisers were relieved by the Court's decision of a policy they had come to find increasingly embarrassing. In view of the tenacity with which Mr. Roosevelt held to his major program, there can hardly be any doubt that had he wanted to pursue the major policy objective involved in the NRA codes, as he did, for example, with the labor provisions, he would not have been stopped by the Court's special theory of the Constitution. As to the seven other cases,[10] it is entirely correct to say, I think, that whatever some of the eminent justices might have thought during their fleeting moments of glory, they did not succeed in interposing a barrier to the achievement of the objectives of the legislation; and in a few years most of the constitutional interpretation on which the decisions rested had been unceremoniously swept under the rug.

The remainder of the thirty-eight cases where the Court has declared legislation unconstitutional within four years of enactment tend to fall into two rather distinct groups: those involving legislation that could reasonably be regarded as important *from the point of view of the lawmaking majority* and those involving minor legislation. Although the one category merges into the other, so that some legislation must be classified rather arbitrarily, probably there will be little disagreement with classifying the specific legislative provisions involved in eleven cases as essentially minor from the point of view of the lawmaking majority (however important they may have been as constitutional interpretations).[11] The specific legislative provisions in-

8 Booth v. United States, 291 U.S. 339 (1934), involved a reduction in the pay of retired judges. Lynch v. United States, 292 U.S. 571 (1934), repealed laws granting to veterans rights to yearly renewable term insurance; there were only twenty-nine policies outstanding in 1932. Hopkins Federal Savings & Loan Ass'n v. Cleary, 296 U.S. 315 (1935), granted permission to state building and loan associations to convert to federal ones on a vote of fifty-one per cent or more of votes cast at a legal meeting. Ashton v. Cameron County Water Improvement District, 298 U.S. 513 (1936), permitting municipalities to petition federal courts for bankruptcy proceedings.

9 Schechter Poultry Corp. v. United States, 295 U.S. 495 (1935).

10 United States v. Butler, 297 U.S. 1 (1936); Perry v. United States, 294 U.S. 330 (1935); Panama Refining Co. v. Ryan, 293 U.S. 388 (1935); Railroad Retirement Board v. Alton R. Co., 295 U.S. 330 (1935); Louisville Joint Stock Land Bank v. Radford, 295 U.S. 555 (1935); Rickert Rice Mills v. Fontenot, 297 U.S. 110 (1936); Carter v. Carter Coal Co., 298 U.S. 238 (1936).

11 United States v. Dewitt, 9 Wall. (U.S.) 41 (1870); Gordon v. United States, 2 Wall. (U.S.) 561 (1865); Monongahela Navigation Co. v. United States, 148 U.S. 312 (1893); Wong Wing v. United States, 163 U.S. 228 (1896); Fairbank v. United States, 181 U.S. 283 (1901); Rassmussen v. United States, 197 U.S. 516 (1905); Muskrat v. United States, 219

volved in the remaining fifteen cases are by no means of uniform importance, but with one or two possible exceptions it seems reasonable to classify them as major policy issues from the point of view of the lawmaking majority.[12] We would expect that cases involving major legislative policy would be propelled to the Court much more rapidly than cases involving minor policy, and, as the table below shows, this is in fact what happens.

TABLE 4

Number of Cases Involving Legislative Policy Other than Those Arising Under New Deal Legislation Holding Legislation Unconstitutional Within Four Years After Enactment.

Interval in Years	Major Policy	Minor Policy	Total
2 or Less	11	2	13
3 to 4	4	9	13
Total	15	11	26

Thus a lawmaking majority with major policy objectives in mind usually has an opportunity to seek for ways of overcoming the Court's veto. It is an interesting and highly significant fact that Congress and the president do generally succeed in overcoming a hostile Court on major policy issues.

TABLE 5

Type of Congressional Action Following Supreme Court Decisions Holding Legislation Unconstitutional Within Four Years After Enactment (Other than New Deal Legislation).

Congressional Action	Major Policy	Minor Policy	Total
Reverses Court's Policy	10[a]	2[d]	12
Changes Own Policy	2[b]	0	2
None	0	8[e]	8
Unclear	3[c]	1[f]	4
Total	15	11	26

Note: For the cases in each category, see footnote 13.

U.S. 346 (1911); Choate v. Trapp, 224 U.S. 665 (1912); Evans v. Gore, 253 U.S. 245 (1920); Untermyer v. Anderson, 276 U.S. 440 (1928); United States v. Lovett, 328 U.S. 303 (1946). Note that although the specific legislative provisions held unconstitutional may have been minor, the basic legislation may have been of major policy importance.

12 Ex parte Garland, 4 Wall. (U.S.) 333 (1867); United States v. Klein, 13 Wall. (U.S.) 128 (1872); Pollock v. Farmers' Loan & Trust Co., 157 U.S. 429 (1895), rehearing granted 158 U.S. 601 (1895); Employers' Liability Cases, 207 U.S. 463 (1908); Keller v. United States, 213 U.S. 138 (1909); Hammer v. Dagenhart, 247 U.S. 251 (1918); Eisner v. Macomber, 252 U.S. 189 (1920); Knickerbocker Ice Co. v. Stewart, 253 U.S. 149 (1920); United States v. Cohen Grocery Co., 255 U.S. 81 (1921); Weeds, Inc. v. United States, 255 U.S. 109

It is particularly instructive to examine the cases involving major policy. In two cases involving punitive legislation enacted by Radical Republican Congresses against supporters of the Confederacy during the Civil War, the Court faced a rapidly crumbling majority whose death knell as an effective national force was sounded with the election of 1876.[14] Three cases are difficult to classify and I have labelled them "unclear." Of these, two were decisions made in 1921 involving a 1919 amendment to the Lever Act to control prices.[15] The legislation was important, and the provision in question was clearly struck down, but the Lever Act terminated three days after the decision and Congress did not return to the subject of price control until World War II, when it experienced no constitutional difficulties arising from these cases (which were primarily concerned with the lack of an ascertainable standard of guilt). The third case in this category successfully eliminated stock dividends from the scope of the Sixteenth Amendment, although a year later Congress enacted legislation taxing the actual income from such stock.[16]

The remaining ten cases were ultimately followed by a reversal of the actual policy results of the Court's action, although not necessarily of the specific constitutional interpretation. In four cases,[17] the policy consequences of the Court's decision were overcome in less than a year. The other six required a long struggle. Workmen's compensation for longshoremen and harbor workers was invalidated by the Court in 1920;[18] in 1922 Congress passed a new law which was, in its turn, knocked down by the Court in 1924;[19] in 1927 Congress passed a third law, which was finally upheld in

(1921); Bailey v. Drexel Furniture Co., 259 U.S. 20 (1922); Hill v. Wallace, 259 U.S. 44 (1922); Washington v. Dawson & Co., 264 U.S. 219 (1924); Trusler v. Crooks, 269 U.S. 475 (1926).

13a Pollock v. Farmers' Loan & Trust Co., 157 U.S. 429 (1895); Employers' Liability Cases, 207 U.S. 463 (1908); Keller v. United States, 213 U.S. 138 (1909); Hammer v. Dagenhart, 247 U.S. 251 (1918); Bailey v. Drexel Furniture Co., 259 U.S. 20 (1922); Trusler v. Crooks, 269 U.S. 475 (1926); Hill v. Wallace, 259 U.S. 44 (1922); Knickerbocker Ice Co. v. Stewart, 253 U.S. 149 (1920); Washington v. Dawson & Co., 264 U.S. 219 (1924).

b Ex parte Garland, 4 Wall. (U.S.) 333 (1867); United States v. Klein, 13 Wall. (U.S.) 128 (1872).

c United States v. Cohen Grocery Co., 255 U.S. 81 (1921); Weeds, Inc. v. United States, 255 U.S. 109 (1921); Eisner v. Macomber, 252 U.S. 189 (1920).

d Gordon v. United States, 2 Wall. (U.S.) 561 (1865); Evans v. Gore, 253 U.S. 245 (1920).

e United States v. Dewitt, 9 Wall. (U.S.) 41 (1870); Monongahela Navigation Co. v. United States, 148 U.S. 312 (1893); Wong Wing v. United States, 163 U.S. 228 (1896); Fairbank v. United States, 181 U.S. 283 (1901); Rassmussen v. United States, 197 U.S. 516 (1905); Muskrat v. United States, 219 U.S. 346 (1911); Choate v. Trapp, 224 U.S. 665 (1912); United States v. Lovett, 328 U.S. 303 (1946).

f Untermyer v. Anderson, 276 U.S. 440 (1928).

14 Ex parte Garland, 4 Wall. (U.S.) 333 (1867); United States v. Klein, 13 Wall. (U.S.) 128 (1872).

15 United States v. Cohen Grocery Co., 255 U.S. 81 (1921); Weeds, Inc. v. United States, 255 U.S. 109 (1921).

16 Eisner v. Macomber, 252 U.S. 189 (1920).

17 Employers' Liability Cases, 207 U.S. 463 (1908); Keller v. United States, 213 U.S. 138 (1909); Trusler v. Crooks, 269 U.S. 475 (1926); Hill v. Wallace, 259 U.S. 44 (1922).

18 Knickerbocker Ice Co. v. Stewart, 253 U.S. 149 (1920).

19 Washington v. Dawson & Co., 264 U.S. 219 (1924).

1932.[20] The notorious income tax cases[21] of 1895 were first somewhat narrowed by the Court itself;[22] the Sixteenth Amendment was recommended by President Taft in 1909 and was ratified in 1913, some eighteen years after the Court's decisions. The two child labor cases represent the most effective battle ever waged by the Court against legislative policy-makers. The original legislation outlawing child labor, based on the commerce clause, was passed in 1916 as a part of Wilson's New Freedom. Like Roosevelt later, Wilson was somewhat unlucky in his Supreme Court appointments; he made only three appointments during his eight years, and one of these was wasted, from a policy point of view, on McReynolds. Had McReynolds voted "right," the subsequent struggle over the problem of child labor need not have occurred, for the decision in 1918 was by a Court divided five to four, McReynolds voting with the majority.[23] Congress moved at once to circumvent the decision by means of the tax power, but in 1922 the Court blocked that approach.[24] In 1924 Congress returned to the engagement with a constitutional amendment that was rapidly endorsed by a number of state legislatures before it began to meet so much resistance in the states remaining that the enterprise miscarried. In 1938, under a second reformist president, new legislation was passed, twenty-two years after the first; this a chastened Court accepted in 1941,[25] and thereby brought to an end a battle that had lasted a full quarter-century.

The entire record of the duel between the Court and the lawmaking majority, in cases where the Court has held legislation unconstitutional within four years after enactment, is summarized in Table 6.

TABLE 6

Type of Congressional Action After Supreme Court Decisions Holding Legislation Unconstitutional Within Four Years After Enactment (Including New Deal Legislation).

Congressional Action	Major Policy	Minor Policy	Total
Reverses Court's Policy	17	2	19
None	0	12	12
Other	6*	1	7
Total	23	15	38

*In addition to the actions in Table 5 under "Changes Own Policy" and "Unclear," this figure includes the NRA legislation affected by the *Schechter Poultry* case.

20 Crowell v. Benson, 285 U.S. 22 (1932).
21 Pollock v. Farmers' Loan & Trust Co., 157 U.S. 429 (1895).
22 Nicol v. Ames, 173 U.S. 509 (1899); Knowlton v. Moore, 178 U.S. 41 (1900); Patton v. Brady, 184 U.S. 608 (1902); Flint v. Stone Tracy Co., 220 U.S. 107 (1911).
23 Hammer v. Dagenhart, 247 U.S. 251 (1918).
24 Bailey v. Drexel Furniture Co., 259 U.S. 20 (1922).
25 United States v. Darby, 312 U.S. 100 (1941).

Thus the application of the majority criterion seems to show the following: First, if the Court did in fact uphold minorities against national majorities, as both its supporters and critics often seem to believe, it would be an extremely anomalous institution from a democratic point of view. Second, the elaborate "democratic" rationalizations of the Court's defenders and the hostility of its "democratic" critics are largely irrelevant, for lawmaking majorities generally have had their way. Third, although the Court seems never to have succeeded in holding out indefinitely, in a very small number of important cases it has delayed the application of policy up to as much as twenty-five years.

V

How can we appraise decisions of the third kind just mentioned? Earlier I referred to the criterion of Right or Justice as a norm sometimes invoked to describe the role of the Court. In accordance with this norm, it might be argued that the most important policy function of the Court is to protect rights that are in some sense basic or fundamental. Thus (the argument might run) in a country where basic rights are, on the whole, respected, one should not expect more than a small number of cases where the Court has had to plant itself firmly against a lawmaking majority. But majorities may, on rare occasions, become "tyrannical"; and when they do, the Court intervenes; and although the constitutional issue may, strictly speaking, be technically open, the Constitution assumes an underlying fundamental body of rights and liberties which the Court guarantees by its decisions.

Here again, however, even without examining the actual cases, it would appear, on political grounds, somewhat unrealistic to suppose that a Court whose members are recruited in the fashion of Supreme Court justices would long hold to norms of Right or Justice substantially at odds with the rest of the political elite. Moreover, in an earlier day it was perhaps easier to believe that certain rights are so natural and self-evident that their fundamental validity is as much a matter of definite knowledge, at least to all reasonable creatures, as the color of a ripe apple. To say that this view is unlikely to find many articulate defenders today is, of course, not to disprove it; it is rather to suggest that we do not need to elaborate the case against it in this essay.

In any event the best rebuttal to the view of the Court suggested above will be found in the record of the Court's decisions. Surely the six cases referred to a moment ago, where the policy consequences of the Court's decisions were overcome only after long battles, will not appeal to many contemporary minds as evidence for the proposition under examination. A natural right to employ child labor in mills and mines? To be free of income taxes by the federal government? To employ longshoremen and harbor workers without the protection of workmen's compensation? The Court itself did not rely upon such arguments in these cases, and it would be no credit to their opinions to reconstruct them along such lines.

So far, however, our evidence has been drawn from cases in which the Court has held legislation unconstitutional within four years after enactment. What of the other forty cases? Do we have evidence in these that the Court has protected fundamental or natural rights and liberties against the dead hand of some past tyranny by the lawmakers? The evidence is not impressive. In the entire history of the Court there is not one case arising under the First Amendment in which the Court has held federal legislation unconstitutional. If we turn from these fundamental liberties of religion, speech, press and assembly, we do find a handful of cases—something less than ten—arising under Amendments Four to Seven in which the Court has declared acts unconstitutional that might properly be regarded as involving rather basic liberties.[26] An inspection of these cases leaves the impression that, in all of them, the lawmakers and the Court were not very far apart; moreover, it is doubtful that the fundamental conditions of liberty in this country have been altered by more than a hair's breadth as a result of these decisions. However, let us give the Court its due; it is little enough.

Over against these decisions we must put the fifteen or so cases in which the Court used the protections of the Fifth, Thirteenth, Fourteenth and Fifteenth Amendments to preserve the rights and liberties of a relatively privileged group at the expense of the rights and liberties of a submerged group: chiefly slaveholders at the expense of slaves,[27] white people at the expense of colored people,[28] and property holders at the expense of wage earners and other groups.[29] These cases, unlike the relatively innocuous ones of the preceding set, all involved liberties of genuinely fundamental importance, where an opposite policy would have meant thoroughly basic shifts in the distribution of rights, liberties, and opportunities in the United States—

[26] The candidates for this category would appear to be Boyd v. United States, 116 U.S. 616 (1886); Rassmussen v. United States, 197 U.S. 516 (1905); Wong Wing v. United States, 163 U.S. 228 (1896); United States v. Moreland, 258 U.S. 433 (1922); Kirby v. United States, 174 U.S. 47 (1899); United States v. Cohen Grocery Co., 255 U.S. 81 (1921); Weeds, Inc. v. United States, 255 U.S. 109 (1921); Justices of the Supreme Court v. United States ex rel. Murray, 9 Wall. (U.S.) 274 (1870); United States ex rel. Toth v. Quarles, 350 U.S. 11 (1955).

[27] Dred Scott v. Sandford, 19 How. (U.S.) 393 (1857).

[28] United States v. Reese, 92 U.S. 214 (1876); United States v. Harris, 106 U.S. 629 (1883); United States v. Stanley (Civil Rights Cases), 109 U.S. 3 (1883); Baldwin v. Franks, 120 U.S. 678 (1887); James v. Bowman, 190 U.S. 127 (1903); Hodges v. United States, 203 U.S. 1 (1906); Butts v. Merchants & Miners Transportation Co., 230 U.S. 126 (1913).

[29] Monongahela Navigation Co. v. United States, 148 U.S. 312 (1893); Adair v. United States, 208 U.S. 161 (1908); Adkins v. Children's Hospital, 261 U.S. 525 (1923); Nichols v. Coolidge, 274 U.S. 531 (1927); Untermyer v. Anderson, 276 U.S. 440 (1928); Heiner v. Donnan, 285 U.S. 312 (1932); Louisville Joint Stock Land Bank v. Radford, 295 U.S. 555 (1935).

where, moreover, the policies sustained by the Court's action have since been repudiated in every civilized nation of the Western world, including our own. Yet, if our earlier argument is correct, it is futile—precisely because the basic distribution of privilege *was* at issue—to suppose that the Court could have possibly acted much differently in these areas of policy from the way in which it did in fact act.

VI

Thus the role of the Court as a policy-making institution is not simple; and it is an error to suppose that its functions can be either described or appraised by means of simple concepts drawn from democratic or moral theory. It is possible, nonetheless, to derive a few general conclusions about the Court's role as a policy-making institution.

National politics in the United States, as in other stable democracies, is dominated by relatively cohesive alliances that endure for long periods of time. One recalls the Jeffersonian alliance, the Jacksonian, the extraordinarily long-lived Republican dominance of the post-Civil War years, and the New Deal alliance shaped by Franklin Roosevelt. Each is marked by a break with past policies, a period of intense struggle, followed by consolidation, and finally decay and disintegration of the alliance.

Except for short-lived transitional periods when the old alliance is disintegrating and the new one is struggling to take control of political institutions, the Supreme Court is inevitably a part of the dominant national alliance. As an element in the political leadership of the dominant alliance, the Court of course supports the major policies of the alliance. By itself, the Court is almost powerless to affect the course of national policy. In the absence of substantial agreement within the alliance, an attempt by the Court to make national policy is likely to lead to disaster, as the *Dred Scott* decision and the early New Deal cases demonstrate. Conceivably, the cases of the last three decades involving the freedom of Negroes, culminating in the now famous decision on school integration, are exceptions to this generalization; I shall have more to say about them in a moment.

The Supreme Court is not, however, simply an *agent* of the alliance. It is an essential part of the political leadership and possesses some bases of power of its own, the most important of which is the unique legitimacy attributed to its interpretations of the Constitution. This legitimacy the Court jeopardizes if it flagrantly opposes the major policies of the dominant alliance; such a course of action, as we have seen, is one in which the Court will not normally be tempted to engage.

It follows that within the somewhat narrow limits set by the basic policy goals of the dominant alliance, the Court *can* make national policy. Its discretion, then, is not unlike that of a powerful committee chairman in Congress who cannot, generally speaking, nullify the basic policies substantially agreed on by the rest of the dominant leadership, but who can, within these limits, often determine important questions of timing, effectiveness, and subordinate policy. Thus the Court is least effective against a current lawmaking majority—and evidently least inclined to act. It is most effective when it sets the bounds of policy for officials, agencies, state governments or even regions, a task that has come to occupy a very large part of the Court's business.[30]

Few of the Court's policy decisions can be interpreted sensibly in terms of a "majority" versus a "minority." In this respect the Court is no different from the rest of the political leadership. Generally speaking, policy at the national level is the outcome of conflict, bargaining, and agreement among minorities; the process is neither minority rule nor majority rule but what might better be called *minorities* rule, where one aggregation of minorities achieves policies opposed by another aggregation.

The main objective of presidential leadership is to build a stable and dominant aggregation of minorities with a high probability of winning the presidency and one or both houses of Congress. The main task of the Court is to confer legitimacy on the fundamental policies of the successful coalition. There are times when the coalition is unstable with respect to certain key policies; at very great risk to its legitimacy powers, the Court can intervene in such cases and may even succeed in establishing policy. Probably in such cases it can succeed only if its action conforms to and reinforces a widespread set of explicit or implicit norms held by the political leadership; norms which are not strong enough or are not distributed in such a way as to insure the existence of an effective lawmaking majority but are, nonetheless, sufficiently powerful to prevent any successful attack on the legitimacy powers of the Court. This is probably the explanation for the relatively successful work of the Court in enlarging the freedom of Negroes to vote during the past three decades and in its famous school integration decisions.[31]

Yet the Court is more than this. Considered as a political system, democ-

30 "Constitutional law and cases with constitutional undertones are of course still very important, with almost one-fourth of the cases in which written opinions were filed [in the two most recent terms] involving such questions. Review of administrative action . . . constitutes the largest category of the Court's work, comprising one-third of the total cases decided on the merits. The remaining . . . categories of litigation . . . all involve largely public law questions." Frankfurter, op. cit. supra note 1, at 793.

31 Rice v. Elmore, 165 F.2d 387 (C.A. 4th, 1947), cert. denied 333 U.S. 875 (1948); United States v. Classic, 313 U.S. 299 (1941); Smith v. Allwright, 321 U.S. 649 (1944); Grovey v. Townsend, 295 U.S. 45 (1935); Brown v. Board of Education, 347 U.S. 483 (1954); Bolling v. Sharpe, 347 U.S. 497 (1954).

racy is a set of basic procedures for arriving at decisions. The operation of these procedures presupposes the existence of certain rights, obligations, liberties and restraints; in short, certain patterns of behavior. The existence of these patterns of behavior in turn presupposes widespread agreement (particularly among the politically active and influential segments of the population) on the validity and propriety of the behavior. Although its record is by no means lacking in serious blemishes, at its best the Court operates to confer legitimacy, not simply on the particular and parochial policies of the dominant political alliance, but upon the basic patterns of behavior required for the operation of a democracy.

[19]

African-American Rights After *Brown*

GERALD N. ROSENBERG

The preceding chapters in this volume have focused on the U.S. Supreme Court and African-American rights in the years prior to the mid-twentieth century. That history shows the Court at its worst and at its best—as perpetuating racism and striving to overcome it. In this chapter, I will step back and ask if the Court's attempts to overcome racism made much difference to the lives of African-Americans. In particular, I will focus on the Court's 1954 decision, *Brown v. Board of Education*,[1] which unanimously struck down race-based segregation in elementary and secondary schools as violating the Equal Protection Clause of the Fourteenth Amendment of the U.S. Constitution. *Brown* is an apt case for focus on the Court's contribution to change because it has received praise across the legal spectrum and is celebrated by scholars and social critics as a landmark. As the legal historian Michael Klarman puts it, "constitutional lawyers and historians generally deem *Brown v. Board of Education* to be the most important U.S. Supreme Court decision of the twentieth century, and possibly of all time."[2]

The question I address in this article is whether the decision in *Brown* made the contribution to American society that this comment suggests. In asking this question, I mean to disparage no one. Civil rights lawyers like Thurgood Marshall, Jack Greenberg and countless others dedicated their careers, and sometimes their lives, to a principled belief in justice for all. My question does not challenge their commitment nor their principles. It does ask whether litigation was the right strategic choice to further their goals, whether their understanding of the strengths and weaknesses of courts as agents of social change was subtle enough to guide them to the best strategy for change.

Underlying this question about *Brown* is a broader question about the role of the Supreme Court in the larger society. Since the mid-twentieth century, there has been a belief that courts can act to further the interests of the relatively disadvantaged. Starting with civil rights and spreading to issues raised by women's groups, environmental groups, political reformers, and others, American courts seemingly have become important producers of political and social change. Cases such as *Brown* and *Roe v. Wade*[3] are heralded as having produced major change. Further, such litigation has often occurred, and appears to have been most successful, when the other branches of government have failed to act. Indeed, for many, part of what makes American democracy exceptional is that it includes the world's most powerful court system, protecting minorities and defending liberty in the face of opposition from the democratically elected branches. Americans look to activist courts, then, as fulfilling an important role in the American scheme.

Courts, many also believe, can bring heightened legitimacy to an issue. Courts deal with rights. Judges, at their best, are not politically beholden nor partisan. Rather, they are independent and principled, deciding not what policy they want but rather what the Constitution requires. This gives judicial decisions a moral legitimacy that is missing from the actions of the other branches. Court decisions can remind Americans of our highest aspirations and chide us for our failings. Courts, Bickel suggests, have the "capacity to appeal to men's better natures, to call forth their aspirations, which may have been forgotten in the moment's hue and cry."[4] For Rostow, the "Supreme Court is, among other things, an educational body, and the Justices are inevitably teachers in a vital national seminar."[5] Bickel agrees, viewing courts as "a great and highly effective educational institution."[6] Courts, one commentator put it, can provide "a cheap method of pricking powerful consciences."[7]

In the confines of a single chapter, I can do little more than sketch out an answer to the question of whether *Brown* made a major contribution to civil rights. Readers who wish to see a more fully developed argument might consult **The Hollow Hope** and other work of mine.[8]

Reasons for Caution

Before uncritically accepting this view of the Court as correct, there are at least three reasons to be skeptical. First, it is almost entirely lawyers who make this argument. Although lawyers may be no less self-critical than other professionals, they may be no more self-critical either. That is, they may have deep-seated psychological reasons for believing in the importance of the institutions in which they work. This may lead to overvaluing the contribution of the courts to furthering the interests of the relatively disadvantaged.

Second, there is an older view of the role of courts which sees them as much more constrained. Under this view, courts are the least able of any of the branches of government to produce change because they lack all of the necessary tools to do so. They are the "least dangerous branch" because they lack budgetary or coercive power. That courts are uniquely dependent on the executive branch is a view that was most forcefully argued over two hundred years ago by Alexander Hamilton in *Federalist 78*. Hamilton wrote: the judiciary "has no influence over either the sword or the purse; no direction either of the strength or of the wealth of the society, and can take no active resolution whatever. It may truly be said to have neither FORCE nor WILL but merely judgment of and must ultimately depend upon the aid of the executive arm even for the efficacy of its judgments."[9] As President Jackson reportedly commented in response to *Worcester v. Georgia*,[10] a decision with which he disagreed, "[Chief Justice] John Marshall has made his decision, now let him enforce it." This view suggests that Court decisions furthering the interests of the relatively disadvantaged will only be implemented when the other branches are willing to do so.

The third reason for skepticism about the role of courts as producers of progressive change comes from several decades of public opinion research. If courts are dependent on public and elite support for their decisions to be implemented, as Hamilton suggests, this requires both public knowledge of Court decisions and a public willingness to act based on them. Proponents of an activist, progressive Court assume this. According to one defender of the claim, "without the dramatic intervention of so dignified an institution as a court, which puts its own prestige and authority on the line, most middle-class Americans would not be informed about such grievances."[11] However, decades of public opinion research paint a mixed picture, at best. In general, only about 40% of the American public report having read or heard something contemporary about the Court.[12] As an example, in 1966, despite important Supreme Court decisions on race, religion, criminal justice, and voting rights, nearly half of respondents could not recall *anything at all* that the Court had done recently.[13] And when prompted with a list of eight "decisions," four of which the Court had recently made and four of which it had never made, and asked to identify which, if any, the Court had made, only 19 % of a 1966 sample made five or more correct choices.[14] In 1973, 20% of respondents to a Harris poll identified the Court as a branch of Congress, as did 12% of respondents with college degrees. In a culture in which personality is important, the public, too, is quite ignorant of the Justices' identity. In a 1989 *Washington Post* poll, for example, 71% of 1,005 respondents could not name any Justice while only 2% could correctly name all nine. Somewhat humorously, while 9% named the distinguished Chief Justice of the United States (Rehnquist), a whopping 54%, six times as many respondents, correctly identified the somewhat less distinguished "judge of the television show 'The People's Court'" (Judge Wapner).[15] The Supreme Court is not in the forefront of the consciousness of most Americans.

This lack of knowledge is not limited to Americans in general, as was illustrated by a fascinating 1990 study reported in that great "scholarly" journal, *Spy Magazine*. In a cleverly designed study, the magazine called six Washington heavyweights claiming to be assistants to five other famous Washingtonians and one Hollywood power broker. The magazine then timed how long it took for the phone calls to be returned. Those called included U.S. Secretary of Defense Dick Cheney; Ben Bradlee, editor of the *Washington Post*; Jack Kent Cooke, owner of the football team the Washington Redskins; and Marlin Fitzwater, Press Secretary to President Bush. The caller claimed to be either the individual or an aid to, among others, Georgette Mosbacher (wife of Cabinet Secretary Robert Mosbacher and renowned for throwing the best parties in Washington); Ben Bradlee, the *Washington Post* editor; Oliver North, William H. Rehnquist, and Senator Moynihan. The results were stunning. The caller claiming to be an aid to Georgette Mosbacher was put immediately through to the Secretary of Defense whose secretary "suggested interrupting a meeting" to reach him. President Bush's press secretary, Marlin Fitzwater, returned the call an hour later. Chief Justice Rehnquist, alas, fared much less well. His calls were returned, on average, two days later than Mosbacher's. Jack Kent Cooke's secretary asked what company "Mr. Lindquist" was with. Fitzwater's secretary apologetically asked "Who is he?" Upon being told that he was the Chief Justice of the United States, it still took Fitzwater four days to return the call.[16]

The point of this discussion is that there are good reasons to be wary of claims that the Court can further the interests of the relatively disadvantaged. Lacking the power to implement their decisions, courts are dependent on other elite institutions and the public at large. And given the findings of the survey literature, this is not a comforting thought for those who believe in the efficacy of the courts to further the interests of the relatively disadvantaged. With this background in mind, I return to *Brown*.

Examining the effects of *Brown* raises questions of how to deal with complicated issues of causation. Because it is difficult to isolate the effects of court decisions from other events in furthering the interests of the relatively disadvantaged, special care is needed in specifying how courts can be effective. On a general level, one can distinguish two types of influence courts can exercise. Court decisions may produce significant social reform through a *judicial* path that relies on the authority of the court. Alternatively, court influence can follow an *extra-judicial* path that invokes court powers of persuasion, legitimacy, and the ability to give salience to issues. Each of these possible paths of influence is different and requires separate analysis.

The *judicial* path of causal influence is straightforward. It focuses on the direct outcome of judicial decisions and examines whether the change required by the courts was made. In civil rights, for example, if a Supreme Court decision ordering an end to public segregation was the cause of segregation ending, then one would see lower courts ordering local officials to end segregation, those officials acting to end it, the community at large supporting it, and, most important, segregation actually ending.

Separate and distinct from judicial effects is the more subtle and complex causal claim of *extra-judicial* effects. Under this conception of causation, courts do more than simply change behavior in the short run. Court decisions may produce significant social reform by inspiring individuals to act or persuading them to examine and change their opinions. Court decisions, particularly Supreme Court decisions, may be powerful symbols, resources for change. They may affect the intellectual climate, the kinds of ideas that are discussed. The mere bringing of legal claims and the hearing of cases may influence ideas. Courts may produce significant social reform by giving salience to issues, in effect placing them on the political agenda. Courts may bring issues to light and keep them in the public eye when other political institutions wish to bury them. Thus, courts may make it difficult for legislators to avoid deciding controversial issues.

In 1954, in *Brown v. Board of Education*,[17] the U.S. Supreme Court found that state laws requiring race-based segregation in public elementary and secondary schools violated the Equal Protection Clause of the Fourteenth Amendment. Overturning nearly sixty years of Court-sanctioned racial segregation, *Brown* is heralded as one of the U.S. Supreme Court's greatest decisions. In particular, *Brown* is the paradigm of the Court's ability to protect rights and bring justice to minorities. To the human rights activist Aryeh Neier, *Brown* is the great "symbol" of courts' ability to protect rights and produce significant social reform.[18] For Jack Greenberg, long-time civil rights litigator, *Brown* is the "principal inspiration to others" who seek change and the protection of rights through litigation.[19]

Given the praise accorded to the *Brown* decision, examining its actual effects produces quite a surprise. The surprise is that a decade after *Brown* virtually nothing had changed for African-American students living in the eleven states of the former Confederacy that required race-based school segregation by law. For example, in the 1963-1964 school year, barely one in one hundred (1.2%) of these African-American children was in a nonsegregated school. That means that for nearly ninety-nine of every 100 African-American children in the South a decade after *Brown*, the finding of a constitutional right changed nothing. A unanimous landmark Supreme Court decision had no effect on their lives. This raises the question of why there was no change.

The answer, in a nutshell, is that there was no political pressure to implement the decision and a great deal of pressure to resist it. On the executive level, there was little support for desegregation until the Johnson presidency. President Eisenhower steadfastly refused to commit his immense popularity or prestige in support of desegregation in general or *Brown* in particular. As Roy Wilkins, executive secretary of the National Association for the Advancement of Colored People (NAACP), put it, "if he had fought World War II the way he fought for civil rights, we would all be speaking German today."[20] And Jack Peltason summed up Eisenhower's position this way: "Thurgood

Marshall got his decision, now let him enforce it."[21] Although President Kennedy was openly and generally supportive of civil rights, he took little concrete initiative in school desegregation and other civil rights matters until pressured by events to do so. He did not rank civil rights as a top priority and, like Eisenhower before him, was "unwilling to draw on the moral credit of his office to advance civil rights."[22]

Civil rights were not supported by other national leaders until late in the Kennedy administration. In March 1956, Southern members of Congress, virtually without exception,[23] signed a document entitled a "Declaration of Constitutional Principles," also known as the Southern Manifesto. Its 101 signers attacked the *Brown* decision as an exercise of "naked power" with "no legal basis." They pledged themselves to "use all lawful means to bring about a reversal of this decision which is contrary to the Constitution and to prevent the use of force in its implementation."[24] This unprecedented attack on the Court demonstrated to all that pressure from Washington to implement the Court's decisions in civil rights would not be forthcoming.

If national political leaders set the stage for ignoring the courts, local politicians acted their part perfectly. A study of the 250 gubernatorial candidates in the Southern states from 1950 to 1973 revealed that after *Brown* "ambitious politicians, to put it mildly, perceived few incentives to advocate compliance."[25] This perception was reinforced by Arkansas Governor Orval Faubus's landslide reelection in 1958, after he repeatedly defied court orders to prevent the desegregation of Central High School in Little Rock, demonstrating the "political rewards of conspicuously defying national authority."[26] Throughout the South, governors and gubernatorial candidates called for defiance of court orders. Any individual or institution wishing

A decade after *Brown* virtually nothing had changed for African-American students living in the eleven states of the former Confederacy that required race-based school segregation by law. For example, in the 1963-1964 school year, barely one in one hundred of these African-American children was in a nonsegregated school. That means that for nearly ninety-nine of every 100 African-American children in the South a decade after *Brown*, the finding of a constitutional right to nonsegregated education changed nothing.

to end segregation pursuant to court order, that is, to obey the law as mandated by the Supreme Court, would incur the wrath of state political leaders and quite possibly national ones. The best they could hope for was a lack of outright condemnation. Political support for desegregation was virtually nonexistent.

At the prodding of state leaders, state legislatures throughout the South passed a variety of pro-segregation laws. By 1957, only three years after *Brown*, at least 136 new laws and state constitutional amendments designed to preserve segregation had been enacted.[27] These ranged from depriving policemen of their retirement and disability if they failed to enforce the state's segregation laws (Georgia), to denying promotion or graduation to any student of a desegregated school (Louisiana), to simply making it illegal to attend a desegregated school (Mississippi) to Virginia's massive resistance including closing public schools, operating a tuition grant scheme, suspending compulsory attendance laws, and building private segregated schools. In 1960-1961 alone, the Louisiana legislature met in one regular and five extraordinary sessions to pass ninety-two laws and resolutions to maintain segregated public schools. As the Southern saying went, "as long as we can legislate, we can segregate."[28]

Along with opposition to desegregation from political leaders at all levels of government, there was hostility from many white Americans. Law and legal decisions operate in a given cultural environment, and the norms of that environment influence the decisions that are made and the impact they have. In the case of civil rights, decisions were announced in a culture in which slavery had existed and apartheid did exist. Institutions and social structures throughout America reflected a history of, if not a present commitment to, racial discrimination. Cultural barriers to civil rights had to be overcome before change could occur. And courts do not have the tools to do so. This is well illustrated in the decade after *Brown*.

One of the important cultural barriers to civil rights was the existence of private groups supportive of segregation. One type, represented by the Ku Klux Klan, White Citizens' Councils, and the like, existed principally to fight civil rights. Either through their own acts, or the atmosphere these groups helped create, violence against blacks and civil rights workers was commonplace throughout the South. Spectacular cases such as the murder of Medgar Evers, the attacks on the freedom riders, the Birmingham Church bombing that killed four black girls, and the murder of three civil rights workers near Philadelphia, Mississippi, are well known. But countless bombings and numerous murders occurred throughout the South.[29] During the summer of 1964 in Mississippi alone there were thirty-five shootings, sixty-five bombings (including thirty-five churches), eighty beatings, and six murders.[30] It was a brave soul indeed who worked to end segregation or implement court decisions.

Another tactic used by white groups to fight civil rights was economic coercion. Since whites controlled the economy throughout the South, this was extraordinarily effective.[31] In fact, so effective was this sort of intimidation that as late as 1961 *not a single* desegregation suit in education had been filed in Mississippi.[32]

A totally different kind of private group resisted civil rights by simply ignoring court decisions and going about their business as if nothing had changed. Public carriers, for example, even when owned by non-Southerners, looked to the "segregationist milieu" in which they operated and thus took a "narrow view of desegregation decrees, implementing them minimally, if at all."[33]

The cultural biases against civil rights that pervaded private groups also pervaded local governments. Court-ordered action may be fought or ignored on a local level, especially if there is no pressure from higher political leadership to follow the law and pressure from private groups not to. It was common to find, for example, that where bus companies followed the law and removed segregation signs in terminals, state and local officials put them back up.[34] In the five Deep South states, as a matter of principle no school-board member or superintendent openly advocated compliance with the Supreme Court decision.[35] And despite *Cooper v. Aaron*,[36] and the sending of troops to Little Rock in 1957, as of June 1963, only sixty-nine out of 7,700 students at the supposedly desegregated, "formerly" white, junior and senior high schools of Little Rock were black.[37] Public resistance, supported by local political action, can almost always effectively defeat court-ordered civil rights.

In sum, in civil rights, court-ordered change confronted a culture opposed to that change. That being the case, the American judicial system, constrained by the need for both elite and popular support, constrained change.

The analysis above, however, omits one key institution and one key group: the judiciary, lawyers and their academic counterparts. The South, like the rest of the country, has both state and federal courts as well as lawyers. And the courts have a natural constituency in the American legal profession. Indeed, Justice Frankfurter believed that lawyers' support of the Court's decision in *Brown* would be decisive. As he put it in a letter to a friend, "it is the legal profession of the South on which our greatest reliance must be placed. . . because the lawyers of the South will gradually realize that there is a transcending issue, namely respect for law as determined so impressively by a unanimous court [in *Brown*]."[38] But Justice Frankfurter was to be doubly disappointed; both Southern lawyers and elite lawyers and legal academics throughout the country condemned the case or offered only the most tepid support.

Lawyers and the Legal Profession

While there were undoubtedly some white Southern lawyers who supported the Court, they were few and far between. Opponents, in contrast, were everywhere. And surprisingly, opposition was voiced not merely by white Southerners but also by elite, Northern lawyers as well. A notable example was the American Bar Association (ABA), which is the nation's major professional legal organization. Politically neutral, it claims the legitimacy of professional expertise. However, in the wake of *Brown*, it lent the pages of its journal, the *ABA Journal*, to condemnation of *Brown*, from the vicious to the technical. It published only the most tepid, rule-of-law, defenses of the decision. Not once, in either editorials or articles, was there an argument that *Brown* was morally, constitutionally, or substantively correct.

The ABA was not alone. In 1958, the Conference of Chief Justices of State Courts issued a report on the Court. While the body of the report was careful, the report finished with polemical conclusions that criticized the Supreme Court for legislating. "In the fields with which we are concerned [the report concluded]...the Supreme Court too often has tended to adopt the role of policy-maker without proper judicial restraint."[39] The report continued, "it has long been an American boast that we have a government of laws and not men. We believe that any study of recent decisions of the Supreme Court will raise at least considerable doubt as to the validity of that boast."[40] The report was adopted by a vote of 36-8 and won praise in an *ABA Journal* editorial for its "attitude of careful study, calm deliberation and temperate statement."

Elite legal academics also joined the fray. "[S]peaking the rhetoric of institutional legitimacy, a significant number of northeastern, white, liberal lawyers joined with white, southern, never-say-die segregationists in questioning the Court's authority and legitimacy in *Brown*."[41] Although there was some support for the decision in law reviews immediately following *Brown*, it was found mostly in short pieces. In contrast, elite law reviews repeatedly blasted the Court. For example, the *Harvard Law Review* poured out a torrent of criticism, especially in its annual Forewords. *Brown* was criticized as poorly thought out, insufficient to support other cases, and unprincipled. The most important article was undoubtedly written by Herbert Wechsler, a law professor at Columbia University in New York City. Giving the Holmes Lecture at Harvard, and appearing as the Foreword to the 1959 *Harvard Law Review*,[42] *Brown* was criticized as unprincipled. *Brown* lacked a neutral principle, Wechsler argued, because separate but equal, if truly equal, was itself a neutral principle and there was no neutral way of deciding between it and equality. Wechsler's piece is the second most cited law review article in the period 1957 through March 1985! The popularity of his critique of *Brown* as unprincipled is a powerful indicator of the lack of support elite academic lawyers gave to *Brown*.

Local Courts

Judges seldom stepped in where politicians, lawyers, and the public at large were unwilling to go. The "fifty-eight lonely men" who served the federal judiciary in the South were being asked to dismantle a social system they had grown up with and of which they were a part. Even a judge as pro-civil-rights as John Minor Wisdom was sympathetic, finding it "not surprising that in a conservative community a federal judge may feel that he cannot jeopardize the respect due the court in all of his cases" by vigorously supporting civil rights.[43] Although there were some outstanding Southern federal judges such as J. Skelly Wright, John Minor Wisdom, Bryan Simpson, and Frank Johnson, there were also some who were not. For example, Judge Elliott (M. Dist. GA) stated that he did not want "pinks, radicals and black voters to outvote those who are trying to preserve our segregation laws."[44] Judge Cox (S. Dist. Miss.), speaking from the Bench in March 1964, referred repeatedly to black voter-registration applicants in derogatory language (as "a bunch of niggers") who were "acting like a bunch of chimpanzees."[45] It is important to note that both judges Elliott and Cox were Kennedy appointees. In the Dallas school desegregation case, started in 1955 and still pending in 1960, in which the federal district court was reversed six times, Judge Davidson complained that the "white man has a right to maintain his racial integrity, and it can't be done so easily in integrated schools."[46]

On the state levels judges were even more biased. Chief Justice J. Edwin Livingston of the Alabama Supreme Court, speaking in 1959 to several hundred students and business leaders, announced: "I'm for segregation in every phase of life and I don't care who knows it....I would close every school from the highest to the lowest before I would go to school with colored people."[47] Alabama circuit judge Walter B. Jones wrote a column in the *Montgomery Advertiser* that he devoted to the "defense of white supremacy." In June 1958 he told readers that in the case against the NAACP, over which he was presiding, he intended to deal the NAACP a "mortal blow" from which it "shall never recover."[48] It is no wonder, then, that despite clear Supreme Court rulings, Alabama was able to keep the NAACP in litigation for eight years and effectively incapacitated in the State. As Leon Friedman, who talked with scores of civil rights lawyers in the South concluded, "the states' legal institutions were and are the principal enemy."[49]

The use of the courts in the civil rights movement is considered the paradigm of a successful strategy for social change. Yet, a closer examination reveals that courts had virtually *no direct effect* on ending discrimination in education. Courageous and praiseworthy decisions were rendered, and nothing changed. *Brown* and its progeny stand for the proposition that courts are impotent to further the interests of the relatively disadvantaged. *Brown* is a paradigm, but for precisely the opposite view.

This, however, is not the end of the story. By the 1972-1973 school year, more than 91% of African-American children in the eleven states of the former Confederacy were in a non-segregated school. Eighteen years after *Brown*, Southern school systems were desegregated. How did this occur?

Change came to Southern school systems

The landslide reelection of Arkansas Governor Orval Faubus in 1958, after he repeatedly ignored court orders to prevent the desegregation of Central High School in Little Rock, demonstrated that defying court orders paid off at the polls. The black students pictured above could only safely enter Central High School under the protection of the U.S. Army.

in the wake of congressional and executive branch action. Title VI of the 1964 Civil Rights Act permitted the cut-off of federal funds to programs receiving federal monies where racial discrimination was practiced, and the 1965 Elementary & Secondary Education Act provided a great deal of federal money to generally poor Southern school districts. By the 1971-1972 school year, for example, federal funds comprised from between 12% and 27.8% of Southern state school budgets, up from between 4.6% and 11.1% in the 1963-1964 school year. This combination of federal funding and Title VI gave the executive branch a tool to induce desegregation when it chose to do so. When the U.S. Department of Health, Education, and Welfare began to threaten fund cut-offs to school districts that refused to desegregate, dramatic change occurred. By the 1972-1973 school year, more than 91% of African-American school children in the eleven Southern states were in integrated schools, up from 1.2% in the 1963-1964 school year. With only the constitutional right in force in the 1963-1964 school year, no more that 5.5% of African-American children in any Southern state were in school with whites. By the 1972-1973 school year, when economic incentives were offered for desegregation, and costs imposed for failure to desegregate, in no Southern state were fewer than 80% of African-American children in integrated schools. School desegregation occurred in the years 1968-72, then, because a set of conditions provided incentives for it and imposed costs for failing to desegregate. When those conditions were lacking, as in the first decade after *Brown*, constitutional rights were flouted. What a Court decision was unable to accomplish, federal dollars were able to achieve. The Supreme Court, acting alone, lacked the power to produce change.

Indirect Effects

The judicial path of influence is not the only way an institution can contribute to civil rights. By bringing an issue to light courts may put pressure on others to act, sparking change.

Thus *Brown* and its progeny may have been the inspiration that eventually led to congressional and executive branch action and some success in civil rights. According to one commentator, "*Brown* set the stage for the ensuing rise in black political activism, for legal challenges to racial discrimination in voting, employment, and education, as well as for the creation of a favorable climate for the passage of the subsequent civil rights legislation and the initiation of the War on Poverty."[50] Indeed, most commentators (and I assume most readers) believe this is the case and hold their belief with little doubt. As C. Herman Pritchett put it, "if the Court had not taken that first giant step in 1954, does anyone think there would now be a Civil Rights Act of 1964?"[51]

In the next few pages I examine these claims. What evidence exists to substantiate them? How important was *Brown* to the civil rights struggle? In examining these questions, it must be noted that social scientists do not understand well enough the dynamics of influence and causation to state with certainty that the claims of Court influence (or any other causal claims) are right or wrong. Similarly, social scientists do not understand fully the myriad of factors that are involved in an individual's reaching a political decision. Ideas seem to have feet of their own, and tracking their footsteps is an imperfect science. Thus, even if I find little or no evidence of extra-judicial influence, it is simply impossible to state with certainty that the Court did not contribute in a significant way to civil rights. On the other hand, claims about the real world require evidence. Otherwise, they are merely statements of faith.

Turning to the specifics, I have tried to delineate the links that are necessary for the Court to have influenced civil rights by the extra-judicial path. The bottom line, the last link, is that the action of the President and Congress resulted in change. That is, the passage of the 1964 Civil Rights Act brought about change. I have demonstrated this elsewhere[52] and it is assumed to be true throughout this chapter. The key question, then, is the extent to which congressional and presidential action was a product of Court action.

One hypothesized link postulates that Court action gave civil rights prominence, putting it on the political agenda. Media coverage of civil rights over time could provide good evidence to assess this link. A second link, put quite simply, is that Court action influenced both the President and Congress to act. The Court, in other words, was able to pressure the other branches into dealing with civil rights. A third hypothesized link proposes that the Court favorably influenced white Americans in general about civil rights and they in turn pressured politicians. By bringing the treatment of black Americans to nationwide attention, the Court may have fomented change. A final hypothesized link suggests that the Court influenced black Americans to act in favor of civil rights and that this in turn influenced white political elites either directly or indirectly through influencing whites in general.

Salience

When the Supreme Court unanimously condemned segregation in 1954, it marked the first time since 1875 that one of the three branches of the federal government spoke strongly in favor of civil rights on a fundamental issue. The Court, it is claimed, put civil rights on the political agenda. "*Brown*," Neier writes, "launched the public debate over racial equality."[53] One important way in which the political agenda is created is through the press. Thus, one way in which the Court may have given salience to civil rights is through inducing increased press coverage of it and balanced treatment of blacks.

Press Coverage

Overall, there is no evidence of such an increase or major change in reporting in the years immediately following *Brown*. In general, newspaper coverage of civil rights was poor until the massive demonstrations of the 1960s.

Numerous studies support this conclusion. C. A. McKnight, executive director of the Southern Education Reporting Service, found that in the years following *Brown* Supreme Court treatment of segregation received "minimum coverage."[54] In 1956, Ralph McGill, editor of the *Atlanta Constitution*, chided newspapers for failing to do "a good job of presenting and interpreting the segregation controversy."[55] This was particularly true in the South, where there was a "paucity" of coverage and where the wire services "seldom reported the story in its full dimensions and meaning."[56] And *Time* magazine criticized Southern newspapers for doing a "patchy, pussyfooting job of covering the region's biggest running story since the end of slavery."[57] In general, the Southern press did not greatly increase or balance its civil rights coverage in response to the Court.

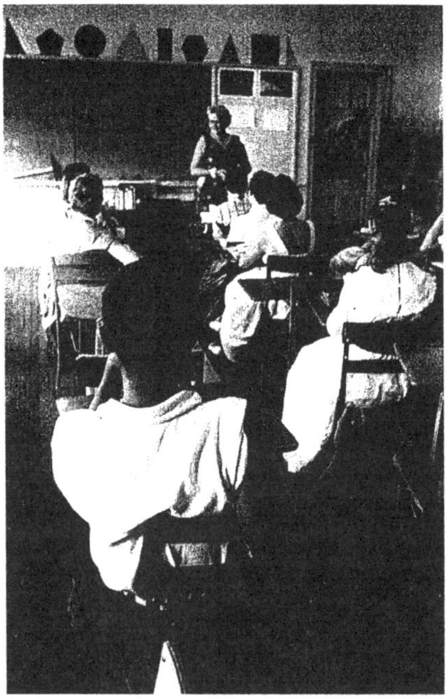

By the 1972-1973 school year, more than 91% of African-American children in the eleven states of the former Confederacy were in a nonsegregated school. The author makes the case that this desegregation did not occur through court battles but in the wake of congressional and executive branch action.

The most powerful way to determine if there was a sustained increase in press coverage of civil rights in response to *Brown* is to actually count press stories over time. The evidence shows that while press coverage of civil rights, as measured by the number of stories dealing with the issue in the *Reader's Guide To Periodical Literature*, increased moderately in 1954 over the previous year's total, by 1958 and 1959 coverage actually dropped below the level found in several of the years of the late 1940s and early 1950s! In addition, if one examines the magazines in America in the 1950s and early 1960s with the largest circulations, *Reader's Digest*, *Ladies Home Journal*, *Life*, and the *Saturday Evening Post*, the same general pattern again repeats. And it was not until 1962 that *TV Guide* ran a story having to do with civil rights. Thus, press coverage provides no evidence that the Court's decision gave civil rights salience for most Americans.

It is possible, of course, that the political agenda is formed more by elites than by ordinary citizens. Thus, it may be that the magazines most likely read by elites would provide increased coverage of civil rights in the wake of the Court's decision. But this is not the case. The magazines most likely to be read by political elites, *The New York Times Magazine*, *Newsweek*, *Time*, and the *New Republic*, show the same pattern. In fact, for each of these magazines there was as much, if not more, coverage of civil rights in several of the years of the 1940s as in 1958 or 1959. The same general pattern holds for civil rights coverage in *The New York Times* as measured by the proportion of pages in the *Times Index* devoted to discrimination. In 1952, there was actually more coverage than in 1954 or 1955. Further, coverage in the years 1954, 1955, 1958, and 1959 was barely equal to or actually less than the coverage allotted to civil rights in four of the years of the 1940s! Here again, there is no evidence that the Court's action indirectly affected elites by putting civil rights on the political agenda through the press.

There was one media outlet that gave enormous coverage to *Brown*; Voice of America! The decision was immediately translated into thirty-four languages and broadcast around the world. In poignant contrast, Universal Newsreels, the company that made news reports for movie theaters in the United States, never mentioned *Brown*.[58]

In sum, press coverage of civil rights provides no evidence for the claim that the Court has important extra-judicial-effects claim. This finding is striking since *Brown* is virtually universally credited with having brought civil rights to national attention.

Elites

The extra-judicial-effects argument claims that the actions of the Supreme Court influenced members of Congress, the President, and the executive branch. The argument might be that because of the "deference paid by the other branches of government and by the American public"[59] to the Supreme Court, its decisions prodded the other branches of the federal government into action. Further, the argument might run that the Court's actions sensitized elites to the legitimate claims of blacks. As Wilkinson puts it, "*Brown* was the catalyst that shook up Congress."[60]

Legislation

A sensible place to look for evidence of indirect effects is in the legislative history and debates over the 1957, 1960, and 1964 civil rights acts, and in presidential pronouncements on civil rights legislation. If Court action was crucial to congressional and presidential action, one might reasonably expect to find members of Congress and the President mentioning it as a reason for introducing and supporting civil rights legislation. While it is true that lack of attribution may only mean that the Court's influence was subtle, it would cast doubt on the force, if not the existence, of this extra-judicial effect.

At the outset, the case for influence is supported by the fact that civil rights bills were introduced and, for the first time since 1875, enacted in the years following *Brown*. While this makes it seem likely that *Brown* played an important role, closer examination of the impetus behind the civil rights acts of 1957, 1960, and 1964, does not support this seemingly reasonable inference. The 1957 and 1960 bills were almost entirely driven by electoral concerns. Republicans attempted to court Northern urban black voters and, at the same time, embarrass the Democrats by exposing the major rift between that party's Northern and Southern wings.[61] The press and political opponents understood the bills as a response to electoral pressures, not to constitutional mandates.

The story of the 1964 act is similar in that there is no evidence of Court influence and a great deal of evidence for other factors, in this case the activities of the civil rights movement. The Kennedy administration offered no civil rights bill until February 1963 and the bill it offered then was "a collection of minor changes far more modest than the 1956 Eisenhower program."[62] When a House subcommittee modified and strengthened the bill, Attorney General Robert Kennedy met with the members of the full Judiciary Committee in executive session and "criticized the subcommittee draft in almost every detail."[63] The President specifically objected to the prohibition of job discrimination that became Title VII, the provision making the Civil Rights Commission a permanent agency, the provision empowering the attorney general to sue on behalf of individuals alleging racial discrimination, and the provisions mandating no discrimination in federally funded programs and allowing fund cut-offs.[64] It was not until the events of the spring of 1963 that the administration changed its thinking.

In Congress, there is little evidence that *Brown* played any appreciable role. The seemingly endless congressional debates, with some four million words uttered in the Senate alone,[65] hardly touched on the case. References to *Brown* can be found on only a few dozen out of many thousands of pages of Senate debate.[66] While much of the focus of the debate was on

President Johnson was the first President to speak movingly about civil rights because neither Presidents Kennedy nor Eisenhower were willing to commit the moral weight of their office to the issue. Yet in signing civil rights acts (such as the Voting Rights Act of 1965 above) Johnson did not mention Supreme Court decisions. Instead, he cited the violence that peaceful black protesters were subject to, the unfairness of racial discrimination, and the desire to honor the memory of President Kennedy.

the constitutionality of the proposed legislation, and on the Fourteenth Amendment, the concern was not with how *Brown* mandated legislative action, or even how *Brown* made such a bill possible. Even in the debates over the fund cut-off provisions, *Brown* was seldom mentioned.[67] This is particularly surprising since it would have been very easy for pressured and uncertain members of Congress to shield their actions behind the constitutional mandate announced by the Court. That they did not credit the Court with affecting their decisions prevents the debates from providing evidence for the indirect-effects thesis. Thus, there does not appear to be evidence for the influence of *Brown* on legislative action.

Reviewing the public pronouncements of Presidents Eisenhower, Kennedy, and Johnson on civil rights legislation, I do not find the Court mentioned as a reason to act. Neither Eisenhower nor Kennedy committed the moral weight of their office to civil rights. When they did act, it was in response to violence or upcoming elections, not in response to Court decisions. While President Johnson spoke movingly and eloquently about civil rights, he did not mention Court decisions as an important reason for civil rights action. In his moving speeches to Congress and the nation in support of the 1964 Civil Rights Act and the 1965 Voting Rights Act he dwelt on the violence that peaceful black protesters were subjected to, the unfairness of racial discrimination, and the desire to honor the memory of President Kennedy. It was these factors that Johnson highlighted as reasons for supporting civil rights, not Court decisions.

In sum, I have not found the evidence necessary to make a case of clear attribution for the Court's effects on Congress or the President. Students of the Civil Rights Acts of 1957, 1960, and 1964 credit their introduction and passage to electoral concerns, or impending violence, not Court decisions. The extra-judicial-effects claim is not supported with Congress or the President.

Whites

The extra-judicial-effects thesis views courts as playing an important role in alerting Americans to social and political grievances. The view here is that the Supreme Court "pricked the conscience"[68] of white America by pointing out both its constitutional duty and its shortcomings. "Except for *Brown*," Aryeh Neier contends, white Americans "would not have known about the plight of blacks under segregation."[69] For this claim to hold, in order for courts to affect behavior, directly or indirectly, people must be aware of what the courts do. While this does not seem an onerous responsibility, I have shown earlier in this chapter that most Americans have little knowledge about U.S. courts and pay little attention to them. The specific question this leaves unanswered is whether this holds true for a case such as *Brown*.

Public Opinion—*Brown* and Civil Rights

Surprisingly, and unfortunately, there appear to be no polls addressing awareness of *Brown*. There are, however, polls charting the reaction to *Brown* by Southerners over time. They show both very little support for desegregation and lessening support throughout the 1950s. By 1959, for example, support for desegregation actually dropped, with only 8% of white Southerners responding that they would not object, down from 15% in 1954.[70]

If there is little evidence that *Brown* changed opinions about school desegregation in the South, perhaps it helped change white opinions more generally. It is clear that throughout the period from the beginning of the Second World War to the passage of the 1964 Act, whites became increasingly supportive of civil rights. Is there evidence that this change was the effect of Court action? The answer appears to be no. Writing in 1956, Hyman and Sheatsley found that the changes in attitude were "solidly based" and "not easily accelerated nor easily reversed."[71] Further, they found that the changes were not due to any specific event, such as Kennedy's assassination, or a Supreme Court decision. They found that changes in national opinion "represent long-term trends that are not easily modified by specific—even by highly dramatic—events."[72]

Another way of examining the indirect-effects claim on white Americans is to look at how the sensitivity of Americans to civil rights changed generally. According to one proponent of judicial influence, the "*Brown* decision was central to eliciting the moral outrage that both blacks and whites were to feel and express about segregation."[73] If the Court served this role, it would necessarily have increased awareness of the plight of blacks. The evidence, however, shows no sign of such an increase. Survey questions as to whether most blacks were being treated fairly resulted in affirmative responses of 66% in 1944, 66% in 1946, and 69% in 1956.[74] The variation of 3% is virtually meaningless. By 1963, when Gallup asked if any group in America was being treated unfairly, 80% said no. Only 5% of the sample named "the Negroes" as being unfairly treated while 4% named "the whites."[75] Most poignantly, in December 1958, when Gallup asked its usual question about the most admired men in the world, Governor Orval Faubus of Arkansas, who had repeatedly defied court orders a year earlier to prevent the desegregation of Central High School in Little Rock, was among the ten most frequently mentioned.[76] As Burke Marshall, head of the Justice Department's Civil Rights Division put it, "the Negro and his problems were still pretty much invisible to the country...until mass demonstrations of the Birmingham type."[77] These results, and the change over time, hardly show an America whose conscience is aroused. If the Court pricked the conscience of white Americans, the sensitivity disappeared quickly.

In sum, in several areas where the Supreme Court would be expected to influence white Americans, evidence of the effect has not been found. Most Americans neither follow Supreme Court decisions nor understand the Court's constitutional role. It is not surprising, then, that change in public opinion appears to be oblivious to the Court. Again, the extra-judicial-effects thesis lacks evidence.

Blacks

The indirect-effects thesis makes claims about the effect of the Supreme Court on black Americans. Here, a plausible claim is that *Brown* was the spark that ignited the black revolution. By recognizing and legitimizing black grievances, the public pronouncement by the Court provided blacks with a new image and encouraged them to act. This assumption is virtually universal among lawyers and legal scholars, and representative quotations can be found throughout this chapter. *Brown* "begot," one legal scholar tells us, "a union of the mightiest and lowliest in America, a mystical, passionate union bound by the pained depths of the black man's cry for justice and the moral authority, unique to the Court, to see that justice realized."[78] Thus, *Brown* may have fundamentally re-oriented the views of black Americans by providing hope that the federal government, if made aware of their plight, would help. Black action, in turn, could have changed white opinions and led to elite action and civil rights. If this is the case, then there are a number of places where evidence should be found.

One area where this effect should be seen is in civil rights demonstrations. The evidence plainly indicates that civil rights marches and demonstrations affected both white Americans and elites and provided a major impetus for civil rights legislation. As Wilkinson puts it, "the Court sired the movement, succored it through the early years, [and] encouraged its first taking wing."[79] If this were the case, if, in the words of civil rights litigator Jack Greenberg, the direct-action campaign would not have developed "without the legal victories that we'd won earlier,"[80] then one would expect to see an increase in the number of demonstrations shortly after the decision. However, there is almost no difference in the number of civil rights demonstrations in the years 1953, 1954, and 1955. There was a large jump in 1956, due to the Montgomery bus boycott. But then the numbers drop. For example, 1959 saw fewer civil rights demonstrations than in four of the years of the 1940s! And the number of demonstrations skyrocketed in the 1960s, six or more years after *Brown*. This pattern does not suggest that the Court played a major role. The time period is too long and the 1960s increases too startling to credit the Court with a meaningful effect.

The Montgomery Bus Boycott

The 1956 Montgomery bus boycott created worldwide attention. Coming just a few years after *Brown*, it is quite plausible that it was sparked by the Court. If this were the case, one might trace the indirect effect of *Brown* to Montgomery to the demonstrations of the 1960s to white opinion to elite action in 1964 and 1965 to desegregation of public schools in the early 1970s. The problem is that there does not appear to be evidence even for this tortuous causal chain. The immediate crisis in Montgomery was brought about by the arrest, in December 1955, of Mrs. Rosa Parks, a black woman, for refusing to give up her seat to a white person and move to the back of a segregated city bus. Parks was the fourth black woman arrested in 1956 for such a refusal.[81] It is unclear why this particular incident sparked the boycott, although Parks was fairly well-known and commanded respect in the black community. Because the Montgomery bus boycott is mentioned by so many civil rights activists, and because it launched both Dr. King's and Reverend Abernathy's civil rights careers, it is worth examining briefly.

In the 1940s and early 1950s there were a number of black civil rights organizations in Montgomery. One of them, the Women's Political Council (WPC), began to focus on bus segregation and lodged complaints with the city at the end of 1953 and again in the spring of 1954, before *Brown*. Before *Brown* the WPC had prepared for a bus boycott by preparing a notice calling on the black community to act and by planning the distribution routes. "On paper, the WPC had already planned for fifty thousand notices calling people to boycott the buses; only the specifics of time and place had to be added."[82] The arrest of Rosa Parks provided the opportunity the WPC was waiting for.

There is another piece of evidence, as well, that suggests that *Brown* was not influential; the nature of the boycotters' initial demands. Despite the efforts of the WPC, and the evident anger of the black community, initially the boycotters did *not* demand an end to bus segregation. Rather, the principal demand called for modified seating by race, with blacks starting at the back and whites at the front. As late as April 1956 Dr. King was still willing to settle on these terms.[83] This led the NAACP to withhold support on the grounds that the demands were too "mild."[84] As Abernathy puts it, "at first we regarded the Montgomery bus boycott as an interruption of our plans rather than as the beginning of their fulfillment."[85] Again, this suggests that a host of local factors provided the inspiration for the boycott.

Finally, four additional parts of the historical context suggest that *Brown* had little influence. First, the idea of a bus boycott was not new, having been used successfully by blacks in Baton Rouge, Louisiana, during the summer of 1953. Dr. Martin Luther King, Jr., the leader of the Montgomery bus boycott, knew the leader of that boycott, T. J. Jemison, from college days, and spoke with him early in the boycott.[86] From the Baton Rouge boycott, Abernathy notes, Montgomery's blacks took "considerable inspiration."[87] Second, Montgomery's blacks "did know that other cities in the Deep South, notably Mobile and Atlanta, had already conceded the 'first come, first served' principle."[88] Third, in November 1955, Representative Adam Clayton Powell visited

This sit-in in Greensboro, North Carolina, which took place in February 1960, started the sit-in movement of the 1960s. Ronald Martin, Robert Patterson, and Mark Martin, students at A&T College, staged a day-long sit-down strike at Woolworth's lunch counter when they were refused service because they were black. The white woman at left decided not to lunch at the counter with them. Within sixty days of Greensboro, sit-ins had spread to at least sixty-five Southern cities.

Montgomery and suggested that blacks use their economic power to force change. Characteristically, the flamboyant Powell took credit for instigating the bus boycott.[89] Finally, King specifically addressed the influence of *Brown* on the boycott. It was clear, he said, that *Brown* "cannot explain why it happened in Montgomery" and that the "crisis was not produced by...even the Supreme Court."[90] Although Montgomery may have inspired blacks, there does not appear to be much evidence that the Court inspired Montgomery.[91]

Sit-Ins

Another possible way in which *Brown* may have sparked change is through providing the inspiration for the sit-in movement and the demonstrations of the 1960s. The decision might have given blacks new hope that the federal government would work to end discrimination. It might have confirmed their own belief in the unfairness of segregation. If this were the case, one might plausibly expect to find participants in, and students of, the demonstrations talking and writing about the Court's decision as one reason for their actions. A review of biographies, autobiographies, and scholarly studies of the civil rights movement provides the evidence for assessing the claim.

The sit-in in Greensboro, North Carolina, in February 1960 started the sit-in movement of the 1960s. Organized by four black college students, it does not appear to have been Court-inspired. After Greensboro, the sit-ins spread quickly throughout the South. Within sixty days of Greensboro, sit-ins had spread to at least sixty-five Southern cities.[92] For black students throughout the South, the inspiration was the action of other students, as well as Montgomery and King. Instead of looking to courts for inspiration and support, the demonstrators "appealed to a higher law" because they "weren't sure about the legality" of their actions.[93] When black students from Atlanta joined the sit-ins, they took out a full-page advertisement in Atlanta's newspapers listing their demands and defending their actions. Entitled "An Appeal For Human Rights," the detailed and lengthy list of grievances was supported by six separate justifications of the sit-ins. No mention of the Court, the Constitution, or *Brown* is found anywhere in the text.[94] The six-year time interval between *Brown* and the sit-ins, the lack of attribution to the Court, the crediting of several non-Court factors, and the rapidity with which the movement spread, all suggest it was unlikely that *Brown* played much of a role.

Why did the sit-ins work? Was it because white business owners, in the wake of *Brown*, saw the constitutional legitimacy of the protestors' claims? The evidence does not support this conclusion. In most places businesses rejected the demands and refused to alter their practices. Constitutional principle did not appear to motivate them. Rather, they tried to outlast the demonstrators. However, sit-ins and ensuing black boycotts took their toll. In Greensboro, for example, Wolff writes of the "tremendous economic pressure put on the stores by the Negroes' boycott, along with the reticence of whites to trade there because of fear of trouble." The Woolworth's store where the sit-ins started registered a $200,000 drop in sales in 1960.[95] Economic pressure, not constitutional mandate, appears the best explanation for the success of the sit-ins.

Dr. Martin Luther King, Jr.

One possible way in which *Brown* might have ignited the civil rights movement is by inspiring Dr. King. His ringing denouncements of segregation, his towering oratory, and his ability to inspire and move both blacks and whites appear to have played an indispensable role in creating pressure for government action. Was King motivated to act by the Court? From an examination of King's thinking, the answer appears to be no. King rooted his beliefs in Christian theology and Gandhian nonviolence, not constitutional doctrine. His attitude to the Court, far from a source of inspiration, was one of strategic disfavor. "Whenever it is possible," he told reporters in early 1957, "we want to avoid court cases in this integration struggle."[96] He rejected litigation as a major tool of struggle for a number of reasons. He wrote of blacks' lack of faith in it, of its "unsuitability" to the civil rights struggle, and of its "hampering progress to this day."[97] Further, he complained that to "accumulate resources for legal actions imposes intolerable hardships on the already overburdened."[98] In addition to its expense, King saw the legal process as slow. Blacks, he warned, "must not get involved in legalism [and] needless fights in lower courts" because that is "exactly what the white man wants the Negro to do. Then he can draw out the fight."[99] Perhaps most important, King believed that litigation was an elite strategy for change that did not involve ordinary people. He believed that when the NAACP was the principal civil rights organization, and court cases were relied on, "the ordinary Negro was involved [only] as a passive spectator" and "his energies were unemployed."[100] Montgomery was particularly poignant, he told the 1957 NAACP annual convention, because, in Garrow's paraphrase, it demonstrated that "rank-and-file blacks themselves could act to advance the race's goals, rather than relying exclusively on lawyers and litigation to win incremental legal gains."[101] And, as he told the NAACP Convention on July 5, 1962, "only when the people themselves begin to act are rights on paper given life blood."[102] King's writings and actions do not provide evidence for the Dynamic Court view that he was inspired by the Court.

Black Groups

The founding of the Student Non-Violent Coordinating Committee (SNCC), the Congress of Racial Equality (CORE), and the Southern Christian Leadership Conference (SCLC), the organizations that provided the leadership and the shock troops of the movement, could quite plausibly have been inspired by the Court. Although SNCC was not founded until six years after *Brown*, and CORE was not revitalized until 1961, it may have taken that long for the effect to be felt.

However, it is quite clear that the Court played no role in inspiring these key groups of the civil rights movement to form. To the contrary, they were formed as an explicit rejection of litigation as a method of social change. The SCLC, for example, was founded in the winter of 1957. The moving force behind it was not the inspiration of *Brown* but an attempt to capitalize on the success of the Montgomery bus boycott.[103] The founding of SNCC in 1960 is similar and was aimed at helping students engaged in sit-ins to create at least some communication and organization network.[104] And CORE was founded in 1942 as a Gandhian-type movement of mass non-violent direct action.[105] As its Executive Director James Farmer told Roy Wilkins of the NAACP in response to Wilkins's opposition to the Freedom Ride, and preference for litigation, "we've had test cases and we've won them all and the status remains quo."[106] The point is that *Brown* is simply not mentioned as a source of inspiration.

If *Brown* is not mentioned by those who sat in, demonstrated, and marched, was anything? The answer is a clear yes. The participants pointed to a number of sources of inspiration for their actions. For some, the emergence of black African nations and the movements that accompanied their liberation had a "profound effect."[107] Over the twelve months from June 1960 to June 1961, eleven African countries gained independence. "We identified with the blacks in Africa," John Lewis of SNCC said, "and we were thrilled by what was going on."[108] Third-world liberation movements were also prominently mentioned by King in his classic **Letter From Birmingham Jail**.[109] For others, the Montgomery bus boycott was an "inspiration."[110] James Forman, a powerful force in SNCC, credits the bus boycott with having a "very significant effect on the consciousness of black people" and a "particularly important effect on young blacks." Montgomery, Forman believed, "helped to generate the student movement of 1960."[111] Participants in sit-ins also pointed to other sit-ins as inspiration, and to Dr. King, either by his actions or his writings.[112] *Brown* and the Supreme Court may have played a role in inspiring the activists of the early 1960s but they did not mention it in describing their inspiration for acting. And given the fact that they did point to other factors as inspiring them, the lack of attribution of *Brown* is all the more telling.[113]

In exploring the case for extra judicial effects with blacks, I looked for evidence in a variety of places, including the Court's ability to inspire black activists, black protest activity, and black leaders. In none of these places was evidence found for the claim and in a number of places the evidence seems to contradict it. Again, the extra-judicial-effects thesis lacks support.

Before I sum up these findings, it is important to note that while there is little evidence that *Brown* helped produce positive change, there is some evidence that it hardened resistance to civil rights among both elites and the white public. I have documented how, throughout the South, white groups intent on using coercion and violence to prevent change grew. Resistance to change increased in all areas, not merely in education but also in voting, transportation, public places, and so on. *Brown* "unleashed a wave of racism that reached hysterical proportions."[114] On the elite level, *Brown* was used as a club by Southerners to fight any civil rights legislation as a ploy to force school desegregation on the South. In hearings and floor debates on the 1957 Civil Rights Act, Southerners repeatedly charged that the bill, aimed at voting rights, was a subterfuge to force school desegregation on the South.[115] When Attorney General Brownell testified before a Senate committee on the 1957 bill, he was queried repeatedly and to his astonishment on whether the bill gave the President the power to use the armed forces to enforce desegregation.[116] By stiffening resistance and raising fears before the activist phase of the civil rights movement was in place, *Brown* may actually have delayed the achievement of civil rights.

The Montgomery bus boycott and Martin Luther King, Jr.'s, writings and actions did more to inspire the civil rights activists of the early 1960s than *Brown* or other Supreme Court rulings. Here Dr. King escorts schoolchildren in 1966 to a formerly all-white school in Grenada, Mississippi, where desegregation had already produced several deadly incidents of violence.

In sum, the claim that a major contribution of the courts in civil rights was to give the issue salience, press political elites to act, prick the consciences of whites, legitimate the grievances of blacks, and fire blacks up to act is not substantiated. In all the places examined, where evidence supportive of the claim should exist, it does not. The concerns of clear attribution, time, and increased press coverage all cut against the thesis. Public-opinion evidence does not support it and, at times, clearly contradicts it. The emergence of the sit-ins, demonstrations, and marches, does not support it. While it must be the case that Court action influenced some people, I have found no evidence that this influence was widespread or of much importance to the battle for civil rights. The evidence suggests that *Brown*'s major positive impact was limited to reinforcing the belief in a legal strategy for change of those already committed to it. The burden of showing that *Brown* accomplished more now rests squarely on those who for years have written and spoken of its immeasurable importance.

Conclusion: The Fly-Paper Court

This chapter has examined whether the Supreme Court's decision in *Brown v. Board of Education* was able to desegregate schools. Surprisingly, the analysis showed the Court's decision, praiseworthy as it was, did not make much of a contribution. This is the case because, on the most fundamental level, courts depend on political support to produce such reform. Thus, political hostility doomed the Court's contributions.

Courts will also be ineffective in producing change, given any serious resistance because of their lack of implementation powers. The structural constraints built into the American judicial system, make courts virtually powerless to produce change. They must depend on the actions of others for their decisions to be implemented. With civil rights, little changed until the federal government became involved. Where there is local hostility to change, court orders will be ignored. Community pressure, violence or threats of violence, and lack of market response all serve to curtail actions to implement court decisions. When Justice Jackson commented during oral argument in *Brown*, "I suppose that realistically this case is here for the reason that action couldn't be obtained from Congress,"[117] he identified a fundamental reason why the Court's action in the case would have little effect.

In general, then, not only does litigation steer activists to an institution that is constrained from helping them, but also it siphons off crucial resources and talent, and runs the risk of weakening political efforts. In terms of financial resources, social reform groups do not have a lot of money. Funding a litigation campaign means that other strategic options are starved of funds. In civil rights, while *Brown* was pending in June 1953, Thurgood Marshall and Walter White sent out a telegram to supporters of the NAACP asking for money, stating "funds entirely spent."[118] Compare this to the half-million-dollar estimates of the cost of the freedom rides, largely due to fines and bail.[119] Further, the legal strategy drained off the talents of people such as Thurgood Marshall and Jack Greenberg. As Martin Luther King, Jr., complained: "to accumulate resources for legal actions imposes intolerable hardships on the already overburdened."[120]

It is important to note here that there were options other than litigation. Massive voter-registration drives could have been started in the urban North and in some major Southern cities. Marches, demonstrations, and sit-ins could have been organized and funded years before they broke out, based on the example of labor unions and the readiness of groups like the CORE. Money could have been invested in public relations. Amazingly, in 1957 the NAACP spent just $7,814 for its Washington Bureau operations. Its entire "public relations and informational activities" spending for 1957 was $17,216. NAACP lobbyists did not even try to cultivate the black press or the black church, let alone their white counterparts. And even in 1959 the public relations budget was only $10,135.[121] When activists succumbed to the "lawyers' vision of change without pain,"[122] a "massive social revolution" was side-tracked into "legal channels."[123] Because the NAACP failed to understand the limits on U.S. courts, its strategy was bound to fail.

If this is the case, then there is another important way in which courts effect social change. It is, to put it simply, that courts act as "fly-paper" for social reformers who succumb to the "lure of litigation." Courts, I have argued, can seldom produce significant social reform. Yet if groups advocating such reform continue to look to the courts for aid, and spend precious resources in litigation, then the courts also limit change by deflecting claims from substantive political battles, where success is possible, to harmless legal ones where it is not. Even when major cases are won, the achievement is often more symbolic that real. Thus, courts may serve an ideological function of luring movements for social reform to an institution that is structurally constrained from serving their needs, providing only an illusion of change.

This conclusion does not deny that courts can occasionally, though rarely, help social reform movements. Sometimes, too, litigation can remove minor but lingering obstacles to change. But here litigation is often a mopping-up operation, and it is often defensive. In civil rights, for example, when opponents of the 1964 and 1965 acts went to court to invalidate them, the courts' refusal to do so allowed change to proceed. Similarly, if there had never been a *Brown* decision, a Southern school board or state wanting to avoid a federal fund cut-off in the late 1960s might have challenged its state law requiring segregation. An obliging court decision would have removed the obstacle without causing much of a stir, or wasting the scarce resources of civil rights groups. This is a very different approach to the courts than one based on using them to produce significant social reform.

Litigation can also help reform movements by providing defense services to keep the movement afloat. In civil rights, the NAACP Legal Defense and Educational Fund, Inc. (Inc. Fund) provided crucial legal service that prevented the repressive legal structures of the Southern states from totally incapacitating the movement. In springing demonstrators from jail, providing bail money, and forcing at least a semblance of due process, Inc. Fund lawyers performed crucial tasks. But again, this is a far cry from a litigation strategy for significant social reform.

These findings also suggest that a great deal of writing about courts is fundamentally flawed. Treating courts and judges as either philosophers on high or as existing solely within a self-contained legal community ignores what they actually do. This does not mean that philosophical thinking and legal analysis should be abandoned. It emphatically does mean that the broad and untested generalizations offered by constitutional scholars about the role, impact, importance, and legitimacy of courts and court opinions that pepper this chapter must be rejected. When asking those sorts of questions about courts, they must be treated as political institutions and studied as such. To ignore social science literature and eschew empirical evidence, as much court writing does, makes it impossible to understand courts as they are.

American courts are not all-powerful institutions. They were designed with severe limitations and placed in a political system of divided powers. To ask them to produce significant social reform is to forget their history and ignore their constraints. It is to cloud our vision with a naive and romantic belief in the triumph of rights over politics. And while romance and even naivete have their charms, they are not best exhibited in courtrooms.

ENDNOTES

[1]347 U.S. 483 (1954).

[2]Michael J. Klarman, "How *Brown* Changed Race Relations: The Backlash Thesis," *Journal of American History* 81 (1994): 81.

[3]410 U.S. 113 (1973).

[4]Alexander M. Bickel, **The Least Dangerous Branch: The Supreme Court at the Bar of Politics**. 2nd ed. (New Haven: Yale University Press, 1962) p. 26.

[5]Eugene V. Rostow, "The Democratic Character of Judicial Review," 66 *Harv. L. Rev.* 193, 208 (1952).

[6]Bickel, **Least Dangerous Branch**, p. 26.

[7]Note. "Implementation Problems in Institutional Reform Litigation," 91 *Harv. L. Rev.* 428, 463 (1977).

[8]**The Hollow Hope: Can Courts Bring About Social Change?** (Chicago: University of Chicago Press, 1991, 1993); "The Irrelevant Court: The Supreme Court's Inability to Influence Popular Beliefs about Equality (or Anything Else)," in **Redefining Equality**, eds. Neal Devins and Dave Douglas (New York: Oxford University Press, 1998): 172-190; "The Implementation of Constitutional Rights: Insights from Law and Economics," 64 *University of Chicago Law Review* 1215 (1997); "The Real World of Constitutional Rights: The Supreme Court and the Implementation of the Abortion Decisions," in **Contemplating Courts**, ed.

Lee Epstein (Washington, D.C., Congressional Quarterly Press, 1995): 390-419; "*Brown* is Dead! Long Live *Brown*!: The Endless Attempt to Canonize a Case," 80 *Virginia Law Review* 161 (1994).

[9]**The Federalist Papers**. Ed. Clinton Rossiter (New York: Mentor, 1961), p. 465.

[10]31 U.S. (6 Peters) 515 (1832).

[11]Ariah Never, **Only Judgment: The Limits of Litigation in Social Change** (Middletown: Wesleyan University Press, 1982) p. 239.

[12]Sheldon Goldman and Thomas P. Jahnige, **The Federal Courts as a Political System**. 2nd ed. (New York: Harper & Row, 1976) p. 145; William J. Daniels, "The Supreme Court and Its Publics," 37 *Alb. L. Rev.* 632 (1973); John N. Kessel, "Public Perceptions of the Supreme Court." *Midwest Journal of Political Science* 10 (1966): 167-91.

[13]Walter F. Murphy, Joseph Tanenhaus, and Daniel L. Kastner, **Public Evaluations of Constitutional Courts: Alternative Explanations** (Beverly Hills: Sage, 1973) p. 53.

[14]Survey cited in Kenneth M. Dolbeare, "The Public Views the Supreme Court." In **Law, Politics, and the Federal Courts**. Ed. Herbert Jacob (Boston: Little, Brown, 1967) pp. 199-201.

[15]Lee Epstein, Jeffrey A. Segal, Harold J. Spaeth, Thomas G. Walker, **The Supreme Court Compendium** (Washington, D.C.: Congressional Quarterly Press, 1994) p. 609.

[16]Findings reported in James Warren, "Hold for Mr. Bigwig," *Chicago Tribune* 12 Ap. 1990, sec. 5, p. 2.

[17]347 U.S. 483 (1954).

[18]Neier, **Only Judgment**, p. 57.

[19]Jack Greenberg, "Litigation for Social Change: Methods, Limits and Role In Democracy," 29 *Record of the Association of the Bar of the City of New York* 320, 331 (1974).

[20]Roy Wilkins with Tom Mathews, **Standing Fast: The Autobiography of Roy Wilkins** (New York: Penguin, 1984) p. 222.

[21]Jack W. Peltason, **Fifty-Eight Lonely Men** (Urbana: University of Illinois Press, 1971) p. 54.

[22]Victor S. Navasky, **Kennedy Justice** (New York: Atheneum, 1977) p. 161.

[23]The only Southern senators not to sign the Manifesto were Johnson of Texas and Kefauver and Gore of Tennessee. And two North Carolina congressman who refused to sign, Charles B. Deane and Thurmond Chatham, lost their seats.

[24]*Cong. Rec.* 12 March 1956: 4460 (Senate), 4515-16 (House).

[25]Earl Black, **Southern Governors and Civil Rights: Racial Segregation as a Campaign Issue in the Second Reconstruction** (Cambridge: Harvard University Press, 1976) p. 299.

[26]Black, **Southern Governors**, p. 299.

[27]Gary Orfield, **The Reconstruction of Southern Education** (New York: Wiley, 1969) pp. 17-18.

[28]Harrell R. Rodgers, Jr., and Charles S. Bullock III, **Law and Social Change: Civil Rights Laws and Their Consequences** (New York: McGraw-Hill, 1972) p. 72.

[29]Peltason, **Fifty-Eight Lonely Men**, p. 5; Southern Regional Council, **Law Enforcement in Mississippi** (Atlanta: Southern Regional Council, 1964) pp. 7-17.

[30]David J. Garrow, **Protest at Selma** (New Haven: Yale University Press, 1978) p. 21; Doug McAdam, **Freedom Summer** (New York: Oxford University Press, 1988) pp. 257-82.

[31]Reed Sarratt, **The Ordeal of Desegregation** (New York: Harper, 1966) pp. 301-2; Peltason, **Fifty-Eight Lonely Men**, pp. 58, 60.

[32]Peltason, **Fifty-Eight Lonely Men**, p. 99.

[33]Catherine A. Barnes, **Journey from Jim Crow: The Desegregation of Southern Transit** (New York: Columbia University Press, 1983) pp. 196, 195.

[34]Robert G. Dixon, Jr., "Civil Rights in Transportation and the I.C.C.," 31 *Geo. Wash. L. Rev.* 198, 213-14 (1962).

[35]Sarratt, **Ordeal**, pp. 99-100.

[36]358 U.S. 1 (1958).

[37]William Brink and Louis Harris, **The Negro Revolution in America** (New York: Simon, 1963) p. 41.

[38]J. Frankfurter, letter to C. C. Burlingham, quoted in Mark G. Yudof, "Implementation Theories & Desegregation," in "Symposium, Judicially Managed Institutional Reform," 32 *Ala. L. Rev.* 441, 450 (1981).

[39]"Report of the Committee on Federal-State Relationships as Affected by Judicial Decisions," *Congressional Record* 25 August 1958: A7782, at p. A7787.

[40]*Id.*, p. A7788.

[41]Gary Peller, "Neutral Principles in the 1950's," 21 *U. Mich. J. L. Ref.* 561, 563 (1988).

[42]Herbert Wechsler, "Toward Neutral Principles of Constitutional Law," 73 *Harv. L. Rev.* 1 (1959).

[43]John Minor Wisdom, "The Frictionmaking, Exacerbating Political Role of Federal Courts," 21 *Sw. L. Rev.* 411, 419 (1967).

[44]Quoted in Note, "Judicial Performance in the Fifth Circuit," 73 *Yale L. J.* 90, 101 n. 71 (1963).

[45] Southern Regional Council, *Law Enforcement* (Atlanta: The Council, 1964) pp.19-20.

[46]Quoted in Sarratt, **Ordeal**, p. 201.

[47]Quoted in Peltason, **Fifty-Eight Lonely Men**, p. 66.

[48]Quoted in Peltason, **Fifty-Eight Lonely Men**, pp. 65, 67.

[49]Leon Friedman, ed., **Southern Justice** (New York: Pantheon, 1965) p. 7.

[50]Henry M. Levin, "Education and Earnings of Blacks and the *Brown* Decision." In **Have We Overcome? Race Relations Since Brown.** Ed. Michael V.

Namorato (Jackson: University of Mississippi Press, 1979) p. 80.

[51]C. Herman Pritchett, "Equal Protection and the Urban Majority," *American Political Science Review* 58 (1964): 869.

[52]See Rosenberg, **Hollow Hope**, chapter 2.

[53]Neier, **Only Judgment**, pp. 241-42.

[54]Quoted in Sarratt, **Ordeal**, p. 263.

[55]Quoted in Roy E. Carter, Jr., "Segregation and the News: A Regional Content Study," *Journalism Quarterly* 34 (1957): 4, n. 4.

[56]Pat Watters and Reese Cleghorn, **Climbing Jacob's Ladder** (New York: Harcourt, 1967) p. 73 n. 10.

[57]"The Press—Dilemma in Dixie," *Time* 20 February 1956: 76.

[58]Taylor Branch, **Parting the Waters: America in the King Years 1954-1963** (New York: Simon & Schuster, 1988) p. 113.

[59]Neier, **Only Judgment**, p. 9.

[60]J. Harvie Wilkinson, III, **From Brown to Bakke: The Supreme Court and School Integration, 1954-1978** (New York: Oxford University Press, 1979) p. 49.

[61]See J. W. Anderson, **Eisenhower, Brownell, and the Congress: The Tangled Origins of the Civil Rights Bill of 1956-1957** (University, Ala: University of Alabama Press, 1964) pp. 3, 47, 133-35; Robert Fredrick Burk, **The Eisenhower Administration and Black Civil Rights** (Knoxville: University of Tennessee Press, 1984) pp. 6, 145, 165, 218; Richard Kluger, **Simple Justice** (New York: Knopf, 1976) p. 754; Steven F. Lawson, **Black Ballots: Voting Rights in the South, 1944-1969** (New York: Columbia University Press, 1976) chap. 6; Roy Wilkins, **Standing Fast**, p. 234.

[62]Orfield, **Reconstruction**, p.24.

[63]Daniel M. Berman, **A Bill Becomes a Law: Congress Enacts Civil Rights Legislation** 2nd ed. (New York: Macmillan, 1966) pp. 21-22; Charles and Barbara Whalen, **The Longest Debate: A Legislative History of the 1964 Civil Rights Act** (Cabin John,. Md: Seven Locks, 1985) pp. 44-45.

[64]Berman, **A Bill Becomes a Law**, pp. 22-23; Jack Greenberg, "Preface. Blacks and the Law," *Annals of the American Academy of Political and Social Science* vol. 407 (1973): ix.

[65]Whalen, **The Longest Debate**, p. 193.

[66]References can be found in the following parts and on the following pages of volume 110 of the *Congressional Record*, 88th Congress, 2nd sess., 1964: Part 4: 4996, 5017, 5087, 5247, 5267, 5342; Part 5: 5695, 5703, 5705, 5935, 6540, 6813, 6814, 6821, 6837, 6838; Part 6: 8052, 8054; Part 7: 8620, 8621; Part 8: 10919, 10921, 10925, 10926, 11194, 11195, 11198; Part 9: 11597, 11875, 12339, 12579, 12580; Part 10: 12683, 13922; Part 11: 14294, 14296, 14447, 14457. Over 40% of these references are by Senators opposing the Bill.

[67]Berman, **A Bill Becomes a Law**; Orfield, **Reconstruction**, pp. 33-45; Whalen, **The Longest Debate**.

[68]Loren Miller, "Very Deliberate Speed." In **The Segregation Era 1863-1954.** Ed. Allen Weinstein and Frank Otto Gatell (New York: Oxford University Press, 1970) p. 281.

[69]Neier, **Only Judgment**, p. 239.

[70]AIPO Poll in Hazel Gaudet Erskine, "The Polls: Race Relations," *Public Opinion Quarterly* 26 (1962): 140, 141.

[71]Herbert H. Hyman and Paul B. Sheatsley, "Attitudes Toward Desegregation," *Scientific American* (Dec. 1956): 38.

[72]Herbert H. Hyman and Paul B. Sheatsley, "Attitudes Toward Desegregation," *Scientific American* (July 1964): 17.

[73]Henry M. Levin, "Education and Earnings of Blacks and the *Brown* Decision." In **Have We Overcome? Race Relations Since Brown.** Ed. Michael V. Namorato (Jackson: University of Mississippi Press, 1979) p. 110-11.

[74]Hyman and Sheatsley, 1956, p. 39.

[75]George H. Gallup, **The Gallup Poll: Public Opinion 1935-1971**. 3 vols. (New York: Random House, 1972) vol 3: 1825.

[76]Gallup, **The Gallup Poll**, vol. 2: 1584.

[77]Quoted in Adam Fairclough, **To Redeem the Soul of America: The Southern Christian Leadership Conference and Martin Luther King, Jr.** (Athens, Ga.: University of Georgia Press, 1987) p. 135.

[78]Wilkinson, **From Brown to Bakke**, p. 5.

[79]Wilkinson, **From Brown to Bakke**, p. 3.

[80]"'Someone Has to Translate Rights into Realities': Conversation with Civil Rights Lawyer Jack Greenberg," 2 *Civil Liberties Rev.* (Fall, 1975): 111.

[81]David Levering Lewis, **King: A Biography** (New York: Praeger Publishers, 1970) p. 48.

[82]Jo Ann Gibson Robinson, **The Montgomery Bus Boycott and the Women Who Started It: The Memoir of Jo Ann Gibson Robinson**. Ed. David J. Garrow (Knoxville: University of Tennessee Press, 1987) p. 39.

[83]Fairclough, **To Redeem the Soul of America**, p. 20.

[84]Wilkins, **Standing Fast**, p. 228.

[85]Ralph David Abernathy, **And the Walls Came Tumbling Down** (New York: Harper & Row, 1989) p. 169.

[86]Branch, **Parting the Waters**, p. 145.

[87]Abernathy, **And the Walls Came Tumbling Down**, p. 178; David J. Garrow, **Bearing the Cross: Martin Luther King, Jr., and the Southern Christian**

Leadership Conference (New York: Morrow, 1986) pp. 26-27; Aldon D. Morris, **The Origins of the Civil Rights Movement: Black Communities Organizing for Change** (New York: The Free Press, 1984) p. x. Morris argues that the Montgomery bus boycott was "partly inspired by the Baton Rouge effort and to some extent modeled after it."

[88]Fairclough, **To Redeem the Soul of America**, p. 12.

[89]J. Mills Thornton III, "Challenge and Response in the Montgomery Bus Boycott of 1955-1956," *Alabama Review* 33 (July 1980): 194.

[90]Martin Luther King, Jr., **Stride Toward Freedom: The Montgomery Story** (New York: Harper, 1958) pp. 64, 191-92. At a news conference in January 1956, King explained the boycott as "part of a world-wide movement. Look at just about any place in the world and the exploited people are rising against their exploiters. This seems to be the outstanding characteristic of our generation" (quoted in Garrow, **Bearing the Cross**, p. 54).

[91]Morris, **Origins**, p. 25 credits the Baton Rouge boycott with more importance than the Court. However, the Supreme Court may have played a vital role in the final victory by allowing the city a way out of a boycott that was costly and damaging. In *Gayle v. Browder*, 352 U.S. 903, (1956), the Supreme Court upheld a lower-court decision prohibiting enforcement of Montgomery's bus segregation law. The Court's decision may have allowed the city to end segregation without "giving in" to the boycotters' demands. On the other hand, without the strength of the boycott, there would have been little pressure on Montgomery to comply.

[92]Southern Regional Council, **The Student Protest Movement Winter 1960.** Revised. (Atlanta: The Southern Regional Council, April 1, 1960) p. 1.

[93]Remarks of Julian Bond, University of Chicago, 10 January 1990. In 1960 Bond was a student leader of the Atlanta sit-ins.

[94]"An Appeal for Human Rights," *Atlanta Constitution* 9 March 1960: 13.

[95]Miles Wolff, **Lunch at the Five and Ten** (New York: Stein and Day, 1970) pp. 173, 174.

[96]quoted in Garrow, **Bearing the Cross**, p. 87.

[97]Martin Luther King, Jr., **Why We Can't Wait** (New York: Harper, 1963) pp. 23, 157.

[98]King, **Why We Can't Wait**, p. 157.

[99]quoted in Garrow, **Bearing the Cross**, p. 91.

[100]quoted in Morris, **Origins**, p. 123.

[101]Garrow, **Bearing the Cross**, p. 78.

[102]quoted in Branch, **Parting the Waters**, p. 598.

[103]Garrow, **Bearing the Cross**, p. 85; Fairclough, **To Redeem the Soul**, pp. 30, 31.

[104]Clayborne Carson, **In Struggle** (Cambridge: Harvard University Press, 1981) pp. 19, 20; Garrow, **Bearing the Cross**, pp. 131 ff; Mary King, **Freedom Song: A Personal Story of the 1960s Civil Rights Movement** (New York: Morrow, 1987) pp. 42-46; Juan Williams, **Eyes on the Prize: America's Civil Rights Years, 1954-1965** (New York: Penguin, 1988) p. 137; Paul Good, "Odyssey of a Man—And a Movement," *The New York Times Magazine* 25 June 1967: 44; Cleveland Sellers, **The River of No Return** (New York: Morrow, 1973) p. 16.

[105]James Farmer, **Lay Bare the Heart: An Autobiography of the Civil Rights Movement** (New York: Plume, 1985) Appendix A.

[106]Quoted in Farmer, **Lay Bare the Heart**, p. 13.

[107]Carson, **In Struggle**, p. 16; Williams, **Eyes on the Prize**, p. 11; James W. Vander Zanden, "The Non-Violent Resistance Movement Against Segregation," *American Journal of Sociology* 68 (1963): 545; Howard Zinn, **Albany: A Study in National Responsibility** (Atlanta: Southern Regional Council, 1962).

[108]quoted in Williams **Eyes on the Prize**, p. 139.

[109]Martin Luther King, Jr., "The Negro is Your Brother" [Letter from Birmingham Jail] as published in 212 *Atlantic Monthly* (August, 1963) pp. 5, 11.

[110]Howard Zinn, **SNCC: The New Abolitionists** (Boston: Beacon, 1964) p. 18.

[111]James Forman, **The Making of Black Revolutionaries** (New York: Macmillan, 1972) pp. 84, 85.

[112]Thomas Gaither, "Orangeburg: Behind the Carolina Stockade." In **Sit-Ins: The Students Report**. Ed. Jim Peck (New York: Congress of Racial Equality, 1960); Minnie Finch, **The NAACP: Its Fight for Justice** (Metuchen, N.J.: Scarecrow, 1981) p. 205; Martin Oppenheimer, "The Genesis of the Southern Negro Student Movement (Sit-In Movement): A Study in Contemporary Negro Protest." Ph.D. Diss. University of Pennsylvania, 1963 p. 103; C. Vann Woodward, **The Strange Career of Jim Crow**. Rev. ed. (New York: Oxford University Press, 1974) p. 197.

[113]For confirmation of this analysis, see, for example, the following works by participants: Abernathy, **And the Walls Came Tumbling Down**; Farmer, **Lay Bare the Heart**; Foreman,**The Making of Black Revolutionaries**; King, **Stride Toward Freedom**; King, **Why We Can't Wait**; King, "The Negro is Your Brother" [Letter from Birmingham Jail]; King, **Freedom Song**; various participants in Peck, **Sit-Ins**; various participants in Howell Raines, **My Soul Is Rested: Movement Days in the Deep South Remembered** (New York: Putnam, 1977); Sellers, **The River of No Return**; Elizabeth Sutherland, ed. **Letters from Mississippi** (NewYork: McGraw-Hill, 1965). Studies of the movement that confirm this analysis include Branch, **Parting the Waters**; Carson, **In Struggle**; William H. Chafe, **Civilities and Civil Rights: Greensboro, North Carolina, and the Black Struggle for Freedom** (New York: Oxford

University Press, 1980); Fairclough, **To Redeem the Soul**; Garrow, **Protest at Selma**; Garrow, **Bearing the Cross**; Henry Hampton and Steve Fayer, **Voices of Freedom: An Oral History of the Civil Rights Movement from the 1950s through the 1980s** (New York: Bantam, 1990); McAdam, **Freedom Summer**; August Meier and Elliott Rudwick, eds. **Black Protest in the Sixties** (Chicago: Quadrangle, 1970); Oppenheimer, "Genesis"; Southern Regional Council, **The Student Protest Movement: A Recapitulation** (N.p.: Southern Regional Council, 1960); Southern Regional Council, **Student Protest Movement**; Southern Regional Council, **The Freedom Ride May 1961** (Atlanta: Southern Regional Council, 1961); Pete Seeger and Bob Reiser, **Everybody Says Freedom: A History of the Civil Rights Movement in Songs and Pictures** (New York: W. W. Norton, 1989); Nancy J. Weiss, **Whitney M. Young, Jr., and the Struggle for Civil Rights** (Princeton: Princeton University Press, 1989); Robin M. Williams, Jr., "Social Change and Social Conflict: Race Relations in the United States, 1944-1964," *Sociological Inquiry* 35 (1965): 8-25; Williams, **Eyes on the Prize**; Wolff, **Lunch at the Five and Ten**; Zanden, "Non-Violent Resistance"; Zinn, **SNCC**.

[114]Fairclough, **To Redeem the Soul**, p. 21.

[115]*Civil Rights: Hearings Before the Subcomm. No 5 of the House Comm. On the Judiciary,* 85th Cong. 806, 1187 (1957).

[116]*Civil Rights–1957: Hearings Before the Subcomm. On Constitutional Rights of the Senate Comm. On the Judiciary,* 85th Congress 214-16 (1957).

[117]Quoted in Leon Friedman, ed., **Argument: The Oral Argument Before the Supreme Court in Brown v. Board of Education of Topeka, 1952-1955** (New York: Chelsea House, 1969) p. 244.

[118]Quoted in Kluger, **Simple Justice**, p. 617.

[119]Sarratt, **Ordeal**, p. 333.

[120]King, **Why We Can't Wait**, p. 157.

[121]Gilbert Ware, "The National Association for the Advancement of Colored People and the Civil Rights Act of 1957." Ph.D. Diss. Princeton University, 1962, pp. 188-89, 189, 190, 13.

[122]Stuart A. Scheingold, **The Politics of Rights: Lawyers, Public Policy, and Political Change** (New Haven: Yale University Press, 1974) p. 145.

[123]Morton J. Horwitz,"The Jurisprudence of *Brown* and the Dilemmas of Liberalism." In **Have We Overcome? Race Relations Since Brown**. Ed. Michael V. Namorato (Jackson: University of Mississippi Press, 1979) p. 184.

[20]

REPUBLICAN SCHOOLMASTER: THE U.S. SUPREME COURT, PUBLIC OPINION, AND ABORTION

CHARLES H. FRANKLIN
LIANE C. KOSAKI
Washington University

The United States Supreme Court has a historical role as a "republican schoolmaster," inculcating virtues in the citizenry. The role as teacher to the republic also serves the interests of the Court. As the "weakest branch," the Supreme Court needs public support if its decisions are to be effective. We investigate the Court's ability to win popular support for its rulings, specifically in the case of Roe *v.* Wade. *The analysis shows that the Court's decision did affect public attitudes but not as previous work would predict. While support for abortions to protect health increased as a result of the Court's decision, the public became more polarized over "discretionary" abortions. The puzzle is what process can account for these disparate reactions. We develop a theory resting on interpersonal influences to explain these results, arguing that the social interpretation of events drives the differing outcomes. This theory is then tested against a purely psychological alternative. The closing discussion considers how these results can be extended to the general problem of public decisions and popular responses, including presidential actions and the influence of the media.*

There is a long tradition of research dealing with the relationship between public opinion and the courts. Much of this research has focused on the impact of public opinion on the behavior of judges. This is a natural result of the problem of the role of the courts in a democratic society. Responsiveness of courts to the views of the public is based on both normative and pragmatic considerations. The courts *should* be responsive in a democratic society. The courts *must* be responsive because of their weakness as institutions. The tools available to the courts to enforce their will on a resistant public are few (Bickel 1962). But if, through their opinions, the courts can instruct the public, enforcement is gentle but effective. We consider this relationship of court and public—the role of the United States Supreme Court as "republican schoolmaster."

Nowhere has the question of the relation between public opinion and the courts been discussed more than in regard to the role of the Supreme Court. The Anti-Federalists recognized and distrusted the power of the Court as ultimate interpreter of the Constitution, but in *Federalist* no. 78 Hamilton argued that the judiciary lacked the power to enforce its decrees and that it was therefore the "weakest branch." Moreover, he argued, the Court would provide a valuable protection against the evils of majority tyranny.

Tocqueville, in his observations on American life, supported Hamilton's argument (Tocqueville 1969, 268–69). Tocqueville saw the judiciary as an aristocracy of sorts and thus a valuable source of the aristocratic virtues that threatened to disappear completely in democratic society. It is clear that the Fed- that threatened to disappear completely in democratic society. It is clear that the Fed- eralists and Tocqueville envisioned a role for the Supreme Court beyond that of servant to the public will. Indeed, the concern at the founding was not only that the Court should respond to public opinion but that it should also play an important role in educating that opinion.

The conception of the Court as republican schoolmaster generally reflects the notion that the Court, through its explication of the law and its high moral standing, may give the populace an example of the way good republicans should behave. Indeed, Lerner (1967) argues that this role was consciously recognized by the justices themselves during the early history of the Court. This concept has a specific application in the belief that the Court can through its decisions confer legitimacy on the claims of disadvantaged groups.

The question of the Supreme Court and public opinion has received much attention in the literature. However, most studies dealing with public opinion and the Court deal with questions of regime support or the response of the Court to public opinion (Dahl 1957; Kessel 1966; Murphy and Tanenhaus 1969). The studies that do deal with the question of the response of the public to Supreme Court decisions generally focus on elite groups (Birkby 1966; Dolbeare and Hammond 1970; R. Johnson 1967; Kemp, Carp, and Brady 1978). While these are important, our concern is with the broader public. If elites attend to public preferences and the Court fails to convince the public, elite support is likely to be tenuous and short-lived.

Public response to Court decisions can have a significant effect on the willingness of officials to comply with the decisions. Should they choose to do so, public officials might move quickly and decisively to implement the policies defined by Court decisions. However, officials' perceptions that an issue is too controversial can lead to inaction, as was the case with school prayer (Dolbeare and Hammond 1970). It may also result in outright resistance to the Court's mandate, as was the case with desegregation (Rodgers and Bullock 1972). Like the Court, public officials "follow th' election returns," but they have far greater incentives than the Court to abide by that mandate.

The question we address in this paper is the nature of public response to Court actions. The argument comes in three parts. First, we present evidence that the Court does influence public opinion but not as expected by most previous work. This section is unabashedly atheoretical. We then develop a post hoc theory of public response to government actions in general and the Court's in particular. This theory accounts for the perplexing findings of the first section. Finally we offer a test of the theory.

Do Court Rulings Affect Public Opinion?

A prominent explanation of the effect of Court rulings on public opinion is the legitimation hypothesis (Adamany 1973; Casey 1974; Dahl 1957; Kessel 1966; Marshall 1987; Murphy and Tanenhaus 1969). According to this line of argument, when the Court rules, it confers legitimacy on the position it favors. The Court's legitimacy allows it to bestow legitimacy on others through its rulings. This leads to increased public support for the position taken by the Court.

There are attractive features to this theory. The Court is held in high regard by many citizens. It is also recognized as the final arbiter of legal questions. Further, it would be perverse to predict the opposite, that the Court's rulings would foster *disagreement* with its position.

Legitimation is one specific mechanism by which the Court may obtain greater support for its position, but there are many other possible mechanisms. Regardless of the mechanism governing individual reactions, the common hypothesis is that rulings increase support for the Court's position. We want to consider these theories as a class, which we call the positive response hypothesis. For our purposes it is not necessary to specify the precise mechanisms that foster support, only to bear in mind that we are considering a broad category of theories, not the legitimation hypothesis alone.

Studies of the positive response hypothesis have focused on changes in the aggregate level of public support for the Court's position. Blake (1977), Uslaner and Weber (1980), and C. Johnson and Canon (1984) all adopt this approach. They compare the level of public support prior to a decision with the level of support after the decision. Marshall (1987) considers 18 Court decisions since the 1930s. In his analysis the shift between predecision and postdecision opinion is taken as a dependent variable to be explained by several independent variables such as unanimity of the Court, liberalism of the decision, and the time lag between the polls. While more complicated than others, Marshall's approach still focuses on the simple shift between pre- and postdecision opinion. The problem with this approach, as Uslaner and Weber point out, is that trends could lead to increased support apart from any direct impact of the Court.

Empirical studies of the Court's impact have produced little support for the positive response hypothesis. Murphy and Tanenhaus (1969) point to the low salience of the Court as a barrier to influence. Adamany (1973) cites a long list of disappointed attempts to demonstrate the existence of such influence. More recently, Marshall's (1987) study of 18 court decisions found that the average shift following the decision was virtually zero. However, Marshall did find some positive evidence in the case of liberal, activist decisions, after a time lag. C. Johnson and Canon (1984, 12–13) show that support for legal abortions increased slightly after the Court's *Roe* decision. The mixed evidence raises doubts about the Court's impact.

Our position is that increased aggregate support for the Court's position is not the best indicator of impact. In the wake of a decision some people may respond positively and some negatively. Both groups are affected by the Court's ruling even if the net effect is no change in aggregate opinion.

Our alternative to the positive response hypothesis is to focus on the *structure* of opinion concerning a ruling; that is, we are concerned with which groups support and oppose a position and how intensely. If support rises (or falls), the decision had an effect. But even if the net effect is nil, while the structure of group support and opposition changes, we argue that the Court still had an impact. We call this the structural response hypothesis.[1] The null hypothesis, then, is that in the wake of a decision the structure of opinion is unchanged. This truly would be evidence that the Court is a poor schoolmaster—not that it fails to convert its pupils but that it leaves them unchanged.

Our position is that theories emphasizing, for whatever reasons, increased agreement with the Court's rulings miss the political role of the Court. When the Court rules on politically controversial cases, it may establish the law of the land, but it does not put an end to debate. It neither converts the opposition nor ends the controversy. A satisfactory theory of Supreme Court impact must recognize that Court decisions do not necessarily

American Political Science Review Vol. 83

bring about agreement and may instead sow the seeds of dissension.

Testing the Structural Response Hypothesis

One problem with the study of public response to the Court is that only a small portion of the public is aware of most Court decisions, and an even smaller proportion is accurately informed about them (Kessel 1966; Murphy and Tanenhaus 1969). Therefore, an examination of Court impact on public opinion is meaningful only in cases where public attention is high. For example, Caldeira (1987) shows that during the Roosevelt Court-packing period the public did respond to Court decisions by adjusting their approval of the Court. This is evidence that when the issues are salient, the public may respond to Court actions. We would expect to see a Court impact in relation to issues of great controversy and public interest, such as desegregation and school prayer, rather than issues of low interest such as antitrust or the commerce clause. Paradoxically, however, the high interest that makes a Court decision salient may also blunt its impact, since these issues are likely to tap relatively well-ordered belief structures.

To test the structural response hypothesis, then, we need a visible issue engaging seemingly well-informed public attitudes. A more visible, controversial, salient decision than the Court's 1973 abortion decision, *Roe* v. *Wade*, could hardly be found.

Roe is easily the most highly debated and criticized decision the Court has made in the last 20 years. Annual commemorative marches are held by those opposed to it, constitutional amendments to overturn it have been proposed, and the author of the Court's opinion—Justice Harry Blackmun—has been the target of hate mail and death threats. Thus, the decision is ideal for a study of public opinion impact. Because of the controversy surrounding it, the level of awareness about the decision should be high.

Of course, this also means that we are observing a high point of Court impact on public opinion. But the emergence of the pro-choice and pro-life movement in the wake of the decision and much of the activism surrounding it occurred after the collection of our data. Our work is concerned with the immediate aftermath of the ruling, not the long-term developments.

Studies of public opinion concerning abortion have examined levels of support in the population but have often ignored the issue of Supreme Court impact (Granberg and Granberg 1980; Plutzer 1986). Where attention has been paid to the decision's impact on public opinion, studies have adopted the positive response hypothesis and found little support for it (Blake 1977; Combs and Welch 1982; Uslaner and Weber 1980). As we have argued above, this conceptualization of public opinion impact is too narrow. In examining the Court's impact on public opinion, we need to consider the structural response hypothesis as well.

The Problem of Attribution

Any study of public response to Court decisions faces a difficult design problem. If we compare opinion before the ruling with opinion after, how do we know that changes we find are due to the Court's ruling rather than something else? For example, Uslaner and Weber (1980) agree that there was more support for some types of abortion after the *Roe* decision than before. But they discount this finding on the grounds that support was trending up before the decision, thus offering a plausible alternative interpretation of the data. How do we sort out the impact of the decision from the spurious influence of

The Supreme Court and Abortion

other factors? To what do we attribute the change?

This problem is not unique to studies of the Court but applies equally to other public decisions and events. The methodological basis of the problem is that we have a quasi-experimental design, with premeasure, experimental treatment, and postmeasure. The problem is that public decisions typically affect all citizens, so there is no contrast group not exposed to the treatment. Thus, any change between measurements might be due to the treatment but might equally be due to something else. It is very difficult to rule out the possibility of spurious influences.

We gained leverage on the problem by distinguishing between those who had heard of the *Roe* decision and those who had not. In order to respond to the Court's action, one must have heard of it. Those who have not heard of it are in effect our contrast group. If long-term trend accounts for change in opinion, those who had not heard of the decision should resemble those who had. If there are shifts among those who heard while those who did not remain unaffected, there is reason to attribute the change to hearing of the Court's decision.

This is not a perfect solution, because respondents are not randomly assigned to the contrast group. Thus, the differences we find could be due to differences in composition between the experimental and contrast groups. For example, those who do not hear of Court decisions are undoubtedly less educated on average than those who do. Since education is also correlated with opinion on the abortion issue, lower support for abortion among those who do not hear may be due to their lower educational level rather than lack of exposure to the decision. However, if we model abortion opinion as a function of several variables, including education, the differences we find are much less likely to be due to composition, precisely because we explicitly include the compositional variables in our model.

Our design is a workable, if not perfect, solution to the attribution problem. By introducing a comparison group we circumvent the problem of such spurious influences as trend. And by explicitly including composition variables we compensate for nonrandom assignment to the comparison group.[2]

Model Specification

The structural response hypothesis we consider concerns the impact of the Court's *Roe* decision on the structure of public support for abortion. As discussed above, the Court's influence may be found in changes in the pattern of support or opposition, as well as in the aggregate level of support that the positive response hypothesis considers. The model we estimate allows both of these potential effects to be specified and tested.

In order to test the structural response hypothesis we need to relate individuals' group membership and personal characteristics to their attitudes toward abortion. The model we estimate uses observations from two cross-section samples, one taken prior to the Court's ruling and the other taken shortly after. The data from these two surveys are pooled and the equation estimated is

$$\begin{aligned} y = \alpha_1 + \alpha_2 d_1 &+ (\beta_{11} + \beta_{21} d_1) Z_1 \\ &+ (\beta_{12} + \beta_{22} d_1) Z_2 + \ldots \\ &+ (\beta_{1k} + \beta_{2k} d_1) Z_k + u, \end{aligned}$$

where y is the respondent's position on the abortion scale, d_1 is a dummy variable equal to one after the Court's decision and zero before, the Z_k variables are personal characteristics of the respondent that influence preferences on the abortion issue, and u is a random disturbance term.

The coefficients in this model are specified so that they may vary between the predecision and postdecision samples.

The β_{1k} coefficients represent the effect of Z_k before the decision, that is, when d_1 is equal to zero. The β_{2k} coefficients indicate the additional influence of Z_k following the decision, when d_1 equals one. Thus, the effect of, say, Z_1 before the decision is β_{11} and its influence after the decision is $\beta_{11} + \beta_{21}$. Clearly if Z_1 has the same influence after the decision as before, β_{21} must equal zero. Conversely, if the effect of Z_1 changes as a result of the decision, β_{21} must be different from zero. This logic is the basis for our hypothesis tests below.

In the equation, α_2 is the coefficient on the dummy variable for 1973 and the β_{2k} coefficients indicate how much change there is in the influence of each Z_k variable between 1972 and 1973. If the structure of preferences was unaffected by the Court's actions, we would expect all the β_{2k} coefficients to be near zero and the effects of Z_k (estimated by β_{1k}) to be constant over the two cross-sections. If each of the β_{2k} coefficients is near zero while α_2 is large and positive, the Court's decision had a uniform effect of raising support for abortion among all population groups represented by Z_k—as predicted by the positive response hypothesis—without changing the structure of the support. If, in contrast, α_2 is small while at least some of the β_{2k} coefficients are large, the primary effect of the decision was to shift the structure of group cleavage on the issue, though producing little net effect on the aggregate balance of preferences. Finally, if both α_2 and the β_{2k} are close to zero, the Court's action had no discernible influence on the public's preferences regarding the issue.

Data

In order to estimate the model we need data taken prior to the Court's decision and again shortly afterward. The National Opinion Research Center's General Social Survey (GSS) provides precisely this. The GSS field work was conducted in February through April of both 1972 and 1973. The Court's ruling was handed down on 21 January 1973. Thus the second cross-section was collected within a short time of the decision, while the first set of respondents were interviewed well before.

The GSS also provides an excellent battery of preference measures for the abortion issue. Each survey contains six relevant items inquiring about approval of legal abortion in cases of (1) threat to the health of the mother, (2) a likely defect in the baby, (3) rape, (4) poor families who cannot afford another child, (5) unwed mothers, and (6) the parents' not wanting more children.[3] In each case the respondent's are asked if they would permit legal abortions in the specified circumstances. We group these into two sets, one including the health, rape, and defect items and the other the poverty, unwed mother, and unwanted cases. We form two simple scales by counting the number of circumstances in which a respondent would permit abortion, one scale for the first three items (the "health" scale) and one for the second three (the "discretionary" scale). Each of these range from zero to three. The distribution of responses on these scales is given in Table 1.[4] These two scales are our dependent variables.

There are several reasons for treating the health and discretionary scales sepa-

Table 1. Distribution of Abortion Scale Responses (%)

	Discretionary Scale		Health Scale	
Score	1972	1973	1972	1973
0	42.1	38.8	10.3	5.5
1	10.9	9.7	7.2	5.3
2	10.2	8.3	10.7	11.9
3	36.8	43.2	71.8	77.4
Number of cases	1,308	1,332	1,308	1,332

The Supreme Court and Abortion

rately. The Court's decision broke major new ground on the discretionary side, while legitimizing the more common justifications based on health. It is possible that the decision may have affected preferences concerning the abortion circumstances differently. Further, the distribution of opinion is markedly different on each scale; the health scale reflects near consensus, while the discretionary scale shows sharp division. This becomes an important point in our theoretical development below. Finally, there is some debate concerning the unidimensionality of the six items and a suggestion that they should be kept distinct (see Clogg and Sawyer 1981).

There are a number of reports of previous research concerning the correlates of abortion preferences, many based on these same data (e.g., Granberg and Granberg 1980; Plutzer 1986). We draw on this research in selecting our exogenous variables. Our concern is to capture the major identified influences in order to test the primary hypotheses concerning the influence of the Court's decision. The variables we have included are education, gender, race, religion, and frequency of church attendance.[5]

Estimation

The ordinal nature of the dependent variables makes an alternative to regression desirable. An appropriate technique is the polychotomous probit model discussed by McKelvey and Zavoina (1975). This technique assumes that the responses arise from an underlying continuous variable representing the respondents' preferences regarding abortion. The actual questions asked in the survey cut this underlying dimension at various points, giving rise to the observed responses. The polychotomous probit model estimates the coefficients relating the exogenous variables to the underlying continuous preference dimension (up to a linear transformation). Thus the estimated probit equation may be thought of as exactly like a regression equation except that the scale of the dependent variable (and hence the absolute size of the coefficients) is arbitrary.

The specification we have proposed demands a test of the hypothesis that the coefficients of the model are invariant across the two samples. Its central test concerns the set of β_{2k} coefficients in our equation. The null hypothesis is that the structure does not change after the ruling. This implies that all the β_{2k} coefficients are jointly equal to zero. The test is readily carried out by comparing the probit model in which the coefficients are unconstrained with a model in which the β_{2k} coefficients are constrained to be zero. The change in the likelihood function provides the test: -2 times the change in the log of the likelihood function is distributed as a chi-squared with degrees of freedom equal to the number of constraints imposed (McKelvey and Zavoina 1975, 110–11). This is analogous to the similar test using constrained and unconstrained regression models (see Johnston 1984, 187–90). If this test leads to the rejection of the null hypothesis, we will have evidence for the structural response hypothesis in the wake of the Court's decision.

Empirical Results

We begin by estimating our model first for the 1973 respondents who had heard of the Court's action, then for those who had not. As discussed above, we need to compare those who heard with the contrast group who had not heard. After comparing the results for each group, we turn to a further check on the effects of differing composition in the two groups.

The estimates on which our hypothesis tests are based are presented in Table 2. Here the equations for abortion preferences are presented for both the constrained and unconstrained models and

American Political Science Review Vol. 83

for both abortion scales. This table contains all the 1972 respondents but among the 1973 respondents only those who said they had heard about the Court's decision.

The estimated coefficients agree with the typical findings of previous work, indicating that those with more education are considerably more supportive of abortion than those with less. Nonwhites are substantially more opposed to abortion than whites, and Catholics more than non-Catholics. Further, as church attendance increases, so does opposition to abortion.[6] The coefficient for women is small, indicating that the responses of men and women do not differ substantially. These results hold true for both abortion scales.

Overall, the equations are highly significant, with chi-squared values of 533.9 and 468.4, with 10 degrees of freedom, for the discretionary and health scales respectively. The chi-squared values are calculated using the standard likelihood ratio test. (For the application to probit see

Table 2. Estimated Abortion Scale Equations for Respondents Who Have Heard of the *Roe* Decision (Probit Estimates)

	Discretionary Scale Models		Health Scale Models	
Variables	Unconstrained	Constrained	Unconstrained	Constrained
Intercept	-.49 (.14)	-.38 (.11)	.78 (.15)	.94 (.12)
1973 dummy	.31 (.21)	.08 (.05)	.58 (.23)	.19 (.06)
Education	.11 (.01)	.11 (.01)	.12 (.01)	.11 (.01)
Education*1973	-.00 (.02)	—	-.02 (.02)	—
Female	.09 (.07)	.00 (.05)	.06 (.08)	.04 (.06)
Female*1973	-.18 (.10)	—	-.05 (.11)	—
Nonwhite	-.12 (.09)	-.23 (.07)	-.46 (.10)	-.49 (.08)
Nonwhite*1973	-.26 (.14)	—	-.06 (.15)	—
Catholic	-.20 (.08)	-.32 (.06)	-.21 (.09)	-.34 (.06)
Catholic*1973	-.25 (.11)	—	-.27 (.13)	—
Church attendance	-.14 (.01)	-.14 (.01)	-.13 (.01)	-.13 (.01)
Threshold 1	.29	.29	.41	.41
Threshold 2	.56	.56	.90	.89
log(L)	-2,651.5	-2,656.6	-1,811.1	-1,814.6
Chi-squared	—	10.2	—	7.0
Significance	—	$p < .05$	—	ns

Note: Standard errors are in parentheses. Number of cases = 2472.

The Supreme Court and Abortion

McKelvey and Zavoina 1975, 110–11).

The test of the structural response hypothesis, comparing the constrained and unconstrained models, is presented at the bottom of columns 2 and 4 in Table 2. The first test considers the discretionary preference scale. Here the chi-squared value of 10.2 with 4 degrees of freedom is statistically significant, indicating that we should reject the null hypothesis of no structural change. The coefficients in column 1 indicate that nonwhites and Catholics became substantially more opposed to discretionary abortion in the aftermath of *Roe*. While the coefficients are not large, there is also a suggestion that women, who had been slightly more supportive of abortion than men, may have become slightly more opposed. There is scant evidence that the effect of education changed.

While it is clear that the structure of preferences for discretionary abortions changed in the direction of greater group differences and conflict, it appears that there was little or no increase in support across all groups. The coefficient for the 1973 dummy variable is positive, but not much larger than its standard error. This suggests that in the case of discretionary abortions, the Court's impact was primarily to increase the polarization of groups on the issue, with little or no increase in overall approval. While consistent with the structural response hypothesis, this result is inexplicable under the positive response notion.

The results are different in the case of the health scale. Here the chi-squared value in column 4 is not significant, indicating that we cannot reject the null hypothesis of constant coefficients. Thus, the polarization effect seen in the case of discretionary abortions is not present in this case. However, there is evidence of an across-the-board increase in approval of health-related abortions. The coefficient for the 1973 dummy is quite large relative to its standard error. This implies that while group differences were not substantially affected, there was an overall increase in approval for abortions in cases of threat to the mother's health, rape, and probable birth defects. This is, of course, what the positive response hypothesis would predict.

As discussed above, a potential design problem is the assumption that the actions of the Court are the only explanation for the change in public attitude, for other trends present before the decision may well have produced the changed coefficients, quite independently of the Court's action. Others have discounted *Roe's* effects on public opinion on the grounds that the trend in the years preceding *Roe* was increasingly favorable to abortion (Blake 1977; Uslaner and Weber 1980; but cf. C. Johnson and Canon 1984). Clearly, our results, too, might be colored by such a trend.

We can test this possibility. There were 168 respondents in 1973 who said they had heard nothing of the Court's ruling. If the structural shifts we find are due to changes independent of the Court's action, these comparison group respondents should demonstrate the same structural shifts as the respondents in Table 2 who had heard of the decision. If they do not, it is additional evidence that the shifts found in Table 2 are in fact the result of public response to the decision.

The results for those who had not heard of the Court's decision are presented in Table 3. There is no evidence for structural shifts like those found in Table 2. In the case of the discretionary scale, there is virtually no change evident at all; and for the health scale, too, the chi-squared falls considerably short of significance. In neither case does the coefficient for the dummy variable for 1973 approach statistical significance. Hence, among those who did not hear of the *Roe* decision, neither the structure of support nor the level of support for abortion changed from 1972 to 1973. This is additional evidence that the shifts found in Table 2 are indeed the result of public reaction to the decision, not the spurious result of independent forces.

But perhaps the Court's influence was felt mainly among the more interested and educated. Not surprisingly, those who had not heard of the Court's decision are less educated than those who had heard and undoubtedly less politically involved. Among those who had heard of the decision, the mean education was 12.0 years of school versus a mean of 10.2 years among those who had not heard. Our finding of little change among those who had not heard of the ruling might be due to their lower interest or education rather than simply to their not hearing of it.[7] This possibility is mitigated by the fact that we include education as a predictor variable. However, it is conceivable that inclusion of the education variable does not capture all education effects. In order to check for this possibility, we can stratify the 1973 sample by education.

We can test the education objection by

Table 3. Estimated Abortion Scale Equations for Respondents Who Have Not Heard of the *Roe* Decision (Probit Estimates)

	Discretionary Scale Models		Health Scale Models	
Variables	Unconstrained	Constrained	Unconstrained	Constrained
Intercept	-.47 (.14)	-.49 (.13)	.69 (.15)	.67 (.14)
1973 dummy	-.20 (.36)	-.04 (.10)	.22 (.34)	.01 (.11)
Education	.12 (.01)	.12 (.01)	.12 (.01)	.12 (.01)
Education*1973	.02 (.03)	—	-.01 (.03)	—
Female	.09 (.07)	.08 (.06)	.05 (.08)	.07 (.07)
Female*1973	-.08 (.20)	—	.17 (.22)	—
Nonwhite	-.12 (.09)	-.10 (.09)	-.46 (.10)	-.43 (.09)
Nonwhite*1973	.11 (.27)	—	.22 (.28)	—
Catholic	-.21 (.08)	-.20 (.07)	-.23 (.09)	-.15 (.08)
Catholic*1973	.02 (.22)	—	.66 (.26)	—
Church attendance	-.14 (.01)	-.14 (.01)	-.12 (.02)	-.12 (.01)
Threshold 1	.33	.33	.39	.38
Threshold 2	.64	.64	.83	.83
log(L)	-1,629.5	-1,629.8	-1,197.5	-1,201.2
Chi-squared	—	.6	—	7.4
Significance	—	ns	—	ns

Note: Standard errors are in parentheses. Number of cases = 1,476.

The Supreme Court and Abortion

reestimating our model for those who have heard but who are below average in education, like those who did not hear. Table 4 presents the results for those who had heard of the decision but had less than 12 years of schooling. The mean education for this group is actually a bit less than for those who had not heard: 8.7 years versus 10.2. The substantive results mirror the findings of Table 2, not Table 3. Even among these less educated respondents, the structural response hypothesis is supported. It appears that the crucial variable is having heard of the Court's decision, not the respondent's level of education.

Discussion

The results presented in Tables 2–4 provide strong evidence of the influence of the Court's actions on the structure of public opinion concerning abortion. In the case of the discretionary scale the result of the decision was to increase the

Table 4. Estimated Abortion Scale Equations for Low Education Respondents Who Have Heard of the *Roe* Decision (Probit Estimates)

	Discretionary Scale Models		Health Scale Models	
Variable	Unconstrained	Constrained	Unconstrained	Constrained
Intercept	-.11 (.21)	-.14 (.17)	.88 (.20)	.91 (.17)
1973 dummy	.09 (.34)	.20 (.08)	.41 (.33)	.28 (.09)
Education	.04 (.02)	.05 (.02)	.10 (.02)	.09 (.02)
Education*1973	.05 (.04)	—	-.02 (.04)	—
Female	.12 (.11)	-.04 (.08)	.04 (.11)	.08 (.09)
Female*1973	-.35 (.16)	—	.08 (.17)	—
Nonwhite	-.16 (.15)	-.22 (.11)	-.55 (.13)	-.53 (.10)
Nonwhite*1973	-.14 (.22)	—	.07 (.21)	—
Catholic	.22 (.13)	.05 (.10)	.09 (.13)	-.03 (.10)
Catholic*1973	-.39 (.20)	—	-.29 (.20)	—
Church attendance	-.11 (.02)	-.11 (.02)	-.11 (.02)	-.11 (.02)
Threshold 1	.31	.31	.46	.46
Threshold 2	.64	.64	.98	.98
log(L)	-962.1	-966.9	-864.1	-865.7
Chi-squared	—	9.6	—	3.2
Significance	—	$p < .05$	—	ns

Note: Standard errors are in parentheses. Number of cases = 871.

American Political Science Review Vol. 83

Table 5. Predicted Discretionary Scale Response Probabilities

Respondents	Scale Category 0	1	2	3
Characteristics				
White, Catholic, 1972	.51	.11	.10	.28
White, Protestant, 1972	.34	.11	.11	.44
White, Catholic, 1973	.53	.11	.10	.26
White, Protestant, 1973	.28	.10	.11	.51
Nonwhite, Protestant, 1972	.52	.11	.10	.27
Nonwhite, Protestant, 1973	.55	.11	.09	.25
	Differences between Group Response Probabilities			
Contrast Groups				
Catholic-Protestant, 1972	.17	.00	−.01	−.16
Catholic-Protestant, 1973	.25	.01	−.01	−.25
Nonwhite-White, 1972	.18	.00	−.01	−.17
Nonwhite-White, 1973	.27	.01	−.02	−.26

differences between groups. In the case of the health scale, the impact was a general rise in approval for such abortions, with little evidence for structural shift.

The most striking result from Table 2 is the general tendency for group differences to increase in response to the decision. For both nonwhites and Catholics the coefficients become larger in absolute value, indicating greater differences with the contrast group. This raises questions about the role of the Court as a legitimizing agent for policy positions. If the major impact of Court decisions was to bring citizens into agreement on fundamental constitutional issues, our coefficients would have been smaller in absolute value, not larger. The results suggest that the impact of the Court decision was, instead, to crystallize issue preferences further and to lead to greater homogeneity of within-group beliefs.

We can illustrate the changes in group preferences by using the equations in Table 2 to estimate the probabilities that respondents with particular characteristics will adopt particular preferences. We are most interested in the differences between groups and how these differences changed between 1972 and 1973. Table 5 presents the predicted probabilities of each discretionary scale response option for four groups and two years. The top panel gives the predicted probabilities. We are interested in the contrasts between these groups over time. This is presented in the lower panel of the table.[8]

The first row of the lower panel shows the difference between a white Catholic and a white Protestant in 1972. The table shows that the average Catholic was .17 more likely to oppose *all* forms of discretionary abortion (a scale score of zero) than an average Protestant. Similarly the Protestant was about .16 more likely than the Catholic to support all cases of discretionary abortion. Compare these figures with the same differences in 1973, shown in the second row. In 1973 the differences have grown by more than 50%, to about .25 and .25, respectively. This is a rather substantial divergence of the two groups. The third and fourth rows of the panel show that similar divergence occurred between white and nonwhite citizens.

The results presented here are both statistically significant and substantial in their implied effects. The changes shown

The Supreme Court and Abortion

in Table 5 should allay fears that our findings are statistical curiosities lacking substantive import.

A Theory of Court Impact on Public Opinion

What theory can account for our results? It is apparent that any theory falling into the class of positive response hypotheses will not be able to explain the findings for discretionary abortions. Likewise, a theory predicting greater polarization in every case must fail in light of the results for the health scale. Our results show that sometimes public support for the Court's position increases and sometimes opinions become more polarized.

When public decisions are made—whether by the courts, the president or Congress—the individual's psyche processes the information and comes to some conclusions regarding it. If people were atomistic, the process would stop here. But they are not. Much of the meaning of public decisions rests on their interpretation, and interpretation depends on others. Individuals may react to decisions, but they must also consider the reactions of those about them. In this way they test their own interpretations of what has happened and modify their conclusions in light of the communal interpretations.

So when the Court rules, initial reactions may be entirely individualistic; but within a short period of time the individual is exposed to the reactions of others in the social environment. These environmental inputs may change or reinforce both the interpretation of the public decision and the individual's reactions to it. This process leads to a classic contextual model of political attitudes. As John Sprague (1982) puts it, "Consequences for individual political behavior arise from the embedding of the individual in . . . microenvironments—environments which are likely to be both informationally biased and interpersonally reactive. It is in these politically nonneutral and interactive contexts that political information is received, nurtured, matured and ultimately brought to bear on individual acts of political participation, public policy support, and partisanship" (p. 108).

The informational and evaluative biases of different social groups lead to different patterns of response to public decisions. We assume that members of microenvironments are positively affected by the group norms. Thus the effect of group interaction is to increase agreement with the modal response within the immediate social environment. When between-group variance is high, we would expect group members to move in opposite directions, leading to greater polarization. When between group variance is low, then more uniform shifts in the population are the likely result. (See Sprague 1982 for a detailed account of how such a process might work at the micro level).

In the case of abortion preferences, there was high between-group variance on the discretionary side prior to the Court's decision. Catholics and nonwhites were considerably more opposed to such abortions. On the health scale, however, there was much less between-group variance. Even among Catholics and nonwhites, there was majority support for abortions in cases of threat to the mother's health, rape, or probable birth defects. This is compatible with our finding of increased polarization on the discretionary scale but a uniform increase in support for the health scale. In each case, group members moved in the direction of the group norm.

The nature of the contextual effect also depends upon the homogeneity of opinion within the social environment. If the environment is consensual, the individual is likely to encounter a stream of reinforcements consistently favoring the modal position. If, however, the social environment is heterogeneous, there will not be consistent reinforcement of a single interpretation of events. This will reduce any contextual effects and produce a response more dependent on the individual alone.

We should consider an alternative theory that does not demand the contextual effect we posit. Individual proccesing of information alone could account for our findings if those who were predisposed to favor the ruling came to favor it more while those predisposed against became more opposed. Clearly, this is consistent with the results on the discretionary scale. It is also consistent with the health scale estimates, considering that majorities in all groups favored legal abortions for reasons of health. The psychological process underlying such a result might rest on effective counterarguing with discrepant information and willing acceptance of congenial data.

If both theories explain the same phenomena, Occam's razor would steer us towards the simpler, individualistic, explanation. However, there is a testable difference between the theories, which we take up in the next section.

A Test of the Theory

Because of the post hoc development of our theory to account for the patterns in our earlier data analysis, we cannot consider those results as a test of the theory. We need, therefore, to consider the merits of the theory when confronted with a new and proper test.

The contextual theory clearly predicts that homogeneity in the social environment is the key variable in attitude change in response to court decisions. The theory would predict that those who are more solidly embedded in an environment—who have more of their interactions within the group—are most likely to be affected by the group norms. Those peripheral to the environment should be much less affected.

While the General Social Survey is not rich in contextual information, we do have one opportunity to test this prediction of the theory. As we have seen, Catholics moved further away from non-Catholics on the discretionary abortion scale in the wake of the decision. A clear prediction of the theory would be that Catholics who are most firmly rooted within the Catholic community would be the most affected by the group norms following the decision. While the level of interaction with fellow Catholics can vary with neighborhood and choice of friends and acquaintances, it is clear that the most intense association with other Catholics is through the church. Those who are highly involved in the church would necessarily have greater contact with others like themselves than those who seldom attend services.

There is an obvious problem here. Catholics who attend most frequently are undoubtedly more devout than those who attend less regularly. Therefore they might be closer to the group norm and thus more strongly opposed to abortion even before the Court ruled. In order to prevent this confounding of the analysis, we include it in the specification of the model.

This is also a chance to test the alternative explanation for our findings, the purely individualistic reaction theory. If reactions to Court decisions depend only on internal processes, increased interaction with others would have no effect. Frequency of attendance would have no effect on adjustments after the decision.

This is a clear difference in predictions between the two theories. However, high-attendance Catholics might still react more vigorously to the decision if they were more extreme before the ruling. If we find that these highly involved Catholics already prior to the Court's ruling were much more strongly opposed to abortion than were less involved Catholics, increased opposition from this group

The Supreme Court and Abortion

after the fact might be due to purely individual processes. However, if this group was not substantially more strongly opposed prior to the ruling, the contextual theory provides an explanation the individualistic theory does not. In this way we hope to replace Occam's razor with a more modern decision rule.

The new model is much like the previous one, with this exception: where the previous model contained only the variables Catholic and Catholic*1973, the new model adds two new variables: high-attendance Catholic and high-attendance Catholic*1973. High attendance is defined as attendance "nearly every week" or more. This represents the top third of respondents. We can write this fragment of the model as

$$y = \ldots + (\beta_1 + \beta_3 A)\text{Catholic} + (\beta_2 + \beta_4 A)\text{Catholic*1973} + u,$$

where A is a church attendance dummy with one indicating high attendance, and zero lower attendance.

In this specification, β_3 indicates how much high-attendance Catholics differ from less frequent churchgoers prior to the decision. This is crucial to distinguishing the individualistic theory from the contextual theory. A large negative value would be consistent with either theory, and the test would become inconclusive. If, however, the coefficient is small, large effects of attendance after the decision must be due to contextual effects, and we can distinguish between the models. That issue rests on the β_4 coefficient. This indicates how high-attendance Catholics reacted to the decision. The contextual theory predicts that β_4 should be large and negative. The individualistic theory predicts this only if β_3 is also large and negative. Thus a small estimate of β_3 and a large estimate of β_4 is unambiguous evidence for the contextual theory and against the individualistic one. A small value of β_4 is evidence against the contextual explanation, regardless of values of β_3. Finally, if β_3 and β_4 are both large, we cannot distinguish between the theories, and the results would be consistent with either explanation.

Once more we estimate the model using the combined 1972–73 GSS data, using only those who have heard of the decision. The results are presented in Table 6.

The estimated coefficients offer strong support for the contextual model and little support for the individualistic one. For the discretionary scale the estimate of β_3 is considerably less than its standard error (a t-value of .62), indicating that high-attendance Catholics were not significantly more opposed to such abortions prior to the decision. The estimate for β_4 is, in contrast, quite large and negative, with a t-value of 1.94. This accords with the contextual theory's predictions but contradicts the individualistic hypothesis.

The health scale results fall into the familiar pattern of a uniform increase in support ($\alpha_2 = .55$, $t = 2.4$) with no structural change. While high-attendance Catholics were more strongly opposed to abortions for health than lower-attendance Catholics, they did not react differently to the decision. In a consensual environment this is what we would expect: the opinion environments are uniform, and so is reaction.

These results are very important for our argument. They show that in the case we are able to test with these data, the contextual theory's prediction is supported. If the theory had not found support in a proper test like this, we could have claimed only that it accounted for the results of our prior findings. But we have shown that it makes predictions not made by a competing explanation.

Interpretation

Our theory explaining reactions to the decisions of the Supreme Court is equally applicable to other public decisions. It would be highly desirable to test it in other settings. Other settings would provide different, and perhaps better, contextual measures and opportunities.

Actions by the president offer one such opportunity. Reactions to foreign crises have long been known to produce a "rally-round-the-flag" effect that raises presidential approval in the immediate aftermath but is often followed by a more sober—and less favorable—assessment (MacKuen 1983; Mueller 1970). The theory developed here suggests a possible explanation for this. In the immediate aftermath of a crisis most reactions are based on individual information processing alone. The crisis event evokes deeply inculcated feelings of regime support and patriotism, producing a short-term gain in approval of the president's actions. In the aftermath, however, social communication processes become the dominant influence. The reaction to events is modified

Table 6. Estimated Abortion Scale Equations Including High Attendance Catholics Variables (Probit Estimates)

Variables	Discretionary Scale	Health Scale
Intercept	-.52	.72
	(.14)	(.15)
1973 dummy	.27	.55
	(.21)	(.23)
Education	.11	.12
	(.01)	(.01)
Education*1973	-.00	-.02
	(.02)	(.02)
Female	.08	.07
	(.07)	(.08)
Female*1973	-.16	-.05
	(.10)	(.11)
Nonwhite	-.13	-.48
	(.10)	(.10)
Nonwhite*1973	-.26	-.06
	(.14)	(.15)
Catholic	-.18	-.01
	(.10)	(.12)
Catholic*1973	-.11	-.29
	(.14)	(.17)
High-Attendance Catholic	-.09	-.39
	(.14)	(.15)
High-Attendance Catholic*1973	-.38	-.00
	(.20)	(.21)
Church attendance	-.13	-.12
	(.01)	(.01)
Threshold 1	.29	.25
Threshold 2	.56	.90
log(L)	-2,646.7	-1,805.2

Note: Standard errors are in parentheses. Number of cases = 2,472.

by the social environment, as a within-group consensus arises as to the interpretation of actions during the crisis. The groups favoring the president interpret events favorably and approval remains the dominant reaction to the crisis within the group. But in groups that are predominantly unfavorable to the president, social communication leads to a reevaluation of the initial response. The result is a lowering of approval as the within-group effects become dominant. The end result is greater polarization between the president's supporters and opponents.

We can also compare our results with those focusing on media's effect on political attitudes. Iyengar and Kinder (1987) say that the media do not "tell people what to think," as a variant of the positive response hypothesis would suggest the media do. Iyengar and Kinder's research indicates that media coverage has a substantial and consequential effect on problem salience, however. We suggest that this may be the first step in the process of public reaction to public decisions. Media coverage increases salience. In the case of mundane news—the sort that Iyengar and Kinder consider—this effect is likely to stop with the individual processing component of the theory (much as they find). If the news is less mundane, however, the increased salience leads to discussion with others, and the contextual part of our theory comes into play. While the simple presentation of news does not lead to attitude change, discussions with others in the environment may. Public reaction, then, depends on news salient enough to provoke discussion. The nature of the reaction depends on both the stimulus and the discussion environment.

Finally, consider the types of reactions that are likely following rulings of the Supreme Court. First, most rulings probably have no effect at all. They are of sufficiently low salience and visibility that most of the public remains unaware of them. We are not concerned with these rulings. We are concerned with the rulings where the Court most needs public support—highly visible and probably highly controversial rulings. There are several likely outcomes, depending on the distribution of group opinion among the public.

If the public homogeneously favors the Court's position prior to the ruling, support will rise across all groups. Similarly, if the populace was uniformly opposed to the Court's position beforehand, support will actually decrease in the aftermath. In both cases, the mechanism is the same: individuals are moving in the direction of their (homogeneous) social context.

Different results occur when public opinion is heterogeneous. In such a case groups differ in their reactions, and greater polarization is the most likely outcome. The net effect on aggregate support is indeterminate. Support will rise or fall depending on the relative sizes of the groups and the relative effects within groups. In such cases we should neither be surprised if the net effect is nil nor mistake this for no effect.

The abortion issue's unusual salience and ability to arouse unusually deep feelings may restrict the range of application of our findings. How generalizable are our results? While the abortion decision is unusual, it is not unique. Other decisions of the Court—such as school prayer, the death penalty, and desegregation—also tap deep feelings and relatively well formed public attitudes. The difference between the abortion case and these others is one of degree, not of kind. In this sense *Roe* was not unique, and we think our results have direct applicability.

Not all of the decisions the Court hands down are like these, however. Many cases that arouse public debate—such as redistricting or the rights of the accused—do not have the same moral overtones, and it would not be surprising if citizens were more willing to be convinced on these issues. While the positive response hypothesis might fare better on issues like these, the evidence is against it. As we noted earlier, previous research has not found much support for the positive response hypothesis even when considering these more prosaic decisions. If the abortion issue is unusual, it is not because the public is more responsive to the Court's rulings on other issues.

We think our findings' limitations have more to do with the salience of Court decisions than with their subject matter. *Roe* is unusual because of the widespread attention it received. In more routine landmark decisions the public rarely approaches the levels of interest and involvement that followed *Roe*. This means that the social interaction process we discuss may never come into play, simply because the decision does not become a topic of discussion at home, church, or neighborhood saloon. In these cases we would not be surprised if the Court had no discernible impact on public attitudes. Our theory is of reaction to salient government decisions; therein lie both its limitations and its strengths.

Conclusions and Implications

We began by considering a role of the Court envisioned by some of its early commentators—the "republican schoolmaster." Our results suggest that citizens do listen to the schoolmaster but they also talk in class. While we found evidence for the persuasive powers of the Court in the case of the health scale, reflected in a general increase in support for the Court's position, we also found that in the case of discretionary abortions the Court only increased differences among groups. In each of these cases it is clear that the Court's action had an impact—that the public responded to its decision. However, the public response is not a simple matter of increased support for the positions taken by the Court majority. This result offers a warning that efforts to consider the effect of the Court—or other institutions—on public preferences must not rely simply on aggregate support for policies as the sole measure of impact.

The effect of decisions on the structure of preferences also suggests that decisions may have consequences not apparent from the aggregate level of support for Court-backed policies. For example, we find that Catholics and nonwhites became considerably more likely to oppose all forms of discretionary abortion following the Court's decision. Even if the aggregate percentage in favor of discretionary abortions remained unchanged, this shift may have been quite important. The concentration of religious and ethnic groups in communities and congressional districts suggests that elected public officials may have found themselves confronted with constituents more strongly committed on the abortion issue than before. As a consequence, representatives from heavily black or Catholic districts may have felt more pressure to support antiabortion measures, such as the Hyde amendment, in the Congress. To the extent that geographic constituencies coincide with demographic groups that are strongly affected by Court decisions, these shifts in public opinion may have exaggerated consequences for elected officials (Jackson and Vinovskis 1983). The effect of *Brown v. Board of Education* is an extreme example of such a situation. Southern white opposition naturally coincided with a major geographic bloc of representatives.

We have focused on the immediate impact of the Court's decision on the preferences of the mass public. In so doing, we have shown that the public is responsive to the actions of public officials. However, we should be careful not to construe the impact of the Court too narrowly. We present evidence concerning the influence of a decision on public attitudes; yet the Court's influence is surely not confined to the immediate aftermath of its decisions.

The Supreme Court and Abortion

In the months and years since the *Roe* decision was handed down there have been increased levels of debate, group mobilization, and political action (Luker 1984). These activities in turn have no doubt influenced citizens' preferences as well. These effects are also an impact of the Court. While our results are important in their own right, we do not suggest that the Court's influence is properly measured only in the immediate effects on public attitudes. By the same token we would suggest that there is no simple standard of "impact." Efforts to reduce the role of the Court (or any other institution of government) to a single summary of its influence are naive. Instead we consider here a single facet of the problem of assessing the responses of citizens to the actions of institutions.

The theory we have proposed to account for public reaction to the Court's decisions is also applicable to the actions of other institutions. We have suggested how this may be applied to actions of the president and how it may be integrated into research on the media. The fundamental message of the theory is that public responses involve both individual and collective components. The observed responses involve the distribution of group opinions as well as individual attitudes. The salience of the stimulus has a profound effect on how the information is processed. Since group discussion takes time, there is also an implicit dynamic process involved that may produce different reactions at different moments. We hope that such notions will enhance our understanding of the interplay of government decisions and citizen reactions.

Notes

We are especially grateful to Larry Baum, Lee Sigelman, John Sprague, and John Zaller for their very helpful comments on earlier versions of this paper.

1. Note that the positive response hypothesis is a special case of the structural response model in which the "structural" change is simply an increase in overall support with no change in group alignments.

2. For a complete discussion on these issues see Mohr 1988, esp. chap. 4. Like many who discuss design issues, Mohr emphasizes the problems with the design we are using; but he also recognizes its potential when randomization is impossible, as it is here.

3. The exact wording for questions on abortion were: "Please tell me whether or not you think it should be possible for a pregnant woman to obtain a legal abortion if

a. there is a strong chance of serious defect in the baby?
b. she is married and does not want any more children?
c. the woman's own health is seriously endangered by the pregnancy?
d. the family has a very low income and cannot afford more children?
e. she became pregnant as a result of rape?
f. she is not married and does not want to marry the man?"

Responses to items a, c, and e comprise the "health" scale; items b, d, and f make up the "discretionary" scale.

4. A glance at the table makes it clear that more people supported legal abortions in 1973 than in 1972. As Uslaner and Weber (1980) point out, however, it would be wrong to attribute this unthinkingly to the Court's action alone. They show that the trend had been toward greater approval of abortions and conclude that this alone accounts for the increase in support. Part of our task is to convince the reader that the effects we find are due to the Court's ruling and not some other plausible explanation, such as trend.

5. Education is measured in years of school. Gender is a dummy variable contrasting females with males. Race is a dummy indicating nonwhites. Religion is a dummy indicator for Catholics. The frequency of church attendance variable ranges from zero (never) to eight (several times a week) with a median of four (about once a month).

6. The church attendance variable is specified with a fixed coefficient because preliminary analysis showed absolutely no tendency for this effect to change following the Court's ruling.

7. This difference is only faintly mirrored in concern over the abortion issue, however. While 94% of those who had heard were able to place themselves on our scale items, 89% of those who had not heard were also able to place themselves. Thus, there appears to be relatively little difference between the groups in their willingness to respond to the abortion preference items.

8. The values of the education, gender, and church attendance variables were set to the mean for

American Political Science Review Vol. 83

the group in constructing this table. Thus, we are comparing average white Protestants with average white Catholics, for example, rather than hypothetical Protestants and Catholics with the same education, gender, and church attendance. This is necessary because we want to present a realistic picture of group differences rather than illustrate the influence of a single variable, holding all others equal, which is the more common practice.

References

Adamany, David. 1973. "Legitimacy, Realigning Elections, and the Supreme Court." *Wisconsin Law Review* 1973:790–846.

Bickel, Alexander M. 1962. *The Least Dangerous Branch: The Supreme Court at the Bar of Politics*. Indianapolis: Bobbs-Merrill.

Birkby, Robert H. 1966. "The Supreme Court and the Bible Belt: Tennessee Reaction to the *Schempp* Decision." *Midwest Journal of Political Science* 10:304–19.

Blake, Judith. 1977. "The Abortion Decisions: Judicial Review and Public Opinion." In *Abortion: New Directions for Policy Studies*, ed. Edward Manier, William Liu, and David Solomon. Notre Dame: University of Notre Dame Press.

Caldeira, Gregory C. 1987. "Public Opinion and the U.S. Supreme Court: FDR's Court-packing Plan." *American Political Science Review* 81:1139–54.

Casey, Gregory. 1974. "The Supreme Court and Myth: An Empirical Investigation." *Law and Society Review* 8:385–419.

Clogg, Clifford C., and Darwin O. Sawyer. 1981. "A Comparison of Alternative Models for Analyzing the Scalability of Response Patterns." In *Sociological Methodology 1981*, ed. Samuel Leinhardt. San Francisco: Jossey-Bass.

Combs, Michael W., and Susan Welch. 1982. "Blacks, Whites, and Attitudes toward Abortion." *Public Opinion Quarterly* 46:510–20.

Dahl, Robert. 1957. "Decision Making in a Democracy: The Supreme Court As a National Policy Maker." *Journal of Public Law* 6:279–95.

Dolbeare, Kenneth M., and Phillip E. Hammond. 1970. "Inertia in Midway: Supreme Court Decisions and Local Response." *Journal of Legal Education* 23:106–22.

Granberg, Donald, and Beth Williams Granberg. 1980. "Abortion Attitudes, 1965–1980: Trends and Determinants." *Family Planning Perspectives* 12:250–61.

Iyengar, Shanto, and Donald R. Kinder. 1987. *News That Matters*. Chicago: University of Chicago Press.

Jackson, John E., and Maris A. Vinovskis. 1983. "Public Opinion, Elections, and the 'Single Issue' Issue." In *The Abortion Dispute and the American System*, ed. Gilbert Y. Steiner. Washington: Brookings Institution.

Johnson, Charles A., and Bradley C. Canon. 1984. *Judicial Policies: Implementation and Impact*. Washington: Congressional Quarterly.

Johnson, Richard M. 1967. *The Dynamics of Compliance: Supreme Court Decision-Making from a New Perspective*. Evanston: Northwestern University Press.

Johnston, John. 1984. *Econometric Methods*. 3d ed. New York: McGraw-Hill.

Kemp, Kathleen A., Robert A. Carp, and David W. Brady. 1978. "The Supreme Court and Social Change: The Case of Abortion." *Western Political Quarterly* 31:19–31.

Kessel, John. 1966. "Public Perceptions of the Supreme Court." *Midwest Journal of Political Science* 10:167–91.

Lerner, Ralph. 1967. "The Supreme Court as Republican Schoolmaster." In *1967 Supreme Court Review*, ed. Philip B. Kurland. Chicago: University of Chicago Press.

Luker, Kristin. 1984. *Abortion and the Politics of Motherhood*. Berkeley: University of California Press.

McKelvey, Richard D., and William Zavoina. 1975. "A Statistical Model for the Analysis of Ordinal Level Dependent Variables." *Journal of Mathematical Sociology* 4:103–20.

MacKuen, Michael B. 1983. "Political Drama, Economic Conditions, and the Dynamics of Presidential Popularity." *American Journal of Political Science* 27:165–92.

Marshall, Thomas. 1987. "The Supreme Court As an Opinion Leader." *American Politics Quarterly* 15:147–68.

Mohr, Lawrence B. 1988. *Impact Analysis for Program Evaluation*. Chicago: Dorsey.

Mueller, John. 1970. "Presidential Popularity from Truman to Johnson." *American Political Science Review* 64:18–34.

Murphy, Walter F., and Joseph Tanenhaus. 1969. "Public Opinion and the United States Supreme Court: A Preliminary Mapping of Some Prerequisites for Court Legitimation of Regime Changes." In *Frontiers of Judicial Research*, ed. Joel B. Grossman and Joseph Tanenhaus. New York: John Wiley & Sons.

Plutzer, Eric. 1986. *Attitudes toward Abortion: A Study of the Social and Ideological Bases of Public Opinion*. Ph.D. diss., Washington University.

Rodgers, Harrell, and Charles Bullock III. 1972. *Law and Social Change: Civil Rights Laws and Their Consequences*. New York: McGraw-Hill.

Roe v. *Wade*. 1973. 410 U.S. 113.

Sprague, John. 1982. "Is There a Micro Theory Consistent with Contextual Analysis?" In *Strategies of Political Inquiry*, ed. Elinor Ostrom. Beverly Hills: Sage.

The Supreme Court and Abortion

Tocqueville, Alexis de. 1969. *Democracy in America*, ed. J. P. Mayer. New York: Doubleday, Anchor.
Uslaner, Eric M., and Ronald E. Weber. 1980. "Public Support for Pro-Choice Abortion Policies in the Nation and the States: Changes and Stability after the *Roe* and *Doe* Decisions." In *The Law and Politics of Abortion*, ed. Carl E. Schneider and Maris A. Vinovskis. Lexington, MA: Lexington.

Charles H. Franklin is Assistant Professor and Liane C. Kosaki is Visiting Assistant Professor of Political Science, Washington University, St. Louis, MO 63130.

Name Index